Pachlu, the great gunia of Baihar.

THE BAIGA

Verrier Elwin

Foreword by

J.H. Hutton

GYAN PUBLISHING HOUSE
New Delhi-110002

THE BAIGA

ISBN : 9788121200547

Verrier Elwin

Published in 2007 in India by
Gyan Publishing House
5, Ansari Road, Daryaganj
Delhi - 110002
Phone : 47034999, 9811692060
E-mail : books@gyanbooks.com

First Published in London
John Murray, Albemarle Street, W.

To

JOHN AND PAMELA STENT

TABLE OF CONTENTS

APPENDIXES

ILLUSTRATIONS

PLATES

An asterisk * against a plate means that the subject has been specially posed for the photographer.

ILLUSTRATIONS IN TEXT

SKETCH MAPS

NOTE

The spelling of the Chhattisgarhi-Baigani words has been made as simple as possible. As pronunciation varies from district to district, it has not been easy to obtain consistency: in the main the form of the words is that given them by the Bhumia Baiga of Pandaria and Dindori. Indian readers especially must not expect to find words spelt in the way that is familiar to them, for Baiga pronunciation frequently differs from the ordinary—thus they say *mamā* for the usual *māma*, *kakā* for *kāka*, *narāyan* for *nārayan*. and they always say 'Nanga Baigin', regardless of grammar.

A number of common words like gunia, mantra, bewar, etc., and the names of trees, birds and animals have been printed in roman type. Long vowels are not shown in these or in any proper names (except in the Appendixes), but only in the italicised words.

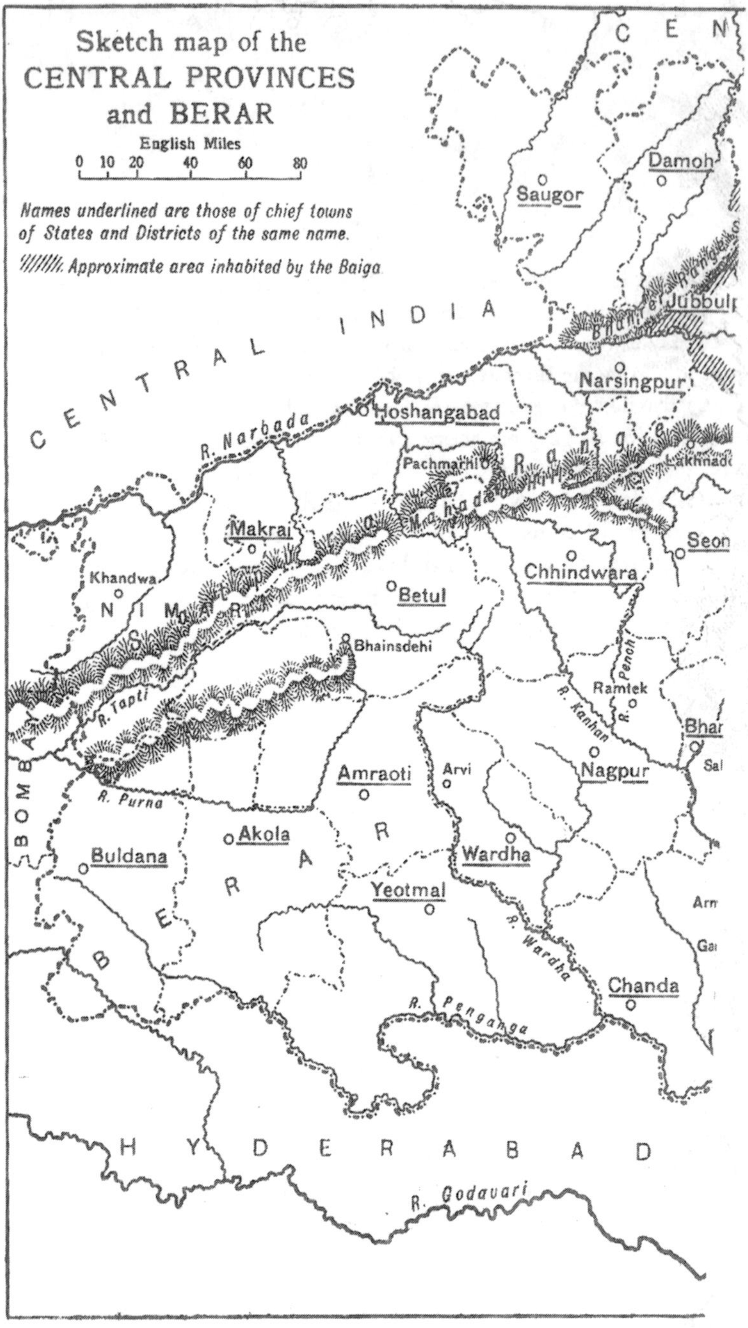

Sketch map of the
CENTRAL PROVINCES
and BERAR
English Miles
0 10 20 40 60 80
Names underlined are those of chief towns of States and Districts of the same name.
Approximate area inhabited by the Baiga
CENTRAL INDIA
C E N
Saugor
Damoh
Jubbul
Narsingpur
Hoshangabad
R. Narbada
Pachmarhi
Lakhnad
Seon
Makrai
Khandwa
NIMAR
Chhindwara
Betul
Bhainsdehi
R. Tapti
BOMBAY
Ramtek
R. Pench
R. Kanhan
Bhar
Sal
Amraoti
Arvi
Nagpur
R. Purna
Akola
Buldana
Wardha
BERAR
Yeotmal
R. Wardha
Chanda
R. Penganga
HYDERABAD
R. Godavari

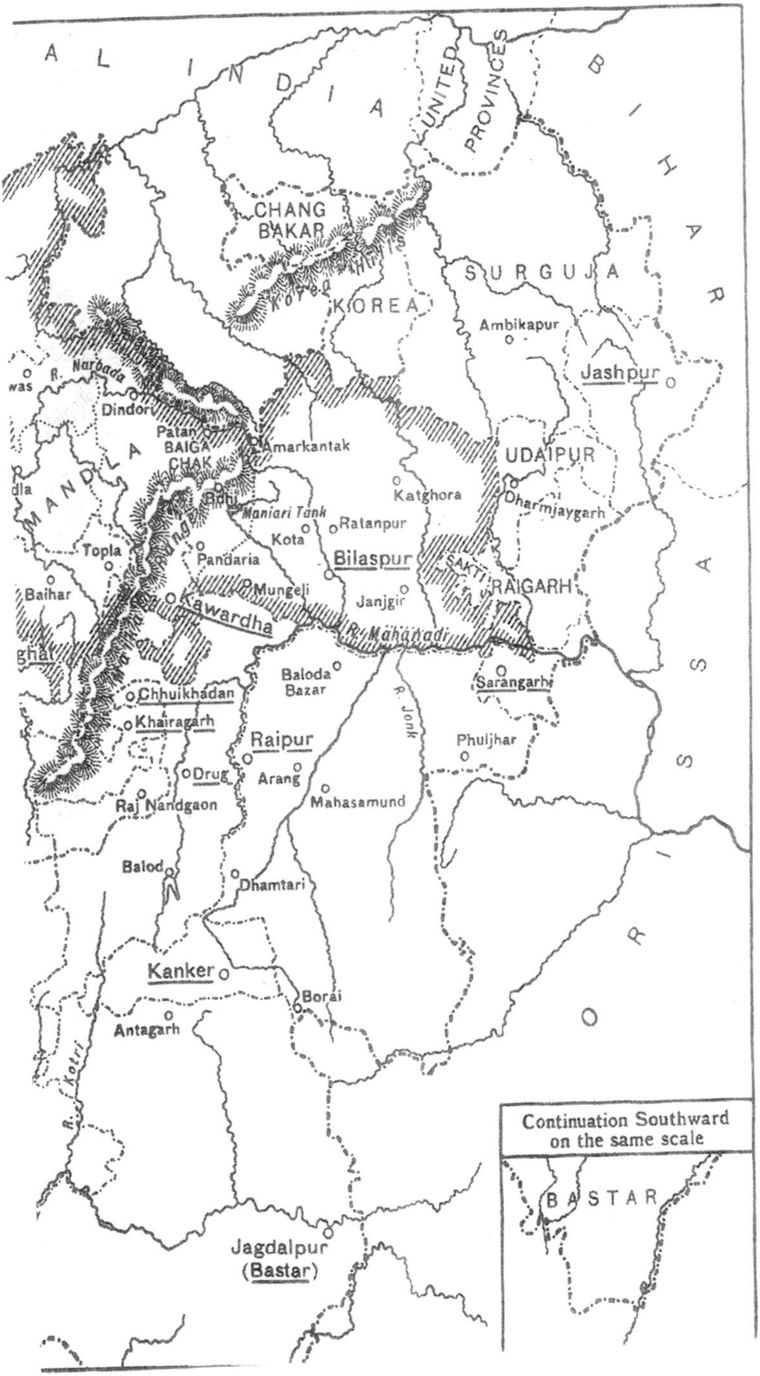

CENTRAL INDIA
UNITED PROVINCES
BIHAR
CHANG BAKAR
Korea Hills
KOREA
SURGUJA
Ambikapur
Jashpur
R. Narbada
Dindori
Patan
BAIGA CHAK
Amarkantak
MANDLA
UDAIPUR
Katghora
Dharmjaygarh
Bohi
Maniari Tank
Ratanpur
Kota
Topla
Pandaria
Bilaspur
SAKTI
RAIGARH
Baihar
Mungeli
Janjgir
Kawardha
R. Mahanadi
Maikal Range
Baloda Bazar
Sarangarh
Chhuikhadan
Khairagarh
R. Jonk
Raipur
Phuljhar
Drug
Arang
Raj Nandgaon
Mahasamund
Balod
Dhamtari
ORISSA
Kanker
Borai
Antagarh
R. Kotri
Jagdalpur (Bastar)
Continuation Southward on the same scale
BASTAR

FOREWORD

ANTHROPOLOGY has waited a hundred years for a full account of the Baiga, but Mr. Elwin has paid the debt as fully as any single author could who had to work on a tribe after its tribal life and organization had largely gone. Even the tongue the Baiga now speak is not their own, for there seems to be no doubt but the Chattisgarhi speech which they carried with them from the plains to their fastnesses in the hills, and that mixture of Dravidian Gondi with Indo-Aryan Hindi and Marathi which is known as Baigani, are both of them the result of linguistic borrowings which have supplanted and effaced an earlier Kolarian language. Language, of course, is no safe indication of race, and the primitive tribes of India, even if the Mongolian fringes be eliminated, show very great variation when examined by the test of the Coefficient of Racial Likeness. The Coefficient of Racial Likeness is by no means an entirely satisfactory criterion of racial affinity, but one would have expected a greater degree of propinquity between such tribes as Bhils, Gonds, Chenchus, etc., than is actually found. In any case the Baiga clearly belong to one of the oldest strata of race in India. Russell's hypothesis of two separate settlements of Kolarian-speaking races is probably sound as far as it goes. There is much to suggest that Kolarian tongues entered India both from the north-west and from the east, and it is possibly significant that, as among the Nicobarese for instance, two distinct methods of making fire are practised by the Baiga apart from the use of flint and steel, and matches, of course. Both the vertical fire-drill is used and the fire-saw, the latter method being typically Indonesian, though found here and there in India proper, as among the Paniyan of Madras.

Other items of culture appear among the Baiga which are also found sporadically among other tribes in India, sometimes very distant, suggesting isolated survivals of some very ancient culture or cultures now submerged except in remote corners of the continent, many of which offer links with similar survivals in Indonesia or Oceania. Thus the use of stilts at one of their festivals of the agricultural year, possibly originating in an attempt to make the crops grow high by the force of goodly ensample, appears again among the Lepcha of the eastern Himalaya, the Angami Naga of Assam, in the Indian Archipelago, and as far to the south-east as the Marquesas. The use of tattoo with the idea that it is necessary for the sake of recognition in another world appears again in Chota Nagpur, in Assam and in Borneo. Probably, if it were known, this association of tattoo is frequent in India. In Burma human victims for the foundations of royal cities had to be free from tattoo, no doubt because the victim, unable to rejoin his relatives after death, would thus give greater permanence to the foundation which he informed. The Baiga use of leaves for purposes for which Hindus and Muslims alike use water associates them with the hill tribes of Assam and Burma, as does the practice of enlarging the lobe of the ear and of regarding a torn lobe as a 'major social disaster'. A big and pendulous ear seems to have once been greatly admired at any rate from Assam to Formosa and south-eastwards far into the Pacific,[1] while at a later period it has been a butt for ridicule. The practice of obtaining fish by beating toxic fruit, leaves or creepers into the running water is worldwide; and the practice of suckling children for long periods—Phulmat the Baiga *gunia* was suckled till she was married at twelve years old—is common among primitive tribes, but the incident recounted in Yogi Dewar's life story of an order for universal marriage being issued by the local god and everyone in the village being married before morning, suggests the otherwise unique practice of the Kadva Kunbis. This Gujarati caste marry only when "the goddess speaks", that is on a date determined by lot in the temple of Umia Mata at Unjha, when all the unmarried of whatever age must be married, no further marriages taking place till the goddess speaks again some ten or even twelve years later. The obloquy incurred by the misfortune of being found to have live vermin in a festering wound is possibly due to some idea that the sufferer's life principle has got misdirected either through his fault or the wrath of god so that it produces life in the wrong place, while the taboo which prevents a pregnant woman from crossing a river is no doubt due to the common belief that spirits cannot cross the water and the tender soul of the unborn child may get left behind.

But perhaps the most striking of these survivals of ancient culture among the Baiga is the social organization which makes it proper for grandparent to marry grandchild. The occurrence among the Chota Nagpur tribes, for instance, and in other societies in India, of a 'joking relationship' between grandparents and grandchildren, which makes possible a freedom and even licence in conversation that would be quite improper between parent and child, has led to the inference being drawn that at some earlier date a marriage system was in force which, like the four-class system of Australia, made marriage between grandparent and grandchild not only permissible but

[1] *Vide* my note on p 308 of Mills's *The Ao Nagas*.

socially approved. It has been supposed by some anthropologists that inequalities of age were enough to make actual unions between grandparent and grandchild impossible even under the four-class marriage system, and that such unions when they did take place were between persons whose classificatory status was grandparent and grandchild, but whose biological relationship was more remote. Others have gone further and have held that the apparent possibility of marriage between even classificatory grand-parents and grandchildren was merely accidental: the four-class system, it was argued, was, in effect, an eight-class system in that a man married, for instance, his father's father's sister's son's daughter, while a woman married her mother's mother's brother's daughter's son, and the four-class system, under which he could, at least in theory, marry his own grandchild, was a purely hypothetical stage which had never, in fact, existed. But here among the Baiga we find a man still marrying not only his classificatory granddaughter—generally, it seems, his wife's sister's son's daughter (Pachlu, pp. 151, 180)—but actually his own daughter's daughter (Yogi Dewar, p. 141), while the union of a woman with her son's son is also mentioned as a regular practice, and three specific instances are given (p. 180), in one of which the grandmother bore two children to her son's son.[1] In other respects the Baiga marriage system appears to be in a state of disruption or at least of transition. There is a division into localized and to some extent endogamous groups which are spoken of by the word ordinarily used by Hindus for caste. These endogamous groups are divided into exogamous territorial divisions, but also into clans which are theoretically exogamous but practically not so. Mr. Elwin considers that the exogamous clan is a recent borrowing from the Gond and that the territorial division is the older exogamous grouping, but he also finds traces of an older exogamous clan which, like those of the Gonds, is totemic, while even among the Gond totems there seem to be traces of two systems, for the Markam clan is named, we are told, after the mango but has the tortoise for its totem. Perhaps it is of some significance that the Gond totems seem to be all animal while the Baiga totems that survive are vegetable.

The remarkable thing about the Baiga endogamy is that it exhibits some of the features of the caste system in what is perhaps a more ancient form than that familiar to us from Hinduism. Thus, as between the more or less endogamous groups referred to, the women of one group are much more strictly debarred from eating with the women of another group than the men appear to be. This does not seem to be a recent loan from

[1] It would have been interesting to have known whether the grandson is regarded as the reincarnation of his grandfather and is therefore his grandmother's husband reborn.

Hinduism. If it were one would expect the men to be stricter than the women, who are generally more conservative in social customs, whereas one of the occasions of male intercommensality for two clans at any rate is a meal of roast monkey. Nothing Hindu there. Again, the men of one group may take wives from another group provided always that they have not been married before, while after marriage such a wife severs her connection with her own group and may not even revisit her mother's house. In some cases, it is true, this practice smacks of Hindu hypergamy, since wives are taken but not given, but in others the practice is reciprocal and hardly analogous, therefore, to the hypergamous practices frequently found among the subcastes of a Hindu caste. Generally speaking the rules of commensality and intermarriage between Baiga tribal groups suggest rather the sort of society from which the caste system may have taken rise, than the society which is characterized by and is dependent on caste to-day. Even within the rules of intermarriage, we are told, to marry the member of another group is dangerous: "it gives your enemies a handle to use against you. It may, or may not, entail supernatural penalties." All this rather suggests a primitive system of taboos such as may have contained the origins from which caste as we know it has developed. A feature of Baiga sex relations rather remarkable in a primitive community is the comparative tolerance of incest. To marry within the exogamous group is a venial sin; intercourse with a mother, a step-mother or a parent-in-law is no doubt held in some horror, but that between other prohibited degrees is considerably less, and forms a subject of song and jest on marriage and other festive occasions. Even intercourse by a man with his mother can apparently be atoned for by a four-day fast and five rupees' worth of liquor in at any rate one section of the tribe.

Interesting, however, as the sociology and psychology of the Baiga are, the most important part of Mr. Elwin's work is probably to be found in that part of his book which deals with the future. For the saving of the Baiga he advocates the establishment of a sort of National Park. His proposals are reasonably concrete and have definite reference to existing conditions. If made by an anthropologist pure and simple they would immediately be suspected or at any rate accused of being a selfish if not satanic scheme for the establishment of an ethnological zoo, but no one who knows Mr. Elwin and his work could accuse him of that. For years he has lived among the Baiga and the Gond as nearly as may be under the conditions under which they live, working for their betterment through his school, his dispensary, his leper asylum. Readers of his *Leaves from the Jungle* will know just a few of the hardships, the dangers and the very narrow escapes from death by sickness and even by poison which he has suffered in the course of such work and in the full knowledge of the risks he runs. Readers of this book will as easily appreciate his unqualified affection for his Baigas as his intimate knowledge of their life. Neither could for a moment accuse the friend whom the Baiga know as 'Big Brother' of advocating their segregation for exhibition purposes or as specimens for scientific inquiry. His plea for their protection, therefore, and in particular for their establishment in a reserved forest area, carries no less weight than his pleas for their protection from the callous but too familiar rapacity of the subordinate officials of the forest, police, excise and revenue departments, and for their administration by more suitable codes than those of the Indian law courts. It carries no less weight than his protest against the equally familiar but if possible even more infuriating practice by which any subordinate 'who has proved himself a blackguard or incompetent elsewhere' is posted to some inaccessible tribal area (where his opportunities for evil though far greater are less lucrative) as a punishment for his misdeeds or as a means of obliterating him, and them, from an inconvenient publicity. Strongest of all perhaps is his plea for the Baigas' enjoyment of reasonable rights in the forests that have been their home from time immemorial and were their property till British administrators deprived them of it. The latter have no longer the power to make amends. That power lies in the hands of the Baigas' Indian compatriots, but whether they have the will to use it remains to be proven.

An account of the Baiga has been long delayed, but in proportion to that delay is the one we have here detailed and thorough. One can only hope that the no less lengthy delay in measures for protecting them may find an equally complete and thorough determination.

J. H. HUTTON.

Cambridge,
July 25th, 1939.

PREFACE

The Baiga tribe is one of the few remaining in the Central Provinces of India that has not yet been greatly affected by civilization. Neither the propaganda of Christian missions nor the influence of Hindu culture has touched a people who may still be described, in Forsyth's words, as 'less raised above the condition of the mere hunting savage than any, and clinging to the most secluded solitudes'. No Indian tribe can be altogether unaffected by the prevailing Hindu civilization, yet on the whole it is astonishing what little effect this has had upon the Baiga's mind. It has had more influence on their material culture which has almost disappeared before the highly organized and efficient trades-unionism of the Hindu caste-system. The modern Baiga hardly make anything for themselves. Their cloth is woven by Mehera and Panka, their shoes and sandals are made by the Chamar, their pots by the Kumbhar, their arrow-heads and axes by the Agaria. The Bania provides them with their ornaments, the Badnin comes to do their tattooing; even the basket-work which has been their speciality for centuries is now being taken from them by the Basor who lay claim to a caste monopoly.

In this book I have not devoted a great deal of space to matters which have already been fully described in authoritative works, such as the geography of the country and the nature of its forests, language, village economics and ordinary agriculture. I have also little to say about the early history of the tribe—for we do not know anything about it; or its racial affinities—for the comparative ethnology of the Province has not yet been put upon a scientific basis; or its anthropometric characters—for these can only be of real value if combined with a survey of many other tribes.

On the other hand, I have treated fully of all those things which the Baiga have made specially their own—the cult of bewar, magic, the diagnosis and cure of disease, the knowledge of the legendary past, the art of recreation, the art of love. This is, I think, one of the first books in which the sexual life of an Indian tribe is discussed with any kind of intimacy. For though India is rich in sexological literature, its ethnographers have generally been too much under the influence of the prevailing Puritan conventions to treat the subject freely. Yet it is essential that we should do so. Our picture of tribal life will be devoid of all contact with reality if we omit what is to the Baiga the most important and most enthralling thing in life. Nor should Indian readers fear that so frank an exposure will lower their prestige in the eyes of the world. On the contrary. For, as Margery Perham has said of Africa, 'the younger anthropologists are doing much to sap that ignorance of Africans which is chiefly responsible for the disdain in which they are held'. My own book has been written out of deep admiration and affection for the Baiga in the hope of stimulating similar emotions in others. I do not hold up their sexual philosophy or practice to imitation, but their simplicity and frankness, their goodness and fundamental decency has much to commend it.

This book has been shortened (partly for the sake of shortness, partly that it may appeal to the general reader and not only to the specialist) by the omission of a good deal of my documentation of Chapter VIII, many charms and tales, many pages of village gossip, many dreams that might offend (and perhaps rightly offend) the reader who was not making a scientific approach to these things. In particular I have reserved my material concerned with the curious and little-known Vagina Dentata legend and sexual deviation for future publication.

I have also omitted the bulk of the Folk-tales. I hope one day to publish a representative collection of these from all parts of the Central Provinces. I have, however, printed in full the short and simple autobiographies of representative men and women, for these give a clear and immediate insight into those things which the Baiga themselves consider memorable.

My qualifications for writing this book are these. Since January 1932 I have been living, with my colleague Mr. Shamrao Hivale, in the heart of the Baiga country, in that Mandla District which contains half the total population of the tribe.

During these six years I have talked freely with hundreds of Baiga in their own language, made many intimate friends, overheard a great volume of village gossip, settled a host of quarrels and disputes, and assisted at nearly all the ceremonies described in this book. I have also made many lengthy tours in other parts of the Baiga country. My first was in 1933, among the bewar-cutting Baiga of Pandaria and the Baiga Chak. This I have thrice repeated. I have twice visited the Baihar Tehsil, home of the wild Bharotia and Narotia Baiga. I have also visited Kawardha State, and know many Baiga from Rewa who have come to see me from across the border. I have made several tours in the Bilaspur District, and in the Mandla, Niwas and Jubbulpore Tehsils. Living as I do in Dindori, not far from the Pandaria border, the home of the Bhumia Baiga, it is of them that my knowledge is most intimate. But these are the most primitive and characteristic of all the Baiga.

At my headquarters I had the immense advantage of a regular settlement, a shop and bazaar, dispensary and leper-home, schools and rest-house, to which people came from far and near. My nearest English neighbours were a hundred miles away: I was thus compelled not only to work but to relax in tribal company.

I had the further advantage of being neither an official who might seem too alarming, nor a missionary who might seem too respectable. I was simply regarded as an amiable and eccentric person who was interested in everybody and everything, and to whom people could say anything that came into their heads. I was the 'Bhumia-sahib'.

One of the greatest compliments an ethnographer could be paid was given me by a Baiga in Pandaria. We had visited his village and been received with great friendliness but none of the fuss and deference which the touring officer generally receives. One of my company was annoyed at this and said to the villagers: "Here is a sahib: he must be someone important. Why don't you make proper arrangements for his reception?" The Baiga laughed at this. "We know it's only *bara bhai* (the usual name for me). He is such an ordinary man (*māmuli admi*) that when we see him coming we say, Oh, it's only *bara bhai*, there's no need to bother!"

During the latter part of my enquiries, however, there went abroad a rumour that I had established a new Baiga-raj, with a Baiga King, unlimited opportunities for hunting and the freedom of the forest. Would that it had been true!

I could have done little without the help of my colleague, Mr. Shamrao Hivale (*chhota bhai*), who established himself in terms of great intimacy with many Baiga, and became an admirable interpreter of their thought. Few people have served these aboriginals with more devotion, or won such great affection in return. Mr. Sunderlal Narbada Prasad (nicknamed Sunderlal Bhumia) certainly knows more about the Baiga than any man living. He toured with me in all parts of the Baiga country, and made many lonely and exhausting journeys on my behalf. To him I owe most of the Folk-tales, which he recorded in the original dialect and helped me to translate. He has now been under training for three years, and I could not have had a more devoted or efficient assistant.

I am also indebted to Pandit Gayadin Prasad, who often helped in the elucidation of an obscure song or mantra; to Sjt. Sunderlal Baghel and Sjt. Kartik Gond who collected songs and folk-lore in Baihar and Niwas respectively; and to Mst. Ahilya Baghelin who frequently threw light on matters where a woman's knowledge was required.

But all these were intermediaries. It is to my Baiga friends that I owe the real making of this book and, in passing, some of the happiest hours of my life spent in their company. I cannot name them all, but at least I must not forget my *mahāprasād* Mahatu (my 'family magician', a great adept, though his love-charms are faulty) and his sons, Mithu and Jantri; Jethu, the lame gunia of Bohi, and those entrancing boys Panku and Charka; Hothu, who was my generous host in Taliyapani, and Bahadur who entertained me at Hirapur; Dhan Singh and Thaggur who have often brought the mysterious benefits of their magic to my own village; Pachlu, the 'professional savage' of Jholar; Rawan, the great hunter of Bilaspur; Lahakat, the Don Juan of Amadob; Dasseru, dreamer of strange dreams; the mild and gentle Ketu; Yogi Dewar, the Mutiny veteran, whom I have not yet seen sober; the many-husbanded Mahi, a perfect 'Cockney' type, coarse and irresistible; the old and knowledgeable Baisakin and her co-wife Malho, just a little jealous; and the children, Phagni and Gondin, Mangli and Bhairi, Goru and Jhingra.

Among those who encouraged me in this work, the chief was Dr. J. H. Hutton who read the manuscript, saved me from many errors, and has contributed a Foreword which adds greatly to the value of the book. Nor can I fail to recall the names of Dr. and Mrs. Seligman, under whose roof at Toot Baldon I have spent unforgettable hours, or that of Dr. Edwin Smith, who will long be remembered, with no less affection, by his friends Mahatu and Yogi Dewar.

I am also indebted to Mr. G. C. F. Ramsden, I.C.S., who lent me some Baiga files from his office and whose photographic genius has provided two of my Plates; to Mr. W. V. Grigson, I.C.S., author of a brilliant monograph on the Maria Gond, with whom I have discussed many details and in whose house I wrote several of my chapters; to Mr. H. N. Jollye, I.F.S., who lent me some old files about the Baiga Chak; to Mr. V. K. Maitland, I.F.S., who arranged my tours in Balaghat and instituted an exhaustive search for the Kondwan and Gondwaina Baiga; to Mr. M. I. Rahim, I.C.S., who, when Deputy Commissioner of Mandla, directed his officials to provide me with some useful statistical material; and to Mr. C. D. C. Caldecott, I.F.S., who sent me the map of the Baiga Chak. I am grateful also to the Rani Saheba of Pandaria and the Raja of Kawardha (under whom the Baiga live in exceptional content) for permission to visit their domains.

To Mrs. Marguerite Milward I owe a special debt. She spent a fortnight in Sanrhwachhapar in January 1938, and modelled two beautiful Baiga heads. She accompanied me on an arduous journey to Bohi, and later went with me to Amadob, Tengradabra and Lamni. In spite of the great pressure of her own work she found time to make all the line drawings and gave me several photos.

Articles on 'Baiga Dreams' and 'The Functional Character of Baiga Mythology' have appeared in *The British Journal of Medical Psychology* and *The Journal of the Anthropological Society of Bombay*, and are partly reproduced here.

Part of my expenses in conducting this research was covered by a grant which, through the sympathy of the Trustees of the late Sir Dorabji Tata, came to me through the Sir D. Tata School of Social Studies, Bombay, of which I am a Research Associate. After the book was completed, the Trustees still further increased my debt to them by a most generous advance which made its publication possible.

I am in debt to the Government of the Central Provinces and Berar which has demonstrated its interest in this beginning of an ethnographic survey of the Province by assisting in its publication. To Viscount Wakefield of Hythe's sympathetic support I am also in debt.

For all this encouragement, as well as for the kindness of a number of personal friends, I am deeply grateful.

Nor can I forget the unfailing goodness and forbearance of all my friends at 50, Albemarle Street. No writer could have been happier in his publisher or found an office staff more sensitive to his necessities.

Perhaps I ought to add that none of those who have so generously assisted me are responsible for the measures I have advocated for the future benefit of the Baiga. I am afraid that my advocacy of a more liberal attitude to bewar and the freedom of the forest on the one side, and a much stricter policy of protection on the other, will not be everywhere acceptable. These are, indeed, desperate measures, but I am convinced that unless something of the kind is done, there is no future for the Baiga, one of the most ancient, most remarkable, and most delightful of the peoples of India.

VERRIER ELWIN.

Sanrhwachhapar,
Mandla District, India.
The Cherta Festival, 1939.

SKETCH MAP ILLUSTRATING THE DISTRIBUTION OF THE SUB-SECTIONS OF BAIGA

Chapter I

GENERAL INTRODUCTION

1. THE BAIGA

THE earliest account of the Baiga that has come down to us is as recent as 1867, when Captain Thomson, in his Seoni Settlement Report, briefly described them as 'the wildest of the tribes, inhabiting the most inaccessible hills and the remotest forests; living on what they can secure with their bows and arrows, in the use of which they are very skilful, and on the forest produce, and the small crops which they raise on the hill sides. . . . They are extraordinarily shy, so much so that it is often difficult to get hold of them, unless you are accompanied by someone they know. They fly out at one end of the village as you appear at the other, and you can see them scrambling up the hill sides amongst the stones and bushes, or hiding and peeping at you from behind bushes like wild animals.' [1]

Colonel Ward was the first to investigate the life and habits of the tribe in any detail, and he has some interesting pages on the subject in his Mandla Settlement Report, published in 1870. He seems to have found the Baiga a great deal easier to get hold of, and soon had them eating with him, and even offering him wives. 'Wild as the forests they live in . . . they are independent, high spirited . . . very well behaved, ready to oblige, and deserving every consideration for their orderly manner of life. Conspicuous for their absence of dress, they live in much better huts, and more orderly villages, than their namesakes (near Mandla). A Baiga village in the heart of the Mykul range is a sight worth seeing.' [2]

About this time Forsyth's classical *Highlands of Central India* appeared. He too was greatly taken by the Baiga. 'Far superior to the Gonds in every respect,' he says,[3] 'are the still utterly unreclaimed forest Bygas. . . . A few of these have somewhat modified their original habits, and live, along

[1] W. B. Thomson: *Report of the Land Revenue Settlement of the Seonee District*, 1867 (Bombay, 1867), p. 39.

[2] H. C. E. Ward: *Report of the Land Revenue Settlement of the Mundlah District*, 1868–69 (Bombay, 1870), p. 36.

[3] J. Forsyth: *The Highlands of Central India* (London, 1871), p. 359.

with the Gonds, in villages lower down the valleys. These have been slightly tainted with Hinduism, shave their elfin locks, and call themselves by a name denoting caste. But the real Byga of the hill ranges is still almost in a state of nature. They are very black, with an upright, slim, though exceedingly wiry frame, and showing less of the negretto type of feature than any other of these wild races. Destitute of all clothing but a small strip of cloth, or at most, when in full dress, with the addition of a coarse cotton sheet worn cross-wise over the chest, with long, tangled, coal-black hair, and furnished with bow and arrow and a keen little axe hitched over the shoulder, the Byga is the very model of a hill aborigine. He scorns all tillage but the dhya-clearing on the mountain-side, pitching his neat habitation of bamboo wicker-work, like an eagle's eyrie, on some hill-top or ledge of rock, far above the valleys penetrated by pathways; and ekes out the fruits of the earth by an unwearied pursuit of game.'

Fifteen years later, Colonel Bloomfield, who had been Deputy Commissioner of Balaghat and Bilaspur for various periods between 1868 and 1885, and had a great affection for the Baiga and knew a lot about them, wrote his *Notes on the Baigas* (1885), an appeal to the missionary societies of Britain to send out men and women to reclaim the tribe to religion and civilization.

This was the last serious piece of writing about the Baiga. Russell[1] has a few pages on them, admirable as far as they go, and there are some rather inaccurate notes in the 1931 Census Report for the Central Provinces.[2] But in writing this book I have had a bare two dozen pages of previous investigation to guide me. This is a loss to science, for a full account of the tribe as it was eighty or a hundred years ago would be invaluable.

II. AFFINITIES OF THE BAIGA

The Baiga appear to be a branch of the great Bhuiya tribe, which still numbers half a million in Bengal and Bihar, and is to be found chiefly in Jashpur and Serguja in the present neighbourhood of the Baiga. The Bhuiya, who are also called Bhumia, are—as their name implies—'lords of the soil'. This title is also claimed by the Baiga who call themselves Bhumiaraja or Bhumijan, and Bhumia is the name given to the most important sub-section of their tribe. Russell deals with this matter very fully, and I cannot do better than quote him in full.

'There appears to be considerable reason,' he says, 'for supposing that

[1] Russell and Hiralal: *Tribes and Castes of the Central Provinces* (London, 1916).

[2] *Census of India*, 1931. Vol. XII., pp. 403 ff.

the Baiga tribe of the Central Provinces are really a branch of the Bhuiyas. Though the Baigas are now mainly returned from Mandla and Balaghat, it seems likely that these districts were not their original home, and that they emigrated from Chhattisgarh into the Satpura Hills on the western borders of the plain. The hill country of Mandla and the Maikal range of Balaghat form one of the wildest and most inhospitable tracts in the Province, and it is unlikely that the Baigas would have made their first settlements here and spread thence into the fertile plain of Chhattisgarh. Migration in the opposite direction would be more natural and probable. But it is fairly certain that the Baiga tribe were among the earliest if not the earliest residents of the Chhattisgarh plain and the hills north and east of it. The Bhaina, Bhunjia and Binjhwar tribes who still reside in this country can all be recognized as offshoots of the Baigas. . . . Some of the oldest forts in Bilaspur are attributed to the Bhainas and a chief of this tribe is remembered as having ruled in Bilaigarh south of the Mahanadi. They are said to have been dominant in Pendra where they are still most numerous, and to have been expelled from Phuljhar in Raipur by the Gonds. The Binjhwars or Binjhals again are an aristocratic sub-division of the Baigas, belonging to the hills east of Chhattisgarh and the Uriya plain country of Sambalpur beyond them. The zemindars of Bodasamar, Rampur, Bhatgaon and other estates to the south and east of the Chhattisgarh plain are members of this tribe. Both the Bhainas and Binjhwars are frequently employed as priests of the village deities all over this area and may therefore be considered as older residents than the Gond and Kawar tribes and the Hindus. Sir G. Grierson also states that the language of the Baigas of Mandla and Balaghat is a form of Chhattisgarhi, and this is fairly conclusive evidence of their first having belonged to Chhattisgarh. It seems not unlikely that the Baigas retreated into the hills round Chhattisgarh after the Hindu invasion and establishment of the Haihaya Rajput dynasty of Ratanpur, which is now assigned to the ninth century of the Christian era; just as the Gonds retired from the Nerbudda valley and the Nagpur plain before the Hindus several centuries later. Sir H. Risley states that the Binjhias or Binjhwars of Chota Nagpur say that their ancestors came from Ratanpur twenty generations ago.'[1]

Russell goes on to argue that the Chhattisgarh plain and the hills north and east of it belong to the same tract of country as the Chota Nagpur States which are the home of the Bhuiya. There is thus no geographical difficulty in supposing the Baiga to be a branch of this tribe.

Again, the name Baiga means a sorcerer or medicine-man. It is applied in this sense to the priests of the Chota Nagpur tribe, the Khairwar. The

[1] Russell and Hiralal: op. cit., ii, pp. 310 ff.

Bhuiyar of Mirzarpur, who seem to be identical with the Bhuiya of Chota Nagpur, are also called Baiga in so far as they perform the function of propitiating the local and ancient deities as their priests. The name Baiga is also applied in the Central Provinces to anyone who serves as a village priest—the Pardhan, the Ghasiya, the Kharwar, the Gond and many Hindu castes use the word in this sense.

'The Baigas of Mandla,' Russell continues, 'are also known as Bhumia, which is only a variant of Bhuiya, having the same meaning of lord of the soil or belonging to the soil. Both Bhuiya and Bhumia are in fact nearly equivalent to our word "aboriginal", and both are names given to the tribe by the Hindus and not originally that by which its members called themselves. It would be quite natural that a branch of the Bhuiyas, who settled in the Central Provinces and were commonly employed as village priests by the Hindus and Gonds should have adopted the name of the office, Baiga, as their tribal designation; just as the title of Munda or village headman has become the name of one branch of the Kol tribe, and Bhumij, another term equivalent to Bhuiya of a second branch.

'Another point of some importance,' he concludes, 'is that the Bhuiyas of Chota Nagpur and the Baigas and the tribes derived from them in the Central Provinces have all completely abandoned their own language and speak a broken form of that of their Hindu neighbours. As has been seen, too, the Bhuiyas are commonly employed as priests in Chota Nagpur, and there seems therefore to be a strong case for the original identity of the two tribes.'

If we accept this, as I personally am inclined to do, it means that we must class the Baiga as a Munda or Kolarian tribe.[1] What little evidence we have, moreover, suggests that the Baiga represent the earliest settlement of all; their Koḷ and Gond neighbours regard them as priests knowing the original secrets of the local soil; they accept their decisions on boundary disputes—Colonel Ward found the help of the Baiga invaluable when he was making his settlement; and they look up to them as an older race. This makes me think that another suggestion of Russell's should be accepted—that there were two separate settlements of the Kolarian or Munda race, the first represented by the Bhar, Bhuiya, Baiga and kindred tribes who have entirely lost their own languages and have names given to them by the Hindus, and the second represented by the Kol or Munda and their related tribes, whose languages and tribal religion and organization, though in a decaying state, can be fully recognized and recorded.

[1] On the Munda or Kol classification of the Bhuiya, see S. C. Roy: *The Hill Bhuiyas of Orissa* (Ranchi, 1935), pp. 20 ff. The 1931 Census classed the Baiga, Bhuiya, Bhaina, Binjhwar, Bharia, Bhumia, Bhunjia, Chatwar, Kadar, Khetwari, Naiya and Rao as members of this group. *Census of India*, 1931. Vol. I. Part II. Imperial Tables, p. 523.

The word 'Kolarian', of course, is not properly applied to an ethnic unit. The term, however, is convenient and familiar, and Baron von Eikstedt's new classification, interesting as it is, has not yet won universal acceptance. He himself appears to class the Baiga as 'Gondid', but this is surely a slip: the Baiga are obviously distinct from the Gond and should be placed in the 'Kolid' group.[1]

III. TRIBAL DIVISIONS

The primary allegiance of every Baiga, whatever his sub-caste may be, is to the Baiga tribe itself. The tribe is strictly endogamous, although as we shall see, women of other tribes who marry Baiga may be admitted after the appropriate rites have been performed.

But further, the tribe itself is divided into a number of more or less endogamous *jāt*—I say 'more or less endogamous' because the rules about intermarriage vary from place to place, and members of some *jāt* may intermarry while others never do so.

Colonel Ward was the first to give a list of these *jāt*; the three 'sects or castes of the Bygas,' he says, 'are the Binjwar or Binchwar, Mondya, Bheronthya'.[2] Colonel Bloomfield, writing of Balaghat, also knew of only three—the Narotia, Bharotia and Binjhwar. Russell gives the names of seven—Binjhwar, Bharotia, Narotia or Nahar, Raibhaina, Kathbhaina, Kondwan or Kundi, and Gondwaina.[3] It is curious that Russell omits the important and characteristic Bhumia. And Colonel Ward also, who was well acquainted with the Bhumia country, fails to mention them—perhaps because in his day there was no very careful distinction drawn between Bhumia and Bharotia. Even to-day in parts of the Baiga Chak some Bhumia Baiga are known as Bharotia. On the other hand, the two sections were distinguished in the Census of 1891.

To-day, we must add to the list the Kurka Baiga, the Sawat Baiga and the Duhd-bhaina. These subsections have probably arisen from intermarriage with other tribes, or perhaps a leading member of a group of villages has committed some tribal offence and been supported by his fellows with the result that they have been cut off from the main stock and taken a new name. The Chhota Bhumia of Niwas are coming into existence in this way. They are Bhumia who clean themselves with water instead of leaves, and dress in Gond fashion, so that the other Bhumia refuse to eat with them.

[1] See. A. K. Iyer, *Mysore Tribes and Castes* (Mysore, 1935), Vol. I, Chap. I.
[2] Ward, op. cit., p. 154. [3] Russell and Hiralal, op. cit., ii., p. 80.

The main difference between these *jāt* is one of distribution.[1] In the main, each *jāt* occupies a separate block of country, and inevitably takes some colour from its neighbours, the geographical situation, the attitude of the administration. Thus the Binjhwar of the comparatively civilized country near Lamta, Nainpur or Jubbulpore, are naturally Hinduized to some extent. The Bharotia in the wilds of the Supgar Range retain most of their tribal customs; the Muria of Niwas who live in predominantly Gond villages resemble the Gond in dress and outlook. To find Baiga life in its fullest and unchecked development we must go to Pandaria or Kawardha where the villagers are still allowed to practise bewar without too much restriction.

Each *jāt* naturally considers itself to be the highest. This is a Bhumia ruling on the matter. 'The Bhumia were born from *dharmi-dharti* (the good earth); the Binjhwar from *lāhuri-dharti* (the young earth); the Bhaina from *pāpi-dharti* (sinful earth); the Bhuiya were born last of all, after the whole world was made. The Binjhwar are a low race—we don't eat from their hands.'

In Niwas, Ketu the Muria put it this way. 'When Lohar Sur was living he called all the Baiga to a great feast, but he gave each separate food. He prepared cows-flesh in one place, roots in a second, rice and kodon in a third. The Kurka and Bharia Baiga ran to eat the cows-flesh and became the lowest of the *jāt*; the Binjhwar and the Muria ate the fruit of the plough, and they were only a little raised off the ground; but the jungly Bhumia and the Bharotia who only ate the fruit of the jungle—these became the greatest of all. That night they all slept in Lohar Sur's house, and in the morning went to relieve themselves. Those who ate the fruit of the jungle, the Bhumia and Bharotia, cleaned themselves with lumps of mud and leaves—hence they are honoured as the highest of the *jāt*. The Binjhwar who used water are regarded as a low *jāt*. We all think the jungly Bhumia are the highest.'

Pachlu, a Bharotia, was very bitter about the conceited ways of the Binjhwar. 'They think themselves superior to us, but we know better. The Bharotia are the highest, then the Binjhwar, then the Narotia, and lowest of all the Gond-bhaina who eat monkeys.'

But the Binjhwar also consider themselves to be the highest. 'We are the real Bhumia, not the Bharotia.' They look down on the Bharotia and Narotia who eat gaur and jungle buffalo—though a Binjhwar once admitted

[1] Among the Dhanwar of Uprora and Matin I found a tradition of primal unity among all the tribes. The Dhanwar give great honour to Nanga Baiga who they regard as the father of their tribe. Nanga Baiga had six grandsons whom he named Bhumia (because he lived on the ground), Dhanwar (because he would never move without his bow and arrow), Dudh-bhaina (because he drank the milk of every animal), Lodha, Bhuiya and Paharia.

to me that if they could only get them, they would not hesitate for a moment.

The Bhumia, wild, handsome, lightly-clad, their hair beautifully dressed, still adept with the bow and arrow, still for the most part practising bewar, live in Dindori (most of the inhabitants of the Baiga Chak are Bhumia), Pandaria, Kawardha and Rewa.

The Bharotia, who live mainly in Baihar, are very like the Bhumia, and a few who live in the Chak and practise bewar are indistinguishable from them.

The Binjhwar Baiga are the most civilized in the Hindu sense. Some of them dress like ordinary low-caste peasants, use the plough, and observe some Hindu feasts and customs. The Hinduizing process has not, however, proceeded very far; the Binjhwar remain primitive at heart and many long to return to the old life of hunting and shifting cultivation. A branch of the tribe has split off and taken the name of Binjhwar; they are now about 60,000 strong and form an important land-owning class in Chhattisgarh. They are not to be confused with the Binjhwar sub-division of the Baiga, though they are probably of the same stock. The Binjhwar Baiga live in Baihar, Mandla, Niwas, Jubbulpore and Rewa, that is to say they occupy a solid block of country to the North and West.

The Muria Baiga who live in Niwas and Mandla distinguish themselves from other Baiga by shaving their hair—'Ordinary Baiga wear their hair as long as your arm: we shave it off.' They have been greatly influenced by the Gond among whom they live. Men and women dress and even look like Gond, they build their houses in Gond style.

The Narotia or Nahar live in Baihar, but in villages separate from other Baiga. They are very like the Bharotia, but are a little more civilized; they consider that the Bharotia are rough and uncouth, talking a vulgar dialect.

The Bhaina Baiga are to be found in Bilaspur and Rewa. They are distinguished from the Bhaina tribe, which inhabits the same locality and is generally believed to be derived from irregular unions between Baiga and Kawar. The Bhaina sub-division of the Baiga may in turn be derived from irregular unions between Baiga and Bhaina. There are three kinds of Bhaina Baiga—Dudh-bhaina, Kath-bhaina and Rai-bhaina. There is little difference between them, and they are all, in habits and appearance, like the Bhumia. Most of them still practise bewar wherever it is permitted in Bilaspur.

The Gond-waina and Kondwan Baiga of Balaghat eat monkeys and beef, and are looked down on by other Baiga in consequence. These two *jāt* are said to live in Baihar and on the Kawardha border, but I have been unable to locate them. Exhaustive enquiries by the Deputy Commissioner and Forest Officer failed to discover any in Balaghat. Yet all Baiga talk about them, though they generally admit that they have not themselves seen them.

Colonel Bloomfield's observations on the Baiga are always interesting Writing of the Binjhwar, Bharotia and Narotia, he says, 'These are different tribes in every way. They neither intermarry nor intermix, and are seldom, if ever, found living together in one village. The Binjhwar appear to be slightly Hinduized[1] and observe sundry petty rules of caste, as if, apparently, they desire to distinguish themselves from the other two tribes, between whom and themselves there is, in physique, language, etc., but little difference. They will not eat the flesh of the ox, bison, nilgai, and many other things—rats, ant-eaters and squirrels—which are readily devoured and much appreciated by the other tribes. . . . The Bharotias are the wildest of all. I believe that not one of them has yet taken to the plough and all who have come to me steadily maintain that they can never bring themselves to it.'

A glance at the map will show that to-day the Baiga all belong to one bit of country. The Baihar Tehsil of Balaghat is geographically and ethnographically part of Mandla District. The northern part of Kawardha and the north-west portion of Pandaria Zemindari belongs to the high forest-covered country of south Mandla and Dindori. The Pendra Zemindari and the Lormi Range of Bilaspur belong more properly to Mandla than to Chhattisgarh. The boundary dividing the Baiga of Jubbulpore and Niwas is purely artificial. In Rewa it is in the hills overlooking the Narbada (which forms the boundary between the State and Mandla) that the Baiga live.

This country is wild and beautiful. It has broad stretches of cultivated lands in its valleys, but most of it is mountainous and covered with dense forest. The Bhumia Baiga, most primitive and characteristic of all, live along the rugged uplands of the Maikal Range which runs from Amarkantak to the Saletekri Hills. From the edge of these hills are splendid views across the Maniari Lake and the foothills of the Lormi Forest, and the traveller can trace the glittering ribbon of the Son winding its way through almost endless jungle.

But no less attractive are the magnificent sal forests of the Supgarh and Baihar Ranges, the quaint rocky hills near Lamta, the milder scenery of Niwas, the uplands of Mandla which the blossoming of the trees turns into a fairyland, the lonely reaches of Jagmandal.

[1] Ten years later, in 1891, the Census figures showed that while 85·5% of the Mandla Baiga were 'animist,' only 44·4% of the Balaghat Baiga could be so classified. The low figure in Balaghat was due to the 'Hinduization' of the Binjhwar. The other sub-divisions showed 70% 'animist'.

The Baiga have been happy in their home; it would be hard to think of a tract of country more suited to their needs. It would make an almost ideal National Park. It contains no towns at all, for Mandla lies on the extreme western border, Kawardha and Pandaria to the south of the tribal areas in their respective domains, and a line could easily be drawn round the Baiga country which omitted even the railway along the western boundary of Balaghat.

IV. APPEARANCE AND PHYSIQUE

Everyone is struck by the charm and distinction of the Baiga, at least of those who live along the Maikal Hills. It is very easy to distinguish them among a crowd of Gond or Hindu cultivators.

'A Baiga,' wrote Mr. J. Lampard, a former missionary in Baihar, 'is speedily discerned in a forest village bazaar, and is the most interesting object in it. His almost nude figure, wild, tangled hair, innocent of such inventions as brush and comb, lithe wiry limbs and jungly and uncivilized appearance, mark him out at once. He generally brings a few mats or baskets which he has made, or fruits, roots, honey, horns of animals, or other jungle products which he has collected, for sale, and with the sum obtained (a few pice or annas at the most) he proceeds to make his weekly purchases, changing his pice into cowrie shells, of which he receives eighty for each one. He buys tobacco, salt, chillies, and other sundries, besides as much kodon, kutki, or perhaps rice as he can afford, always leaving a trifle to be expended at the liquor shop before departing for home. The various purchases are tied up in the corners of the bit of rag twisted round his head; unlike pieces of cloth known to civilization which usually have four corners, the Baiga's headgear appears to be nothing but corners, and when the shopping is done, the scrap of rag may have a dozen minute bundles tied up in it.'[1]

Both Forsyth and Ward found the Baiga better looking and of a finer physique than the Gond, and—so far as the men are concerned—I agree with them.

'The Bygas to the eastward,' says Ward, 'on the Mykul Range, are much finer specimens of humanity than those nearer Mundlah; in habits too they are superior; they are a fine manly race, and better looking than their brethren near Mundlah. They have not the flat head and receding forehead so common among the Gonds, nor the broad flat nose; the head is longer, and the features more aquiline; their hands are peculiarly small. Some

[1] *Balaghat District Gazetteer* (Allahabad, 1907), pp. 98 f.

among them have all the types of low civilization—flat heads, thick lips, distended nostrils; but on the whole, I was much struck with the appearance of these Bygas of the Eastern Ghauts, as much superior to their brethren in other parts.'[1]

Baiga men are far better looking than their women. The young men are often strikingly handsome, with strong, slim, shapely bodies, fine but gentle features, magnificent black glossy wavy hair, and a great vitality. The older men have a certain distinction both in their bearing and appearance.

The reader will get a far better idea of the appearance of the Baiga by studying the illustrations in this book than by any description I can give. But I may briefly note that the colour of the skin varies greatly, from the exquisite golden brown of a boy like Charka, through the dark heavy brown of the average Bharotia in Baihar, to the dead black of old Jethu. On the whole, their skin is a lighter brown than that of the Gond. The hair is black and thick and long on the head, but generally scanty elsewhere, moustaches are worn, and in Pandaria little straggly beards. White hair is not uncommon. Ward wrote that he had found four or five woolly crops like an African's in the Mandla District, but I have never seen this among Baiga, though I have noticed it among Gond and Panka.

The custom of moulding the head and nose shortly after birth may possibly have some slight effect on the facial characters. Once when I was examining the head of the headman's son at Daharkata, his father-in-law Deo Singh suddenly exclaimed: "His nose is all right now, but once it was flat as a *chapāti*. He doesn't like my telling you, but when he was born I saw his silly little nose, and my sister working on it, making it big and a good shape. She did his head as well."

There are two quite distinct types, both among men and women. The first type, of which Panku of Bohi is a typical example (see p. 160), has a long head, high cheek-bones—sometimes very high cheek-bones, a fine pointed face, pointed chin, small almost delicate nose not depressed at the root, narrow eyes and straight eye-slits, lips of medium thickness, and a slightly emphasized under-jaw.

The second type may be seen in the Plate facing p. 10 (Muria man). It is marked by a square head, and much coarser features. The cheek-bones are not so high, the nose is large with wide nostrils and is slightly depressed at the root. The eyes are larger, the lips of medium thickness but coarser, and there is a markedly retreating chin.

Baiga women are not attractive. They are dumpy, heavy, squat, with enormous thighs and calves, thick ankles, too short and stout for beauty.

[1] Ward: op. cit., p. 155.

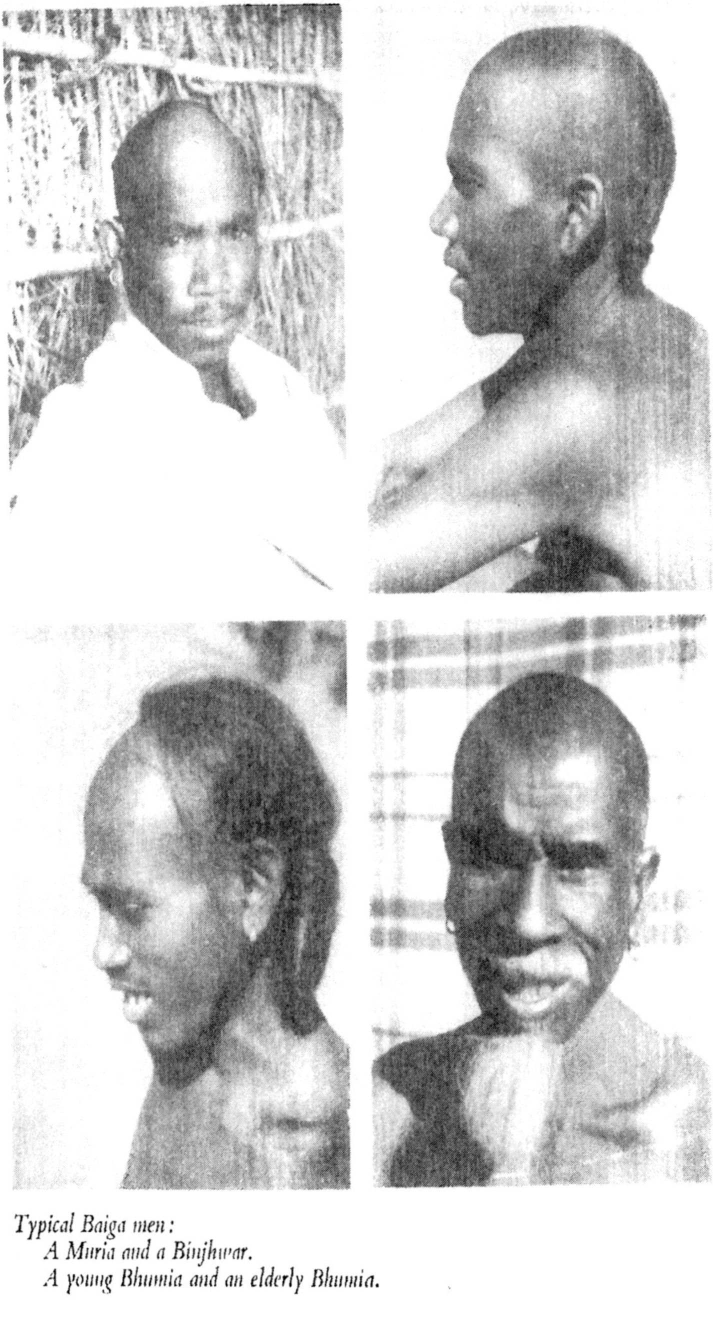

Typical Baiga men:
A Muria and a Binjhwar.
A young Bhumia and an elderly Bhumia.

They have in them more of Audrey than of Tess. They too fall naturally into two types. The first has an oval face, a fine nose not depressed at the root, a good pointed chin, medium cheek-bones, pretty mouth with medium lips, and small attractive eyes.

The second type, of which an excellent example is Mahi (see p. 160), has a square head and a noticeably flat face. The cheek-bones are not prominent. The forehead is flat, and low to medium in height. The nose is coarse and has a depressed root. The eyes are small and narrow. The mouth is sensitive, the lips not very thick. The chin is definite, and a little square.[1]

Of course, among so many women, some must be beautiful. A slight mixture of Gond blood makes a great difference to a Baigin's charms. Here and there you may see Baiga girls who are really lovely. The gentle charm of Pharria (a Muria of Amtera), the startling and unexpected beauty of Lumpi (another Muria, of Barkera), the troubled loveliness of Jindwa (a Bhumia of Mangela), the fresh vitality of Junhi (a Bhumia of Chauradadar), the exquisite carriage of Adri of Silpiri, Champi of Bohi, Baisakia of Lamni, little Phagni Bharotia of Jholar—these need no love-magic to reinforce their charms, and would hold their own with any Gond beauty. In any case, the Baiga admire Audrey as much as Tess. 'Even a young donkey,' they say, 'is lovely to its mate.'

V. CLOTHES AND ORNAMENTS

The clothes and ornaments of the Baiga have no special significance, for they neither spin nor weave, but buy their clothes from the local Panka or Mehera who weave cloth with mill-made yarn, and their ornaments from the bazaars. But I must give a brief account of what they wear, for in this they generally differ from their neighbours.

The orthodox Baiga tradition is to wear as little as possible. Bhagavan, it is remembered, gave Nanga Baiga a piece of cloth nine hands[2] long, but Nanga Baiga returned all but a hand and a half as unnecessary. Some of the older Baiga trace their present poverty to the wearing of clothes and shoes. The wilder Baiga, however, still wear exceedingly little. The men put on a very small dhoti, often it is only a *lingoti* with a broad flap which hangs down in front. This is sometimes made of the same pink-coloured

[1] I am indebted to Mrs. Milward for helping me to distinguish the two types of Baiga.

[2] A 'hand' or *hath* is the length of the fore-arm, measured from the elbow to the finger-tips. In English a 'hand' is 4 inches—the breadth of the extended palm; the Baiga 'hand' is a cubit.

cloth as the woman's *lugra*. In the cold, they tie a thick double cloth—the *kapchi*—round their shoulders. On the head is usually a rag called *patka* or *pharria*, but some of the well-to-do have a regular turban twenty hands long. Some, but very few, wear rather elaborate sandals called *bhadai*, or country shoes, made by the Chamar, but the majority go unshod. Boys wear a *pharria* rag round their loins.

In Niwas and Mandla, it is common now to see the *bandi* or *waskut*, a small waistcoat of white homespun or cheap black Japanese cloth. The Muria Baiga wear a small cloth round the loins but without the flap in front, after the Gond custom. The Binjhwar of Baihar dress in more or less Hindu fashion, in dhoti, shirt, coat or waistcoat, and wear the small round cap, the bamboo lining of which they make themselves.

Bhumia women wear a long strip of cloth called *chitra* or *lugra* tied round the waist, carried up across the breasts, over the right shoulder, and tucked in at the back. The skirt thus formed is often very short, not reaching to the knees. The head is left bare. Bharotia and Narotia women also wear the *lugra* like this, but Binjhwar and some Muria cover themselves up a bit more, wearing the *lugra* over both shoulders, sometimes over the head, and they tie the *kānch* in Gond fashion.

The wearing of the *kānch* is the most generally discussed difference between the various sections of Baiga. To wear the *kānch* means that one end of the *lugra* is brought down between the legs and tucked firmly in at the waist. It is tied very strongly. It is in fact worn something like a man's dhoti. The other method is to tie it like a skirt. The Baiga wear the *kānch* wherever Gond influence is strong. It is not a specially Hindu custom. The Hindu women of Gujerat and many women of the higher castes in the Baiga country do not tie it. Maharashtrian women do. The reason probably is that while Gujerat has been mainly a land of peace, Maharashtra has been the scene of many wars, where women might be raped or abducted and where the *kānch* might give them a slight additional protection, a chance to escape (for with the *kānch* it is much easier to run), or at least some psychological security. In the same way the Gond, an ancient and warlike race, made their women tie it, but the Baiga living in peace in the security of their jungles did not until some of them came under strong Gond influence.

Bhumia women do not wear the *choli* or bodice, but in Niwas some put on a jacket called *jhulāwa*. During the menstrual period they wear a small strip of cloth called the *chindhi* between the legs. It is tucked in at either end through the *kardhan* (relic of the old leaf-dress), the cord that is always worn about the waist, and is thus held in place.

Young girls wear a *lugri*, a small strip of cloth tied skirt-wise round the waist. After puberty, they throw the end of the *lugri* over the right shoulder. This is the *khandela*, and the girl is called *khandlāhin*—she is mature.

For ornament, men wear iron or silver bracelets, one on each wrist, called *chūra*. On the third and little fingers of either hand they may wear a *mundri* (ring) of brass, aluminium, silver, copper or gold. In their ears, they wear the *bāri* in the upper part, the *bāla* in a hole through the middle, and the *lurki* through the lobe. The *bāri* consists of blue and white beads strung on a circle of fine wire. The *bāla* is much the same only larger. The *lurki* is a small ring of gold or silver.

Old men do not usually wear anything; others dress up for festivals. Mahatu wears only an iron *sakri*, or chain, in which his deity resides. Yogi wears a necklace of black and red beads. Jethu has long since sold all his ornaments for liquor.

At dances the men wear a *kalgi* of peacocks' feathers stuck in the turban, and *chhūta*, a necklace of gay-coloured beads, round the neck. On their feet they put *paijna*, anklets with little bells. Sometimes they wear the *chhīt*, a red cloth tied round the head like a turban, and a special shirt called *jhanga*. Some wear a *neur* made of peacocks' feathers on the chest and back. But the young men may wear almost anything at a dance. They may put on any ornaments they can find; the *hawel* is specially popular.

Bhumia women wear the *dhār*, but without its characteristic chains. In the same hole in the lobe of the ear from which the *dhār* is worn, there is also put the *pola*, a thick round bit of wood, with a hole through the middle, which keeps the aperture open when other ornaments are not being worn. The *pola* may be made of leaves, the thin stock of a *tuma* gourd, or the stalk of maize. The *tarki* is a similar ornament but is faced with *lac*. The Baiga of Bilaspur sometimes wear the brass umbrella-shaped *kinwa* in their ears. To take these ornaments, the hole in the ear is very slowly enlarged. First, a single bit of grass is inserted, then another, then another. The little bundle may go on growing from three months to a year.

The Baiga never wear nose-ornaments. This is an important rule distinguishing them from other tribes, and the suggestion that a Baiga girl might perforate her nose is always treated as a huge joke.

For tying the hair, they use the woollen *phundara* or sometimes the silk *jhela*. Very rarely they wear a silver *mangchirni* across the head in the manner of the Gond *bindia*.

Round the neck is the *chhūta*, a necklace of vari-coloured beads, worn rather tightly: the *sutia*, a large round silver torc; the *hawel*, a necklace of silver coins—lucky coins which bear the king's head—which hangs down to the breasts. Other necklaces are the *kanthi*—of black beads; the *latkania*—of red, blue and yellow; and the *guria bichuli*—a series of coloured squares.

They wear *mundri* on the fingers and bangles called *chūra* or *pattā*. On the feet, *chūra* are also worn; these are called *tin-kor*, they are heavy brass anklets with wide rings. The *pairi* are often celebrated in the songs: ornamented brass or silver anklets that slip down over the heel—they have *ghungru*, or little bits of metal inside to make them tinkle. On the toes are worn *chutki*, and a *chutka* on the big toe.

Different sections of Baiga may easily be distinguished by their ornaments. The Bhumia wear least of all—for though the above list is a description of their standard decorations, they rarely wear more than one or two of them. Only the Bhumia generally wear the heavy brass *tin-kor* round their ankles. The Bharotia are distinguished by wearing only brass bangles, a lot of them; the highest up the arm, bigger than the others, is called the *darakna*. The others are the *kaknāhi*.[1] They do not wear the *tarki* or any ornaments faced with *lac*. The Narotia, however, do wear the *tarki*, but only very rarely brass bangles. They prefer coloured glass which is never worn by Bharotia. Muria and Binjhwar wear ordinary glass or aluminium bangles. The Kath-bhaina wear brass bangles with a single glass bangle for variety.

In Niwas the Chhota Bhumia wear the *tikli* or spangle on the forehead, but I have never seen a Bara Bhumia or a Bharotia with it.

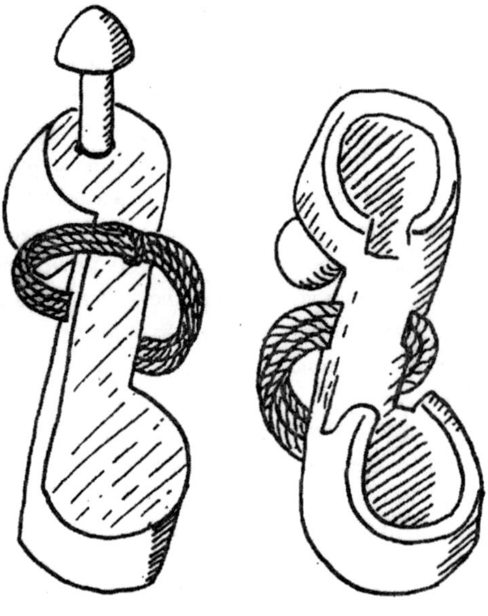

FIG. 1. *Kharaut.*

[1] Perhaps from the Gondi *kaikana* (belonging to the hands) or the Sanskrit *kankan* the wristlet worn at the time of marriage.

These are, I think, the main differences in dress and ornament between the various sub-tribes of Baiga. These depend, in the main, not on Hindu, but on Gond influence. I have not described them at great length since except for the customs regulating the tying of the *kānch* and the avoidance of nose-ornaments, there is little that is specifically Baiga in character. That is to be expected of a tribe which has never had a tradition of clothing or personal adornment, but has obviously taken to these things as a result of contact with Gond and Hindu civilization.

For protection from the rain, a wicker hood lined with mohlain[1] leaves, the *khumra* or *khumri*, is worn over the head, and a rough blanket is tied across the shoulders, with a big knot just below the chin.

In the rains, wooden clogs called *kharaut* are worn. These stand about two and a half inches off the ground, and are hollow underneath. The toes grip a peg, and the foot is held in position by string. This is shown in Fig. 1.

For carrying money or tobacco, the Baiga use a number of little bags. Women wear the small knitted 'secret' *gupti* round their necks: they make this themselves, and put money in it. Men also use the *gupti*, but the long knitted *basni* tied round the waist is more popular. The *thaili* is another kind of bag for money: it is made of woven cloth or of sambhar skin.

For everything to do with smoking, the *pissai* pouch (made of skin, cloth, or woven string) is the Baiga's invariable companion. Less common is the *thondi*, a length of hollow bamboo closed at the lower end, which is hung from the waist. Tobacco may be kept in this, and sometimes money.

VI. HAIR-DRESSING

In a later chapter we will see the very important part that the hair plays in the erotic life of the Baiga. Here we will briefly examine their customs of hair-dressing.

It is the Bhumia who pay the greatest attention to their hair. Their habit is either to wear it long, allowing it to fall freely over the head, or to shave the front part of the crown, cutting it back into a perfectly straight line. In both cases the hair at the back is allowed to grow very long and is tied into a *jūra*, or bun, which hangs down on the left side of the head. Some of the older Baiga have immensely long pig-tails that are tied up in this way. Latti of Rupnidadar has a long tail of dead-looking brownish hair, in strong contrast to the dark-black colour of the rest. 'It is always growing by the power of the gods,' he told me. 'Once I watched it growing before my eyes one night. All kinds of

[1] *Bauhinia rahlii*

different hair are mixed up with it by magic.' And Pattu of Ajghardaba said to some young men, 'How will you ever get hair like mine if you part it and try to show off before the girls?' The Bharotia have the same custom, but they allow the bun to hang down straight behind.

The Narotia and Binjhwar do not tie the hair in a bun, but simply keep a small tuft or *chutti* hanging down in Gond fashion. The Muria shave the head altogether, leaving a small tuft. This is knotted as a protection against snake-bite and the attacks of evil spirits. A gunia must undo the knot before beginning his work, or no spirit will be able to approach him.

The hair is cut with a razor obtained from the local Agaria. No Nai (barber) may touch a Baiga's head. Only a fellow Baiga, and sometimes a Gond, may shave it on pain of excommunication. The chin is usually shaved, but at present little goatee beards are fashionable among the Baiga of Pandaria. Moustaches are generally worn.

Women do not cut their hair. The younger women have a special method, different from the Hindu or Gond, of tying their hair. Parting it neatly in the middle, a girl lets it fall down behind. She gathers it in one hand and ties it round, high up near the head, two or three times with a coloured woollen *phundara* or a bit of cord. Then she folds the hair upwards, so that the fold covers the neck. She puts the *kakai* (comb) inside the fold, and continues to tie the hair in the same place. Finally she allows the rather untidy flap (*jhela*) of hair to fall back over the bun thus formed.

Old women simply twist their hair round and round, in male fashion, into a little knot (*jūra*).

Baiga girls are very fond of their little wooden combs. Often a girl hangs two or three of these round her neck, tokens from various admirers. *Ghī* is rubbed into the hair to make it glossy, but oil is seldom used. Armpits are shaved and the pubic hair removed, by both men and women: otherwise a man's virility passes into it, and is lost. The pubic hair is not shaved: wood-ash is rubbed in, and a few hairs are removed at a time. Women generally do this for one another.

The comb is useful for removing lice. A wife often examines her husband's head for lice. If she catches one she kills it between her two nails. This is illustrated by the riddle—'Ten went for the hunt, but two did the killing.'

The Baiga do not generally use either hair or nail-parings in magic, and so they are not concerned about throwing away cut ends of hair. It is only the *chutti* that has a magical significance.

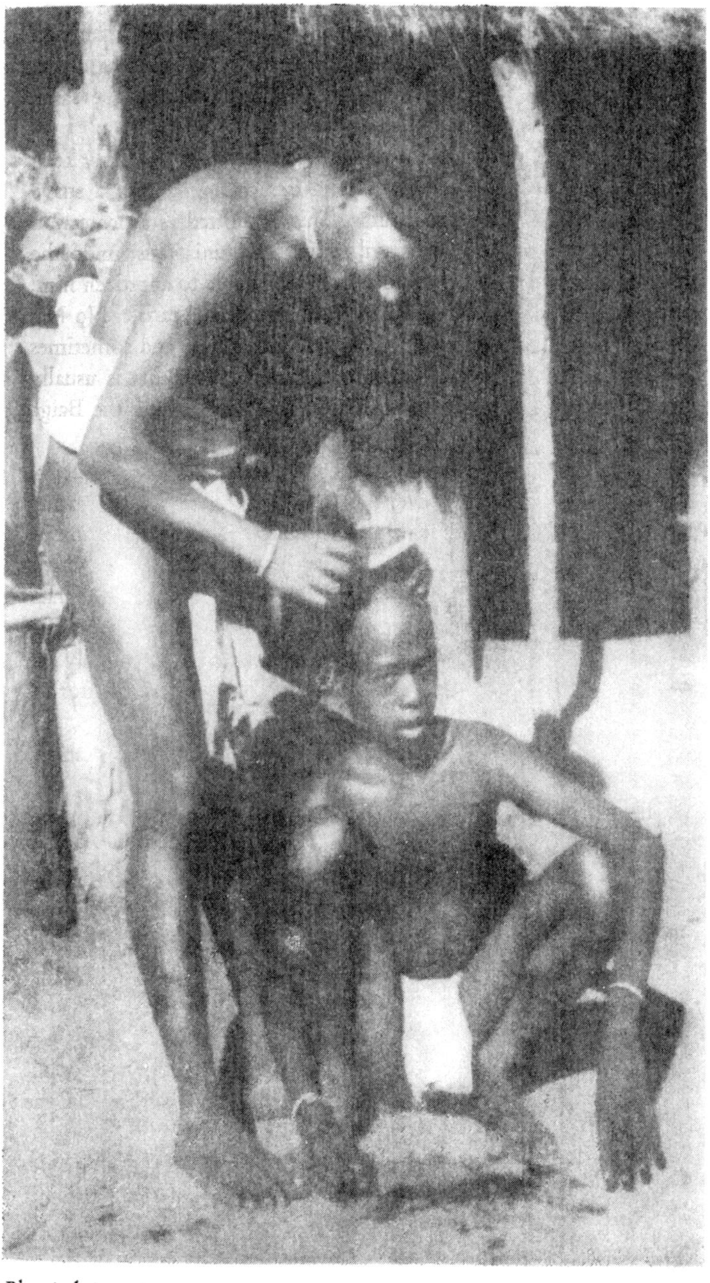

Bhumia hair-cutting.

VII. BATHING

The Baiga are generally credited with the belief that if they wash they will be eaten by tigers. 'One article of a Bygah's creed,' says Lawrence in his Settlement Report, 'is that if he washes himself tigers will eat him or snakes will bite him.'[1] And Thomson, writing about the same time (1867) says that 'they hardly seem to understand the use of water except for drinking, and are filthy in their persons'.[2] A lawyer who had many dealings with them told me that 'their bodies are as dirty as their hearts are clean'.

I myself have not found that their hearts are so clean or their bodies so dirty as is generally supposed. The Baiga certainly do not believe that they will be eaten by tigers as a punishment for washing. What they do believe is that if they wash themselves with water after defecation, they may be eaten by a tiger. This is one of their most particular beliefs; it comes down from the days of Nanga Baiga himself who always cleaned himself with leaves and won the heart of Thakur Deo by showing him the result.[3] Some of the Muria and Binjhwar Baiga now use water like the Gond, but they admit they are inferior to the true Baiga on account of it.

The Baiga generally gives an impression of cleanliness. The younger men who are in the hey-dey of their erotic adventures are indeed very careful about their personal appearance and keep themselves scrupulously tidy. The older people are more careless. The general rule is that 'we bathe when our hair becomes matted. That is the sign. Then we go to the stream, undo the bun and clean it with white mud'. They wash by throwing water over their shoulders, with their hands or a gourd. Where the river is deep enough they have a swim; but generally only those who live near a river learn how to swim, 'like dogs, patting the water'. They can swim about fifty yards; 'then our thighs get weary'. It is common for Baiga to be drowned during the rains. Women bathe at least once every month, at the close of the menstrual period. It would probably, however, be safe to say that nowadays both men and women bathe every four or five days. 'We used to bathe only once a year,' Jethu told me. 'Then we were full of magic.'

The morning toilet is often performed with the help of a gourd. It is filled with water from a pitcher and the stem is held between the chin and

[1] A. J. Lawrence: *Report of the Land Revenue Settlement of the Bhundara District* (Bombay, 1867), p. 54.

[2] Thomson: op. cit., p. 39.

[3] See p. 322.

shoulder, the head on one side, and the water is tipped out by appropriate movements of the body on to the hands or feet. In the old days, the Baiga never cleaned their teeth. Now they use twigs of sarai[1], jamun[2] or harra[3]—but not saj[4]: 'for the saj is the home of Bara Deo, and we were born beneath it.' If they break a twig for this purpose and lose it, they do not break another on the same day. 'We take the first from the tree with love: if we take another, it will be an injury.'

Many of the Bhumia do not wash their hands before food. But the Binjhwar do, and so do those Muria and others who have come under Gond influence.

The Baiga wash their clothes about once a month. They do this by putting the cloth into a pot with water and a few handfuls of fine wood-ash. They allow this to boil thoroughly, and then take the clothes to the nearest stream and wash them out, pounding them with their hands and—if the cloth is very thick—beating it against a stone, or with a stick called the *kutela*.

They cannot afford to wash their clothes more frequently, for fear of wearing them out. The result is that those who wear many clothes suffer greatly from itch. The real naked Baiga are much the healthier.

VIII. TATTOOING

The ethnographer who hopes to find tribal or esoteric significance in the tattoo-marks that so liberally adorn the bodies of Baiga women is doomed to disappointment.

'One thing is certain,' says Luard on tattooing in Central India generally, 'and that is that the wearers of these devices only look upon them as ornamental and decorative devices, with no deeper significance'.[5] If by 'deeper significance' are meant such fancies as that the tattoo-marks represent totem animals or are a form of sympathetic magic to save the wearer from the animals portrayed on her body, this is probably true. But for the Baiga the marks have another and much more serious significance. They are a form of sexual expression and a powerful sexual stimulant.

This is partly indicated by the fact that a girl's arms and breasts are not tattooed until she is adolescent, nor her legs until her marriage. There is also no doubt that tattooing greatly enhances a girl's beauty in the eyes of Baiga menfolk. 'When she is well tattooed, then our sinful eyes declare

[1] *Boswellia serrata.* [2] *Eugenia jambolana.* The wilder Baiga call it *jām.* [3] *Terminalia chebula.* [4] The saj (*terminalia tomentosa*) is the traditional home of Bara Deo.

[5] Luard: *Tattooing in Central India* (Bombay, 1905), p. 1.

her beautiful.' 'It is instead of ornaments, it is to make her beautiful.' 'A light-coloured girl needs it; how lovely she looks when she wears bangles that match the line of tattooing!' I asked a girl once what her marks meant, and she replied in one word 'Desire!'

It is possible also that tattooing has to do with the skin-eroticism which is a strong sexual agent in Baiga love-making.

Women themselves take a great pride in their tattoo-marks. Mahi[1], who only was able to spend five rupees on hers, yet boasts frequently of her mother who paid twenty-five and was apparently tattooed from head to foot. Women like being tattooed, partly because they know it increases their attractiveness to their men, and partly because of its permanence. This, I think, is a quite genuine sentiment; one thing at least is lasting in a world of changing husbands, changing settlements and shifting cultivation. A Dadaria says,

> If you buy bangles, my daughter, they will break in a few days;
> But if you are tattooed, it will last for ever.

Among the Dhandha, tattoo-marks are described as 'eggs laid by a black bird which we can't pick up', 'a black dog that casts no shadow,' and 'a jacket that can never be taken off'. 'These marks,' said Phulmat, 'are the only things that are certain to go with us to the grave and beyond it.' There is also a theory that the ornaments tattooed on the body can be sold after death. On the back appears the figure called *dhandha* which is simply six dots joined together by lines. Malho told me that after death Bhagavan took everything from them, but if there was one *dhandha* on the back he couldn't solve, then he had to put that mark on the child into whose body the *jīv* would be re-incarnated.

Men are seldom tattooed, but they sometimes put the *chandrama* (moon) on the back of the hand and the *bichhu* (scorpion) on the fore-arm. Sometimes they tattoo themselves on the affected parts in order to cure rheumatism; they say that the treatment is effective.

The operation itself is performed by a Badnin, whom the Baiga call Godnaharin, though both men and women do the *chandrama* and the *bichhu* for themselves. The Baiga also prepare the ink; they take the cast skin of any snake (though the *domi* snake is preferred) and burn it; then they burn black til[2] and mix it with some ramtilla[3] oil and the powdered snake-skin. The needles are bought at any bazaar. The process is, of course, very painful, and part of the pride shown by the Baiga women in their adorning may be due to the memory of suffering courageously endured. 'They

[1] The life-stories of most of my informants will be found in Chapter IV.

[2] *Sesamum indicum.* [3] *Guzotia abyssinica.* The ink may also be made with soot mixed with the burnt bark of *pterocarpus marsupium.*

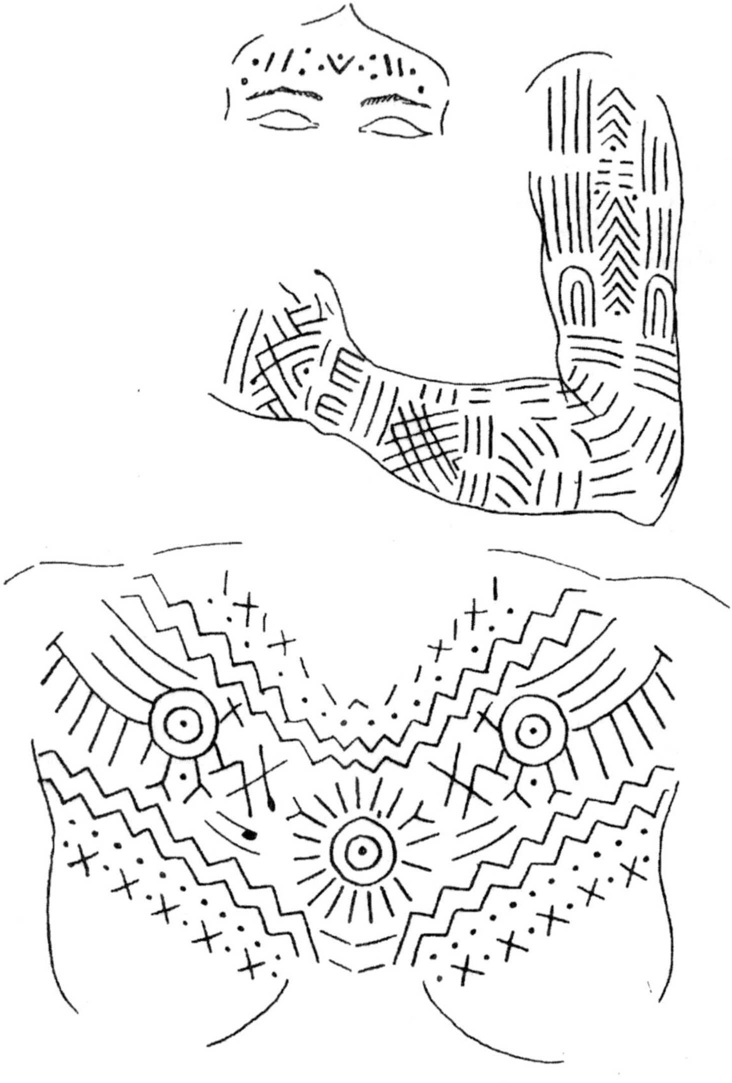

Characteristic tattooing on a Bhumia woman.

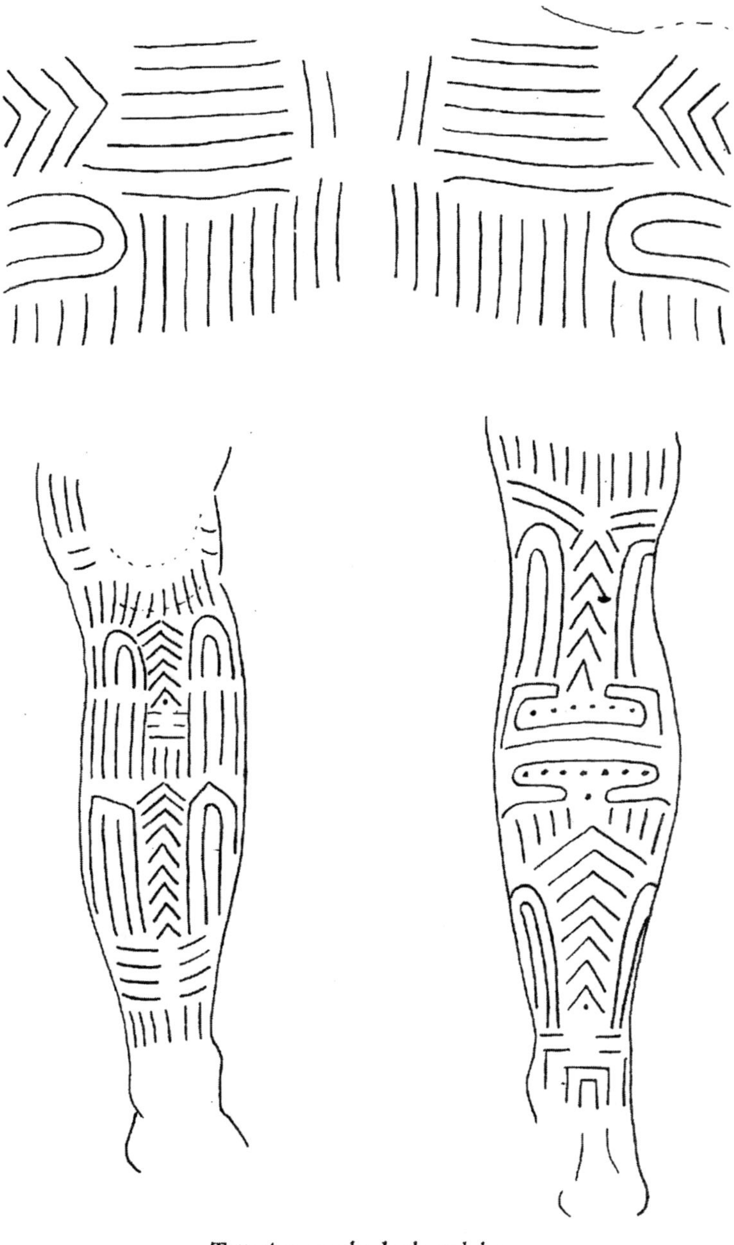

Tattooing on the back and legs.

scream hard,' observed old Malho with grim satisfaction. 'We don't give them any drugs. It hurts for seven or eight days and swells up. Then it gets all right, and they find they have something that no one will ever take away from them.' When a girl screams, the old women laugh at her and say, 'If you cannot bear *godan* (tattooing), how will you endure *chodan* (intercourse)?'

A curious rule forbids the husband to watch the operation. The girl is treated as though she were in her monthly period for two days afterwards. Then her body is covered with turmeric and oil, and she bathes. If her husband watches her, or if she fails to get tattooed at all, Bhagavan will dig holes all over her body with an iron bar after her death.

The usual marks tattooed on a Baiga woman are these: a triangular decoration is made on the forehead when a Baiga girl is about five years old. On the breast is a peacock, or a *dauri* (basket) and on the arm the *haldi-gāth* (the turmeric root). These are done when the girl reaches puberty. At the time of marriage or later, a *jhophari* (a pattern of any kind) may be made on the back of the hand, the lines of dots known as *palāni* or *kajeri* on the thighs, and in between the *palāni* the *bail ankhi*. On the knee is the *phulia*, round like a flower, and on the back are flies, men, the *sakri* or magic chain, and the *dhandha* which we have already described. On the legs are fish-bones and the *chakmak* (steel).

Up to marriage the cost of all tattooing is born by the girl's mother. She pays one anna for the mark on the forehead, four annas for each arm and four annas for the breasts. After marriage, it is the father-in-law who pays for the girl, eight annas for each thigh, four annas for each leg, and five annas for the back. In view of these low prices it is not easy to see how Mahi's mother managed to spend twenty-five rupees on herself, but possibly there is a higher tariff for fancy work.

The drawings on pp. 20 and 21 show the markings on the strapping light-skinned Jitho of Bohi village, and were recorded for me by Mrs. Milward. They may be taken as fairly typical, certainly for all Bhumia, though the other *jāt* have slightly different patterns of the forehead.

IX. THE BAIGA VILLAGE

A typical Baiga village gives an impression of a strong and vital corporate life. It is not bound together by an exacting code of reciprocal obligations between kin, nor by a common loyalty to some dictatorial chief; but it is vitalized by a vivid consciousness of the tribal idea, a devotion to Mother Earth, and an adherence to Baiga law.

Elaborate Binjhwar house (Bondhwa).
Corner of Bhumia village (Bohi).

The plan of the village fosters this impression of energy, equality and corporate loyalty. Unlike the Gond, the Baiga build their villages either in the form of a large square, or with houses lining the sides of a broad street some thirty feet across. The Gond build their houses in separate enclosures; each home is the embodiment of their individualistic, litigous, suspicious, secretive character. The Baiga village expresses the friendly, open-hearted, honest, communistic nature of the tribe.

The Baiga have an eye for a good site. They set their villages in places convenient for bewar, but it is hard to believe that aesthetic considerations are ignored; it would be difficult to find places more charming than Bohi by its waterfall with a view of undulating hills dense with forest, Ledra Taliapani on the edge of the cliff looking down on the distant Maniari Lake, Daharkata on its heaven-kissing hill with clear and open distances around, Rupnidadar visited by every wind, vistas of great beauty just visible between its surrounding trees, Amadob in the quiet forest glades.

The ordinary Bhumia village is always remote. 'Buried as they are in the heart of the jungles,' says Colonel Ward, 'these villages are very difficult to find; for one is on the top of a high hill, and the next will be low down in the valley between two ranges of high hills. Inspection among these people was no easy work.'[1] That was one reason why the Baiga went there. If possible they build their villages at the top of some steep, almost perpendicular pass, reached only by narrow foot-paths along which a party must walk in single file. Often, in order to avoid making obvious tracks leading to their villages, Baiga avoid the paths.

The village boundary is usually marked by a strip of cleared land twenty or thirty yards broad, emphasized at critical points by piles of stones. The boundary, *mero*, as it is called, is the Baiga's special province. In most villages, the *marghat* or burying-place is just inside the boundary. It is to the boundary that all the diseases are carried at the Bida ceremony and thrown away. It is at the *mero* that nails must be driven to shut the mouths of tigers. The Baiga, in fact, must reinforce the official boundaries by a magic wall which he builds against the raids of wild animals and the spread of disease.

The Bhumia village is built round a large square. Generally three sides of this are closed by houses, and the fourth is open to the air, but fenced with bamboo or a cactus-hedge. Often there are little groups of houses at some distance from the main square. Sometimes, the shape of the village is a long rectangle, as in Lamni; sometimes, as in Daharkata, there are two large squares joined by a road. Each side of the square consists of six or seven huts, which look at first sight as if they were all built on to one another.

[1] Ward: op. cit., p. 159.

But this is not so. Each house is a detached residence, with a narrow passage separating it from its neighbour. This is the *godri* which leads to the *nakni* where people go to urinate by night.

All round the square outside are the strips of garden-land known as the *bāri*, where the people grow tobacco, sweet potatoes or maize. The *gūda*, or pigs' houses, are not in the garden, but inside the square, often in front of the houses and built on to them. The *sār*, or cattle-sheds, form part of the line of huts in the square, and it is not always easy to distinguish them from the human habitations.

There is no house for the gods, though sometimes a tall pole is erected in front of the chief gunia's house. If there is a *madhia* or a shrine for Dharti Mata or Thakur Deo this is generally built at some distance from the village. There are no bachelors' dormitories or corporate houses, no menstruation huts and no special granaries. There are often, however, tall platforms (*mācha*) erected in the middle or at the side of the square for drying and storing maize. Tobacco is spread on the roof and dried there. Other grain is put out on cots in the sun.

Outside the square is a small hut, or *chatti*, for the use of travellers or officials. It generally consists of two rooms, without doors, and a small stable. It stands in its own compound fenced with bamboo.

These squares are generally very clean, and in spite of the tumbledown houses have an attractive appearance. There may be a slight odour of pigs'-dung, but the pigs themselves play a large part in keeping the village clean and sanitary. From time to time the children make piles of rubbish which they burn with great delight. Refuse is normally thrown behind the house into the compound, where it serves as a manure.

This is the normal arrangement of a Bhumia village. But the Bhaina villages of Bilaspur follow the same model, so do many Bharotia and Narotia villages in Balaghat. Col. Ward found this plan common throughout Mandla.

Very often these squares are dominated by one family, and most of the other households are related to it. Those who are not related build their houses in little groups at some distance from the main centre.

For example, in the accompanying plan (Fig. 2), we have a sketch of the Baiga square in the predominantly Gond village of Hirapur in Baihar. House A is occupied by Bahadur himself and his three wives and adopted son. House B belongs to the brother of Bahadur's middle wife. He lives here with his wife and five children. House C is for cattle belonging to Bahadur. House D belongs to Namu, Bahadur's son-in-law, who lives here with his mother's elder sister's daughter, his father and mother (who are Bahadur's *samdhi* and always useful in emergency) and his three sons

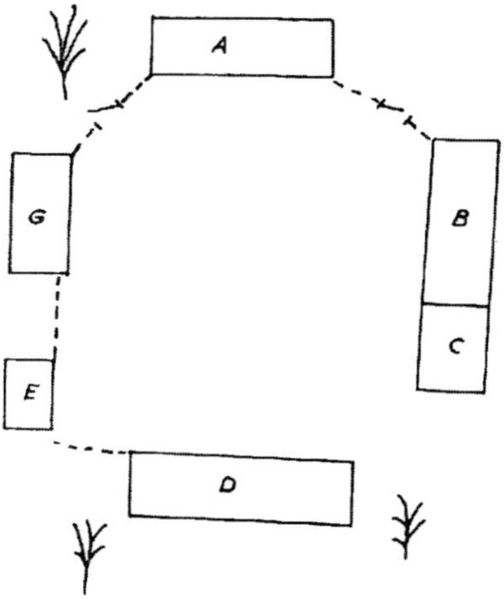

FIG. 2. *Baiga-Tola of Hirapur.*

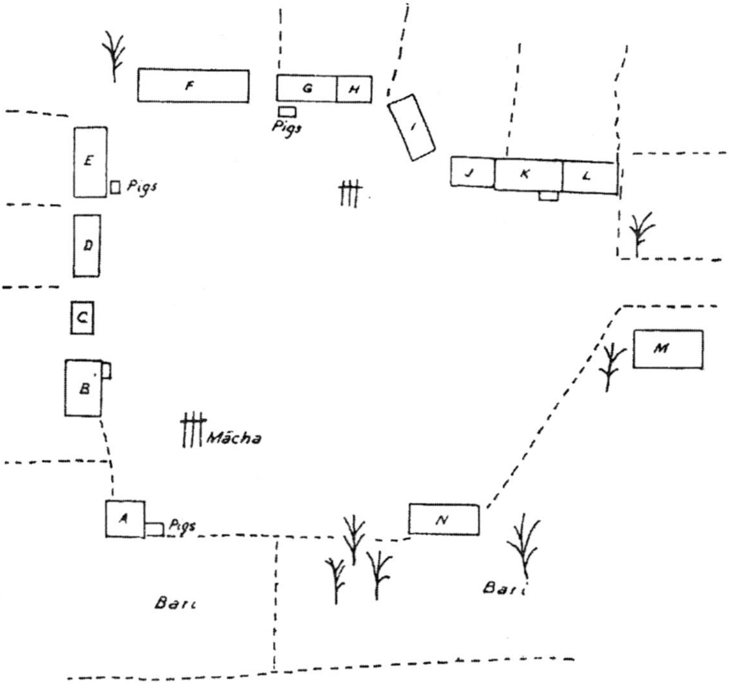

FIG. 3. *Rough Plan of Rupnidadar.*

(who are Bahadur's classificatory grandsons). In house E lives Bahadur's son-in-law's brother Karu and his wife and two children. House F is a Guest House built by Bahadur for important visitors. All these houses belong to Bahadur, for they have all been built on a piece of ground belonging to him. But each of the three families who occupy them own their own bits of land for which they pay rent direct to Government. Bahadur has no right to take rent from his relations for their houses, but though he denies it I have very little doubt that he does so. The compound belongs entirely to Bahadur, and everybody has to work for him in it.

The second plan (Fig. 3), illustrates the lay-out of Rupnidadar, a Bhumia village in Pandaria. Here the main square is entirely dominated by Chidi the headman. The houses are distributed as follows:

House A. The headman's son-in-law, Tok.
House B. The headman's son, Mahutu.
House C. Cattle.
House D. The headman's son-in-law, Nandwa.
House E. The headman's eldest son, Buka.
House F. Cattle.
House G. Chidi the headman.
House H. The headman's youngest son, Banu.
House I. The headman's son, Pirtu.
House J. A servant, Gela.
House K. Cattle.
House L. Buka, an old man, no relation.
House M. The *chatti* for officials.
House N. Dhan Singh, a classificatory 'brother'.

Here each of the headman's relatives owns his own property, the house is his and he has his own *bewar*. The headman's house is in no way distinguished from the others, but he is recognized as the secular head of the village, and as such commands a good deal of authority and respect.

The plan of Bohi (Fig. 4), illustrates not only the lay-out of a typical Baiga village, but shows how each section of it centres round some leading individual. Houses 1–14 are all related to Jethu, 16–20 to Badu, 21–25 to Bijare.

Where Gond influence has been strong, the Baiga lay out their villages and plan their houses in Gond fashion. Most Binjhwar and Muria villages, and some Bhumia villages in Niwas, together with some Bharotia and Narotia villages are formed on the Gond model. That is to say, each house stands in its own compound, entirely separate and aloof from other houses. Sometimes there is a family group of houses approaching the Baiga model.

FIG. 4. *Plan of Bohi*

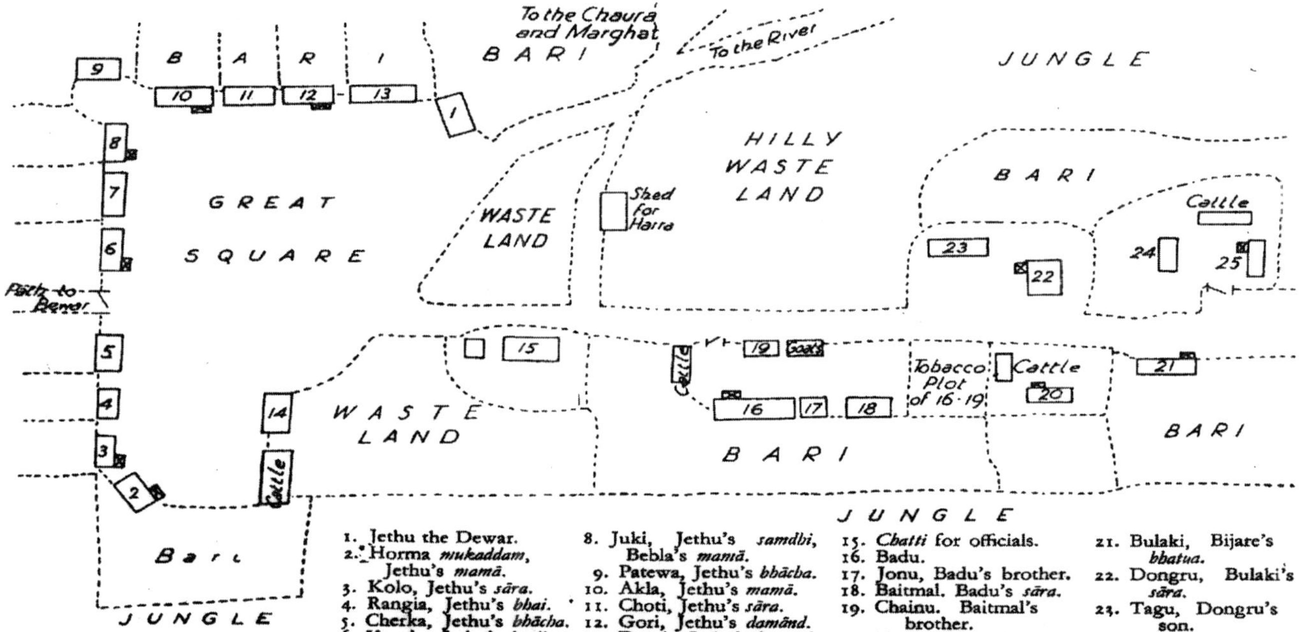

1. Jethu the Dewar.
2. *Horma *mukaddam*, Jethu's *mamā*.
3. Kolo, Jethu's *sāra*.
4. Rangia, Jethu's *bhai*.
5. Cherka, Jethu's *bhācha*.
6. Konda, Jethu's *batija*.
7. Bebla, Jethu's *bhai*.
8. Juki, Jethu's *samdhi*, Bebla's *mamā*.
9. Patewa, Jethu's *bhācha*.
10. Akla, Jethu's *mamā*.
11. Choti, Jethu's *sāra*.
12. Gori, Jethu's *damānd*.
13. Deruja, Jethu's *damānd*.
14. Tanwa, Jethu's *bhai*.
15. *Chatti* for officials.
16. Badu.
17. Jonu, Badu's brother.
18. Baitmal. Badu's *sāra*.
19. Chainu. Baitmal's brother.
20. Torri, Baitmal's brother.
21. Bulaki, Bijare's *bhatua*.
22. Dongru, Bulaki's *sāra*.
23. Tagu, Dongru's son.
24. Bijare, the *Diwan*.
25. Chamra, Bijare's son.

Sometimes, as at Arhwai in Baihar, there is not even a street connecting the houses; sometimes, as in Amtera, the houses are all on top of one another, the compound being grouped round the main mass of buildings.

In the Lamta Zemindari, I saw some Binjhwar villages, Khaira for example and Salang Tola, which were almost exactly like the Gond villages I have seen in Betul and Chhindwara. A narrow street runs through the village, and on either side are houses, raised a little from the level of the street, and standing well back from it, each with a small fenced compound in front and a garden behind.

In the majority of cases the Bharotia houses, even when scattered, have one house to each enclosure. The Binjhwar and Muria, like the Gond, build three or four houses in a small square and enclose it.

Shifting cultivation means shifting villages, and in the old days the Baiga were constantly on the move. Even to-day they not infrequently change the sites of their villages, though they have been considerably restricted by the organization of the country under its successive settlements. When they decide on a new site, they measure out the land for the first house with string. If the string is too short or too long it means that 'Dharti Mata is not willing to grant the land and we must go elsewhere'. When they have found the right spot they 'settle which side shall be the cook-room and see where the rubbish can be put out'. Then they fix a pole with a thorn-bush tied to it, and in the hole dug for it, they put five grains of rice, some turmeric and a pice, saying, 'O Dharti Mata, give us one pice worth of land!'

X. THE BAIGA HOUSE

Unless you put a pillar in the middle of the house, and poles on the side, can the gunia build it by his magic?—Baiga Proverb.

The Bhumia or Bharotia house, indeed the typical Baiga house everywhere, is very simple, generally tumbledown and dilapidated. This is due to the fact that the Baiga never seem to think it necessary to finish off their walls properly with the coating of mud and whitewash which makes even the poorest Gond house attractive. The miserable look of a Baiga house is not due to poverty, but to indifference. In the forest villages, all the simple materials that are needed for a large and imposing building may be taken from the jungle free of charge—a few heavy wood pillars, some poles, split bamboo, some lengths of bark, a quantity of thatching grass, mud, cow-dung and white earth—the majority of Baiga can obtain these things without payment. But they are of nomad blood. They cannot take a building seriously. In the old days they pulled down a house and built a new one every few years. Even to-day they are always on the move. There is no incitement to build. And so while Gond of equal financial position build large and comfortable houses, the Baiga are content with hovels, with broken walls and uneven floors.

The ground plan (Fig. 5) of a typical Bhumia house in Pandaria, Kawardha and Dindori, which holds good also throughout the Baiga country for the more nomadic families, is very simple.

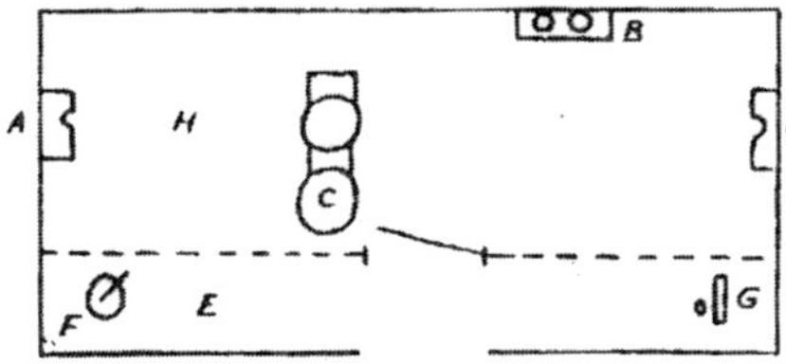

FIG. 5.

A. Hearth for cooking.
B. Stand for water-pots.
C. Row of grain-bins dividing house into two rooms.
D. Hearth for fire used for light and warmth.
E. Verandah.
F. Grindstone.
G. Rice-husker.
H. Inner Room.
I. Outer Room.

In other parts of the Baiga country there are variations on this plan, especially where the Baiga have come under Gond influence.

The chief differences between a Baiga and a Gond house are these: the Baiga house is generally part of a row of buildings and is separated from its neighbours by a narrow passage two or three feet wide. The Gond house stands in its own compound, separate from others. The Gond make substantial walls of mud and plaster them with cow-dung and white earth. The Baiga do not use whitewash, sometimes do not even use cow-dung, and often plaster only the inside of their walls or leave them altogether bare.

The Gond generally build three little huts in a square, one for cooking, one for eating and one a bedroom. They do not like to sleep and cook in the same room. Every married couple should have a separate room, so that if a son and his wife are living with the parents, they build on a fourth house, thus completing the square. The Baiga generally have only one house to a family, and everyone must cook, sleep and eat in the same place.

In the settled Binjhwar and Muria villages, in those Bharotia and Narotia villages that are laid out on the Gond model, and even in some Bhumia villages in Niwas, the houses often tend to conform to the Gond type. For example, this (Fig. 6) is a plan of Baghela Muria's house at Barkera in Niwas.

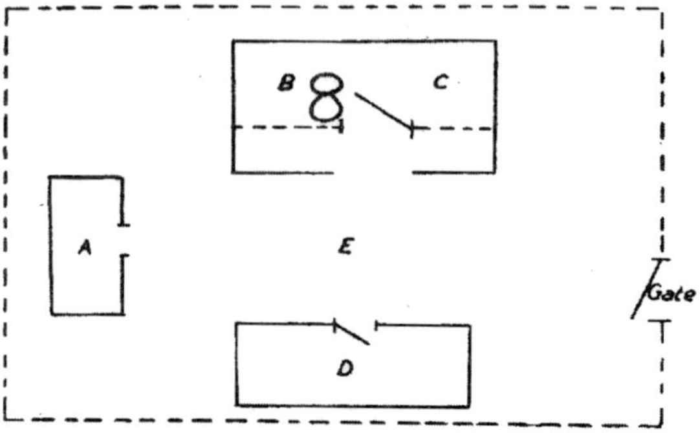

FIG. 6.

A. Cattle-shed.
B. Kitchen.
C. Eating-room.
D. Room for sleeping, etc.
E. Courtyard.

In the following sketch (Fig. 7) is represented the house of a Bhumia Baiga of Niwas. It is Har Bhajan's house at Mangela. He has his two sons and their wives still living with him. Gond influence is seen in the fact that the house stands by itself in its own compound, and the three families have separate rooms, with a common water-supply and kitchen. In a Bhumia village in Pandaria, they would all be living in one small hut. The walls of Har Bhajan's house are thickly plastered with mud and white-washed. They are decorated with animals, and the door-posts have a zigzag ornamentation in red. The doors are all of solid wood and are fastened with chains and padlocks.

In Baihar the Binjhwar and Bharotia houses are distinguished by the fact that they have doors both back and front and some have quite large windows. The ground-plan of Bahadur's house is given below (Fig. 8). It will be noticed that the house has two verandahs, in front and behind, two wooden doors, and a large roofed-in space in front where people can sit and talk. On the roof is tobacco, maize and grass drying; the maize is sheltered by leaf-covers called *puri*. Here there is no pigsty (for Bahadur does not approve of pigs), but a *dongi*—a small trough on a trestle—provides food for his cows. To one side are two tall poles decorated with peacocks' feathers for Matia Deo and Marhai Deo.

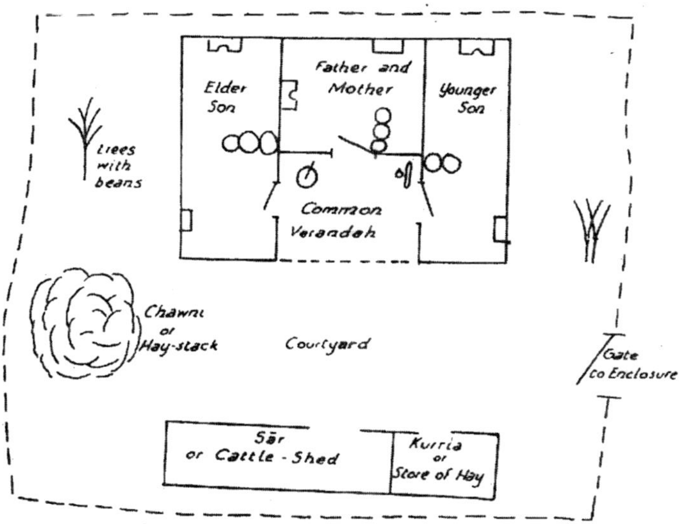

FIG. 7. *Plan of Bhumia house in Niwas.*

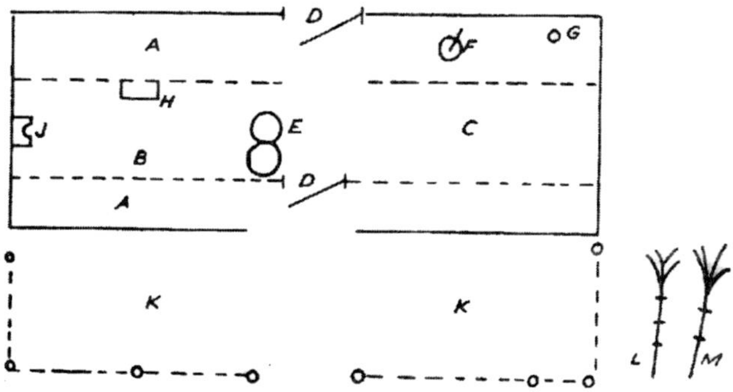

FIG. 8. *Plan of Bahadur's house.*

A. Verandahs.
B. Kitchen.
C. Bedroom.
D. Doors.
E. Earthen bins that divide the house into two.
F. Rice-husker.
G. Grindstone.
H. Stand for water-pots.
J. Hearth for cooking.
K. Open but sheltered meeting-place.
L & M. Matia and Marhai.

One of the most attractive Baiga houses I have seen is in Bhondwa in Balaghat (Fig. 9). It belongs to a very dignified old man named Ghuri Binjhwar, and has a Deogarh in its compound, a thing I have not seen elsewhere.

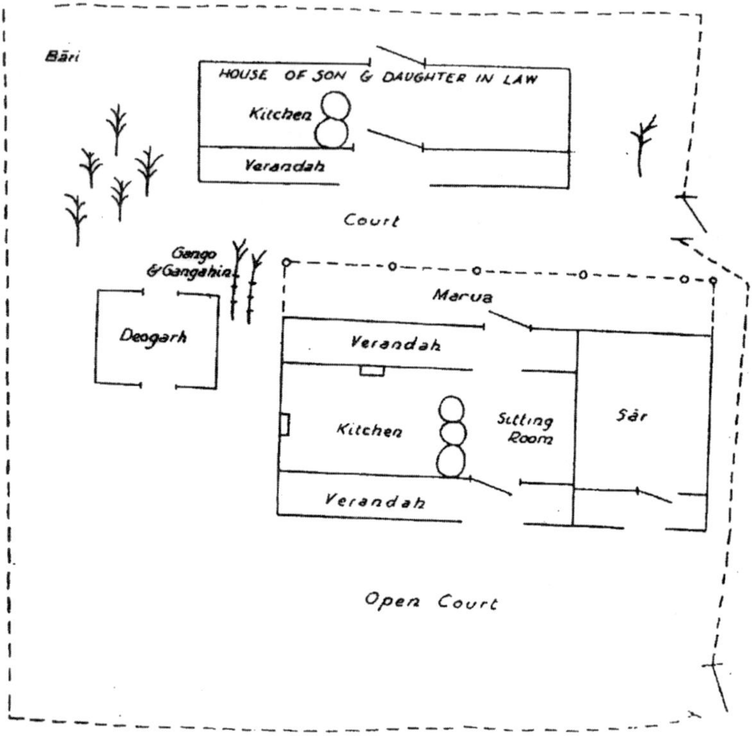

FIG. 9. *Plan of Ghuri's House at Bhondwa in Balaghat.*

But of these only the first is a typical Baiga house. In describing the details of construction, I will confine myself to what seems to me the standard Baiga house, whose plan appears on page 29, a simple rectangular box with a small verandah in front and a single door.

This kind of house is built up round a single central pillar, the *barendi-thūnhi*, which has a forked top. Resting on this is a long pole, the roof-tree, or *churla*, which is supported at either end by the *dadawaria thūnhi*. These three central pillars are seven or eight feet high. The side walls which are four or five feet high, are supported by *dābi thūnhi*, small stout poles three or four feet apart, with forked tops on which rest the *patotī* poles. From the *churla* to the *patoti* poles are laid a number of *malga* or *karoti* poles, about one foot apart, to carry the roof or *thāth*.

The roof consists of a bamboo framework called *bhadri* which is generally made on the ground, and then hoisted into its place where it is supported by the *malga*. Once in position a thatch of grass,[1] known as the *sapsen*, is tied on to it with the bark-rope called *bandhna*. To prevent the roof being blown away, it is tied down with this rope or weighed with heavy logs and stones called *ladna*.

The walls are made of long pieces of *chhirra* straw neatly arranged in lines and tied in place with strips of bark, or of split bamboo roughly interwoven, and tied together in the same way. They are called *tāntī*. In Amtera I saw a beautifully made wall of *birhol*[2] branches, but the Baiga do not usually spend much time or trouble on their walls. The walls are sometimes left open and give little protection from the wind. More often, they are roughly plastered with a mud made by mixing *lālmāti* (if available) water and *pirosi* (rice or kodon chaff) or *paira* (heavier rubbish from the threshing-floor). Often only the inside of the wall is plastered. When the mud dries it is given a wash of cow-dung. There is often a hole high up in the wall to allow smoke to escape.

The walls of the front verandah, which is seldom more than four or five feet broad, are often only three feet high and are seldom plastered.

Inside the house a floor is made of stones, covered with loose earth, and then plastered and cow-dunged.

The house is generally divided into two rooms by a row of *kothi* or *khursa*, round bamboo grain-bins plastered with mud that are set on their *chachara*, stand. Sometimes the bins are not more than waist-high, sometimes they reach to the roof. The poorer Baiga who have no grain to put in a bin if there was one, divide their houses by a rough bamboo wall. I have seen many such houses with no store of food save a little kodon[3] or kutki[4] in baskets.

In the first room there is a low stand for the water-pots; this is the *parhendā* or *ghinaunchi*, and a *chūlha* where a fire is kept burning for light and warmth. In the inner room is the hearth which is used for cooking, and the *deosthān*, or place of the gods, behind the hearth. The *deosthān* is a place rather than a tangible object, and the visitor who enters a Baiga house hoping to see a number of godlings in an inner room will be disappointed. Anybody may enter the first room and sit there, but it is improper for an outsider to go into the second. I have never put my foot over the threshold of the inner room, even in the houses of my most intimate friends, though I have often peeped over the wall.

[1] Five kinds of grass are used: gonchi (*pollinea argentea*), rusa (*andropogon schoenanthus*), sena (*ischoemum laxum*), moya (*pennisetum alopecuros*) and sukla or lampa (*heteropogon contortus*).

[2] *Indigofera pulchella* [3] *paspalum scrobiculatum.* [4] *panicum psilopodium.*

Carving on a door at Lamni.

On the verandah is the rice-husker—a hole in a beam sunk in the ground, called the *okri* or *kāndi*, and a pestle, the *mūsar*. In one corner is the grindstone which may either be a proper *chakia*—a stone mill used for husking rice or grinding flour, or a *jāta*—a similar implement, but fashioned of earth and kodon chaff, which can only be used for the preliminary husking of rice or kodon.

The door is generally a rectangular frame of bamboo wickerwork that slides to and fro on a horizontal pole fixed above the door-frame which in turn is simply a gap left in the wall. On the inside of the door-frame is a loop of bark-rope and from inside this can be fixed in place by closing the door, passing a stick through the loop and allowing it to catch the sides of the doorway. From the outside the door is shut in a way that would only be possible outside the boundaries of civilized society: a forked stick is propped up against it to hold it in place, and sometimes a couple of poles are laid crosswise against it. No Baiga will ever break into a house thus protected, or hardly ever. Some houses have a number of logs called *patni* in front of the door as a protection against mud during the rains.

Sometimes, a wooden door of two leaves is used. Each leaf is cut so as to leave a projecting peg in the top and bottom corner. This fits into a hole in the door-frame. The doors are very rarely carved. In Lamni, a Baiga craftsman has decorated a number of doors, one of which was sketched for me by Mrs. Milward, and is reproduced on page 34.

In front of the house or at the side is the *gūda* or pigsty, a roomy and very clean little building, made either of bamboo wicker, or of logs laid horizontally between vertical stays. Each sty has a small doorway which is closed by dropping a number of logs down between two horizontal parallel poles at top and bottom. The sty has a sloping roof of grass thatch. Outside the house is a trough called the *kotna*, and this is filled twice a day with *pej* or other leavings of the household.

The *sār* or cattle-shed often forms part of the square. It is built in the same way as an ordinary house, but without a verandah and the walls are not plastered.

The Baiga house is very small, but it is often cosy enough and always scrupulously clean. Most of the household goods are hung from the roof, oily and black from the smoke of constant fires. I remember the extraordinary medly of things suspended from Hothu's roof in Taliyapani (Pandaria). There were a dozen little bundles of various spices and herbs, packets of tobacco, jungle medicines carefully wrapped in bits of cloth, clothes stored in a *jhāpi*, gourds, bows and arrows, traps of every kind, bundles of drying maize, brooms—both the bamboo *kareta* and the grass *bahari*, a *kāwar* for carrying loads, and the *karchāri* or *sujia* for transporting bundles of hay or straw. Hung from the roof, also, by loops of grass is the *adgasnī*, a bamboo pole which serves as a clothes-line, and over which is hung most of the household's clothing.

On the walls you may find axes, sickles, a *khanta* for dibbling holes for seed, more bows and arrows, the larger traps like the *bissera* or *khujji-phānda*, bundles of hemp for string, strips of bark, drums, the bamboo frame for making a tobacco *thailī*. Standing in a corner may be a bed, and every kind of basket in various parts of the house. In the inner room are a few cooking-pots, probably simply an earthen *handi* for *pej*, an earthen *tilai* for vegetables, a *paina* for steaming rice. In a corner is an earthen *dohni* full of *pej* to be kept till evening. Standing against the wall there may be a *chatāi* or bamboo mat for sleeping. By the fire is a *māchi* or *pīdha*, little seats—the *māchi* may have legs of sambhar horns, the *pīdha* is a flat square of wood. There are also two or three *gursi*, shallow earthen pots for holding fire; these are put under the beds at night.

Such is the Baiga home, dark, cosy, smelling eternally of wood-smoke and food cooking, a place of warmth and affection, not a permanent abode, but a good tent on life's journey.

XI. HOUSEHOLD POSSESSIONS

The Baiga has few other possessions, for he makes very few things. He makes his own bed, a simple frame of wood with a string mattress. The frame is generally made of bamboo, tinsa[1] or khamara.[2] The string is of *bagai* grass or hemp. The Baiga gets his iron from the Agaria, the black-smith who is to be found throughout Mandla, or from the Lohar elsewhere. Among his iron instruments may be a *pharsa*—a sort of battle-axe, the serviceable *tangia*—axe, the sickle or *hassia*, some arrow-heads, a *khanta*, a *kudāri* for digging, a *basula* for planing wood, a *bindhna* for making holes in wood, a long pointed *sābar* for digging, a *rāphi* for clearing grass. The prices charged by the Agaria for these things are usually:

Tangia	As. 4
Pharsa	As. 9
Hassia	As. 3
Arrow-heads	As. 1 each
Khanta	As. 4 or 5
Kudāri	As. 4 or 5
Basula	As. 8
Bindhna	As. 2 or 3
Sābar	As. 8
Rāphi	As. 8

[1] *Ougeinia dalbergioides*. [2] *Trewia nudiflora*.

The Baiga make a large variety of baskets, generally for their own use, only excepting the *dauri* which for some reason they all avoid. Only the Bhumia make the *jhāpi*, and only the Binjhwar make *sūpa* (winnowing fans). Otherwise all the Baiga make the following:

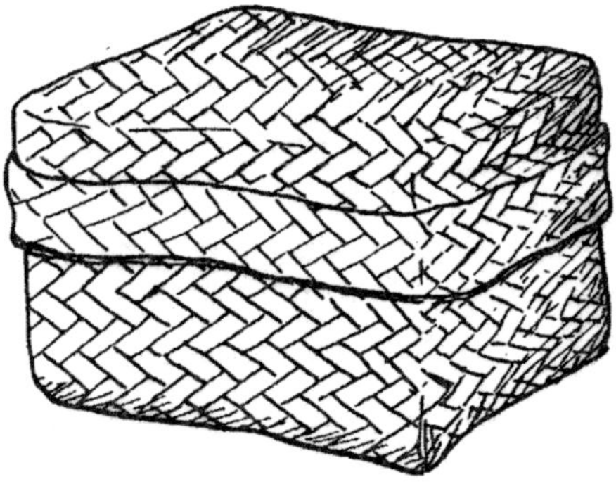

FIG. 10. *Sikosi.*

Sikosi (Fig. 10). A square basket of broad twilled bamboo strips, 14 inches square and 6 inches high. A cover is made to come right down over the basket, and is 15 inches square and 3 inches deep. The result is a double basket very useful for storing clothes.

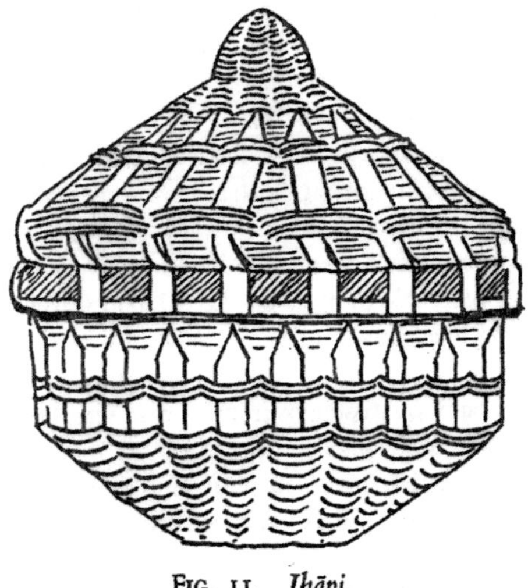

FIG. 11. *Jhāpi.*

Jhāpi (Fig. 11). A beautifully made basket for storing clothes, ornaments and dresses for the dance. It is about 16 inches in diameter and stands 14 inches from the ground. It is made of strips of bamboo of various sizes. It will be best appreciated from the illustration.

FIG. 12. *Mora.*

Mora (Fig. 12). A shallow open basket, 9 inches square and 5 inches deep, of bamboo strips 1 inch broad plaited checkwise, used for baling out water from a stream which has been damned for fishing.

Dāli (Fig. 13). A circular bamboo basket about 16 inches in diameter, 14 inches high, with an aperture at the top of 9 inches for storing grain. It is plaited with warp and weft of very thin bamboo strips, and covered with mud and cow-dung.

Dhūti (Fig. 13). A small triangular basket of ½-inch strips of bamboo, plaited checkwise. It is 12 inches long at the bottom, and the aperture at the top is 3½ inches. It has a little string handle, and is used for bringing fish home from the stream.

Dauri (Fig. 13). Baiga use but do not make this. It is a circular basket of fine construction, 14 inches in diameter at the mouth, with a narrow base of 4 inches. Thin strips of bamboo are woven checkwise through broad warps outside, and the inside is lined with a twilled lining of ½-inch strips of bamboo. The mouth of the basket is strengthened with a broad belt 1¼ inches wide of bark held in place by the bamboo warps which are taken up and over it and fixed down inside. The *dauri* is used for cleaning rice.

Kikrahi (Fig. 13). A circular basket 15 inches in diameter and 8 inches deep, fine wefts of bamboo passing over inch-broad warps checkwise. Used for carrying grain or vegetables.

Tukna. The same, but plastered with mud and cow-dung.

Pitla (Fig. 13). A small basket 6 inches high and 3½ inches in diameter of strips of udar[1] bark ¾ inches broad plaited checkwise. Ramtilla or rye is put in this and it is squeezed slowly till the oil is expressed.

Bijni. A bamboo fan of ¼-inch strips of bamboo plaited twill fashion, 8 inches square and attached to a 11-inch handle, used for getting up a fire.

[1] *Sterculia villosa.*

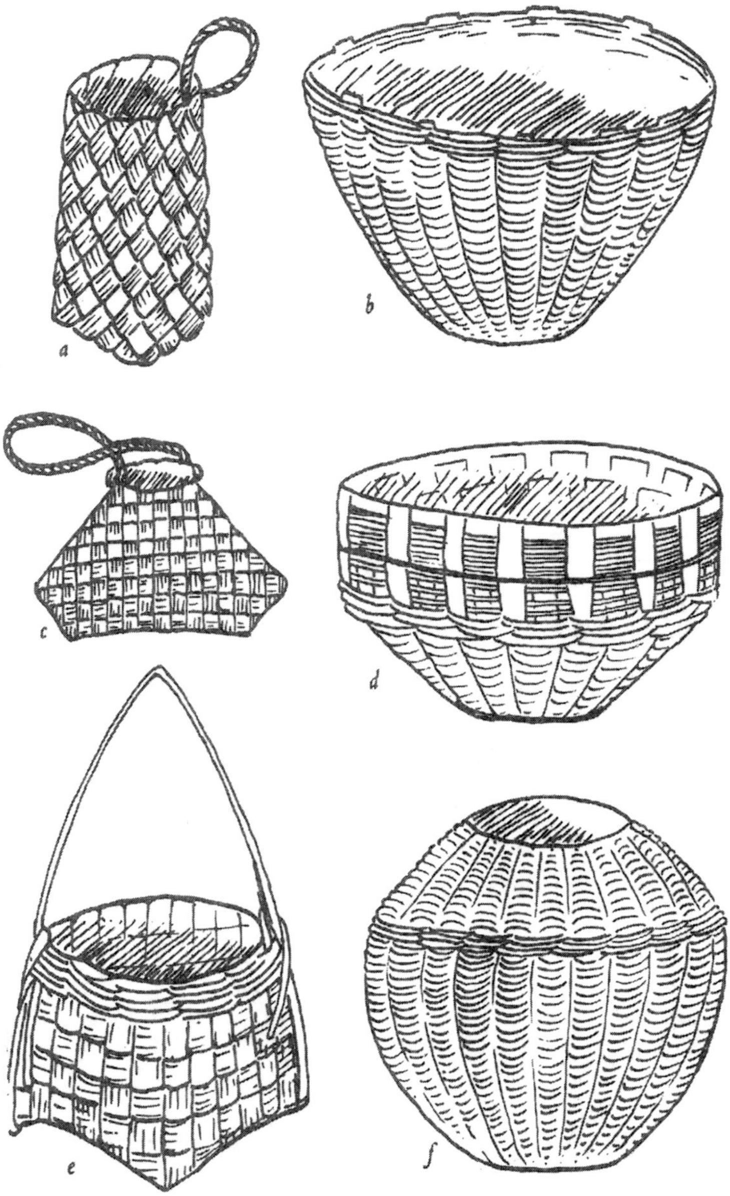

FIG. 13. *a Pitla.* *b Kikrahi.* *c Dhūti.* *d Dauri.* *e Chalgi.* *f Dāli.*

Churki. A circular basket, 7 inches in diameter and 6 inches high, swelling in the middle. Eight ½-inch slats are placed across each other, are bent upwards, and very thin hoops of bamboo are woven through them. The *churki* is useful for storing vegetables.

Chalgi (Fig. 13). A basket almost of a Western type, with a handle. It is used for carrying food to the bewar, and is often brought back full of roots. It is 6 inches deep and 9 inches in diameter, woven of broad ¾-inch strips of bamboo, and strengthened round the top by a band of very thin horizontal slats.

Chīttī. A bamboo lid which is placed on top of earthen cooking-pots. Broad 1-inch strips of bamboo form the basis of the lid, which is 8 inches in diameter, and thin slips of bamboo are woven through them, the wider slips being neatly tucked in at the ends.

Sūpa. The winnowing-fan of the usual Indian pattern.

The Baiga also make a leaf-basket called *pūri*, of mohlain leaves roughly stitched together, for carrying roots and grain, leaf-cups called *dona*, and leaf-plates called *patri*. The *dona* and *patri* may be made of mohlain, sarai, or parsa[1] leaves.

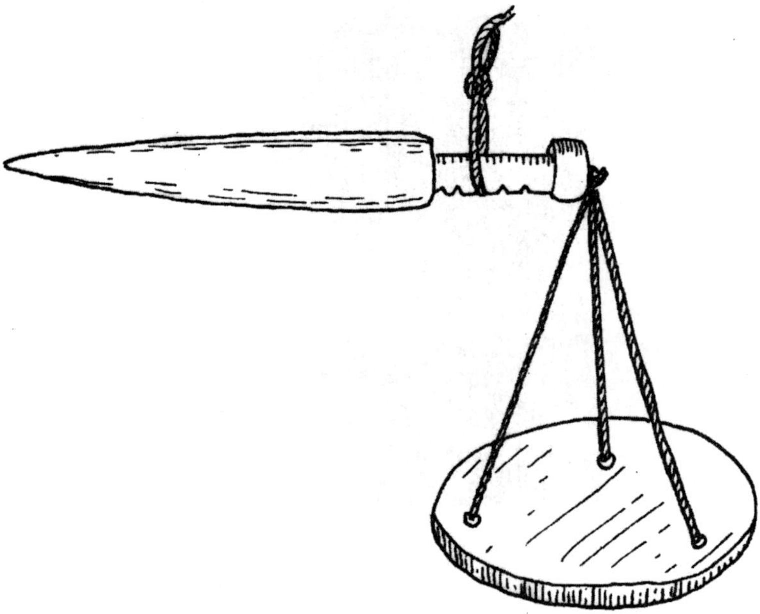

FIG. 14. *Narja.*

The string is, for the purpose of illustration, in the half-seen notch, but the narja would not, of course, balance like this without a weight on the pālwa.

[1] *Ficus retusa.*

Carrying roots in a leaf-basket.
Weighing roots in the narja.

For measuring small quantities, say of roots or tobacco, the Baiga use the *narja* (Fig. 14), a balance in which a circular bit of khamara wood called the *pālwa* is attached by strings to a counterweight of tinsa wood, the *dāndi*. There are notches in the *dāndi* for $\frac{1}{8}$, $\frac{1}{4}$, $\frac{1}{2}$, 1 and 2 *seer*,[1] and as the string is fitted into one or other of the notches it gives these weights.

[1] A seer is about two pounds. The table of weights in Mandla is:

40 tola	=	1 paili
2 paili	=	1 seer
5 seer	=	1 kuro
20 kuro	=	1 khandi

XII. DOMESTIC ANIMALS

The Baiga are very fond of pigs. They look after them well, give them clean and roomy houses and feed them properly. The dedicated Laru pig is treated with great honour. For pigs are necessary for marriages, for many sacrificial rituals, for most serious penalty feasts. As breeders of poultry the Baiga are almost equally successful; chickens are also in constant demand for religious or magical ceremonies. Goats are kept and are cherished as a valuable form of property.

The bewar-cutting Baiga have very few cattle. They do not use bullocks for threshing or any other purpose; but they sometimes keep a few cows for milk. When the Government stopped bewar-cutting in Balaghat and Mandla, they had to supply the Baiga with bullocks for ploughing. A number of Baiga sold their bullocks and reported that they had been eaten by tigers. But nowadays many Baiga have cows and bullocks and a few have buffaloes. At one time they all ate beef. Now the various sub-sections accuse one another of doing so, but all deny it. But I believe that many Bhumia, Bharotia and Muria still continue the practice secretly, and the Kondwan, Gond-waina and Kurka Baiga openly. The Baiga give their cattle names—a bullock with black circles round its eyes is called Kajra; a white line down the forehead earns it the name of Patna; a white bullock is named Dhaura, a black and white one Lilwa, a brown one Kosa. A bullock with *chapra* horns hanging between eyes and ears is unlucky; it should be kept apart from the herd or it will die. A *korri-gai*, with crooked horns curving over the eyes is also unlucky. 'If you keep it in your house, it will soon see your bones.' It is also wise to 'keep a squinting cow out of your shed'.

Dogs and cats are kept—or at least are permitted to live—about the house.

Dogs are given names 'according to their character'—Bucha,[1] Kabera,[2] Banra[3], Baghia.[4] In Hirapur, Bahadur had an offensive-looking cat without a tail of which he seemed very fond. He called her Junhi.

The appropriate way to call animals is as follows. A cat, *minu minu minu*. A dog, *udro udro udro thū thū thū*. A goat, *harrr-o harrr-o!* Hens, *kuru kuru kuru kuru!* Buffalo, *ariya ariya ao!* Pigs, *aur-r-r aur-r-r lāru lāru a-u-r-r-r-r!* A cow is addressed by name; *dhaura bachhiya bachhiya ao ao heu heu ao ao!* A dog is driven away by a simple *dur-rē dur-rē!*

I describe elsewhere the killing of the Laru pig. A small pig to be killed for domestic use is caught by the hind legs, whirled in the air and smashed down head first upon a stone. If the pig is too large for this, its head is broken by a heavy blow from the *mūsar* (rice-pounder). At sacrifices I have seen the gunia cut off the head of a small pig by carving it with a pharsa-axe. A goat is decapitated by a single well-aimed blow with the axe. Small chickens have their heads twisted off, larger ones are strangled by constriction of the windpipe, or are smashed on the ground.

Barbaric as they sound, these methods kill quickly and certainly with a minimum of pain. On the whole, Baiga are very good to their animals who live almost as members of the family and share its gains and reverses.

XIII. TOBACCO

The most treasured part of the Baiga's *bāri* is his tobacco patch. It is very carefully fenced off, placed near the house for fear of thieves, watered and weeded with a care that no other crop can claim. This care reflects the Baiga's great attachment to tobacco. 'I can go without liquor for five days,' says Pachlu, 'but I can't do without my *chungi* for five minutes.' And so the pipe is an almost sacred object: it is handed as a mark of consideration from friend to friend; no one who is of another tribe or excommunicate can share it. No social sanction is more powerful than the fear that a friend may refuse one's *chungi* at a feast or funeral. Curiously enough the earthen pipe, the *chīlum*, has no such tribal significance, but may be shared with anyone.

The *chungi* is made of sarai or mohlain leaves. A fine strip is pulled off from the back of the leaf and made into a little ring. A strip is also removed from the bottom and made into a small cylinder. Then the leaf itself is carefully rolled into a long thin pipe, the little ring is slipped round it to hold it together, and the cylinder is put inside to prevent the tobacco slipping down too far. The pipe is preserved by being stuck into the

[1] Earless. [2] Spotted. [3] Tailless. [4] A wandering bitch.

hair above the bun, or into the folds of the turban. You may sometimes see a youth with half a dozen pipes sticking up all round his head.

The Baiga grow several kinds of tobacco. The *dīhaī* is the most common. After it has been dried, it is rubbed in the hands and the fragments that fall to the ground are called *bhaski*. *Sulki* has long narrow leaves. It is quickly harvested and is comparatively mild and sweet. *Kijra mākhur*, on the other hand, is very strong and burns the throat, even the Baiga throat. *Māndor mākhur* has very large leaves so has *aindmāl mākhur* whose leaves twist as they ripen. Finally the tobacco you buy in a shop is called *bangli tamāk*. The Baiga seldom need to purchase it, for their crop is planned to last them through the year.

XIV. FIRE

The Baiga use both the fire-saw and the fire-drill for making fire. The latter is more common in Pandaria and Dindori, the former in Baihar. The fire-drill is generally worked by two men. They make a small hollow in the middle of a flat piece of bamboo, and put a few pieces of grit into it. One of the men holds this hearth firmly by its two ends with his feet, and the other takes a thin dry, sharpened bamboo, inserts the pointed end in the hollow, and revolves it rapidly by rubbing it between the palms of his hands. His fellow takes turns with him. The friction makes wood-dust in the hollow and this soon smoulders into fire.

For the fire-saw, a piece of bamboo is split down the middle for a third of its length and wedged open with a bit of stick, to form the hearth. Another bit of split bamboo is sharpened all along its length. The hearth is placed slanting slightly against a stone and under it is placed the tinder, dry leaves or cotton from the semur[1] tree. One man holds the hearth firmly with his hands and feet, while another saws across the split bamboo with the sharp edge of his saw, pressing down as hard as he can and sawing as rapidly as possible. Very soon smoke rises, and soon a spark falls on the wood-dust and other tinder. The sawing is stopped then, and the men blow carefully on the spark till the tinder is well kindled.

A good way of preparing cloth for tinder is to burn some til[2] stalks, and rub bits of old cloth in the hot ashes. It then becomes slightly oily and inflammable.

The Baiga also use the steel and flint, especially for lighting their pipes. They carry a little bag known as the *pissai*, either home-made of string, or of leather from the bazaar. It contains the *belhari*—a small gourd filled

[1] *Bombax malabaricum.* [2] *Sesamum indicum.*

with semur cotton, a small spike of tendu[1] wood for shaping the pipe, and a *chakmak-pathra* (steel and flint), and some sarai leaves and tobacco.

I have only seen matches once in a Baiga village, in a Binjhwar's house at Lamta near the railway station.

XV. LIQUOR

Bhagavan himself sent the great giant Bhimsen to find mahua liquor before the foundation of the world, and thus established it as a necessary ingredient in all Baiga worship.[2] It is sprinkled on the seed at the Bidri ceremony so vital to fertility, on the mud images at the Mati Uthana rite, on the nails that keep the earth in place or bind the mouth of the tiger. It is drunk at the Bida which drives away disease from the village, and at the sacrifices which protect the bewar. Mourners take it at a funeral, and revellers at a wedding. It is an essential item in the gifts at the *sagai* (engagement), it is generally levied as part of the fine to be paid for readmission to tribal penalties after excommunication; it is a convenient way of paying a gunia for his services.

It is not true that the Baiga drink only to get drunk. Liquor not only has a solemn ritual significance, but its flavour gives an exquisite pleasure. The Baiga are very particular about the quality of their liquor, and sometimes go many miles to a shop where a finer flavour may be obtained. But they do, of course, enjoy the sensation of being drunk. It is an escape from an often all too grim reality. It is a stimulus that releases their most ready wit and choicest stories. 'When our mouth is full of liquor,' says Ketu, 'we talk like kings. But when it is empty, we remember the money we had to borrow to pay for it!' Drunkenness is not, however, very common. The headman of Bohi, and the former headman of Daharkata are habitual drunkards, but I know of few others. Most Baiga have steadier heads than the Gond. I remember ninety-year-old Yogi Dewar putting down two bottles without much effect, and Mahatu, Jethu, Bahadur and many others have a remarkable capacity.

The Baiga depend entirely on the spirit distilled from the corolla of the mahua[3] tree, now supplied mainly from licensed out-stills throughout the country. These stills are generally in the hands of Kalar and Punjabi adventurers, though an attempt has been made lately to persuade the Gond to take them. In Daharkata, in the Baiga Chak, the contract has been held for many years by a Baiga family, and in Jaldar it is held by Yogi Dewar.

In the old days, Jethu told me, 'we made liquor ourselves, and were

[1] *Diospyros tomentosa.* [2] See p. 311. [3] *Bassia latifolia.*

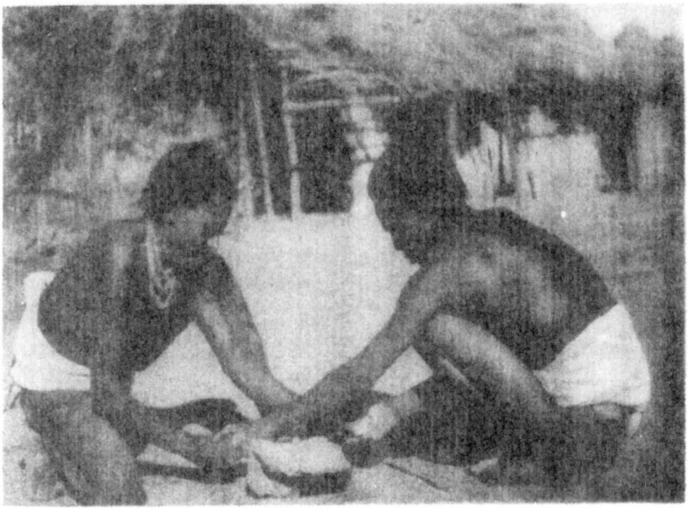

The fire-drill.
The fire-saw.

afraid of no one. I used to make it in this way. I took five *seer* of mahua, and put it in a big earthen pot full of water. So long as it tasted sweet, it was not ready. When it began to go sour, then we knew we could begin. We would pour it into another earthen pot and place it on the fire. Then we had a third earthen pot ready, with two holes in the side. We put this upside down on the first, mouth to mouth, and tied it with mud and rags. Then we fitted hollow bamboo tubes into the two holes of the upper pot, and let these run down into two other pots. The steam from the boiling mahua would run down the tubes, and turn into liquor. The first three bottles are always very good and strong.' Inspired by this recollection, he began to sing an old *matwāri*, drinking song:

> The landlord swanks about his village.
> The tenant lords it in the field.
> The Kalar is master of the liquor-still.
>   At a wedding the bottle with the broken neck
>   Goes round and round and round.

The liquor in the first few bottles is called *phuli*; it is very strong and costs about eight annas. The rest is *rāsi* and costs from one and a half to three annas a bottle.

The liquor is drunk out of neat little cups of folded sarai or mohlain leaf. When a number of people are drinking together, they sometimes pour a corporate libation to Dharti Mata before serving it. The stricter Baiga, however, each pour a few drops on the ground before raising the first cup to their lips, and repeat the following mantra:

> Sirseti! Karseti! Panseti! Raktburar! Barburar! Malset guru Malset guruain! Chima guru Chima guruain! Alpha guru Alpha guruain! Tusar guru Tusar guruain! Mindra Pat Mindra guruain! Buchi guruain! Jilmili! Four times eighty-four are the mountains! The four-mouthed monkey says tan tan! Talmuchi guruain! I salute you O Earth! Again I salute you O Earth! Sanja guruain! O lady of the Evening, stand with your hair dishevelled! O Sirseti Mai, stand on my throat as I drink.

They then salute everyone present, stretching out the right hand towards each in turn very solemnly, raise the cup to the lips, generally spilling a little in the process, and swallow the liquor in one gulp.

The Baiga sometimes take *gānja*, but seldom *bhang* or opium. They drink water both during and after meals, from a brass pot if they have one, or from a gourd dipped into the water-pot. They do not usually drink milk, but, when they get it, make it into *ghī*. But when they can, they mix milk into the children's *pej*.

XVI. FOOD

Ek bīta jag jīta: sānjh khay bihana rīta. The stomach is a span broad: you go throughout the world for it. Eat in the evening: empty again in the morning. —Baiga Proverb.

'If I were to be given a hundred rupees,' said old Thaggur, with a meaning look at me, 'I would spend it on buying a bit of jungle for bewar. If I couldn't get that I would spend it on food. If I had enough food, I would buy a young and lovely wife.' Food is less important than the bewar, but it matters more than sex. I think that is the general view, though there is a pleasant story from Mandla which suggests that liquor may rank with food in attraction and importance. A Baiga shikari, who was given a present of twenty-five rupees, was asked how he intended to spend it. He replied that thirteen rupees would go to the money-lender, two rupees on food and clothing, and the remaining ten on liquor.[1] On the other hand, when Bukwa, landlord of Ufri, sold some of his timber for a hundred rupees, he spent it all in a couple of months on clothes and really heavy eating.

'As long as you've five mouthfuls in your belly,' declares a proverb, 'you can forget both god and ghost.'

The songs testify to the importance of food. This is the theme of many Karma and Dadaria. I will quote a number of them here, the obscurer references will be explained later in the chapter.

Karma

i

O Bhagavan, the maize has grown.
We are going to roast and eat it.
Kutki Rani has come.
We shall touch her feet. It is she that saves our lives.

ii

All night long I have been shivering with cold.
Cover me now with your blanket.

[1] *Mandla District Gazetteer* (Bombay, 1912), p. 72.

Youth and age with leaf-cups.

For supper there was *dāl*[1] *bhāt*;
You poured *ghī* all over it.
But even then, in my little dhoti,
I was shivering with cold.
So now, at midnight, cover me with the end of your *lugra*.

iii

The wind is blowing hard,
There is a fire outside the house.
The stranger has come,
He is smoking his pipe.
Cook *chapāti* with *marria* flour,
Prepare a curry of *singni* fish.
Get ready a dish of vegetable and water.

iv

However hard it be, you must remove the fish's skin.
Where did you get the *lāl-bhāji*?
Where did you get the young shoots of bamboo?
Where did you get the *kānda*-fish?
How hard it is to remove this fish's skin!
We got the *bhāji* in our garden.
We brought the bamboo-shoots from the jungle.
We caught the *kānda*-fish in the river.
How hard it is to remove this fish's skin!

v

Near our garden grows a munga tree.[2]
O neighbour girl, tell him to pick some munga fruit for me!
He picks it with his left hand, he holds it in his right.
You have given me this munga; how am I to cook it?
Boil it in water; put oil in a pot.
Make the oil hot; put the munga in it.
Then it will be ready, give it to your husband.
But at supper-time, the husband curses her and says,
I saw you cooking munga fruit,
But all you give me is vegetable from the river!

vi

Which is the fish that lives under the stone?
Which is the fish that you like to eat?

[1] Generally channa (*cicer arietinum*), urad (*phaseolus radiatus*), masur dal (*ervum lens*) or rahar dal (*cajanus indicus*).
[2] *Moringa pterygosperma.*

The *gewari* lives beneath the stone.
The *kusuwar* is good to eat.

vii

Make a leaf-cup of mango-leaves!
Make a plate of pipar leaves!
O girl, your waist is slender,
You will break beneath that load.
You must eat rice and mango chutney.
Then you will be strong.
When the bar tree ripens and the pakhri,
O boy with small mouth and long hair,
If your mind and mine agree,
We will run away together.

viii

There was a brinjal in the garden.
I picked it for my supper.
I made some curds from milk.
I made some buttermilk from curds.
I cooked the brinjal in the curds and buttermilk.

Dadaria

i

The *bhāji* of gram is fried in *ghī*.
Open your heart, my friend; tell me where we can sleep together.

ii

Come to my house, and I'll make you some *lapsa*.[1]
O my *jawāra*, you have taken my *naksa* (honour).

iii

It is noon; it is time for food.
But if you eat rice, you feel all the hungrier.
Let's drink a little *pej*!

iv

He cooked his *khijri*[2] in milk with dirty half-ground *kodai*.
It is all his own folly that he has been ruined.

[1] Half-ground wheat prepared with *gur*.
[2] The Baiga make *khijri* by cooking rice or kodai with salt and water. It is kept very moist.

v

I put the half-ground *kodai* in the pot for cooking
For love of you I have left my family.

vi

Are you going to eat the *akri-kodai* or no?
Tell me the truth: are you coming or no?

vii

She ate *marria*[1] roti with honey.
Now she has eaten that, she will be in my power.

viii

At night, rice; in the morning *dāl*.
She who gives it to me is an old friend of mine.

ix

She was cooking the rice, but she fell asleep.
O girl, when I don't see you, I feel very lonely.

x

We caught the fish, but there was no buttermilk to cook it in.
Speak to me with open heart; there is no one here.

xi

I killed some fish, but had no salt to eat with them.
Who has taken the fish? Tell me, or I'll take your life.

Yet the staple food of the Baiga is the simplest and coarsest possible. There is a legend to account for this.

'Long ago, Bhagavan called all the tribes of mankind to a feast. On one side he put rice and *dāl*, vegetable and meat curry for the Hindus; on the other side he put *chapāti*, *ghī*, and sugar for the Baiga and Gond. When everyone had come, Bhagavan asked them to sit down and eat. But at that moment, a rat came out of its hole, and ran across the floor. As Bhagavan had provided no meat for the Gond and Baiga, they all jumped up, and chased the rat so that they could add it to the feast. But they couldn't catch it, and when they came back they found that the Hindus had come and taken all their *chapāti*, *ghī* and sugar, and there was nothing left for them at all. Then Bhagavan brought the water in which the rice had been boiled and gave it to them. "This is *pej*," he said, "and you will eat it for ever."'

[1] *Eleusine coracana.*

Forsyth, however, strongly recommends two of the items of the Baiga's diet.[1] Near Amarkantak, he was given 'numerous delicacies' of the wilds, 'among which two were particularly acceptable, namely, a fine pure arrowroot (*tikur*) made from the roots of the wild *Curcuma Angustifolia* and a beautiful small grain called *siker*, which is nothing but the produce of old plants of the grain called *kutki*, generally cultivated by those hill tribes in their *dhya* clearings. After a clearing has been abandoned, the plants of *kutki* rapidly degenerate, and in their third and fourth year the grain has become this *siker*. It is much smaller than the fully cultivated grain, but also much sweeter, and with a nutty flavour about it, which is particularly delicious. . . . It made the best porridge I have ever tasted'.

But the bulk of Baiga food is poor and monotonous enough. The Baiga eat three times a day. First, in the early morning about eight, at the meal they call *juāra*, they usually drink *pej* of *kodon, kutki, siker* or rice. The second meal, which also consists of *pej*, is taken about four in the afternoon and is called *marraiya:* and the third, at night, rather late, called *biyāri*, may consist of *kodon* and *dāl*, with vegetables and sometimes bread of wheat or *marria*. In the Mandla Tehsil, these meals are known as *murgal, marria* and *biyāri*.

Pej is prepared by first boiling a quantity of water, two *seer* for each adult. When it is bubbling, rice, *kodon* or *kutki* is thrown into the pot—one *seer* of grain for every six of water, and is left to boil. Then it is taken off the fire, and two or three more *seer* of cold water are poured on to the rice. This is known as *pej bhedna*. *Kodon* requires more water than rice; in all a *seer* of *kodon* needs to be mixed with ten or eleven *seer* of water. Well-to-do people, sick people or pregnant women take *pej* without adding cold water.

Kodon passes through three stages on its way to the cooking-pot. It is first partially husked in the *jāta* and becomes *akri-kodai*. It is then fully husked and partly cleaned by the *mūsar:* it is now *bhagri-kodai*. Finally, it is cleaned and washed, and is *kodai* proper. But it is eaten at all three stages. *Bhagri-kodai* is preferred because of its flavour.

But *pej* is only the basis and foundation for other food. In the *kānda-bāri*, only sweet potatoes and maize are cultivated, but the Baiga go out and gather every kind of jungle leaf and herb. Popular among these are the leaves of the chinch (*corchorus olitorius*), the munga (*moringa pterygosperma*), the chakaora (*cassia tora*), the pipal (*ficus religiosa*), phang (*rivea hypocrateri formis*), kawa keni (*combretum nanum*), kajra (*phoenix sylvestris?*), khatua (*antidesma diandrum*), pakhri (*ficus infectoria*), amara (*spondias mangifera*), the flowers of the birhol (*indigofera pulchella*), the young shoots of the

[1] Forsyth: op. cit., p. 417.

bamboo and the kachnar (*bauhinia purpurea*), and the small tender leaves of the amli (*bauhinia malabarica*). These are nearly always boiled with a little salt and chili.

The *karīl-chena* (bamboo shoots) are a great delicacy. They are prepared by removing the outer skin, and boiling. Then all the water is squeezed out of them and they are pounded a little. Then they are again boiled with salt, turmeric and chili. Pipal leaves are first boiled, and then dried in the sun. Afterwards they are rubbed in the hands, and cooked in buttermilk.

A large variety of roots are collected in the forest. The best of these are the *kanhiakānda*. Other popular *kānda* are *kirchi*, *kundru*,[1] *jalia*, *jarungi*, *sua*[2] and *saidu*. They are washed and scraped, then boiled and often eaten without salt or spices. Sometimes, they are cut up and made into curry; or they may be dipped in the sour curry of gram, or *pej* a few days old.

Among fruits the most popular is the mango. At the mango season, everybody goes to the jungle, and gathers baskets of the small green fruit: often they take it to the bazaar, and sell them at 100 an anna, but they eat a large proportion themselves. Other fruits are jamun (*eugenia jambolana*), char (*buchanania latifolia*), khamer (*gmelina arborea*), tendu (*diospyros tomentosa*), gular (*ficus glomerata*), bar (*ficus bengalensis*), bel (*aegle marmelos*), bohar (*cordya myxa*) and many others. The mahua (*bassia latifolia*) is so valued by the Baiga that they never cut it in their bewar. Its sweet and sickly flowers are dried and made into a gruel or chutney. Its seeds yield an oil that can be used for cooking. The corolla are made into liquor.

Many varieties of fish are mentioned in the songs. Some Baiga do not care for fish; they regard them as unsatisfying. 'He who eats meat spends two days digesting it; he who eats fish is only made hungry for something else.' The Baiga do not attribute any aphrodisiac qualities to fish—it is meat that rouses lust—but they believe it to be good for the eyes. Fish is prepared in various ways. The fish is washed but not cleaned. Oil is put in a pot and heated, buttermilk is mixed in, and further heated, then the fish is added, and all are boiled up together with turmeric, chili and salt. If they want to preserve the fish for a day or two they burn it, and keep the parched and shrivelled flesh for future use.

'But our minds,' says Bukwa of Ufri, 'are never satisfied without meat. Even if Government make a hundred laws that we are not to hunt, we will do it. One of us will keep the official talking, and the rest will go off to the jungle and get a good fat deer.' 'Secretly,' said Rawan, 'we kill

[1] *Coccinia indica.* [2] *Dillenia pentagyna.*

sambhar,[1] hiran,[2] gutri,[3] hares,[4] lil,[5] chital,[6] mangwari,[7] mongoose, peacock, and bring them home and eat them with great delight.' Almost every kind of meat is acceptable. Most people prefer the haril[8] or the flesh of the sambhar, though Mahi likes a nice boiled chicken, and her husband a plump jungle pig. Mahi's chicken must of course be a jungle fowl, which is much more tasty than a domestic fowl. But even a domestic fowl is better than a rat.

The Baiga are said to distinguish twenty-one different varieties of rat, though I have only been able to collect the names of seventeen. These are the black hairy *balod mussa*, the black hairless *kaparia*, the red and beautiful *parbat mussa*, the spotted *chiddi* squirrel, the *tola mussa* with pointed mouth, the white *dhodaria*, the long-haired black *tareli mussa*, the *karanda mussa* with its black back and white belly, the small *kanjeli*, the light-brown *sabkatti* that kills small house mice, the *neola* or mongoose, the brown *bijnori*, the large musk rat, the *ghuns*, the tiny *chotē* that lives in the fields, the brown *gururia*, the *chhūchu*—the ordinary musk rat with a long face and evil smell, the *bundurchotia* that lives in trees. The Baiga eat all these, save the house rats and even these are eaten by children. To cook a rat, a stick is thrust through its mouth into its belly, and it is held over the fire till all the hair is singed off. Sometimes it is then cleaned and cut up, fried in oil, and boiled in rice water; sometimes it is roasted as it is, and eaten on the spot.

Meat is generally prepared by being first boiled in water, and then either cut up and made into curry, or fried in *ghī* or oil. A haril or fowl is put on the open fire till all the feathers are burnt off, and then roasted. A very small chick is roasted like a rat with a stick thrust into its mouth. The Baiga eat the skin and the entrails, even the bones if the bird or animal is small. They specially delight in a roast goat, which is prepared for special occasions. The whole party sits quietly drinking round a great fire, and a goat is suspended above it. Then as it roasts, the company pull bits of the flesh out of the flames and eat them while drinking.

Eggs are boiled, the shell is removed and they are made into curry with *haldi*, chili and any vegetable available. Eggs are also put in balls of fresh cow-dung and placed in the glowing embers of a fire till they are ready.

Children eat crows; the flesh has a good effect on the eyes, for the crow is very sharp-sighted.

[1] *cervus unicolor* or *equinus*. [2] *antilope bezoartica*. [3] *cervulus muntjac* (the barking deer). [4] *lepus ruficaudatus*. [5] *portax pictus*. [6] *cervus axis*. [7] Probably *memimna indica* (the mouse deer). [8] *crocopus phoenicopterus*.

Cooking a rat.

XVII. LANGUAGE

It has often been remarked as a notable fact that the very tribes that are usually regarded as the true autochthenes of the country, such as the Kamar and Baiga, have lost all traces of the older Austro-asiatic languages and have entirely assimilated the speech of the Aryan invaders of their land. This very fact is, of course, some evidence of the antiquity of the Baiga who probably lost their own tongue even when they were still inhabitants of the Chhattisgarh plain, and took the new Chhattisgarhi speech with them up into the wild hill retreats whither they fled before the approach of civilization.

To-day the Baiga speak the language of their neighbours. In Bilaspur and along the Maikal Hills they talk ordinary Chhattisgarhi; in Mandla and Jubbulpore they talk Eastern Hindi with Awadhi modifications and a few words borrowed from Gondi; in Balaghat, they talk Marathi, Hindi and Gondi—or a mixture of all three—and the mysterious language called Baigani.

Baigani is now recognized as a corrupt form of Chhattisgarhi, but it was once supposed to be a real language with a large number of speakers. The 1881 Census recorded only 237 of these speakers in Balaghat and 24 in Seoni, but there were 4,977 in Mandla, 3,389 in Raipur,[1] 2,047 in Bilaspur, 2,399 in Sambalpur, making a total of 13,073. Ten years later only 2,616 Baigani speakers were returned, and Sir B. Robertson, the author of the Central Provinces section of the Report, already casts doubt on the validity of the classification, and quotes the opinion of the Tehsildar of Ramgarh, who had so much to do with the settlement of the Baiga Chak, as saying 'that he had found the language the Baigas speak was not a separate language, but a corruption of Hindi'.[2] Colonel Ward also considered that the only language known to the Baiga was Hindi, and Sterndale noted with some astonishment the number of Sanskrit words with which they were acquainted.

The classical description of Baigani is in the Linguistic Survey. As far as I can tell, what is described there is now regarded by the Narotia and the Binjhwar of Balaghat as the wild and uncouth tongue of the Bharotia. The other sub-divisions of the tribe rather pride themselves that they do not speak the *Bharotia boli*. In their turn the Bharotia affect to despise the smooth and mincing language of the Binjhwar.

Baigani, as Grierson shows, 'is a corrupt form of Chhattisgarhi, but

[1] The 1881 Census gives the number of Baiga in Raipur as 7,316, but these must have been Binjhwar.

[2] *Census of India*, 1891, Vol. XI, p. 142.

is freely mixed up with words and idioms taken from other languages, including on the one hand Gondi, and on the other Bundeli. From Gondi it borrows a portion of its vocabulary, and, from Bundeli, the most noticeable idiom which is borrowed is the occasional use of the Agent case with *ne* before a transitive verb in the past tense.

'In another important point it has borrowed from Gondi in rather a peculiar way. The termination of the first person singular of a verb in that language, ends in *na* or *n*. Baigani has borrowed this *na* or *n* and adds it indifferently to all persons of any verb. Similarly many cases of Gondi nouns end in a termination containing the letter *n*, and there Baigani seems to have borrowed here and there in a very capricious manner. This is specially noticeable in the case of the Gondi genitive termination *na*. The result is that the language of a Baiga is full of the syllable *na*, repeated over and over again as a kind of expletive.'[1]

Chhattisgarhi is fully illustrated in the *Linguistic Survey*,[2] and has been described in the authoritative *Grammar of the Chhattisgarhi Dialect*, by Hiralal Kavyopadhyaya.

XVIII. THE BAIGA PANTHEON

Before 1921, the Census of India classified the religion of the Baiga and allied primitive tribes as 'animistic', but in that year the Census Commissioner, J. T. Marten, changed this designation into 'Tribal Religion' as being more accurate.[3] For, as a more recent, and greater, Census Commissioner, Dr. J. H. Hutton, has shown, the beliefs held by the tribes are not 'mere vague imaginings of superstitious and untaught minds, but the debris of a real religious system, a definite philosophy, to the one time prevalence of which the manifold survivals in Hinduism testify, linking together geographically the austro-asiatic and austroloid cultures of the forest-clad hills where the isolated remains of the original religion still hold out in an unassimilated form.'[4] In this section, however, I do not propose to discuss this religion, but simply to give an account of the various deities who play a part in Baiga life.

The Baiga pantheon is exceedingly varied and elastic. It differs from village to village. There is no exclusiveness about it. The Baiga naturally worships everything he can, in order to be on the safe side. When the new

[1] *Linguistic Survey of India*, Vol. VI, p. 235.
[2] Ibid, pp. 184–257.
[3] *Census of India*, 1921. Vol I. Part i, p. 111.
[4] *Census of India*, 1931. Vol. I. Part i, p. 417.

Satpura Railway first made its way into the hills, a Baiga was found offering coconuts and chickens to the engine. It may be said, in fact, that the pantheon of any one Baiga Dewar will be more or less coterminous with his theological studies. For Baiga theology is directed, not to knowing more about God, but to knowing about more gods.[1]

Moreover, the Baiga has to perform religious ceremonies for other tribes and even for the Hindus. He thus gains a very Catholic view of things. It is indeed astonishing that his pantheon has not been swamped by the Hindu deities; yet even the Binjhwar Baiga have adopted very few. The test, therefore, that was proposed in the Census operations of 1901 and 1911 that 'if a man said he worshipped Mahadeo, he was to be recorded as a Hindu, and if he revered the tribal gods, the name of the tribe was to be entered in the column of religion'[2] was most misleading. On this test every Baiga might be classed as a Hindu, for he worships every god that he has ever heard of—even the 'stranger Mahadeo that comes from far', as a Baiga once described him. His special and private concerns are with his tribal gods, but he would invoke Christian, Mussalman, Buddhist or Hindu saints and deities if he thought it would make for safety.

Another point that must be remembered is that the Baiga have lost their own language, and can thus only describe their deities by Sanskrit or Hindi words. This gives their pantheon a spurious air of civilized theology and Hindu respectability. Bhagavan is worshipped by Hindus, but he is a very different being from the Bhagavan of the Baiga legends. The Baiga Mahadeo, deceitful and cowardly, bears no resemblance to the mighty being of Hindu theosophy. Dharti Mata is not unknown to popular Hinduism; she has suffered a heavy change into the fierce destructive Durga. This has happened throughout the aboriginal districts: old shrines to Dharti Mata or Thakurain in Chanda, Bastar and Mandhata have been transformed into temples of Kali. Already, forty years ago, 'Thakurani Mai, the "blood-thirsty tutelary goddess", to whom on the 1st May, 1868, the Hill Bhuiyas of Keonjhar offered the head of the obnoxious Dewan of their chief, has been transformed in Singbhum and Lohardaga into the Hindu Durga, to whom a Bhuiya priest makes offerings of goats and sheep.'[3]

BHAGAVAN

The Baiga does not generally show very great reverence towards his deities. He laughs and jokes, very obscenely sometimes, during

[1] The Baiga divide supernatural beings into *deo* (gods) who are usually benevolent and *bhut* (spirits) who are usually hostile to man. I have used the conventional translations, but it must not be supposed that the Baiga have clear-cut notions corresponding to our own.

[2] *Census of India*, 1901. Vol. XIII, p. 95.

[3] *Census of India*, 1901. Vol. XIII, p. 401.

the ceremonies, interrupts them at critical moments for a few pulls at his pipe, abuses those gods who fail him in the roundest terms. I remember a Baiga *pujāri* in Jubbulpore getting impatient with a worshipper who was making deep reverences before the cairn outside the village, and giving a hearty kick to his conveniently bending figure. The Baiga does perhaps show a certain respect for the deity whom he now calls by the Hindi word 'Bhagavan'. Bhagavan is the Creator, and it is to him that many aspects of the social and economic life of the tribe trace their origin. He instituted bewar. He settled the Baiga in the jungle. He gave them seed. He established the rules of exogamy. He provided the tribe with the taboos that would maintain its integrity and prestige. He did indeed murder Nanga Baiga in a particularly cowardly fashion, and afterwards tricked his sons out of most of their magical inheritance. Yet to-day, he is regarded as benevolent and harmless. His functions are mainly concerned with life and death. He sends his chaprasi to call men when their term of life is ended. Every *jīv* goes to him. He lives 'far away', but somewhere on the earth that he has created for his pleasure, in a great palace on an island guarded by two rivers of fire. There he cares for the souls who come to him, punishing the worst of them, sending the rest back to earth to be born again. All birth and death is in his hands. Apart from this, he does not interfere seriously with the affairs of men. He is not invoked in mantra, and there are no places associated with his name, not even a stick or stone to do him honour.

BARA DEO OR BUDHA DEO

The present position of Bara Deo or Budha Deo is an interesting example of the effect of an administrative measure upon theology. Bara Deo has always been regarded as the chief deity of the Baiga and Gond. 'Their principal deity,' says Russell of the Baiga, 'is Bura Deo, who is supposed to reside in a saj tree; he is worshipped in the month of Jeth (May), when goats, fowls, coconuts, and the liquor of the new mahua crop are offered to him.'[1] So an old bewar-cutting Baiga of Taliyapani told me: "Bara Deo is older than Narayan Deo. He is of our family. He belongs to us. At first, he lived in an anthill. Then he went to Nanga Baiga in a dream, and began to live with him. Nanga Baiga took him to the forest, and put him in the stump of a saj tree. From that time, we have never cut the saj down to the ground; we always leave a stump."

But some modern Baiga, who have taken to the plough, have a very different opinion of this ancient god. Bara Deo's temple was the bewar, his shrine the saj stump carefully preserved. But with the passing of bewar,

[1] Russell and Hiralal, op. cit., ii, p. 85.

Bara Deo lost his temple and his power. After being for many centuries the chief of the deities of the open air, he has in many villages sunk to the position of a mere household god, sharing Narayan Deo's kicks on the threshold, or living with Dulha Deo behind the hearth.

"At first," the Dewar of Kotalwahi told me, "Bara Deo lived with Annadai in the belly of a Chamar. She was the first to break out of it, and Bara Deo followed her. He went to live in a saj tree. But now bewar is stopped, we have brought him into the house, and he lives with Narayan Deo. He is the same as Narayan Deo." Mahatu will have nothing to do with Bara Deo at all. "He is a Gond god; he is not for us Baiga." He is very emphatic about it.

THAKUR DEO

Thakur Deo is the lord of the village, and its headman. He is a jovial old god, with a white beard nine hands long, fond of a bawdy joke, wholly benevolent, almost a Pickwickian character, though I fancy Mr. Pickwick would not have approved his curious interest in excreta. Among the world's deities he is an individual and striking figure. He lives, on earth, in the pipal tree. He sometimes rides abroad on a white horse.

The Baiga have given him a fantastic genealogy. Marra Deo and Marra Luati were born, one from the earth left on the edges of a grave, and the other from the wood left over from a funeral pyre. These two went to live in Deo Muni Pahar, and they had two children, Bijeye and Ijeye. Bijeye's wife was called Jalmotin Kanya, and their son was Brahma. Brahma's wife was Sri Bhadavan, and their son was Thakur Deo. Thakur Deo's own wife is Dharti Mata, who is sometimes called Thakurani. The Bhaina, however, say his consort is Nakti Devi, goddess of the fields. In Hindu hands he becomes Bhairon, the terrible consort of Kali. But where the old fertility beliefs are strong, he is transformed instead into Kama, the god of love, and Dharti Mata into his mistress Rati! No such romance has gathered about the original figure of Thakur Deo, but he is greatly liked and honoured. He is such a thorough Baiga, so good-humoured, always ready to do a man a good turn, always on the right side! In Ajwainbar, I heard a friendly and affectionate Karma song about him:

> An old, old man is Thakur Deo.
> Where does he cut his bewar?
> Where does he kindle his fire?
> Where does he hang his *khumri*?
> He is the Thakur of the whole world.

He cuts his bewar on a rocky hill.
He kindles his fire in the river.
He hangs his *khumri* on a rusty nail.
He is the Thakur of the whole world.

"Thakur Deo," says Ketu, "is the oldest and the most honoured of the gods. We worship him with fire and sarai gum. Then he rides on a man, and we tell him all our sorrows, and he explains things to us, who are evil, why they suffer, what ghost or witch is troubling us, and what we ought to do. When he has given all his advice, he leaves the man and goes away."

Ward describes how, 'in Ramgurh, this deity is held in great reverence; but there he is supposed to occupy more than one shape. One village, Jata, in the Shahpore talooqua, is said to be very highly favoured, as one of the residences of their deity. I was shown there a few links of a roughly-forged chain, which the superstitition of the people had gifted with the power of voluntary motion. This chain looked very old, and no one could tell me how long it had been at Jata. It is occasionally found hanging in a ber tree, sometimes on a stone under the tree, from which it was said to have descended four days before. Each of these movements is made the occasion of some petty sacrifices, of which the attendant Baiga priest reaps the benefit.'[1] I have myself witnessed the miracle of the increase of the three stones of Thakur Deo.[2]

DHARTI MATA

Dharti Mata, or Mother Earth, the mother of the Baiga, is loved as well as worshipped, for to her alone among the deities is given the capacity for love, and the Baiga believe that she loves them, her children. They were born from her womb, and so long as they do not insult her by lacerating her breast with the plough, she tells them all her secrets. To her the month of Jeth is sacred, for then—just before the rains—she lies ready to be impregnated. She is worshipped at the Bidri ceremony, remembered at the Bida, invoked in many mantra. A Baiga will not take a drink of liquor without dropping a few drops on the ground in her honour. If the Dewar considers that her cult is decreasing, he may order a special offering of black pigs, black chickens, and black goats, once in three years.

The Baiga often identify Dharti Mata with Annadai or Kutkidai, goddess of food, and worship her with love and gratitude. For she is the ancient mother of the world, and is adored by every tribe, not only in India, but all

[1] Ward, op. cit., p. 133.

[2] In some villages of Jubbulpore, Thakur Deo is regarded as having first claim on the rents. The *malguzar* goes to him and asks his permission before beginning to collect, and the first rent realized is placed before him for a short time. *Jubbulpore District Gazetteer* (Bombay, 1909), p 87.

over the face of the earth. Frazer has studied, in greatest detail, the worship of the earth among the Vedic Indians, the Greeks, the Romans, in China, in modern India, in Africa and in America (See *The Worship of Nature*, Chapters VI to XI).

BHIMSEN

Bhima or Bhima-sen, the second of the five Pandava, and son of Vayu the Wind, is a prominent figure in Hindu legend. Huge of stature, strong, ill-tempered, abusive, brave, coarse, sometimes cruel, he was a gigantic eater, and earned the nickname of Vrikodava, wolf's belly. He naturally appeals to the aboriginal mind and was adopted under the name of Bhimsen into the Gond and Baiga pantheon. He is the Falstaff of Baiga mythology. He is less honoured by the Baiga than the Gond; both in Kawardha and Bilaspur his cult is indifferently maintained. But elsewhere he is worshipped along with Thakur Deo. He is the giver of rain. Dhan Singh says: "We give Bal Raja Bhimsen some incense at the time of Bidri; at other times we think little about him. But when there is no rain we offer him a red cock and a red chick."

GANSAM DEO

The widespread cult of Gansam Deo[1] has had its influence on the Baiga, and in some villages they erect a pole and build a platform in his honour, for he is powerful to drive away tigers. He is not, however, quite so popular as the following Karma song would suggest:

> O babu Gomshan, where were you born?
> Where are you going to live?
> You were born in Serguja, now you live in every village.
> When you come to a village, where do you make your home?
> At the entrance to each village a *chaura* is built for you.
> On the *chaura* a pole is put,
> And from the pole a flag is flown.
> The rice is made black and yellow for you;
> A horned goat is killed,
> And a river of blood is made to flow on the *chaura*.

In Balaghat, Gango and his consort Gangahin are more popular. In Binjhwar and Narotia houses, they are represented by a couple of tall bamboo poles. Gango's pole has zigzag lines made with red ochre, and a splendid bunch of peacocks' feathers. Gangahin is represented by a

[1] Crooke, rather surprisingly, calls Gansam Deo 'the chief Gond deity', and refers to a legend which derives him from an actual Gond chieftan. There has been an attempt to Hinduize him into Ghanasyama, 'black as a rain cloud', an epithet of Rama and Krishna. Crooke: *The Popular Religion and Folk-lore of Northern India* (London, 1896), i, p. 118.

bamboo pole which is divided by three horizontal wooden crosses. The ends of these are tied to one another by strings which are decorated with flowers. The pole itself is decorated with zigzag lines drawn in red and black, and at the top are peacocks' feathers and a red flag.

The Binjhwar call Gango Matia and Gangahin Marhai. They carry the poles round the village at Diwali and beg at all the houses.

In other districts, poles are set up to represent almost any deity. Near the village, a little hut called the *madhia* is built; inside it is a *chaura*, a raised earthen platform, and on this a lamp, an earthen pot, and perhaps an iron *tirsul* are placed. In front of the shrine, there is sometimes a wooden swing from the movements of which the presence and approval of the god can be recognized. Often, there is only a platform, with a couple of poles beside it. On the poles you may find a *dhaja* (flag), *tirsul*, a *sarria* (iron necklet), a *tikli*, *bandan*, bangles or iron scourges. It is here that the gunia generally make their offerings.

Where wild animals are troublesome, a shrine may be built for Baghesur Pat, and a mud image of a tiger placed inside it.

HOUSEHOLD GODS

In addition to the great gods of the tribe, every family honours a number of household gods. Chief among these are the AJI-DADI, the ancestors, who live behind the hearth. Also located behind the hearth is DULHA DEO, the deified ghost of a young Gond bridegroom who was killed by a tiger on his way to the bride's house. He guards and blesses the *sagai* (engagement) and the marriage-bed. In some houses, Bara Deo lives with him and shares his worship.

NARAYAN DEO, who is now often identified with Bara Deo, lives on the threshold, and as explained in Chapter XI, it is a good thing to kick him every time you go in or out of the house. The Laru pigs are dedicated to him, when it is suspected that he has caught a man by the throat and made him ill. His friend, ANDHERI DEO, lives with him on the thresholds of houses in Bilaspur.

RAT MAI, goddess of night, lives in the house, and makes children happy. When they go anywhere, they say to her, "Go before us!" and when they come back, they say, "Follow us home!" If she is angry, she may give you fever, but is easily appeased by the offering of a black cock. The lower Hindu castes have a quite different idea of Rat Mai. In the dark fortnight of Magh they fast all day, and in the evening make lines on the walls of their houses with lamp-black. They sacrifice a black she-goat or sow, every part of which must be consumed inside the house, even the refuse being buried there.

PANIHARIN lives by the water-pots in a corner of the house. When the women go to get water she protects them. She stops people touching the earthen pots and defiling them. The Baiga offer her pulse and new rice sprinkled on the fire.

In the *madhia*, the sacred mud shrine made on the walls of some houses, where they keep a *tirsul* and peacocks' feathers, lives SATDHARI, who protects the household from disease. MASWASI, lord of the chase, lives in the bow and arrow. So do SUTTIBHAVANI, RAKTIPURBI, ALOPURBI, and KOLIN SUTTI BHAVANI. Others say that Maswasi lives in the bow with the twelve Lodha brothers who catch deer. They are all worshipped before a man goes to hunt, and if he is successful, he smears a little of his victim's blood on the bow and arrow. The four goddesses always accompany the hunter to the jungle, but Maswasi himself stays at home.

In the *lota* (pot) or *thāli* (brass plate) lives KANSASUR MATA; in the axe is LOHASUR MATA; sometimes NARBADA MAI lives in an iron chain hanging from the wall; BASINLAIYA finds a home in a bit of bamboo. Sacred and dangerous are the *battisbandan*, the thirty-two corners of the house, and the little *orcha*, or verandah-roof, that juts out over the front wall. BEHARBASU or PHARKAIN lives in the gate. In the midst of the cattle-shed is KHUT, god of cattle. In a Muria Baiga's house I saw a small *khumri* with a string made of hair from a cow's tail hung on the outer wall of the cattle-shed. This was HOLERA DEO, who protects the cattle.

All these deities are, in relation to man, benevolent or at least neutral. Here they differ from the often more significant and powerful spirits described in Chapter XIII, all of whom are hostile, ready to obey the least whim of a witch or sorcerer, whom it is necessary to propitiate, but whom no one would revere.

Now the essence of Baiga religion is to mobilize these forces of neutrality or benevolence against the forces of evil. Baiga religion is not a dogma, it is a war. The Dewar or gunia is not so much a priest as a warrior. He is a noble and heroic figure, fighting a desperate battle against the unseen powers of disaster and disease. His allies are the great guru and the more benevolent deities; these he must keep friendly by worship and reverence. His enemies must be either defeated outright by the power of his allies, or propitiated by himself. Here is a new reading of his religion—a great battle that divides the supernatural world, that calls out the noblest of mankind to give themselves to the heroic task of saving their fellows from the invisible and unknown.

XIX. FESTIVALS

Nothing is so infectious as a celebration. We will not therefore be surprised to find the Baiga observing a number of their neighbours' feasts, or rather keeping festival on the same days. They often have a quite different idea of what the festival is and sometimes no idea at all, but they do not like to be left out. Thus the Baiga observe the Holi and Dasahra festivals of the Hindus, but they know nothing of Kamadeva's attempt to rouse Shiva's desire for Parvati, they have no idea of propitiating Holika. The Dasahra gains its importance by being the occasion for the Baiga Bida ceremony; none of the Hindu rites or theories are associated with it. It is the same at Diwali. It would be more accurate to say, not that the Baiga observe Dasahra or Diwali, but that they observe a festival at these times.

The first festival of the year is in January. This is the children's feast of Cherta or Kichrahi. The Baiga probably took it from the Gond. Boys dress up as sadhus or put on masks, and go round the village begging, with the song, *Cherta! cherta! Mai, murgi, mārta! Kothikē dhān herta.* When they have got enough, they go down to the riverside, and the girls cook. They make one of the boys represent a crow, and when all the others are served, he gets very little. He must eat first, and while he is eating, a girl throws a blazing brand from the fire at him, and he jumps up and runs away. Then the others can begin their meal. Parents observe this day as a fast.

In March the Baiga keep Phag, as you would expect. They could hardly be expected to pass by so admirable an excuse for getting drunk. But the feast is no more to them than that. "It is not for the gods," they say. "It is for men."

The Bidri ceremony occurs in June, and the Hareli is observed at the beginning of August, in the early part of the rains. The Bhumia believe it to be the festival of Annadai, who is Kutki Dai, goddess of the crops. They bring four kinds of twig, hasiadaphar (*baliospermum axillare*), yogilatti (*asparagus racemosus*), bhawarsal (*hymenodictyon excelsum*), and bhilwa (*semecarpus anacardium*), make them into little bundles, and put them above their doors and in the fields. They believe that these bundles represent the 'crest' of the kodon or kutki, and will ensure good crops.

The Bharotia do the same but make the 'crest' only of bhilwa. In the evening they have a feast.

The Narotia and Binjhwar of Balaghat make stilts on this day, and the children begin to walk about on them. This is called the Geri.

Mask and dancers at the Cherta festival.

I found the Binjhwar and Muria of Mandla and Niwas, however, keeping Hareli in honour of the cow. They feed their cows, take out their ploughs and wash them, put a basket of earth under their ploughs and feed them with *chapāti*. Then they drink in honour of the cow. "It is a Hindu feast, not ours," they told me.

The Pola, two months later, is a sort of sequel to the Hareli. The Bhumia and Bharotia simply put branches of the bhilwa or bhoir trees above their doorways and have a feast. The Narotia and any others who make stilts take them down to the nearest stream, pile them up and burn them. They believe that they are blowing away all the diseases of the village as the wind carries off the smoke. They also decorate their houses with branches of the bhilwa or with bamboo leaves.

At the end of the rains comes the Nawa feast. This is a sort of Harvest Thanksgiving. First they take a handful of rice-stalks, remove the beard and offer this to Thakur Deo. "O Dharti Mai, O Thakur Deo, these are yours! O Nanga Baiga, Nanga Baigin, these are yours!" When they return to their houses they each tie a little bit of the rice-beard above their doors. The women prepare the new rice. The head of each household fasts, for he himself must do the cooking. In Pandaria he sits down before a pot full of boiling water bubbling on the fire, and throws the new rice into it, handful by handful, calling on the names of gods and ancestors. Elsewhere he takes seven saj or parsa leaves, puts a little of the cooked food on each, and offers it near the hearth to a god or ancestor. "All food eaten that day must be of the new harvest, nothing of last year."

The Dassera or Dasahra falls in October. For the Baiga this is chiefly important for the Bida ceremony which I describe in another chapter. It also initiates a month of dancing: the men dance the Dassera, a kind of Saila; the women dance the Rina. During this month which sees the end of the rains, villages exchange visits, and they feast whenever possible.[1]

A little later comes Diwali. Only the very Hinduized Baiga observe it. Bahadur lights a few little lamps and makes offerings to his cattle. They take Gango and Gangahin—represented by tall poles crowned with peacocks' feathers—round the village, begging at every house.

In Mandla I was told: "At Dewari the gunia wake up their *sūpa-tuma* by sacrifices to them. It is now that the witches dance secretly and bring back all the evil spirits we had expelled at the time of the Dassera."

[1] The Hindu Dasahra, which has been called the autumn Saturnalia, celebrates the return of fertility. Its more picturesque features include these customs: they look for the auspicious nilkanth bird; they compose quarrels; each caste worships the implements of its trade. There seems to be no connection between this and the Baiga festival held on the same date.

The Baiga usually observe these two last festivals on dates different from the Hindu calendar.

The Baiga do not usually observe the Jawara ceremony so popular among the Gond.

XX. OMENS

'Like other superstitious people,' says Russell, 'the Baigas are great believers in omens.' But on the whole, in my experience, I have found the Baiga paying far less attention to omens, times and seasons than, for example, their Hindu neighbours. They do not regard an eclipse or thunder and lightning as inauspicious. They do not normally observe days and seasons. It was only in Daharkata, in the Baiga Chak, where the Baiga have for decades been under Hindu influence, that I was able to discover some sort of a time-table of days and seasons. There they told me that:

Sunday was good for work in bewar or forest.

Monday was good for extracting oil.

Tuesday was a bad day for starting a journey.

Wednesday, on the other hand, was a good day for starting a long journey.

Thursday was the day for lovers' meeting.

Friday was a day of rest, for washing clothes, drinking, and dancing.

Saturday was good for work in the forest.

More generally it is held that a marriage may begin on any day but Saturday, but must not be celebrated during the months of Jeth and Pus. A *mohini* or a *thūa* should be prepared on a Sunday or Wednesday, the Laru-kaj should begin on a Saturday, the Bidri on Wednesday or Friday. The *jawāra*-friendship should be initiated on a Monday, the *māhaprasād* on a Monday, and the *sakhi* on a Thursday.

But none of these rules are kept strictly and they vary considerably from place to place.

Such omens as the Baiga consider important follow the usual conventions. Sneezing is always of significance. If a Baiga sneezes once or thrice at the beginning of a journey he goes back home: if he sneezes twice, he knows all will be well. If he strikes his foot against a stone he returns home; one of the most tragic deaths I have ever known was attributed to neglect of this precaution. If a man meets a snake or a gutri crossing the road in either direction, he returns home and sends for a gunia who tells him which god it was. He sacrifices a chicken and sets out again. But some Baiga believe that so long as the deer crosses the road from left to right, there is no danger. It is very bad for a bear to cross the road in front of you, or if you hear the kiddari pigeon as you are starting out. If a jackal 'cuts the road', you must prepare a *thūa* on the spot. Put the branch of any bush on the path, and a big stone above it. The branch represents the enemy who sent the jackal, the stone is his grave. You may then go on your way.

If your left eye twitches it means variously that a stranger is coming to the village, that you are going to meet a bear or tiger in the jungle, or that some disaster is threatening the house of your mother-in-law. The twitching of the left eye gives greater hope: it means that the sick will recover, or that a friend or relation is coming to see you.

If the palm of your hand itches, it is a sign that a hare or gutri has been caught in a trap away in the jungle. "If your right hand itches," Mahatu once said, "it means that someone is going to give you money; but if your left itches, you'll spend the whole day washing your own bottom." If the sole of your foot itches, it means someone is talking about you. If it tickles unbearably, then someone must be abusing you. If you want to find out who it is, begin to recite slowly the names of everyone you know. If the itching ceases as you repeat any name, then you know that it was that person who was discussing you. It is also possible to discover when a visitor will come. Take a pipal leaf and cut it so that it exactly fits the mouth of a small water-pot. Fill this with water, close it with the leaf, and turn it upside down. Begin to say, "To-day So-and-so will come. To-morrow. Thursday. Friday," and the water will break the leaf and gush out as you mention the day on which your visitor will come.

It is very bad to see a crow bathing alone in a stream. It means that some relation who lives far away has died and no message has yet had time to reach you. So also if your right arm throbs, it means that some relation is in trouble.

But the Baiga rely more on dreams than on omens to reveal the future. I have recorded a large number of prophetic dreams in the Chapter on that subject.

The Baiga also claim to be able to read as an open book the great volume of Nature. "We Baiga," says Mahatu, "understand everything from trees and fruit and flowers. If we see a parrot eating a mango only in the middle, then we know there will be rain for two months but not in Bhadon (September). But if the parrot eats the whole mango, and drops the stone on the ground, then we know that there will be good rain every month."

Similarly Dhan Singh declared that "the Brahmin can read his sacred books, but we are children of Dharti Mata, and she loves us and whispers her secrets in our ears. In the partridge's nest, if all the eggs lie together, then rains will be good. But if they lie apart, it will be poor. And if one egg lies separate from the rest, in that direction there will be famine."

XXI. OATHS

As a tribe the Baiga are exceptionally truthful and straightforward, especially in their dealings with one another. There are certain subjects, however, on which they are always prepared to lie—a girl will take any oath to prove that she has not committed adultery, though a man will freely confess it, the penalties for him being, of course, much lighter; and they generally lie when accused of having broken one of the forest laws. They do not seem to regard an oath as specially dangerous or binding, though to break a promise made to a *deo* or *bhut* is often fatal. They are prepared to swear by their relations, the gods, and the things of everyday use around them. In fact there is hardly anything a Baiga is not prepared to swear by. I once heard one swear "by the Magistrate Sahib's pen".[1]

The Baiga swears by the blood of his mother and by the blood of his sister; he promises to commit incest if he has not spoken the truth. He lays his hand on his child's head, saying, "May he die if I tell a lie." More emphatically still he may declare his readiness to eat the flesh of his son and daughter or of his father and mother. Finally he professes himself ready to eat the excrement of his wife.

Less frequently the Baiga invokes the gods. "May Jal Deo, the water-god, drown me, if I am lying!" "May Agin Deo (the Fire-god) burn me!" "May the Earth devour me!" "May the Wind carry me off!" "May Raja Bastar Rai destroy me!"—and so on.

He also swears by any sacred object—by the sarai tree, by the bier of a dead man, by the little roof that is added to the wall of a house to make a verandah, by the sacred forest herbs, by the dry bamboo, by the lumps of salt,[2] by the Narbada River. Sometimes he goes under a tree and says, "May this tree fall and crush me, if I am not speaking the truth!"

A husband who wants to find out what his wife has been doing puts to her a series of oaths of a gradually ascending scale of seriousness. First he asks her to swear by the gods, by Agin Deo or Anna Dai. She does it willingly. Then he demands, "Say 'I will eat your flesh if I did it'." This too is granted, though less willingly. He then puts to her an oath on the head of her child or her child's flesh—and she takes it, even if guilty, but with a bad conscience. Heaviest oath of all, he makes her swear by the earth.

The offer to eat human flesh or human excrement probably derives from

[1] This was in my own Court, a most unfortunate oath, as my pen had just finished writing a hundred thousand words of fiction!

[2] Meaning that 'as the bamboo dries standing in the clump, so may I dry and wither' and 'as the lumps of salt dissolve in water, so may I disappear if I tell a lie'.

the days when there drifted across the whole of the Baiga country grim stories of the Birhor and Bhunjia who were rumoured to eat human flesh and of the mendicant Aghori who even to-day eat excrement.

It is unfortunate that in the Courts the oath is administered in a form that is meaningless to the Baiga, and not only to the Baiga but to most other litigants. Witnesses are asked to say that they will *imān sē*, or really and truly, speak the truth. If after making this solemn affirmation, they perjure themselves they are liable for a criminal offence, but the almost universal practice of perjury in the Indian Courts seems to indicate that the purely legal oath is inadequate.

Section VIII of the Indian Oaths Act allows 'any party to, or witness in, any judicial proceeding to give evidence on oath in any form common amongst, or held binding by, persons of the race or persuasion to which he belongs, and not repugnant to justice or decency.' The Court may also ask any party or witness whether he will make an oath proposed by the opposite party. The Court cannot compel the party to make it, but if 'he refuses the Court shall record, as part of the proceedings, the nature of the oath or affirmation proposed, the facts that he was asked whether he would make it, and that he refused it.'

It is not, however, within the competence of the Court itself to propose such an oath. It would be a good thing, at least in tribal areas, if this were allowed, as the following experience recorded by Risley in the 1901 Census suggests.

'In a small sub-divisional court, where I used one to dispense what was accepted as justice in the surrounding jungles, there was tied to the railings which fenced off the seat of justice from the multitude a fragment of a tiger's skin. When members of certain tribes, of whom the Santals were a type, came into court to give evidence, they were required to take a peculiar but most impressive oath, the use of which was, I believe, entirely illegal. Holding the tiger's skin in one hand, the witness began by invoking the power of the Sun and Moon and after asseverating his intention to tell the truth he ended up by devoting himself to be devoured by the power of the tiger in case he should tell a lie. . . . The reality of these ideas, the effectiveness of the sanctions which they invoked, was sufficiently attested by the manifest reluctance of a mendacious witness to touch the magic skin, and by the zeal with which the court usher insisted upon his taking a firm grasp of it.'[1]

[1] *Census of India*, 1901. General Report, p. 357.

XXII. PROVERBS

The Baiga are not very well provided with proverbs (*ahna*), but such as they have are often shrewd and amusing and throw some light on their psychology and daily life.

Many proverbs make fun of the pretentious or boastful man. 'The boastful man goes everywhere talking, talking; but he ends up in the little hut where he started.' 'In his house, there is nothing. When he goes out, he wears his dhoti down to his knees.' The ordinary dress of a Baiga is a small lingoti, and a full dhoti covering the knees is a mark of unusual prosperity. Another sign of wealth is the use of betel nut; few Baiga can afford it. 'His father and grandfather never tasted betel; but he takes it once, and must show his reddened teeth to everyone.' The pauper who pretends to riches is ridiculed. 'He begs and begs from house to house, then goes and belches in the bazaar,' as though he had just stuffed himself like a Brahmin.

Ingratitude is castigated. Once we were discussing the treacherous behaviour, the *bandar ki doshti*, the monkey's friendship, of a certain Gond, and old Mahatu exclaimed, "A Gond, a Woman, and a Dream—never say that any of these three belongs to you." A *khawai-mit* is one who remains your friend only as long as he expects to get something out of you.

Another proverb about Gond contrasts their behaviour with that of the Baiga when a chaprasi comes to the village to exact *begar*. 'The Gond hide here and there; the Baiga creeps behind his own fireplace.' The Gond generally scatter in the forest, but the Baiga hide inside their houses and pretend they are not at home. 'Even a fool can escape danger by hiding behind a tree.'

Another proverb throws light on the conflict between the Baiga and the authorities. 'All eat the stolen food; but one gets indigestion.' This was said when a whole village of Baiga enjoyed a feast off a sambhar killed by one of their hunters. But he himself was fined heavily under the Game Act. "What fools we Baiga are," they sometimes say humorously at such times, "to go on living in the forest!" and "The Baiga sees an animal and shoots at it. If he misses, the animal kills him; if he hits, the Government kills him." The moral is that nowadays it is safer to leave your bows and arrows at home.

There are several proverbs about idleness and stupidity. A man who always says he will do something, but doesn't—'His mouth is always busy, but what are his hands and feet doing?' and 'Wherever he lives, he causes loss to his host.'

The idle fellow is well described.

"Where have you been? Nowhere. What have you brought with you? Nothing."

And this is a boy who never does anything properly. 'He troubles the whole world. Instead of urinating at night in the earthen pot, he does it in the lid,' and of course makes a mess of the floor.

The man who wastes his time during the busy months: 'The man who kills fish in Asad, and visits his relatives in Kartik has no leaves or plates in his house.' Another idle man is rebuked: 'All you can do is stretch your hands and feet, and bring your plate at meal-times.'

The difference between rich and poor, is often—and rather pathetically—expressed. 'To a rich man a dhoti is nothing. To a poor man a lingoti is everything.' But the difference between a dhoti and a lingoti, between a rich Baiga and a poor one, is only a matter of a few yards of cloth.

Yet rich and poor are never treated alike. When a well-to-do man, his whole body covered but his face, comes to a house, his treatment is very different from that of his poor neighbour, who comes naked but for his lingoti which barely covers his privates.

'See his face, give him betel!

'See his buttocks, seat him anywhere!

A stingy man is one who 'wants to offer *konda roti* (the cheapest kind of food) to the *bhut*,' who won't spend money even for his soul's safety.

A hungry man sits with whoever will feed him. 'Where there is food, there his eyes do service.'

A calculating lover is satirized:

'If you've any money, run away with me;

'But if you're in debt, run away with someone else.'

A greedy man says, 'I've such a big stomach that I can't spare a scrap for anyone, or I won't be able to fill it.'

A handsome man who is difficult to live with is addressed: 'To look at, you are ripe enough. But when I come to eat you, you are raw.'

Scandal is well described. 'Once it is sown outside the house, the harvest fills all the world.'

There are many proverbs about impotence. 'It is all one to me, whether my husband is at home or in another village.' 'The sarai leaves are reddening; daily you come and give me nothing.' 'How hard his mouth works; how idle are his loins.'

But whenever there is real love, the Baiga proverb-maker is merciful. He never attacks any kind of sincerity, however foolish. "They are united as kodon and buttermilk," said Jethu to me once of a couple who had run away, driving their little pig—their only possession—before them through the jungle.

'The girl's life is in her boy's heart:

'His life is in hers.'

And they also say, 'The housewife always uses a *mūsar* to pound rice, the Dewar always talks of wisdom, the lover always talks of love.'

Beauty, however, does not always spell enjoyment. 'Her face is lovely as a parrot. But her vagina is wide as a well.' Or again: 'What is the use of a pretty face, if she has the brains of a buffalo.' And the Baiga cynic sums up his experience of womankind. 'Outside, how beautiful! But go in and there's nothing but a mouse's hole.' But this is no argument against romance. Necessity drives everyone. When Mithu took his elderly leprous wife to his bed, they said, "When you're hungry, you'll make a full meal of a cucumber. When you're burning hot, you'll have even an old woman."

A good man is the real divinity. 'He who gives a stick to the blind, a rag to the naked, water to the thirsty, food to the hungry, a son to the childless—he is a god.'

And in the end, old age! The boys tease their grandfather and ask him if he ever did anything naughty when he was young. 'In times past I did deeds past. Now I rest on my elbow, my hand to my cheek.'

And again: 'In youth, he never thinks of consequences: in age he remembers the next morning.'

XXIII. BAIGA GALI

The most striking thing about the bad language of the Baiga is the very wide field from which they draw no material. The realms of theology and eschatology, of prostitution, bastardy and homosexuality are but indifferently exploited: it is from the sciences of anatomy and sociology that the Baiga draw their main inspiration. This fact is very important for a proper understanding of the Baiga mind, for in no way does a people reveal itself so readily and so directly as in its swearing.

The most obvious omission in Baiga *gāli* is the absence of the religious oath. There is nothing to correspond with the full-blooded 'Gog's bones' or 'Od's blood' of the Elizabethan Age, or even the somewhat more agnostic and tepid 'O God' and 'O Lord' of our own. No one would ever think of swearing by the bones of Thakur Deo or the sacred heart of Nanga Baiga. The exasperated Baiga does not call the Forest-guard who has caught him poaching a 'creeping Bara Deo'. Moreover, the Baiga's extreme vagueness about the after-life deprives him of the invaluable expletives 'hell' and 'damnation', for he believes in neither. He cannot even use some jungle equivalent of 'Good Heavens' or 'Goodness Gracious', for he has no real conception of either grace or heaven.

The Hinduized Baiga does sometimes say "I'll pay you out in your next birth!" or "May you be re-born as a pig in my house!" but this is a cumbersome and remote-sounding substitute for the compendious, immediate and effective 'damn you!' Sometimes at the height of a quarrel, those who are artists in these matters call down the vengeance of heaven upon their adversaries. 'May Suraj Narayan destroy you!' 'May Rat Mai kill you!' 'May Pawan Deo carry you away!' But this is not common. On the whole, religious oaths are absent, and this fact is, I think, an indication of the comparatively light hold that religion—as distinguished, of course, from magic—has on the interests and affections of the tribe.

Magic is of absorbing interest, but it is far too dynamic and explosive a subject to be referred to without great risk in ordinary life.

We may also remark the absence from the Baiga vocabulary of some of the commonest Indian *gāli*. The Baiga never employ, for example, the word '*sālāh*', in such frequent use by Mussalmans. 'Bahinchod badmash', popular among Hindus, is rarely used by Baiga. 'Sūr ka bachcha' (son of a pig), perhaps the favourite *gāli* of the Police Station or Range Office, is unknown to the Baiga, and would appear to them a rather weak expression as the pig is one of their most useful and favourite animals.

Homosexual expressions are not common—here again is a wide divergence from Western practice. At all events it does not seem to annoy the Baiga very much to be accused of homosexual practices, perhaps because these, though not so rare as is generally believed, are devoid of any deep emotional content. There is at all events no one term which corresponds to the famous English expression which was defined by Dr. Johnson as 'a term of endearment between sailors'.

The imputation of bastardy also gives no offence, if indeed it is ever made. The Baiga do actually have a word for bastard, 'bhūla larka', but Mahatu in the course of a long life and many wanderings told me that he had only heard of two cases where it could properly be applied. Here then is an interesting sidelight on Baiga affairs. The bastard has no social stigma attached to him—'If anyone was at fault it was the mother. What did the child do?'—and indeed matters are so arranged that the unmarried mother is hardly ever to be found.

The Baiga do not accuse their women of being whores or strumpets. The word 'randi' is not one of their terms of abuse, for they hardly know what it means. There are no Baiga whores. The expression 'chhinal chodri', meaning a woman of free morals, is, however, sometimes used.

It is from the field of sexual physiology that the Baiga draws the bulk of his material. It is here that he is really at home, and there is hardly anything that he cannot produce and use with devastating effect. The most common word in his vocabulary is 'bhosri', which almost corresponds to the Western 'bloody' and has the same advantage—that nearly everyone has forgotten what it means. It actually refers to the male or female genitals and has a wide range of usage. It is often employed in the genitive, and then means, 'You who are born of a penis!'—a simple affirmation of faith in physiological paternity which generally causes a quite disproportionate outburst of rage. Children are specially enraged at being abused in this way: many times I have known boys in tears, sometimes trembling with passion, on account of it. Adults, however, take this *gāli* less seriously.

Then what a fascination the pubic hairs have for the Baiga, the more mysterious because they nearly always pull them out! Hair is, of course, an object of high sexual attraction to the Baiga, but this hardly explains the explosive character of the word *jhāt*. 'My *jhāt* doesn't want it,' is one of the rudest possible ways of saying 'No'. 'I'll make you eat my *jhāt*!' 'I'll stuff your *jhāt* up your vagina!', 'I'll cut off your *jhāt*!'—the word is capable of a score of uses, each more insulting than the last.

References to the excretory functions are often made, for this is a subject on which the Baiga may fairly claim to be specialists. Their custom of cleaning themselves with leaves instead of water, the signal success of Nanga Baiga in attracting the attention of Thakur Deo with a dirty leaf, mark them out from all others. The words 'hagru' and 'hagri' which are applied to persons and 'tatti' and 'gu' which are applied to excreta itself, are useful *gāli*. I have, by the way, a good friend who was called Hagru by his parents to frighten away the *bhut*, and I call him this a dozen times a day without any feeling of embarrassment at the use of such a curious appellation. *Hagri* is more commonly used than the masculine form, and is regarded as a greater insult. I well remember a husband referring to a wife who had betrayed him with the utmost bitterness as 'that *hagri*'. An oppressive landlord or policeman may be described as one 'who urinates liquid fire', and threats may be made to urinate or excrete in an opponent's mouth. 'You'll eat my mother's excreta' or 'I'll make you eat my excreta' are *gāli* of a very explosive nature.

Direct references to the private parts are more common. The words are generally used in the genitive implying that the subject is 'born of' or 'belongs to' the organ mentioned. The penis, vagina, rectum, clitoris, labia majora and labia minora are all employed in this manner. A man will also threaten to cut one or other of them off, or to stuff something into them, generally salt or chili.

Then there are the inevitable threats to copulate with any and every member of your opponent's family. But where the Hindu or Mussalman generally accuses his enemy of incest, shouting *bahin chod* (copulator with your sister) at him, the Baiga does not generally say this, perhaps thinking that it would not be regarded as a very great insult. What the Baiga says is that he himself will copulate with his opponent's sister, mother, aunt, or daughter. The most insulting reference is to the daughter.

When a husband abuses his wife, he can add insult upon insult by addressing her as sister or daughter. "*Bhosri!*" he may begin. "Why do you give me *gāli?*" she screams in reply. "Are you my sister or daughter that I shouldn't abuse you? Very well. From to-day, you are my daughter. I won't say a word." Kundia left her husband's house because he lost his temper and called her 'Kundia Beti' (daughter).

The scope of this kind of abuse is, of course, greatly widened by reference to the animal world, and here the Baiga falls back on conventional methods and accuses his enemy of committing bestiality with every possible animal. It is interesting to note that here too the word 'bitch' is considered particularly insulting.

But to a woman the most rage-making expression of all is 'tonhi,' witch. I have listened to quarrels in which women have been getting along very bouncingly with the most violent reflections on their own honour and the morals of their families, in which the obscenest expressions have been used with entire good humour: but no sooner has the fatal word 'tonhi' been uttered than there has been screaming, passionate tears, and the initiation of a life-long feud. For the word 'tonhi' is not only disreputable, it is dangerous; witchcraft and its punishment are still far too real to be referred to lightly.

To a man any abuse implying impotence is highly annoying, for a Baiga's potency is his honour. So 'murdār' and 'nāmarad' are valuable additions to the Baiga's vocabulary. Equally insulting is a curious expression, 'Massager of the feet of women', implying, I suppose, a gigolo or henpecked husband. The rules about not eating another's leavings give point to the *gāli*, 'Eater of my leavings!'

There are also a large number of miscellaneous expressions such as: 'May there never be a light in your house!' or 'May a tiger eat you!' or 'You were born of a mad womb!' or 'May fire burn you in your sleep!' Two are regarded as of special potency. 'I'll see you going, but I'll not see you returning,' was the curse that gave Mahatu a nasty attack of epididymitis; and 'Go and tell your father,' or 'Does this belong to your father?' seems to excite unusual annoyance.

A study of bad language in connection with tribal institutions immediately reveals its sociological significance. It shows us the comparatively limited hold of the gods on the imagination of the tribe, and the powerful interest still controlled by magic and witchcraft. It reveals the fact that homosexuality is not very seriously regarded, that prostitution is non-existent, that bastardy is almost unrecognized. It betrays the extreme sexual freedom of the tribe and the dread of impotence. It finally emphasizes, here as everywhere, the great gulf between the Baiga and the rest of the population.

XXIV. THE OUTSIDE WORLD

The average Bhumia or Bharotia Baiga of Pandaria, the wilds of Mandla, Kawardha or Baihar, have only the vaguest notion of the civilized world. In Bohi I found they believed that the Rani of Pandaria was the queen of India; they had never before been visited by an Englishman. Elsewhere, they think that Mandla or Balaghat is the centre of Government. Many have never heard of Nagpur, Delhi or Bombay. The Baiga, more than other tribes, however, have strong opinions about the English owing to their conflict with the Government about the cutting of bewar. Most of them know something also about Mahatma Gandhi.

Gandhi is 'a god like the other gods'; he is 'a great and powerful raja'; he is 'a very rich man who has made a lot of money by fighting the English'. Forest-fires are generally due to his curse which will make the English poorer. He is 'the incarnation of Bhagavan. One day his wife had twins, and on that day he drove out the English and established Hindu-raj'. 'The English fought against him, but when they put handcuffs on his hands they turned into flowers and fell off, and when they put him in jail, he flew away in a chariot over the walls.' Not many are so uninstructed as an old man in Jholar who thought the Mahatma was 'something to eat'. There is no nationalist feeling among the Baiga; Congress and English alike are hostile to the Baiga-raj, though in the end this will triumph over the mightiest empires. The Mahatma is revered as a saint rather than as a politician, though recently there has been a revulsion of feeling against him on account of Prohibition. 'How can he take away the best thing in our lives?'

The Baiga find it rather difficult to make up their mind about the English. On the one hand, 'the English are our brothers, we belong to their family'. Individual Forest Officers, like Baiga Thompson and the 'Lungra Sahib' were very popular. Yogi Dewar still remembers Colonel Hogg, handsome and well-dressed, with affection as 'the best we ever had'. Mr. C. E. C. Cox made a great impression in Baihar a year or two ago; the Baiga were astonished that 'the lord of eighteen talukas' could be so genial and simple. In Amadob, Mr. Ramsden is remembered as the 'sahib with shining spectacles' and his generosity has often been held up to me as an example.

Although thousands of Baiga have never seen a train, and even a motor car is a matter of excitement and astonishment, they sing a number of songs about the Westerner's power of making these things.

> The train comes puffing into the jungle.
> In one car rides the King;
> In another car rides the Queen;
> In the third is the sahib with shining spectacles.
> The train comes puff-puff-puff.
> The sahib with shining spectacles
> Gives presents to the Baiga.

That was from Amadob. The next is also from Bilaspur District, from Ajwainbar village.

> Be careful where you go,
> For the English are kings.
> Who has ever seen the boundary of their kingdom?
> They have taken all the best hills.
> In the sweet forest they have built their bungalows.
> They have big guns.
> When the tiger and tigress see them,
> They run away for fear.

Shahpura in Niwas is near the telegraph line, and hence the following:

> The ever-touring Englishmen have built their bungalows
> All over our sweet forest.
> They drive their trains with smoke.
> O look at them, how they talk on wires to one another!
> With their wires they have bound the whole world together for
> themselves.

And this from Pondi, where the railway now runs:

> O Englishman, marvellous is your brain that makes the engine run,
> With iron nails and iron plugs and coal you make it run,
> With fire and water you created smoke; by your brain you make it run.

The Baiga, of course, find it very difficult to forgive the English for stopping bewar-cutting and hunting, and a legend has grown up about the conquest of the Baiga which may be symbolically correct but has no basis in history. Ketu told me this story one evening by the fire in Amtera.

"The English Raja came into the forest and the Baiga Raja went out to meet him. The English Raja said: 'Bring out your army.' The Baiga Raja said: 'Prepare your army and I'll bring mine.' The Baiga Raja went into the jungle and called every kind of tiger, and the leopard, the panther, the bear, the elephant, monkeys and deer, jungle pig and porcupine, and led them against the English. They all were killed—only the Baiga Raja escaped with his life.

"As he was alone, the English Raja let him go. The Baiga went to the bazaar, and got many earthen pots. In every pot he put bees and wasps, hornets and stinging flies, and closed the mouths of the pots. He filled nine carts with them and came to the English camp.

"'Well,' said the English Raja, 'why don't you bring another army?'

"The Baiga Raja said: 'I have no army. I have just come with my few possessions in these carts. Now you must fight with me alone. Prepare your army!'

"So the English army got ready, and when they had all come together, the Baiga Raja threw the pots one by one into their midst. As they hit the ground they broke, and the wasps and bees came out and bit the English army, and they all ran away.

"But the English came back again afterwards and conquered us with their laws when we were not looking."

Pachlu gave me another version in Baihar.

"At first the English came like sadhus to us. They had staffs in their hands and begging-bowls. But under their arms was paper and pencil. They went from village to village, begging their way, and singing. Wherever they went the people fell in love with them for their goodness and their sweet singing. So they made many friends, and learnt all about our country and our jungle. Secretly they wrote it down in little books.

"Very soon they came in a far different fashion, riding on horses, and by the help of their servants they measured the land, and gave new laws to the Baiga.

"And at last they came in their motors. They were kings now and the whole country belonged to them."

A few Baiga go to the tea gardens in Assam. Those who go bring back good accounts of their pay and treatment. But the experience does not seem to enlarge their horizons very greatly. On the whole the Baiga know little of civilization and think little of it. In Niwas I met two Baiga who had been to Jubbulpore to see what it was like. One was Lakgan of Rangaon. He went to 'see the tamasha and cinema' of which a constable had told him. But the day he arrived he was run over by a motor-bus, and spent his holiday in hospital. The other, Bhagela of Barkera, after being thoroughly frightened and confused by the traffic, went to bed in the sarai. In the middle of the night he got up and went outside to relieve himself. But he could not find his way back. He wandered about a bit, and at last found himself in the wrong house. He was immediately apprehended as a thief, and the police were sent for. Bhagela explained vigorously that he was a jungly Baiga, and the word was sufficient to secure his release. But the police sent him back to his village the following morning.

Few Baiga have become Christians. In 1882, two hundred of them came to Col. Bloomfield's bungalow to meet Bishop Johnson, of Calcutta—but they returned to their jungle. Mr. A. W. McMillan, in his *Jungle Pioneering in Gondland* (London, 1906), says something of the 'score or so' Baiga who had then joined the Christian Church. He gives high praise to his own cook, Yohan Badaru, a Christian Baiga (p. 50). He took Yohan to Bombay where he thought the houses were like mountains, and 'on seeing the sea innocently asked whether it flooded the city in rainy weather.' 'In comparing the Gond who is supposed to have come *from* Heaven,' says Mr. McMillan, 'with the Baiga who has undoubtedly gone *to* Heaven, one cannot help glorifying God for the wonderful power of His transforming grace as displayed in this erstwhile dark and superstitious son of one of the semi-wild and untutored races of mankind.' (p. 53).

Chapter II

THE BAIGA'S LIVELIHOOD

I. POSSESSION AND OWNERSHIP

THE Baiga naturally have rather vague ideas about property and inheritance. They are *gai-nanga*, naked as cows. They live from day to day on what they can get; often there is no store of grain in their dilapidated houses. They are nomadic by tradition and habit, and even in these more settled times find it hard—as a glance at Chapter IV will show—to remain in any one place for long. The practice of bewar does not foster the sense of attachment to particular bits of land or require the accumulation of cattle. A few axes, some cooking-pots, a little store of ornaments and cash—this is the fortune of an ordinary Baiga.

Small wonder then that discussions about ownership, partition, inheritance, do not greatly excite them and that they rarely appear in the Civil Courts. Yet their customs are fairly definite, though often modified by kindness.

First, as to ownership. Within the home, everything, from the building down to the cheapest cooking-pot, is the property of the husband or father of the family. Once a wife has entered his house, everything, even what she 'earns by her own sweat', belongs to her husband. The ornaments he gives her are hers for the using only; should she leave him and marry another man, they must be returned. She cannot give them away as presents. But anything she brought with her from her parents' house is regarded as her own. Sometimes a widow manages to retain a share of her husband's property. This also remains hers after she remarries.

The son and daughters must hand over to the father anything they may earn. If the boy makes a fish-trap, for example, and sells it, he must give the money to his father. Even his axe does not belong to him, but to his father.

When the boy marries, if his father approves of the union, he may give him some cooking-pots, an axe, a little cloth, to begin his new life, and help him build his house, if he intends to live separately. But if the father does not approve, the son cannot claim any 'partition' as of right when he

Bhumia youth spinning string.
A platform for storing maize and kodon in a corner of Rupnidadar.

sets up a separate establishment. If, on the other hand, the son decides to continue to live with his wife in the father's house—as sometimes happens when the parents are old and need support—then the old arrangement obtains. All the earnings of both the son and his wife must go to the father, and all their everyday possessions are vested in him. If, after a year or two, they set up house elsewhere, the father will probably give them something to start with, but he is not obliged to.

The Baiga 'joint-family' is thus quite different to a Hindu joint-family under the Mitakshara law, in which all the male members lineally descended from a common ancestor are coparceners in the property. If a member of such a family demands partition and his share, he has a right to have it. But this is not in Baiga law. There are no coparceners in the property, for it all belongs absolutely to one person, the head of the family, and it remains within his discretion how he shall partition it during his lifetime.

A son or a wife, however, may secretly keep a store of money. They may keep back part of their earnings; a wife or daughter may receive presents from admirers. This is known as *pogri*. It is this that often enables a son to marry against his father's wishes, or a wife to elope with a new lover.

II. THE SOURCES OF INCOME

What are the sources of Baiga wealth (I am confining myself here, as everywhere, to the bewar-cutting Baiga, as the others in no way differ from the ordinary Indian cultivator)? This is very hard to estimate. I would not attempt to give any idea of a Baiga's income, for so much of his livelihood depends on the forest, and comes to him in the most haphazard way. For example, take Rawan's household during a good month. His daughter has come to stay from her husband's house. Everyone is well. His unmarried son of seventeen years is with him and his third wife has not yet run away. He has been successful in killing a gutri, a sambhar, two hares and a green pigeon. His women-folk have been industrious in picking mangoes and digging roots. He has had no overhead expenses. This month he is prosperous. But take a bad month. His son has just got married and left him. His third wife has run away. His daughter has gone home to her husband. His second wife has been involved in a scandal with a Panka and he has had to pay a heavy tribal fine. He has only killed a couple of hares with his bow and arrow. He himself has been ill for fifteen days, and his one faithful wife has been largely occupied in nursing him. A storm has ruined half the crop. This month, his income is down to nothing, his expenditure has eaten up all his savings. And it is difficult to take an average of good and bad months, for these things go in a run, and no one knows what may happen.

But we may briefly indicate the main sources of a Baiga's income, though this, of course, will only be partly in money; most of it is in kind.

In 1878, Colonel Bloomfield recorded a report of the Ṫehsildar of Baihar that 'the Bygahs eke out their existence by the following means:

1. Cutting *dhya* and thus obtaining the *kharif* crops.
2. Village pūjāriship, exorcism, and herbalism.
3. Bamboo matting and baskets.
4. By collecting and selling honey and jungle produce such as harra.[1]
5. By labour.
6. By jungle fruits and roots.
7. By killing wild animals, and on fish.'

We will consider No. 1 at length in a moment. 'Village pūjāriship' is rich in promises but in little else. Bahadur's experience is instructive.[2] It is the custom to sneer at the village priest for being so anxious about his 'collection'. This is most unfair. The gunia often has to leave all other business to devote himself to works of mercy, and he would starve unless he took what he could from his patients. At the most this is not more than his expenses and a bit of cloth. Colonel Ward records a Baiga receiving Rs. 80 for freeing the town of Mandla from an epidemic. But such windfalls come only once in a lifetime, and then only to those who live near a town.

The Baiga have almost lost their income from bamboo work. This is partly due to an agitation by the Basor who claimed that the Baiga were infringing their caste or 'Trades Union' rights, so that many Baiga now only make baskets and mats for their own use, and partly due to the corruption of minor officials who catch the unhappy Baiga on the way to the bazaar and, on the pretext that the bamboo was stolen, take all the fruits of the tribesmen's labour for their own profit.

The collecting of honey is subject to the same disadvantages. I remember how a Sub-inspector of police forbade anyone to remove honey from a famous clump of trees, where there were no fewer than eighty hives, on the ground that all honey belonged to Government and therefore to himself. He privately arranged that the honey was to be removed and brought to him, and so made considerable profit. The Baiga are generally afraid to offer honey for sale for fear some official will take it from them; indeed they are afraid to go to the bazaars at all, for fear their goods will be taken and

[1] *Terminalia chebula.*

[2] See Chap. IV, p. 155.

their labour impressed by some jack-in-office. But when they do gather honey, this mantra should be repeated at the foot of the tree where the hives are:

> Mahadeo Parvati, when my pot is full, then into the seven seas and sixteen rivers I will make a river of honey to flow.

Alhough Government laid down in 1890 that labour for harra contractors should normally be given to the Baiga, this provision has been largely forgotten.

Labour is more profitable. Every family in a Forest Village has, by agreement, to provide the Department with one able-bodied working man a day. Although some Baiga grumble at this, it is really a great boon to them. They receive three annas a day in wages, and it provides them with certain and regular work for part of the year. Unhappily there is not enough work to give employment to the Baiga all the year round. Those who become sawyers earn a great deal more, but only a few Baiga avail themselves of the opportunity. They are not generally very happy in regular employment. Some of them take the work of fire-watchers on Rs. 6 a month, but this only lasts for two months of the year. I personally only know of two Baiga forest guards—Jumaria in Kisli-Belwani and Ram Singh in Banjar—and both resigned, though there must, of course, have been others.

The more civilized Baiga work in the fields for Gond and other well-to-do villagers. But it is not unknown for the more conservative Bhumia to employ Gond cultivators to work their fields for them. There are several different kinds of contracts into which they may enter. The first is known as *adhiya*: here the lender advances land, seed, and cattle on condition that the borrower pays half the land revenue and gives him half the crop. The exact terms may vary according to the fertility of the soil. In this there is a sharing of risk between lender and borrower.

In the *bādhi* and *bijāhi* systems, however, there is no such risk to the lender. On *bādhi*, he advances grain or food to a cultivator on condition of receiving one and a half times the amount at harvest-time: on *bijāhi*, he receives double the amount.

Būhi is a system of borrowing bullocks; a bullock is taken for two harvests, and four and a half *khandi* of grain is given in return.

The best Bhumia Baiga, however, have little to do with such arrangements. Jungle fruit and roots are plentiful; the time spent in gathering them is the happiest and most romantic of the Baiga's life. He sometimes sells the fruit—mangoes, twenty-five for a pice, a hundred for an anna, other fruit like jamun, ghui, wild guavas, by *keja* (exchange), *seer* for *seer* of kodon or kutki.

But the chief economic interest and the staple source of income for the Baiga is the bewar, and this we will study in another chapter.

III. FISHING

The seventh source of income was hunting and fishing. The little mountain streams that flow near the Baiga villages do not contain much that is worth eating. Yet old Jethu at Bohi was able to distinguish over twenty varieties of fish—the *saur*, the long snake-like *bāmi*, *kusuwa*, *kotri* and *kotra*, *jimta*, *enda*, *kharhari*, *tengua*, *padina*, *ganda*, *dandai*, *rehu*, *munda*, *singan*, *phalia*, *galāj*, *pariyans*, *kokia*, *kusra*, *mohrāli*. The *pariyans*, *kotri* and *kokia* are the most common; the most popular are the little *kotri* which, fried, tastes rather like whitebait, the large *saur* from which you can get large fleshy fillets, and the *enda*. River prawns are also popular.

Both men and women go fishing and enjoy it, especially in the hot weather. In the cold weather they are generally afraid of chills and fever, and during the rains not a few are drowned in the floods. There are no ceremonies connected with fishing, but as the Baiga go to and fro in the water they sing such songs as these:

> Her legs are moving.
> The *bansi* is moving.
> Her *chutki* are tinkling.
> Which hand do you use to put the bait on the hook?
> Which hand do you use to kill the fish?
>   With my left hand I bait the hook.
>   With my right I kill the fish.

The most common method of catching fish is to dam up a stream and throw all the water out of the pool thus formed. This is described in the song:

> We dam up the river above and below,
> From the midst we throw out the water.
>   As we go on throwing out the water,
>   Our backs begin to ache,
>   So we go to rest in the cool shade.

Poison is fairly often used—the powdered bark of the chirechar,[1] or guhalari,[2] or tinsa[3] are said to be effective. So is the unripe fruit of the

[1] *Fluggea microcarpa.* [2] *Milletia auriculata.* [3] *Ougeinia dalbergioides.*

Bhumia with jhumar fish-trap.

mainhar[1] and the fruit of the bheri.[2] The poison is thrown into the water, and the people beat the surface with sticks so that it becomes well mixed into the current. Gradually the fish become stupefied and may easily be collected by another party waiting lower down the stream.

The Bhumia rarely use nets, but they make a number of different bamboo traps. The *kumni*[3] is a long tapering trap four feet long made of thin strips of bamboo not thicker than one sixth of an inch and with a mesh of the same size. The mouth is nine inches in diameter, and two inches from the top is the *ānkhi*, a wall closing the mouth with a small aperture three inches wide opening into a sort of corkscrew funnel. There are three of these *ānkhi*, and when the trap is placed in the stream the force of the water carries the fish through one aperture after another into the tail where the bamboo strips are tied together with a bit of string. The fish cannot find their way out again, and when enough are caught the tail is undone and the fish removed.

The *jhitka* is a trap of the same pattern, but much smaller with only one *ānkhi*.

The *bissera* is used in the same way, but it is made of a single piece of bamboo which is slit up into a large number of strips which at last open out into a mouth eight inches wide. Sometimes a *jhitka* which is then called a *kurru* is placed inside the trap for greater security. As the tail of the trap is simply the original stump of bamboo, there is no way of opening it, and the fish have to be shaken out on to the ground. The *bissera* is much easier to make than the kumni, but it is easier for the fish to escape from it.

The *gābhi* is very similar to the *bissera*.

The *chhāpa* is like a candle extinguisher,[4] with a wide, open bottom and a small hole in the top. It is pushed down through the water on to a shoal of fish, and a few of them may be caught and can be removed through the hole in the top.

The *gira* is a net strung across a large wooden frame. This is held by two people, placed at an angle in the stream, and slowly moved through the water.

The *jhumar* is a very elaborate bamboo trap, with a number of small apertures out of which the fish cannot escape.

The Baiga also fish with a line, using hooks which are called variously *chatuwa*, *bansi*, and *gāra*. The *gāra* is the largest and is baited with small frogs to catch *saur*. The *bansi* is baited with worms and catches *bāmi*, *tengna* or *kotra*. The *chatuwa* is the smallest; it is baited also with worms and catches the tiny *kotri* and *karri*.

[1] That is, mainphal (*randia dumetorum*) [2] *Caesaria tomentosa.* [3] This resembles the *bubu roya* of Malay which also has lobster-pot divisons. [4] This is akiu to the *ottal* or plunge-basket of Malabar. See *Madras Fisheries Bulletin* (Madras, 1938), Vol. XXVII, p. 19.

IV. HUNTING

The Baiga, says Forsyth, 'ekes out the fruits of the earth by an unwearying pursuit of game. Full of courage, and accustomed to depend on each other, they hesitate not to attack every animal of the forest, including the tiger himself. They possess a most deadly poison wherewith they tip their little arrows of reed; and the most ponderous beast seldom goes more than a mile, after being pierced by one of these, without falling. . . . The flesh is discoloured and spoilt for some distance round the wound. This is cut out and the rest of the carcase is held to be wholesome food. Their bows are made entirely of the bamboo, "string" and all; they are very neat, and possess wonderful power for their size. A good shot among them will strike the crown of a hat at fifty yards. Their arrows are of two sorts; those for ordinary use being tipped with a plain iron head, and feathered from the wing of the peafowl, while those intended for poisoning and deadly work have a loose head, round which the poison is wrapped, and which remains in the wound. . . . A Byga has been known to attack and destroy a tiger with no other weapon than his axe. This little weapon is also used as a projectile, and the Bygas will thus knock over hares, peafowl, etc., with astonishing skill.'[1]

There is so little left of this ancient skill that it will be well to call another witness to it. Colonel Ward, writing about the same time, says, that the Baiga are 'first-rate sportsmen . . . very expert in all the appliances of the chase; good shots with their small bows and arrows—the latter being usually poisoned with the juice extracted from the *aconitum ferox* growing in the jungles they inhabit. . . . They are very cunning in laying snares for small deer, birds, etc., and occasionally kill tigers and panthers in the rough traps they erect round their fields and bewurs. Clever trackers and indefatigable few animals, once touched, escape them, for they follow the track of blood from morning till dark.'[2]

The game laws of modern times have pressed almost as hardly on the Baiga as the restrictions on bewar, and have helped to alter their whole character. A nomadic tribe, living on the fruits of the chase, the rich harvests of shifting cultivation, and the natural gifts of the forest, is slowly being changed by administrative action into a low and degraded caste of Hindu cultivators.

The golden days are gone. The old skill is largely perished. But so strong is the Baiga's love for meat, so deeply rooted in him the instinct of pursuit, that he still maintains some of his former hunting customs. 'Even

[1] Forsyth: op. cit., p. 360. [2] Ward: op. cit., p. 155.

Setting the kumni trap.
Using the chhāpa plunge-trap.

if Government passes a hundred laws, we will do it. One of us will keep the official talking; the rest will go out and shoot a deer.' Even the Binjhwar Baiga say, 'We love meat so much that we often go and secretly get it in the forest.'

Almost all animals may be hunted, though not all are eaten. The tiger and the bear are not eaten, but the tiger's fat is extracted and used for lamps and massage. Only the Kondwan and Gondwaina Baiga hunt monkeys—'they look like men, and when they are dead they have a bad smell'. The Binjhwar and Muria do not kill gaur[1]; this is not such a sacrifice as it sounds, for these animals are now very rare. All Baiga avoid sparrows, owls, parrots, kites and vultures. Cranes are spared because they go about in pairs, and it is believed that if you kill one, you will soon lose your own mate.

A few, rather attenuated, ceremonies have survived. Maswasi is the god, or goddess, of the hunt, and lives in the bow and arrow. Raktipurbi, Alopurbi, Sattibhavani, and Kolin Sattibhavani also live with him in the arrows. Before going to hunt the Baiga promises these deities a coconut or a cock if he is successful, and he says this mantra over his bow and arrow.

> O Raktipurbi! O Alopurbi! O Sattibhavani! O Kolin Sattibhavani! I am going to the thick jungle. Turn all the tigers and bears into stone. Turn the thorns into wax. Turn the snakes into sticks. Bring out the deer and make it stand before me.

The result of this is that the goddesses go with the hunter, and drive away all the carnivora, leaving only deer and birds. Another mantra refers to the various kinds of arrows.

> *Saktibān, dhanusbān, aginbān, chirribān, bittabān, andriban chakarbān, sabdavedibān!*[2] Who takes these arrows in his hand? Nanga Baiga takes them. Bhuiphor Baiga, Bhuiphor Baigin, come from Nanga Parbat where you live, and take them. O the four quarters of the earth! O the eighty-four drivers of game! To-day Nanga Baiga goes forth to hunt. Whether I kill bear or tiger, sambhar or chital, I will give their blood and the water from their eyes.

This was how Pachlu went to hunt in his youth. I have only once found anyone speak of the need of abstinence before going out to hunt, in fact most Baiga explicitly deny the necessity. "In the old days," said Binja,

[1] *Gavaeus gaurus.*

[2] The powerful arrow, the bow and arrow, the arrow of fire, the thin arrow, the blunt arrow, the arrow that kills in the dark, the arrow that goes like a wheel, the arrow that kills by its sound.

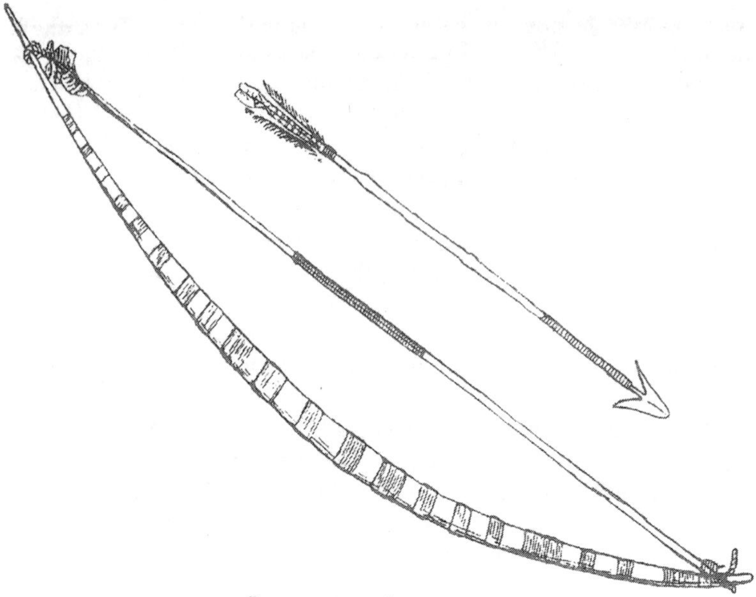

FIG. 15. *Baiga bow and arrow.*

a Muria of Niwas, "when we went to hunt, we lay on one side and did not approach our wives, and spoke to no one. At night in our dreams, our *jīv* would go out and see where game was to be had. In the morning, we bathed and gave fire to the bow and arrow, and went out to hunt. All day we fasted. Then we would certainly get whatever we saw in our dream. When we killed a sambhar, we put some of the water from its eyes and its liver on the bow and arrow, and we drank its blood, and smeared some of it on our foreheads. Then we gave the bow and arrow a red cock and a coconut. But one day a sadhu cursed us that we would never get anything, and since that day our hunting has failed."

For hunting, the Baiga use spears and bows and arrows. The spear may be entirely of iron, when it is called *sāng*, or it may consist of a bamboo shaft to which an iron spearhead is attached. This is called a *barchi*. The *barchi* may either have a single-bladed head into the socket of which the shaft is inserted, or a three-bladed head the tang of which is driven into the bamboo shaft.

The Baiga bow is generally a little over five feet long; the stave is made of dhamin[1] or bamboo, the string of bamboo. When the string is made, a stop is left at either end, and the string is attached to the stave by bits of cord

[1] *Grewia vestita.*

that pass over the stops and round notches cut in the horns. The string is strengthened in the middle by sambhar or hiran sinew which is bound to it by kosa silk. The stave also is given a binding of kosa every time anything is killed. Some twenty birds and animals have thus been killed by the bow in Fig. 15.

The arrow is made of katai[1] or dhamin wood. A notch is cut in the shaft-butt and sinew is bound over the notch and along the shaft with kosa, and feathers of almost any bird are attached straight along the shaft in the same manner. The arrow-head has its tang driven into the shaft and is tied firmly with kosa, and poison is spread on the tang immediately behind the head.

The Baiga holds his bow perpendicularly, his left hand grasps the stave, his thumb against the belly, four fingers round the stave. The arrow is placed to the left of the stave and rests above the fingers. The first and second fingers of the right hand are placed across the string, and the arrow held lightly between them.

It is a delightful sight, in Pandaria, to see the Baiga carrying their bows and arrows through the jungle, happy and excited at the chance of game. A people's stature grows when it has the freedom of its traditional customs. In the Mandla District, where the Baiga are forbidden to carry their bows and arrows, they have lost something of the freshness and vitality of their life. They can only follow the ancient way in penalty of heavy fines.

It is safer, therefore, for the modern Baiga to rely on his traps which are unlikely to be found. These are often, and quite legally, placed round the bewar for its protection; if an animal enters a cultivated field or clearing it does so at its own risk. One such trap is the *suri*, which is made by placing a number of long knives and spears in any place over which animals are likely to jump, or in any gate or aperture. Then if an animal comes into the bewar, the Baiga frighten it and sometimes send it dashing to its death on the spears.

The *dāng-phānda* (Fig. 16) is a real trap. A small triangular piece of plaited bamboo is placed over a hole in the ground underneath some supple-branched tree. A string is tied to the narrow end of the piece of bamboo, and attached to a branch which is bent down almost to the ground. A noose is arranged round the hole, and the piece of bamboo fixed in place with a stick. Some food is scattered about as bait. If a gutri or other small deer happens to tread on the bamboo covering of the hole, the stick is broken, the noose tightens round its foot, and the branch of the tree flies into the air, carrying the creature with it.

The *phatki* is a hare-trap. A bamboo cage is made with a self-acting noose over the door. Rice or kodon is placed inside the trap and when

[1] *Flacourtia romontchi.*

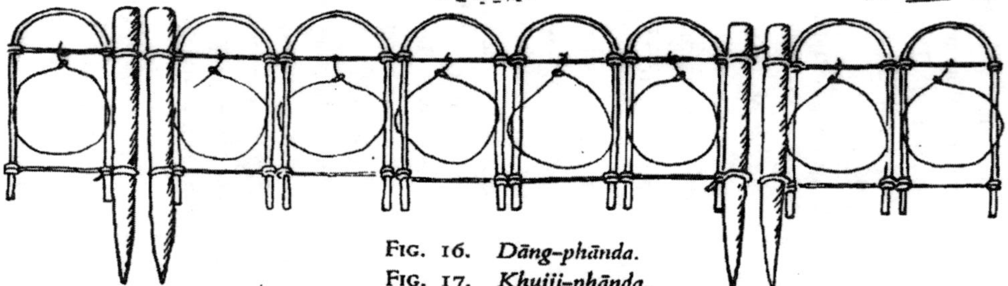

FIG. 16. *Dāng-phānda.*
FIG. 17. *Khujji-phānda.*

the hare pushes its head through the noose to get at the food the cord tightens and it is caught.

The *dāya-phānda* consists of a long rope to which a number of small nooses made of cows' hair are attached. Kodon and kutki are scattered about behind the row of nooses, and phadki[1] come along, poke their heads through the nooses and get caught.

The *khujji-phānda* (Fig. 17) is very similar, except that the nooses are suspended from little bamboo triangles that are fixed in the ground, and are smaller in order to catch lawa.[2]

Choph is simply birdlime. It is made of the milk of the *thūa*[3] tree cooked with *ramtilla* oil, and is used as birdlime is always used.

The *thonga-phanda* (Fig. 18) is used to catch small pigs, procupines and hares. Two heavy logs, weighted still further with stones, are supported above a rough cage. Inside, food is put on an arrangement of sticks, and when the animal treads on these, they release a string which in turn releases the supports on which the logs have been resting. These fall with a heavy crash and crush the victim.

There are three kinds of rat-trap in common use. The *dabka-phānda* is a long rectangular box, six inches wide, eight inches high and two and a half feet long, open at the ends and top. A heavy block of wood fits in to it, and is held in place by a piece of bamboo running vertically through a hole in the centre. The ends of the block are connected by a string which passes over the top of the bamboo and is attached to another stick the end of which rests on the top of the bamboo. From the other end of this stick, which projects at right angles from the box, another string goes down to the bottom of the trap. When it is set, the heavy block is raised three inches, and the string that holds it up is kept in position by a bit of wood caught by a ring that in turn is attached to a piece of plaited bamboo inside. Food is put on this. When the rat treads on it, its weight lowers it and with it the ring, thus releasing the stick that holds the string, and the block comes down on the rat and kills it.

Two other kinds of *mussa-phānda* have no special names. The first (Fig. 19) is made from a single bamboo, two and a half feet long, cut into narrow strips which are tied together with string that goes round and round in a spiral at two-inch intervals up to the mouth. Food is placed at the narrow end, the trap is placed over the rat's hole, and when the rat goes in, the trap contracts about it and it is unable to back out.

The third trap is very elaborate, like a cross-bow. Its construction and

[1] *Columba intermedia.*

[2] The bush quail (*perdicula asiatica*).

[3] *Euphorbia tirucalli.*

FIG. 19. *Rat-trap.*

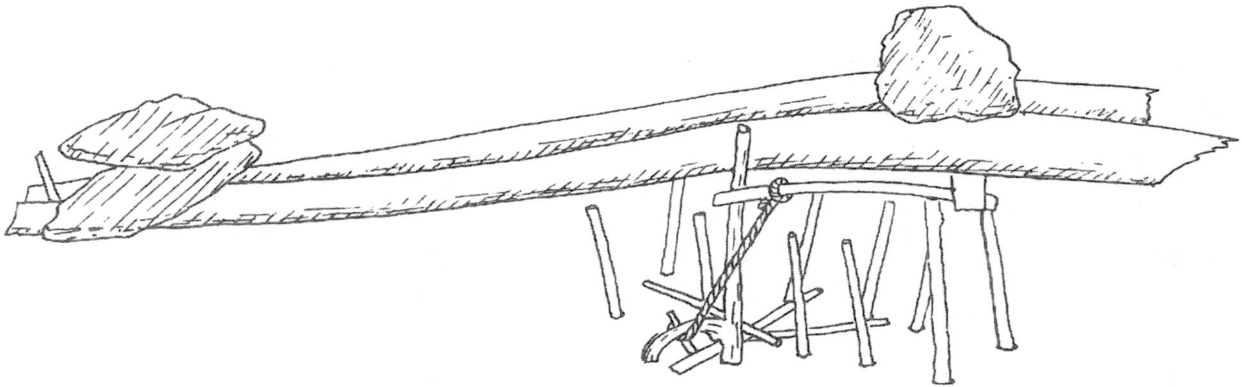

FIG. 18. *Thōnga-phānda.*

plan is made clear in the drawing (Fig. 20). The rat enters the little hole and its weight releases the 'arrow' which pierces its body. The trap is three feet long.[1]

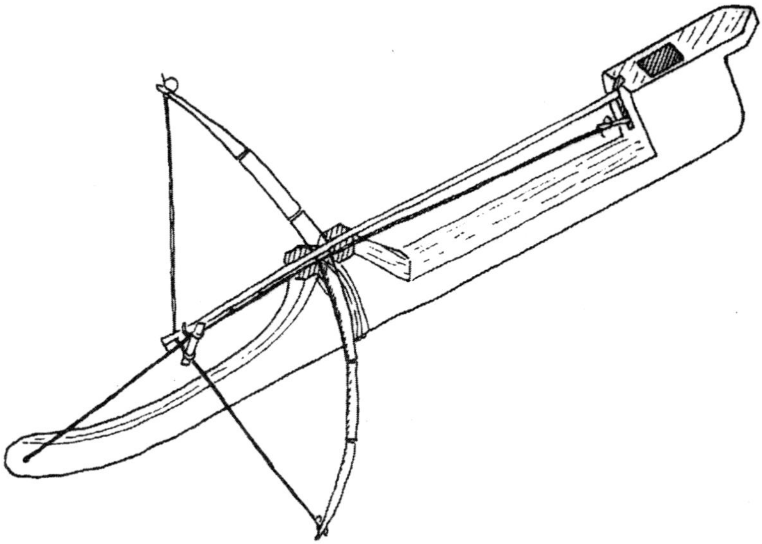

FIG. 20. *Rat-trap.*

V. EXPENDITURE

Apart from the business of keeping alive, a Baiga's expenses are not great. He grows enough tobacco in his garden to fulfil life's primary need. Liquor, when he can get drunk on half a bottle, at two or three annas a bottle, is not very expensive. Most of his food is home-grown or gathered in the forest. He has to buy salt, a little cloth, some ornaments for the better progress of his intrigues, an occasional blanket. His heaviest regular charges are the taxes. These vary from place to place.

In Pandaria, the Baiga pay Rs. 4 an axe for bewar. This allows them as much forest as one man can cut. They also pay Re. 1 for *nishtār* which covers the right to use every kind of forest produce. Each head of cattle costs 4 annas, each goat 2 annas, each buffalo 12 annas. Once a year every villager must take a load of *khumri*, grass or bark to Pandaria, and must contribute to the tribute of one rupee which the headman of every village offers to the Rani. The taxation in Kawardha is similar.

[1] In the British Museum there is a similar cross-bow trap from Malay, but this catches its victims in a loop. Another, from Perak, impales the rat, but the Baiga trap seems simpler and more lethal.

In the Baiga Chak the Baiga pay Rs. 2 an axe, Re. 1 for every plough, no *nishtār*, 4 annas per bullock after the first 8, Rs. 2 for a buffalo, 3 annas a goat. They may take as much wood, grass, bark, etc., from the forest as they need for personal use. But in the Baiga Chak they have to pay Rs. 2 for the *kānda-bāri*, which is a heavy additional burden upon them.

In Bilaspur, the Baiga pay 8 annas an acre for their bewar, which is more or less equivalent to the Rs. 2 an axe in Mandla.

Elsewhere, the Baiga pay the same taxes as the rest of the population.

The extraordinary expenses of a Baiga are as follows:

At the birth of a child, one rupee's worth of liquor when it is named.

For a marriage with the full ritual, from Rs. 5 to Rs. 25. This is how a well-to-do family of Rupnidadar spent its money for the marriage of Bharat and Churki.

Liquor	Rs. 10
Cloth	Rs. 20
Kodai	1½ *khandi*
Dāl	10 *kuro*
Pigs	1
Drums and band	Rs. 14

At the time of the engagement, the bridegroom's family paid Rs. 7 as *sukh* or bride-price. At the wedding, they paid Rs. 3 to the girl's family and the *panch* of her village 'for keeping her chaste up till now'.

Out of the money spent on cloth, gifts were made as follows:

For the *āji-bondri*	Rs. 2
For the *mai-odna*	Rs. 3
For the *bhai-bānti*	Re. 1
For the *dosi*	As. 8
For the *suāsīn*[1]	As. 4

This was a fairly expensive wedding. The more parsimonious Deo Singh did it much cheaper. He spent on:

Cloth	Rs. 2
Liquor	Rs. 5
Kodai	10 *kuro*
Pigs	1 (rather small)

The engagement cost him Rs. 3, and he gave Rs. 5 for *sukh*, Rs. 2 for liquor to the *panch*, and Rs. 2 to the girl's family, 'to keep them quiet'. Presents could not be avoided, so he spent for:

[1] These terms are explained in Chapter IX.

Shaking fish out of the bissera-trap.
Fishing with the gira in the Seoni river.

The *āji-bondri*	Re. 1.4.0.
The *mai-sari*	Rs. 2
The *bhai-bānti*	As. 12
The *dosi*	As. 4
The *suāsīn*	2 pice

The *haldi-pāni* marriage is one of the cheapest in the world. It can easily be managed within two rupees. Yogi Dewar married his six wives at a minimum of expense after the inevitable outlay of fifteen to twenty rupees on the first one.

Funeral expenses also are not heavy. 'To destroy sorrow, we drink when a friend has died.' Wood must be obtained, or helpers to dig the grave, the corpse must be wrapped in new cloth, the mourners must be feasted. The whole expense, however, need not exceed Rs. 5 and this is chargeable on the dead man's estate. Those of his heirs who contribute, moreover, receive a larger share of the inheritance. The neighbours are also very considerate. When a man is poor, they may refuse to eat or drink with him so as to avoid devouring the whole of his inheritance. Daulu, of Rupnidadar, for example, was very hard up, and when his old mother died—from whom, of course, he had no expectations—the villagers agreed not to accept a funeral feast from him, but to drink a rupee's worth of liquor in memory of the old lady and so make an end.

VI. PARTITION AND INHERITANCE

There is rarely any dispute among the Baiga about the succession to their exiguous goods; a lawyer of long experience at Dindori told me he had only heard of one case where a Baiga had appeared in a Civil Court. Few Baiga could draw up a complete Code of Inheritance, and cases are generally settled by agreement or argument as they arise. Particularly on such a point as a woman's right to inherit, the personality of the widow seems to count for a great deal more than any general principles. The only safe way to discover the rules governing Baiga practice is to give a number of actual cases bearing on the different situations that arise, and that is what I now propose to do.

In every case, the first charge upon the estate is the dead owner's funeral expenses. Anyone, even a daughter, who contributes to the funeral feast, is entitled to a small share of the property.

In Tilaidabra, when Pandu's father died, his elder married daughter helped with the funeral, and got a calf and a sari. In Amadob, when

Gahania's father died, his two sisters helped with liquor and *kodai*, and were given an axe and a sari apiece.

When a man dies leaving only a son or sons to survive him, his property goes entirely to his son if there is only one, or is equally divided among the sons of the whole blood. Sons of the half blood get a slightly smaller share, and under special circumstances sons of the whole blood also may receive larger or smaller shares.

In Ranjki, Sadhu died leaving three sons, all of whom were living with him at the time, and his property was divided equally among them.

When Rawan's father died, he left Rawan and two other sons and a daughter who was unmarried. Rawan had quarrelled with his father and refused to touch his property which was divided into two equal shares for the two other brothers. Each brother gave one eighth of his share to his sister.

In Basulalat, Samaru's property was divided among his five sons equally, except that the eldest son, who had to maintain his three sisters till their marriage, received a slightly larger share.

When Pirtu's father died in Rupnidadar, "everything was taken by my elder brother who had to look after three of us younger brothers. When he died without sons, the property came to me. Then my third brother died, and when the youngest married and went to live separately, I gave him four sickles and two axes—we had nothing else to share".

Pattu of Ajgar said: "When my father died, we were three brothers. We each took equal shares, though I was the eldest and had to maintain my mother."

Sons who are still living with their father at the time of his death, and to a greater or less degree helping to maintain him, receive a slightly larger share than those who are living separately and have probably received some portion of the family goods already.

In Bakal, Kewal had five sons. Two were living separate and each of them got a one-anna share[1] less than those who were living with their father.

In Amadob, Lahakat was living separate and his three brothers were with their father. Lahakat's share was one anna less than the others.

In Chulpani, when Chamru's father died, he left seven sons, four living separate, and three with their father. Those who were separate got a one-anna share less apiece.

A son of the *dūsara bīj*, or of the half blood, receives a little less. If a man has two sons, one by a first wife and one by a second (married only by *haldi-pāni* rites), the property is divided in the ratio of 9 to 7. But the

[1] Shares are usually described in terms of annas and a rupee. Sixteen annas is the whole property, an eight-anna share is half, a one-anna share is one-sixteenth.

grandson of the second wife has equal rights. If a woman with two sons by another man takes a new husband and he dies, leaving one son from her, the sons of the first husband rank as adopted sons of the second and receive a *bālpos* share, and the property will be divided in the ratio 5 and 5 and 6.

Bukwa's father was the landlord of Ufri. He died, leaving two sons, Bukwa from his first wife, and Rigla from his second. Bukwa received a nine-anna share and Rigla a seven-anna share of the property. But Bukwa's sons and Rigla's sons will inherit equally.

Baihar, a Baiga girl, with two sons from a former husband, married a new husband with two sons from a former wife. When he died, his possessions were divided into two three-and-a-half-anna shares and two four-and-a-half-anna shares, the smaller shares going to Baihar's sons.

The fact that a son is excommunicated for some tribal offence, even for a serious one like marrying a Pankin or eating with a Mussalman, does not bar him in any way from his full rights of inheritance.

Dubla of Bohi was excommunicate for having had intercourse with his 'classificatory' sister, at the time of his father's death. He inherited equally with his brothers.

When a man dies leaving not only sons but a widow, much depends on the personality of the widow. If she is thinking of marrying again, she will probably try to secure a share of the property, a moveable share like a cow for preference, so that she can take it with her to her new home. But if she is old and uninterested in further matrimonial ventures, and if she is wise, she will demand to be maintained out of her husband's estate and cared for by one of her sons. This is, actually, by far the most profitable course for a widow to take. Where the property is generally so small, her share of it is not likely to exceed a few rupees in value; but by not pressing her claim to inherit she has a life-annuity in the services of one or other of her sons.

The official view is that a widow should be maintained on the estate until she dies or remarries. But actually she can and does inherit a share equally with her sons and absolutely in her own right.

In Pandpur, Dhan Singh looked after his mother, and received a two-anna share more than his brother for doing so.

In Amtera, Bangi died leaving three sons and a widow. The widow wanted to live on her own, and the property was divided into four equal shares, of which she received one.

When Deo Singh's father died in Dengurjam, he was a boy. His mother took charge of everything and looked after him, till he was old enough to begin looking after her.

In Saraipani, when Tikaita's father died, he left three sons and a widow.

The property was divided into four equal shares, and the three brothers and the widow took one each. In this case, the widow was not their own mother, but her younger sister whom their father had married.

Latti of Rupnidadar was an only son, and inherited everything. "But I had to feed my mother till she died, as she didn't marry again."

Chidi, also of Rupnidadar, said: " When my father died, my mother took half and kept us two younger brothers, and my elder brother took half and went to live separately. Then my mother died and I took what she had. When my younger brother grew up and married, I gave him nothing. When my elder brother died, he left a little son. His wife took everything—3 sickles, 2 axes and a *khanta* and brought up the child."

Ojha of Arhwai told me, "I live with my widowed mother. Everything belongs to her. If she marries, it will come to me. If I go and live separate, it will remain with her."

The following illustrates the importance of the widow's personality.

When Buka's father died in Banga, he left two small sons, a small daughter and his wife's younger sister, whom he had married and who was now his widow. She began to make the children work for their living, probably hoping to drive them away, and so get all the property for herself. Buka told his brother and sister: "We must go and live separately, but we are too small to work." But the brothers went to graze cattle, and the sister stayed in the house. Then the widow married a new husband. The sister ran away. When Buka was grown up, he claimed the property. But he could only get a half-share which he divided with his brother. The widow claimed the rest, for, she said: " You have failed to support me in my widowhood."

The adventures of Baihar seem to point the same moral.

In Tilaidabra lived Judan with his unmarried daughter Baihar and two small sons, and his wife Andyar. He died, and Andyar took all the property and married again. The new husband took all the property, but soon died, so Andyar took back her own and took possession also of her second husband's property. Then Andyar died. Baihar, still unmarried, and her two little brothers divided the double property. She lived with the elder of the two brothers and they put what they had together. The youngest boy lived separately, but after a time conceived a guilty love for Baihar who was so alarmed that she ran away and married someone at once. She took a two-anna share from her brothers. Then Baihar's husband died, leaving two sons.

Then Baihar married again, and the new husband got all Baihar's property and all her first husband's property. But they soon quarrelled, and Baihar left her husband and took everything back from him. Soon she married a new husband. He had two sons from a former wife. She still had her two sons from her first husband. When he died—no one survived marriage with Baihar for very long—the total property was divided into five shares. His own sons and Baihar herself got a full share apiece. Baihar's sons got a smaller share (one anna less) each.

Baihar now married a fourth husband. Her two sons were now grown up, and they were angry with her for remarrying. They took everything from her and sent her to her husband. From him she had a daughter. Then he tired of her and left her, taking the daughter with him.

So Baihar married a fifth husband. Soon afterwards she heard that the fourth had died. So Baihar left her fifth husband and went and found her daughter, and took possession of the fourth husband's property.

Then Baihar's two sons decided to live separately, and when they came to divide up their property and saw how much of it they owed to their mother's enterprise and courage, their hearts were softened towards her. So they divided it into four parts, one for each of them, one for their mother, and one for her daughter.

So Baihar lived comfortably to a great age, and when her daughter was married, she persuaded her sons to bear the expense.

A daughter, even if unmarried, is not supposed to inherit, for 'she will soon be cooking *pej* in another man's house', but in practice she often receives a small share, either through the generosity of her brothers, or as a reward for helping at the funeral.

When a man leaves no son or sons of his own, but only grandsons, that is sons of predeceased sons, or nephews who are sons of predeceased brothers, the Baiga seem to follow the same tradition that has been codified in the Hindu Law of Mitakshara. I have not been able to obtain any actual examples of this, but I have discussed the matter with landlords like Ketu and Bukwa, and elders like Mahatu and Bahadur, and they agree in saying that when, for example, Bagla has a family of three sons, Amru, Chirbu and Biru; and Chirbu has two sons, Gumma and Hattu whom he predeceases; and Biru has a son Dhandha, whom he predeceases; and Dhandha in turn has three sons, Lotara, Karhai and Kamu whom he also predeceases; and at last Bagla himself dies, then his property is divided *per stirpes* into three equal shares of which one goes to Amru, one to Gumma and Hattu together, and one to Lotara, Karhai and Kamu together. The Baiga call this division *bhai sē hisāb*, in opposition to the *per capita* division which they call *beta sē hisāb*. The *bhai sē hisāb* can only occur, according to the Hindu law, under the doctrine of representation, where the son, the grandson whose father is dead, and the great-grandson whose father and grandfather are both dead, succeed as representing the rights of their parents to their shares. The Baiga follow the same rule.

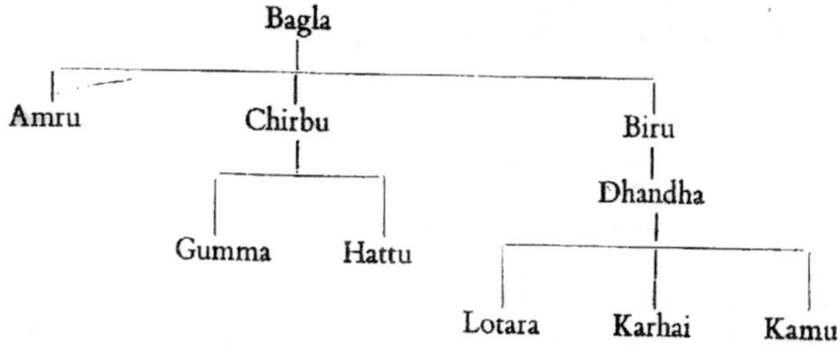

But suppose we have a family in which all the survivors are of the same relationship, that is nephews, to the deceased. Then, according to both Hindu and Baiga law, they will inherit *per capita.*

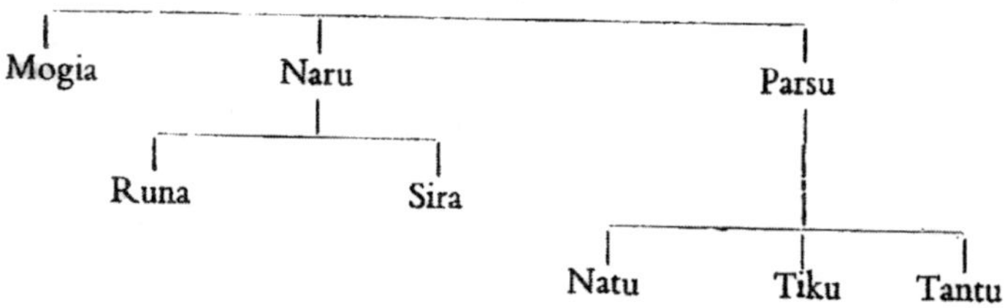

Mogia, Naru and Parsu are brothers living separately, and Mogia has become fairly well-to-do. Naru has two sons whom he predeceases, and Parsu three sons whom he predeceases. If Mogia had no sons, it would be the usual Baiga custom for him to adopt one of Naru's or Parsu's sons, who would then inherit the whole of Mogia's property. But if he did not do that, then on his death his property would be divided equally among his five classificatory 'sons', who all look on him as their father, and who inherit, not as representing their parents, but in their own right.

Baiga adoption differs from the *dattaka* adoption of the Hindus in having no religious significance. The Hindu, believing with Vasistha that 'there is no heavenly region for a sonless man', adopts a son to ensure him spiritual benefit after death by performing the proper funeral ceremonial, as well as to be his heir and perpetuate his name. The Baiga adopt boys, even in addition to their own sons, when they need more workers in the bewar, or simply because they like them. The Baiga, unlike the Hindu,[1] may adopt an orphan and indeed generally does. There are no ceremonies connected with Baiga adoption, but in order to avoid possible disputes about

[1] Except where custom authorizes the Hindu to adopt an orphan.

the property, the father generally makes a formal announcement of the adoption before the village *panch*.

Where there is no son of the whole blood living, the adopted son inherits fully *ex parte paterna*. If there are sons, the adopted son gets what is called a *bālpos* share, not exceeding one eighth of the whole, and his marriage expenses. But adoption is not common. The following cases are all I have met in the past five years.

In Boira, the son of Tetha and Kondi was left an orphan when only two months old. His father's sister, Ramli, who had a little daughter at her breast, adopted him and fed him as her own child. He lives with the family as their own, and will inherit a *bālpos* share, as there are other sons.

In Koteli, Dhiru adopted a boy called Chutti, for he only had a daughter, and did not want his goods to pass to her and thus to her husband. But Chutti was killed by magic soon after Dhiru's death, and as no one else would take it, the girl got the property after all.

In Bokrakachar, Saunu adopted a boy though he had two sons already. When he died, the adopted boy got one plough of bullocks and his marriage expenses. The rest was divided between the two sons.

In Hirapur (Balaghat), Bahadur has adopted his sister's son, for in spite of marrying three wives he has had no sons of his own. He proposes to declare before the *panch* that all his property is to go to this boy.

Chapter III

BEWAR CULTIVATION

I. SHIFTING CULTIVATION THROUGHOUT THE WORLD

WHAT is known to the Baiga as bewar is extensively practised throughout the tropical and sub-tropical regions of the world. It is the common method of cultivation in the forests of South America, in many parts of Africa and Mauritius, in Melanesia and the Atlantic Islands, in Assam, in Ceylon, and in the remoter forest areas of South and Central India. It is known as *sartage* in the French and Belgian Ardennes, as 'farming' in West Africa, as *kohola* in the South-east Solomon Islands, as *chena* by the Vedda. In India, the *dahi* and *koman* cultivation of the Bhuiya of Orissa, the *penda* of the Bastar Maria, the *jhum* of the Assam hill tribes, the *podu* of the Khond of Jeypore, the *beora* of the Pahari Korwa of Jashpur, the *taungya* of the Burma hill tribes, are all, with some variations, akin to the bewar of the Baiga.

Before proceeding to discuss the Baiga's practice, I will give some examples of shifting cultivation throughout the world. The plough is so established a feature of European civilization that it is remarkable to find a form of shifting cultivation practised in the French and Belgian Ardennes, in the oak coppice forests, which are grown to produce bark for tanning and small poles and firewood.[1] Here it is called *sartage* or *essortage*. If the wood and weeds to be burnt are spread uniformly all over the area, the process is called *sartage à feu courant*. If the fuel is collected in separate heaps and then fired, it is called *sartage à feu couvert*. *Sartage*, however, differs from bewar as commonly practised by the Baiga. In the Ardennes, the greatest care is taken to preserve the vitality of the stools by cutting them flush with the ground, and not spreading over them any of the stuff to be burned. But the Baiga fire every bit of wood that is felled, they cut the

[1] Roheim: *Riddle of the Sphinx* (London, 1934), p. 18, refers to a Scandinavian legend in which a fairy child betrays his great age by crying "Seven times have I seen the forest of Lessö felled." Similarly in a Corinthian song a child says:

"Now I am already so old
That the meadows by yonder house
Has been nine times meadow and nine times wood."

Mr. J. P. Mills: *The Rangma Nagas* (London, 1937), p. 76, suggests that here there may be 'a faint memory of a time when shifting cultivation was practised in Europe'.

stools high, and often pile combustible matter all over them. In the Ardennes, again, when the crop is weeded or harvested, all damage to the shoots that come up from the stools is carefully avoided. But the Baiga lop the coppice shoots even while the crop is still standing, or if they spare them then, they lop and spread them over the ground after the harvest, so as to be ready for the next firing and sowing.

We may illustrate the South American practice by a description of the customs of the Bakairi Indians on the Upper Xingu. Dr. Schmidt tells how he 'was a witness of the method pursued. First of all, the undergrowth and low thicket were cut down. Then the individual trees were notched so as to determine the direction in which they would fall. Lastly, one large tree on the edge of the area was felled. In its fall this tree knocked down the trees immediately adjacent to it; these in turn brought down those next to them, so that the whole section fell together with one prolonged crash. The fallen trees are left for months in the dry season, and when they have dried up fire is kindled throughout the area. All the brushwood and the smaller branches are burned, and the charred trunks are left on the ground. The soil is neither hoed nor worked in any way, but at the beginning of the rainy season holes for the seeds or cuttings are made, and the earth surrounding them is slightly loosened with a pointed 'planting-stick' or dibble.[1] The Indians of South America have hitherto used the ground stone axe with a wooden handle, but this is being supplanted by the European steel axe. The Africans seem always to have used the iron axe. The Bakairi use as dibble the claw of the great armadillo.

In West Africa, shifting cultivation, there known as 'farming', is universally practised. Professor Stebbing, a former member of the Indian Forest Service, has recently investigated the situation there in relation to the degredation of the forest, the dessication of the countryside, and the sand encroachment of the Sahara. The shrinkage of forest along the Sahara border has created a serious position.

'The people are living on the edge, not of a volcano, but of a desert whose power is incalculable and whose silent and almost invisible approach must be difficult to estimate. But the end is obvious; total annihilation of vegetation and the disappearance of man and beast from the overwhelmed locality.'[2]

This is not wholly due to shifting cultivation. Great havoc is caused by the annual firing of the countryside, either for shooting purposes or for

[1] Schmidt, *The Primitive Races of Mankind* (London, 1926), p. 112.

[2] Stebbing, *The Forests of West Africa and the Sahara* (London, 1937), p. 16. See also Faulkner and Mackie, *West African Agriculture* (Cambridge, 1933) and Jones, "The Earth Goddess: A Study of Native Farming on the West African Coast." *Royal Empire Society Imperial Studies*, No. 12 (London, 1936).

grazing, by the promiscuous cutting of fuel, and by uneconomic exploitation by timber contractors. 'It is important', says Professor Stebbing, 'that the process of what may be termed the extinction of the mixed deciduous forest by man should be understood.'[1] First of all, as a result of 'farming' the forest becomes pock-marked with little patches of the former sites of the shifting cultivator. These soon become clothed with the more rapid-growing light-demanding species of trees. This growth gradually deteriorates in height and density. Thus, in Sierra Leone, the old forest has almost disappeared; in Ashanti, in the Gold Coast, there is country where only the tall elephant grass remains; here the farming is restricted to this material for its ashes from the burning. At last this type of degraded forest is no longer capable of providing an agricultural crop, and the herds and flocks of the nomadic shepherds invade it. For some time it is capable of affording ordinary browsing and pasturage. But after a time, when the forest degenerates still further into open savannah conditions, the nomads treat the area under a rough system of pollarding, the material cut being fed to the goats. 'Under this system of treatment the final extinction of the savannah forest takes place, when the weakened roots and vanishing rainfall result in the death of the trees.'[2]

Thus, shifting cultivation, the firing of the forest, over-grazing and the pollarding of the savannah, has largely destroyed the forest barrier which protected West Africa from the ever-encroaching Sahara. To remedy this, Professor Stebbing has advocated the extension of forest reserves, the re-organization of the forestry staff, less wasteful management of timber concessions and, especially, the introduction of the Indian system of *taungya* cultivation.

'The method of raising new crops of forest trees,' he writes, 'by what is generally known as the *taungya* method (termed *chena*, a Ceylon word, by the Director of Forests, Nigeria) has been very successfully inaugurated in Nigeria as also in the Gold Coast and Sierra Leone. The French in the Ivory Coast have also made a commencement with the method.

'In principle, it merely consists in felling a piece of forest in more or less thefashion under which farming is practised in West Africa. The agriculturalist who undertakes the felling is granted by the Forest Department this piece of forest land rent free for a couple or more years to raise agricultural crops, on the condition that he plants out young forest trees, or sows the seed, in such a manner (usually in lines at a stipulated distance apart) and in such a year of the lease as may be laid down by the forest officer. Thus, when the land is vacated by the agriculturalist, a young forest crop of trees remains *in situ*.'[3]

In Africa, this system has achieved considerable success, especially in Nigeria. At Sapoba, as Mr. Kennedy, the silviculturlist there, wrote in

[1] Ibid, p. 20. [2] Ibid, p. 21. [3] Ibid, pp. 48ff.

A Bhumia archer in the Pandaria jungle.

1928: 'The system has been on the whole very successful... every reasonable concession has been granted and no irksome regulations have been framed to worry the cultivators in any way.'[1] The method at Sapoba was to put in the young trees during the first year. In the second year the *taungya*-cutter beat up the area, and replaced dead young trees. The silviculturlist then took back the area. The cultivator moved on to the next area. A bonus of £3 per four households was granted if the area was successfully planted up, i.e., about 98 per cent success. The size of a *taungya* for four households is ten acres.

The Oba of Benin visited these plantations in 1933, and was very taken with them. He wished that a Benin name should be used instead of *taungya*[2] and coined the word 'ugbiwego', and in every way gave encouragement to the scheme.

In Northern Nigeria, in spite of the suspicion of the people of Zaria, *taungya* was very successful at Katsina and Sokoto. It was equally so in the Bosomoa Reserve in the Gold Coast. In Sierra Leone, in spite of many difficulties, progress has been made. In the Ivory Coast, *taungya* was not adopted by the French till 1933, but it has been worked with considerable success, especially in the De La Rasso Reserve. The French have decided that two years is the maximum for which a *taungya* lease should be granted for any one area.

I have described this method and its success at considerable length because of its possible bearings, which we will consider later, on the future of bewar among the Baiga.

In the meantime, we must return to our general survey.

The methods of the Melanesians of the South-east Solomon Islands, to take but one example from this ethnographical province, are not unlike bewar. After getting permission from the Chief, the people clear a piece of ground in the virgin forest. This is called 'opening the forest'. Felling for the new crops continues during July and August. The ground chosen for the yam garden is spoken of as being 'full grown'. It is first 'brushed' (they use the Queensland term nowadays), that is, the undergrowth is cleared and the hanging vines are cut. Many trees are left after being ring-barked; they will do as poles for the yam vines, branches being hung on the lower limbs to serve the same purpose. Then everything is fired and the ground raked over by hand. On a given day a summons calls the people to dig the yam holes. These are mere scratchings a few inches deep, the digging being done with sharp stakes. New ground is cleared and fired

[1] Ibid, p. 165.

[2] Mr. L. Dudley Stamp also regrets the use of the word *taungya* to describe "what is really a regular system of rotation." He prefers to speak of "bush fallowing", since periods of cultivation are separated by periods of fallowing. See L. Dudley Stamp: "Land Utilization and Soil Erosion in Nigeria." *Geographical Review*, Vol. XXVIII, No. 1, p. 35.

for the yams and hanas every year, and the same ground is never planted twice, fertilizers being unknown. The chief difference from the Baiga's method is that the Baiga use the same piece of ground for three years in succession, and thus cause much less damage to the forest.[1]

In British North Borneo, the hill Dusuns and Muruts cultivate rice by clearing and burning the virgin forest for every crop until within five or six years all the available land in the neighbourhood of their villages is exhausted. Then they shift their villages.[2] The Kayan and Bahau tribes have actually moved right across Borneo, and are drifting down into Sarawak as a result of these migrations. Government has now restricted the tribes to secondary jungle that has lain fallow for some time. It is said that great damage has been done; but after centuries of such cultivation, there are still more than two million acres of commercial forest within two miles of the coast.[3]

In Indo-China, the Moi fell a large tract of forest, enough for the whole village, in November at the end of the rains. They leave the fallen trees till April and then fire them. After the first rains have washed the ashes into the soil, they begin to sow rice. Women take a large part in the operations; they hollow trenches in the soil with pointed sticks and the men throw in the seed.[4]

Coming now to India, we find shifting cultivation under the name of *jhum* practised all over Assam. Of the Sema Naga, Dr. Hutton writes: 'Although terraced and irrigated cultivation has been adopted by a few Sema villages on the edge of the Eastern Angami country, and an attempt is being made with gradually increasing success to introduce it among the other Sema villages farther north, it cannot yet be regarded as more than an occasional and exotic form of cultivation, and the villages that have adopted it from the Eastern Angamis have generally either taken to Angami custom and dress entirely, like Swemi, or are in the process of taking to them, like Hebulimi. . . . The genuine Sema method of cultivation is jhuming pure and simple.'[5]

The Sema custom is to use the land for two successive seasons, and then leave it for seven years as a minimum, for ten to twelve years on an average, and for fifteen to twenty years as the ideal.

'In jhuming the Semas do not, as some tribes do, first burn and then clear, but they clear the land, cutting down many of the trees, and then burn, afterwards cutting down the burnt trunks of the remaining trees, and then

[1] Ivens: *Melanesians of the South-east Solomon Islands* (London, 1927), p. 356.
[2] Rutter: *British North Borneo* (London, 1922), pp. 58, 226.
[3] Hose and McDougall: *The Pagan Tribes of Borneo* (London, 1912), p. 112.
[4] Baudesson: *Indo-China and its Primitive People*, p. 18.
[5] Hutton: *The Sema Nagas* (London, 1921), p. 59.

clearing up the fields and digging the ashes into the soil. Neither do they all imitate, at any rate to the same extent, the excellent Lhota practice of stripping the trees of all their branches and leaving a bunch of green leaf at the top so that the tree does not die, but branches out again when the two years' cultivation is finished. On the contrary, many of them cut the trees down and burn them entirely.'[1]

The Lakher also grow all their crops in *jhum*. 'The jungle, whether it be bamboos or trees, is all cut down, and left to dry. When thoroughly dry it is set on fire, the fiercer the blaze the better, as the fire kills all insects and destroys their eggs and renders sterile the seeds of weeds and jungle plants, while the wood or bamboo ashes form a valuable manure. The logs that have not burnt are then cleared to one side and used for fencing the field, which is then ready for sowing. Though this method of cultivation is very wasteful of timber and bamboos, it is the only form of cultivation that can be followed in this country. The hills are too steep and water is too scarce to allow of terraced cultivation.'[2]

The fields are used for only one year at a time, and if possible are left for eight or ten years. But in other parts of the Lushai Hills, where the population is denser, fields have to be used every two or three years. But here the eupatorium grows very rapidly and is a welcome alternative to thatch grass which cannot be used for *jhum*.

The Magh of the Chittagong Hill Tracts are taking to the plough with enthusiasm, though they continue to practise *jhum* as well. They also only use the land once, and then abandon it.[3]

In Assam *jhum* land cannot theoretically be held in ownership by the tribesmen. It is a ruling of Government that '*jhum* land, which the owners have bought or inherited as immovable property which can be validly held by an individual or a clan, is all unclassed State forest at the absolute disposal of Government on which there is no liability to pay compensation in the event of its being taken over.'

As further examples of the custom in India we may take the Bhuiya of Orissa and the Maria of Bastar. The Bhuiya practise two kinds of shifting cultivation. In the *dahi* method, they clear a more or less level patch on a hill slope. All the trees are cut down and piled one upon another in rows. Bushes and shrubs are also cut and piled about them. When they are dry, they are fired, the land is dug up, and upland rice is planted.

By the *koman* process all bushes and shrubs are cut and placed in heaps round the trees. After a month or two they are fired. The fires destroy

[1] Ibid, p. 60.

[2] Parry: *The Lakhers* (London, 1932), pp. 74 ff.

[3] *Census of India*, 1931. Vol. I, Part III, B. p. 120.

[4] Ibid, p. 147. Note by J. P. Mills.

the branches and twigs of the trees, leaving only the scorched and naked trunks. The ashes are then spread all over the *koman*. In one part, upland rice is sown and elsewhere other crops. Beans are sown round the tree-trunks and allowed to climb up them.[1]

Mr. W. V. Grigson has described the system of shifting cultivation in Bastar State in his book on the Maria Gond. In Bastar the system of cutting trees or brushwood and spreading them over a field for burning is called *dahi* in Halbi and *parka* by the Maria. This system obtains, not on hill-slopes but on more or less level ground. In Halbi the word *marhan* is applied to shifting cultivation on the flat ground; it is called *dippa* by the Muria and Hill Maria, and *erka* by the Bison-horn Maria. These flat lands are only cultivated for two years. When they are exhausted, they are used for *dahi* or *parka* cultivation.

Penda cultivation is practised on steep hill-sides. 'Beyond roughly distributing the unburnt material over the slope, and, wearing wooden clogs or strips of saja bark to protect the soles of his feet, poking unburnt logs into a burning patch with long bamboo poles, he does not try to spread the ashes evenly, or use the *parka-lathi*, and consequently adjacent patches of crops vary greatly in height and density.'[2]

II. THE BAIGA CULT OF BEWAR

We have now briefly surveyed, by means of typical examples, the practice of shifting cultivation in different parts of the world. But so far as I have been able to discover, the only people who have exalted this type of cultivation into a regular cultus, and have adopted it as the symbol of their tribe, differentiating them from all others, are the Baiga.

The Baiga were established in the practice of bewar[3] by Bhagavan himself who, when he called all the tribes of the world together to make a king, at first chose the Baiga. But Nanga Baiga begged that the Gond, his brother, might be king in his place. Bhagavan was pleased at this request, and, as a mark of his favour took Nanga Baiga by the hand and placed him on his throne by his side. He granted his prayer to make the Gond king, but he gave the Baiga an even greater blessing.

'All the kingdoms of the world,' he said, 'may fall to pieces, but he who is made of earth and is Bhumiaraja, lord of the earth, shall never forsake it. You will make your living from the earth. You will dig roots

[1] S. C. Roy: *The Hill Bhuiyas of Orissa*, pp. 69 ff.

[2] W. V. Grigson: *The Maria Gonds of Bastar* (Oxford, 1938), pp. 126 ff.

[3] The word 'bewar' is used to describe both the practice of shifting cultivation and the patches of forest which are so cultivated.

and eat them. You will cut wood and carry it on your shoulders. Your wife will pick leaves and sell them. You must not tear the breasts of your Mother the Earth with the plough like the Gond and Hindu.[1] You will cut down trees and burn them and sow your seed in the ashes. But you will never become rich, for if you did you would forsake the earth, and then there would be no one to guard it and keep its nails in place.' Then Bhagavan showed Nanga Baiga how to cut bewar and sow seed in the ashes of burnt trees; and when he had taught him everything, he called him to receive gifts of seed.

This legend is told, and believed, throughout the length and breadth of the Baiga country, in Mandla and Niwas, in Rewa and Dindori, in Baihar, in Bilaspur, in Pandaria. In the old days it was the foundation of the economic and social life of the tribe. Every Baiga who has yielded to the plough knows himself to be standing on *pāpi-dharti*, on sinful earth, or as we would say, is in a state of mortal sin. 'When the bewar was stopped, and we first touched the plough,' says Mahatu, 'a man died in every house.' And Hothu of Taliapani confessed to me that he had at one time used a plough. 'But my children have always been weak and sickly on account of it. If even one Baiga in a village touches the plough, we are all affected!' This is a perfectly genuine religious belief, which the most vigorous propaganda has left unshaken. Dhan Singh of Pandpur once told me that if some magician were to come to him and ask him to choose the three things that he most wanted and that the Baiga most wanted in the world, he would say, 'First give us back our jungle. Then let us have free *kāndabāri* (root-plantations). And third, let us hunt freely once more. We do not want riches, only these three things.'

I have found the same attitude among all the sub-tribes of Baiga. Ketu, a Muria of Niwas, said to me: "The English are giving swaraj to everyone but the Baiga: why can't they give us bewar-swaraj?" A Narotia Baiga of Balaghat said: "It is because we commit the great sin of driving the plough that we now wear tattered clothes and have become slaves to others." In Arhwai (in the Supkar Range) Jaggan, an old Bharotia, said: "When we break the belly of the earth we break our own belly and all the food falls out. By stopping bewar, the English have turned us into naked sadhu." And even the Binjhwar I met near Lamta sighed for the good days of bewar cutting and hunting.

[1] There is a curious parallel in the history of an American Indian messianic cult. Smohalla, the prophet of the Columbia River Basin, addressed his followers in 1870: 'You ask me to plough the ground. Shall I take a knife and tear my mother's bosom? You ask me to dig for stone. Shall I dig under her skin for her bones? You ask me to cut grass. But how dare I cut off my mother's hair?'—*Bureau of American Enthology*, 14th Annual Report, 1892–3, p. 716.

It is commonly believed that the present poverty of the tribe is due to their disobedience of Bhagavan's command; Mother Earth is insulted when her children tear her breasts, and now refuses to supply their needs. For this reason, their magic has decayed, the crops fail, and they are subject to the vengeance of wild beasts.

Bewar, however, is still practised by the Baiga of Kawardha State, of Pandaria Zemindari, in many parts of Bilaspur, in the Baiga Chak of Mandla, and until quite recently in Rewa. The methods they adopt are not unlike those we have already described. To-day, they mean by bewar the custom of felling and burning trees *in situ*; they give the name *dāhia* to the practice of dragging logs and brushwood into a clearing, distributing it over the space available, and then firing it. In the Mandla Settlement Report of 1868–69, Colonel Ward has given an interesting account of how bewar (though he calls it *dhya*) was practised in Mandla seventy years ago.

'With no other instrument of agriculture but their axe and a small sickle, it is astonishing to see the extent of clearing one village of Bygas makes on the sides of the hills of which their village is located.

'Until lately, it was their habit to select the spots for their dhyas with an utter disregard for all the rules of forest conservancy. Where the trees are largest and most numerous there will the Byga resort, and in the cold weather months will cut down sufficient wood to cover pretty closely the whole of the area he means to bring under cultivation. In May and June, just before the setting in of the rains, this wood and the brushwood in which it has fallen, is set fire to; and almost before the fire is out, the Bygas may be seen taking up the ashes and spreading them over the whole surface of their field; this is done either with a bundle of thorns, or with long bamboos, until there is a superstratum of about an inch of ashes spread over the ground.

'In these ashes they sow kodon, koodkee, and, occasionally, a poor specimen of rice, called here 'bygana'. From being on the side of a hill the ashes are cut up into furrows by the action of the rains, and often much of the seed must be washed away altogether; but sufficient seems to remain for the Byga's wants. When sown, the field is fenced round very roughly, and strongly, small trees being felled so as to fall one on to the other; the interstices are filled in with bamboos, and the boughs are carefully interlaced, so that the smallest kind of deer cannot effect an entrance; in addition to this, where there is any danger of the crops being eaten up by buffaloes or bison, which push through any ordinary fence, the Bygas bury a line of broad-bladed spears, called "dansas", in the ground at about the spot where these beasts would land if they jumped the fence. They then watch their opportunity, and, sneaking round to the opposite side, give a series of yells, which send the cattle off terrified over or through the fence. Generally more than one is wounded, and often one killed on the spot; the rest, once started, make straight away, and never visit that field again. In the fences round these "bewurs", as these patches of cultivation are called, are usually two or three cunningly-contrived traps for small deer, something on the principle of the old figure of 4; and several nooses for peacocks, hares, etc. These the Byga carefully examines every morning; and great is his delight when occasionally he finds a panther crushed under one of the figure of 4 traps.

'One of these "bewurs" lasts the Byga, at the outside, three years. He usually leaves sufficient wood on the ground the first season to last for a second season's burning. The third year, if by chance he should make up his mind to stick to one field for so long, his labour is much enhanced, as he has to cut and drag the requisite wood for some little distance and lay it over his field; in addition to this the outturn of the crops falls off every year; so that, altogether, the Byga has every inducement to change the locale of his cultivation, and, where no restriction has been put on his movements, as a rule he does so.

'It takes six or seven years before one of these old "bewurs" is sufficiently covered with wood again to make it worth the Bygas' while to cultivate it a second time. In three years it is probably densely covered with brushwood, but this, if burnt, leaves so little ash that it has to be largely supplemented with timber; and as this has been previously cut all round the clearing, it becomes a work of supererogation to take up one of these old plots before the wood has well grown when other and more suitable land is available.'[1]

The modern Baiga prepares his bewar in very similar fashion. The family first goes into the jungle and selects a suitable site. When they have found one, they take some rice and throw it over a tree in the middle of the new bewar, and fell it with a single stroke of the axe. The head of the family takes a leaf from the tree, folds it in four, and ties it on the standing stool. This is accepted by other Baiga as evidence of occupation.

A little later, they return and cut all the grasses and brushwood. Fifteen days afterwards, they worship their axes, promising Kutki Dai or Anna Dai that if the crop is good, they will make special offerings at harvest-time. They turn the axe with the blade downwards, and recite over it a short mantra invoking the aid of Nanga Baiga and Nanga Baigin. Then they go to the bewar. Before felling, they offer a coconut to the jungle-dwellers, whose home they are now going to despoil, and then they proceed to fell all the trees within the area chosen, leaving stools about a foot high.

In May they go to burn the now dry wood and undergrowth. In the

[1] Ward: op. cit., p. 38.

interval they have distributed the stuff fairly evenly over the bewar, but they have carefully observed the original tree that was felled. It is here that they are to make the Virgin Fire. It is forbidden to kindle the fire with flint and steel; it must be made by twirling a bamboo stick in a hole made in another, split, bamboo. When the fire has kindled, the bamboos are cut up, and each member of the family takes a bit and lights it. They set fire first to the original tree, and then go all over the bewar firing it.

The next duty is to fence the bewar, which they do with logs and brushwood cut round the edges, and they put snares and traps for deer and other animals.

After the first rain has fallen, they take their seed to the bewar, and perform a variation of the Bidri ceremony, offering special gifts to Dharti Mata. The men fill the folds of their dhoti with seeds, all mixed up together and scatter them anywhere and everywhere in the ashes.[1] After a few days, they return and dibble the lines for *rahar dāl* across the middle of the field; they drop three seeds into each hole. Round the stools of the trees, they sow beans and cucumbers.

At harvest-time, they make a small imitation threshing-floor for Thakur Deo, and offer to him and Anna Dai the first-fruits of the crop and a cock or pig, whatever they had promised at the time of felling. It is vital to implement these promises; there are many grim tales of tigers devouring those who failed to do so.

The first year, the crop is gathered rather than cut; only the tops of the plants are removed, and the stalks left for next year. The second year, they burn any trees that may be left, and all the dry stalks of the previous harvest. The third year, the crop is generally poor, for there is little left to burn.

They may, however, use the third-year bewar as a *dāhia*-clearing, and drag logs and brushwood from the surrounding forest and spread it over the field.

Little huts are erected in the bewar. These are called *lāri* when they are built on the ground, and when raised on poles, *mācha*. Here the people watch their crops, and protect them from wild animals. 'We must sleep there every night; we both, husband and wife, sleep there, otherwise we would die of cold. But our wives never watch in the bewar during their periods.'

A threshing-floor is prepared in the bewar-clearing itself, or on the nearest piece of fairly level ground. The Baiga do not usually thresh with bullocks, but a line of men and women, boys and girls, go round and round in a circle stamping with their feet.[2]

[1] See footnote on p. 131.

[2] The Maria of Bastar erect a thick bamboo railing on posts and the men (women do not take part—unlike the Baiga) range themselves in two rows on either side of the railing and holding it with their hands. Then they dance up and down, rubbing the ears of corn between their feet. Some of the Korku on the Betul Border of Hosbangabad, C.P., thresh in the same way.—Grigson: op. cit., p. 136.

Sometimes, when the crop is poor, a bundle of kodon is taken to the house and threshed there. In Jholar I saw a woman threshing kodon with her feet, on the kitchen floor. "There was no life in the crop this year," she said.

The winnowing is done in the usual way. A man takes the kodon in a *sūpa* and holds it up as high as his own head. He gently shakes it so that the grain falls to the ground and the chaff is blown away.

III. WEANING FROM THE AXE

The first serious attempt to put an end to bewar-cultivation was made during the Settlement operations of 1867-69. It was decided that 'according to all positive law, according to the Settlement Code, and according to the custom of the country', the Baiga had 'no title to proprietory right or to occupancy right in the tracts over which they roamed'.

What the then Chief Commissioner, Sir Richard Temple, desired was, not so much to save the forests from destruction, as 'to civilize these people and make them useful members of the Commonwealth'. In the opinion of Mr. J. H. Morris, the Settlement Commissioner for the Central Provinces, and for a time Acting Chief Commissioner, this could only be achieved by inducing them to take to plough-cultivation. 'So long as these people do nothing but grow kodo or koatkee on dhya patches for their own food; so long as they produce nothing at all for sale or barter to other people; and so long as they actually consume nothing except a few grains of salt from the outer world, they can never improve, they can never rise in the human scale, but must continue to be wild men of the woods as they are now.'

Under Sir Richard Temple's administration the policy was 'to take one tract at a time, and bring these people down from the hill sides on which they roamed, and settle them to cultivate lands in the valleys'. But proposals to forbid bewar absolutely were resisted, and Temple refused to adopt a policy that would 'improve these poor people off the face of the earth'.

In Seoni, Captain Thomson had reported that the Baiga there 'never use the plough or till the land; but sow in the ashes of the jungle which they cut down'. In Raigarh, however, 'having been by the waste land rules somewhat restricted in their wanderings, they had in several places taken to the use of the plough'.[1] He had proposed stringent measures for checking bewar altogether, but was criticised by the Chief Commissioner for 'not treating with sufficient consideration the claims of communities belonging

[1] Thomson: op. cit., p. 39.

to the aboriginal tribes, who, in the midst of the jungle, have established some kind of village and brought under cultivation a certain amount of land'. The Chief Commissioner himself was concerned to protect 'the material interests of the wild tribes', while hoping that 'they would gradually be induced to settle down permanently into closer communication with the more civilized inhabitants and adopt more civilized ways'. He arranged, therefore, that the bewar-cutting tribes should be assigned tracts of country averaging a square mile or so, 'their hills being specially reserved from sale, and their right to reside and cultivate recognized in any usufruct lease granted over these hills'.[1] I do not know how far this policy was actually carried out.

In Balaghat, the Baiga met the new rules restricting bewar with stubborn opposition; the District authorities moreover were not very energetic in enforcing them, and even continued to take a tax of one rupee an axe; so that ten years later only about forty families out of over four hundred had taken to the plough.

In Mandla, Colonel Ward reported that 'it had been found quite impracticable, as well as hard and impolitic, to force the Bygas to give up their dhya cultivation and take to the plough; so that the settlement with them has been simply the attempt to confine their destructive propensities within a ring fence'.[2] Some of the Mandla Baiga, however, had already taken to the plough, 'through force of example' and were themselves 'setting an example to their wilder brethren'. But in the Ramgarh Tehsil, 'the Byga country par excellence, at the head of the Borhneyr, and the rivers which water the Pertabgurh talooqua', the situation was quite different, great damage had been done, and nothing would induce the Baiga to change their habits. However, says Colonel Ward, 'if carefully looked after, the injury they cause to the forests there, may be made more negative than positive, by placing certain restrictions on their wandering habits, and keeping them within the boundaries now fixed for them; which have been selected so as to allow them wood enough for their wants, but in situations where, owing to their previous devastations, or the inaccessibility of the locality, the timber is of little value'. In Pertabgurh and Mokutpore, 7,794 acres of land were allotted to the Baiga of twelve villages. 'The amount of their present cultivation roughly measured is 1,431 acres, so that a little over five times its area of cultivation has been allotted to each. Formerly the area claimed by these people amounted to over 30,000 acres. They have expressed themselves quite satisfied with the arrangement made for them. But if the country was opened up to trade, and the value of money became more known, the Bygas would soon learn wherein their

[1] Ibid, Memorandum, p. 12.

[2] Ward: op. cit., p. 35.

Baiga threshing by foot.
Winnowing kodon.

own advantage lay, and would do as their brethren have done in other parts of the country—drop the axe and take to the plough; but until we have shown them what benefit it is to them, and, in fact, have created wants which their present primitive habits will not enable them to provide for, we cannot expect them to change their nature'.[1]

Ward records an amusing conversation which he had with some Baiga on this subject, in which 'he was rather put to it to reply to some of the pertinent questions of the shrewd old men' and was once entirely 'shut up' by one old grey-beard. But the Colonel evidently handled the situation with great tact, for the talk ended with his 'receiving a deputation from the tribe, requesting me to live among them, promising that I should want for nothing, and that they would supply me with four Byga wives to attend on me, and that, doubtless, under my tuition they would soon learn the art of plough cultivation. This flattering offer was declined of necessity'.[2] Had the Colonel only been a little more adventurous, it is obvious that there would have been no problem of the Baiga Chak!

We will now trace briefly the progress of 'civilization' among the Baiga during the next twenty years. The fact that 'the marketable value of forest produce rose in something like geometrical proportions' during those years probably accounts for a shifting of emphasis from Sir Richard Temple's policy of benevolent improvement for their own sake to a frank and simple desire to better the Provincial budget. The interests of a small and savage tribe were of little account beside the necessity of commercializing the forest. The struggle between the Baiga and the administration was joined in Mandla and Balaghat. For some reason, a more liberal policy has always been followed in Bilaspur.

Balaghat is largely populated by Binjhwar Baiga, the most Hinduized section of the tribe, and even before 1868 several families of these in Pondi, Gudma and Sonkar in the Man Valley, had taken to the plough. Pondi was the earliest settlement of the kind in the whole province. But every attempt to carry out the Chief Commissioner's policy met with vigorous opposition. Up to 1870, the only new convert to the plough was Ganu, headman of Goara. He was followed by Mutira Pujari of Jaldidhar who, however, insisted on maintaining his bewar at the same time, "even," he said, "if the Deputy Commissioner cut his throat". In 1871 a 'lucky chance' helped Colonel Bloomfield to win over a whole village of Narotia Baiga. Government had offered a reward of Rs. 200 for the killing of a dangerous elephant; and the Khandarparhi Baiga headed by Ranjar Pujari, helped Bloomfield and Naylor to hunt the mad creature down, and were given the reward. As a result of this Bloomfield persuaded them to come down from the

[1] Ward, op. cit., p. 39. [2] Ibid, p. 160.

rocks of Khandarparhi and take to the plough in the good lands of Karwahi.

Colonel Bloomfield, of course, was very deeply in earnest about the uplift and civilization of the Baiga. He wrote a little pamphlet called *Notes on the Baigas* and circulated it to a number of missionary societies, his belief being that if they could be converted to Christianity all their problems would be solved.

By 1878, only about 40 families, out of 441, in the Balaghat District, had been settled, and the Deputy Commissioner, Major H. M. Repton, determined to speed matters up. His view was that the slow progress made hitherto had been due to the fact that though bewar had been nominally forbidden, Government had continued to collect the tax of one rupee per axe, and that this had meant that the practice had in effect been winked at. In 1877, for example, no fewer than 280 axes were taxed. Major Repton determined to stop this. He abolished the tax; he forbade bewar throughout the district; he even went so far as to destroy standing crops on some existing bewar. He also obtained sanction from the Chief Commissioner for the expenditure of Rs. 2,000, in Mandla and Balaghat, on the settlement of the Baiga. But the Chief Commissioner advised a policy of proceeding slowly to 'wean' the Baiga from the axe. The destruction of crops was not approved. It was proposed to mix the Baiga with Gond who would teach them the new methods of cultivation, and not to settle Baiga in villages by themselves. It is almost a tribal law, of course, that Baiga should live in separate settlements, and not mixed with other communities. The new scheme of civilization, however, was not based on anthropological principles.

By March of the following year, 33 families had come down into Gond villages and were putting up huts, for which they had been allowed to collect grass and bamboo free of charge. That year, a further sum, bringing the total to Rs. 3,500 for Balaghat, was sanctioned for the purchase of seed and plough-cattle; and subordinate officials were ordered to see that the Baiga were not harassed, but gently persuaded to come down to the ordinary villages.

By May, 1881, 75 families had been settled with land, grain, bullocks and implements, at the cost of about Rs. 3,000. Forty other families settled without assistance, and 485 families remained 'unreclaimed'.

In September, 1881, an annual expenditure of Rs. 2,500 for four years was sanctioned.

By the end of September, 1882, the Deputy Commissioner had spent Rs. 2,280 in helping 190 families to settle down to the plough, and these included a few Bharotia.

By September of the following year, this number had risen to over 300 families, and Rs. 6,250 had been spent. These families were settled in 23 different villages, in 220 houses, and numbered 325 men, 329 women, and 488 children, a total of 1,142 persons. They were cutting 788 acres of land, and possessed 476 Government cattle in addition to 11 of their own. The majority of the new settlers were Narotia Baiga, though 20 families of the wild Bharotia were included. But that year, in face of Government pressure, many Bharotia took fright, and 57 families, together with 24 families of Gond migrated to the Saletekri Zemindari. However, in 1884, the Deputy Commissioner of Balaghat was able to congratulate himself that on the whole the scheme had been successful, and to report that 'the Baiga I have in hand are more happy and contented than they have been for a long time'.

In Mandla some of the more civilized Binjhwar Baiga in the Mandla Tehsil had already, before 1868, taken to the plough, as is common when a tribe becomes semi-Hinduized. But, as in Balaghat, progress was slow until in 1879 a sum of Rs. 800 was advanced to 40 families who were settled in lands in three villages. This money was spent on bullocks, seed, implements, and the settlement of trifling debts. In their first year, these families got Gond to teach them to plough, but the next year they were able to do it for themselves. They paid one rupee per plough for the first two years, then three rupees until the Mandla Settlement expired in 1889, after which they were assessed as ordinary villagers.

In 1880, at the beginning of the cold weather, another effort was made and Rs. 2,000 was spent in settling 33 families in Silpuri near Bichia, and 65 families in the lands near Changaon and other villages round about Ramnagar. But as the propaganda against bewar increased, many Baiga fled into Kawardha State and the Zemindari of Chhattisgarh.

Thereafter the march of civilization continued year by year. In 1882, 32 families were settled at a cost of Rs. 1,200; in 1883, an expenditure of Rs. 1,550 was sanctioned. In 1884, 127 families were settled in six villages, and cost Government Rs. 2,805. They had 521 acres of land, 226 cattle and 132 houses. Most of these were said to have been Bharotia.

In fact, by 1885, the Mandla Tehsil was largely free of bewar, and even as early as 1880 the Deputy Commissioner was able to report that the new Baiga village of Chaugaon was 'quite indistinguishable from an ordinary village of this district'.

The Ramgarh Tehsil, however, presented a much more serious problem, and it was another ten years before a solution was attempted. Shortly before 1890, however, the schemes adumbrated by Colonel Ward twenty years earlier began to be reconsidered. He had suggested confining the bewar-cutting Baiga within a ring-fence, and allotting to them tracts of country where, owing to previous cuttings or the inaccessibility of the locality, the timber was of little value. The forest officers did not want to prohibit bewar-cutting altogether, for fear that they would lose the valuable assistance of Baiga labour. For, as a Divisional Forest Officer (Mr. M. Muttanah of Mandla) of the time observed, 'We are entirely dependent for our labour supply on these Baiga who are by far the best wood-cutters we have in the district. Indeed it appears to me that we can scarcely get on with our work, should we lose this valuable source of labour supply. Collection of harra and minor products, and line clearings, would be impossible without them.'

It was therefore decided to repeat Colonel Ward's experiment of setting aside one particular area in which bewar would be allowed, and to prohibit it elsewhere in the district. The original suggestion was that portions of forest known as Blocks 44 and 52 should be set aside for this purpose, but they were found on enquiry to be unsuitable, and instead a tract of 23,920 acres was carved out of Block 54. The Deputy Commissioner of Mandla at this time was Colonel Hogg, who was 'inclined to treat the Baigas liberally, and say to them, "You have got all that you may expect, and now you will get no more."'

IV. THE BAIGA CHAK

The tract chosen was in the wild uplands of the Mandla Hills, and was described by Colonel Hogg as 'a hilly tract practically hemmed in on all sides by wild and uninhabitable hills. It is perfectly inaccessible and is therefore useless as a timber-producing area'. This Baiga Chak, as it was now to be called, was bounded on the east by the Narbada and Rewa State; on the south by Bilaspur District; on the west by Mandla Tehsil; and on the north by ryatwari areas only recently excised from Government forest. The Chak was established by a letter (No. 2,860/221 of the 13th May, 1890) from Mr. L. K. Laurie, officiating Secretary to the Chief Commissioner, to the Commissioner of the Jubbulpore Division.

'After much discussion'—so runs the text of the letter—'it is now proposed to confine all the bewar-cutting Baigas to an area to be carved out of Block 54, amounting to 23,920 acres (of the Ramgarh Tehsil).... This is the only tract in Mandla in which bewar cultivation shall in future be permitted. The area will be known as the "Baiga Reserve". All the bewar-cutting families now residing outside that area must be warned forthwith that, if they wish to practise bewar, they must move into the Reserve before the next cultivating season; and bewar must be put a stop to in all other parts of the Tehsil. None but Baigas must be allowed to settle in the Reserve.

'The Chief Commissioner entirely agrees that it should be the policy of the Administration to convert the Baigas—so far as they can be induced to settle to regular cultivation—into forest-workers; and that their management should therefore be entrusted in the main to the Forest Department.... The Baigas should be told that though they are to be allowed to practice bewar within the Reserve, they can only do so in such localities as may from time to time (and as required) be pointed out to them by the Forest Officer. The latter will be responsible that bewar is not allowed on ridges enclosing the head waters of important streams, or where it would be detrimental to the water supply of the country.

'Furthermore, the Baigas should be made to understand that the Administration, while permitting the practise of bewar within the Reserve, does not look with favour upon this form of cultivation. As an indication of its disapproval, it will demand—and recover through the Forest Department—a tax of Re. 1 per annum for every axe employed in felling wood for bewar. As an encouragement to them to seek other means of support, plots of land within the Reserve will be allotted on ten years' leases—of which the first three will be rent-free, and the remaining seven at the rate of 4 annas per acre—to all the Baigas who are willing to settle down to regular cultivation. Any Baiga family wishing to take up land outside the Reserve, will be given plots on the same terms. Advances of money, free of interest, for the purchase of plough-cattle and seed will be given by the Deputy Commissioner to any Baigas who take leases of plots (either within or without the Reserve) upon these conditions. Employment will also be found by the Forest Department for all who may agree to work in the forests under the orders of the forest officers. Baigas undertaking to work in this way will be settled in forest villages, helped to build, and given plots for home cultivation.

'In order to provide labour for those who are willing to work, it should be arranged that in the extracting of timber for the Department and for purchasers, and in the collecting of harra and other minor produce, Baigas should be preferentially employed. All contracts relating to the produce of the forest in the neighbourhood of the Reserve must stipulate for this preferential employment.'

Malguzars were also to be encouraged to accept Baiga in their villages. When Baiga cultivators had been settled for five years, the Malguzar would receive a sanad entitling him to have such lands valued at half rates at settlement. In Mandla Tehsil, all the bewar-cutting Baiga lived in Malguzari villages, and though in Mandla the clause (XVI) in the Wajib-ul-arz regarding forests did not bind Malguzars to manage these in accordance with the directions of Government, it did prohibit the cutting of sal, teak and shisham without permission. 'This restriction, if properly insisted on, would probably suffice to stop bewar in Malguzari villages. It should be enforced by the Deputy Commissioner universally, so far as the conditions of the Settlement allow: and bewar-cultivation should be stayed, wherever possible, in the Mandla as well as in the Ramgarh Tehsil.'

The Chak was not, therefore, as sometimes has been supposed, a sort of National Park where the Baiga would be allowed to carry on their ancient tribal life, but a Reformatory where the Baiga, under strict supervision and increasing official pressure, would be slowly 'weaned' from their primitive habits.

Inside the area demarcated for the Chak there were already a number of Baiga villages, Daharkata, Silpuri, Dhaba, Ajgar, Jhilung, Lamota and Rajni Sarai. Here 1,551 Baiga were living. Outside the Chak, all the Baiga were ordered either to abandon bewar or move into the Reserve. It is notable that there was practically no migration into the Reserve, though many Baiga went into the neighbouring States. The rest refused to leave their villages, and agreed to adopt plough cultivation if advances of money for seed and cattle were given them. These Baiga were now definitely settled in seven forest villages, specially constituted for the purpose, Chauradadar, Karadih, Dadargaon, Daldal, Udhor, Jagatpur, Pandpur; and at the same time three villages of Gond were established at Tuichidih, Pandripani and Tirchula. The first five of the Baiga villages were already largely occupied by Gond, who were in possession of the best land. Udhor and Pandpur had only poor land, and Udhor was soon closed. Pandpur remains a fairly flourishing Baiga settlement.

Unfortunately, it does not seem to have been agreed whether the Forest Department or the Deputy Commissioner was really responsible for the reformation of the Baiga, and for the next three years very little was done beyond the enforcement of the order prohibiting bewar. The Secretariat Letter we have just quoted had contemplated a generous scheme of compensation for Baiga both within and outside the Chak, but for three years this was not forthcoming. During these years the condition of the Baiga of Ramgarh Tehsil was deplorable. Suddenly deprived of their ancestral means of livelihood, threatened with expulsion from the forests they had known from childhood, prevented even from growing root-crops for fear this should divert their attention from the plough, forced to adopt a mode of cultivation forbidden by their religion, yet unprovided with the means of purchasing ploughs and cattle, these Baiga endured some years of utter poverty and destitution. Those days are still vividly remembered. "There was no food, there were no bullocks, there was no money. The Ranger tried to help us, but what could he do?" It is good to note that the names of Mr. Muttanah, the D.F.O., and Mohan Lal, the Ranger, are still gratefully remembered by the Baiga for the sympathy and help they gave during those hard years. Ranger Mohan Lal in fact sent a letter to the D.F.O., Mandla, which by its quaint humanity brightens the dull pages of the official file in which it is preserved.

'The poor Baiga,' he wrote, 'is a race that is admitted on all hands as living from hand to mouth, and having even no sufficient cloth to cover their loins with. They could not be allowed to make new bewars nor have they been supplied with other means of support. So death is staring these poor helpless people in their faces as it were, and these innocent loyal creatures are at the mercy of district authorities.' Mohan Lal proposed that the Baiga should be allowed to sow their old bewar for one year at least so that they should not fall into the hands of the money-lenders. But though Colonel Grace now came to advise Colonel Hogg, nothing was done.

At the end of 1892, a number of Baiga, 11 in Pandpur, 34 in Udhor, 12 in Karadih and 7 in Dadargaon, began cutting bewar again, saying that otherwise they were faced with certain starvation. They were severely reprimanded, but under the circumstances criminal action was not taken against them. It was not until 1894 that, after a great deal of correspondence, a sum of Rs. 800 was advanced and 56 bullocks were supplied to the Baiga. One pair of bullocks was given on loan to every two families, together with as much seed as they wanted.

Progress, however, had been slow. After three years, only 17 out of the 94 families in Block 62 had settled to plough cultivation, and of these only 7 owned their own bullocks. The administration of the Chak was strongly criticised by Colonel Grace. In 1893, therefore, the Chief Commissioner decided on a new drive to free the country of bewar altogether. He transferred the management of the Chak—to its great advantage—to the Forest Department; he decided not to extend the Reserve, but 'to take up in real earnest the work of settling Baigas down to a regular plough cultivation in forest villages', and asked for the submission of a scheme that would effect this purpose.

At this time there were 94 Baiga families in what was known as Block 62, 30 families in Block 54, some 60 families in the surrounding Malguzari villages, and 362 families in the Chak. The greatest difficulty was experienced in dealing with the families living in Malguzari villages, the Deputy Commissioner reporting that 'they clung like a spoilt child to their axe and fire'. To combat this, a policy was adopted of mixing Gond with Baiga; Gond were encouraged to settle among the Baiga and given advantageous grants of land when they did so, and they were asked to take Baiga as agricultural labourers and train them to the plough. In the end, however,

SKETCH MAP OF

BAIGA CHAK, KARANJIA AND DINDORI RANGES

MANDLA DIVISION

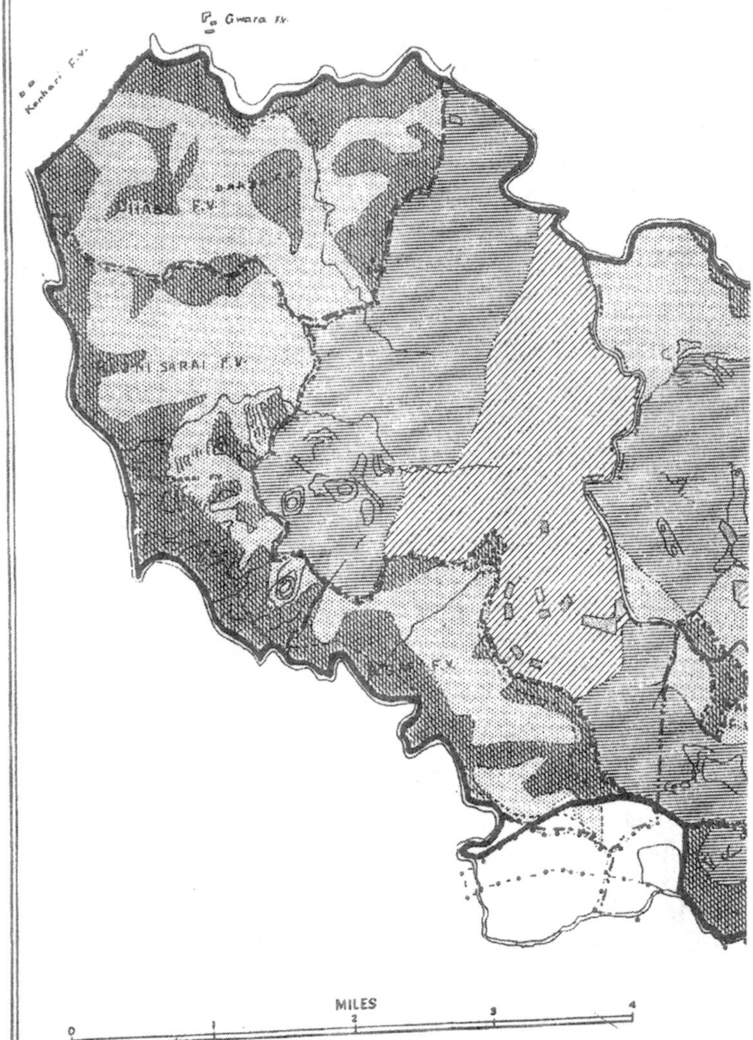

Area in Acres	References	
—	*Boundary of Baiga Chak*	
194 acres	*Existing Bewar cultivation*	
5,500 ,,	*Area available for Bewar cultivation in future*	
4,740 ,,	*Area in which Bewar have already been cultivated and not fit for such in future for at least 20 years to come*	
4,124 ,,	*Existing field cultivation*	
8,300 ,,	*Poor forest not fit either for Bewar or field cultivation*	
Total area of Baiga Chak } 22,858 acres		
	Forest village boundary in Baiga Chak	
	Range boundary	

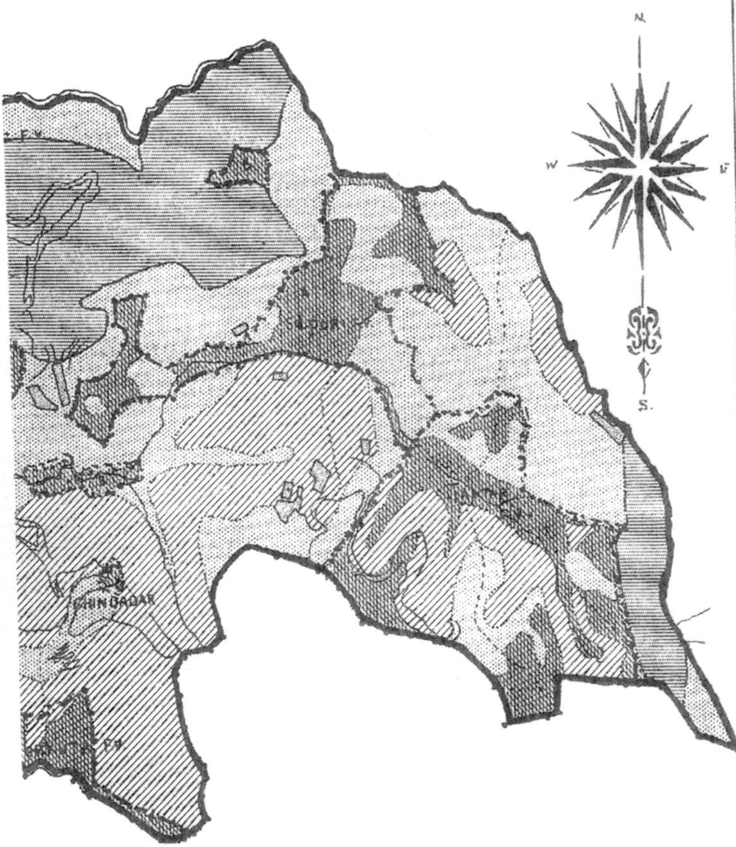

we find many Baiga who have nominally accepted the plough, never actually touching it, but employing Gond as their servants, while they themselves carry on their ancient duties of sorcery with an occasional excursion into the woods for roots.

This policy succeeded almost everywhere, though in the Ghugri Malguzari, from 1894 to 1898, bewar was permitted over an area of no less than 6,172 acres, being cut by 610 families who made 1,153 clearings at one rupee four annas the axe. Elsewhere, however, by 1895, the Baiga had generally settled down to the new conditions—the name of Forester Mannu Tiwari should be remembered as one of the apostles of civilization in the Mandla District.

Within the Chak itself, the Baiga were put under discipline. A Forester was placed in charge of the Chak, and the bewar-plots were strictly delimited. The Baiga seem to have been found rather difficult to manage; they could not understand why they could only cut bewar in the plots allotted to them. They claimed that they could go anywhere they liked. They seem to have resented the propaganda against bewar. A famous Dewar named Mahtu, the headman of Dharkata, set his face against all change; and although the leader of Silpuri village, Dewan, and a number of others came round to the official side, they dared not do anything for fear of Mahtu's curses. At the same time, some of the officials were hardly sympathetic. But whatever the reason, the population of the Chak dwindled alarmingly in the course of the next ten years. In 1891 it was 1,551; in 1901 it had sunk to 700; or from 362 families to 132. In 1903 there was a further drop of 100, for in that year Rajni Sarai was totally deserted, the Baiga fleeing in a body on an attempt being made to move them to the Banjar Reserve for sleeper work. Rajni Sarai was later peopled by Gond, and is now an entirely Gond village with a population of 114. To-day the Baiga population of the Chak is 601—the numbers have remained stationary for over thirty years.

In 1895 the policy enunciated in the Secretariat Letter of 1890 was apparently altered, as it was felt that if Gond and other cultivators were allowed to mix with the Baiga in the Chak, it would be easier to wean the latter from their axes. Accordingly, a number of other settlers were admitted. To-day there are 81 Dhoba, 37 Ahir, 18 Agaria, 102 Panka, 132 Gond, and 10 others settled in the Chak. This is a very high proportion of the total population of 1,076; there are 475 others to 601 Baiga.

The amount of bewar cut has also greatly decreased. In the ten years, 1892 to 1901, 3,354 acres were burnt for bewar, and at that time it was estimated that the limitations of the Reserve were such that only 1,000 acres remained for use. To-day there are only 194 acres under bewar

Ramsden

Dudh-Bhaina woman with khanta for digging roots.
Man with rain-hat.

cultivation, an area that is changed every three years according to an official programme. This means that about 70 acres a year are all that are required. On the other hand, the area has recouped itself remarkably since 1901 when there were only 1,000 acres available for bewar. It is now estimated that 5,500 acres are ready for immediate bewar, and a further 4,740 acres will be available after twenty or thirty years. There are also 4,124 acres of fields under plough cultivation.

In Daharkata, out of 28 families of Baiga, 22 bewar are cut by 21 families. In Silpuri, out of 23 families, 12½ bewar are cut by 15 families. In Ajgar, out of 29 families, only 13 cut bewar. Less than 50 bewar are thus being cut throughout the Chak.

No new Baiga are allowed to enter the Chak, and once a Baiga has surrendered his bewar, he cannot recover it. Only those who have the hereditary right are now allowed to practise it.

We have now almost reached the end of our survey. It remains to state that to-day bewar is permitted in certain States, notably Kawardha and Bastar—it has recently been prohibited in Rewa to the great distress of the Baiga there—and in some of the great Zemindari. It is permitted in the Southern Circle of Bilaspur, on condition that only bamboo and mixed forest areas that are free of sal are used, that notice is given before firing, that the Baiga are responsible for clearing a line round their bewar to prevent the fires from spreading, and that they keep to each bewar for three years.

V. THE CASE FOR BEWAR

What is the real case against bewar? Sir Richard Temple thought that so long as the Baiga practised it, they would remain wild men of the hills and never rise in the social scale. Forest officers have very naturally deplored the destruction of the trees—Mahatu recalls how Mr. Muttanah and his wife visited a bewar clearing in Karadih about 1890 and actually wept at the sight of such devastation. His wife embraced the trees and said they were her children. 'It is sad,' says Colonel Ward, 'to see the havoc that has been made among the forests by the Baiga axes. . . . In many places the hills have been swept clean of forests for miles; in others, the Byga marks are tall, blackened, charred stems standing in hundreds among the green forests; these are the trees killed by the Baiga for the sake of the resin.' And again: 'It is really difficult to believe that so few people could sweep the face of the earth so clear of timber as they have done.'[1] Forsyth says: 'The Byga is the most terrible enemy to the forests we have anywhere in these hills. Thousands of square miles of sal forest have been

[1] Ward: op. cit., p. 161.

clean destroyed by them in the progress of their dhya cultivation.'[1] Others fear the possible effects of bewar on rainfall and the rivers. Desiccation and erosion have long been the bugbears of the administration. Bewar is also condemned as a lazy method of cultivation.

Waste and idleness, erosion and the failure of the water supply, a primitive and uneconomic method—these are the expressions that the course of time have transformed into clichés, representing unquestioned and unquestionable facts.

What is there to say on the other side? In the first place we must remember that shifting cultivation is regarded in other parts of the world as the mark of a comparatively advanced stage of civilization. Tribes like the Punan of Borneo, the Kubu of Sumatra, the Sakai of Malay, many Indian tribes in America, most of the Australian aboriginals have no form of cultivation at all, and live by hunting and gathering food. The Government of Ceylon actually put pressure on the Vedda to take to *chena* shifting cultivation in order to raise them in the scale of humanity. The 'mound-culture' of America and the 'ditch-culture' of ancient Peru and the hoe-tillage of Africa and the South Seas are all more primitive than bewar. In fact, the plough is characteristic only of the European and the dominant Asiatic civilizations; in opposition to bewar it has been exalted into a sort of fetish. The plough is undoubtedly the mark of the ever-advancing Hindu-European civilization which will soon finally overwhelm the old culture of the axe.

Authorities are by no means agreed about the extent of the damage done to the forest by bewar-cultivation. The opinions of Ward and Forsyth are undoubtedly exaggerated. Waste there is, but much of that waste is recouped in time.

'There is much misconception', says *The Mandla District Gazetteer*, 'as to the amount of permanent damage done to the forests by the axe cultivation of the Baigas, which has been blamed for the denudation of the sources of the Upper Nerbudda and her tributaries. Mr. Bell discussed this matter at length with many Baigas, and the allegation is not in accordance with either their assertions or his own observation. They claim that the jungle only grows the thicker and stronger after the abandonment of a bewar, and they have shown not one, but fifty abandoned bewars where the sal reproduction was strong and luxuriant enough even to impede progress. It is the dahia cultivation of the Gonds, they assert, which has denuded the forests. The reason for this is that the Gonds cultivate only below the line of frost. The sal once cut in those regions can only reproduce small shoots, which are destroyed by the annually recurring frosts. As frost comes as early as the middle of November, the Baiga crops, which as a rule are late ripeners,

[1] Forsyth: op. cit., p. 364.

must be sown where they will not suffer from it. The Baigas therefore choose a site well above the line of frost for their bewar, and in such sites the sal can freely reproduce. The Gond inflicts a permanent, the Baiga only a temporary, injury to the forests.'[1]

In 1909, a noteable report was written on this subject by Mr. A. P. Percival, who had been D.F.O. in Balaghat for several years and was then in Mandla. 'I think', he says, 'that the importance of the whole matter has been exaggerated, and there is a general want of perspective when so much can be talked and written about the Baiga Chak, and far more important and urgent questions such as the fire protection and working of several hundred square miles of pure sal forest, and the truly serious state of affairs in the reserved forest in and around Dindori plain are ignored or passed by without comment, or any serious attempt to improve matters.

'The old bewars are invariably situated on dadars, on tops of hills, and on the middle and upper slopes, always well above the frost zone. The reason is that their wild crops do not ripen before frost, and to bewar no low ground means frost-ruin. Also, on lower ground a dense coarse grass grows up and chokes the crop. The lower ground also has not enough tree-growth. It is thus certain that the ruined aspect of many low-lying frost-bitten areas and the black cotton *maidan* lands below them, are in no way due to the Baigas; occasionally they may be due to the Gonds, but in my own opinion it is mainly a question of soils.'

Percival considered that an area was fit to be re-bewared after twelve to fifteen years. 'I had some difficulty in getting through the dense thickets of sal saplings on twelve-year-old bewars on an elephant. Nobody can possibly inspect past bewar areas as I have done, and not be struck with the extraordinary regrowth that springs up within a few years.'[2]

If bewar leads inevitably to denudation and ruined forests how can we explain 'the often wonderful regrowth of sal in all stages from seedlings through saplings to poles that is to be seen stretching in an almost unbroken line of forest from the Baiga Chak to Karadih towards Amarkantak, say twenty square miles, the like of which I have rarely seen in the whole of the Balaghat, Motinala or Banjar Sal forests, and of which there is no possibility of doubting that the majority are old bewar areas?

'Up to three years after an area has been abandoned the regrowth is scanty, by the end of six years it is freely filling up, at the end of twelve years regeneration is usually complete. If there are any exceptions it is on

[1] Op. cit., p. 73.

[2] 'There is a popular idea that jhuming tribes fell and destroy virgin forest every year. This is, of course, absurd. All suitable land in the Rengma country was taken up generations ago, and now lies fallow under secondary jungle for the six to twelve years rotation on which each block is cut.'—J. P. Mills: *The Rengma Nagas* (London, 1937), p. 76.

comparatively small areas where rocky ground is to be found and the Baigas say there never was forest growth nor bewar, which is obviously correct, as on recent low-lying bewar given out on wrong principles by the very people who are inveighing against the damage wrought by bewar.'

Percival concludes by pointing out that if it were a matter of exploiting the forest commercially, and cutting timber on a large scale, no one would say anything about the damage and denudation of the forest. 'Perhaps I can best make my point by saying that were the Chak situated near a railway station with a demand for timber and fuel, we should not professionally hesitate a moment in constituting felling series and working over a fixed area of probably 200 to 300 acres annually.' But all that the Baiga in the Chak at that time required was 161 acres, and Percival thought at least 5,000 acres were available.

Ten years earlier, the illicit bewar-cutting in the Ghugri estate in Mandla had attracted the attention of Government. The manager, Narbada Prasad, acting for his aunt, Parbati Bai, the Malguzarin, had allowed bewar to be cut from 1894 to 1898. No fewer than 610 people had taken advantage of the opportunity, and had cut 1,153 bewar between them. Narbada Prasad levied a tax of Re. 1.4.0 per axe from the Baiga and something a little in excess of the usual plough rate from the Gond.

The bewar-cutting came to a natural end as a result of the famine of 1897, when over half the Baiga population of Ghugri died, and the orders of Government prohibiting it were hardly necessary. But Mr. C. M. McCrie who was then D.F.O. of Mandla sent a competent Ranger to examine the estate and see how much damage had actually been done. McCrie reported that 'the figures clearly show that bewar-cutting does not entail the permanent extinction of forest growth on the areas on which it is practised. Indeed it would probably do little harm or permanent damage if old bewar were allowed sufficient rest before being again attacked, and if due precautions were taken to prevent the whole forest being burned annually at the time when the bewars for the year are fired'. He considered that the bewar did have an adverse effect on the commercial value of the forest, as the trees grew up again in a pollard state and were not fit for working, but he did not think they had any real effect in causing denudation and the ruin of the water-supply.

I will call three more witnesses in the Baiga's defence, Dr. J. H. Hutton, Mr. W. V. Grigson and the late Sir Bampfylde Fuller. Dr. Hutton places the problem on the broadest basis.

'Afforestation,' he says, 'is a frequent grievance, and in forests which were common property under a tribal regime it becomes a punishable offence to exercise what the tribe regards as an inalienable right. Thus, under the Assam Forest Regulations tribal land used for jhuming is held to be Unclassed State Forest, and as such at the absolute disposal of Government. It can be taken and its possessors ousted without any sort of compensation. But this land has by the great majority of hill tribes been regarded for many generations as their most valuable real property. . . . In the Madras Agency Tracts again the same attitude has been taken towards *jhum*, there called *podu*, and has been carried to the extent of the prohibition of cultivation, twice bringing the Sawara tribe to the verge of open rebellion. *Dahia* (or bewar), as it is there called, is similarly forbidden in the Central Provinces, compelling the forest tribes to cultivate only under the Land Settlement system which is in many cases unsuited to them. Primitive systems of agriculture are frequently extremely wasteful of forest land and may in hill country prove damaging to adjoining plains on account of denudation, the too rapid escape of rain, and consequent inundation below. At the same time, wasteful cultivation of this kind is often the only known means of subsistence. It cannot be abandoned in a day for other methods with which the cultivator, whose knowledge is traditional, is unfamiliar.'

Mr. W. V. Grigson, writing about the Maria Gond of Bastar State, points out that even if there has been damage to the forest, most of this has occurred in places so inaccessible that they could not be exploited for commercial purposes.

'This shifting cultivation,' he says, 'is criticised from two points of view. The forestry enthusiast laments the passing of much fine forest, and foretells desiccation and erosion. Others condemn *penda* as a lazy method of cultivation. The former forgets that in most of this area the forests have been too remote and inaccessible ever to be exploited, and that, even though some fine timber has been sacrificed, much that has gone was hopelessly over-mature. . . . Few signs are apparent of erosion, save in the more open parts of the Bison-horn country where *erka* has cleared the plains below the hills of forest, and there are no signs of any reduction in the heavy rainfall. . . . It is a superficial criticism that condemns *penda* cultivation as lazy. The clearing of the land, especially if it be covered with heavy timber, is most arduous. Remote and sometimes almost perpendicular slopes two or three miles from the village have to be cleared; the wood and scrub spread over the ground; field-houses, sheds and watching platforms have to be built on the *penda* slopes. The firing of the *penda* is particularly arduous: the stumps have to be cleared of the shoots that spring up when the rains have set in: and where deer or bison are numerous the clearings have to be fenced with heavy timber fencing.'[1]

[1] Grigson, op. cit., pp. 128 ff.

Life in the bewar, in fact, is not only arduous, but dangerous, as the long roll of Baiga killed by bear, panther, or tiger testifies. The bewar calls out the best in a man; he is summoned to a desperate battle with the forces of nature; the bewar preserves something of the romance and adventure of the days of old.

No administrator, not even Ward or Bloomfield, has shown greater or more intelligent appreciation of the needs of the Baiga than Sir Bampfylde Fuller. From 1893 to 1901 and afterwards he was actively interested in their problems. At the end of 1893 he was Commissioner of Settlements and Agriculture in the Central Provinces. In that capacity he toured widely among the Baiga of Mandla and the Lormi Range in Bilaspur, and also among the Muria of Bastar. 'I believe,' he says, 'that the settlement of bewar-cutting Baigas to cultivation will be a far more difficult task than has sometimes been anticipated. Baigas will be found to take land. But they will rarely be of the bewar-cutting class.'

'The recent orders of Government,' he continues, 'have really brought the bewar-cutting Baigas of Mandla and Bilaspur to a state of destitution. Their cultivation with the axe and mattock is of an entirely different type to plough-cultivation, and they cannot more reasonably be forced to a plough than a weaver can be forced to service in a cotton mill.

'The Bhumias of Bilaspur complained bitterly to me of the hardships they were put to for bare subsistence. . . . When I was in the Mandla uplands tigers were giving great trouble and I was told that the current report was that the Baigas in revenge for their treatment by Government had withdrawn the spells by which they keep the tigers in check and that numerous deaths from tigers might be expected. The Bhumias of Lormi obliged me by an exhibition of dancing, but they refused for some time my presents of money, eagerly asking instead for their lost bewars.'

Fuller goes on to doubt whether the reasons for stopping bewar were as clear and cogent as they were usually assumed to be. He suggested that the timber cut was of no great value and was situated in so remote and difficult localities that it would never pay to transport it. Secondly he questioned 'whether bewars under certain conditions of soil and rainfall do denude the hills provided that they are not concentrated on too small an area. In this matter,' he adds, 'a great deal too much has been taken for granted.

'I have been told that in Mauritious the forests are regularly cut and burnt. . . . The people I asked declared that in some respects forest growth was improved by bewar, and that a bewar-clearing would ordinarily be under dense jungle in eight or ten years. I was shown hills in Mandla which were said to have been stripped by bewar twenty-five years ago, but were now thickly clothed with high forest. In Bastar where jungle is almost universally cut and burnt as a preparation for plough-cultivation, I saw really fine patches of young sal forest on land which I was informed had been cleared only three years previously, and looking to the number of years during which bewar has been practised unchecked it seems necessary to conclude that almost the whole of our Forest Reserves have been under bewar-cultivation at some time or other.

'There are circumstances which justify a Government calling on its subjects to reform or perish. But the reform must be supported by very strong reasons, and the more numerous the people affected the stronger must be the case against them. With these people there are, moreover, sentimental reasons for kind treatment. They are relics of old time; they live in places which no others would dare to inhabit; and it seems hard to deny them their customary food in order to lengthen the life of valueless jungle.'

Again, when Commissioner of the Jubbulpore Division in 1898, Fuller returned to the charge.

'I am under the impression, that in the past rather exaggerated ideas have been entertained of the injurious effects of bewar, especially in a country of heavy rainfall where its effects seem often to be not the permanent denudation of the land, but the substitution of one kind of forest growth for another.'

And finally, most cogently of all, in 1901, he said:

'It is of much more importance that a tribe of people should live in peace and comfort, than that a certain area of land should grow trees of one sort or another, or indeed should grow trees at all.

'The practise of bewar undoubtedly changes the character of the jungle, substituting bamboos for trees. But bamboos are, speaking generally, the most useful forest product we can grow.'

I have quoted enough to show that there is, among those who have served the Baiga best and loved them most, a considerable body of opinion that considers that bewar should not be regarded as quite the bogey that it has been assumed to be, that the damage it causes has been exaggerated, that given proper conditions the forest often recovers itself in time, and that in the case of a small tribe like the Baiga the effect on erosion and the rainfall is not a very serious danger. After all, there are only some 40,000 Baiga, and even if all of these began to cut bewar again, they could hardly—spread as they would be over a very large area—make a great deal of difference to the climatic conditions of the country.

On wider grounds, it may be argued that the Baiga have a very legitimate grievance. It is sometimes said that no one has ever criticized the justice of the anti-bewar policy. This is not correct. For the last seventy years, the Baiga have constantly and bitterly criticized the inequity of their treatment.

But they have had no champion to fight for them, no spokesman to voice their grievances. When the Chak was first founded a great many petitions were sent to Government, of which the following is a specimen. It was presented by Dholi Baiga of Udhor in 1892. Now that bewar has been stopped, he says, 'we daily starve, having had no food grain in our possession. The only wealth we possess is our axe. We have no clothes to cover our body with, but we pass cold nights by the fire-side. We are now dying for want of food. . . . We cannot go elsewhere, as the British Government is everywhere. What fault have we done that the Government does not take care of us? Prisoners are supplied with ample food in jail. A cultivator of the grass is not deprived of his holding, but the Government does not give us our right who have lived here for generations past'. And in the famine of 1897, Guhra and Ramsingh, Baiga of Kukrapani, begged that at a time when Government was helping everyone, they might be allowed to cut bewar in the forest near their village. 'We are dying of starvation. Beside bewar we have no other profession'. Both these petitions, and most of the others that were received, had to be rejected in accordance with the accepted policy.

I have recorded two songs which vividly describe the feelings of the Baiga when their bewar-cutting is prohibited.

Such a calamity had never been before!
Some he beats, some he catches by the ear,
Some he drives out of the village.
He robs us of our axes, he robs us of our jungle.
He beats the Gond; he drives the Baiga and Baigin from their jungle.
The police come with orders to catch us like dogs.
O such a calamity had never been before!

And again:

In this Raja's reign we all are dying of hunger.
He robs us of our axes, he robs us of our jungle.
The Baigin says to the Baiga, Come let us dig some roots.
We will fetch them in a small basket,
And feed our little children,
But secretly or else the police will take them from us.
From village to village go the Raja's men,
They make roads, but not for us; the roads are for the Raja.
He steals the Baiga's bewar.
We are all dying of hunger during this Raja's reign.

Both these songs were entirely spontaneous, and were not prompted by any political agitation, of which the Baiga are wholly ignorant.

Throughout this book we shall see again and again the extraordinary importance of the bewar in the social, religious and economic life of the tribe. It is their own special possession; it makes them different from all others; it is their right and duty, laid on them from the beginning of the world. The contrast between a bewar-cutting village and a 'civilized' village is astonishing; the social and religious life of the latter is emasculated, void of reality and vigour. Materially, it may be better off, but the inner life of the people is dying, and the Baiga of these villages will soon sink to the dead level of apathy and futility of their semi-civilized neighbours. Even Colonel Ward, hostile as he was to bewar, was struck by the difference between the Baiga of Mandla who were 'getting over gradually their dislike to ploughs and cattle, and where they have the means, show no objection to the plough' and 'the real Baigas' of the hills of the Maikal Range. 'Wild as the forests they live in, they have none of that cringing fear of people in authority which is shown so much by the Gonds and Bygas of Mundlah. They are independent, high-spirited, finer specimens of humanity than their brethren farther west, very well behaved, ready to oblige, and deserving every consideration for their orderly manner of life.' And this is only to be expected, for it is impossible to deprive primitive people of a vital part of their economy,[1] to tear a page out of their mythology, to force them into a way of life repugnant to them by tradition, inclination, and tribal law, without irreparably injuring their life and spirit.

[1] Experience in Africa has emphasised the great caution needed in any interference with old-established tribal customs: there may well be a sound technological basis for their survival. For example, Mr. Dudley Stamp has shown that the African has probably discovered in his 'dirty farming' the most efficient method of cultivation in a climate where "it is almost impossible to protect the long plow farrow from the most destructive and virulent forms of soil erosion." (Stamp: op. cit., p. 44). "It is to be hoped that Southern Nigeria may long be spared the dangers of the plow" (p. 39). And Dr. Leakey has defended the Kikuyu method of irregular planting of different crops mixed up, in precisely Baiga fashion (see p. 112) in the same patch. He shows how this custom, condemned by the European agriculturalist, conserves the moisture and prevents soil-erosion. See Leakey: *Kenya Contrasts and Problems* (London, 1936), pp. 118 ff.

Chapter IV

THE LIFE-STORIES OF TYPICAL BAIGA

I.

It was reading Margery Perham's *Ten Africans*, written 'so that English readers might obtain a sense of that intimacy which few of our people can achieve in life', that suggested to me that it would be useful to collect similar accounts of the lives of Baiga. It has been extremely difficult to obtain autobiographies that are in any way complete, but the fifteen lives contained in this chapter are, I think, the most valuable part of my book. They take us direct to the realities of Baiga life, and reveal to us the things that are important to the people themselves.

Most of the characters in this chapter appear again and again as informants throughout the book, and their life-stories thus form a useful background to their statements that are recorded elsewhere. This is specially so in the case of dreams.

These short and simple stories will repay careful study.

II. MAHATU

Mahatu was one of the best of my informants and his name appears frequently in these pages. He is my own *mahāprasād* and can therefore speak very freely to me. He has on several occasions, when I have been ill, come to divine the cause. In 1937 he performed the Bida ceremony for my own village. His son, Mithu, lives with his wife and family in my Leper Refuge. Mahatu is much respected, though there is some doubt about the efficacy of his love-magic. He has an excellent memory; once I came across a list of the loans advanced by Government to the people of Karadih over thirty-five years ago. To test him I asked Mahatu the amounts received by each villager, and he was able to tell me exactly.

I was born in Dutirawar in Kawardha State. My mother was Baisakin and my father, who was a great magician, was Punna. When I was five

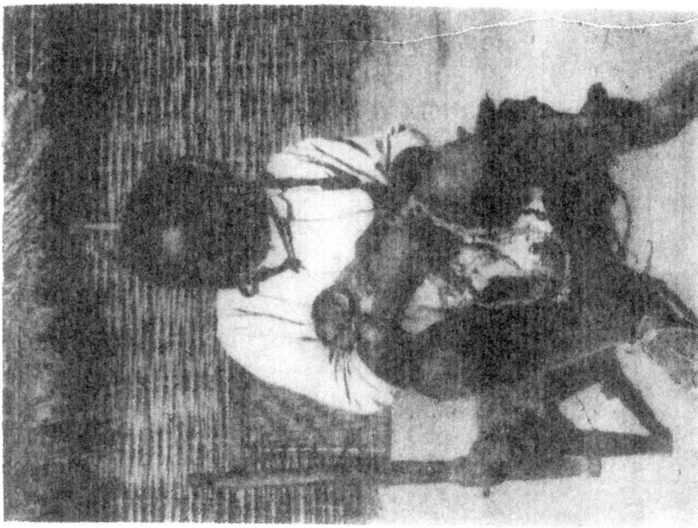

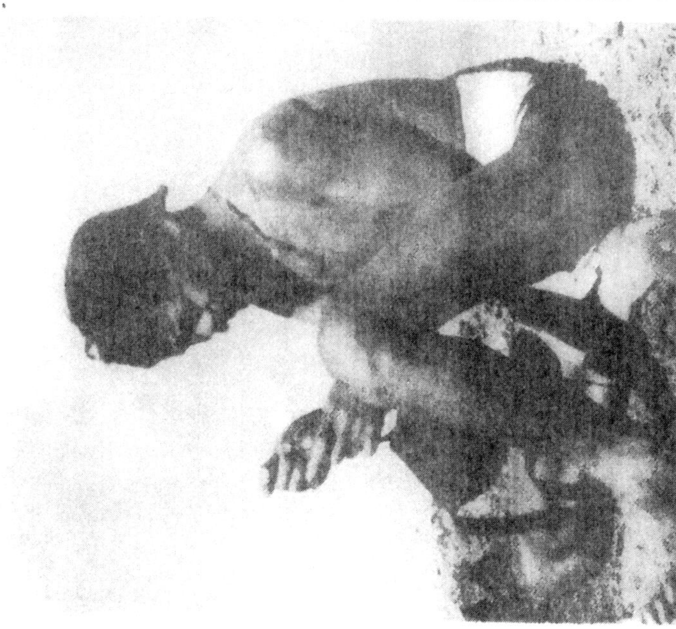

Mahatu, with materials for a smoke
A Dudh-Bhaina with pet.

years old I took my axe and sickle and went with my father to his bewar.

At that time we went to Ajnu and cut bewar there also. We lived seven years there and then came to Kapripani where we also cut bewar at two rupees an axe.

In those days there was a Raja in Ramgarh. Then came the English when I was twelve years old and robbed and beat us. So we went to Damin Tola and lived there for two years, living on our bewar.

In Damin Tola lived a witch, Maniaro. She and my father were friends. But when she tried to marry him, my father sent her away. So she was angry and made a snake and sent it to bite my father. It came into the bewar and bit him, and in two and a half days he died.

After my father's death, we lived six years in Damin Tola, then we went to Karadih. There my mother took a new husband. In Karadih I cut bewar for seven years. Then came the Utarna Sahib[1] with his wife and children. He called all the Baiga to him. I went with the others. We met in a bewar where the trees had just been felled. There were many trees everywhere, some were so big that the Sahib's wife couldn't climb over them. When she saw them lying there, she wept and embraced them, calling them her children. Then she said to us: "From to-day your bewar is stopped; you are never to cut it again." The sahib tried very much to let us continue, but his wife prevented him.

So then I went to Chauradadar and lived there five years. When bewar was first stopped we had a very hard time. In Karadih in the bewar days twenty-five drums used to come out for the Karma dance. Afterwards there would be only two or three, and there was no more joy. We were all broken up, some ran away to one place, some to another place. We had little food, for we didn't know how to plough and we believed it to be a sin. So what were we to do? We went to the Gond and they put their hands upon ours and taught us to plough. But they robbed us in every way. By the time we had paid them for their work we had hardly a *khandi* of grain left in each field. They used to steal our seed. There was a school in Karadih then, and I went to it and learnt a few letters. But when the famine came, the school closed.

In Chauradadar, my uncle, whom my mother had married, went to his own daughter. Two or three days later a tiger killed and ate him. After his death I became headman of Chauradadar. I did that work for three or four years. Then I ran away with a married girl to Karadih, and

[1] So called because he wore a ring in the upper lobe of his ear. This was apparently Mr. M. Muttanah, then D.F.O. of Mandla, who was in charge of the resettlement of the Baiga, after bewar-cutting had been stopped in 1890.

married her there myself. She stayed with me for a little while and then ran away with someone else. That was the first time I had kept a girl.

Then I made a *mohini* for another girl, and she came to me and stayed for a year and then ran away with someone else.

So I went back to Chauradadar and got another girl and married her. From her I have had five sons and a daughter. Then she too ran away and married another man.

I went to live in Ranjki and cut bewar there for a year, and then came back to Karadih to sing Dadaria. That was the time when there was great sickness in all the villages round (the influenza epidemic of 1918?). The night we arrived my new wife suddenly fell ill. There was not one gunia in Karadih. All night I sat helpless by her side, holding her pulse. In the morning she died. The next night Thakurain came to me in a dream and told me that I was to be the gunia of Karadih. She showed me what to do and taught me to play on the *tuma-bāja.*[1] I began to play at once and the sick people heard it and were encouraged. Then said Thakurain: "You must give me a red goat." Then I was frightened, for I had no goat and I was afraid she might kill me. "At least give me something," she said. Then in my dream I saw a woman coming from the river with a pot of water on her head. I knew she was a bad woman, a witch. So I said to Thakurain: "I give you that woman." The next day the woman died. But now I was a gunia and I began my work, and not one other person died in Karadih.

Shortly after this my brother Tiktu stole my bullocks. I had gone to cut wood in the forest, and my brother took my bullocks to Jankhi and sold them there. I went searching everywhere; I thought they had been killed by a tiger. But at night I went to listen outside my brother's house, and I heard his wife say: "If Mahatu hears of this, he'll beat you." Then I discovered the whole matter, and found my bullocks had been sold for forty rupees. I told the Forest Guard and he sent a report. The police came and said: "He is your brother, why quarrel with him? Take the money and let him go." But I said: "No. There must be handcuffs and he must be punished, or he'll do it again." Then he was put in jail for six months. When he came out, I gave a feast for him—ten rupees' worth of liquor, a *khandi* of rice, a goat two feet high and a pig one foot high.

I was greatly deceived by a Panjabi. He lived in Gorakhpur. He had taken the harra contract, and he paid three rupees to each house for gathering it. But I didn't want to do it, so I returned the six rupees I had received and said: "Remove my name from the list." Six years later that Panjabi came back and said: "You owe me a hundred rupees." He took three bullocks, six cows and twenty rupees from me. Then my uncle cursed him and said:

[1]A fiddle made by attaching a bit of bamboo to a gourd resonator: strings are stretched across it.

"O Panjabi, go! You have robbed my son of all he has. May you die in a stranger's house!" And he did die, not long afterwards, far from his own home, in Pendra. Then I held both my ears and I said: "I'll rob a dead body of its clothes and wear them, but never more will I have dealings with a Panjabi."

I saw a very bad thing once in Karadih. Hatkadi Baiga was a friend of mine. He tried to get some land from a Panjabi. The Panjabi lent him a hundred rupees. Hatkadi paid him forty and then another forty. Then the Panjabi came and said he had received nothing, and demanded the whole hundred. How could Hatkadi give it to him? The Panjabi beat him; then whenever the Panjabi came to find him, Hatkadi hid himself. At last the man came and slept outside Hatkadi's door. In the morning that poor Baiga came out and the big Panjabi caught him and beat him. Hatkadi said: "My money is in the headman's house. Let me get my cloth and we'll go and fetch it." So he went in and hid some ***māhur*** poison from his arrows in his loin-cloth. As they went along to the headman's house, Hatkadi secretly ate the poison. When they got there, he said: "I can only give you twenty rupees." The Panjabi struck him with his stick. "Well, let me smoke first," said Hatkadi. As he began to smoke, the poison worked inside him, and he leapt in the air and fell down. The Panjabi seized him and beat him again. Then Hatkadi jumped three times in the air, and fell dead. We all took the Panjabi to the police, and he was put in jail for six years.

I am always being called to help sick people, and after I have 'looked' in my *sūpa* and told them what to do, they often get well. They don't always get well, but they do often.

Once in Pakripani, many people were ill. They sent their own Dewar to fetch me with three bottles of liquor. I went and stopped that sickness. Then in the night all the gods came to me in a dream; they were very angry; they said: "You've driven us out of this village, now we're going to eat you." I was sleeping near the fire. The gods pushed my head into the fire and all my hair was burnt. I shouted and the people came and drove the gods away. Then in another dream the goddess said to me: "For three years, you must not smoke or eat meat or go to a woman. You are not to accept any reward for your work as gunia." Hearing this, I gave up meat and tobacco for three years.

In Chauradadar once, all the people came to me about their fields. I took my *sūpa* and saw what was wrong, and ever since they have had good crops.

In Ladra Taliyapani a Baiga had no children. After he had called me, he had a child.

In Lamni the headman got very ill, and no one could help him. They sent me two bottles of liquor and five rupees. I drank the liquor but sent the five rupees back. A few minutes before I reached Lamni the man died. But I brought back his life, and he became well.

I go as gunia, and to do the Bidri and Bida ceremonies, to Jigri, to Sagar Tola, to Banjar, to Saraiya, to Chauradadar, to Gwara, and to Karadih.

Now my wife has left me I am not very happy, but I live with my son Jantri in Chauradadar, and come from time to time to see Mithu and his wife in the hospital at Sanhrwachhapar.

III. PHULMAT

The story of Phulmat is the almost unique record of a woman gunia. I am told that there is another woman gunia in Rewa State, but she does not seem to enjoy the same dignity and position as Phulmat of Kotalwahi. Phulmat to-day is a motherly, rather sweet-looking woman of about sixty: she is greatly respected and enjoys as large a practice as any of her male rivals. She has a very strong character and can dominate even the vivacious Mahi, her daughter-in-law. Her story is of special interest and importance.

I was born in Belki; my father's name was Tika, my mother's Kotli. In those days we all cut bewar. While I was still a baby, my parents moved from Belki to Karadih. There we lived till I was nine years old. We then went to Dadargaon.

In Dadargaon I was forcibly married to Marru. None of us wanted the marriage. I was too young, only ten years old, and my father didn't like Marru. But my brother Chaitu had run away with Marru's wife, and Marru said that he must have a girl in return. So I was married to him, but I never went to him or even touched him.

In Dadargaon I lived with my parents for one year. Then we all came to Kotalwahi. It was then that I stopped drinking my mother's milk. She suckled me till after my marriage, till I was twelve years old.

After we had been in Kotalwahi for two years the famine[1] came, and my mother died of hunger.

[1] There were famines in Mandla in 1868 when the Baiga were only slightly affected, in 1896–97 when they suffered severely, in 1900, in 1908 and in 1921. The famine to which the narrators refer in these histories is that of 1896–97. The *Mandla Gazetteer* says: 'The shyness of the Baigas led them to such lengths in the first great famine of 1897, that many died of starvation with relief at their very doors, overlooked by their Gond and Hindu fellow-villagers, and themselves afraid to apply; and even later when their first shyness had been overcome, it was no uncommon thing for the whole male population of a village to flee in the jungles on the approach of a relief officer, leaving their women and children to treat the intruder as best they might' (p. 70).

After the famine, though there was a 31% decrease in the Banjar Range, no villages were actually deserted. The low mortality among cattle was very striking.

After my mother's death I went with my elder brother back to Dadargaon. When I reached there Marru caught me and dragged me by force to his house. But that same evening I escaped and ran back alone to Kotalwahi.

In Kotalwahi lived Garhu who had a wife already, but I liked him and became his *chhotki*. After fifteen days Marru came and made a quarrel in the house, and demanded money for me. Garhu gave him twenty-one Rupees for me. I lived with Garhu very happily; my co-wife was kind to me and there were no quarrels.

A year after that my father and brother and my brother's wife went to dig for *tikur kānda* in the jungle. A tiger caught my brother; he shouted for help and my father ran and hit the tiger who ran away in fear, for my father was a great Dewar. They took my brother home, but the next day he died.

I lived five or six years with Garhu and I had a baby boy from him. After the birth of the child, my co-wife began to trouble me, so I took the child and ran away to Dadargaon. There I lived with Marru's younger brother Hagru. After eight or ten days Garhu came there and took ten rupees for me from Hagru. He also took my child away from me and went home.

But I had ten children from Hagru. Of these, six boys died.

From Dadargaon I went with Hagru to Umaria and stayed there for ten or twelve years. After that we went for two years to Dadargaon again, and then came to Kotalwahi. Here my husband has become old and deaf, so I work to earn money to keep us, and I look after him.

When I was twenty or twenty-one years old, I saw in a dream all the twenty-one Mata and all the *devata* coming to visit me. They wore golden ornaments, and a Mata took the form of a Chamarin. They said to me: "We have come to you. You are to be our servant. You must obey us." I said: "I am only a poor woman and I have to work daily for my living. What can I do for you?" They said: "If you don't obey us, we will beat you and carry you away." Then they disappeared and I awoke.

Another day, not long afterwards, they came again and said the same things. After that I fell very ill. All the gunia came, but they could do nothing. Then my father-in-law came and he said: "I cannot save her. Take her to her father." So they carried me to my father, and when I saw him I fainted. Everyone began to weep. But when I recovered, my father looked in his *sūpa*, and he said: "You are ill because you didn't obey the gods when they came to you in your dream." So then I decided I would do whatever the gods told me, and I recovered.

After that, every Monday the god (*deo*) came to me. At the time of my second son's wedding, the god rode on me, but he told me nothing.

Then Hagru took me to Karadih. We lived happily there. A man in Karadih fell ill and the gunia went to him. The god came to ride on his brother, and came on me also. From that day I have been a gunia. Every Monday the god rides upon me.

Since then I have cured two men, three women and three children of their diseases.

When he first came the god spoke very clearly to me. But then one day my husband's brother's wife went to the *deosthān* during her period and since then the god has been dim.

At that time I had two dreams. In the first my *jīv* went flying up into the sky to catch the sun. I had nearly reached it, and was stretching out my hand to grasp it and pull it down when I fell down, down, down into a lot of mud. I stuck in the mud and couldn't get out. But an Ahir boy came and pulled me out, and brought a lot of water and washed me. Then he sent me home. When I got there my husband took his sickle and made it red-hot in the fire and burnt my vagina with it so that I awoke.

Another day I dreamt that I fell very ill and died. I met many gods and they treated me with great honour and put me in a chariot and took me to Bhagavan's house. The chariot stopped on top of a tree. Then the tree caught fire and the chariot flew up into the air. I caught hold of one of the wheels, but my hand slipped and I fell down, and so awoke.

Once a man was very ill. They called five gunia to save him, but they could do nothing and he died. Then the god rode on me, and I brought that dead man back to life.

So nowadays in Kotalwahi, whenever anyone is ill, they bring coconuts and some liquor to me on a Monday, and the god comes upon me, or I 'look' in *bahari kāri* or my *sūpa* and tell them what is the matter, and the sick person gets well again.

IV. YOGI DEWAR

The astonishing old gentleman who is known as Yogi Dewar is a Mutiny veteran, at least 105 years old. He was over 20 when Captain Waddington suppressed the rebels of Ghugri and Ramgarh, and about 35 with ten fine sons at the time when the second mad elephant terrorized Mandla, and went across to Balaghat where it was killed by Colonel Bloomfield in 1871. He is still full of life and energy, can face a thirty-mile walk without flinching, and is as eager as ever for romantic adventure. He is not nearly so much the 'professional savage' as Pachlu or the hardened shikari as Rawan. He is simple and delightful, and when I gave him some new clothes he executed a dance of triumph before my house—though the gift was small enough. He came to see me with a young Bharotia boy who was technically his father-in-law. Yogi is a solitary Binjhwar living in a solitary Barotia village—Jaldar of the Baiga Chak—in a predominantly Bhumia area. He has thus had to marry Barotia girls. The boy who came with him had married Yogi's daughter, and Yogi had married the boy's daughter. So they were actually fathers-in-law of one another! I do not know how much of his life-story is true, but it is very interesting.

I am a Binjhwar Baiga, of the Durwa *goti*, and my father's name was Rai Singh—though these things do not matter. I was born in Kamera, and my family cut bewar.

When I was two years old, I got small-pox, and all the village ran away into the jungle. My parents left me alone. Once a day they used to come and look at me. When I got well after fifteen days, my parents came and took me to the forest. We lived there on roots and mahua for some time.

By the time I was five years old I had twelve brothers and one sister. Then came an order from the god that all who were unmarried must be married by the following dawn or they would die. So that night we didn't sleep; we built booths, we prepared *haldi*, we married some of the boys to cats and dogs, a girl was married to a rat. I and my four brothers were all married to one girl. By the morning everyone in the village had been married. Only one of my brothers who was deaf remained—we had forgotten him. In three days he was dead.

In my boyhood, there were only Baiga in the world. There was no Gond, Hindu, Mussalman, Pardhan, or Panka. So no one ever laughed with another man's wife. If they did they were thrust through with a spear in the chest. We Baiga lived on roots and mahua. We had to pay three rupees for one *seer* of gram in those days. This was so all the time that the Mad Raja was the scarecrow of Ramgarh.

I was more than twenty years of age when the English came. When we heard of their army we ran and hid in the hills. The Mad Raja for fear went down to Patal Dip, ruled over by the Nizam Shah. Gajar Patan, the Mad Raja's Diwan, for fear jumped into the fire and died. The English army came and took Ghugri, and then they came to Ramgarh, where the Mad Raja had his fort. Here was his Rani, and when she saw the English coming, she stabbed herself with a sword. The Baiga fought for the Mad Raja with stones and arrows, but when the Rani died she said that no one should be punished and the head of the English army said to us: "We won't trouble you more; let every man go to his own house." Then the English went away, and sent Rahtan Sahib who built the police stations and courts all over Mandla. With the English came the Mussalman, Panka and Hindu—and Ramgarh was no more the home of the Baiga.[1]

When I was about thirty-five a witch killed my father, and his property was divided between us twelve brothers. I got the largest share for I had to look after my mother.

After this I left my brothers and went to Teliapani where I worked as a Lamsena for four years. Then I paid ten rupees, and was married. I was 40 years old then.

In the next three years, I was busy getting new wives. In all I married six girls. They lived together very happily. Every day I used to go to each of them, so they had nothing to grumble about. They never quarrelled with me or with one another. From them I had twenty sons and six daughters.

Once I went to Jubbulpore. There I saw, in one row many cows, in a second row pigs, in a third row goats, in a fourth row white sahibs, and then nothing but motors. From there I went to Allahabad and saw big houses. From there I went to Raipur, and saw a dance and tamasha. From there I went to Bombay and saw a real city at last. There were motors and bicycles and a sahib four feet wide who took my photo and gave me ten rupees. From Bombay I went to Cawnpore, but there was nothing there. Then I came home.

When I was a boy the first mad elephant came. It had a chain on one leg. Two years later it returned, and now it had chains on two legs. When it came to Samnapur we fled into the houses and shut the doors. Then the elephant went to Mangabeli, there my father-in-law lived. He was very strong and he caught the elephant and tied it up and fed it every day. I went there to see it. I said to my father-in-law: "Now it is in your hands, let us give is poison." So we made some poison from *massna kānda*, gave it in its food and it died. When the Mandla Raja heard of it, he called us there and gave us a feast and five rupees each.

[1] Many Baiga still refer to the Dindori Tehsil as the Ramgarh Taluka, its former name. Before the Mutiny this belonged to a Lodhi Raja, Gaji Singh, who was invested with the title by Nizam Shah when the latter was Raja of Mandla. The Mad Raja was Raja Bikramajit who went mad a few days after coming to the throne. He was the first Raja's grandson. The Raja's wife was chiefly instrumental in rousing the Ramgarh Taluka to rebellion. The Mutiny in Mandla was not very serious, and Captain Waddington, who was in charge of the British forces, easily captured Ghugri, where there was a rebel outpost, on March 31st, 1858, and then advanced on Ramgarh. The Rani fled with her troops and the fort was captured without resistance, but before she could be captured the Rani killed herself. She declared that she had been the sole cause of the rising, and a general pardon was proclaimed. In its main points, therefore, Yogi's memory is astonishingly correct.

Above: Yogi Dewar and Bansi, the ruined panda.
Below: Ketu, the landlord and Rawan, the great hunter.

When I was about thirty-five, another mad elephant came. In the mornings it used to rush out of the jungle and catch people and split them in half. My *kāki* was living in Gaura. One day as she was carrying *pej* to her husband in his bewar—she had her child in her arms—she saw the elephant far away. She ran to hide in a stream. But the elephant chased her and went into the stream and pulled her out and split her body in two, but left the child. Then it went away to Baihar, and there it was killed by Bullumfail.[1]

I have seen many sahibs visiting this jungle. There was Rahtan first, then Buruk[2] who was small and fat, then Hogg[3] who was handsome and wore fine clothes, the best sahib I have ever seen, then Muttaneh[4] who was always asking for chickens. I remember Kenny, Tam, Lod, Mukri, and the Christian sahib. Kenny was very good. Thamsen stopped our bewar. Hogg was my friend. He went to hunt with me, and was so pleased that he opened the Baiga Chak in my name.

Five years ago I married my daughter's daughter. As I had had twenty sons, I was reborn as a young boy. I went three times with her, then I made her go four times with my son's son, round the pole at the wedding.

V. BAIHAR

Baihar, the old Kath-bhaina woman of Taliyapani, was a famous beauty in her youth, and even to-day, in spite of the ravages of disease and age, she is a fine and impressive figure. She is shrewd also, with a strong interest in property as will be seen by a reference to p. 96.

I was born in Ranjki (Bilaspur). My father's name was Juran, my mother's Andhyar. When I was only a year old my mother died. My father married another wife. I had two elder brothers and a sister. My brothers were married and living in separate houses in the same village, we had kept a Lamsena boy for my sister. Our new mother was very unkind to us. She gave us bad food, and one day she picked me up, beat me and threw me down on the floor. So I was hardly ever in our house, I used to spend half my days with one brother, and half with the other.

When my breasts were formed, I was fourteen years old, then my second brother took me to live in his house. Once as we were going through the jungle, desire came into his eyes, and he threw me down on the ground and went to me. I was so angry that I left the village and went to Karadih.

[1] Colonel Bloomfield. [2] Colonel T. H. B. Brooke, D.C. of Mandla at various periods from 1875–88. [3] Colonel T. W. Hogg, D.C. Mandla, 1888–91. [4] D.F.O. of Mandla about 1890.

After I had been in Karadih eight days a man forcibly married me. The next day my father and elder brother arrived to take me home. There was a great quarrel about me, and at last my husband gave Rs. 20 as bride-price for me.

One day I went with two girls to work in the Dak Bungalow. A forest guard took me by force. He gave all three of us eight annas each. At that time I was very pretty. Many men wept for me, and sent me messages. When will you come to me? Why don't you talk to me? What present would you like?

One day my husband went for *begār* to Karanjia. I was sleeping alone. Three boys came into my house, and all three of them attacked me. When my husband came home, I told him, and we were so angry that we went from Karadih to Chauradadar. There too we cut bewar.

In the year my first child was born (i.e. about 1890) the Inspector Sahib came with his wife and looked at the jungle and stopped all the Baiga cutting bewar.

When bewar was stopped we left Mandla district and went to Ranjki again. There every man was soon dying with love for me. I made friends with two of them. That year I had another son, who knows who his father was? The next year many of us went to pick mangoes. I went with my husband. He climbed a tree, fell down and died.

Six months afterwards I made a new husband. We were very happy together. But soon afterwards I made friends with another man. My husband knew about it. One evening he said he was going to another village, but secretly he hid under the grain-bins. My lover came, and when we were fairly at it, my husband came out and seized a blazing log from the fire and drove my lover out of the house. Then my husband beat me, so I let him go to sleep and, when he was snoring, I crept out of the house, and ran off with my lover.

But that husband of mine was a magician. He took my cloth and buried it down by the river. So my period lasted for three months, and my lover was not pleased. He called many gunia, and at last I was well again.

Then we went to Kukripani, and took my two sons. There a daughter was born. Even then with three brats pulling at my breasts, I was still very pretty. For fear of men, I never went anywhere alone. But one day my second husband came along, and caught me and put chili in my privates. After that I never flirted with any man again. Whenever a man tried I gave him a lot of *gāli*. But my third husband soon died, and I took all he had and gave it to my sons.

Then I married a fourth husband, and he died in three years. I was going to make a fifth husband, but my two sons took everything and went away from me. So I took my daughter and made a fifth husband. He soon died, and I took all he had and went back to my sons.

At last we came to Tilaidabra, and there I married my daughter and my elder son, and invited the people of twelve villages.

VI. LAHAKAT

Lahakat is a Dudh-Bhaina Baiga of Amadob in the Pendra Zemindari, a person of great charm and a certain coarse distinction. Wrapped in a tattered green blanket, he is a fine figure of a man, and was a famous Don Juan in his youth, boasting that he had seduced no fewer than fifty different girls before he was twenty-five. Even now he is not quite a drawing-room character, but he is most attractive.

I was born in Kannat-chak, and when I fell from my mother to the ground I lay out of my senses for an hour.

I was about ten years old when my life began. I had gone to the jungle to get honey. There were two little boys and three little girls with me. I climbed up the tree and brought down honey for all of them, and we three boys made friends with the three girls. I went to each of the girls once, but one of them was frightened, and I was frightened too and ran away to my mother's brother's house at Tadpatra. After fifteen days my father came to fetch me and I went home. Then I often went to get honey or wood or mangoes with those little girls.

Once when I was out grazing goats, I was playing with a she-goat. A Brahmin came by and caught me. He said he would take me to the police, so I went with him to my father who gave him three rupees to keep quiet. Then my father, not for the goat but for the three rupees, beat me so much that blood flowed from my nose.

When I was fifteen I was sleeping alone one night in the bewar when a tiger came. I hid inside the hut. The tiger sniffed at the wall and went away.

That same year when I went to pick mangoes I met a girl whom I loved very much, and we left our mangoes and ran away together to Pharisemur. But the girl's uncle lived there and he drove me away, so I had to leave the girl and go home.

After living in Amanalla for fifteen years we went to Damgarh, and there too we cut bewar. There I used to meet another girl in the jungle, and she became pregnant. She was unmarried, so I married her and we were very happy together.

Two years later came the famine, and my father died of hunger.

We lived ten years in Dumgarh, then went to Tawadabra and again cut bewar. A month after we got there my mother died. At that time I was very poor.

A year later we were singing Karma one night. I got very drunk and lay down to sleep on the verandah of somebody else's house. There was a girl—she too was drunk—she came and pulled me up. I caught her and threw her down on the verandah and took her then and there. A man saw us and tied us together in our own clothes. I didn't know what had happened, being drunk. Then the girl's husband came with two or four friends and they all beat me. When I felt better I got up and dragged the girl to my house and threw *haldi-pāni* over her.

After that everyone used to give me *gāli* in that village, so I went with this new girl and my old wife to Mai. There we made a house and cut bewar. Now I began to love my new wife very much. At the time of sleeping, I used to sleep face to face in her arms. I didn't look at my elder wife. In two or four days I would only go once to her.

So for sorrow she used to make love to another man. I heard about it, but at that very time I too was in love with a third girl. I used to give her liquor. So I said nothing.

One evening I was drinking with my two wives and this other girl. My wives got drunk and went to sleep. Then I went to the other girl. But my elder wife woke and seeing us began to scream and abuse me. After that I married the third girl. I gave twenty-five rupees in cash for her. I always used to sleep in the middle of the three. I loved the two younger wives most.

My elder wife was very unhappy, poor girl, and soon she ran away with another man. Soon afterwards, my second wife died. So I went from Mai to Keonchi with my third wife, but on the way we met a tiger. It sprang on me and threw me down. I had an axe and hit the tiger with it and it ran away. But we returned home to Mai.

Two or four days later, two sahibs and their memsahib came to Kabirchabutra, which is three miles away. The sahib asked for a shikari, and they told him about me, so he sent for me. But I could not walk. They brought me in a litter. Then the sahibs and the memsahib looked at the wounds made by the tiger, and the memsahib bound me up with bandages. They put medicine for five days in a bottle. The sahibs each gave me five rupees and the memsahib gave me three, and sent me home.

We went from Mai to Gwara. There we had to plough, and I became the servant of a Gond. I took a new wife there, but she died in two years. Then we went back to Amadob, and cut bewar.

VII. RAWAN

Rawan is a very celebrated hunter and gunia of the Bilaspur District. He is a Bhumia Baiga, and regarded with a good deal of awe by his fellows, but—like Pachlu—he is too well aware of his prowess to be very popular.

I was born in Saraipani. My father was Sahina, my mother Chaito. In my childhood they said of me "*Hāth gōd jhiti, pet dhūti*". My hands and feet were sticks, my stomach was a fish-basket. I was so weak that when I played with other children, they used to hit me and throw stones at me. Once a boy cut my head open.

When I was about eight years old, my stomach got smaller and my hands and legs stronger. My father made me a bow and arrow, and all day I used to wander in the jungle. I became so good at it that when I shot at a bird I never missed.

I was about twelve when one day sitting by the river with my bow and arrow, I saw a pretty girl with a pot on her head come for water. I shot at it and broke it. She was angry and gave me *gāli*, but I caught hold of her, and threw her down and had her. Whenever I saw a pretty girl come to the river for water, I shot at her pot and broke it, and then I played with the girl. None escaped.

Once I was sleeping with a girl out in the bewar under the open sky. A tiger came and sniffed at my ear. I gave it a punch on the nose and said: *Dur-rē kutta*, and the tiger ran away.

When I was sixteen, my father arranged my marriage. After that I had a very bad disease in my loins, and the gunia saved my life with difficulty.

At this time whenever I went to hunt, I never came back without something. I loved to sing the Karma, and when girls saw me dance they fainted for love of me, and came to me of their own accord.

Soon I had four wives. But I never slept with them, but always separately to avoid quarrels. But I went to each every night. I never failed.

Then one night I saw some god in my dream and he told me that I should never fail in my hunting, but that I was always to eat the liver of the animals I killed before anything else. Another night, he came and told me some mantra for my hunting. Then I was frightened, and left my house and went to sleep in the jungle. For three nights I slept in a hollow tree. My wives were afraid I had been killed by a tiger. Then I came home.

At that time I used to go grazing cattle. One day I was sitting on the stump of a tree with my comb and mirror and was doing my hair. Suddenly a tiger jumped on one of the cows. I gave it *gāli* and told it to go away. Then it left the cow and jumped on me, knocking me off the tree and sitting on me. In those days my hair was very long. The tiger seized it and began to drag me away. I caught its privates in my hands and squeezed them. The tiger dragged me fifty yards, then I got up and kicked it, and took hold of it and dragged it fifty yards to the jungle, kicked it again, and sent it away. I told no one about this for fifteen days.

From Saraipani I went to Sarpani. There my father fell ill and died. I had two brothers. I had quarrelled with my father. So I gave all the property of my father to my two brothers. In Sarpani we cut bewar.

One day I went to hunt. I told my wives that if I was still alive, I would return in fifteen days. There I stayed fifteen days, and on the last day I killed a sambhar with my arrow. I took out the liver and ate it, and drank the blood. Then I cut it in half, and brought it home.

After ten years we went to Umania. There we both cut bewar and ploughed. Once I was sleeping alone in the bewar when a tiger picked me up and carried me to its den. Suddenly I awoke, and found the tiger carrying me off. I gave it a good smack on the face, it roared and ran away. I went back to the bewar, lay down and went to sleep.

Once I was going by night from Umania to Pandaria through dense jungle. In the road I met a tiger. We began to play with each other. It kissed my privates, and I kissed his. We were enjoying ourselves very much, but it scratched me with its paw, so I gave it a smack and it ran away. Then I went on my way to Pandaria.

One day Tam Sahib came for a *hāka*. He made a very big *hāka*, but he got no tiger. He called for me. I said, I could do nothing sober. So Tam Sahib sent for a tin of liquor and, when I had drunk that I felt better, and I took him to the jungle. I made him sit in a tree, and I stood below and called the tigers. Three tigers came together. Tam Sahib was so frightened that he couldn't do anything.

Then Uking Sahib came. When he had given me his tin of liquor to drink, I got him a tiger, and he did kill it. He made me sit on it and took a photo and gave me three rupees.

Then Kumar Sahib came. He shot a tiger. It wasn't killed, only wounded. He was going after it to find it, but I stopped him, and took a stick and went ahead and tracked it. Then Kumar Sahib shot it. He gave me eight annas.

Then the Lal Sahib came. He became my friend. I taught him all my mantra. He killed three of my tigers, and took me to Kawardha. The Lal Sahib and the Diwan and the Raja and the Rani and the Diwan's wife all came out into the jungle. I made them sit in a tree, and I stood below, and called the tigers. Three tigers came, but the women saw them and screamed, so the tigers ran away. Then they took me to Lohara and shot two of my tigers. They gave me fifteen rupees.

In my village no tiger has ever killed anyone since I have been there. I have one tiger who is my adopted son. He always feeds me with sambhar and chital, and I never let anyone kill him.

Now I am old. Any tiger could eat me and enjoy it, for my hands and feet are tender now.

Once the Deputy Commissioner called me to Bilaspur. I said: "Keep your money in your house. My home is the jungle."

Government has tried hard to take away my bow and arrow. But I said: "The day my bow leaves my hand I will die."

But I must drop it soon, for I am very old.

VIII. HIRONDA

Hironda is a very old woman, belonging to the Bharotia sub-clan, who lives with her enterprising and prosperous son, Bichi Shikari, in Jholar (Baihar Tehsil). She claims to be a hundred years old, and she may well be, for she is considerably older than Pachlu of the same village and regards him as a young boy.

I was born in Kumnijhiria, in Raigarh. While I was still drinking the milk of my mother, she died, and my father only saved me by making me drink *passia* (the water strained from the *pej*). Wherever he went, he took me also; he was my mother. When I was born, in those days my father cut bewar. I had to work very hard in my youth. When I was about five, my father took a new wife. That year we left Kumnijhiria and went to Daldal. There too we cut bewar. When I was five or six I had to look after my little brothers and sisters. I used to feed them and bring them water in tiny earthen pots.

Soon after I became *khandlāhin* I went to Manhapur. When I was thirteen, my father made my *sagai-barokhi*. A year later I was married.

My husband, Saunu, loved me very much for two years. Then he began to spend his nights with another girl. For a year he did this. I abused him, but he beat me. I waited a year, and then I quietly made friends with another man, and planned to run away with him.

But just at that time, a snake bit Saunu's girl and she died. Saunu began to love me very much again. Only when he was drunk he beat me and cursed me. When he did that I got very angry and ran away to Jholar, alone, through the forest. After fifteen days came Saunu to bring me home. I said I wouldn't go. Then he brought all his possessions, and followed me and lived with me. We cut bewar together. I lived five years in Jholar, then went to Bijagarh. There a Baiga witch troubled me. I was pregnant and I went to the jungle. The witch met me and said, "How big your belly looks!" and touched it. The third day, my child died in the womb. I was very ill, ready to die. The gunia looked in his *sūpa* and said: "We must give medicine to bring out the child." I was ill for three months.

That year a man-eater came to the village. He ate my husband's elder brother. We were all afraid, and I came with Saunu back to Jholar. That was the year Government stopped the cutting of bewar. Saunu got bullocks from Government, but he sold them. The Government sepoy came to our house, but I hid my husband in the grain-bin, and said he had gone to the jungle, and that he was going from there to his sister's house. Then the sepoy went away. That year we cut the jungle for the Raja's road.

Now my father died of leprosy. Then the mad elephant came. I had five children then. For fear of the elephant I never went out alone for water, nor did I sleep with my husband, for he slept alone—and I only slept where there were many people. We did our work when we found ourselves alone in the daytime.

Once I went to get char, and climbed a tree to pick it. I fell down and was senseless. Blood flowed from my breast. Those who were with me put me on a bed and brought me home. It was fifteen days before I was well.

Once again I fell very ill and was out of my senses for three days. Seven gunia came and I recovered.

My husband died of some disease of his stomach. I wanted to make a new husband, but who would have me with five children?

Once as I was going to my brother's house, two men met me in the way and caught me and threw me on the ground. Both of them went to me. Then I came home. One or two months later I was very ill. I was pregnant; it was from my husband. A boy was born. He died. The gunia offered three chickens and five coconuts for me. So then I had seven sons and three daughters. But they all died save one daughter and my three sons during the famine.[1]

I have never quarrelled with anyone in my life—save sometimes with my husband when we were drunk.

IX. PACHLU

I do not know whether Pachlu has a very nice nature, but he has great distinction. He is an old Bharotia Baiga, and now lives in the pleasant village of Jholar high up in the great sal forest of Baihar. He claims to be 140 years old. Unhappily, the mad elephant killed by Colonel Bloomfield in 1871 still ranges through history destroying the older Baiga's claims to great antiquity. For this is a date by which stories can be checked, for all remember it. "At the time", says Pachlu, "I was only twelve years old. I was not really ready for girls. I had been once or twice with them to the jungle—that was all." Pachlu is thus about 80 years old, as you would guess from his looks and conversation.

When I saw him, Pachlu had still not altogether recovered from the social exaltation excited in him by a visit from the Chief Conservator of Forests who had taken his photo. "Ever since he talked to the Lord of Eighteen Talukas", said the disgusted headman of his village, "the old man wants to drink liquor as if it were water. We are being pestered by tigers, but he does nothing."

But that apart, Pachlu is a charming and remarkable old man, a fascinating and humorous talker, still overflowing with vitality, an acute and vigorous critic. "When we greet a Brahmin, he looks up to heaven in pride. We

[1]These two famine songs have a pathetic interest.

(i)

This is a year of famine.
We are all dying of hunger.
  Where shall we get our *kodon-pej*?
  Where shall we get *sikia-pej*?
Take a leaf-cup of *pej* and be content with that.
Find a root here or there: you must be content with that.
We can't get *bādbi*: we can't get *bijābi*.
Let us go slowly, with our empty *sikka* swinging.

(ii)

In time of famine it is hard to borrow even *sikia*,
Even if you go weeping from house to house.
You can't get it for money, you can't get it on loan,
You can't get it for *bijābi*, you can't get it for *bādbi*,
Even if you go weeping from house to house.

don't ask him to eat our pigs, so what business has he to despise us? These Binjhwar also think they are above us, and won't eat with us. But we are many and they are few, so what does it matter?" He was almost equally hostile to the British Government and the Congress—neither had done anything for the Baiga. "You will bring your Raj here", he said to me, "and you'll take it away. But we are the Bhumiaraja, the lords of the soil, and we will go on for ever." And again: "What are the English doing that they allow the Congress to oppress us? If Gandhi stops us drinking, he can search all over the world for his swaraj, but he won't get it."

I was born in Chhindpuri, and when I was two days old my mother put some chaff in a basket, and laid me on it. My cord had still not dropped. She carried me away, with the other villagers, to Lodhabarra, for the bewar-lands were used up in the old village. There in Lodhabarra, my cord dropped off, and my mother buried it in our new house. That village was in Mandla District, and my parents cut jungle. As I was born after five sisters, I was called Pachlu.

Three years later, we went to Chilphara. We cut bewar there also. When I was six years old I went to the bewar, running along behind my father. Once I went alone. My father had gone ahead. A monkey caught me and carried me up into a tree. I sat screaming on a branch. When my father came home in the evening, he heard the noise, and went to the tree. He joined his hands and said to the monkey, "Sir, that is my son. I am a poor man, Sir. Give him back to me." When he heard that, the monkey brought me down from the tree. Very slowly and carefully he came, and from that day my father has worshipped all monkeys as gods.[1]

A year later, we went to Kusera, and cut new jungle. Then my father died. I didn't know what it meant to be dead. I was playing with the other boys, but when they took my father to bury him, my mother's brother took me with them. But when I saw my father's body lying there, and the fire round it, I ran away and began to play again. The boys asked me where I had been, and I said, "My father is ill: they took him down to the river, and lit a fire to warm him."

For a year I lived there with my mother, but we had a lot of trouble. My father's eldest brother took away the house from mother. I stayed seven years in his house in Mutukpur. There I cut bewar myself for seven years. Then I went to Balaghat District.

It was then that Government closed the jungle, and called all the Baiga

[1] Mathu, a Kath-Bhaina of Bilaspur, had a similar experience as a child. A monkey carried him up into a mango-tree beside his house. His father offered rice and a coconut on the place where the child had been sleeping, and the monkey left him, and went away.

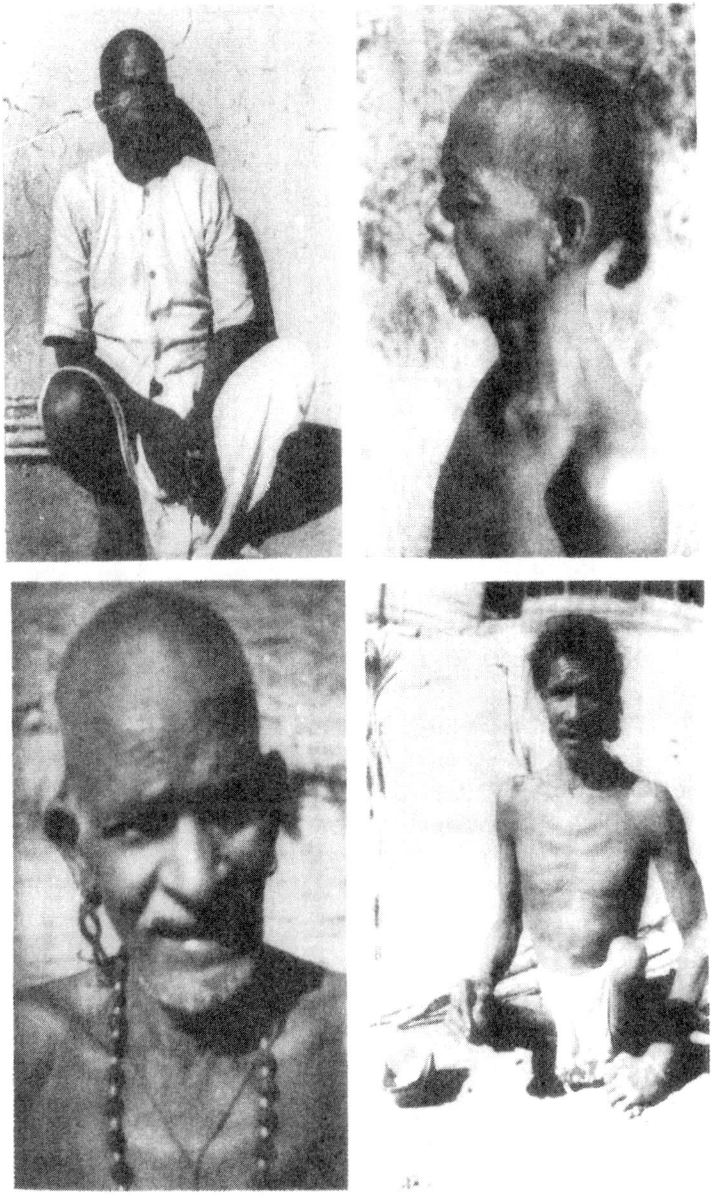

Above: Bahadur and Dhan Singh.
Below: Lahakat and Jethu.

to Balaghat. The big sahib came from Nagpur and told us that the jungle was closed. "You must plough like Hindus," he said. He gave us each two bullocks and some seed. We didn't know what ploughing was, so some of the Government's men came and taught us. For a time we ploughed, then we sold our bullocks and reported that they had been killed by a tiger. But when Government found it out, we were called to Nagpur, and the sahib asked us where our bullocks had gone. We said that some had died of disease, and others had been killed by tigers. Then the sahib made those that had sold their bullocks stand before him. He threatened to send them to jail for seven years. Then we stood up and said, "Send us to jail, for now the jungle is closed all the world is a jail to us. Take back your bullocks, for we don't need them." Then the sahib forgave us the imprisonment but he took back the bullocks. Since then we have been slaves to the Gond cultivators. But I and my father's elder brother went to Patela in Kawardha, for we were afraid of the English. There I cut a great deal of jungle.

I was fifteen years old when I was married. My wife was older than me. Everyone told me not to marry her. But I said, "Let her run away if she wants to; then I'll marry someone else." But my wife didn't run away, she was happy, and more or less faithful.

I stayed nine years in Patela, and then went to Tharma. There my father's elder brother and his wife and my mother all died together of cholera. Whatever property they had came to me. I lived seven years in Tharma, and it was there that I began to use the plough.

One day I arranged to meet a girl at night. But her husband found it out and dressed in her sari and went and sat in the place. I came creeping, slowly, softly along; I could just see the sari. Then he coughed, and I knew it was a man. I jumped up and ran for my life. After that I went away to Banania. There I got very angry with my wife and took poison. But my wife put excreta and worms in my mouth, and I vomited all the poison out.

Then I left Banania and came to Jholar. By now my wife was old. She said, "I am an old woman now, I can't do all the work. Get another wife." Now I had already made friends with a girl during the Karma, and when my wife said that, I married her. But that girl stayed with me five or six years and then ran away with another man.

Then I married my grand-daughter, my wife's sister's son's daughter. Five years later, my elder wife died. I had five sons and five daughters. I am still living with my grand-daughter. I love her very much.

Once I went to see my sister. I had a load of maize. The river was in flood, and I tried to cross. I had a sickle tied to my waist. A log came floating down and the sickle caught in it, and cut my *lingoti*, and it was carried away. I came out of the river naked. I saw two women and a man coming. I hid in the jungle. They thought I was a thief and chased me. I sat behind a tree, holding my privates with my hands. I told them what had happened and they went away. I went from tree to tree in the jungle, and at night came to my sister's house, and sat outside till they gave me a bit of cloth.

In my lifetime I have killed fifteen bears, five or six jungle buffalo and two tigers. Once I went to hunt. I had a spear, an axe and a bow and arrow. There were three bears in the jungle. I thought they were pigs. They all three attacked me at once. I drove one away with my spear, one with my axe, and I gave the third a mighty kick on the rump, and it went even faster than the others.

Once a tiger ate three of my cows; each cow had a calf. That tiger had three cubs. I was very angry and I went and took away the cubs. One of them bit my hand. I fed them with milk and took them to Balaghat. The Chhota Sahib sent me to the Laihibari Bungalow. There were seven sahibs, each with his wife, sitting on the verandah drinking seven glasses of English liquor. I gave them the cubs. Each sahib got up, gave me a slap on the cheek and handed me seven rupees. I said, "You may hit me again if you'll give me another seven rupees." Since that day my name has been famous throughout the world.

When I came home I fell so ill that I thought I was going to die. Five gunia came and took ten rupees from me. But it was no use. So I stopped them, and got well of my own accord.

Every sahib that comes here loves me and comes to see me, but in the name of a gift they don't even give me their *jhāt*. Once a sahib gave me four annas, and another gave eight annas.

Whenever a tiger kills a man, I go out and call him and stop him doing it again. Once in Kawardha a tiger ate seven men. No one could do the rites. Lallu Sahib went there. He called me, and I went and made a mud image and threw it into the air. The tiger was hiding in a bush, and my image stuck on its back, and it ran away. In Bagheli a tiger had been eating people for five years, and none of the Baiga there could do anything. The road ran through a pass and the tiger used to sit above the road and jump down on people. I saw in a dream that this was happening, so the next day I took a chicken in my hand and went there. When I arrived, everyone knew that a great Dewar had come, and they gathered round me, calling me *pujāri*. I soon settled their business. Once again in Jholar when two or three men were dying I saved their lives. In Bondar-Bholia I saved two men.

If people want children, they must come to me on a Sunday. That day I sleep on one side, and ask Bhagavan to send a *jiv* to this or that woman. Bhagavan listens to my words. A little while ago I was talking to Bhagavan in a dream, and my wife woke me. Since then I have been unable to do anything. But I didn't beat her. I love her too much. And she is a young man's wife. Yet she stays with me.

X. BAHADUR

Bahadur is perhaps the most enterprising and prosperous Baiga I have met. He is a Narotia or Nahar, of the Durwa *goti*, and now lives in Hirapur, a small village five miles from Baihar on the Balaghat road. I have already described the plan of the little village he has established where he lives in patriarchal dignity, surrounded by relatives. His own house is a monument to the skill and energy of his wives. Bahadur is an ugly man, a quarrelsome man, but he has a quality of largeness: he entertains nobly, has built a comfortable little guest-house: he is afraid of no one, there is not a trace of servility in him. He has a bad reputation in Baihar, the merchants are afraid of him, even the forest guards are careful what they say to him. This is turning the tables with a vengeance! Once, when I went to stay with him, I drove my car along a footpath about a quarter of a mile from the road right into his house. This excited him beyond measure, and I heard him shouting to the villagers, "To-morrow morning everyone must come and make the road fit for cars, and we'll have a notice-board up by the road saying that this is the way to Bahadur's house."

Bahadur is in the direct descent from the famous Ranger Pujari who helped Colonel Bloomfield kill the mad elephant in 1871. Bahadur claims that Colonel Bloomfield gave his family three villages, but that a later Deputy Commissioner took them back again.

I was born in Karwahi. My father was Santu, my mother Ujiarin. In those days we cut bewar. Once when I was playing with the other boys I broke open a boy's head with a stone, but no one dared to beat me.

When I was about ten years old, my mother died of cholera. I had two little brothers and two sisters. I loved them very much and looked after them. The following year we left Karwahi for Gohara and it was there we first took to the plough. We were sick all that year on account of it. After we had been there a few months, my father took another wife, and she gave us all a lot of trouble. Sometimes I got no food for two days at a time. I had to beg from house to house. She gave me no clothes either. Then my mother's father took me to his house. There I used to graze his cattle and lived happily.

When I was fifteen my elder brother arranged my marriage, and I was very happy. One day we went to see my father, but he beat my wife for his wife had told him that she never did any work. However, we stayed with my father for a year. We were happy, we had good clothes, my wife was pregnant. My father's wife could not bear to see us. She went to Kairagarh Devi and brought her back to injure my wife. While my wife was bathing, my father's wife wrung out her clothes, and let one drop of water that contained the magic fall on her. Then my wife was ill for six months. During the illness a boy was born to her. My wife lived only five months after that. I did everything I could. I called all the gunia, I brought medicine, I offered sacrifice to all the gods, but it was no use. Every gunia that came fell ill himself. On the day that my wife died I saw in a dream that it was my father's wife who had brought Kairagarh Devi and put a spell on my wife in the river. But I said nothing. I fed my child with milk through a rubber I got from a merchant in Baihar. But after twenty days the child died also.

Then I lived alone for two years. During that time a girl began to be very fond of me. She used to stand far away and watch me at work. She would stand in the doorway and peep at me while I was doing gunia. Then she sent me messages, to meet her in the jungle, in the river-bed, by the roadside. So at last I married her.

In the year my father died, a forest guard came to the village and abused someone about a bamboo-cutting licence. I came home just then and heard him. I can never endure *gāli.* I took the forest guard's stick and beat him, then I picked him up and threw him on the ground. Next day the police came to arrest me. I said what I had done, and they made me hold my ears and get up and down two or four times, and after that they let me go.

A year later I made friends with another girl in the bazaar. I gave her little presents of fruit and parched gram. Soon I made her my *chhotki.* I gave her husband twenty rupees for her.

That year I went to the court. The headman of Gohara had caught an Ahir and put dung and some drops of menstrual blood in his mouth, because it was believed that he was a magician. So the Ahir made a case against the headman, and I was one of the Ahir's witnesses. The headman was very angry, and said he'd beat me. I said that if I got him alone I'd kill him.

Once I went to the Baihar bazaar and got very drunk. The headman of Kopro was drunk also. We went home together. Soon we began to quarrel. I picked him up and threw him on the ground. I went home very happy, but they carried him home on a litter.

I am a very great gunia. Once two men had died. I was away at that time, but I came home after they had been dead two hours and I brought them back to life.

The Gohora headman's son was ill. He wouldn't call me at first, and sent for three or four other gunia who did nothing but take his money. At last he had to send for me, and I made his son well at once. But what I did cost him five sucking-pigs, a coconut and some *sendur*.

A Gond had no son. All his children died when they were born. I went to him for two years, until at last children began to live. Now he has two sons and two daughters. He promised to give me a calf, but he hasn't yet.

In Kopra, a Baiga girl's child came too soon. Many gunia tried to do something. When I came everything was all right at once. The husband promised me a dhoti, but he hasn't given it to me yet.

Once in Baihar, the Revenue Inspector's wife was very ill, ready to die. She took all the hospital medicines, but what could they do? Then they called the gunia. At last they sent for me, and within a day she was well. I also told them who was the witch who had caused this trouble. It was Jogaru Ahirin. She used to bring water for the household and wash their clothes. She put the magic in the water. So the police arrested the witch, and the Sub-Inspector and Munshi gave her a lot of *gāli* and said they'd put her in jail. The woman came running to me and fell at my feet saying, "Drive the magic out of my body, and I'll give you a bullock and three bottles of liquor." Then I said to the police, "Don't trouble her. I'll do it all." So I took a castor-tree branch, and a stick of tamarind, and with these drove the magic out of her body. I placed a stick of castor against each of her eyes, and made her hold them there. Then I struck her knees three times, twice on the left knee and once on the right knee, with the tamarind stick, and as I did so all the magic passed out of her body into the sticks. Then I tied her eyes with her own *chindhi*. I pissed through the hollow castor sticks and threw them all away into the river. The Revenue Inspector promised me a coat, but he hasn't given it to me yet.

I have done the earth ceremony for men killed by tigers ten or fifteen times. I have met twenty tigers in the jungle, but I have always driven them away with my mantra. I am not afraid of tigers, but I am very much afraid of bears.

Once I was embanking a field and a snake bit my foot. Baisasur was god of that field and he was angry because I had made no offering that year.

So he sent the snake. I ran home and fell there senseless. When I recovered I was all right, so I gave a coconut to Nang Deo and a pig to the field.

Once I got drunk in the headman's house in Hirapur. There was a *sutia* hanging from the wall. I took it away home with me. The headman's wife followed me and asked for it back. I got angry and dragged her into the house and forced her. The woman ran home weeping and told her husband what had happened. Then we had a great quarrel. The headman tried to turn me out of the village. But what could he do, he is an inferior person.

I have had two wives in order to have children, but there has been no result. I have adopted a boy. We all live together very happily.

XI. KETU

Ketu, a Muria Baiga of Amtera, in the Niwas Tehsil, on the Dindori-Jubbulpore road, is an old man of gentle and unassuming charm. His father used to be the *mālguzār* (landlord) of the village, and Ketu is still called *mālguzār* and has a good deal of influence of a purely secular kind.

I was born here in Amtera. My father's name was Bakeria, my mother was Bundai. I was very happy as a child. But one day when I was about four years old, a snake bit my brother as we were playing in the fields, and I ran home screaming.

When I was a boy I used to take the cattle out to graze. Out in the fields I used to play *ghar-gundia* and *gai-gai* with the other children. One day I made a long penis out of a leaf and put it into the vagina of a girl. She ran crying to her parents. They told my father and he beat me. They put in iron pincers and pulled out the leaf.

I was only eleven when I was married. In that year I forced a girl in the field, but I hurt her and she told her mother. My father heard of this also and beat me again. Although my wife was so small my father made me begin to sleep with her. Two or four years later, my wife became mature.

When I was eighteen I had my first son. My father was very pleased and gave a feast and liquor to all the Baiga. At that time we had eight ploughs of bullocks.

Three or four years later there was the famine. My father got very poor and said he was dying of hunger. My son went to eat in the Government kitchen. My wife went to beg. But my father and I lived on roots.

About this time the Deputy Commissioner came and stayed in Bargaon. He called my father. My father went with all his papers and said, "My *mālguzāri* cannot go on. My son is a boy. I cannot collect the taxes. So I give my village to Government".

But the Deputy Commissioner said, "Don't give up your village, or when your son grows up he'll curse you".

But my father took no notice and the Deputy Commissioner agreed. When my father came home I had a great quarrel with him. The next year the D.C. came to Dongaria, and I went to see him. On the way I met a chaprasi and he said, "Amtera is lost". So I went home again.

Then when the D.C. came to Bargaon, I did go to him, and asked him to give my village back. He said, "Government has taken your village. Your father has hidden much treasure underground. Dig that up and live on it". When I heard that I took the rope of the tent and tied it to a tree, and said, "Huzoor, hang me here". The D.C. said, "No, you can hang yourself with your own hands. I'm not going to do it. Go away".

After that I tried to go to Nagpur to see the Governor. I took two men with me and we got as far as Mandla. But there they said, "You must give us ten rupees each, and go on alone." So I came home.

That year my father fell ill and died. The bullocks also died—all but two or three. The crops were ruined by frost. I began to be very poor.

Two years afterwards I went to my sister's house in Silgawa. I was wearing a good coat, shirt and dhoti. We sang Karma and afterwards I lay down alone to sleep. But a girl came and lay down beside me. I was frightened, not knowing why she came. "Why are you here?" I asked her. "For love of you," she said. Then I was pleased and stayed with her. But the next day she followed me home and even came into my house. I tried to turn her out, but she said: "If you drive me away, I'll hang myself and die." So I kept the girl and paid her husband a cow and a calf.

A year later my married wife died in childbirth. My mother was still alive. My new wife didn't feed the children properly, so my mother took care of them instead. I was very angry with this girl, so I took two men with me and went to search for guavas.[1] On the way the girl turned herself into a tiger and sat in the road. When she saw me she stood up on her two hind-legs and roared at me. Then I ran home. The girl was not in the house. So I knew then that it was she who was the tiger. That evening when she came home, I drove her from the house.

The next morning all my children were dead.

A year afterwards, I married a new wife and we were very happy together. I had two sons from her. That year it was that my mother

[1] An expression meaning 'to search for the breasts of a new girl'.

went out to the fields in the rains, and was drowned in the floods as she came home.

Now I live here in my father's village and pay rent for the land that is really mine. My sons and daughters live near me, and when there is food and some liquor and it is not very cold, we are happy.

XII. BANSI

Bansi is an elderly Muria Baiga, about sixty-five years of age, who now lives in Dhangaon in the Niwas Tehsil. He was once a famous gunia, but his wife's mistake in going into his *madhia* during her period ruined his life.

My father's name was Sadhu, my mother's Sunia. I belong to the Morabi-*goti*. In my childhood we used to cut bewar. Once when I was a little boy, running along behind my father on the way to the bewar, we met a tiger, and had to run for our lives. A few days later when we were digging roots a snake bit my foot. The reason was that there was a god living in the bewar and we had given him nothing before going to dig for roots. That was why the snake bit me. When my father had discovered the cause, he offered a cock and a coconut in the bewar and I got well again.

When I was nine or ten I got very ill with a pain in my stomach. A Chamarin massaged me, and I got well again. The next year I went as a servant in a man's house, but I quarrelled with him and left. When I was thirteen there was famine. My father was blind, my mother's head was always shaking, so they went begging and fed their children. I went to eat in the Government kitchen. That year my father died of cholera. I had three other brothers at that time. They lived apart from us.

When I was twenty I married. I lived six years in Kamaria. Then there was a quarrel, and I came to Dhangaon, and began to use the plough.

Twice the Revenue Inspector took me for *begar*, he did not even give me my food for two days.

Once I went to the jungle for bark-rope. I climbed a tree and fell. I was ill for a month with my waist broken. I took jungle medicine and recovered.

At the time of my first son's birth, I had a dream. All the gods, the twelve Dewar and fifty-six Guru took me by the hand and raised me up saying, "You will be a *panda* and we will live in your house. Whatever you say we will obey you". So saying they went away and I awoke. I lit a lamp and searched everywhere in the house. There was nothing there! There was no wife, no child, everything had disappeared. I took a coconut in my hand and went to the door. I looked towards the jungle, and called the gods to come back again. But all round the house there was nothing but the growling of many tigers. I was afraid and shut the door. Then I lay down and slept. Then I dreamt again, and the gods came back. They washed their feet and gave me the water to drink, and sat down round me in the house. Then I got up again, and now my wife and child were back again in the house.

The next day I went to a gunia and began to learn mantra. That night the gods said, "Prepare twenty-one pillars and twenty-one *tirsul*". So the next day I made them, and then I was a *panda*. You may see my little *madhia* down by the river where every Sunday the god rides on me. In the old days my shrine used sometimes to turn all golden, sometimes gods and goddesses danced there. Sick people came and asked about the future. I would tell one that he had two years to live, another that he had five. A Mehera came to me whose nose had rotted away, his face was broken, he had foul discharges. He was ready to die. I laid my hand on his face, and he became well. He grew a new nose. For that he gave me ten rupees.

Another day a merchant came to me. His waist was broken. I seized his feet and dragged him towards me and he recovered. A Baiga woman had a child in her belly and it died. She was very ill. They could not bring it out. They brought her to me. I rubbed her belly and the child became water and disappeared. The woman recovered.

On the day I perform *dhām*, I don't go to my wife, and I take food from someone else's hands. I don't look at anybody. I only drink *ulta dhār* water (water that is scooped out in the same direction that the river is flowing and drunk facing downstream).

But one day my wife went to clean the shrine. At that very moment she began her period but she didn't know it. As she went into the shrine the pillar of the hut broke of its own accord, and her child whom she was carrying began to go mad. The place had been clean—in a moment it was foul and stinking. My wife was terrified, she ran home and told me all about it. I went to the shrine, and there a voice came to me, "I am going to destroy you, Bansi", it said. "Not one child will remain to you."

As the voice spoke, all the mantra went from my mind. After three days when my wife washed her head, I fasted for two days. I got some water from a virgin girl and went to the shrine with a coconut. I sprinkled the water there and broke the coconut. Then the pillar was restored and the place clean once more. That night I had a dream. "You were a great *panda*. Now you will be an ordinary gunia. You have driven all the gods away. Every one of your children will go mad."

Within two years all my children had gone mad and died. Then we had another son. He too is mad. He wanders sometimes in the jungle, he goes into people's houses, he takes food out of their pots. I am mad too sometimes. I have kept three other women beside my wife. None stayed for long. Each of them too went mad.

One day a sadhu came to me and he said, "When you yourself are dead, then all these others will recover."

XIII. MAHI

Mahi is a small, lively, good-looking, talkative woman of about thirty. She is very charming, flirtatious, and 'modern'. She is, for example, quite prepared to ignore the tribal rules of exogamy. At the same time she is very motherly, and always has one or two children with her; she has even taken 'milk-medicine' so as to be able to nurse someone's child. She is at present married but has declared that she wants a change, and that if anyone else would like to marry her, they have only to let her know.

I am a Bhumia Baigin, of the Durwa *goti* and the Rathoria *garh*. My father's name was Manohar, my mother's Kondi. I was born in Kapoli, the youngest child of the family. My eldest sister was Kari, my eldest brother is Bharua who has kept Baisakin. When I was a baby my father died.

The thing I remember most in my life is hunger. I have always been hungry. I was happy as a child, but I was hungry.

When I was five or six years old we went from Kapoti to Dadargaon. I was going along with my mother with a small pot of pulse on my head. But some Lamana frightened me, and I dropped the pot on the ground and began to scream. The pot broke and the pulse was scattered all over the ground. My mother beat me, and I went weeping to Dadargaon.

After four years we left Dadargaon and came to Andha. There we couldn't cut bewar; we had no bullocks; so we worked for other people.

There was a boy called Badu there. He was kept as my Lamsena. I was married to him. Then I was tattooed, but only eight annas worth, not like my mother who cost twenty-five rupees and was very beautiful. But after Badu had only worked for one year, the rascal ran away. I didn't like him, so what did I care?

Then I went to Ledra Taliyapani and lived with my sister. There we lived for two years together. Then my mother came and took me to Jaknadi.

Busts modelled by Mrs. Milward:

Panku, son of Jethu.

Mahi, whose life-story is recorded on p. 160.

In Jaknadi we worked for our food, cutting wood, picking leaves, grinding for other people. I used to meet a Binjhwar Baiga called Jarhu of the Parteti *goti* in the jungle, and at last I decided to keep him. I slept with him for a year, and had a daughter from him.

When the girl was two or three months old, she died. I stayed one month longer with Jarhu. Then he began to trouble me. He said, "You are only a Bhumia, I am a Binjhwar. I won't eat with you". He stopped giving me good food, so I went back to Ledra Taliyapani, and stayed for a month with my sister there.

Then one day I went for water to a stream where there were trees all round and no one came near. I met Chaitu. He was a Morabi of the Kumania *garh*. We made friends there in that jungle, and so I decided to keep him. I made him my husband with *haldi-pāni*. I lived with Chaitu for fifteen or twenty days, then I got tired of him and I said, "You are an old man, I won't live with you any longer". So I ran away from him to Marradabra.

In Marradabra there lived a very handsome man called Buti. He was of the Morabi *goti* and Saradia *garh*. I was mad for him. I made love-magic for him. After a few days he could not sit still; he was restless as gram in the frying pan or a fish in a dried-up stream. He soon came to me. I lived with him for a year, and he gave me a daughter.

After the child was born, I couldn't work properly, and Buti began to trouble me; he didn't give me enough to eat. After two months the child died. Then Buti's mother and sister quarrelled with me and Buti pushed me out of his house with his hands.

Then I came to live in Kotalwahi with my elder brother. I stayed with him a month. In Chait of that year a Gond *panda* came to sow the Jawara. I went to see it. There I saw Kaddar who had also come from Umaria. We made friends with each other. But we were both of the Durwa *goti*, though he was a Libraria and I a Rathoria. So my mother and Kaddar's mother discussed the matter, and my mother said, "What does it matter if they are of the same *goti*; they are of different *garh*; let them marry". But my brother said, "Kaddar always beats his wives". Then Kaddar said, "No, I'll never beat her". His mother said, "I'll be responsible if he beats her". So I made him my husband and went with him to Umaria and we stayed there for a month.

Then we went to Ledra Taliyapani and lived there for five or six years. We cut bewar there.

Then we went to Ajwainbar and we cut bewar there also. One day I went to the bewar, and in the grass on the border there was a snake and it bit me. I fell down senseless. I was ill for a month, I thought I would die.

The gunia came and saw in his *sūpa* that it was my father-in-law who had sent Alobhavani who eats raw meat and who had spread grass in the bewar and turned it into a snake. So we offered her a pig, a she-goat, a hen and coconuts, and I got well again.

After a year we returned to Kotalwahi. There a witch attacked me and I fell ill again. But my father-in-law looked in his *sūpa* and saved me, though he was my enemy.

Two or three years later I went to Bhoira to see my friend. Jonu's wife had died leaving a baby. I said I would take the child. I got milk-medicine, and milk filled my breasts and I fed the child. Her name is Phagni and I have adopted her.

In my life I have had a lot of dreams, but I always wake up too soon. Once I was giving my husband a good beating. How pleased I was, but I awoke. Another day, in my dream my husband died, and I said to myself, "Now I must make a new husband". I went to a Karma dance to find one, but the noise of the drums woke me.

Another time, I ate a big cucumber and died. My husband threw it away, for it had poison in it. He wept very much and all the village stood round me weeping. Then I awoke.

Once I dreamt that a bear had bitten my husband very badly. He had made a *mācha* in the bewar and was watching the crops. He shouted, and I awoke.

I once had a very long dream. There was a tall straight mango tree without any branches. I climbed up it and picked some mangoes from the top. A Brahmin came by, and he called up to me, "Girl, give me some mangoes, and I will bless you". So I gave him five mangoes and he asked me to come to his house. The next day I went to his house. He was sleeping inside. I stood in the courtyard and called to him. He asked me to come in and I went and sat on his bed. So we became friends. He said, "If you want a child, get someone to tattoo you in your *okh̃a-kokha*". As he said that, he poked me in the ribs and with the tickling, I awoke.

Once I dreamt that a man had made love-magic for me and was taking me away to the Tea Gardens. On the way I hit my foot against a stone and woke.

I always laugh when I remember the dream in which I turned into a monkey and danced on the branches of a tree. At last the branch broke, I fell down, and woke.

XIV. DHAN SINGH

Dhan Singh is the headman and Dewar of Pandpur, a forest-village in the Karanjia Range. He is a very respectable old man of about fifty, usually rather grave and reserved, though on occasion he can unbend and become extremely lively. Then he takes a drum and dances the Karma or plays the Tapori which he does very well, and makes hilarious jokes. He is courteous and intelligent. He comes from time to time to perform ceremonies in Sanrhwachhapar; in May, 1937, he came to repair the magic boundaries of the village which had been broken and a tiger had been killing a number of cattle.

I was born in Rampur, near Samnapur in the Dindori Tehsil. My father used to cut bewar. We had two bullocks, but we didn't know how to plough and so we used to hire them out on *būhi*, which means that you get three *khandi* of kodon for each bullock. I used to go to the bewar to guard it, and when I came home I brought wood for the house. My parents never beat me; they loved me very much.

When I was ten or twelve years old I went for the first time to dig for roots in the jungle. Then it was that the mad elephant came to our bewar and ate all our crops. Then it came into the village and pulled one of the houses to pieces.

For fear of the elephant we left Rampur and came to Kapripani. We used to cut bewar there also. I was about fourteen at that time. We lived there for twenty-five years. Then the women of the village proclaimed the Stiria Raj[1] and they killed my pig. I was very sad over the loss of the pig.

I had a little sister. In Damin Tola we had friends who wanted to exchange a girl for my sister. So this was arranged, and I was married when I was about eighteen.

Before we were married I went with her to the forest to get mahua. There I went to her; it was the first time I ever did it. It was a good thing I knew my wife before marriage; we knew we would suit each other, and we have remained together for our whole life.

Six or seven years after my marriage a daughter was born, but she died the same day. A witch had caused my wife's womb to be burnt up. I went to several Dewar, but they could do nothing. And again, three years later, my wife was greatly troubled by a witch in Lalpur called Titri. My wife was all dried up inside. Titri tried also to steal my wife's liver. I went to beat her, but she cried, "Your wife will recover, I swear it!" So I let her alone.

[1] See p. 238.

Ten years after my marriage I married a second wife. Her father had said to me, "If you don't marry my daughter, I'll make you walk between her legs". So I took her and married her. It was a proper marriage; the first wife sat on one side and the second on the other. I felt very important with two wives. I gave three tins of liquor at that marriage.

I used to sleep in the middle of the house, with the new wife in one corner and the old one in the other. I would go to one side or the other as my desire led me. But I only slept with my new wife for one night. Five days after our marriage, she went to dig *sakal kānda*. She found great fat ones and roasted them and ate them all. Then in the middle of the night she ran away to Lalpur, and from there to her mother's house in Ranjki. I ran after her for a little way, but I met a bear standing in the middle of the path. It stood upright and opened its arms to me. I shook my axe at it, and it went away, but after that I thought I would come home.

I didn't love the girl very much. She was fat and ugly. Her breasts were big as a gourd. A girl with big breasts is always bad. She belongs to many men.

It was while we were living in Kapripani that Hoblal Jamadar came and told us that we were not to cut bewar any more. So half of us went away to Mangarh Malguzari and half to Pondi. I went to Mangarh for we could cut bewar there so long as we didn't cut jamun or fruit trees.

In Mangarh my father caught a very bad cough and cold and died. My bullock also died there. My mother had two small sons and one daughter. I had to look after them all. So we went to live in Damin Tola.

Then came the famine. In Damin Tola we couldn't cut bewar, so for hunger we had to learn to use the plough. But when we sowed our seed, the Gond came and stole it. Every day we went to the forest to dig for roots. Rich men used to pretend that there was no food in their houses and sat hungry all day, but at midnight they would cook and eat. Government offered us taccavi loans but we were afraid to take them. They opened kitchens, but we didn't go; we preferred to eat our roots. Everyone who was blind, or lame, or stupid, and all the children, went and were fed by Government. But I wouldn't let my mother's children go; I fed them on *girchi kānda* and *kanhia kānda*.

When the rains came, we ate *kodela* (the wild kodon), and *sawar* and *chichmi* (a small grain like kutki), and every kind of jungle vegetable. We brought basketfuls to our house. We got a little salt and tobacco by selling wood. Whenever we went to borrow anything, people shut their doors when they saw us coming. Many Baiga died of hunger in those days.

After that came the influenza and twenty to twenty-five people died in every village. We buried them all, but we only spent one rupee on the liquor for each of them.

Then my mother's hands and feet swelled up and she died.

I have never had a child, but I adopted my wife's sister's son Hagru. He won't inherit my property, my brother's son will get it. But if my wife is still living, she will have it. Though really it will all have to go to pay my debts.

Ten years ago I came from Tala, where I had moved from Damin Tola, to Pandpur. Government asked me to be the headman. In Pandpur we pay one rupee a plough and eight annas for the *kāndabāri*. If we have more than eight cattle we pay four annas for each. We have to give *begar*, but we are paid three annas a day for it. In Kapripani we used to pay two rupees an axe for our bewar.

In Pandpur I have been happy, but we were much better off when I was a young man. When we cut bewar we got good crops of every kind; now we have broken the breasts of Mai Dharti and we get nothing. Also in my youth we were always hunting, but now we are afraid. I once caught a bear in my trap. Its leg was caught in the noose and it was hung up in the tree.

In Pandpur I was once very ill for a whole year with asthma. I have never had venereal disease. This year I was nearly drowned in the Seoni river, and I lost all my clothes.

I once went to Mandla and liked it very much. I wanted to live there always. I have never been in a train or motor-car. The ruler of this country lives in Mandla; I don't know who is the Raja of India. Perhaps Gandhi is the Raja, but who he is or what he does I have no idea. But I have heard that he wants Hindu-Raj in India.

Once in Kapripani I saw a *churelin*. A woman had died with a child in her belly. They took her out to bury her, but afterwards they decided to burn her body. But when the fire was lighted, another *churelin* like a big kussera bird came and beat with its wings all round the pyre to put out the flames.

In our house we worship Maswasi who lives in our *orchha* (roof above the verandah), and Narayan who lives on the threshold. Inside the house are Aloha Deo, Lodha Deo, Dulha Deo and the Ajidadi (ancestors) all living in the hearth. Rat Mai and Dudia Khut are in the cattle-shed. When Dudia Khut is angry, our cow refuses to give milk to her calf. We don't worship Bara Deo or Mahadeo.

In our house there lives a *raksa* and we love him very much and do him honour. He is the grandfather of my grandfather on my father's side who died without being married. He lives by the hearth. When we cook we put a little food on a bit of coal for him. He is a good *raksa* and never troubles us, but of course he is always wanting girls. One day a visitor came to stay with us, she was young and pretty, and the *raksa* went to her in the middle of the night. Another day when the house was empty a thief came, but the *raksa* caught him by the hand and held him till we returned. Another time, when we were all out in the bewar, a girl went into the house to steal grain. She put her hand into the bin, and the *raksa* caught hold of it and she couldn't pull it out. When we came home, there she was, caught.

It is twenty years since I became a gunia. My father-in-law was my guru. He showed me which gods to worship and what to do and taught me *sūpa-tuma*. Ever since I have done the work of a Dewar. I used to go to Jarasrung, Bahapur, Bondar, Sukulpura, Bartola, Dokadongri and Kilari. Now I am old, my brother's son whom I taught and who lives in Sarai, does the work for me. When I go to a sick man, he gives me liquor; and if he recovers, then a present of cloth or a goat. But if he dies they give nothing.

If some magician came and asked me to choose the three things that I most wanted and that the Baiga most wanted in the world, I would say, "First, give us back our jungle. Then give us free *kāndabāri*. And third, let us hunt freely once more. We do not want riches, only these three things."

XV. BAISAKIN

Baisakin is a very handsome old lady of about sixty, the elder wife of the Dewar of Kotalwahi, a Bhumia. She is not herself a gunia, but she acts as a sort of 'control' to her husband who can get no good results of his divination without her. She is an excellent story-teller, and very witty, and must have been a remarkable beauty in her youth.

My father and mother lived in Dadargaon. There I was born. At that time, my father cut bewar and also had fields. He had twelve cows and twelve ploughs with twenty-four bullocks, and twelve more bullocks for carrying loads.

When I was a baby, my parents went to Andha. There they used the plough. I had five elder brothers and one sister.

When I was four or five I had to spend all day looking after my eldest brother's son. I had no time to play.

When I was eight or nine, my parents took me to live in Kamarkodra. There also they used the plough.

When I was eleven or twelve, my mother died. A year later we went to live in Karadih.

When I was fifteen or sixteen, my father died.

When I was twenty, I was married. My eldest brother arranged it. I lived for one year in my father-in-law's house in Karadih. Then my husband went to Kursi in Rewa State to marry a second wife named Bhairi. I was angry and went to live with my brother.

For a year I stayed with my brother in Karadih. Then my husband came with his father and they took me away to Kursi. I stayed there happily for a month and then I got very ill. My father-in-law was a gunia, and he 'looked' in his *sūpa* and saw what was the matter, and they made offerings and I recovered. But I was very weak and my husband wouldn't give me proper food because I didn't do enough work. So I ran away back to Karadih.

There I stayed for another year in my brother's house. While I was there I made friends with Bukwa the landlord of Ufri which is very near that village. When our love had grown, Bukwa kept me in his house, though he had a wife already. For two or three years I lived with him. Then came the famine. We ate boiled sarai fruit and channa flour thinly mixed with water. But Bukwa didn't give me proper food and abused me and beat me.

So I ran away from him and went back to my brother's house and lived a year with him again.

Then Giru, a very famous Dewar, fell in love with me and kept me. He took me to Kotalwahi. For ten or twelve years I lived happily with him. He never beat me or abused me or went to other women. He taught me all his mantra. But one day his cow fell ill, and he said, "If my cow gets well, I'll give a speckled cock." The cow got well, and I said, "Now you must give a speckled cock." But he said, "No, it doesn't matter. The cow is all right now, and what can they do?" But that very day be began to vomit and to have many motions. On the third day he died.

When he was dead, I lived alone for two years. Then one day when I was in the jungle I met Bharua Dewar who had gone there alone to pick leaves. I met him on the bank of a stream and we got to know one another. Often we met there. After a time the people in the village began to suspect that we were doing something, and they said to me, "You must keep Bharua as your husband." So I married him with *haldi-pāni*. For a year I lived happily with him. Then I had a dream that I had sunk deep into the river. The fish bit me and I woke screaming. Bharua said the fish were witches. At that time a witch stole my cloth while I was bathing during my period and buried it in the mud. Then I was in my period for a whole month. There was no stopping it. So my husband 'looked' in his *sūpa* and saw what had happened and we dug up the cloth and cleaned it with ashes, and I was well again.

For five or four years we lived happily together. Then Bharua made Malho his *chhotki*. After some time Malho had a child. I have never had a child. But I dreamt then that a daughter was born from me. All my clothes were covered with blood and the child died. I wept and my husband woke me.

Then last year I had a great quarrel with Bharua and his Malho, and I made a separate house. Bharua lives with Malho, their child and one cow and a calf. I have no child, but I have five bullocks and four cows. We all live together, but I won't go into his house. He has to come to me in my house. At this time I dreamt that I went to Bhagavan and sought for some place to live. But I could find no home anywhere, so I came back to earth.

Three months ago Bharua beat me very violently. Since then I have refused to let him have my bullocks for his field. He has not come into my house since then. But he cannot do his gunia work properly, for I won't help him. I dreamt after that that there were two nights to every day. I sat in the dark, and then went for water. But there was a lot of frost on the road, and I slipped and fell.

I live happily, for I give offerings to Mother Earth for everything, and I have never injured her breasts as Bharua and his Malho have.

XVI. JETHU

Jethu, the crippled Dewar, lives in a little hut in one corner of the great square of Bohi. With him are his wife, his wizened bent old mother, his amazingly handsome son Panku, his daughter-in-law and two grandchildren. Next door are his daughter and her husband with their children. Jethu rules over his family and the whole village. He is far the most intelligent man there, the most cheerful, the most courageous, the most enterprising. His deformity—his legs are two withered sticks—makes no odds; he is far more respected than the drunken headman of the village or any of the other elders.

I am a Bhumia Baiga, of the Durwa *goti* and the Telasia *g̃arh*. I was born in Chiyadad. My father's name was Suna, my mother's Sauni. When I was a little boy my father climbed up a semur tree to get the honey from a bee's-nest, but the branch broke and he fell down and was killed.

After my father's death, we went to live in Chata with my grandfather Tedga Dewar. There was my mother, my brother Chaitu and my two sisters Budwari and Cheri.

Tedga, my paternal grandfather, had two wives. My father was the son of his elder wife. But his younger wife had no son, and when she saw her partner had not only a son but a grandson also, she was very angry She was a witch, and she determined to ruin me.

One day, when I was about twelve years old, I went with my mother to the bewar. Now that witch had made a snake and sent it to the bewar saying, "When Jethu comes, bite him". So when I reached the bewar, a small snake with its head raised attacked me and tried to bite me. But I escaped and the snake ran into the stump of a chhindi palm. I dug up the root of the tree, but was unable to find the snake. The same day, I found a bird caught in the rat-trap in the bewar. The bird was alive, and when I tried to take it out, it escaped and flew away. That very night, my illness began. I had fever, and my mother put me in a pot of hot water to bathe me. But when she took me out, my legs were dried up, and my head flung back and helpless. From that day I have been lame as you see me now.

While I was still a boy I became a gunia. My grandfather was very fond of me and taught me everything. At first he made me sit with the *sūpa-tuma*, and he himself sat beside me to see if there were any mistakes. From my boyhood I have been a *barua*. When the god comes, all men look very small to you, about three feet high. You don't know what you are doing. When the god comes violently, you don't recognize anybody. You feel as if you were drunk. Afterwards you feel very tired and your head and shoulders ache all night.

After some time, my grandfather died, and we left Chata and went to Silpuri in the Baiga Chak where we were allowed to cut bewar. For ten or twelve years we lived there very happily. There was no trouble there, for soon after we arrived a bat came to live in my house and the bat brought me good fortune, as it always has done during my life.

In Silpuri there was a young unmarried girl whom I desired. I made love-magic for her, and after a few days she came to my house. At night her relatives came to take her away and beat me. But at the back of my house the wall was broken. I slipped through, and escaped into the jungle. The people broke down the door and took the girl home. The next day I made them all drunk, and after some time they agreed and I married the girl with bangles.

In Silpuri there were many witches. Once a witch there turned my semen into water. When I discovered through my *sūpa* who the witch was I made her turn the water back into semen again. Another time a witch turned into a tiger. Her hands, feet, head, everything became a tiger's. She had no tail. She went with her sister-in-law to the bewar, for she wanted to eat her. She went into the *lāri*-hut and became a tiger inside. Her sister-in-law heard her growling and ran to call the neighbours. They all came and gathered round the hut and cried, "Remember what you really are. You are a human being. Come back to us again". When she heard that the witch became a woman again.

From Silpuri we went to live in Belki. There a son was born, but died after eight days, and then a daughter who died also. Then Panku was born, and after him Phagni who later married Deriya.

In Belki I once met a girl in the jungle. What is there to tell? We did our work and came home. I made love-magic there for another girl, and for a long while she could not be happy apart from me. She loved me very much. But when we went to live in Tanta, the *mohini* lost its power.

From Belki we went to live in Tanta. While we were there cholera came to the village and twenty-one men died. The Ranger called me for gunia. The Lame Sahib also came, and I made afresh the boundary of the village and the sickness stopped. I made a cart and put bangles and a *tikli* on a goat, and performed the Bida and drove the cholera out of Tanta. The cholera went on to Tonchi, so I went there also, and got a rupee's worth of liquor, and I drove it out of Tonchi also. Where it went then I do not know.

After that, my fame spread and I had to go to many places. I used to get very tired dragging myself along on my hands. In Chitalbahara a man was killed by a tiger, and I had to go there and drive the nails to shut the tiger's mouth. In Jankhi, there was a Mehera who couldn't get a child. I went and saw the Samduria sisters dancing in my *sūpa*. I offered coconuts for him, and his wife became pregnant. He gave me cloth and liquor. In Silpuri I got a girl from Ajghar for my brother-in-law through my *mohini*. In Bohi years ago, the bewar gave no crops. I did gunia, and since then the harvest has always been good. A Baigin was pregnant but the child could not be born. I looked in my *sūpa* and saw the Samduria sisters, so we offered coconuts and the child was born. When I work for other people I get some cloth, a coconut and some liquor. When I work for other Baiga I get a cup of *pej* and a bottle of liquor.

We came to Bohi eleven years ago. It is a good place. We like it very much, but there are many witches. There is a witch called Raju; twice she has sent snakes to bite my son, once in the bewar, and once while he was reaping the kutki crop. Raju troubles everyone in Bohi. It is she who sent the tiger who killed Deriya's son. She hates me especially because I once saved a man who had been bitten by one of her snakes.

Now I have two she-goats, one Laru pig and my house and *bāri*. That is all my property. My son and his wife give me food whenever I have nothing to eat. I earn a little money by going to help sick people, and by doing the Bida and Bidri for this village and Jumor. When officials come here they are always very good to me; they sit and talk with me; no one gives me any trouble.

I have never been to Pandaria. The Zemindarin rules over our country. I know of no other ruler. I have heard of Gandhi. He is a god like any other Raja.

I do not often dream. Once in a dream my *jīv* took wings and flew through the air till it fell down. It saw the whole world while it was flying. It went as far as Jankhi (about twenty-five miles from Bohi). Another time I dreamt that I went to bathe and the fish in the stream bit me. This meant that the *bīr* of the witch Raju were after me. Another time, my *jīv* went to a girl, and she cut off my penis with a knife.

Here in Bohi, five years ago, I made love-magic for a woman with five children. She became mad for me, and was always saying, "I want to live with Jethu". It is all over now.

Chapter V

THE SOCIAL ORGANIZATION OF THE BAIGA

I. EXOGAMOUS DIVISIONS

THE JĀT

We have already, in Chapter I, discussed the different divisions, or *jāt*, into which the Baiga tribe is divided. These divisions are more or less endogamous. As each *jāt* usually lives separate from the others, there is seldom any temptation to intermarry. The problem arises chiefly in Niwas, where Binjhwar, Muria and Bhumia live side by side. There are a number of rather complicated rules governing social intercourse between the *jāt*.

The women of one *jāt* are absolutely barred from eating with members of any other *jāt*.

Bhumia men eat from the hands of Binjhwar in Rewa State, but not elsewhere. They eat from Bharotia on the borders of Mandla and Balaghat, but from no one else. In Niwas, however, the decadent Chhota Bhumia eat from Muria, Binjhwar and Bhaina.

Binjhwar men eat from Bhumia in Dindori, and with Muria in Niwas. Elsewhere they are very strict about this.

Bharotia men eat from Bhumia, Binjhwar and Narotia.

Narotia eat from Bharotia and Binjhwar.

Bhaina Baiga eat from Bhumia and Binjhwar in Bilaspur and from Muria in Niwas.

Kondwan, Kurka and Gond-waina are said to eat together if occasion arises. It is said to be not uncommon for Kondwan and Gond-waina to sit down together to a feast of roast monkey.

There are also rules of intermarriage. I think it is safe to say that in general men will marry the virgin girls of any other *jāt*, with the idea that the girl thus becomes a member of her husband's *jāt* and severs all connection with her own. She ought not even to visit her mother's house after marriage. Girls who have been already married are not accepted. But this custom is not observed in every case.

The Bhumia, for example, take Dudh-Bhaina girls, but refuse to give their girls in return. They also take Binjhwar girls, but it is a disputed point how far they ought to give their girls to Binjhwar. In Mandla, the Bharotia desire intermarriage with the Binjhwar. "We give our daughters to the Binjhwar", they say. "We don't accept them", the Binjhwar reply.

In Baihar, Bharotia and Narotia intermarry, provided the girls on either side are virgin.

In Niwas, although Muria, Binjhwar and Bhumia eat together, they do not intermarry, and very serious consequences follow any breach of the rule.

But even under the above rules, to marry a member of another *jāt* is dangerous. It gives your enemies a handle to use against you. It may, or may not, entail supernatural penalities. It is safer to marry within the *jāt*. The endogamous rules, enforced as they are by geographical conditions, are generally observed.

The Garh and the Goti

The *jāt* are again subdivided into a very large number of exogamous *garh* and *goti*. The *garh*, which are the more important of the two, are based on residence. The idea is that every Baiga originally belonged to a particular hill or jungle, and that he must marry his daughters to men belonging to a different hill or jungle, a sound and logical basis for exogamy. "The *garh* were made to prevent brother and sister from sleeping together," say the Baiga. This arrangement undoubtedly makes for health and variety, and protects from incest, to which the Baiga seem somewhat prone.

These *garh* derive from Nanga Baigin herself. She gave her twelve sons the names of the first twelve *garh*—Binjhwar, Sawat, Chituria, Damgharia, Ghangaria, Dawaria, Pachgaiha, Salgaia, Kumaria, Massania, Chanania, Chandgaria. The names Binjhwar and Sawat are given to both *jāt* and *garh*, but only rarely to the latter. From these twelve came the great multitude of *garh* that exist to-day.

These *garh* are territorial. They are exogamous, but not totemic. They represent the original division of the *jāt*, and were adequate for their purpose.

But the organization of the Baiga seems to have been thrown into confusion by contact with the Gond. The Gond have no territorial exogamous divisions, but they have a number of very strict, highly developed, totemic, exogamous *gotra*.[1]

[1] 'Gond names are found most frequently,' says Russell, 'among the Gondwanias and Narotias, and these have adopted from the Gonds the prohibition of marriage between worshippers of the same number of gods. Thus the four septs (Markam, Maravi, Netam and Tekam) worship seven gods and may not intermarry. But they may marry among other septs who worship six gods.'—Russell and Hiralal, op. cit., p. 81. I have not myself found any examples of this.

The Baiga, seeing their Gond neighbours fully equipped with *gotra*, seem to have felt that to obtain real tribal respectability, they ought to have them too. So they borrowed a few *gotra* from the Gond, which they called *goti*. In Baihar, the Bharotia say that only five *goti* are real, "the rest will pass away"—these are Morabi, Durwa, Markam, Parteti and Potta. In Kawardha, I found Morabi, Durwa, Parteti, Potta, Baghel and Nangbansi. The Niwas Baiga have twelve *goti*—Morabi, Markam, Tekam, Netam, Syam, Kusro, Sindram, Uika, Udde, Chicham, Potta, Pendo. In parts of Mandla they have no *goti* at all, only *garh*—and this undoubtedly reflects the original organization of the tribe.

The fact that the *goti* are borrowed, and borrowed comparatively recently, has caused them to be regarded very lightly. You ought not to marry within your *goti*, it is true, but if you do a bottle of liquor will atone the venial fault. Provided you marry within your *jāt* and outside your *garh*, it does not matter very greatly if you marry inside your *goti*.

This liberal attitude to the *goti*, as we shall see, has had its reaction also on the integrity of the *garh*, and has reduced the exogamous fidelity of the tribe to great confusion.

Totemism

Among the Gond, the *gotra* are totemic. The Markam *gotra*, named after the mango, has the tortoise as its totem, the Netam has the dog, the Parteti the crocodile. But in strong support of their own tradition that the *goti* are merely borrowed, is the fact that among the Baiga is no real totemism. Some Dudh-bhaina Baiga once told me that the Parteti never killed the crocodile, the Markam never killed the tortoise and the Baghel never killed the tiger. "We can't kill our animals. Even if we shoot at them, we are sure to miss. And they will never trouble us." In Kawardha I found some Nangbansi who revered the snake.

But elsewhere, with one exception, I have not been able to find any such customs, save that the tiger is sometimes regarded as a sort of totem of the whole tribe. Some Baiga—but by no means all—dislike taking part in a beat for a tiger, and they believe that if they are forced to tie up a 'kill' for a tiger the shikari will never get it, and that in return a tiger can only injure them if they are on *pāpi-dharti*.[1]

But in one village I discovered, quite unexpectedly, a belief in totemism that was alive, and obviously not borrowed. This was in Amtera, in Niwas, among a very old family of Muria. Here they confessed to seven

[1] I remember the gloomy satisfaction with which the Baiga of Chauradadar related to me how they were forced by a certain official first to take part in a tiger-beat and then to tie up a buffalo under his machan, and how he was completely unsuccessful on both occasions.

exogamous *goti*, each with a different tree as totem, with special rites which were obviously taken very seriously. The seven *goti* were these:

Belgaria Durwa. "We believe the bel tree[1] to be our Bara Deo. We call its fruit virgin coconuts. Once a year we break a branch of the bel, and burying it sacrifice a coconut over the place."

Karraiya Durwa. "We believe the karra[2] tree to be Bara Deo. We take the cooking-pan called *karaiha* to the karra tree, and cook *roti* there. Then we sacrifice the *roti* to the karra tree."

Tiljaria Durwa. Their totem is the tilwan.[3] They grind some of it, make it into bread, and offer it.

Bartaria Durwa. The bar[4] tree is the totem. They offer a *barhai* (she-goat) to the tree.

Sachera Markam. The totem is the sachera or saj[5] tree. They cook its leaves in fresh rice and offer this to the tree.

Thaurgaria Markam. The totem is the thaur[6]. They also make fresh rice mixed with its leaves and offer it.

Jhinjhigania Markam. The bamboo *jhinjhi* (clump) is the totem, and bamboo shoots are offered to it.

II. ATTITUDE TO UNTOUCHABILITY

"In the old days," say the Baiga, "we knew nothing of untouchability. It is only since the Hindus so greatly increased that we have begun to observe it." Colonel Ward, speaking of the Mandla Baiga of seventy years ago, says, "A Gond will gladly eat food cooked by the Byga, though the latter will not touch food prepared by the Gond; yet the Byga can hardly be said to have any caste prejudices, as he will eat or drink with Europeans if allowed."[7] The story of the Magic Feather, another version of which is current among the Santal, illustrates the older attitude to untouchability. Even to-day the Baiga have none of the conventional abhorrence for an untouchable, but in order to be on the safe side, and to save themselves from the reproach of their neighbours, they avoid him as much as possible. This story is from Niwas Tehsil.

'In a certain village lived a Baiga with his wife and only son. All day long the boy used to go hunting, and his wife used to quarrel with him. So at last he said, "I can't stay here, for I can't leave the house without being troubled by my wife. So I shall go to the war, and I'll die there." He refused to listen to his family, and went away to fight. When he reached

[1] *Aegle marmelos*: a tree sacred throughout India. [2] *Holarrhena antidysenterica.* [3] *Wendlandia exserta.* [4] *Ficus bengalensis.* [5] *Terminalia tomentosa.* [6] *Bauhinia variegata.* Also called kachna. [7] Ward: op. cit., p. 162.

the battle-field, he first took a bath in the river, and said, "How I wish I could get some food." There was a *deo* there who heard him, and it turned into a crow and flew up and away to where a girl was cooking. The crow became a cat, and stole some bread. Then it became a crow again, and flew off to the boy and gave him the bread. The boy thought, "God has sent me food." The crow sat in front of the boy who gave it a bit, and then a dog came and he gave it another bit, and he had half for himself. Then he went to the battle-field, but the war was just over and everyone was dead. The boy hid under the corpses. Then came Rai Gidal flying from the sky. But she didn't eat any of the good corpses, only one dried-up rotten body. When the boy came near, he said, "Why do you only eat the rotten and not the good corpses?" She said, "Come and look through my wing." The boy looked through the wing across the battle-field, and could see nothing but the dead bodies of pigs, dogs, cats, donkeys, she-goats, frogs; there was not a human being to be seen. Then the vulture said, "I only eat those who will be reborn as human beings in their next birth. That is why I don't eat all these corpses." So saying, she pulled out one of her feathers and gave it to him. He took it and went home. There he looked at his mother through it. He saw a she-goat. Then he looked at his wife. He saw a bitch. When he looked at his father he saw a bull. Then he sent away his wife, and went to the bazaar to try to find a human being to marry. He looked at everyone through his feather, but there was not a single human being there. At last a Chamar's daughter with shoes tied in her cloth came to the bazaar. He looked, and saw a lovely human being. So he caught her, and said he would marry her. All the people began to laugh. But he took her home, his father also looked at her and saw she was human, so they gave a tribal feast for her, and he married her, and they lived happily together.'[1]

III. RULES OF SOCIAL INTERCOURSE

The Baiga, however, have probably always been rather strict in matters of food and drink; if they ate with Colonel Ward, that was a sign of their diplomatic acumen rather than a proof of tribal liberality.

Baiga now consider it safer to avoid social intercourse with people who openly eat beef. They have no real objection to eating beef, and many Bhumia and Bharotia eat it privately, but they have become sensitive to the scorn of neighbouring Hindus.

[1] The Santal have a similar tale of a Brahmin who married a Chamar girl, but the Baiga story has more point. Bompas: *Folklore of the Santal Parganas* (London 1909), p. 408, and Bodding: *Santal Folk Tales* (Oslo, 1929), iii. p. 89.

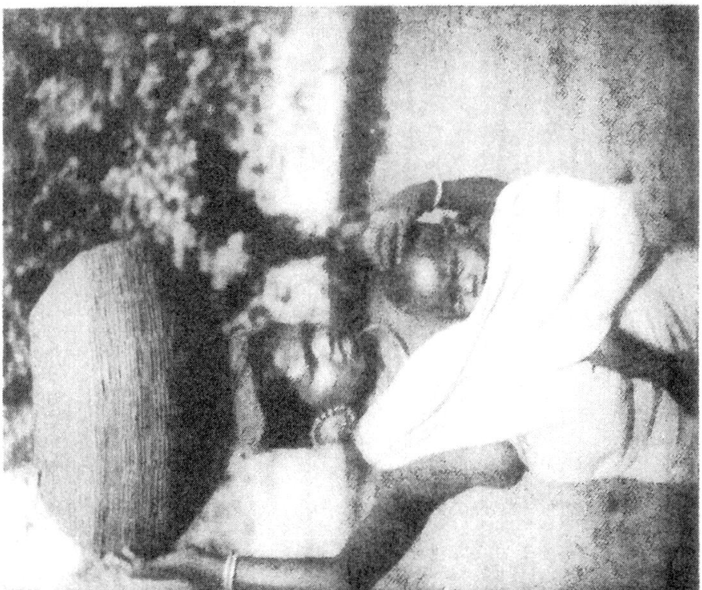

Bhumia girl carrying baby and dali-basket.
Bhumia girl washing clothes.

A Baiga, however, may take certain kinds of nourishment from anyone, even from a Mussalman. In this they follow Hindu custom, and accept boiled milk, cooked sweetmeats, fresh fruit, mahua liquor, tobacco and cigarettes and, of course, all kinds of dry and uncooked food.

Children can eat with anyone and anywhere until they are married or—in the case of girls—till they put the *khandela* across the shoulder which is a sign that puberty has been attained.

Women are much more strictly guarded. They must not only not eat with anyone outside the tribe, but also avoid eating with anyone outside their own sub-tribe.

On the whole, it is a more serious offence to eat with a non-Baiga woman than to seduce her. Marrying a non-Baiga would not matter very much if the kitchen did not have to be shared as well as the bedroom. There are, however, two schools of thought regarding extra-tribal marriages. The rigorist school considers that tribal purity must be maintained even at the cost of a little personal frustration. "How can we admit a Gond among the Baiga?" a leading Binjhwar once asked me. "He is on the opposite bank of the river; how can we bring the two banks together?" I well remember how annoyed a group of Dudh-bhaina were when Mahatu the Bhumia told me in their presence that on payment of the appropriate fees, Gond could be admitted to the tribe. I remember an almost exactly similar scene when at an Anglo-Catholic Church Society at Oxford, it was proposed to admit Free Churchmen to Communion. Even a man like the rather liberal-minded Yogi Binjhwar who would, grudgingly, admit a Gond girl, insists that she must be a virgin, that is to say she must not have been married already. "The Gond," he says patronizingly, "eagerly take even our married women into their homes; we might possibly accept a virgin or two." But he will go no further than that; after all the Gond is the younger brother of the Baiga, one might stretch a point for them. But no Brahmin can ever be admitted, nor can an Agaria, a Mussalman, a Christian, a Chamar. If a Baiga marries a Panka girl he is excommunicated and never readmitted. In Belki, this happened, and the Baiga husband is now regarded as a Panka.

But there is a liberal party, almost a proselytizing party, which delights in making as many new Baiga as possible. This is probably how the Bhaina-Baiga, the Gondwaina-Baiga, the Kurka, Sawat, Nahar Baiga came into existence, by intermarriage with the tribes whose names they still bear. Others, after paying the proper fees and enduring the not very pleasant ceremonies, are admitted into one of the larger sub-divisions of the tribe. "Thousands of Gond girls become Baiga," I was told enthusiastically in Niwas. The Folk-tales are full of these conversions. A Brahmin girl marries a Baiga prince and is admitted to the tribe. Girls from the Ahir, Gond and even (in the old days) Panka tribes all enter the Baiga fold through the gate of marriage. Virginity is a desirable, but not essential condition.

In Menjkadadar (Rewa), a Gond became a Baiga. In Kohka (Rewa), a Gond girl became a Baigin. "That Baiga was servant to the girl's father, and they ran away to Toneapani, and gave two goats and two rupees worth of liquor and a good feast and the girl was made a Baigin." In Bendi, a Gondin has become a Baigin, but she is not fully accepted for only men will eat from her hands. In Bijori (Dindori Tehsil) a Gond named Pithu fell in love with a Baiga girl, and became a Baiga in order to marry her.

The procedure of bringing a wife or more rarely a husband into the tribe through the gate of marriage—and there is no other way in—is by the same ceremonies and with more or less the same expense as is involved in a penalty feast after excommunication. In fact the ceremony is a penalty feast. The Baiga takes his Gondin or Ahirin to his house and marries her by *haldi-pāni* rites. He is automatically excommunicated. He asks for readmission, and gives a feast in the manner I describe in another chapter.[1] When the husband is readmitted, the girl is automatically admitted by his side. "Now her faith in her own tribe is broken, and she is purified. But if she runs away to another man, he will have to give a feast for her again. We can all eat from her hands, but she must remain in that house, and not change."

IV. THE LAWS OF KINSHIP

The kinship system of the Baiga is of the usual classificatory type although, owing to the fact that they speak a dialect of Hindi and in consequence use some of the customary Hindi words for their relations, this is not immediately apparent. The Baiga's attitude, however, is entirely 'classificatory'; he regards everyone whom his own father would regard as a brother as his father, all the women whom his father might marry are his mothers, and so on.

Baiga social custom has obviously had its influence on their terminology.[2] Thus, the same kinship term *mamā* is used for the father's sister's husband and the mother's brother; where there is a cross-cousin marriage, these relationships are combined in the same person. The father-in-law is also called *mamā*.

[1] See p. 204.

[2] A full list of kinship terms will be found in Appendix.

The father's sister, mother's brother's wife and mother-in-law are also as we would expect, described by the same term, *māmi*.

The step-father, the father's younger brother and the mother's younger sister's husband are all called *kakā*. This is probably due to the facts (i) that when a man marries the widow of his elder brother, he is both step-father and uncle to his brother's children, and (ii) that when a man marries a younger sister of his elder brother's wife, his brother's children have to accept him as at once their father's younger brother and their mother's younger sister's husband.

It will be noticed that the mother's brother's daughter and the father's sister's daughter are called *mahina bahin*, and similarly the father's sister's son and mother's brother's son are called *mahina bhai*, for these cross-cousins may marry. But a man's mother's sister's daughter, father's brother's daughter and wife's younger brother's wife are called *bahin*, for he may not marry these.

Different terms are often used for the same class of relatives, according to their age. Most men of the same generation, a man's own brothers, his mother's brother's sons, his mother's sister's sons, his father's brother's sons, his father's sister's sons, are classed together as brothers. The term *bhai* is used if they are younger than the speaker, *dadā* if they are older. A woman calls her husband's elder sister's husband *sadhua*, and his younger sister's husband *bhai*.

For all practical business, there is no relationship more important than that covered by the Hindi term *samdhi*. This is the relation between certain members of families united by marriage. Thus, if a man marries his son, the following members of his daughter-in-law's family will be his *samdhi*:

His son's wife's father.
His son's wife's father's younger brothers.
His son's wife's father's elder brothers.
His son's wife's mother's sisters' husbands, both younger and elder.

The women of the family will be his *samdhin*, that is:

His son's wife's mother.
His son's wife's mother's sisters.
His son's wife's father's brothers' wives.

His own wife will, of course, also be related as *samdhin* to the appropriate persons in the other family.

"My *samdhi*'s duties are many and varied," says Jethu. "He acts as *dosi* in the marriages of my other children. If there is a death in my house, he comes to serve food and shave my head at the Daskaram. If I am excommunicated, he is the first to eat from my hands at the penalty feast."

The right to marry within the circle of relatives is regulated both by clan-exogamy and by the usual Indian laws prohibiting the union of close kin. The Baiga, however, recognize two exceptions to the general custom; they allow the cross-cousin marriage and they accord a remarkable permission to the union of grandparents and grandchildren and other relations who belong to these generations.

This custom is by no means uncommon among the Baiga. Some of them indeed feel a little ashamed of the sometimes striking incongruities involved in such unions, and try to cover it up by declaring it a mere formality. When I discussed it with some Narotia Baiga, for example, they tried to make out that it was a Gond practice unknown to themselves. But they admitted that the old people at least joked about it with their 'grandchildren'. "He calls his grand-daughter his *chhotki* and says he is dying with love for her. The grandmother calls her grandson her *danni*, her *mālik*, her lord and master, and asks him what his wishes are, for she is ready to obey."

Others say that the custom is a formality to prevent a very old man turning into a *raksa*[1] after his death. "When a man cuts a third set of teeth", Deo Singh told me, "then he has entered on a new birth, he is a new man. But he must get 'married', for if he dies 'unmarried' he will turn into a *raksa*. So he marries the daughter of his wife's sister's son. An old woman marries her son's son. They have a regular marriage with the *sāt-bawar*, for they are virgins again once they have cut their third set of teeth."

But this is not the whole story. The danger of relying on general statements instead of concrete examples was illustrated during my visit to Jholar, where one evening the people gave me the 'third set of teeth theory', but assured me that even this practice was unknown among the Bharotia. The very next morning I discovered that Pachlu, the leading Dewar of that very village, was himself married to his wife's sister's son's daughter, a charming young girl who seemed quite devoted to her classificatory grandfather.

In Amadob (Bilaspur), when the mother of Nohari was widowed, she married Nohari's son by *haldi-pāni*. They were Dudh-bhaina.

In Udhor (Dindori), Ketu Patal a Bhumia and relative of Mahatu, died leaving a widow. She married her son's son by *haldi-pāni* rites. She was not very old and bore her grandson two children.

In Karadih (Dindori) my friend Righu married his mother's mother and is still living very happily with her.

[1] See p. 369.

Yogi Dewar has married his daughter's daughter. "Once I had had twenty sons, I was re-born and became a young boy again."

Cross-cousin marriages are also common. It is noticeable that the same kinship term *mamā* is applied to the mother's brother, the father's sister's husband and—significantly—the father-in-law. Of course, in a cross-cousin marriage, the mother's brother and the father's sister's husband are combined in one and the same person.

The cross-cousin marriage means that I can marry the daughter of my mother's brother, or the daughter of my father's sister. But I cannot, of course, marry the daughter of my father's brother—for she belongs to the same *goti*. Nor can I marry my mother's sister's daughter, presumably because my father can marry his wife's sister, whose daughter is therefore my *bahin*.

Fairly common also is the *sāta-palta* marriage which is a reciprocal cross-cousin marriage. In Amtera, for example, Ketu's son had married Ketu's sister's daughter, and Ketu's daughter had married Ketu's sister's son. In this way the marriage expenses were much reduced; there was no outlay on dowries and one celebration served for both weddings.

The Baiga do not observe a very strict code of avoidances. For example, there is no taboo surrounding the persons of the father- or mother-in-law. But there are a few relationships that are fairly strictly regulated, though a breach of the rules does not involve a severer penalty than a coconut or a bottle of liquor.

The most important rule of avoidance separates a girl from her husband's elder brother. He is her *jeth*. She must not look directly at him, or speak to him. She should cover her face in his presence. She must not allow herself to be alone in the same room with him, or give him food or even wash his pots. She should not remain in his company even when other people are present.

A similar, perhaps slightly less rigorous, rule governs a man's relations with his *ded-sās* (wife's elder sister). He may take water from her, but at a distance. He may talk to her, but only through a go-between. He must never be alone in a room with her.

There are few special rules of conduct before parents or parents-in-law. A man does not joke or make love to his wife in their presence, and he ought not to tell a dirty story or use excessive abuse, at least before his mother-in-law. It is considered bad for a man to see the breasts of his mother-in-law. The Baiga do not stand or show any special respect to their parents. If a man is smoking by the fire and his father-in-law is there he should offer him first puff at his pipe. If the mother-in-law comes to fetch her daughter home for any reason, the son should go to her and formally offer her hospitality for the night.

But though there are no rules of avoidance, there is a tradition of hostility between a man or woman and the mother-in-law. In Tilaidabra, when we were sitting by the fire in the evening, the acrid smoke was very troublesome, and however often we moved it followed, perpetually blowing into our eyes. One of the company remarked, "How your mother-in-law loves you!"

A very favourite theme of the songs is the unhappiness of the young wife in a household of her husband's relatives.

> How hard it is to live here!
> My *māmi*[1] hits me with her fists,
> My *nanand*[2] twists my cheeks.
> Only one there is who keeps me happy,
> And that is my handsome young *dewar*.[3]

A man has the right to bully his wife's younger brother. In Amtera I noticed a boy run and hide in real alarm when his uncle suddenly arrived in the house.

The solemn business of relationships is sometimes tiresome, but on the whole the Baiga get a great deal of amusement out of it, especially from the time-honoured and licensed subjects for ribald comment. These are the relations between a man and his elder brother's wife, a girl and her husband's younger brother, a man and his wife's younger sister, a girl and her elder sister's husband, a man and his granddaughter, a woman and her grandson. The point is, of course, that any of these pairs can and perhaps some day will marry one another, and their relationship not only provides much amusement but is the source of a good deal of romance.

A man will have the right, for example, to marry his elder brother's wife if she should be widowed; what wonder if he sometimes anticipates that event and enjoys a pleasant intrigue during the brother's lifetime! And this intrigue, even if discovered, is not taken very seriously. If it were the other way about, if the elder brother intrigued with the younger brother's wife, it would be taken very seriously. And again, a man can at any moment take his wife's younger sister as his *chhotki* if he can get her, and his wife allows him to. If he can't, he has some licence to enjoy her as she is, and his wife is generally complaisant. This relationship is not a matter for jealousy but for jest.

These relations provide constant motives for the songs, of which the following are typical.

[1] Mother-in-law. [2] Husband's younger sister. [3] Husband's younger brother.

i

O my *bhauji*,[1] listen, though I am inconstant,
I am loved by those who care to love.
Listen, give your ear, my *bhauji*, I would sleep with you.
How I want to love you; clasp me to your breast.

ii

In Srawan the rain drenches us with water.
My young *dewar*[2] is combing my wet hair,
And now he spreads his hands over my young body.

iii

Near the bed a lamp is burning.
Look, look, he is with his *bhauji*.
A-re-re! A-re-re! My *dewar* is enjoying me.
He has torn my jacket.

iv

O friend, pass me your pipe,
And let my mind be satisfied.
My mother's brother's daughter is very pretty,
And so my heart is ever hungry.

V. RULES OF ETIQUETTE

Names

Certain rules of etiquette govern the conduct of relations towards one another. The first controls the use of proper names.

A husband must never, except perhaps in Court, use his wife's name, nor may a wife use her husband's. If they do, people say, "Look they've become brother and sister!"

A man should not use the names of his daughter-in-law, his younger brother's wife, or his elder brother's wife.

A woman should not use the name of her husband's elder brother, his younger brother, or her father-in-law.

It is not usual to use the names of dead relatives, 'to stop the memory of sorrow', but there does not seem to be any actual taboo on their use or fear that there is danger in it.

Food

Another set of rules covers the use of *jūtha*, or food left over on the plate, an important matter to a people so hungry and so ill-provided.

[1] Elder brother's wife. [2] Husband's younger brother.

A wife and children may eat the husband's leavings, but he may not eat theirs.

Younger brothers may eat the leavings of elder brothers; younger sisters may eat the leavings of elder sisters; a junior wife may eat an elder's leavings; but not vice versa.

All children before they are mature may eat anybody's leavings. A son and daughter, even after they are married may eat a father's.

Samdhi may eat one another's leavings.

These rules have their bearing on who may eat from the same plate. It is only because a husband may not eat his wife's *jūtha* that they do not eat together from the same plate. They may eat at the same time, and facing one another. The Baiga custom is to serve all the food at once—there are no second helpings—and so there is no need to wait till the husband is finished. A son and daughter may also eat at the same time and in the presence of their parents-in-law.

A father allows his children to eat off his plate while they are young, but not later. Thus it is only *samdhi*, in the end, who can take one another's leavings and eat together off the same plate.

This rule also applies to liquor. A father may give his little son a sip from his leaf-cup, but otherwise the only person with whom he may share it is a *samdhi*.

Salutations

The mode of greeting and salutation is regulated to some extent by kinship. When two *samdhi* meet, they catch each other's arms, pull them to and fro three times and say, *Rām Rām*, stooping slightly and touching each other's knees with the right hand. If they are drinking, they greet one another with *Johar*, instead of *Rām Rām*.

When a son meets his father he touches his feet, and the father raises him and touches him lightly under the chin, making a slight clucking noise with his tongue. When two brothers meet, they clasp each other's arms, the younger touches the elder's feet, and the elder touches the younger's chin. When a son-in-law meets his father-in-law, the greeting is the same, but he says *mamā-jī-rām*.

The proper greeting, by man or woman, to a mother-in-law, however, is to touch her feet and she responds by touching the chin, the Baiga's exiguous substitute for a kiss.

When a girl comes home after a long journey, she falls at her mother's feet, the mother kisses her lightly on either side of the head, and then they sit down opposite each other and both weep loudly for some time.

Son greeting father.
Friend greeting friend.
Father greeting son.

Two women, if they are *samdhi*, clasp each other's arms and touch each other's knees, but do not kiss each other.

When a husband meets his wife, he gives her no greeting and takes no notice of her whatsoever if other people are about.

VI. THE BREAKING OF THE LAWS

The background of the 'incest-situation' among the modern Baiga is the gradually weakening hold of the laws of exogamy upon them. This is not to say that the Baiga regard clan-incest and kin-incest as identical. They are similar in kind, but vary greatly in degree. 'The law of exogamy', says Malinowski, 'the prohibition of marriage and intercourse within the clan is often quoted as one of the most rigid and wholesale commandments of primitive law, in that it forbids sexual relations within the clan with the same stringency, regardless of the degree of kinship between the two people concerned. . . . It lumps together all the men and all the women of the clan as 'brothers' and 'sisters' to each other and debars them absolutely from sexual intimacy. A careful analysis of the relevant facts in the Trobriands completely disposes of this view. It is one of these figments of native tradition, taken over at its face value by anthropology and bodily incorporated into its teachings. In the Trobriands the breach of exogamy is regarded quite differently according to whether the guilty pair are closely related or whether they are only united by bonds of common clanship. As kinship receded, the stringency lessens and, when committed with one who merely belongs to the same clan, the breach of exogamy is but a venial offence, easily condoned.'[1] This passage might equally well have been written as an account of the Baiga.

We will now proceed to a survey of the entire 'incest-situation' in the tribe, beginning with clan-incest, which gives the key to the whole and proceeding to those offences which are treated with greater stringency.

The Baiga offer us an unusually clear example of the functional character of myth and legend. Only those institutions that are vitalized by myth have any living reality to-day. The accounts of the origin of exogamy given in Chapter XI are not very convincing. The stories are not widely known, and they are not very good stories. The most popular of them attributes the foundation of the *goti* to a trick played on Nanga Baiga by Bhagavan. But an institution that was founded in deceit can be evaded by deceit. Partly as a result of this, partly as a result of the bewildering complexity of the Baiga's system of *jāt*, *garh* and *goti*, and the real social

[1] Malinowski: *Crime and Custom in Savage Society* (London, 1932), pp. 82 f.

and economic difficulties of observing them, the Baiga find themselves to-day in a great muddle over their exogamous divisions. A common view is that 'we adopted them because everyone else had them, but we care little for them'.

This applies specially to the *goti*, which were clearly an adaptation of the Gond and Hindu *gotra*. The territorial *garh* are regarded more seriously. Every Baiga, as we have seen, belongs to an endogamous *jāt*, a territorial *garh*, and a rather artificial social division, the *goti*. Geographical conditions ensure that marriages outside the *jāt* are uncommon; where they do occur, the wife is accepted, after the prescribed penalty of a tribal dinner has been paid, into her husband's *jāt*. This is not regarded as a serious offence, but it has far-reaching social consequences, for it completely separates the woman from her family, brings her into a new environment, and probably necessitates her migration to a new district.

It is chiefly in Niwas that problems about 'inter-caste' marriages occur, for here Binjhwar, Muria and Bhumia live side by side. Intermarriage between these *jāt* is regarded with disfavour and merits both social and supernatural penalties. Bisram, a Binjhwar who married a Muria, only suffered a certain loss of social standing—when his house was burnt down, no one would help him because of the Muria girl—but it had no effect on him, for a little later, he married a Bhumia girl as well.

Chagna, Muria of Berkera, however, had a much harder time. He ran away with a Binjhwar's wife. "As we were going through the jungle, we met a tiger—for I had taken a girl of another *jāt*. A week later, a tiger sprang on me in my field, but the neighbours saved me. But that very night, the tiger dragged my two cows out of their shed and killed them. A month later I fell very ill. Baghesur Pat spoke to me in a dream. 'You have married a Binjhwar girl, although you are a Muria; so a tiger has eaten your cows, and will soon eat you.' The next day we killed two goats for Baghesur Pat and I gave a goat to the village, and I got well again."

The division of the tribe into *garh* is based on a sound psychological principle, that the most successful marriages occur between strangers, or at least between people who have not been brought up together. The prohibition of marriage within the *garh* means that a man must take a girl from another village. So Havelock Ellis points out that in regard to incest, 'there is no anti-incestuous instinct, no natural aversion; but a deep stirring of the sexual impulse needs a strong excitement, and for this a new object is required, not one that has become commonplace by familiarity.... It is noteworthy that the most pronounced cases of incestuous love occur between brother and sister who have not been brought up together, so that the influence of familiarity is absent.'[1]

The *goti*, however, are merely artificial; they were borrowed from the Gond, and are less seriously regarded. The *goti* have a sociological, but the *garh* a psychological, basis. And so we find throughout the Baiga country the rule that where two lovers have a different *goti* and the same *garh*, they can marry or have intercourse only with great difficulty. But where they have the same *goti* and different *garh*, they can marry with ease.

Thus, in Niwas there is no penalty at all for breaking the *goti*, but a small penalty for breaking the *garh*. In Kawardha, the Pandripani Baiga said that if two members of the Durwa *goti*, one a Jajulia and one a Ghatia, wanted to marry, they could give their village two rupees' worth of liquor and do so. At Bodai also, the Baiga said that the *goti* could be broken with a bottle of liquor. In Taliapani, it costs two rupees to break the *garh* and only eight annas to break the *goti*.

"We don't bother about the *garh* very much nowadays," said Dasseru of Bondar. "We are told not to marry here, not to marry there. But we must follow where our eyes lead us."

And Mahatu told me that "nowadays many Baiga go to girls of their own *goti*, but we don't consider it a very great sin. Since bewar was stopped all our life has been sin, so why should we worry about a little sin like the breaking of the *goti*."[2]

There are, of course, stricter views. A Dadaria song from the Binjhwar country in Baihar taunts a girl—"You have lovers from your own *goti*." One of the few cases of Baiga suicide that I have known comes from Bilaspur and was apparently due to shame and anger over a breach of the *goti*.

"Kuhutu's father and Bukiya's father are brothers, so Kuhutu and Bukiya are of the same *goti*, Durwa. One day, Kuhutu's wife, Mahaki, accused him of going to Bukiya. He took no notice and continued to do so. One day Mahaki went with the other women of the village to the forest to get mangoes. She lagged behind, and when no one was looking, climbed up a tree, tied a rope round her neck and the other end round a branch, jumped down and died.

"Kuhutu then took Bukiya openly to his house. He had to give a feast for her, and then they were both admitted to the tribe."

[1] Havelock Ellis: *Psychology of Sex* (London, 1934), p. 80.

[2] There is a reference, which I have not had the opportunity to verify, in the 1911 Census to the Poyam Gond of Betul who disregard the rules of exogamy, and allow brothers and sisters to marry. There is also a sect of Ganda in Chhattisgarh who broke away from the main tribe, and deliberately abandoned the idea of exogamy, allowing the union of brother and sister.—(*Census of India*, 1911. Vol. x, p. 134.)

But it may be that the suicide was due to simple jealousy.

I once had a good instance of the way the official attitude is put before, not only the ethnographer, but even a member of another tribe, though actual practice may be in glaring contradiction to it.

One evening in Bohi I was talking to Jethu. He observed that he belonged to the Durwa *goti*. I tactlessly exclaimed, "But your son-in-law Deriya is also Durwa; your daughter is a Durwa-beti and she has married a Durwa-beta."

A Gond there began to laugh when he heard this. "Look at these Baiga," he said. "They break everything, even their *goti*." But Jethu was not put out. He smiled in a superior manner and said, "What does Deriya know about his *goti*? His parents died when he was a boy. He is really a Morabi. How could I marry my daughter to a Durwa-beta?"

But everyone present knew that was just what he had done. Yet not a word was said, probably because Jethu was too important.

On the other hand, the rather insignificant Kath-bhaina Marhu had a very bad time through marrying a girl of his own Korcho *goti*. There was no other girl suitable, even this girl was much older than he, and his father arranged the wedding. There was a big pot full of liquor, four rupees' worth. When the visitors came, they picked up the pot and smashed it, and went away, refusing to take any part in the marriage. But the very first night that Marhu slept with his elderly wife, he was so disgusted with her erotic technique that he turned her out of the house, and his family were forgiven.

From clan-incest it is an easy step to kin-incest, though the latter is much more seriously regarded. The Baiga themselves say that the *garh* were instituted to "prevent brothers and sisters sleeping together". With the breakdown of the rules of exogamy, we will not be surprised at finding a fairly liberal attitude to kin-incest.

Here again we find ourselves faced with many differing degrees of guilt. A connection between mother and son, which is very rare, is regarded with real horror; it is almost as bad to have intercourse with your father's younger wife. In the same class comes intercourse between a man and his mother-in-law, and a woman and her father-in-law.

These are the major crimes. After them, comes a connection between father and daughter, between a brother and his younger brother's wife (against which there are very stringent, but, I think, purely social restraints) and between a man and his father's sister.

Brother-sister incest is held to be bad, but not so bad as the relations I have just described.

For a man to go to his mother's sister, is regarded as a small fault easily condoned by a tribal feast.

The Baiga do not regard it as bad for a man to have intercourse with his wife's younger sister, or his elder brother's wife.

Let us first of all consider the official Baiga attitude to incest, the attitude which will be explained to the casual traveller and accepted by him as normal for the tribe. In the first place, the Baiga will say that incest, in its more serious forms, never occurs; they will then declare that it could not occur because of the severe social and supernatural sanctions which forbid it. For, in the first place, incest is the cause of earthquakes, of the loosening of the nails which Nanga Baigin drove into the earth to keep it steady at the beginning of the world. It brings leprosy, broken eyes, and worms in the feet. It is punished by social ostracism, it breaks up the family, it leads to barrenness and sterility.

"Even if they offer us fifty feasts," Mahatu once said, "we would never re-admit them to the tribe." And Lahakat declared that "Bhagavan could never give a child as the result of such a union".

The Folk-tales have many references to incest and generally condemn it. A story from Rewa describes how a man takes his own daughter away from her husband and lives with her, though she has a child from her husband. When the villagers ask who the girl is, and whose is the child, he says his daughter is his wife, and the child is his. But one night, his cow speaks to him. "You have lived with your own daughter", she says. "You will become a leper." And so he does, and worms devour his feet till he dies.

In a Bopsa story, an old man falls in love with his daughter-in-law, and after several attempts succeeds in seducing her. But his son finds out what has happened and says, "Father, you've been to my wife; I'll go to your daughter, my sister". The child is so small that she dies. Three times more does the father go to his daughter-in-law, and after that a kind of madness comes upon the family. The son cuts off his penis with an axe, the father burns off his with the fire. The girl continues to live with the two impotent men, and is known as *bāp beta ki dauki*. Soon she is drowned, the father falls from a tree and is killed, and the son is eaten by a tiger. This highly moral story reveals what everybody knows never happens as a result of incest!

In a Pondi story, father and son are rivals for the same girl. The father marries her, but the son says, "You may be my father, but one day I'll carry off your wife". The girl also prefers the boy to his father. In the end the son murders his father and carries off the girl. We are not told what happens to them, but the general tone of the story is disapproving.

The myths generally are favourable to incest, but the story of Banbindra Raja and the origin of seed[1] seems to condemn it. Banbindra has so much seed in his belly that his wife cannot contain it all, and so he goes to his daughter, who for shame turns herself into a bamboo. The Mandla legend of the Sun and Moon condemns brother-sister incest, for the bed of sin on which the Sun and Moon have slept together runs away to hide beneath the ocean, but is thrown by Nanga Baiga up into the sky.

The words *bahinchod* and *daichod* are not part of the Baiga's vocabulary of abuse; but it is very common in marriage songs, and in the songs that accompany the Laru-kaj, for people to accuse each other of incest. This is generally, however, taken with the utmost good humour.

A few songs also openly and freely refer to incest.

i

You may sow *masur dal* in a field or in a marsh,
According to your mind.
So the father slept all night with his son's wife.
He enjoyed her dhoti.

ii

Kodon is growing on the borders of the village.
My uncle is enjoying his own daughter.
See how he tugs at her breasts!

iii

The boy is weeping, he longs for his wife.
But it is his father who enjoys her all night.
So take me away, away from here,
Away to another land.

Two stories may be quoted as illustrating the stricter view of incest. The first, from Bohi village in Pandaria, was told me as a true history.

'An old Baiga named Dariya had a son Dasseru and a daughter Ledhi. They were all very poor; they had nothing to wear, nothing to eat. The children grew up and became mature. In one corner of the hut the father used to sleep with his wife; in the other corner Dasseru slept with Ledhi. Each was ready for a mate, but where was the money for the marriage? So as they slept together under the one blanket, the boy used to go daily to his sister.

'Then one day they left their parents, and ran away together to another village. They had children. But almost at once Ledhi grew old and ugly, and was always ailing.

[1] See p. 319.

'After some time, their daughter in turn became mature, and the mother being old and ugly, Dasseru caught his own daughter and went to her. She at once began to scream, "Look, mother, what my father is doing!"

'But Ledhi said, "He is not doing anything, child. He's only putting you to sleep". Then when Ledhi had gone to sleep, Dasseru again went to his daughter, and now the child's vagina became swollen and bleeding. When he saw that, Dasseru knew he had done a great wrong, and he took poison and died.'

The second story, which comes from Kawardha State, is obviously fictitious. It is interesting to note that I was told the same tale by a Gond woman. In her version, the 'marriage' was not consummated; the children died to save themselves from the crime. This is entirely in the Gond tradition, which regards incest with far greater severity than the Baiga.[1]

'A Baiga and his wife had seven sons and one daughter. Six of the sons were married, but not the youngest. One day the youngest boy went to the bewar and brought a mushroom. He put it in the house and said, "Whoever eats this will be my wife". No one ate it, but his little sister did so by mistake. Then the six sisters-in-law said, "Who has eaten it?" "I have", said the little girl. "Then you'll have to be his wife". But the girl thought they were only joking. When her brother came back from the bewar, however, he told her that she would really have to marry him. When she heard that, she was very angry. She took the seed of a semur tree in her hand and went to the jungle. There she sowed it, and said, "If you are truly a semur tree, grow at once". Immediately it was as high as her waist. Then she said, "If you are truly a semur, don't break when I sit on you." So she sat on it, and it didn't break. Then she said, "If you're truly a semur, climb up into the sky". The semur at once grew up into the sky carrying her with it.

'Then all the family came to find her. Her mother called to her. "Tell me, am I to call you *beti* (daughter) or *bahu* (daughter-in-law)?" The girl called down, "How can I tell, am I to call you *dai* (mother) or *māmi* (mother-in-law)?" Then came the father. "Am I to call you *beti* (daughter) or *bhai-bahu* (daughter-in-law)?" he cried. She answered, "How do I know—are you my *mamā* (father-in-law) or my *dadā* (father)?" Then her elder brother asked, "Are you my *bahin* (sister) or my *bahu* (younger brother's wife)?" She replied, "Are you my *bha* (brother) or *jeth* (husband's elder brother)?" Then her sisters-in-law cried, "Are you our *nanand* (husband's

[1] It is interesting to note that in the Santal version of the story the 'marriage' (as in the Gond version) is not consummated. After the death of the brother and sister, their blood, though it flowed in the same ditch, was never mixed. And though their bodies were burnt on the same pyre, the smoke went in different directions, indicating that "it will never do to marry brother and sister." Bodding: op. cit., pp. 369 ff.

younger sister) or our *dharāni* (husband's younger brother's wife)?" She replied, "Are you my *bhauji* (elder brother's wife) or my *jethāni* (husband's elder brother's wife)?" At last the youngest brother called to her, "Are you my *bahin* (sister) or my *dauki* (wife)?" And she answered, "How do I know—are you my *bhai* (brother) or my *dauka* (husband)?" Then they all went home.

'At night there was heavy rain. They took their food and slept. The girl climbed down from the tree and came to the house. She stood at the door and cried to everyone in turn, but only when she took the name of the little brother did anyone hear. He got up and let her in, and cooked for her. When they had eaten, they slept together on one bed and he went to her. Then with his axe, he killed her, and afterwards himself. In the morning they all thought they were sleeping late and laughed at them until they went in and saw what had happened.'

But the general day-to-day attitude is comparatively lax. "It is not a very great sin", said a 'civilised' Bhaina Baiga of Bilaspur, "to go to your mother or sister. The real crime is to kill a cow."

"When a horse neighs"—this was how Lahakat of Amadob explained it—"you must give it something to eat. So when a boy or a girl is excited with desire, they must be satisfied, no matter how. Let it be father and daughter, brother and sister, mother and son. They will go off into the jungle together. Then if they are caught, they will be ostracized, but if they give a feast they will be taken back into the tribe."

The Binjhwar Baiga of Baihar, as we would expect, take the Hindu view that the killing of a cow is the greatest of all crimes. "To go to your mother or sister", they told me in Baihar, "is less a crime than to kill a cow. The penalty for the first is a four days' feast, and five rupees' worth of liquor. But for the second you must give five days' *ghī-chapāti*, twelve days' *dāl bhāt* and ten rupees' worth of liquor". They quoted a case of a man who lived with his sister and had to give only five rupees' worth of liquor. In the same village a Baiga killed a cow. He not only got worms in his hands and feet, but he had to spend forty rupees on a tribal dinner.

In Niwas the Baiga say that incest is as bad as murder if a man does it by force. 'But when both brother and sister are happy and think nothing of it, then it doesn't matter at all'.

We have so far considered the stricter aspects of the Baiga attitude to incest, taking the word in its narrower sense of such intercourse with close kin as custom forbids. We may now proceed to examine how far a more liberal attitude prevails.

Nanga Baiga and Nanga Baigin were brother and sister. "What were they to do?" asks the legend. "What is the harm of it?" asked Nanga Baiga. When they were old enough they desired each other. "What need of marriage?" asked Nanga Baiga. They were both naked. He used to go and bathe in a pond and his sister went to watch him. He came to her on the bank and said, "If you're ready, let's do it". She answered, "If you have a mind to it, I'm ready". So they became mated among the trees on the bank of the pond. Thus simply did incest come into the world.

Further, Gunshian and Gunshiain, the children of Nanga Baiga, were brother and sister, and they married, apparently without disastrous consequences. In another story, Mahadeo was Amardevi's son; he married his own mother, and she was transformed into Parvati.

A Niwas folk-tale describes how the hero marries his deceased wife's three sisters, after they had murdered the wife, and all lived happily afterwards.

The Baiga discuss the matter without embarrassment, and are always willing to provide information about it. My impression is that most of them have little or no innate repulsion towards incest, and they avoid it chiefly for fear of the social sanctions with which it is associated. There is also a vague idea that it may be dangerous; earthquake or disease may come upon the guilty pair. There is no clear picture. I will quote a number of examples which will illustrate the very varied reactions that the same thing may produce on different minds, and the danger of attempting in such a case to make definite rules or offer dogmatic statements.

'In Dumgarh, a brother and sister, children of the same parents, ran away together. Their names were Gunju and Jethi. They went to Pendra and lived, apart from us all, until they died. They never returned.'

'In Dumgarh also, there lived Mahatu and Keji, brother and sister they were, born of the same parents. Mahatu was always looking out for a chance to copulate with Keji. One day he was standing on the bank of the river, and Keji came for water. He asked her for some, but she refused to give any, so he broke her pot and carried her under a mohlain tree and copulated with her there. Then they ran away together to Gurridadar. Keji's husband and father went and brought her home. They gave four days' feast for her and five rupees' worth of liquor, and she was taken back.'

In Chhindpani, Saranja lived with his wife Jethi and his daughter Changu at the same time. This went on for years, till he was an old man. He gave thirteen days *dāl bhāt*, two days *ghī chapāti* and twelve rupees for liquor, and he was readmitted to the tribe. But the girl, though she lived separately after that, could never get a husband, for everyone knew that she would not bear a child.

In Gurridadar, a Binjhwar Baiga lived with his step-daughter, and before his death his hands and feet were eaten by worms.

'In Boira a man lived with his sister. Her eyes broke open. As Bhagavan had punished them, we did not trouble them further. We took no feast from them.'

'In Lamda of Mandla Tehsil, an old Baiga had a son and a daughter. One day, in a dream, Bara Deo came and said, "Marry your son to your daughter. If you don't, you'll die". Next day, the old man went to the *panch* and asked their leave to do so. But he didn't tell them his dream. They all said he was mad. So secretly he married his son and daughter inside the house, and kept a Lamsena to save the girl's name. Then he died as a punishment, and the girl also died. The boy is still living. We did not decaste him; why should we? He had done nothing, it was his father's fault.'

'In the old days, in Bodai, a boy married his own mother after his father's death. It was horrible, we do not care to talk of it.'

'There were two brothers living in Pandripani. One married his father's *chotki*, the other married his own sister. They went to live in Kukarahi, where they still are. One day there was a death in my house. The *chotki*, who is my own sister, came for the mourning, but we all beat her and drove her out. "Don't show your face here, you son-copulator," they cried. But the others said, "Let her go, the sin is hers. It is not your responsibility". Now both these couples are living very happily, and don't feel ashamed. The mother and son have given a feast, but we take food now from all of them.'

'Gahania, Kath-Bhaina, ran away with his father's sister, his *māmi*, to Kapripani. The people there refused to eat or drink with them, and he tired of it, he left her and came home. We did not punish him.'

'Chamru, Kath-Bhaina of Chulpani, a boy of eighteen, married his mother's sister's daughter and lived with her four years till she died of snake-bite. It was wrong; she was his *bahin*; when he came home he had to give a feast.'

Chapter VI

BAIGA JURISPRUDENCE

IN this chapter, I propose to examine the Baiga system of tribal jurisprudence which I will for the moment confine to its negative rulings, to that division of customary rules to which are attached the greatly dreaded sanctions of excommunication.

The Baiga system runs parallel to the Indian Penal Code and the Forest Act, by whose provisions a large part of tribal life is, of course, governed. But it is of the greatest interest to note how completely unimportant these provisions are in the moral and social consciousness of the Baiga. No social stigma attaches to the thief—provided he does not steal from another Baiga. He may even be regarded as a hero if he effects a successful theft from a Government Reserved Forest. Adultery is punishable under Section 497 of the Indian Penal Code, but it is not punishable under the Baiga code unless it has been committed with someone outside the tribe. Even then is is only the woman who is penalized. Kidnapping, or abduction of women, is very severely punished by Sections 365 and 366 of the Indian Penal Code, but a tribe which for centuries has practised marriage by capture is not likely to take such laws seriously. Conviction for an offence involves no penalty or even discredit; but to go to prison does, for it is believed that no one can observe his tribal rules in jail.

But in fact hardly any Baiga have been to jail, and it is the rarest thing for them even to appear in either a Criminal or Civil Court. They are frequently convicted of offences against the forest laws, but these are nearly always compounded by the department and are very rarely taken into court.[1]

The existence of a strong and all-pervading system of official jurisprudence has to some extent determined the nature of the Baiga's code of customary rules. It is, of course, inaccurate to speak of this as a code, although the primitive Indian mind shows a surprising readiness to codify its customs, and I should not be surprised if sooner or later some literate

[1] During the past five years in the Karanjia Range 33 Baiga were convicted of illegal felling and removal of trees, 3 of illicit grazing, and 15 of illicitly killing sambhar.

Baiga did not do so. In 1934 a Gond Court was established at Dindori, and produced a hypertrophied list of tribal offences and the fines which breach of them would involve. A drink of liquor would cost the culprit twenty-five rupees, the village that indulged in the Karma dance would be fined fifty, and so on. The Mehera also, a semi-aboriginal caste of Mandla and Bilaspur, allowed their Mahant, or chief priest, to codify a list of laws which forbade them the use of tobacco, turned them all into teetotallers and vegetarians, and imposed the severest penalties for anyone who ran away with another man's legally married wife. It was only when a member of the Mahant's own family committed a flagrant breach of this last regulation that the code was abandoned, though many of the actual rules survive.

Baiga jurisprudence concerns itself mainly with maintaining the integrity of the tribe on the one hand, and its prestige on the other.

For example, if a woman commits adultery with someone outside the Baiga fold, there is a risk that she may bring alien blood into the tribe. This is the real reason for the 'double standard' which is expressed by the Baiga in the proverb—'Man is a brass *batuwa* and woman an earthen *handi*.' This proverb derives from the custom that if anyone outside your caste or tribe touches your earthen pot, it is so completely defiled that you must smash it to pieces. On visiting a Baiga house, you may sometimes be welcomed by the sight of the women hurriedly removing their pots into a place of safety. But if a brass pot is similarly infected by alien contact, it need not be thrown away, a little water frees it of the deed. So if a man commits adultery outside the tribe, he washes and is clean. But if a woman does so, she is excommunicate, and her readmission will depend largely on the social standing of her lover.

Marriage, or living openly with a member of another tribe, is a different matter; but here it is not so much a question of sexual defilement as of domestic complications. The Baiga who marries a Panka girl must let her use his kitchen and cook for him. He is thus excommunicated, not for having sexual intercourse with a Pankin, but for eating from her hands. The rule, which is often in practice disregarded, is that a man can have intercourse with anybody, even a Chamarin, so long as he does not eat with her. If he marries a Gondin, an Ahirin or a Brahmanin, his wife may, after the appropriate penalties have been paid, be admitted into the Baiga fold; though as we have seen, there is much divergence of opinion on this point. A Baiga woman who has been married to or kept by a Gond, Ahir or Brahmin may be readmitted, but if her lover has been a Panka, a Chamar, an Agaria, a Mehera, a Mussalman or a Christian, she can never be forgiven. "If a girl goes to a Mussalman, that is for life and death." We will see shortly how very often this rule is, in practice, set aside. Laws, or the Baiga as for civilized people, depend greatly on who you are. An Abelard can ignore ecclesiastical regulations which would crush a mere curate with a Pass degree.

Tribal integrity is also imperilled when a man goes to jail, so on his release a convict has to give a tribal dinner before he is readmitted to tribal privileges. This is one of the most fruitful causes that makes the tribesmen habitual criminals. They come out of jail and are cast on the world without resources. They have to pay a heavy penalty to their neighbours and as often as not have to steal or cheat to get the necessary funds.

The 'naked Baiga' has few objects of finery; he has little jewellery and scanty clothes. But he does pay a great deal of attention to his hair, which in tribal estimation is one of the most important of the secondary sexual characters. We need not therefore be surprised to find that the Baiga consider that anyone who allows himself to be barbered by alien hands has betrayed the sexual integrity of the tribe and must be punished by temporary excommunication.

Anything that lowers the prestige of the tribe is as seriously regarded as an offence that impairs its integrity. For the Baiga is subject to an immense and delightful vanity. He is Bhumia-raja, lord of the earth; he is the true Pashupati, master of wild animals: he is the child of Dharti Mata, and knows all her secrets, he is the master of magic, the adept inventor of love-charms, the controller of wind and rain and fire. For such a being to allow himself to be beaten is no ordinary disgrace, and is severely punished. Here is a striking divergence from the Indian Penal Code! There is no penalty for inflicting hurt, even grievous hurt, on someone else; there is a severe penalty for letting someone else inflict hurt or grievous hurt on you. In Tilaidabra, the Bhaina Baiga told me that if any one of them allowed himself to be beaten with a shoe by a Panka, a Mehera, a Chamar, or an Agaria he would be excommunicate for ten years and then have to give a six days' feast with four goats before he would be forgiven. A beating by a Gond would be less expensive, and curiously no penalty attaches to a beating by an Englishman, "for we are the wives of the English and so he has a right to beat us". *Sirkāri juta* is also excluded from the operations of tribal law: it is no offence to be beaten by a policeman or a forest-guard —for this happens so frequently that the Baiga would be financially ruined if they took it too seriously.

The maintenance of tribal prestige accounts, I think, for the curious provision that the Baiga must not kill a dog, a cat or a cow. This is not a universal or genuinely Baiga regulation; it has been borrowed by them from their Hindu neighbours because they found that the latter despised them for doing such things. The Hindus are equally emphatic about the wrongfulness of keeping pigs and chickens, but economic pressure has so far saved the Baiga from yielding here.

In the section on menstruation I consider fully both the positive and negative rulings of Baiga law upon that subject. To maintain these rules intact is certainly a point of tribal prestige. In the same way, Baiga credit would suffer if they did not uphold the dignity and order of their rules of exogamy and kinship. These also have been fully considered elsewhere. Bestiality is penalized, partly because it is a practice unworthy of a Baiga, partly because it is aesthetically repugnant and implies that the culprit is unable to obtain normal sexual satisfaction.

Baiga 'Criminal Law' covers also a number of other offences which it is not easy to classify or understand. The most mysterious of these is the dreaded crime of getting vermin in a wound, which must be heavily expiated and is a sure sign of the divine displeasure. Another almost equally serious offence is for a woman to allow her ear to be torn. The Baigin often wear in the lower lobe of the ear a very thick circular bit of wood called a *tarki*, which distends the hole so much that its lower rim is a mere thin pendulous strip of flesh, and very liable to get torn. Should this happen, however, it is regarded as a major social disaster, and Russell has suggested that 'the continuous distension of the lobe of the ear and the large hole produced is supposed to have some sympathetic effect in opening the womb and making child-birth more easy. The tearing of the ear might then be considered to render the woman incapable of bearing a child, and the penalties attached to it would be sufficiently explained'.

A woman with a torn ear is called Buchi, Kantuti or Luti. There is a proverb about a vain and silly woman. "She has a torn ear, but wants to wear a *tarki*."

I confess I have no explanation to offer for the rule that if a Baiga woman makes a hole in her nose and wears a *nathni* she should be temporarily excommunicate.

Another class of offences are those which suggest that a man is impotent or 'unmanly'. A man is socially exiled for allowing his wife to beat him or for allowing her or compelling her to take the lead in sexual intercourse. 'She must not ride upon her husband. Her place is below.'

It will be obvious, therefore, that Baiga jurisprudence is the direct product of Baiga psychology, and is a necessary part of the magical, social and economic system of the tribe. There is nothing artificial or arbitrary about it, and it may be presumed that it is on the whole fairly carefully observed. We will see in a moment how far this is so, but I must first give the regular tariff of penalties and show who is responsible for exacting them.

It is hardly possible to avoid giving a list of the penalties attached to the different breaches of tribal rule that we have been describing, for these are a matter of absorbing interest to the Baiga. The penalties, of course, fluctuate like prices in the bazaar and thus have a similar hold on the attention, but they do give some idea of the relative degree of abhorrence with which various offences are regarded.

Vermin in a wound. Ganja Baiga of Chiklatola got vermin in a wound in his head. He gave two rupees' worth of liquor, one goat, and ten *kuro* of *kodai.* Samaru of Dengurjam, who had vermin in his feet; and Chamru of Chiklatola, who had vermin in a wound on his chest, suffered the same penalty.

Tearing of the Ear. In Ghatabara, a woman's ear was torn, and her husband Bhainu gave a rupee's worth of liquor and a pig by the river, a rupee's worth of liquor and a hen by the gate, and seven rupees' worth of liquor, a goat and twenty *kuro* of *kodai* in the house. Three days later he had to give three rupees' worth of liquor and a feast to visitors from distant villages who arrived late.

Killing a dog, cat or cow. In Mandla Tehsil this seems to be taken very seriously, and the people say that the killing of a cat or dog can only be expiated by a feast costing fifty rupees. In Bilaspur a Kath-Bhaina Baiga had to give a feast of forty rupees in Tilaidabra for killing a cow. In Mandla, in Kajheri village, however, the people only demanded seven rupees' worth of liquor, two goats and a feast.

Going to Jail. In Kajheri also a Baiga named Lerboha broke through the wall of a house to steal, and was given six months imprisonment. For this he had to give a feast costing fifteen rupees. But when Girdhari of the same village went into a neighbour's house to assault his wife, and was fined fifty rupees by the court, he had to pay no tribal penalty, for though convicted he had not actually been to jail.

Bestiality. For intercourse with a goat, a mare or a hen, which is regarded as a very minor offence, only five rupees' worth of liquor, or as we would say, 'Drinks all round' is demanded. "I have often known it happen," says Lahakat casually, "but it doesn't matter very much."

Breach of the Menstruation Rules. In Dengurjam, Chuniya's wife touched the cooking-pots and had to give a five rupees' feast and a rupee of liquor. In Belki, a Baiga took food from a menstruous Gondin and had to give a goat, fifteen *kuro* of rice and three rupees of liquor. If a man has intercourse with his wife at this period, over and above the supernatural sanctions that are invoked, he must give a goat, five *kuro* of rice and a rupee of liquor. In Pondi of Mandla Tehsil, a Baiga who beat his wife at this time had to give five rupees for liquor; had he beaten her with a shoe, they told me, he would have had to have given fifteen.

Allowing oneself to be beaten. A Bhaina Baiga of Tilaidabra who allowed a Panka Kotwar to beat him with a shoe was excommunicate for ten years, and had to give a feast lasting six days and including four goats. An elder wife who was driven from her house in favour of a *chotki*, invited her husband to a party, made him drunk, and kicked him five times in the presence of a *panch*. For this he was excommunicated, but no penalty attached to the woman.

Clan-exogamy and *Incest.* In Pandaria, for breaking the *garh*, two rupees of liquor; for breaking the *goti*, eight annas. For a son to have intercourse with his mother, the penalty is a four days' feast and five rupees for liquor. In Baihar a case of brother-sister incest was penalized by only five rupees for liquor. But in Dumgarh the same offence cost four days' feasting and five rupees for liquor.

Marriage outside the Tribe. In Pondi of Mandla, Renda married a Gondin. He gave a feast of fifty rupees, and they were both received into the tribe. In Satiya village of Dindori, the same offence was expiated by twelve rupees of liquor, three goats, a *khandi* and a half of rice; and in Bilaspur a Bhaina Baiga gave five rupees' worth of liquor, one goat, and ten *kuro* of *kodai*.

Miscellaneous. For all minor offences like piercing the nose, or getting your hair cut by a barber, there is a flat rate of a feast, with a pig or goat, to the immediate neighbours and two or three rupees' worth of liquor.

Such are the official and public penalties prescribed, and not infrequently inflicted, for breach of tribal custom. But Mahatu tells me, "Nowadays we never get what we want. We demand a seven days' feast, with seven goats and twenty rupees' worth of liquor. We think ourselves lucky if we get a three days' feast with a pig, and ten rupees' worth of liquor."

Who inflicts these penalties, and who decides when a man or woman has committed a breach of tribal law? In the first place we must remove from our minds any idea of a tribal court, a trial, a central or presiding authority. This is how Mahi describes the process of excommunication. "Suppose a girl has gone to a Panka. Someone has seen her. She begins to talk. Then one evening, when that girl goes to the well to get water, the women draw away from her, they say, 'Don't touch our water-pots, don't come too near us.' A few days afterwards, when the women have had time to talk to their husbands while they sleep together, perhaps the girl's father or her brother is sitting with the men. They say, 'No, we won't take your pipe, we can't smoke with you.' Then the family knows that the girl has committed some fault. When next the village

The Village Tribunal: women gossiping by the well.
Woman cooking in a field.

gathers together for a festival or a dance, then the girl's father calls out, 'What has my family done that you won't share our pipe or eat with us?' Then all the people tell him, and generally he gives a small feast to the elders of the village on behalf of the family, and after that they share his pipe again. But the girl's fate is decided by the *panch*."

Now the *panch*, in a Baiga village, is not a definite body with members and a President. It is rather a group of important villagers with a quorum of five. There may be many more present to decide the culprit's fate. The headman of the village, the landlord, the Kotwar or village watchman, the leading Dewar or gunia, may not have any influence over them. There is no rule. A certain power of decision, a reputation for integrity, the command of some possessions or many sons, a record of tribal loyalty—these things give a man ascendency in the council. But there is nothing fixed or definite, no rules of procedure, and probably it is the women behind the scenes who really rule.

The real arbiter of tribal destiny is, therefore, tribal opinion. This very rarely finds a single spokesman, though among the Gond and lower Hindu castes dictators do occasionally arise who rule their communities with great strictness. This normally occurs at a time of social awakening and reform.

One more point must be considered, the extreme contagiousness of excommunication. This is, of course, one of its most powerful sanctions, for many a boy or girl who would care little for the bad opinion of the elders of the village is crushed by the domestic commotion that follows on the father's pipe being refused. The rule is that if one member of a particular household group is excommunicate, all the other members—who are regarded partly as being responsible, partly as having inevitably suffered some contagion through food or water—are excommunicate also. Thus when Nanas, the wife of Raunu, who had quarrelled with him and gone to live for a time with her parents in Karanjia, was excommunicated, her husband was not involved, as it was held that he could hardly, under the circumstances, be responsible. But her father, mother, elder sister and brother-in-law, who were all living in the house at the time, were infected and had to give a small penalty feast to the neighbours before anyone would eat or smoke with them. Nanas herself had to give a much bigger feast at a later date.

An unmarried boy or girl living with their parents infects them, and if the boy marries and continues to live at home, his wife may infect both him and her parents-in-law. If he lives separately, only he himself will be infected. When the daughter marries, her parents are free of her unless she leaves her husband and returns home. Contagion operates, in fact, not through kinship but through residence, just as it would in the case of an actual disease.

A very good example of this occurred in Boira. Some time ago a poor Baiga named Raitu, who had already an elderly wife with several children, took a beautiful young girl as his *chhotki*. For some reason the village immediately got suspicious. The elders were jealous that so poor a man should take a second, and attractive, wife; the women could not understand why the girl should marry so poor and elderly a man. Then one day the girl was seen in the early morning near the house of a Mussalman merchant who had established himself in the neighbourhood. Instantly the word went round that Raitu had married the girl on behalf of the Mussalman, and that she was visiting the latter every night. No one dreamt of sitting up to watch to see if this was true; no one thought of asking either Raitu, or the girl, or the Mussalman about it: but when Raitu's wives next went to the well, the other women began to abuse them, and all removed their water-pots well out of their reach. Raitu's elder wife was so angry that the following day she tried to poison the *chhotki* who nearly died. When she recovered she ran away home.

But the mischief was done. Raitu, his daughter, and both his wives were excommunicate. The *chhotki*'s parents were not infected, even though the girl went home to live with them, for they were no longer responsible for her after marriage, and they were careful not to allow her to bring water for the household or enter the kitchen. Raitu gave a penalty feast, but he was so annoyed with the people of Boira for their behaviour to him that he moved to another village and gave the feast there, carefully omitting to invite any of the Boira people. For a month or so all went well. Then came the Dassera festival and some of the people who had taken part in Raitu's feast went to see their friends and relations in Boira. But these refused to smoke with them, and later when everyone was drunk there was a tremendous quarrel. The outcome of this was that the Boira people refused to accept Raitu's feast as valid since they had not been invited and every single person who had taken part in the feast was declared excommunicate. So they all had to give penalty feasts, to which they were careful to invite the people of Boira who for a month or two did little else but go here and there eating dinners, and at the end of that time, Raitu borrowed some money and gave another feast and was forgiven. But since his *chhotki* had left him, this feast did not, as it were, 'cover' her and her father had to give a separate and special feast for her.

What would have happened if Raitu had refused to give the second penalty feast? In the first place, it would have been difficult for him to marry his children later on. He had two little daughters. He might have found husbands for them outside the tribe, but it would have been unlikely. Then, he would never be able to entertain any one in his house. If his own mother came to see him, he would not be able even to wash her feet with water or give her a drink of *pej*. His wife would be continually insulted down by the well, and would come home in a bad temper. He himself would be able to attend all the tribal ceremonies and weddings, even to play a leading part in them, but when the *chungi* was handed to and fro, he would be unable to take it, and he would feel that people were looking at him, strangers asking what had happened, his friends a little ashamed. Furthermore, the excommunicate stands on *pāpi-dharti*, the soil of sin, where none of the magical safeguards of the Baiga operate. He might be killed by a tiger, attacked by evil spirits, his crops might be blighted and destroyed.

Excommunication weighs most heavily on the head of a family. A young girl, especially if she is vivacious and attractive, may hardly notice it except for the constant nagging of her relatives. She is saved from the burdensome duties of cooking and fetching water, the question of the pipe does not arise, even if the women at the well are sometimes rude, all the boys of the village will be after her. For an excommunicate girl has a flavour about her; it is evident that she is no ordinary girl, and is prepared for adventure. She probably enjoys herself more than she has ever done before—for a few years. Then comes the longing for children and a home, and she must either get herself readmitted into the tribe or marry outside it. Generally by now she has established intimate relations with everyone in the village, and the way back is not made difficult.

An ugly or deformed girl has a much harder fate, for here there is the added danger that she may be accused of being a witch. But witchcraft, it is curious to note, is not in itself a thing that brings excommunication. There are many well-established witches who enjoy all their tribal privileges.

Once again, we come back to the fact that everything depends on who you are. Raitu would not have been given nearly so much trouble had he not been a poor man. The case of Ruksa Dewar, a leading magician of the Karanjia Range, also illustrates this. He was excommunicate for having intercourse with his own daughter-in-law. The total cost of this adventure was estimated by his village as two rupees for liquor before they would take his pipe. Then before they would eat with him, they demanded six rupees for liquor, two goats and six *khandi* of rice. Ruksa gave the two rupees of liquor so that he would not be ashamed in public but he declared that he didn't care whether the people ate from him or no. He was an old man, most of his relatives were dead, and he probably thought privately that he would save a good deal of money by not being able to entertain visitors. So Ruksa Dewar is more or less established as a permanent outcaste of a rather special kind. Everyone sits and smokes and drinks liquor with him, but they don't eat in his house. The interesting thing, and the point I want to make, however, is this, that the excommunication has not made the least difference to Ruksa's extensive practice as a gunia. He is in demand everywhere, and his magic seems to be as powerful as ever. He is regarded with great reverence, and his popularity is undiminished. Only a few of his fellow gunia, especially Mahatu, affect to be deeply shocked by his immoral conduct and frequently discuss it.

A great deal depends on whether the crime comes out into the open or not. Sometimes the culprit, or victim, feels bound to confess it. Poor old Sarju the leper got vermin in his feet, and was weeping because he said that the cost of the penalty feast that would be demanded would ruin him. When I pointed out that we could cure him in no time and that there was no need to tell anyone about it, he looked at me in a very shocked manner and said that as the vermin had been sent by Bhagavan himself, he could not commit the further wickedness of not openly confessing that he was a great villain and getting himself purged by a tribal dinner.

But in most other cases, so long as everything can be discreetly hushed up, there is no trouble. For instance, Sukho, another young and pretty girl, had connection with a Panka and then with a Mussalman official. Everybody knew of it, but it so happened that Sukho was not the sort of girl that other women got jealous of, so nothing was ever said down by the well, and Sukho was not penalized.

This is even more common among the Baiga's neighbours, for the Baiga themselves do not have very much connection with outsiders. I know a Mehera girl who was kept by a sub-inspector of police, but the people thought it safer to say nothing about it, and she was never decasted. A Panka girl was kept for years by a Mussalman merchant, but it was done discreetly and never openly admitted and the girl and the merchant were both popular, so no action was taken in her case either. A Pardhan girl had her ear torn open, but all the men in the village were so fond of her that they let her off with a nominal penalty.

Baiga customary law is thus far from the fixed and rigid system that primitive jurisprudence is sometimes supposed to be. It has great influence; it has far-reaching social and economic implications; it is often dreaded far more than the official criminal or civil code; but it is elastic and adaptable to every circumstance.

The ritual of readmission to the tribe is complicated and, as we have seen, expensive. There are, however, two grades of excommunication. A village may refuse to share a man's pipe; this generally happens when a man is infected by someone living in his house. All such cases of what we might call 'secondary excommunication' can be atoned by a small dinner to the elders of the village or one's immediate neighbours and relations.

In more serious cases also, the actual culprit can, without being re-established in all his tribal privileges, have his *chungi*-rights restored by giving two or three rupees' worth of liquor, this being taken as a preliminary to the giving of a proper feast later on. This does not apply to women.

The giving of *roti*, to gain admission to full tribal rights and privileges, is a much more serious affair. It actually involves the giving of three feasts. The first is given by the river, so that the water can carry the offence away. The second is given at the gate of the house, so that the culprit may enter. The third is inside the house, so that the building itself may be purified. For the first two feasts the food is cooked by friends, and the culprit sits and shares the meal, but no one will take food or water from his hands. At the third feast, which is the really important one, the culprit and his family themselves prepare the food, and everybody eats from their hands.

The crux of the whole matter is that obviously some one person must be the first to eat from the culprit's guilty hands. Once this has been done by a responsible person, the guilt is regarded as having passed to him, and all the others are free to eat from the culprit. Now it is socially and spiritually dangerous to be the first to eat, for you not only become automatically outcaste yourself by doing so, but if there is any catch in the business, some deeper guilt, for example, as yet undiscovered, this may recoil upon you. The man who eats must in any case be a *samdhi* of the culprit, and in spite of the fact that there is always a special gift of five or ten rupees 'under the leaf' from which he takes the food, and that all his expenses are paid (for the *samdhi* must himself afterwards give a penalty feast so that he may be freed of the stain of eating at the first feast) there is little competition for the duty. Some years ago in Bondar a *samdhi* was called but his friends said that if he went his only son would die or go blind. So he refused. Nothing actually happened on this occasion to the man who deputized for him, but a little later when the same man went to another village and performed this duty, the eyes of one of his children *did* 'break' and the child went blind. This created a deep impression throughout the countryside.

The proceedings at one of these penalty feasts will be best understood if I give an actual instance. I have myself often witnessed the feasts, but never one so dramatic as the following which was related to me by Mahatu, and which, as it gives his own reactions to the affair, is far more valuable than anything I could describe myself.

"My brother's wife Mandro, Putua's sister-in-law ran away with an Agaria. How can I describe the shame we felt, for our family is descended from Nanga Baiga himself and we have never done such things?

"We searched all over the world for her and at last found her at Ufri, ten miles away. We brought her home with sweet words, but once we had got her in the house at Chauradadar, we began to beat her. Her three sisters beat and beat and beat her, for we were all outcaste because of her. We said, 'We'll never let her back into the tribe, nor will we let her go to the Agaria. She must stay with her husband and they will both be disgraced'.

"But my brother came and her own brother came and they begged me to let her come back. So at last we agreed that if they gave twenty rupees for liquor, ten goats, six *khandi* of kodon, and *dāl-bhāt* for twelve days to the elders of twelve villages, we would take the girl back.

"We argued for days, for days we did no work we had to talk so much, and at last it was settled that they should give fifteen rupees for liquor, five goats, and a three days' feast to the men of twelve villages.

"This is what happened. Those who were excommunicate, Mandro herself, her brother and the three sisters, all tainted by her, fell at our feet and begged to be taken back. 'We have fallen into a ditch,' they said. 'Take us out and set us on a hill.'

"The *samdhi* answered, 'You must feed us all for three days!' 'Yes, yes, we will,' they cried. 'Then come down to the river, and we'll see whether we'll throw you in or put you on the bank.'

"Then we all went down to the river, and Mandro's hair was cut off, and her brother's head was shaved. We sat down and drank twelve bottles of liquor. Then we pelted them with cow-dung and drove them across the river, and so came back to the house.

"Then at the gate we stopped. We drank eighteen bottles of liquor there, and they brought out a goat. Mandro's brother killed it with one blow of his axe. The blood was caught in a dish, and Mandro was made to drink some of it, all hot as it was. When she had drunk we let her into the house, and while we sat round drinking, she and her sisters went to roast the goat and prepare rice.

"When they brought out the rice, we got up and shouted. We took the rice and threw it all over the courtyard and trampled on it, and threw it out into the road, for the girl had been defiled by an Agaria.

"Then we sat down again and drank some more, and at last the *samdhi* agreed to eat first from Mandro's hands, if she put twenty rupees under his plate and he was given a goat and enough liquor for three days.

"Mandro put ten rupees under his plate and the *samdhi* had to be satisfied with that. He sat down, and Mandro and her brother sat down opposite him. They put food into his hand and he put food into their hands, and so they ate together. They put food into each other's mouths.

"Then we all ate the goat, and danced through the night. The next day more people came, and we feasted for three days.

"But now the *samdhi* was himself outcasted, and the twelve villages laughed at him. So on the fourth day he killed his own goat and spent some of the ten rupees on liquor for us all, and we feasted, and he too came back into the tribe."

Note.—The marriage of Baiga women and non-Baiga is very rare. The Baiga girl does not easily adapt herself to an alien household. A Mussalman of Dindori married a Baigin and did his best to 'civilise' her. He dressed her well and gave her rich and varied food: she used to go quietly to the forest and eat roots and wild fruit. He tried to teach her to cook: she refused to learn, so he tied her to the pillar in the middle of the kitchen and forced her to watch him cooking. Fourteen years later he confessed that though he was devoted to her, he had failed to make her into a wife fit for a Mussalman, and she had never learnt to cook.

Chapter VII

THE GREAT CRISES: BIRTH

I. THE BAIGA ATTITUDE TO MENSTRUATION

ALTHOUGH the Baiga have some acquaintance with certain aspects of reproductive physiology, they naturally have no understanding of the morphological changes in the ovaries which constitute the menstrual cycle, they have not even guessed at the process of ovulation. They have observed the oestrous behaviour of the lower mammals, but have no idea that the primates are subject to menstruation like themselves. At the same time, the topic of menstruation is one of absorbing interest and importance, for it not only influences the economic and social life of the home, but it partly regulates the Baiga's attitude towards other castes and tribes.

The Baiga regard menstruation[1] partly as a physical disorder whose origin we will describe immediately, and partly as a preliminary to the birth of children. "This is her flower; later will come the fruit." "Just as the mango and other trees flower before bearing fruit, so does a woman give red flowers before she bears a child." Uterine hæmorrhage has probably never been more gracefully described. A connection with the breasts, here again linking it with childbirth, is recognized. The very common glandular swelling of the breasts, actually due to a congestion of blood caused by tension in the ovaries, is thus described: "Just before she flowers, the blood fills her breasts, and they swell and are tender. Then the blood passes down by a pipe into the womb and runs out through the vagina." It is believed that conception usually takes place on the day that the woman takes her bath at the close of her period.

Curiously enough the Baiga do not trace the origin of menstruation to the attacks of evil spirits or ghosts, though their belief in the *raksa* (who has intercourse with young girls in their sleep) might easily have led them to do so: nor do they associate it with the bite of an animal, though there are hints of this in the folk tales. It is in no sense a wound, and is thus never

[1] To describe menstruation, the Baiga use expressions meaning 'she is outside', 'her head is dirty', 'she is broken', 'she is under the law of women', 'she is not well', 'she cannot touch the pots', and 'she cannot enter the cow-shed'.

confused with the rupture of the hymen—hymeneal blood is entirely distinct, it is a local hæmorrhage, it does not flow down from the breasts, but is due to the narrow and delicate nature of the immature vagina. Still less do the Baiga regard menstruation as in any sense a *purgatorium terrestre et naturale*: it is neither a purification, nor is it wholly natural. For in the beginning, though women had periodic cycles, presumably of sexual desire, no blood passed from their bodies. The cycles were in fact oestrous and not menstrual! The legend is as follows:

"Nanga Baiga and Nanga Baigin lived in the Nanga Pahar near a deep well hidden in the jungle. Nanga Baigin always had to go to a pond for water, it was a long way off. She wanted to go to the well, but Nanga Baiga wouldn't let her. But one morning, when Nanga Baiga had gone to cut his bewar, she took a broom and went to clean the well. For a long time, she couldn't find the way, but after wandering here and there she discovered it, and at last reached the well.

"In those days no blood flowed from women during their period, but it was then that they had greatest pleasure: the blood of all the women in the world was in the well. That blood was like the sea; it was alive, it stirred with waves. When Nanga Baigin saw it, she laughed at the sport and at her laughter the sea of blood fell calm. Then the blood sank down, down, down to the bottom of the sea that is below the world. When the blood was shut down there in the darkness, it began to ask, "Who has imprisoned us here?" It was living blood: it awoke: it rushed up through the earth: it spouted up in the well. It covered Nanga Baigin's face, her nose, her arms, her belly, her legs. She began to have pain in her belly. After that every month blood flowed from her.

"When this happened, Nanga Baigin fainted. When her daughter fainted, Mother Earth trembled a little. Nanga Baiga felt it in his bewar, and he ran home to see what had happened to his wife. There he found a river of blood flowing, so great a flood it was that all the gods were hiding behind trees for fear of it. None dared approach her. Nanga Baiga came to within two miles. But a little of the blood touched him, and he became impure.

"Nanga Baiga took his axe and went away, away, away through the forest, beyond the seven seas and the sixteen rivers, till he reached the place where Guru Binjhwar and his wife were living. They were sitting on a little stone in the middle of the sea, their faces to the sun. When he heard the story, Guru Binjhwar took his *sūpa* and his wife took the *tuma*, and they sought for the reason of the trouble. After three days the Guru said to Nanga Baiga, "You can go now: your wife is well again."

"When Nanga Baiga reached home, he found that his wife had had a bath and was waiting for him, a pot of water in her hand. He took her into the house and said, 'Why did you go to the well? You have spread this disease to every woman in the world.'

"But Guru Binjhwar sent the blood to the moon. That is why it comes to women according to the moon."[1]

Unfortunately we are never told what it was that Guru Binjhwar discovered during his three days' divination, and we are left in ignorance of the nature of the taboo which Nanga Baigin broke when she went to the well. It must have been a serious one to bring so embarrassing a penalty on the whole of womankind!

Another version of the legend finds the origin of menstruation in Mahadeo and Parvati and connects it, as often in India, with the lotus. 'Amardevi wanted to put a flower in Parvati's belly. As she slept, the goddess put a lotus in her mouth. At once she began to menstruate. Wherever a drop of blood fell on the ground, there was a lotus born. The lotus lived three days and died. This went on for three months. Then Mahadeo picked all the flowers and burnt them. But he dreamt then that without flowers there could be no fruit. The next day he saw a fruit in the midst of the lotus.'

Yet another story describes how Mahadeo made a garden and sowed *bīj bhāji* (herbs that had had a 'seed-charm' recited over them). He told Parvati not to visit his garden, but she disobeyed him. At her first visit, she began to menstruate; at her second, she ate the herbs that contained birth-magic and became pregnant.

In a Baiga village, menstruation is a far greater embarrassment than it is in civilized society. Uterine blood is regarded with the greatest horror.[2] The house where a menstrual woman is living is 'a house of night'. The Baiga do not, however, build a separate house for women at this time,[3] nor do they even make a special door which only she may use.[4] The Baiga's attitude is half-way between the excessive strictness of the Australian aboriginals and the Bushmen of South Africa and the comparative laxity of the modern world. The Baiga woman is 'touchable'

[1] Menstruation is more commonly discussed in relation to the sun, whose rays are liable to impregnate girls at this time. In *The Golden Bough* Frazer has collected from all over the world instances of the seclusion of girls from the sun during their period. The Baiga have no such custom, but have recognized the correspondence between menstrual periodicity and the revolutions of the moon. They regard the moon as female because she retires for a 'period' of one day in every month.

[2] But hymeneal blood, or local hæmorrhage caused by friction of the vagina through excessive intercourse with an immature girl, is regarded with comparative indifference.

[3] As do the Maria of Bastar State.

[4] One section of the Deswari Dhanwar of the Bilaspur Zemindaris, known as Dui Duaria for this very reason, have a back door to their houses which are only used by menstruous women.

at this period, she is not entirely segregated, but she must strictly observe the prescribed taboos. Thus, she is forbidden to fetch water, she must not cook or enter the kitchen, she must avoid the cow-shed and the store-room, she must not touch the grain-bin, she must not approach the grind-stone or the place where rice is husked. She is not permitted to clean the floors of the house with cow-dung. She must not go to the *deosthān*. She must not go near the bewar or any cultivated field, or the crops will be ruined.[1] Above all, she must not have intercourse with any man: she must sleep apart from her husband, on the floor or on another bed. She may, however, sleep with her children.

These taboos are enforced by stringent sanctions. We have already seen the appalling disasters that befell the unhappy Bansi (p. 159). A breach of the same rules has caused Phulmat's vision to grow dim (p. 138). The disapproval of society is equally emphatic. For example, three years ago in Dengurjam, Chunia's wife went into the house at this time and touched the cooking-pots. The pots were destroyed and Chunia had to give a penalty feast to the village and a rupee's worth of liquor to the leading inhabitants. Last year, in Chikla Tola, Latta Baiga's daughter-in-law did the same thing, and Latta had to pay a similar penalty. Recently a Baiga of Belki village took food from a menstruous Gondin, and had to give a goat, a feast of rice, and three rupees' worth of liquor. "If we eat from her hands," so Dhan Singh summed up the matter, "then Narayan Deo who lives in the threshold will devour us. If we eat from her hands by mistake, a tiger will attack us or a snake will bite us, but we may escape. But if we do it knowingly, Narayan Deo will kill us that very day."[2]

For a man to have intercourse with his wife during her period is regarded not only as aesthetically disgusting—'It is dirty, it is sinful, it has a bad smell'—but also as highly dangerous for man. In any case he must give a penalty feast: in a recent case in Pandaria a man had to give a goat, rice and a rupee's worth of liquor. But worse, worms may attack a man's feet and he may get an acute attack of gonorrhea. A belief in the toxic character of the menstrual woman, which is old as Pliny, is still

[1] The Halba do not allow a menstruous woman to walk across a ploughed field. The Gond have almost the same rules as the Baiga. It is curious that there is no rule against crossing a river: it is the pregnant woman who must not do that.

[2] Narayan Deo is the Sun God and it is interesting to link this belief in the vengeance he will take on the man who usurps his prerogative at this period with the wide-spread belief that menstruous women must be protected from the sun lest they be impregnated by his rays. For this belief—which the Baiga do not appear to hold—of the power of the sun over a menstruous woman, see Hartland: *Primitive Paternity* (London 1909), i. pp. 25 f., 89 ff., 97 ff.; Crooke: *Popular Religion and Folk-Lore of Northern India*, i. pp. 11, 69; Frazer: *The Golden Bough* (Abridged Ed.), pp. 595 ff. and Meyer: *Sexual Life in Ancient India*, (London 1930), i. p. 37.

widely prevalent in Europe and modern scientists are coming to the conclusion that there is something more in the idea than mere superstition. Van de Velde goes so far as to say that, 'I do not think it any longer possible for an unbiassed doctor to reject the existence of menstrual toxins as without foundation'.[1] He indeed dismisses the theory that the menses contain substances which may cause inflammations of the mucus lining of the male urethra, though there may be urethritis due to dirt, a very likely cause among the Baiga. But gonococci left over from some previous infection may 'renew their virulence in the menstrual secretions and pass with such secretions into the male urethra and there renew acute symptoms of gonorrhea'.[2] In view of the fact, therefore, that gonorrhea is almost endemic among the Baiga and Gond, their taboo on sexual intercourse during the menstrual period may be based not on superstition, but on accurate observation of results.

During his wife's menstruation, the husband also is to some extent secluded. He may cook—that is a social necessity—but he must not approach the *deosthān*, or touch the grain-bin, or go near the grindstone or place where rice is husked, nor may he sow seed in his field or bewar. He must not beat his wife at this time. He must not only abstain from his wife, but from all other women also, for in his semen is a little blood, and if he uses it now all the semen in his body may flow out, and he may become impotent. If he beats his wife, he must pay a penalty of a feast to the village and a rupee's worth of liquor. If he goes near the grain-bin or grindstone, he must offer a coconut to Narayan Deo. He is in fact subject to the rules of a couvade.[3]

A girl's attainment of puberty is not marked by any special ceremonies, in fact she generally keeps the matter as secret as possible.[4] Her attention is chiefly directed to a simple rite whereby she hopes to keep the duration of her period as short as she can. On the last day of her first menstruation, she takes two and a half pīpal leaves and buries them in mud, with the idea that her period will only last two and a half days in future. Other women, on the third day of their first menstruation, take some of the blood on the

[1] Van de Velde: *Ideal Marriage*, pp. 108, 291.

[2] Van de Velde: op.cit., p. 291.

[3] During his wife's period, a Halba man may not plough or sow, and a Kamar must take a special bath before he enters the forest. Russell and Hiralal: iii, pp. 196, 326. Dr. J. H. Hutton, writing about the hill tribes of Travancore, says, 'The Couvade appears to be extended to the menses so that when a woman is in her monthly period her husband s also sick and to a certain extent secluded.'—*Census of India*, 1931, Vol. I. Part B. p. 10.

[4] This absence of special rites and superstitions connected with the beginning of puberty is unusual. Meyer, for example, regards it as 'quite an astonishment' that the Vedda of Ceylon have no such superstitions (See Seligman: *The Veddas*, p. 94), for it is precisely at this time that the girl is 'highly susceptible to magical influences and easily brings mishap on others'. Meyer: op. cit. i, p. 37.

third finger of the right hand, and trace three lines on the wall of the house. Their future periods, they believe, will then only last three days. The normal length of the period, however, among Baiga women is four or five days. This may be due to the very active life they lead and which they hardly intermit at this time. It is often said that the period of a woman who is faithful to one man lasts only two and a half days; other women suffer four, five or seven days according to the number of their lovers. Women are very rarely 'unwell' during their periods, though sometimes congestion in the uterine adnexae causes pain in the abdomen and thighs.

Menorrhagia may be caused by some breach of the menstruous taboos, by witchcraft, by the unsuccessful use of the blood in love-magic, and by the magical vengeance of a disappointed lover.

In the first place then, if a woman enters the house during her period and thus offends Dulha Deo, he may punish her with menorrhagia. If, however, she makes reparation by staying faithfully outside the house, she may be cured. 'Then she goes and touches the feet of Dulha Deo, and that night her husband gives her a child.'

Menorrhagia may also be the result of witchcraft. During the period girls wear a small strip of cloth called the *chindhi* tied between the legs and kept in place by a cord that goes round the waist. This *chindhi* has to be very carefully preserved, for if a malignant witch can get hold of it, she can use it to keep the girl in a permanently menstruous condition.

A similar cause is an unsuccessful attempt at love-magic, always a dangerous undertaking. A gunia of Mandla Tehsil told me how this happened. "You must go and find a *chindhi* that belongs to the girl you desire. Take it, with a black cock, some *phuli* liquor, a coconut, and go to a cross-roads in the early morning. Give incense in the name of Bhavan Jogini, kill the cock and let a drop of its blood fall on the cloth. Cross the cloth also with castor oil. This is the *mohini*. You are to make a line across her threshold with the cloth. She will follow you. But if there is some error, or if she doesn't come to you, then her blood will flow for months at a time."

Mithu once told me how a friend of his took revenge on a girl that refused him. "She promised to meet him in the jungle. He goes and waits and waits and waits, but she doesn't come. He is very angry. He waits till the following Sunday, then goes and hides outside her house. When she throws away her used leaf-plate, he picks it up and buries it somewhere, asking the Samduria sisters to make the girl's blood flow for months and months. So it happens. The girl is driven to distraction. She falls at my friend's feet and promises to give him all he wants. Then he digs up the leaves, her flow stops, she bathes her head, and he takes her to the jungle."

As far as I have been able to discover, there is no attempt to regulate the date of marriage with the bride's period. I have not found any example of a premature menstruation caused by the excitement actually on the wedding night, as sometimes occurs in Europe. I was once discussing this point with some Baiga, and a Hindu who was present seriously argued that this was a very good reason for child-marriage, you never ran the risk of any such embarrassment!

It is rather unusual for a woman to cease menstruating during the period of lactation. But it is impossible to get actual statistics on such a matter, though it is often discussed.

The same difficulty attends the making of any exact statement about sexual periodicity. As far as I can discover from talking to the relatively small circle of my intimate friends, which includes a few women, the height of sexual desire in the Baiga woman occurs at the close of the menstrual period. This is the time when conception—so it is believed—usually occurs, and a wise woman will avoid the consummation of an intrigue on this day.[1] A few friends, say half a dozen, have told me that their wives seem to experience a heightening of desire during the period itself, but the majority say that the very opposite is true. This is what we would expect in view of the stringent taboos laid on intercourse at this time. Finally, about half my informants say that there is an increase of desire just before the period begins. This is fairly in accord with clinical experience in Europe, and though my information (except on the point that desire is heightened immediately after the period, which is very fully attested) is scanty in the extreme, it may be a pointer in the direction of the real facts. The heightening of desire at the close of the period is probably due to the abstinence which precedes it.

So seriously do the Baiga take this subject of menstruation that it partly regulates their relations with their neighbours. For some reason, they believe that the Brahmins eat from the hands of their wives at this time.[2]

[1] When a woman 'washes her head' at the close of her period, she must be careful that the first man she sees on going home is her husband. If another man's shadow falls upon her, her next child will resemble him and not its father.

[2] As regards the 'good' Brahmin this is an entirely libellous accusation. According to the Mahabharata (xiii, 104, 150; xvi, 8, 5, 6), to go to a *rajasvala*, or menstruous woman, is one of the things that costs a man his happiness and his long life. He must not eat any food on which her eyes have fallen; such food is only fit for demons. The Laws of Manu and the Indian Law Books are equally emphatic. Food she has touched must not be eaten (Vasishtha, v, 7; Yajnav, i, 168; Manu, iv, 208: Vishnu, li, 16). She must not go near the ancestral sacrifice: even her glance makes a man unclean: even speech with her defiles. If she touches a twice-born man, she should be flogged with a whip. 'The wisdom, the energy, the strength, the right, and the vitality of a man who approaches a woman covered with menstrual excrement, utterly perish' (Manu, iv, 41). But some of the Brahmins who live in the Baiga country do not obey these laws.

They refuse, accordingly to take water or food from Brahmins and generally regard them as inferior. Certain sections of the Gond are also careless, and the Baiga refuse to eat with them. The Ahir, Dhimar, Pathari, Panka, Agaria and most of the Gond observe the menstrual taboos, and the Baiga therefore are willing to associate with Ahir, Dhimar and Gond, and would with the others were they not debarred from doing so on other grounds. But most Hindu castes, Christians, Mussalmans, Sikhs are believed, often quite wrongly, to ignore the taboos, and the Baiga therefore refuse to eat, drink, smoke or intermarry with them. They have the contagion of menstrual blood upon them, and so must be avoided.

It is clear, therefore, that the taboo on the menstruous woman arose, among the Baiga, as in the rest of the world, from a dread of the uterine blood, and had nothing to do originally with a ban on sexual intercourse.[1] Indeed, according to the Baiga legend, the cyclic period was originally oestrous rather than menstrual, and it was only with the coming of the blood that abstinence had to be observed. At the same time, it is impossible to exaggerate the physical and psychological value of this taboo on sexual intercourse. It is probably the one thing that saves the tribe from complete sexual degradation. Among a people who are accustomed to have intercourse several times a day, who are completely unrestrained in thought and action, such periods of rest as these taboos prescribe are of the utmost value. By them something of the fine and delicate perceptions and delights of a moderate sexuality are preserved. It is the love that is given at the end of the period of abstinence that dwells most vividly in the Baiga's mind and that produces fruit.

II. THE TECHNIQUE OF CONCEPTION

The Baiga are well aware of the facts of physiological paternity; they have their own rough and ready theories of the psycho-physiology of sexual libido; their vocabulary of sexual anatomy is adequate for social, though not of course for scientific, purposes; they have carefully observed, and obviously devoted much thought to the processes of gestation and procreation.

Their sexual vocabulary covers fairly adequately the main points of the external genitalia. We must remember that the Baiga have no opportunity for the dissection of human corpses, though they frequently cut up pigs and other animals, and hence they only have a vague idea of the internal organs. But they have words, for example, for the glans penis (*tippōr*),

[1] Cp. Raglan: *Jocasta's Crime* (London, 1933), p. 115.

the frenulum præputii (*gargatti*), the meatus (*chēd*), and the urethra (*muthni*). They also distinguish the labia majora (*mania*), labia minora (*phokka*) and the clitoris (*tita*), though they appear to be ignorant of the existence of the hymen.

Sexual intercourse between a man and woman is necessary for the birth of a child. That is the normal rule. The Baiga would not, however, go so far as to say that a virgin cannot conceive. It is just possible that she might become pregnant by drinking urine. In the folk-tales one girl drinks a cup of human urine and conceives a son, another girl drinks a cup of jackal's urine and has a litter of jackal cubs. It is not unknown for a girl to become pregnant by licking a cloth which has semen on it. A girl may be impregnated by an animal, but in that case she will not bear a human child; a girl who goes to a dog, for example, will give birth to puppies. More common, nowadays, is the belief in the *raksa*, the ghost of an unmarried man who is always seeking to wreak his lust on the virgin maidens of his village. Phula of Pandpur assured me with the utmost earnestness that she was a virgin and that her child was the son of a *raksa*. Jitho of Bondar took a solemn oath that the gonorrhea from which she was suffering had been contracted in the same way. But even in all these examples, it will be noticed, the role of the male is understood—it must be a man's urine, a male animal, a man's ghost which acts before conception can take place.

The actual process of conception has been frequently described to me, and I will give some typical accounts.

"The day the woman washes her head," says Thaggur, "on that day her husband goes and touches the feet of Dulha Deo. That night he goes to her. Above her stomach is a little bag; its mouth opens and shuts; there is blood in it. His seed rushes in and the mouth of the bag shuts. Her blood and his seed mingle; it becomes the blood of a child; it grows; in three months there is life."

"In a man's water," says Lahakat, "there is flesh. You may go a thousand times to a woman, and there will be no child: you may go once, and she is pregnant. It is when there is blood in the man's water, and blood also in the woman's water, and these two mingle that you get a child. The man's *tej* and the woman's *lār* give strength to each other. The man's *tej* is urine with seeds in it."

"Bhagavan," says Hothu, "cannot give a child as he likes. When a man goes many times to a woman, then one day or another his seed is right. On the day she has washed her head, then he eats food in the evening, he talks to no one, he sees no one's face, he goes to his wife. His seed pours into her bag and her blood mingles with it. Then Bhagavan hears of it,

Bhumia youth. **Milward**
Bhumia girl with dubka-phānda.
Bhumia woman, whose tattoo marks are recorded on pp. 20 and 21.

and after two or three months he sends a *jīv* to that house. The *jīv* wanders round their bed, and when it finds a chance it slips into the woman's belly, it touches the blood that has mingled with the seed of the man. It awakes, there is life; after six months a child is born."

Dhan Singh's account is rather similar. "It begins on the day she bathes after her period. The unborn *jīv* is waiting, seeking for a place of warmth and love where it has friends. After five or six months it comes into the child. Then the child, in the seventh month, awakes. It swims this side, it swims that side, it dives to and fro. As soon as the shadow of the ninth month falls upon it, it is ready to come out."

There is a universal belief, as we have seen, that conception takes place on the day that sees the end of a woman's menstrual period. Mahi, who has long wanted a child, described how "on the day I wash my head I hold my husband to me. After his seed has gone into me, I clasp him to me for a whole hour, I keep him in my womb, so that his seed will not run out".

The great problem of the relation between intercourse and conception is solved by reference to Bhagavan—for the Deity is for the Baiga (as for more civilized people) an admirable refuge from exact thinking. Bhagavan apparently intervenes twice in the process. He first decides when a child shall be conceived, and later he sends a *jīv* to effect its quickening. But the Baiga do not trust only in Bhagavan. In the case of childlessness they use medicine and magic to produce children; they sometimes use medicine to prevent them. Their faith in Bhagavan is largely conventional. At heart they believe that conception is a matter of chance. The man's semen must be 'right'; there must be no interference by a witch or the jealous Samduria sisters; the woman's secretions also must be ready to mingle with the man's seed.

Like the Trobriand Islanders, the Baiga have no idea of the physiological function of the testes. The suggestion that semen originates there is always treated with derision. Semen is manufactured in the chest. "A juice is extracted from the food in the stomach and ascends to the chest, from which runs a tube down to the penis." "Seed is made in a little chamber above the urine-chamber," says Thaggur. "The seed," adds Rawan, "is made in a little chamber in the water-house (bladder). Then it comes by a pipe through the testes into the penis."

The testes are the seat of the *jīv* and the power-house of the penis. "The work of the testes," says Rawan, "is to erect the penis. They have no other business." "The testes," says Lahakat, "are only for erection. They give strength to the penis and raise it by means of a cord. But the seed is not made there. It is made higher up. Otherwise how could there be blood in the seed? You can see how it happens; if you cut off the testes, there is no more erection. If you cut off the testes of a bull, it can't go to a cow any longer. Women also have a discharge, but they have no testes."

III. CONCEPTION AMONG ANIMALS

A sexual dichotomy runs through the whole universe. The sun and moon were husband and wife. Every tree in the forest is a lover. "A tree that bears much fruit is a woman; a tree that gives nothing is a man." It is in the month of Bhadon (August) that trees copulate with one another. "When a great wind blows," says Mahatu, "then the branches rub against one another and you can hear the noise of their copulation. Male trees are red, female are white. Trees are the ornaments worn by the hills."

The Baiga understand fairly well the copulatory technique of the larger animals, though they are curiously ignorant about birds and insects. Some think that fish copulate mouth to mouth, others that they "swim along side by side, turning towards each other and touching bottom to bottom again and again." Mahatu, rather surprisingly, had an idea of fishes' eggs. "In Asad (July) when there is a flood, then the she-fish give eggs. The male comes and touches them and a *jīv* enters and little fish are born."

I met some Dudh-bhaina Baiga in Pendra who were very well informed about fish. "The saur fish copulate as they swim. The wife gives eggs, and the husband comes back and takes them in his mouth; then he hides them in a hole, and little fish are born. The bami fish have coitus mouth to mouth. The wife lays her eggs in a hole: then comes the husband and touches the eggs with his tail, and all the children are born at once and swim away behind their father."

Snakes copulate by intertwining with one another until they change colour. Butterflies mount each other, and are born from eggs. The Baiga do not seem to have observed a connection between butterfly, caterpillar and chrysalis.

Scorpions have no connection with each other, for "who would want to lie with a scorpion? Not even another scorpion". Baby scorpions are created when a crab's claws fall off; the discarded claws turn into scorpions.

The alarming insect known as *ban-bichu* is born "from the belly of the sarai-tree". The *mundri-kīra*, which devours the rice and kodon, is born from the belly of the earth. The locust is specially created by

Bhagavan who puts it in an iron bin and keeps it there till it is dying of hunger. Then he lets it out to go and devastate the world. From the excreta of the locust is born the small red *sonahi-kīra*. The centipede is the Ahir, or cowherd, of all the other insects. It too is born from the belly of the earth. White ants are the children of Budha Nag, and come up to the surface of the earth to make houses for their parents.

The Dudh-bhaina Baiga of Pendra also knew a lot about insects. Leeches are Rawanbansi. When Rawan died, his blood fell in the water, and leeches were born. Leeches never go to one another, but if one of them is killed, and its blood falls into water, scores of little leeches are born.

The *kamra-kīra* (a black hairy caterpillar) is born on the walls of houses. "The husband sits on his wife, and she lays her eggs on the wall. Then the husband goes and pours his seed over the eggs and the children are born."

The butterfly is born in flowers. The female lays her eggs on a flower, and the male, full of love, comes and puts his seed upon them.

The *pun-kīra* is born on leaves in the month of Sravan. When the male goes to the female, he immediately dies.

The cricket, who cries *jhing, jhing, jhing* all night long, is said by some to be born from the nail-parings of Bhagavan, but in Pendra they give a less exalted origin. An Ahirin was once going to sell curds. On the way, she met a cow who was giving birth to a calf. The cow asked the girl to massage her. She refused, saying she was in a hurry. So the cow cursed her and from her menstrual blood thousands of crickets were born.

There are few traditions about birds. In the month of Chait, the peacock displays his tail, and dances before his wives. "His seed drops from his mouth on to the ground, and the peahens run to eat it. As a result, they lay eggs which have a *jiv* in them."

IV. CONTRACEPTION

I have tried very hard to find some tradition of contraception among the Baiga, but with little success. This is, I think, a matter for some surprise, for on the face of it, it would seem inevitable that some such practice must exist. For how is it that this perpetual sexual intercourse, this almost uncontrolled licence, bears so little fruit?[1] The illegitimate child is unknown, unwanted babies are few. Can it be simply that 'the grass that is constantly trodden doesn't grow'? Can it be that the sexual organs are in some way injured by their premature employment? The Baiga themselves explain it by saying that "when a girl is going always to everyone, the mouth of her bag or womb never shuts, and so the man's seed runs in and out. That is why a loose girl never has a child". On the other hand the famous Mandro of Chuktipani, who used to entice four or five boys in a single evening, one day met her destiny in triplets.

The Baiga are thus entirely aware of this problem, and sometimes permit themselves to be astonished at it. But everywhere I have been assured that they have no real methods of birth control. They do sometimes, they say, take medicine; both man and wife take it, before intercourse. "Then there will be flowers, but no fruit."

The katai (*flacourtia romontchi*) is believed to have influence on conception. If a woman eats the root, she will be fertile; if she eats the flower, she will be barren.

"Sukli Baiga, of Khairda," I was told in Niwas, "had ten children. How could he feed them? He took some medicine and his seed went bad. He had no more children." This was twenty years ago. In Niwas I also heard of the *lach-kur*, a small shrub, which is used as a contraceptive. "Pull it up on a Sunday, and when you go to your wife, put the shrub under her waist, without her knowing. This makes her strength less. If you grind a little and put it in her food, she won't have a child." The wife can also make her husband impotent by tying a little of the shrub round his waist.

If, when a child is born, the parents decide that it should be the last, then if they lay the placenta with the foetal side upwards on the ground, the mother will not conceive again.

If there is an unwanted child, there are many ways of procuring an abortion. The most popular is heavy massage. "They ground me as if I were wheat," a girl once told me. Sometimes the masseuse even stands on the belly of the pregnant girl and stamps with her feet "till the child within turns to water". A mixture of gunpowder and *phuli* liquor is considered very effective. Otherwise a mixture of amarbel[2] creeper, tinsa[3]

[1] Dr. Ashley-Montague has assembled a good deal of evidence to show that we ought not to be surprised at this, since there is—both in mammals and human beings—a clear 'sterility interval' between the menarche and first conception. It is wrong to suppose that at puberty a girl normally arrives at the capacity to bear children. For an interesting discussion see Ashley-Montague: *Coming into Being among the Australian Aborigines* (London, 1937), pp. 238ff.

[2] *Cuscuta reflexa.*

[3] *Ougeinia dalbergioides.*

bark and other ingredients is given. The cumulative effect of these measures is nearly always successful.

But generally, when I have begun to discuss contraception, my Baiga friends have quickly changed the subject to aphrodisiacs and the means of obtaining rather than of preventing children. For, in fact, their families are very small. The average size of a tribal family in the Central Provinces is only 3·7 to 4·0. Out of every thousand children born only 687·8 to 891·2 survive. The lower figure is for the plateau division where the majority of the Baiga live. No one can read through the biographies recorded in Chapter IV without being struck by the large number of children that die in infancy, and the desire of the people to have children who will survive them. Deo Singh of Dengurjam had twelve children. "I've thrown six away, but six remain." The famous Yogi Dewar had no fewer than six daughters and twenty sons from six wives.

The idea of *coitus interruptus* as a method of birth control, which is generally practised by the people of Tikopia,[1] was very surprising to the Baiga. "Other tribes may do it," Mahatu assured me, "but no Baiga would ever do such a thing. For the sowing of the seed in its proper field is the happiest moment of our life."

The Baiga do, however, practise a form of *coitus reservatus*. But this is not in order to prevent conception, but to increase their own pleasure and to avenge themselves on some girl who has previously refused them or cast doubts on their potency.

This is what once happened to Jantri. He was very fond of a young girl in Chauradadar. One day he was standing under a wild mango tree and helping her pluck the fruit, and said simply, "Give me, girl!" The girl seems to have been fond of him, but was sexually unawakened. So she said, "Be off with you, you impotent fool!" Jantri said to himself, "All right, you wait." He did nothing that day, but on the following Tuesday—it had to be on a Tuesday—he took some *dāl* and rice in two leaf-cups and sprinkled it on a pipal tree, saying, "You have called me here and I have come." The next morning, very early, he went out, no one seeing him, and picked two and a half leaves from the pipal tree, holding his breath, and tied them round his waist. As he did so he repeated the prescribed mantra.

Jantri wore the leaves all that day, and in the evening he managed to get the girl alone in her room. He caught her, threw her on the ground and went to her. He claims that, as a result of the charm, he was able to continue without fatigue and without interruption all through the night till dawn. "But the girl," he said, "was broken. She never dared say no to me again."

[1] Cp Firth: *We, The Tikopia* (London, 1936), p. 490 ff.

Another method, popular in Kawardha, is this. "If a girl taunts you with being impotent, take a pebble and put a mantra in it. Then tie the pebble round your waist and go to her. Go on till she begs you to stop. Then leave her, remove the pebble, and when you go to her again, you will be able to discharge. But don't tell her about the pebble or she'll pull it off." This is the mantra, which must be repeated while holding the breath.

> On this side is the tilled field, on that side it lies fallow.
> O the *bāri* of Siklal! The stones of a rocky place!
> Who binds it? I bind it.
> I bind the stone in a hard place.
> May my binding be strong and sure.
> May the seed which is the stone be bound as long as I have desire.
> So long let it remain within me!

V. CHILDLESSNESS

It is considered a reproach for a woman not to have a child. It is bad to see her face in the early morning. It is probably a punishment for incest in her family. Or it may, of course, be due to witchcraft. The witch generally gets her chance at the woman's wedding. When the *suāsin* puts turmeric on the bride's body the witch may slip a *bhut* into her womb. Or at the time of *tikāwan-bandāwan*, an enemy may throw a *bhut* at the girl along with her handful of rice. Or when the *beni* is undone down by the river, an enemy may put an evil spell on the girl. If a woman stands on her heels and holding her left cheek with her hand, touches the *marua* pole, there will be no child. The Samduria sisters also watch with anxious and jealous eyes the women of earth, and try to stop them having children.

If childlessness is due to witchcraft or the action of the Samduria sisters, the gunia is called, and he offers coconuts or other sacrifices in the name of Guru Nanga Baiga. He gives three pinches of ash with his fingers to the wife and three to the husband. This method is specially effective if the real cause of childlessness has been the psychological impotence of the husband.

These difficulties never occur in the lives of those girls who were wise enough, at their first menstruation, to go into the jungle, pick a great bundle of leaves, and bring them home on their hips as if the bundle was a child. This simple piece of magic ensures pregnancy within a few years.

Another method is to find the umbilical cord of some other woman's child and to tie it in the fold of the cloth.

A more elaborate means is as follows. In the evening of the day when the wife has washed her head, husband and wife shut up the house and prepare their supper. They sit down opposite one another, and open their clothes. They rub ashes all over their pubic hairs, pull them out, and throw them away. Then they exchange garments and put them on. After that, the husband in his wife's *lugra* and the wife in her husband's *dhoti*, sit down for their supper. The woman eats off a leaf-plate upside down, but the husband's plate is the right way up. They must both eat at the same time. Then, still wearing each other's clothes, they go to bed, and that night conception ought to take place.

I once recorded a curious taunt-song reproaching a woman who could not get a child.

> She cannot get a child, she cannot get a child.
>   She eats a little mouse.
>   She eats a tiny frog.
>   She gobbles up a tiger.
> But she cannot get a child.

The most likely time of the year for conception is December and January, when the spring crops are growing, when the weather is bracing and vigorous, and the cool dry shade of the forest invites the people to love. For the highest number of births, taking the Central Provinces as a whole, is in August, September and October; and the lowest number of births is in December and February. Thus conception is least likely in the hot weather, most probable in the colder months. I have not been able to get separate figures for the Baiga, but all my enquiries indicate that in this they do not differ from the rest of the Province.

The Baiga seem to be quite indifferent to the sex of their children. They do not have the passionate longing for boys so common among Hindus. "Women generally like to have daughters, and men to have sons." But if boys are desired, then if one son is born, his umbilical cord is buried upside down to the way it fell, and after that boys always will be born. If a woman has only had daughters, then if she is given (without her knowledge) a scrap of the umbilical cord of a boy to eat, she will henceforth bear sons.

VI. PREGNANCY

Baiga embryology diagnoses the beginning of pregnancy by the stopping of the menstrual period for two months, and by the swelling of the breasts.

If the nipples grow black, it is believed that a boy will be born; if they turn brown, it will be a girl.

During pregnancy a number of precautions must be observed. The favourite *kanhia kānda* should not be eaten as it is liable to cause abortion, but there are no other food restrictions. A pregnant woman must not cross the rope by which a horse is tethered; if she does there is a danger that as a horse is pregnant for twelve months, her own pregnancy may be similarly extended. In this emergency she should be given a concoction of a little bit of the rope ground and mixed with water. She must also be careful not to step across the little rough threads of the rope that is used to make beds or seats. If she does, though the child will be born, the placenta will not come out and she will die.

She must not sleep on a sack—or the child may get small-pox; nor may she step over a pig-trough, or her child may suffer from rickets; nor may she step across a *sikka*, or her child may be born with six lines across its forehead like the strings of the *sikka*.

If milk comes from the breasts during pregnancy, they think the child will be still-born. "The breasts are weeping for the child."

Sexual intercourse generally continues up to the seventh or eighth month.

There is a very curious Karma song about a pregnant woman which was given me by an old Baiga, Dhundar of Chagda village, which I quote though I do not pretend to understand it.

> The pregnant girl sits anywhere,
> Anywhere but near the fire.
> Her tail has hair growing on the tip.
> There are whiskers on her face.
> She is not afraid of anyone;
> There is only one thing that she fears.
> She will sit anywhere, but never near the fire.

Dhundar said that the meaning of this was that the leopard only fears one thing, and that is fire. So a pregnant woman is half a leopard, she has hair on her tail and face, and is afraid to sit near the fire. The song may be connected with the belief that women can turn themselves into tigers and leopards.

VII. CONFINEMENT

I was able to get some idea of the ceremonies attendant on a woman's travail by an unexpected and surprising offer of Mahi to give a demonstration of them with two of her friends. This gave me a very fair idea of what actually occurred, and I was able to supplement it by information from Mithu and Baisakiya who have had two children born in the Leper Home, almost at my door, and from other friends.

When the mother's pains begin she goes into the house with any women who may be with her and shuts the door. They do not go to a special part of the building, but use the main room without any previous preparations in the way of cow-dunging. The husband and other men sit outside waiting, in case their assistance is required in ways that I will explain presently. They are only allowed inside if no women are available to help.

One of the assistants dips her hand in oil and presses it against the wall. If all five fingers give an equal mark, they believe that the labour will be accomplished without difficulty. Another method of divination is to put a little oil between the mother's breasts. If the oil flows straight down, they know that all will be well. When Baisakiya's last child was born, Mahatu sat outside with his *bahari-kāri* to watch and see that no witch or evil spirit came to interfere. His *churelin*, who lives in his house,[1] came all the way from Chauradadar, about twenty miles, to help.

"Then the woman walks this side, she walks that side. Her friends shake her belly to and fro. If there is much pain they break the cord that is round her waist." When she is about to be delivered they sit her down on the ground; one woman squats behind her and grips her shoulders, another sits in front and puts her feet against her thighs. In this way they hold her steady. They rub her body and thump her back. The parturient woman holds her breath, and bears down on her belly, giving little grunts "as though she were relieving herself". When the *liquor amnii* comes out, they immediately make a *gundhri* out of her cloth and place it under her. On the presentation of the vertex, they remove the cloth, and let the child fall on the floor. No one apparently catches it, the assistants pay more attention to the mother than to the child. If the placenta does not come out immediately, they take the mother's hair and put it into her mouth, the idea being that the effort to expel it will bring out the placenta. Then the mother stands up with her legs apart, and one of the assistants covers her own head with oil and rubs her head against the mother's belly till all the blood has flowed out.

The mother herself, or sometimes her *samdhin*, cuts the umbilical cord with a sharp bit of bamboo or the broken edge of an earthen pot. No Nai or Dhobin, no one in fact who is not intimately related, is allowed to cut the cord or give any help. They then dig a hole in the floor on the very spot where the child was born, and bury the cord there and place fire above it. Sometimes, however, they plaster the cord with mud on to the pillar

[1] See Chap. XIII, p. 368.

in the middle of the house. The mother grinds the bit of the pot into a paste and puts it round the stump of the cord that still projects from the child's stomach. Until this stump separates by a natural process of mummification, the mother may not move from the house. She must lie with her child on the ground; no *sūpa* or broom may be brought near her; she mustn't put her hand against the wall.

When the stump of the cord falls off, then the mother ties a ring of chhindi palm round both the child's feet and places a thorn on its head. She may now go out of the house. She must not take normal food, but she is given khyjri, beans, roots, or the fruit of the okad tree. She must clean her teeth with a stick of katai (*flacourtia ramontchi*) and her friends grind up some katai bark and put it in hot water for her to drink. Another prescription was given me by Gaontia of Bendi village.

> Root of bansem (*cylista scariosa*), yogilatti (*asparagus racemosus*), chhindi (*phoenix acaulis*).
>
> Bark of bija (*pterocarpus marsupium*), kasai (*bridelia retusa*).

All these were to be pounded and the juice extracted, mixed with water and boiled, then given to drink with a little oil.

This is the course of a normal travail. But where for some reason delivery is difficult or delayed, urgent measures must be taken. Sometimes they make a hole in the roof. A virgin girl brings water from the river, and this is passed from hand to hand along a line of men and thus up to the roof. The parturient woman stands beneath, and three mouthfuls are poured into her open mouth. Another method is to take the wood of a tree struck by lightning, set fire to it, and warm her with it.

Or, if there is a gun in the village, the gunia brings it and washes the barrel with water. He gives this water to the woman to drink. If there is no gun, she herself washes the inside of her husband's feet and drinks the water.

If the magician has diagnosed from the colour of the nipples that a girl will be born, the women make a small *sūpa* and put rice in it. They shake this up and down in front of the woman's belly, crying, "Come out, girl, you'll soon be cleaning rice, you'll soon be grinding, pounding, fetching water". If a boy is expected, they take a bow and arrow and cry, "Come out, boy, you'll soon be out in the jungle shooting green pigeon and every kind of bird".

The child is, of course, possessed by the *jīv* of someone who was once connected with the family, and it is important to find out who this is. When the child smiles for the first time, the parents wash its feet with water which has some silver in it, and then drink the water. The gunia then proceeds to find out which *jīv* has been reborn in the child. He takes the names of all conceivable ancestors in his *kāri*. He looks for some swelling of the eyes or head that would remind them of the dead. He offers it rings and ornaments to see if it recognizes any of them.

If the child was formerly a leader of the tribe, it refuses to drink the mother's milk from pride. Then the magician takes a chicken and offers it rice. When the chicken eats, the child goes contentedly to its mother's breast.

VIII. THE NAMING OF THE CHILD

When they have discovered which ancestor has come back to earth in the person of the child, they proceed to name it. This is done by the mother's father or the maternal uncle. First he cuts the child's hair. Then he gives the child his name. This must not be the name either of parents or grandparents or of the ancestor who has been reincarnated. It may be taken from the month or the day of the week or from some physical peculiarity of the child. This is the *pedinām*. Later on, the child is often given a nickname (*daukinām*). A full list of these, many of them amusing and expressive, will be found in Appendix IV. As everywhere in India, bad names are given to frighten the *bhut* or to deceive them as to the child's real value.

Sometimes when a child is about to die, the parents call an Agaria, and give cow's flesh to him and money, pretending that the child is his, so that whatever spirit is troubling it will go away. A lovely little Baiga girl in Andha was sold for a pice to a Gond because the parents thought she would die. Her name is now Gondin.

The name Lamu or Lamia is given to a child who is conceived so soon after the birth of the previous child that the mother has not had time to have a menstrual period. The Lamu child is dangerous, for he may cause the house to be struck by lightning. During a thunderstorm everyone runs away from him. For his protection, soon after birth they put him in a basket and wave a blazing torch of *chirra* round it saying *Lāmu jal gaya; taur kalank kat gaya*—the Lamu is burnt; your cord is cut. Later, a ring is made of virgin iron, a virgin must blow the bellows for the Agaria as he makes it. In July and August, when the worst thunderstorms are expected, they put the immortal chhindi leaves on a bamboo *khumri* and fix the ring on the top. If the boy wears this whenever he goes out, he will be safe.

Twins are welcomed. Two girls are called Chita Kota, the name Kota being given to the elder. Two boys are called Ram Lakshman. A boy and a girl are called Ganga Jamna. "It runs in the family," said Mahatu. "If the mother bears twins, the daughter will bear them also." Triplets however, are regarded with distaste. "She is a woman, but she produces a litter as if she were a bitch." A picture of the Quins roused long and ribald laughter. The Baiga do not seem to share the Hindu horror of brother and sister twins as *pāp-pāpi* who have shared the same bed inside their mother's womb.

If a child is born with teeth, the Baiga call it Rakshasa. They put it in an earthen pot and bury it alive, for otherwise it would eat the mother. When it has been buried it is called Bhandar, food for the earth. I have not personally come across any example of this, but the people say it is done or used to be done.

A breech-presentation (especially with extended legs), is unlucky. The people are afraid the child will be struck by lightning.

When a mother first feeds her first-born child, both her breasts "should stand up straight and full. If one falls down," says Mahi, "it means the child will die."

IX. THE CHILD'S FUTURE

There are many magical charms and practices designed to better the child's future. To make him walk better the parents put little bells on his ankles or round his waist. They put hare's dung taken from a stone on his instep to stop it tickling and to help him to run swiftly.

They throw the first teeth on to the roof and cry, "O cat, carry away these teeth, and give us some of your sharp ones instead".

To make him a good dancer, they cook rice and *dāl* together with milk in a wooden spoon so that as the milk dances in the spoon and makes it wriggle to and fro, so the boy will dance wriggling his body.

To make the child swim well, a little chip of wood is taken from a boat and washed in water which is given to the child to drink.

If they want the child to be expert in climbing trees, they give him a squirrel (*sciurus palmarum*) to eat.

If a child is dumb, they give him the ever-trembling pipal leaves mixed with milk and rice, so that his tongue will begin to tremble.

When the child first eats, they give him bitter water from a gourd to make him vomit, and thus be protected from poison and magic.

The child is suckled for two or three years, then weaned by being separated from the mother. Sometimes cow-dung or chili is put on the nipples. Should the child die, the flow of milk to the breasts is stopped by

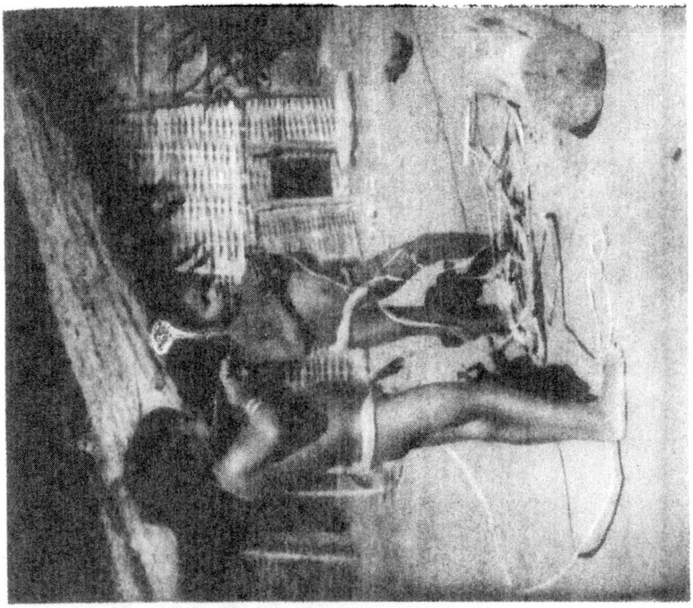

Bhumia boy.
Bhumia boys making bark-rope.

sympathetic magic. A friend takes two and a half leaves, touches the mother's breasts with them, and puts them in the roof above the hearth. Then as the leaves dry in the heat, so does the milk in the breasts. Sometimes, they mix the milk with cow-dung, make two and a half cakes and stick it on the wall to dry with the same object.

I have come across a number of cases of artificial lactation. Mahi had not had a child for twelve years. "My breasts were completely dry. Then my husband's relation died leaving a baby behind. So I took milk-medicine and the milk gushed out of my breasts, and I suckled the child." Mahi herself showed me the milk flowing from her breast.

"Beyond the Narbada, a three months' child was left an orphan. He was the son of Gurha Baiga. Bhoin, Bhadao's wife, of Bondar, took milk-medicine and suckled the child." In Ranjki, a child of two months was left an orphan. Bigri his uncle decided to adopt him. His wife had had no child for eight years and her breasts were dry. He secretly got milk-medicine and put it in her food. Within three days, milk had filled her breast and she was able to feed the child. Chamrin of Tikera Tola had never had a child, but she took milk-medicine, and with a little trouble was able to feed her sister's child.

The milk-medicine itself is made by grinding the root of the *dudhi bel* (a creeper, the *doemia extensa*?) and mixing it with water.

Note.—Primitive ideas about the menopause have seldom been recorded. The Baiga have few to record. They do not recognize a definite, inevitable period to which they give a name. Menstruation ceases, "for as a tree withers with age, so does the blood-stream slowly dry." Capacity for child-bearing is impaired, but this is not due to any change in the woman but to the incapacity of an elderly husband. The disappointments of the climacteric can be cured by a young lover. Mahatu's mother-in-law had passed the menopause, then she left her old husband for her daughter's son and bore him a child. The Baiga, then, do not regard the climacteric as terminating their sexual life or even their capacity to bear children; hence they are not afraid of it; indeed, they look forward to it as initiating a time when they will no longer suffer the social embarrassments of menstruation. "While the stream is drying there is trouble; then we get well and are very happy."

Chapter VIII

THE DEVELOPMENT OF THE SEXUAL CONSCIOUSNESS

I. THE SEXUAL LIFE OF CHILDREN

BAIGA children grow up free and unrestrained. They are underfed and often diseased; they suffer from itch and every possible affection of the eyes; not a few have hereditary or acquired venereal disease; but on the whole they have a happy life, for it is free.

Their sexual consciousness is developed very early. Parents may insist on their children going to work and to work hard, but they rarely interfere with their pleasures. "The child is the god of the house," says Phulmat. "The greatest love in the world," says Hothu, "is the love of children." You may often see a Baiga father carrying his child in his arms, kissing and fondling it. Even when they see their children indulging in erotic play, they simply laugh tolerantly. "Sometimes we say, 'Why do it now? Wait a little'. But the children grow excited, so what should they do?" Lahakat might be expected to adopt this tolerant attitude; but Dhan Singh, a much stricter and chaster man, echoed it. "If a child of seven goes to a girl, what does it matter? It does no harm. But of course when they are grown up and go to the bazaars, then there is something in it." Sujji of Kawardha told me that "if I catch my young daughter with a boy I let her alone. I don't beat her or abuse her; otherwise the neighbours may say, 'Is she your wife or your daughter that you are so jealous? Why are you making trouble, you impotent old man? Let her do what she likes'".

Not all Baiga parents are equally tolerant. Bukwa, the present landlord of Ufri, was well beaten as a child. His father Ramoli was a very strict man; he never ate with Gond friends or even drank liquor with them. He maintained all the tribal taboos. "He beat me," recalls Bukwa, "till there was not a shoe or a stick or a hand in the whole house that had not struck me. But my mother thought me a god"—and old Bukwa shouted with laughter at the idea—"and she used to protect me."

There is no regular initiation into the mysteries of sex; no *gotulghar* (children's dormitory) where the child may learn. There are no ceremonies at puberty. The child simply picks up its knowledge in the ordinary casual way. "The penis and the vagina are our two teachers." Sometimes, I was told in Kawardha, "an old woman gets a boy; she teaches him". I have been astonished by the number of people whose first sex experience was with old and unattractive women who seduced them.

Unlike the Gond, who have a tradition that every married couple must have a separate house to sleep in, the Baiga only have one house to a family, and the child has every opportunity of watching the 'primal scene'. The experience of Buka, a Bharotia of Pandaria, is illuminating. When he was about eight years old, he went to sleep with his father in their little hut in the bewar. At midnight, the father went out to meet a girl from another bewar. The child, frightened, ran after him and found him with the girl. He flung his arms round his father's neck, and held him till he was taken home. His father gave him something to eat, and returned to the girl. Then Buka called his mother, and there was a great quarrel.

Children are also often used as go-betweens and chaperones in intrigues. A women going to meet her lover in the jungle or by a stream often takes a child with her, the convention being that no one would do anything improper in its presence. The child has to sit behind a tree or bush, but often watches what is going on. In this way children get accustomed not only to married love, but to the more romantic adventures of the jungle.

The Baiga themselves believe that children are born with a complete equipment of phallic knowledge. Certainly the language of even the youngest children is amazingly well-informed. "Soon after the child is born, directly it is able to talk, it says, I'll copulate with your mother." I know a small boy of about four years old who drives the cattle to the accompaniment of a stream of sexual *gāli* of which you would not expect his father to be competent.

When the children are out in the fields or forest, watching the bewar, or grazing cattle, they play a good many impromptu games. The official recreations of the tribe are described elsewhere, and do not have any special sexual meaning. But here in the privacy of the jungle, the children quickly improvise such entertainments as Cow and Bull, Horse and Mare, Cock and Hen, Pig and Sow, and play them with a wealth of realistic detail which reveals considerable physiological knowledge. Sometimes the part of the hens, cows, mares is taken by little girls, sometimes by the younger boys. Once in Amadob I saw a little boy catch hold of a little girl and play at being a goat in front of everyone.

Another favourite game is Houses, and a number of Baiga have told me that it was during this game that they had their first sexual encounters. This is played when boys and girls wander together into the jungle. They pair off and make little huts out of leaves and branches. They make mud hearths and grain-bins, collect roots and fruit and pretend to cook them. They 'marry' one another with a strict regard for their exogamous obligations, and invent relationships between the various houses. The married couples make a purdah and sleep behind it. It is then that they make their first clumsy attempts at intercourse, though more experienced children manage very well.

They also greatly enjoy a dance that they call the tamasha. A boy makes a cloth penis of enormously exaggerated length and goes round and round with obscene movements and gestures, wagging the cloth against everyone he meets. Sometimes all the boys dance together, round and round, each holding his penis in his hand, while the little girls look on, screaming with affected embarrassment and delight.

The experience of the rupture of the hymen is practically unknown among the Baiga. They have no dread of hymeneal blood, for they hardly know what it is. They have no fear of deflowering virgins, for there are no virgins. Each little girl has slowly, almost imperceptibly, had her vagina enlarged, and by her wedding-night she is already an experienced lover.

"When two or three little boys go to bathe in the river, then they play with the little girls, and do what they can."

Dhan Singh was only nine years old when he had his first sexual experience. "We were plucking mahua. I was laughing at her. I seized her and had her under the tree. There was no blood. I came to love her and married her in the end."

It is never wise for parents to interfere. "There were two young girls. Their breasts had just begun to grow. Their parents were very jealous of them. They never let them go alone anywhere. They took them away from the Karma after half an hour. All the boys desired them. They desired it also. One day while they were fetching water, two boys took them to the jungle. After that they went every day. The parents thought they were fetching water, they didn't know. After two months all four ran away together."

As among other tribes where pre-nuptial licence is permitted, there are no ceremonies observed by the Baiga at puberty. Among girls, the beginning of puberty is diagnosed by the onset of menstruation, the development of the breasts and the growth of hair in the arm-pits. When this happens the child is, in a curious expression, *hushiyār*, literally 'clever' perhaps meaning that she now knows her way about. The boy also becomes *hushiyār*, at about fourteen, when his pubic hair begins to grow. "We know he is mature, when he starts flirting with every girl he meets."

Puberty makes no difference to a boy, but a girl now loses some of her freedom. She is more carefully watched. She must wear the *khandela* over one shoulder to hide her breasts. She must no longer eat from all and sundry. She must do nothing that would reduce her value in the marriage market. In practice, however, she continues to do what she likes, only she has to be a little more careful.

II. A TRADITION OF FRIENDSHIP

The Baiga are capable of the most passionate and faithful friendships. In Bohi, Charka and Panku, Latchi and Chatla, are all devoted friends. They are always to be seen about together: they twine their arms round one another's necks without embarrassment; sometimes they sit in each other's laps, their legs intertwined. Charka, especially, loves to come up behind his friends, fling his arms round them, and rub his nose and cheeks against the naked back.

Under such circumstances, it is not surprising to find among the Baiga —as indeed among several other primitive tribes such as the Gond, the Oraon and others—a highly developed theory and organization of friendship.

Baiga society is bound together by these friendships or alliances. They are more enduring than the marriage tie; they last till death and beyond it; they even break down the harsh barriers of tribal exclusiveness.

These covenants of friendship are of two classes. There are the five great friendships, the *mahāprasād*, the *narbadajal*, the *sakhi*, the *jawāra* and the *bhajli*; and there are the lighter, more easily achieved, *phūl* friendships.

These alliances must normally be made between members of the same sex, though old men and women sometimes become *sakhi*, and young people occasionally break the rule, more or less in fun. But this is not normally approved. On the other hand, if I am a man's *jawāra*, then my wife is his *jawāra*, his wife is my *jawāra*, and my wife is his wife's *jawāra*.

The friendships may be made only between members of different *goti* and different *garh*, that is between people who could be *samdhi* of one another. Once the friendship has been inaugurated, neither party may take the other's name. A Baiga may make a covenant of friendship with members of other communities, even with a European or a Mussalman, but nowadays it is not considered correct to do this with an Agaria or a Chamar.

For the greater friendships, the ritual of initiation is standardized. The two friends call together their neighbours, and in the middle of a room or out in the compound, women prepare a patch of cow-dunged earth. One of them traces a patterned square with *marria*-flour in the middle of it. The friends then sit down, one on either side, and the two senior people present complete the square. A piece of smouldering cow-dung is brought and one of the elders puts a few drops of *ghī* upon it. Then the two friends stand up, each holding in his hands a brass dish containing gifts—some rice, *dāl*, salt, tobacco, matches, a coconut, and a rupee, perhaps even a bit of cloth. They exchange their gifts three times, put them down, and embrace each other, saying, "*Johār, jawāra*," or "*Johār, mahāprasād*," or *sakhi*, or *bhajli*, as the case may be. Henceforth, they are never to address each other by their personal names, but only by the title of their friendships. They sit down, and one of the elders smashes a coconut. The two friends place a small bit of coconut in each other's mouths. If they are entering on the *jawāra* or *bhajli* friendships, they put some wheat or *juār* shoots over each other's ears. Then they distribute coconut to everyone present, and if they can afford it they all have a little liquor.

The *phūl*-friendships have a simpler ritual of admission. Two friends may be going through the forest or the fields; they feel a sudden wave of affection for one another. They pick a flower, a creeper, some vegetable, put it over each other's ears, and greet each other by the appropriate name. Such friendships as these are often made by children, and often lightly and laughingly. Yet they are real enough, and may last as long as the others. They are of many different titles, though there is no difference in degree or quality between them. Among them may be mentioned the *kodon-karīl* (shoot of the kodon), *chār-maur* (flower of the *buchanania latifolia*), the *lāl-bhāji* (red spinach), the *gulāb-phūl* (flower of the rose), *amarbel* (the never-dying creeper), the *kelapān* (leaf of the plantain), the *gondā-phūl* (flower of the marigold), the *āmā-maur* (the flower of the mango), the *tilwan-phūl* (the flower of *wendlandia exserta*).

But between the five chief covenants there are certain differences.

The *mahāprasād* is the chief of all. In theory a man may only have one *mahāprasād*, though this rule, like all Baiga rules, is often broken. Thus Mahatu, my own *mahāprasād*, has also, very shrewdly, as he is a Forest Villager, entered into this covenant with a Mussalman Ranger.[1]

The *narbadajal* or *gangājal* ranks next in importance and solemnity. It is usually made between women, and sometimes initiated by the friends going down to a stream, and sprinkling water on one another.

The *sakhi* comes next. The Baiga, unlike the Gond, do not attach much importance to this grade of friendship. To the Gond, *sakhi* are made in

[1] The Baiga do not observe the Chattisgarhi custom of lending your wife to your *mahāprasād* when he comes to stay with you.

heaven. Rama and Bhagavan are *sakhi.* It is the most sacred of the friendships. But the Baiga are less enthusiastic, perhaps on account of the very curious belief that if in a village two households have an equal number of children, all the children of one house must become *sakhi* to all the children of the other. If they fail to do so, then Bhagavan will make them his *sakhi*, that is, they will die. To such a length is this belief carried that once when a sow littered seven male and one female piglets, in a village where there was a family of seven boys and one girl, the children were solemnly and formally constituted the *sakhi* of the little pigs!

When a man's *sakhi* dies, he has to give a dinner to the elders of the village. There is no restriction to the number of *sakhi* anyone may have.

The *jawāra* is the most romantic of these engagements. It is usually celebrated in spring, when the new crop is fresh and green. It is sometimes, though not necessarily, made between people of the same name. The *bhajli* is the least of the chief covenants. It is a union of good companions, who will stand by one another and back each other up.

Friends who begin as *bhajli* may advance to greater intimacy. They may later become *jawāra* or *mahāprasād.*

I doubt if there is a homosexual basis to any of these friendships. The only one that has an emotional setting is the *jawāra*; the others are alliances, smoking and drinking partnerships, rather than sentimental romances. In any case the wives—or husbands—have a share in them. Friendship is a fine art to the Baiga, but its grosser perversions are regarded with scorn and horror.

III. THE POSITION OF WOMEN

Before proceeding to study the two sexes at love with one another, we must give some consideration to the background against which the sexual life of the tribe is set. We have said something about the life of children: we will now describe the position of women.

In Baiga society women enjoy an excellent position. Theoretically, in so patriarchal and priestly a tribe, men should be in the ascendant: actually women have great freedom and no little authority. The Baiga woman may go about alone; she generally chooses her own husband and changes him at will; she may dance in public; she may take her wares to the bazaar and open her own shop there; she may own property; she may drink and smoke in her husband's presence; she often eats in his company. In the Baiga *Genesis* it is not the woman who brings death into the world and all our woe; Nanga Baigin drives the nails that hold the world steady—woman stabilizes and does not shake the world.

Baiga women may not generally, however, officiate in magical or priestly ceremonies. I think it probable, however, that before they became taunted with the reproach of witchcraft, women were priestesses both among the Baiga and in many Hindu castes. The long hair of the Gosains and other ascetics and their long robes may be relics of the old priestly functions of women. Traces of this survive among the Baiga. Phulmat of Kotalwahi is a fully recognized gunia and her very interesting autobiography may be read in another chapter. There is another woman gunia in Rewa State. The Dewar of Kotalwahi never ventures out without one of his wives who acts as a sort of 'control' in his divinations. Without her he is helpless. Mahi, far more intelligent and well-informed than her husband, generally tells him what to do when he is summoned to perform a ceremony. Dhan Singh takes his wife on circuit with him, but denies that she gives him any help. All the same he feels lost without her.[1]

Women play a leading part in the marriage ceremonial, and—where it is practised—in the Jawara ceremony. At the birth of a child, it is the maternal relations who conduct the ritual. Women as well as men may be *barua*, 'horses', on whom the god rides at times of inspiration. On the other hand, women are absent at the actual burial or cremation of the dead —though they perform their own funeral rites separately—and at the Bidri and Bida ceremonies.

But it is her reputation for witchcraft that is the strongest element in the position of the Baiga woman. You have to be very careful with her, as though you were dealing with a sadhu. For her curse may be well as powerful as his. Major Repton, when Deputy Commissioner of Balaghat in 1878, observed that the 'Baiga females seem to have a reputation as exorcists and herbalists'. Even those who are not official exorcists may have an expert knowledge of love-magic, and may reinforce their husband's incantations by the sick-bed with discreet doses of jungle medicines.

There is not so clear a division of labour between men and women as in other tribes. Both men and women cook—the husband, of course, often has to see to the dinner during his wife's period. Both men and women fetch water and go fishing. Only men, however, go out hunting and take part in a beat. Women may cut wood and are almost as expert as men in the use of the axe. With a few exceptions, in fact, women may do everything men can do. But they must not make *khumri*. They must not thatch the roofs of houses. Some say, however, that this rule only applies to the sacred months of Jeth and Baisakh—if women climbed on the roof then the rains would fail; but they may do so at other times provided

[1] That fine old lady is now dead, after months of pain most courageously endured, and 'the god has gone dim' for her husband.

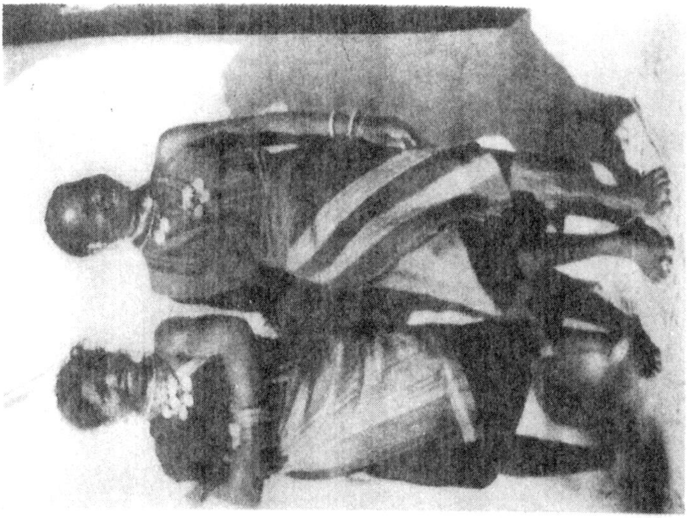

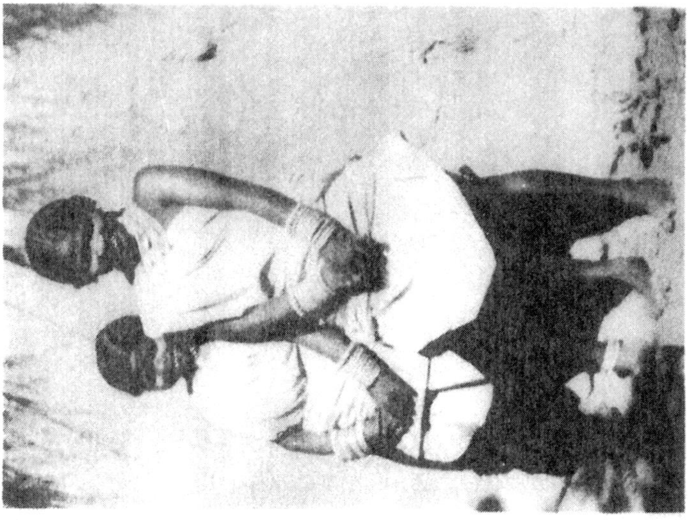

Bharotia women. (Note the brass bangles.)
Narotia women: The two wives of Bahadur.

no men are present. Colonel Dalton noted (in the *Indian Antiquary*, Vol. X, p. 364) that Baiga women were not allowed to sit or lie on any four-legged bed or stool. But this provision seems to be no longer in force.

Women may clear and fire the bewar, but they must take no part in sowing, for Earth is a woman. For this reason also they must never touch a plough or the crop will be ruined.

Women may kill fish, but not pigs, goats or chickens. If they happen to do so, no man may eat them.

We should not be deceived by the proverb, 'Man is a brass vessel; woman is an earthen pot', into thinking that there is a double standard in sexual matters for men and women. The meaning of the proverb is that while anyone, even a Mussalman, may touch a brass vessel without spoiling it, no one may touch an earthen pot without defiling it and necessitating its destruction. So, it is said, a man may go where he will for his amorous adventures, but if a woman allows herself to be touched she is defiled and severely penalized. But this is a social, not a sexual, regulation. It is intended to govern the relations of the Baiga with other tribes and castes. It has nothing to do with sexual freedom within the tribe. Here women are as free as men, perhaps in some ways freer, for the man may sometimes have to take the responsibility for his acts, which the woman rarely does.

We see therefore that in the general social life of the tribe there is a very great measure of equality between the sexes. In the intimate life of the home, however, man must be the master. In Kenda Zemindari I heard a story that well illustrates this attitude.

"A Baiga called Bir-Bakaria and his wife lived together in their village. They did plough-cultivation. At night, when he came back from the fields, Bir-Bakaria used to take a lamp in his hand and go from house to house begging a little oil. When he got some he would go home and massage his wife's legs with the oil. When they went to bed, the wife would force her husband.

"In that village lived a very poor Gond, and one day he went to Bir-Bakaria's house to steal his bullocks. He hid in the shed by the house. There was a crack in the wall so that he could see all that went on inside.

"Bir-Bakaria came home with a plough on one shoulder and a bundle of wood on the other. When she saw him his wife cried, 'Come, my lord, with a plough on one shoulder and wood on the other; come and serve your queen.'

"So Bir-Bakaria came in and put the wood and the plough on the ground. Then his wife said, 'Go and fill this pot with water. And afterwards with pleasure eat your food.' Her husband went and got water. Then his wife said, 'Go and get fire and a sieve for the wheat-flour, and then with pleasure eat your food.' So Bir-Bakaria got fire and brought a sieve for the flour. Then said his wife, 'To-day I will make *roti*.' So she made seven *roti*, and when she had finished, she sang, 'He who sits warm by the fire shall have five. He who sits afar in the cold shall have two.'

"Then the wife made her husband sit far from the fire and she herself sat down in its warmth. She gave him two *roti*, and ate five herself.

"Then she said to her husband, 'Now get the bed ready.' Bir-Bakaria ran to make the bed. His wife lay down and said, 'Now massage my legs.' Her husband did so. Then he lay down and his wife had the mastery.

"All this time the Gond was watching. When he saw what the woman did, he could not contain himself. He broke into the house, and first he beat the woman and then Bir-Bakaria. Then he tied up Bir-Bakaria with a rope and took his wife before his eyes. When he had finished, he took a burning log from the fire and thrust it into her.

"In the morning Bir-Bakaria and his wife ran to the police. They called the Gond and he said, 'I was drunk with anger. I saw this impotent fellow bring oil and massage his wife's legs. Then he brought her wood and water, fire and a sieve for flour. When food was ready he went and sat in the cold, and only ate two *roti* while his wife ate five by the fire. Then he spread the bed, and massaged his wife again. But when I saw the rest, I could not stop myself. I went in and beat them.'

"When they heard that, the police were very pleased, and they sent a report to the Government who gave a bullock to that Gond as a reward. So he went to his house and lived happily. But what happened to Bir-Bakaria I have not heard."

Perhaps the most curious tradition in the relation of the sexes is the old story of the Stiria Raj. Dhan Singh remembers it vividly when he was a young man in Kapripani fifty years ago. A great company of Baiga women were filled with one of those 'inspirations' that descend from time to time on primitive tribes. They dressed up as men, adorned themselves with men's ornaments and tied turbans on their heads. Carrying spears and bows and arrows, they went out as an army. When they came to a village, they beat all the men, and drove them to take shelter in their houses. Then they caught a pig, cut off its ears and tail and gave them to the headman. They took the pig and marched home. Then the women of the village they had visited took the ears and tail from the headman and themselves formed an army and marched to the next village. There they repeated the process with another pig. Meanwhile the women of the original village captured a man and made him their servant. They made him kill the pig and roast it. Then they had a great feast and ended all with the Karma.

"We men were very frightened," says Dhan Singh. "For the women had spears and they were mad. Who knew what they would do? I was only a young boy and I wept very much when my pig was killed."

Perhaps some memory of this survives in the custom which still allows women to beat men at the Phag Festival. The Gond, but not (so far as I have observed) the Baiga, play the game of Gur Torna, when women beat their men as they climb up a slippery pole for a lump of *gur*. The Baiga do not observe Phag and have no idea of its meaning. But they see all their neighbours enjoying themselves, and so their women go out to beat any man they can find and extract a present from him.

IV. THE PLACE OF SEX IN TRIBAL LIFE

We have seen so far that the phallic life of the Baiga, so long as it is confined within the borders of the tribe and observes certain fundamental conventions, is free, warm and spontaneous. A study of the biographies recorded in Chapter IV will not suggest, however, that sex is the primary interest of this tribe. Husbands are changed, not because they are sexually unsatisfactory, but because they do not provide sufficient food. A woman may be turned out of the house, not because she has lost her beauty, but because she is not a good cook. Food, magic and the bewar are, I think, the predominant concerns of the Baiga; but sex must not be underrated. It forms a necessary inevitable background. Warm, vigorous, direct, phallic enjoyment is as necessary as food, but as it is more readily available, it does not seem so important. So far as my observations have gone, I would not say that erotic interests engross the whole attention of the Baiga in the sense, for example, that they engross the attention of the Gond. But they are absolutely necessary. Celibacy is unheard of, continence is never practised. "Without a wife, a man pines away, O friend!" "When love is done with, what shall I do with this body of mine?" The theme recurs again and again in the Karma, Dadaria and Jharpat songs.

> Without my girl, my life is wasted.
> As the insects eat the *channa*,
> As the frost kills the *masur dāl*,
> As the *senduri* weed grows up amid the wheat,
> So is my life wasted without my girl.

And this, from Boira Village in Bilaspur:

In this life, in this life, you must have someone with you.
Take any girl, any girl you can find, to be with you.
Take a Bhumnin girl to live with you.

And again:

In some houses there is food,
In other houses there is money,
But in every house there is youth and desire.

Love is as necessary to the Baigin as to the Baiga.

A girl's life lives in the heart of her boy:
His life is in hers.

And:

The *pej* is cooking in the pot.
Unless I see my lord, how sad I feel, O friend!

In Silpuri in the Baiga Chak I heard a Karma song which expressed the desire to take all that life can offer before it is too late.

Come, boys, and let us play!
Life is only for two days.
Take whichever girl you like.
Life is only for two days.
Her hips sway like a young bamboo.
Life is only for two days.
His body wriggles like a rice-stalk.
Life is only for two days.

It is not expected that a widow will remain faithful to the memory of her dead husband. Indeed, were she to do so, and stay unmarried, the gravest doubts would be cast on her moral character. So a cynical Karma describes the readiness of a Baiga girl to take a new husband.

If your husband has done a bunk,
Clean your teeth with a saj twig.
Wash your feet and wash your hands,
And soon you'll get another man.

It is, in fact, considered wholly impossible for anyone to live without a *jōdi*, or mate. That is a simple law of nature that must be obeyed.

Charka, Bhumia youth of Bohi.

V. THE BAIGA'S IDEA OF EROTIC ATTRACTIVENESS

Baiga women are not, as a rule, attractive to Western eyes, in this differing from their Gond and Pardhan neighbours. They are often stout and stumpy, with thick limbs and coarse features. The Gond themselves consider Baiga girls to be distinctly inferior in erotic attraction. "No one would sleep with a Baiga woman." I well remember the incredulous and amused astonishment with which a Gond village once greeted the rumour that a certain Mussalman Forest Guard had seduced a Baiga girl.

There is a proverb that distinguishes three kinds of girls. '*Khumri mudh ki gondin, sālhō mudh ki pankin, mul mulhin baigin.* A curly-headed Gondin, a beautiful Pankin, a grinning Baigin.'

But in the eyes of their own menfolk, Baiga women are beautiful and romantic enough, while the men themselves are entirely charming. Even the old men are often strikingly handsome, and the young men, particularly those of from fifteen to twenty-two have a gentle beauty which is most attractive, even though it may be criticized as being over delicate and feminine in quality. I do not think I have ever seen more handsome youths than Charka and Panku of Bohi village or Mahatu's younger son Jantri.

In attempting to surprise Baiga opinion of what causes a man or woman to be aesthetically beautiful or sexually attractive, I have made considerable use of the songs, in which they reveal in a natural and unforced manner their real ideas.

> If you want to know the story of my life,
> Then listen to my Karma.

Without these we might easily be misled into thinking that lust rather than love, bestial craving rather than the desires of the phallic consciousness, ruled the Baiga mind. It has been interesting, and often amusing, to check these results by discussing with the Baiga the illustrations in the works of European anthropologists.

The first thing that strikes one in discussing a person or a picture with these tribesmen is that they seldom take the impression of the thing as a whole. They analyse it, giving as it were so many marks for each feature until from the aggregate they can say whether it is beautiful or no. "The nose is good," they cry. "But the lips are too thick. That forehead is broad and fine, but the ears should not be so."

In *The Sexual Life of Savages*, Malinowski has pictures of two women, one a Melanesian beauty, the other of a type not generally admired. The Baiga entirely approved the Melanesian's choice. Of the first, Lahakat exclaimed, "She is slim, her breasts are lovely, her nose is straight. But the other is too fat; her nose is snub, her nipples point earthwards". The vivacious Mahi was very down on the less attractive Melanesian. "Look, she is fat as a basket: her cheeks are broad as a tiger's buttocks; her nose is like a *dongi*, a pig's trough; her shoulders are too broad for a woman; she is *buglo*, fat-faced; her whole face is puffed out." On the other hand old Baisakin considered that she was not too ugly, though a little fat.

But everyone who has seen her has preferred Vaikiteraki of Tikopia (Plate VII of Firth's *We, the Tikopia*). She is considered more beautiful than her sister Foraurakei, though she too is lovely, with perfect breasts and of the right colour. But Vaikiteraki is a miracle of beauty; she has made a deep impression on my Baiga. Jantri has even gone so far as to make love-magic for her, so that he can at least visit her in dream. He is not sure whether he has been successful, but he has met someone very like her. When Dhan Singh saw her picture, he exclaimed, elderly and dignified ecclesiastic as he is, "O I could live for ever between those breasts!" And Phulmat declared that "she is truly beautiful. Her nose is like a grain of channa, with a small straight tip".

The other woman of Tikopia in Plate VI of Dr. Firth's book did not meet with approval. "She is *khokhli*, her lips are thick and protruding, she is *pachki*, her cheeks are fallen."

Mahi was very excited by the portrait of the Sema chief Vikhepu in Dr. Hutton's *Sema Nagas*, and said he was just what she wanted for a new husband (her affection for the present occupant of the post is apparently growing a trifle thin) and she thought that the little daughter of the Chief of Philimi would do admirably for me!

I was a little doubtful how far the Baiga would appreciate African beauty. I once showed a group of them the photos in Richard Wyndham's delightful book *The Gentle Savage*, especially his studies of the young Niam-Niam Rafa. Wyndham himself says of her that 'her appearance was savage. As is the custom with these cannibals, her front teeth were filed. Her face was scarred by tribal markings. But her body was sublime'. My Baiga agreed.

But they thought the Zande women terrible.

On the whole, the Baiga liked the pictures of African men. They thought they looked very virile. Curly hair is apparently not always displeasing to them, though it is generally despised when it occurs among the Baiga themselves. I expected that they would be greatly taken with the men of Tikopia, but I was disappointed. Afirna of sa Fasi (Plate V) had *jabar-tepra* eyes. "They are not good." He was too fierce for them, a very different type from the gentle Baiga. But they liked Pa Fetauta (Plate V) for his fine moustaches. They thought his son Fakaokokava too was handsome, with his fine forehead and splendid arms. His nose was perhaps a thought too flat.

As we have seen, the Baiga rarely describe a person as a whole, but proceed at once to analysis, taking the parts of the body one by one. In considering what it is that the Baiga find attractive in one another, we may follow the same course.

The primary sexual characters are, of course, only revealed to the eyes of intimacy. The genitals should be well developed and regularly shaped. A large penis is admired in men, a small vagina in women. The Baiga distinguish between a vagina that is *tip-tip* or small and tight, and one that is *gus-gus*, enlarged by frequent intercourse and child-bearing. There are many references to this in the Folk Tales, and there is no doubt that women have a dread of becoming *gus-gus*, as they will then lose much of their sexual attractiveness. In one story the hero could only find one girl out of a whole village of maidens who was *tip-tip*—and thus presumably chaste. In another, a woman has herself sewn up with wire in order to be more pleasing to her husband. In one of the Vagina Dentata tales the woman has her teeth removed from the vagina, and henceforth can get no pleasure in intercourse, as she cannot tell whether she has been penetrated or not. She seeks satisfaction from a horse, and dies.

Among the secondary sexual characters, the breasts must have first place. Before anything else a Baiga looks at a girl's breasts. Plainness of feature, a stocky figure, a dark colour—all these can be forgiven if the breasts are firm and rounded. They must not however be too broad or fat. The Baiga distinguish different kinds of breast—the *bajar-dūdh* are firm and hard; *kumha kumha dūdh* stand up strong and straight; *ūncha dūdh* are too big and prominent; *bhoir ke tarah dūdh* are small and undeveloped like *bhoir* fruit; *oram-dūdh* are breasts that fall down a little, "being shy"; *budhia dūdh* are wrinkled and flabby. A woman who has no paps at all is described as having *chatka dūdh*. Other descriptions are *gobarchhattia*, "as big as cow-pats"; *tuma-dūdh*, "the shape of a gourd"; *mirigthani*, "small as a deer"; *panhi dūdh*, "long and pendulous as a country shoe". It is said that if a child puts on shoes, her breasts will go like this. If the breasts are unequal in size, they are called *mamā-bācha*, "uncle and nephew", or *kāni dūdh*, "squinting breasts". The most characteristic breast among the Baiga is that called by Jayle *sein à tête de brioche*. The areolæ are generally large and clearly marked.

"The breasts must stand up," says Lahakat, "strong and firm, ready to be caught." And old Mahatu says, "It is the breasts that matter. So long as she has good breasts, I don't mind how black she is." His younger son Jantri echoes him. "In youth it is the breasts that thrill us. We could live for ever fondling them." It is a glimpse of the girl's breasts, followed perhaps by actual mammillary contact, that leads to intimacy. The breasts may be seen at the bathing-place.

> At the time of bathing my breasts are bare;
> That is when you look at me and desire me!

A man cannot forget what he has seen.

> When a cow dies, the kites circle in the sky above it.
> I have seen your breasts and my mind is fixed upon them.

During the Karma dance, when the girls bend forward in the rhythm of the movement, the breasts are often visible beneath the lightly worn cloth. "When a beautiful girl dances in the Karma, her breasts tremble to and fro: when she bends forward in the dance and draws near to the men, her lover's hand shoots out and touches them." Thus Jantri, and his brother says much the same. "When she wears a many-coloured necklace, and has firm young breasts, and you hold them in your hands, how happy you feel! You want to live there, between her breasts, for ever and ever."[1]

In the songs the breasts are called oranges—the same synonym is used by the Muria of Bastar State—mangoes or guavas. For example, the real meaning of the following lines is that the girl is seeking another lover who will catch her breasts and carry her away.

> The mango tree is laden with many a ripe mango.
> But where is my love, who will come and eat my mangoes?

The same meaning attaches to the oranges in this song.

> In the midst of the river, the tree is full of leaves.
> Among the leaves, monkeys are hiding—
> They are eating the fruit that grows there.
> O when will I meet my true love
> Who will put aside the leaves,
> And pluck the oranges that grow
> So round and firm upon my tree?

[1] Compare D. H. Lawrence: *Song of a Man who is Loved.*

> Between her breasts is my home, between her breasts . . .
> So I hope I shall spend eternity
> With my face down buried between her breasts;
> And my still heart full of security,
> And my still hands full of her breasts.

The breasts play an important part in the mechanism of tumescence and intercourse. The fondling of the breasts is generally the only tactile contact that precedes coitus. "We don't kiss. We just press the breasts till she cries out, 'Stop! Stop! I can't bear it any longer!'" The posture adopted by the Baiga also gives them every opportunity to observe and handle the breasts. They do so—"so long as they are firm and rounded as a fig; but when they fall like a sack, we leave them alone".

Curiously enough, the eyes—which are so important to Western lovers—are almost ignored by the Baiga. This may have an entirely practical cause; I do not remember ever having seen a Baiga with beautiful eyes. "The face," says Lahakat, "should not be too fat or too thin, it should slope straight downwards. The nose must be straight. A snub nose is bad. The forehead should be broad. The lips should not be very thick. The ears must be thin and fine, the throat slender. The eyes should not be as big as a cow's, nor yet so small as a frog's. The eyelashes should not be very big. Eyebrows must not join in the middle." This may be taken as an authoritative and representative statement of what the Baiga expect of the human face.

A slender waist, with broad hips, is much admired. Baiga women are generally on the stout, stumpy, gross side; hence delicacy is always delightful.

> The girl's waist is so slender,
> She might break beneath her load of mangoes.

The body should be straight and slim, the bearing dignified. Moderation is chiefly admired. You must be not too fat, not too thin, not too short, not too tall. Men should be taller and stronger than girls—though many Baiga women are much more muscular and well-developed than their husbands. The thighs should be round, strong and fat; in most Baiga girls they are.

Another secondary sexual character almost as important as the breasts is the hair. This has a very strong erotic attraction for the Baiga, the men especially pay a lot of attention to dressing it in the most becoming fashion. In women it is the loosened hair falling about the shoulders, or tied firmly back and fastened in a bun with a bright-coloured *phundara* that alternately excite delighted attention. Mahatu says, "A girl whose hair falls to the waist! When she is combing it, with a gleaming *dhār* in her ears, and a bright *phundara* in her hand, how lovely she looks!"

> The girl whose beauty captures the mind
> Stands beneath the tree.
> Her hair is all about her shoulders.
> She glances down the forest-path to see who comes.

And again:

Her long hair is all scattered on the ground.
I am going to pick the flowers.
At sunset her hair is all scattered on the ground,
And I am going to pick the flowers.
At bed-time her hair is all scattered on the ground.
I have picked a lovely flower.

Long hair tied in a bun is also attractive.

O where did you get your *chutka*?
O where did you get that *phundara*?
It is your hair that stirs my love for you.

Long hair is also attractive in men.

That boy with his small mouth and long hair looks very handsome.
I will run away with him.

Men also tie their hair into a bun with gay-coloured wool. The ornaments in the hair are very important.

In her hair are tied two *jhopa*.
Her lover too has tied a *jhopa* in his hair.

Flowers are also tied in the hair, and a Karma from Shahpura illustrates this custom very charmingly.

I went to the hill to pluck leaves from the forest, mother.
I looked here and there and I picked good leaves, mother.
Then I saw a flower of seven colours, mother.
I picked it and hid it in the fold of my dress, mother.
I stuck it in my hair for my adorning, mother.

Hair on the body is regarded as ugly, both in men and women, and is usually removed.

Every boy and girl carries a little wooden comb, which is home-made and often a present between lovers.

Like most people in India, the Baiga are attracted by a light brown colour. They themselves vary greatly, from almost black to a beautiful golden brown. It is sometimes hard to believe that a Mahatu with his dirty dead black body and Charka, whose exquisite colouring is universally admired, can belong to the same tribe. The Baiga, however, are less

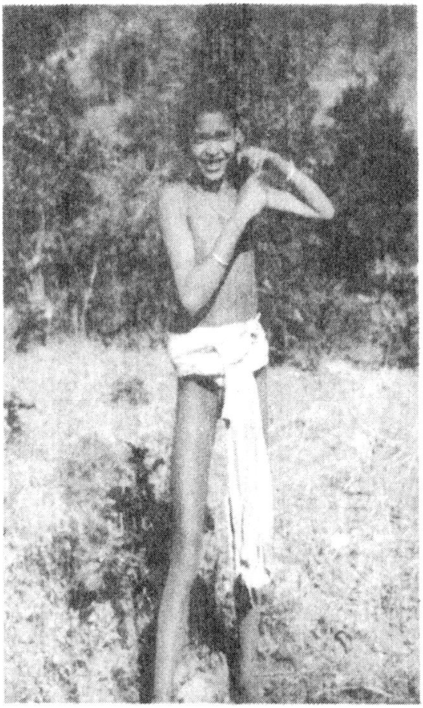

Hair-dressing in youth and age.

inclined to take colour as a primary criterion of beauty than their neighbours. They have a proverb, '*Kāri la sāju gori la godna*', or 'For a dark girl, ornaments; for a fair girl, tattooing'. A dark-coloured girl is very well provided she has plenty of gleaming ornaments and a bright *phundara* with flowers in her hair. A blonde girl needs a lot of tattooing to emphasize her charms.

The pure red and white colour of the European is not attractive to the Baiga, though most of them are polite enough to praise my own appearance. If I had a good bust, they say, I would make a fairly pleasant woman, though perhaps a trifle large; as a man, apart from my colour, I am satisfactory. They admired the photo of Dr. Malinowski in his *Sexual Life of Savages.*

Erotic charm is not complete without a profusion of ornaments. When we see the cheap, tawdry and sometimes quite unsightly ornaments worn by Baiga women, the broad brass *toda* burdening the legs, the clumsy brass bangles, the ill-fitting *sutia* round the neck, we find it hard to imagine how attractive they make a girl in the eyes of her lover, or with what eagerness and excitement a girl anticipates a gift of even the least of them.

Consider these word-pictures, all sung in the Karma dance, which give us in the Baiga's own words, what they expect their girls to wear.

> She is kneading flour and shyly looking up at me.
> There are *paijna* on her feet,
> A yellow cloth round her waist,
> About her breasts a coloured jacket,
> A *kanthi* on her neck.
> In her mouth is betel.
> There's a *kundal* in her ear.
> She is going to the bazaar.
> She looks back; her eyes meet mine.
> O girl, walk slowly, we are coming to the woods.

And again:

> Slender and beautiful she hides her face.
> She peeps out now and then.
> Round her neck is the *munga-moti.*
> In her ears are *kundal-moti* that glitter in the sun.
> They swing to and fro as she turns her head to look at me.

And:

> Under the pipal tree there is a little bed.
> She is wearing many bangles; her breasts are large.
> On all eight parts of her body she wears red necklaces.
> She is slender and beautiful; she stands beneath the pipal.
> Beside her is a little bed.

A gift of ornaments is a sure way into a girl's heart.

The leaves of the palm-tree are trembling in the breeze,
And my heart trembles with love for you.
You went to the Muki bazaar to buy me *chutki*,
And when I see those *chutki* my heart is filled with love for you.

The sound of tinkling ornaments, specially if they blend with a lovely voice, is almost irresistible.

The rings tremble in her ears.
She is like the maina.
Her voice is sweet as the maina's.

And:

Her *chura* and *pairī* tinkle as she goes.
In the shade of the mango she waits for me.
She goes on, then looks back to see if I am coming.

And:

The beads in your *ganthi* are shining like gold.
Your juice has fallen from you.
You are looking at your *chutki*.
You make them tinkle by shaking your feet.

And:

The bamboos are sounding *rui-chui* in the wind.
The girl wants *chutki*; she is gazing at her lover with love from head to foot.
The girl wants *pairi*; she is gazing at her lover . . .

and so on through the entire catalogue of ornaments.

Boys also pride themselves on their dress and rings. "In the upper lobe of his ear, the *bāri* trembles; in the lower is the *lurki*."

I am wearing a turban,
Its end hangs down my back.
O girl look behind you,
And your whole life will be changed.

In men, as we would expect, physical beauty is less important than strength, energy, sexual potency, vitality.

Your horse is like the moon,
Its rider shines as the lightning.
Your body is bright as the sun.
My heart weeps for love of you.

A girl may seek everywhere to find a man strong enough to master her.

You have been to three houses in search of a real man.
But where will you find one who is strong enough for you?

A facility for telling witty stories, however obscene, the ability to imitate animals, especially in their sexual functions, achievement in song and the dance, are powerful factors in a lover's success. "To get a girl," I was once advised by Sujji of Kawardha, "First send someone to her to tell her how you love her. Then joke with her, tell her dirty stories, help her when she goes to cut wood or draw water, give her little presents of jamun and char fruit, above all make her laugh—and you'll get her in the end."

A very effective method is to imitate the sexual activities of animals. A man covers his face with his hand, puts his head on one side, and imitates a goat in heat. "*Le-le bo-bo-bo-bo,*" he cries over and over again. Then if the girl answers "*Meār,*" he knows she is ready for him. This was recommended by Dasseru of Bondar, whose skill in the amusing Tapori game has also been invaluable to him.

Sujawal, an ugly, undersized little fellow, has had enormous success with girls because of his distinction as a dancer. Directly he slings the drum round his neck, the Karma is transformed; a shock of erotic energy possesses it; there is not a girl present who is not thrilled by him.

He comes from the house as lightning flickers in the sky.
His hair is tied in a knot on one side.
He stands shining in the court.
What is he doing standing in the court?
What is the boy doing? He is shining like the lightning.
He is standing on tip-toe playing on the flute.
He leaps in the air as he beats on his drum.
Come, let us go and listen to his flute.

It is hard to be indifferent to the music of the flute heard in the fields.

Out in the fields a boy is playing on his flute.
    If you have ears you may hear him.
    If you have eyes you may see him.
    And know if he is for you or no.

The boy is playing on his flute.
Who is walking in front?
Who is walking behind?
Who is that hiding in between?
The boy is playing on his flute.
The big girls go ahead.
The little girls walk behind.
Their lovers are hiding in between.

A man too loves to see his girl in the dance or at work, picking mangoes, gathering mahua flowers, drawing water from the well.

When she draws water from the well,
She has to struggle with the heavy bucket.
But how beautiful to watch her doing so!

I have only found one song that seems to deal with ugliness rather than beauty. The lover has met a girl in the dark, and pretends that he does not know who she is. But he will recognize her the following day by her ugliness.

On your broad forehead is a *tikli*.
Wait till the dawn; I'll recognize you then.
How thin your legs are! The hair on your head is curly.
Your eyes are small and full of dirt.
The skin of your back is hard and rough.
Wait till the dawn. By these signs I will know you.

VI. A BAIGA'S WOOING

How does a Baiga fall in love and how does he set about his wooing? Does he usually marry the girl of his choice, or do tribal conventions and his parents' circumstances intervene?

More among the Baiga than among the Gond, marriages are based on love. In both tribes, men and women live with the partners they desire, defying all law and custom; but the forces of tribal convention and social position operate more strongly among the Gond. The result is that for the Gond marriage does not matter very much. Many a girl, in fact, treats marriage simply as the door to romance: once marriage has made a respectable woman of her, she begins her erotic life in earnest, and sooner or later elopes with her real lover. I have known several Gond girls

Milward

Bhumia girls.

who have run away on their wedding night, not because they have been married in tears against their will, but because they needed the marriage ceremony for their credit and position. It was more convenient to have it with the boy of their parents' choice—perhaps he was a Lamsena, perhaps the families had a long-standing agreement. There was no ill-feeling about it: marriage was simply the door to a new erotic life, no matter with whom. Thus the beautiful Lamia of Karanjia, the despair of the whole village, refused to elope with her real lover Kuar Singh, until she had been legally and expensively married to a quite insignificant person named Tiblu. That done, away she went with Kuar on her wedding night.

Kalarin, the famous virgin of Bohi, would not consent to live with her lover Motiram, until she had been properly married. Her parents would not marry her to Motiram because they had kept a Lamsena to whom the girl was bound. So she was married to her Lamsena, but on her wedding night, she bit and scratched the unfortunate boy and drove him from the house. A week later she was living happily with Motiram.

The same thing happens among the Baiga, though not so commonly. But both men and women must be married—formally—sometime or other. Often marriage initiates the life of romance; sometimes it takes place much later. Phulmat was forced to marry Marru, because her brother had run away with Marru's wife and he demanded a girl in return. But she refused to live with him, and soon found herself kept by someone else of her own choice. Mahi had to marry her Lamsena, but there was no love in it, and they soon separated, and each married someone else according to their own desire. Very often, I think, the Baiga marry the girl who has captured the fancy of their youth. Thus Dasseru married the girl whom he had loved from childhood, whom he first seduced by the bank of a stream while she was drawing water. Dunda caught a young virgin girl in the great forest that lies beyond Chauradadar, and seduced her. They were only ten years old, and *prima coitio est acerrima*. But afterwards it was different, and in the end they married. Bukwa, the landlord of Ufri, was in love with a young girl in his village when he was only twelve years old. But she was afraid and would not go to him. So one day he took her to the sal forest of Ufri to pick mohlain leaves. There he made her naked and enjoyed her. "After that she was quite happy. We were always meeting in the jungle. After a year I asked her father, and the engagement was arranged."

An important aspect of the Baiga theory of the erotic approach is that it is not considered improper for the girl to take the lead in the matter. A girl must never ask a man actually to have intercourse with her, a wife must never suggest it to her husband (though if he fails in his duty, she may accuse him of going to another woman) but she may in a general manner initiate the process of seduction.

This is how Jantri's wife, little Theko, won him. "She was dying for me, her mind was fixed on me. But I took no notice. So she got an old woman and sent her to me. She said, 'You have pricked her with the thorn of your love.' I said, 'You liar, I've never had anything to do with her.' 'No, no, she's mad for you.' 'Very well then,' I said, 'if she really loves me, let her meet me in the jungle.' The next day I went for wood, she went for leaves. I was very shy. I just went on cutting wood. She said, 'Come and help me pick these leaves.' I looked here and there; I was very young; I didn't know what to do. 'Why don't you help me,' she said again. 'No, I'm afraid of your father and mother.' 'What have they to do with it?' she said. 'They are not my masters. Come here at once.' But I was afraid and ran away.

"Then she sent me another message. She said, "I'll tell the *panch* that you caught my hand in the jungle and went to me by force and that I've your child in my belly.' But I thought she would be ashamed to do that, so I took no notice.

"And then one day she went to the headman. She had eaten so much that her stomach had swelled out. She opened her cloth and said, 'Look, a man has done this!' So the headman called all the boys and made us stand in a row before him. He said to the girl, 'Show us who it was.' I was very frightened then and tried to hide behind the others. But she came and caught my hand and said, 'This is the impotent rascal who took me by force in the jungle.' Then they made me marry her. I am very happy with her now, for she really loves me."

Dhan Singh had a less agreeable experience. "I was never one to run after girls," he told me. "But once a girl came of her own accord to my house. I said that I had no money. But that made no difference. She said she wanted to live with me, and she wouldn't go away. Then her husband came with his friends to fetch her. I said, 'Go and fetch her.' They went into the house, but she took an earthen pot in her arms, and said, 'If this breaks, I'll go to the police and say you forced me!' Then they were frightened and went away. After a few days she got tired of me and went to another man."

Of a girl who forces her company on a man, the Baiga say, "A Paithu has jumped in." A girl who can't make up her mind about any permanent association is called Jaidin—"she stays as many days as she is inclined for." A girl of many husbands is called Satrahin, "the wife of seventeen men". A girl who is audacious enough to get twice married officially is called Chaudahin, "she has been fourteen times round the pole".

The Baiga are not a jealous people nor do they gravely censure sexual freedom so long as it obeys the exogamous and endogamous customs of the tribe. But a faithless partner is not applauded. The men have a proverb: 'A rat scatters the grain all over the village: it is only the owner of the grain-bin that can never eat it.' And the women retort: 'The goat pastures all over the village: the woman of the house can never bring it home.' Other proverbs satirizing the relations of men and women are these: 'Everyone calls a simpleton's wife *bhauji*.' 'Directly you appear at the gate, she undoes her sari.' 'As the grindstone roars continually, so her mouth never ceases nagging her husband. But as the peg stands in the grindstone, though she may break his eyes, he takes no notice.'

VII. THE QUALITY OF A BAIGA'S LOVE

We have now studied the general background of the sexual consciousness of the Baiga, his early initiation into the mysteries of love, the strong position and large freedom of women, the conventions governing the erotic approach. How far does this freedom, this continual gratification of desire with anyone who happens to be about, dull the keen edge of passion and turn love from a wonder and a wild desire into a mere lust for physical gratification? If we may refer for a moment to a distinction made by D. H. Lawrence, I think it is safe to say that anyone who had been brought up in the 'cerebral-sex-tradition' would find his erotic life completely ruined by these conditions. But we must not apply our Western and 'civilized' ideas to Baiga conditions. Here perhaps Lawrence is right; the 'phallic consciousness' does not seem to be impaired by this state of affairs. It remains warm and generous, spontaneous and romantic. No one can deny that the songs quoted in this chapter breathe the very breath of love. Many Baiga have assured me that they extract the keenest delight from their erotic adventures.

> O my love, when I see your beauty,
> I laugh aloud for joy.

We must be content to accept a situation that is almost entirely different from our own. 'There is nothing roundabout in a Trobriand wooing,' says Malinowski, 'nor do they seek full personal relations with sexual possession only as a consequence. Simply and directly a meeting is asked for with the avowed intention of sexual gratification. If the invitation is accepted, the satisfaction of the boy's desire eliminates the romantic frame of mind, the craving for the unattainable and mysterious. If he is rejected there is not much room for personal tragedy, for he is accustomed from childhood to have his sexual impulses thwarted by some girls, and he knows that another intrigue cures this type of ill surely and swiftly.' This would serve as an accurate description of the Baiga.

But over and above these fleeting memories of delight or frustration, nearly every Baiga seems to have had one or two experiences of a much deeper character. One girl has above all others caught and held his imagination; one girl has filled his memory so that for years afterwards his body will quiver *ting-ting ting-ting* as he thinks of her. And these are the experiences that have left their mark on the songs, from which so much erotic knowledge may be extracted.

The Karma songs, for example, present us with a hundred vivid pictures of the intimate life of the Baiga. They show us a girl creeping across the room at night to sprinkle water on a sleeping man to rouse him to adventure. We see the lover coming in the rains and his eager welcome.

> Softly, softly the rain is falling.
> The yard is full of mud and slush.
> Beloved, here is water; wash your feet,
> And softly creep into my bed.

In a Karma of Silpuri, the lovers are pictured as going out to the edge of the village beneath a mahua tree.

> To-night you took me under the mahua tree.
> Once you beat me,
> Twice you beat me,
> Thrice you beat me with a strong arrow.
> O this very night you took me beneath the mahua tree.

The Baiga is not often frustrated in his desires, but he is sometimes, and then—until he can cure himself with a new attachment—his suffering is very real.

> I begged you to come to me last night.
> All my body was hungry for you.
> But you never came.
> My heart is breaking to pieces for your sake, my love.
> But you never come.

And again:

> O girl, I threw my *lota* on the ground.
> You heard it fall, but you took no notice.
> I called to you with my eyes,
> But you never came.

Love from the heart, is thus described:

In my garden is a well;
All round it hang the mangoes.
How deep and cool my well is.
But you are deeper far in love.
The sun beats down and you are thirsty,
But you care not for my water.
You know the deep love of the heart.

Most illuminating of all are the Dadaria, for the longer poems in this kind give us, by means of a dialogue between a girl and her lover, an account of the entire course of an intrigue from its beginning to its successful consummation. I will first quote a Dadaria from Bhimlat village. This shows us two lovers whose lives have from childhood hung together like clothes on a bamboo pole. It is a very beautiful account of the love 'that hurts the heart like the longing for a drink of mahua' and the desire to make it lasting and eternal. The meeting in the mango-grove at the end and the shy revelation of the secret mysteries of love remind me of Carew.

BOY: O silly girl, why do you always look behind you?
Take care! There is a ditch, you may fall into it.
GIRL: This chironji that we're eating will last only for two days,
But may our friendship be eternal.
BOY: A desire is pricking you for the mahua along the road,
So does the friendship of lovers hurt the heart.
GIRL: How lovely is my silver ring! But we are such a perfect pair, I fear
That someone may cast on us their Evil Eye.
BOY: I have bought a cloth in the bazaar,
Our lives have always hung together on the bamboo pole.
GIRL: See how swiftly the river rushes by!
The love we have created! Never alter it, my friend.
BOY: The leaves of the tamarind are very sour,
But this silver belt is lovely in your eyes.
GIRL: How bright our garden is with flowers,
But fairer still the mango-grove.
BOY: I asked you, girl, for water in a pitcher,
But let us go and see the mango-grove.
GIRL: There is a pitcher full of water.
I will come, my love, for your sake.
BOY: As we pick the mangoes we pull down the boughs around us.
Tell me where in your body is the hiding-place of love.

The next Dadaria that I will quote is a typical *banbhajan*, or forest song, with its refrain 'I've come to the jungle' which incidentally reveals the very varied reasons for which people go to the forest. This is a real intrigue poem, and it is interesting to note that it is the girl who takes the initiative, asking the boy to listen to her songs, wondering why he is sad, expressing her longing for a faithful lover, then—very characteristically—pointing to some monkeys on a tree near-by—"O little brother, they suspect us." In the end, they find harmony and intimacy. The girl offers to hide her lover in the folds of her dress and offers him a life-time of enjoyment, and he begs her to hug him so close that no air can pass between them.

GIRL: Come, take your axe and we'll go to the jungle.
Listen to my songs with your left ear.
BOY: I've come to the jungle for jamun berries,
O girl, they all say that you are a teacher of songs.
GIRL: I've come to the jungle to find kerela.
Tell me why you are sad, O friend.
BOY: I've come to the jungle for khamer fruit.
How I long for you! Come and sit with me.
GIRL: I've come to the jungle to gather thorns.
I weep with desire for a faithful lover.
BOY: I've come to the jungle to kill a wood-pigeon.
My love, I will leave everything for you.
GIRL: Look, on that dry tree the monkeys are sitting.
O little brother, they all suspect us.
BOY: I've come to the jungle to dig for roots.
Don't be frightened, I'll pay a bullock for you.
GIRL: O the mango in the valley and the creeper on the hill!
O love, come to me and I will hide you in my dress.
BOY: I've come to the jungle to gather leaves.
It is in our youth we must take delight.
GIRL: O my love, come drink some water and enjoy me.
As much as anyone could enjoy in all their life-time.
BOY: I've come to the jungle to kill a porcupine.
We'll sleep together by the mango-tree.
Hold me so close that no air can pass between us.

The next Dadaria is an altogether more serious affair. Here a youth seduces an already married woman from her allegiance to her husband. We miss something of the freshness and innocence of the first two poems. There are some very practical references to the financial situation and the

Milward

Bhumia girl with characteristic hemispherical breasts and large sharply defined areolæ.

police. The poem is divided into two 'Nights'. In the first, the girl has not yet made up her mind, and there is a good deal of preliminary skirmishing: the lovers are still, as it were, manœuvring for position. In the 'Second Night', however, the girl decides. She is still young, anxious rather for adventure than security. She cannot face the great heap of kodon that awaits her and the endless grinding of wheat. She decides to go with her lover. As they creep out of the village, she is thrilled by the beauty of the forest, standing magnificent and silent in the moonlight.

First Night

BOY: You have drawn water from the well, you are standing in your garden.
How am I to come to you, my friend?

GIRL: Wrap up your supper in parsa leaves,
And come and sit with me, O friend.

BOY: I want to cut my bewar, but I can't find an axe.
I have searched through all the village,
But there is not one girl unmarried.

GIRL: When you take your pipe, how the smoke puffs out of your mouth!
On yonder hill two Baiga boys are fighting over me.

BOY: When I drive an arrow, I do not miss.
To-night I will make you cry, holding your head in your hands.

GIRL: I can see your bones sticking through your skin.
Who are you to make me cry?

BOY: Whenever I go to cut wood in the forest,
I will always think of you, my friend.

GIRL: In my red sari I go there every day.
But all you remember is that I belong to another.

BOY: I'm going to the forest to get a bee-hive.
You have lovers inside your own *goti*.

GIRL: I'm going to the bazaar to buy a *lugra*.
You think of nothing but your own pleasure.

BOY: I'm going to the forest to dig *kanhia-kānda*.
Tell me truly, will you come or no.

GIRL: You have climbed half-way up the hill.
And now for weariness you throw yourself down.

BOY: How silent and lonely is this jungle.
Who is there to see anything we do?

Second Night

BOY: To-night the moon lights up the road.
I looked everywhere for you to see if you would come.

GIRL: Out in the channa field there is a little hut.
The girl is weeping for her necklace.
Her love has robbed her of it.
BOY: Keep the liquor safely in the hollow *thondi.*
When I hear your voice my mind burns like fire.
GIRL: Look how the roof is blackened by the smoke.
My love grows a little stronger.
But if we part my body will grow weak.
BOY: See the bright moon which lightens every path.
Why do you lie to me so often, friend.
GIRL: When we live at home there is rice and curd to eat.
When we run away to the forest, there is nothing but berries.
BOY: When the path is not used, it is overgrown with jungle.
You only want my money, but I want
A girl who will love me for ever.
GIRL: Ah! He was smoking his pipe, but now he puts it down.
This is a secret between you and me.
Don't make me scream or all the world will hear.
BOY: In the waters of the well I see the image of a palace.
Go and ask the police how many rupees are in my *basni.*
GIRL: Look at that heap of kodon. I have got to pound it.
I'll run away instead. No one will pursue us.
BOY: Why go on grinding wheat for another man?
Come away with me. I'll make a report to the police.
GIRL: How beautiful is the hem of the forest in the moonlight.
My heart is fixed on you, my friend.

In the two following songs, one a Karma of Boira, and one from Umaria, we have condensed pictures of the actual crisis of an elopement.

It is very cloudy, but no rain is falling.
She says, No it is too dark!
All around it is so dark!
I cannot see my hand.
The wind is blowing strongly.
Why are you crying, my darling?
Take your rings and your cloth,
Put on all your ornaments,
And come. Don't fear the dark.
Come as the lawa to its mate,
And we'll run away together.

In the second Karma, the husband is more anxious to see if his wife has left the ornaments behind than if she is there herself.

> The mangoes and the tamarind are thick with fruit in spring.
> At midnight my lover sends for me.
> O why does my lover send for me?
>
> She takes off her tinkling anklets and goes quietly to him.
> O why does my lover send for me?
>
> Her husband wakes. He takes a lamp
> And searches in the house.
> Has she left those silver anklets or no?
> O why does my lover send for me?

VIII. THE BACKGROUND OF ROMANCE

The Baiga have the advantage of a perfect setting for their romances. The forest, the *madhuban*, the sweet forest, the *nandanban*, the forest of delight, is his natural home. What lover could fail to be inspired by its remoteness, the sweet smell of flowers, the murmuring of the wind in the branches of uncounted trees? Here the simple, natural and direct passions of the Baiga come to perfect maturity.

The forest, then, is the trysting-place of lovers. A party of Baiga goes out to dig for roots. Gradually they break up and separate. A boy follows his girl, and helps her; his greater strength removes a stubborn root. "Then she is pleased, they find a bush, she lets him do it" (Sujji of Kawardha). Sometimes the boy teases her, tells her she doesn't know how to use her axe, tries to take it from her. "She struggles, they hit one another—in a moment they are embracing" (Panku of Bohi). Or perhaps the girl is cutting wood. The boy comes up behind her, tells her she is not doing it properly, threatens her with his axe. "She seizes it, they struggle to and fro; she is in his arms, they are alone in the forest." If the girl is obstinate, the lover waits till the sun is high in heaven and she thirsty; then he comes with a *thondi* (hollow bamboo used as a bottle) full of liquor. I am told that this is a love-charm that never fails of its effect.

One of the songs describes how a boy climbed a mango tree, and cried "hoop-hoop, hoop-hoop," like a monkey, to attract his girl. But her mother-in-law came along at just the wrong moment, and the girl ran away, crying out that she was frightened of the monkey.

Often it is the girl who takes the initiative.

The girl who stands in the shade of the mahua tree.
By her eyes alone can make you restless.

She sets out to trap her lover.

For the turtle-dove I have set a snare.
To trap my lover I have put roots in the fold of my *lugra.*

Sometimes she throws stones from the shelter of a thicket to attract his attention.

I was going quietly on my way,
Why did you throw stones at me?
Why did you wink at me?
This is a forest, so take care.
I'll catch you by the neck,
And throw you down among the bushes.

In this way the lovers play a sort of hide-and-seek, hiding little presents in their clothes, so that they have to go very near each other, and struggle to get them.

How can I console my mind and body?
I'll get *chutki* for her feet.
I'll hide them in the fold of my *dhoti.*
She'll have to hunt for them.
Thus will I console my mind and body.

No wonder that the Baiga loves his forest, which supplies him with food and with some of the most vivid experiences of his life. So he can sing of it with real love, as in this Karma from Boira village.

Which is the tree that is green and dear to you?
Which is the flower that makes the whole forest red?
The trees on the hill are green and dear to me.
The flower of the semur is red.

The wooded banks of the streams that flow everywhere among the hills provide what is perhaps the most beautiful scenery in the Baiga country. Here too is a perfect setting for the encounter of lovers.

Down by the river, I can just see her sari,
And my heart is full of hope.

A girl always has an excuse to go and fetch water from the well or a stream, and it is a convention that she may go alone.

> On the bank of the river, my Ratnu is working.
> His girl passes by, she puts her pitcher down
> She winks at him with her left eye
> And goes down to the water's edge.
> Ah, look how secretly she beckons him.
> She crosses the sunlit water
> To the shade of trees beyond.

In another song a young Baiga is trying to persuade his girl to fetch him water. He will go with her to the lonely shaded river; he will bear her company as she goes to the mango-grove.

> O water-girl with tinkling anklets,
> You are walking to and fro.
> Go and fetch water, for the dusk is falling,
> I will meet you at the lonely well.

And:

> Sing how your girl spilt the water from her pitcher,
> And how you went laughing together to the river.

In another song, the boy goes down to the river, on an evening when a cold wind blows, and he bathes near his girl.

> The evening breeze blows chill across the water.
> My girl has gone to bathe.
> But it is cold; she only splashes water on her legs.
> And I too am cold in the waters of this stream.
> If I can get you, my girl, I'll warm you at my fire.

Hitherto we have watched the Baiga in the remote solitude of the forest, but the crowded arena of the bazaar or dance is as good a trysting-place. Or rather this is the place where attachments are begun and trysts are made. The bazaar is the place for the first shy gifts of love and admiration. 'Give her a pice or two of parched gram in the bazaar, and she will give you everything,' is a proverb in Kawardha. Gifts are not essential to the success of an intrigue; there is no idea that the man must give some kind of equivalent to the woman for her services to him in intercourse. But little gifts are treasured as tokens and proofs of love, and a wise lover will always invest in a few bangles or a basket of fruit. "Give me the ring from your finger; it will be a love-token that will last till death."

The Baiga seem quite indifferent to the monetary value of these gifts. In one of the songs a girl is described as having lost an armlet worth five rupees and a *hawel* worth seven rupees eight annas.

> But the ring you gave me,
> Though it is only worth one pice,
> Is precious to me as my life.

A gift, however small, will cure most ills and bring an end to any quarrel.

> Beneath the mango tree my queen is weeping.
> Don't cry, my little queen. I'll bring a *bichhia* for you.
> Surely I will bring it.

And when a secret lover comes to the house by night, his girl must welcome him with gifts. "See how many things I have made ready for you. Here is fire in a dry cake of dung, water in a pitcher, rice in a basket, sweets on a plate. Come, eat, my love. And see how beautiful on my arms are the bangles you gave me." Then the man sings softly:

> My girl went to the bazaar and bought new bangles.
> She came back home and showed me her breasts.

The Karma dance is a natural invitation to love. The rhythm and excitement of its movements, the close proximity of men and women, the erotic nature of the songs, the countless opportunities of the night, inflame the senses and lead to many lasting romances.

During the Karma, as the girls bend forward in the dance, and their breasts sway to and fro, a man's hand shoots out for momentary contact with his beloved. It is a sign. After a little while, the girl says, "I'm getting fever," or "I've a bad headache," and she slips away. Five minutes later the man says, "My waist is breaking, I must go and rest," and he follows her into the jungle on the borders of the village.

The girl treads on a man's heel when his back is towards her in the movement of the dance. This is a sign. Another sign is for the girl to walk on her heels when the man is looking. Sometimes a girl makes up songs, which they all sing, but only her lover understands.

> O the swing of a shoe!
> Let us sing together,
> And we will soon be friends.

And then at last, the girl yields to her lover, or wins him to her side.

O my love, drink as much water as you can,
And enjoy me.
As much as anyone could enjoy in all his life-time.

And again:

Cut a green bamboo.
Pull off the bark.
Get a bed ready;
A bed with four legs.
At midnight there's a lovely girl
Sleeping on the bed.
At midnight her lover
Mounts his horse and rides away.

And then, provided he has found real love, a man is utterly and unfeignedly happy. His gifts have borne fruit; those meetings by the river or in the forest were not merely transitory; the girl he loved has come to him, and will remain.

His body is like gold.
His soul is all pleasure.
Like a blazing fire his face.
He looks at his love and feels nor thirst nor hunger.
You may abuse him to your heart's content;
He takes no notice of it.

IX. THE EROTIC APPROACH TO INTERCOURSE

We have now traced the course of a Baiga romance to the very threshold of its consummation. We must now draw even nearer and try to watch two Baiga at the most intimate and delightful moment of their lives.

I do not think it is unfair to say that the Baiga are unusually deficient in all the accessories of erotic culture. Their approach to the sexual act is immediate and direct; they know no refinements of approach; they adopt one position only for the sexual act itself, and regard all others as unnatural; in a normal man tumescence occurs almost immediately—the only tactile contact preparatory to it seems to be some form of mammillary excitation. If a Baiga could read such books as Forel's *The Sexual Question*, or Krafft-Ebing's *Psychopathia Sexualis*, he would not only be puzzled, he would be horrified. The variations described by Krafft-Ebing would seem to him purely bestial, the refinements discussed by Forel would appear wholly unnecessary.

The kiss, for example, both among Baiga and their neighbours the Gond, plays a very small part in love-making, though it is more commonly practised by the Panka and Pardhan.[1] Nor do the Baiga have any tactile substitute for it; they do not louse, or scratch, or bite, or nip the eyebrows; *fellatio* is unknown, and *penilinctus* very rare. Even an erotic expert like Lahakat assured me that he had never kissed a girl in his life. "Our bodies kiss," he said, "so why should we use our mouths?"

The position adopted during intercourse does not favour kissing. Dhan Singh has kissed, but very seldom. Mahatu once saw an Englishwoman kiss her husband, a forest officer, and thought it disgusting. In Kawardha, however, I was told that young people do kiss, though they stop the practice after the birth of a child. "They bite the cheeks with their teeth. While the girl is lying before him, he lifts her up, he kisses her, he puts her down again." They even kiss on the lips, but it is not a long protracted kiss, and the tongue plays no part in it.

It is significant, however, that in the whole range of the songs, riddles and folk-tales that I have recorded—although sexual matters are freely and frankly discussed throughout—there is only one reference to the kiss.

A very practical reason for the low value set on kissing may be the filthy mouths and foul breath of the Baiga. I remember once discussing this point with a group of Baiga and suggesting that a man whose mouth stank of stale tobacco could hardly expect to be a successful lover. The next morning, three of the company declared that they had abandoned smoking for ever!

The Baiga discuss the sexual act simply and naturally; they are neither embarrassed nor excited. Their method of intercourse is similar to that of the Trobriand Islanders.

"They lie down together and the man holds his girl tightly in his arms; their legs are interlaced, he rubs his face against hers." The woman may sing quietly to her lover a refrain from a Karma such as:

> Let us sleep together in a beautiful bed.
> Hold me so tightly that no air can pass between our bodies.

And:

> These two are playing together.
> Thigh to thigh, breast to breast.
> Their legs are intertwined.
> Slowly, slowly he presses into her.

[1] Psychologists may trace the connection between the long period of suckling (pp. 136, 228), devotion to the breast and indifference to the kiss, the mouth having lost much of its erogenous character.

Muria girl.
Bhumia girl in dance-attire.

There is little conversation; the Baiga have practically no vocabulary of endearment; almost directly after the clothes are removed, the normal healthy man enters the state of tumescence, and commences the sexual act.

The woman lies on her back, her legs apart and raised, the knees bent. The man squats or kneels in front of her, taking her legs under his arms and against his waist. Then "he swings to and fro, as the green bamboo swings in the wind". Or "his body wriggles to and fro like rice-stalks in the breeze".

"We sleep," says Dhan Singh, "on separate beds. The Gond always sleep in each other's arms, not so the Baiga. If I go to sleep without doing it my girl wakes me up. 'What are you sleeping for?' she asks. 'Whom have you been with to-day?' But if I am awake, we wait till all is quiet. Then a ripple passes between us. She coughs to show she is ready. Then we go on to the floor together. She doesn't remove all her clothes. She lies on her back with her legs in the air. I kneel against her. It knows its place; it makes no mistake. Like an arrow it goes straight to its home. If it misses, the man is impotent. She puts her legs round my waist. She makes no response. She wants it, but she mustn't show it. So long as her breast is round like a fig, you hold and press it; when it is loose as a sack, you let it go. Once you are there, you want to live there, stuck there, pressed to her, for ever."

"There is no other way of doing it," adds Lahakat. "Only in this way can you have pleasure. If you want to enjoy your *pej*, you must sit properly for eating it, or you won't be able to digest it. So with this you must sit properly. In my youth I wanted to live always doing it."

Sometimes, however, intercourse is effected side by side. The woman's legs then embrace the man and he clasps her to him. But this method is not popular, and is adopted mainly at times of sickness and weakness.

Dr. Malinowski has emphasized the difference between this mechanism of coitus and the European. He has also drawn attention to the fact that the Queensland aborigines copulate in a very similar manner. In India, so far as I know, the method is fairly common,[1] though not exclusively adopted as by the Baiga and Gond. The Baiga are emphatic that no other way is possible. The astride attitude recommended by Martial is described and ridiculed in one of the folk-tales; in another, the averse position is dismissed as only worthy of a goat.

It is naturally very difficult to discover what the woman feels about these

[1] I notice, for example, that the Lepcha of Sikkim appear to follow the same method. See Gorer: *Himalayan Village* (London, 1938), p. 330.

things. But some of the Karma songs, all composed and sung by women, provide us with a few authentic documents.

i

Long, long are the pumpkins!
They are milky and long.
He sleeps all night with me,
But in the day he calls me sister.
Often, often he plays with my firm breasts.
They are his playthings.

ii

The brinjal is growing round the borders of my court.
O I am a young calf, and he is a bull.
He is pushing me against my will.
He is tugging at my breasts.

iii

O wheaten is the bread, from the coconut the oil!
He has filled his belly with thick wheaten bread.
He is playing roughly with me.
Now he has attacked my breasts.

iv

I asked him for a little love.
But he gave so much that he wore me out.
Even the crows began to talk outside.
For he wouldn't let me leave the bed.
The whole night long he hugged and hugged and hugged me.

v

The chutney's made of mango,
The curry's made of bohar flowers.
My lover's lust is up.
Come let us go to bed.

The curry's made of karela.
The *pej* is made of *kutki*.
All night my lover slept with me.
Now take me to the big bazaar.

He gave me *pairi* at the big bazaar.
And that night too my lover slept with me.
All night the *pairi* tinkled, tinkled.
Now take me to the river for a bathe.

X. FREQUENCY OF INTERCOURSE

One of the things that it is difficult for the alien mind to understand is the extraordinary frequency of intercourse indulged by the Baiga. Of course, we have to discount a little the Baiga's own claims to potency: he believes that he belongs to the most virile race in the world; in fact, before bewar was stopped, the penis of the Baiga was five times larger than anybody else's. So when a Baiga tells you that he has intercourse three or four times a day, you are not bound to believe him.

Not always—but sometimes you should. "The first few days after marriage," says the young and charming Jantri, "we go three or four times a day. To quench my thirst and to quench hers, I had to do it six times a day. But now she has had two children, and my life is normal again." But by 'normal' Jantri does not mean Luther's 'twice a week', but 'twice a day'—once at bed-time and once at cock-crow.

This is the universal minimum. Even old Thaggur, chapfallen and wizened as he is, says, "Twice a day is enough!" But Sujji declares that "in youth we do it three or four times a day, but when children are born, then once or twice. Sometimes we even rest for a day". Lahakat, as we would expect, boasts a higher standard than that. "Three times in the day, five times at night—that is the least a true Baiga should do!" But Mahatu, in his old age, has fallen back on the Lutheran standard and contents himself with dreams.

The Baiga theory seems to be that you must always gratify a desire when it arises. "I may starve for three days," says Lahakat. "But I won't keep away from my wife." "If the Finger of Fire says Come," said Mahatu once with the full approval of his audience. "You must follow. This little finger is our master. Not the English Government, not the Police Captain, not the Ranger, they are not our masters; we are ruled by the Finger of Fire."

This continual intercourse undoubtedly places a great strain on the usually under-nourished and often diseased husband, and leads to the impotence and dread of it that we will discuss in the chapter on Dreams. For if he fails, not only is he no true Baiga, but his wife will accuse him of having betrayed her during the day, and if he fails often will certainly leave him.

The Baiga do not generally observe times of ritual continence. Bausi claims to do so (p. 159) and Mahatu was ordered in a dream to be celibate for a time (p. 135). But normally the gunia preparing to begin his magic rites, the hunter setting out to shoot, the fisherman on his way to the river, are not bound to abstinence. They do not, however, seem to have any idea that coitus may help the fishing or hunt to be more fruitful. No, it is simply that "when the horse is thirsty, you must let it go to the river".

The only times of abstinence are during menstruation, in advanced pregnancy and immediately after birth. During his wife's menstrual period a man is forbidden to go either to her or anyone else; if he has intercourse at this time, he may lose all his semen. This rule is, of course, of the utmost benefit to the Baiga; it ensures him a regular period of rest and sexual recovery.

During pregnancy, says Lahakat, "a man should not go to his wife more than three times a week, and after the sixth month not at all. After birth he must give her rest for three months if the child is a girl, for four months if it is a boy. On the day his wife washes her head and first brings water to the house, he may take her, but only if she agrees".

Not everyone, however, would agree with Lahakat's moderation. Many Baiga continue to go to their wives up to the eighth month, though most of them observe the rules after birth.

XI. THE PREVALENCE AND CENSURE OF SEXUAL DEVIATIONS

When I first began to make discreet enquiries about the prevalence of sexual deviations among the Baiga, I was hampered by the belief that these were very rare among aboriginal, and especially among Indian aboriginal, peoples. I had long been told by my Indian friends that masturbation was rarely practised in India, that homosexuality was regarded—except by one community—with horror and disgust, that bestiality was unknown, and that sadistic and masochistic tendencies could not flourish among so gentle and restrained a people. At first also my own researches tended to confirm this view, and I regarded such examples to the contrary as came to my notice as interesting exceptions. For in the first place, most normal people are genuinely ignorant of these matters and in any case are not likely to discuss them with strangers. If, for example, a Confucian psychiatrist were to question a Bishop about the possible prevalence of pæderasty among churchwardens, I doubt if he would receive a very polite or detailed answer. In the second place I was greatly impressed by the general sexual hyperæsthesia of the Baiga, and was constantly tempted to classify it as here satyriasis and there nymphomania. I resisted, and rightly resisted, the temptation, but the facts before me were not likely to convince me that anything but normal, if excessive, hetero-sexual activities were ever practised. One is hardly encouraged to look for deviations, when one discovers that even a slight variation from the conventional posture in coitus is regarded as indecorous!

But just about the time that my Baiga friends began to feel that they knew me well enough to speak freely in my presence, they also dropped hints that they had more to say about sexual deviation than they had hitherto revealed. Soon, to my astonishment, I learnt that masturbation was widely practised, that nearly all women were masochistic and loved being beaten by their husbands, that homosexual practices (however detested) were not unknown and erotic pedophilia comparatively common, and that bestiality was sufficiently frequent to have been made a tribal offence and to be penalized by tribal sanctions.

I remember overhearing a discussion by a little gathering of Baiga one evening. There was a good fire, and when they had got warmed inside and out, they got talking—quite spontaneously—on this very subject. The gist of their conversation was that sexual aberrations were of two kinds. They were either a substitute—compensatory as we would say—or an experiment. I believe this classification to be correct. I have never found a case of excessive masturbation or one that was not immediately cured by the coming of a woman, nor have I found any example of congenital homosexuality.

Sexual aberrations are first, then, compensatory, a very second-best substitute for the real thing. If you can't get a girl, they were saying in a tolerant, rather amused, fashion, if you can't get a girl even in a dream, then of course you may masturbate. It is not very manly—because, of course, a Baiga, being the most adept lover in the world, ought never to be without *some* girl. But if he is, and "his seed boils within and troubles him", let him masturbate. There is no harm in it, it doesn't affect his health, it breaks no tribal taboo, it incurs no penalty.

But if a man is not satisfied with that, and none of my old Baiga seemed to think very much of it, then he may get a young and pretty boy and sleep with him instead of with a girl. But I think that they did not really mean sodomy by this; they thought of the frustrated Baiga playing with the boy and consoling himself with his company. Or if he can't get a boy, there are goats and mares, sows and cows to be had everywhere. But if you are caught with an animal, you are a social outcaste, you must stand drinks all round, or no one will smoke with you or share your food.

But, of course, directly you can get a girl, you give up everything else and go to her.

Children, from the age of six to sixteen, must make experiments. A child knows very little about its own body; let it explore. No one, said my old gentlemen, is going to take any notice of that. If little girls want adventures, let them have them; if little boys like to play with each other, it doesn't matter very much.

I have tried to reproduce the rather flippant and tolerant way in which the Baiga discuss these things. Their censure of them is not generally severe.

But homosexuality, in the full sense of the word is regarded with real horror and disgust. Baiga who will discuss with freedom and even with zest the general licence of their tribe, who will mention actual cases of incest and bestiality without embarrassment, grow ashamed and awkward at any mention of sodomy. "It is unheard of; no one could do it."

Chapter IX

THE GREAT CRISES: MARRIAGE

I. THE SOCIAL SIGNIFICANCE OF MARRIAGE

MARRIAGE is of great social significance, though it has little sexual importance, for the Baiga. Before marriage, which generally is celebrated some time after puberty—in 1931 only 590, or 4·2 per cent of the whole female population had been married before thirteen—both bride and bridegroom will have had many erotic adventures, some with one another, and some with other girls and boys. Nor does marriage initiate either a permanent or an exclusive relationship. The husband may at any moment add a fresh wife to his establishment, and the wife may at any moment run away to someone else.

But socially and economically marriage is very important. The necessity of paying a 'bride-price' is an incentive to family thrift, and a stimulus to youthful labour. There can be no economic progress without the creation of wants: marriage supplies one of the chief wants in Baiga life. Socially, an unmarried woman is unheard of: the spinster does not exist: there is a mere handful of widows: the unmarried man is doomed to become a *raksa* after death. For a woman, marriage is specially important; although pre-nuptial intercourse is common, she passes through the door into a new erotic life; she gains a new freedom—hitherto a whole family has watched her movements; now she has to conceal them only from her husband. Marriage makes a respectable woman of her; it licenses her to bear children; it establishes her as a responsible member of the community.

For a man, marriage is chiefly important because permanent sexual association is impossible without it. Otherwise it neither limits his erotic activities, not extends them. For both sexes, the formal and official marriage does not usually initiate a life-partnership. That comes later, after further sexual experiment. I do not mean that the Baiga are ignorant of the joys of a permanent and more or less exclusive relationship; many of them have experienced it. What I do mean is that it is not generally inaugurated by the formal and official ceremony that we are about to describe.

II. THE ENGAGEMENT

A boy and girl may be formally engaged at any age, sometimes in childhood, more frequently soon after puberty. A Birha song from Bhimlat runs—

> O Bhavani, write it, write it in my fate!
> A daughter twelve years old, a son of sixteen—
> These two will make a perfect pair.

The boy's party approaches the girl's house. Five friends of the family go ahead and say to the girl's father, "To-day, visitors are coming to your house!" They are followed by the boy himself, his father and mother, and other relatives, with gifts of chickens, coconut, cloth, bangles and some bottles of liquor. "Why have you come?" asks the girl's father. "I have come to find a gourd in which to put my seed. Have you a gourd here?" If the girl's father answers "Yes", the party enters the compound and sits down.

Then the girl's father takes a cupful of liquor and carries it into the house. He offers a few drops to Dulha Deo, to Bhitraha Deo, to Karirat, to Bhavani Mata, to Narayan Deo, to the ancestors living by the hearth, to whatever there is of holy and numinous in the house, and says, "This boy and this girl belong to you: show us what we are to do!"

Meanwhile the girl has been watching the scene from behind the door or some other secluded place. The father goes to her and says, "Shall I drink or no?" The girl probably knows her prospective husband all too well, and if she likes him, she says "Yes!" If he is a new boy, however, she may take some time to decide. But her decision is final. When she gives her consent, her father goes out and begins to drink with the boy's party, his *samdhi*, belonging if possible to a different *goti* and *garh*. We have seen that the rules of exogamy are not always observed, but their breach is comparatively rare in formal engagements and weddings.

This is the normal procedure in Dindori. In Kawardha, I was told, the boy and girl have a talk together first, though not in private: and if they like one another, they tell their parents, "Drink your liquor!"

In Bilaspur, the Bhaina Baiga have a more elaborate approach. Outside the house, the two fathers sit opposite each other on the ground, and after a little talk, the girl's father takes the boy's father on his back, and carries him into the house. They eat together on that day, but not otherwise

Bhumia with thonga-phānda.
Preparing the marriage elephant with three cots, winnowing-fans and baskets.

until the marriage. In the evening, they let the boy and girl sleep together, and in the morning they ask the girl if she liked him. If she says "Yes," her father offers a chicken and a pair of bangles to Dulha Deo, saying, "Trusting in thee we have arranged a marriage. Do not spoil it!"

In Mandla, when the girl has given her consent, the boy's father greets his *samdhi*. "*Johār samdhi!*" To which the reply is "*Johār purkha!*" Then the girl's father asks, "Is it to be one leg or two legs?" meaning "Are we to have one or two rupees' worth of liquor?" All the villagers come together, and they celebrate the *sagai*.

There remains the delicate matter of the 'bride-price'. The two *samdhi* settle this together with a good deal of miscellaneous advice from everybody. This is called *sukh* in Mandla and Bilaspur, and elsewhere *kharcha*. It generally amounts to Rs. 18 or Rs. 25, and is often paid in kind. At the time of payment, in whole or part, the boy's parents give a feast known as the Barokhi. It is now that they fix the date of marriage. This may be celebrated at any time save the sacred months of Jeth and Pus, specially in Jeth when Dharti Mata lies waiting to be impregnated, and even the Agaria refuse to put nails in a bed or fix the share in a plough.

Russell gives a slightly different account, which may represent the custom in Baihar twenty years ago. 'Three ceremonies,' he says, 'should precede the marriage. The first, which may take place at any time after the birth of both children, consists merely in the arrangement for their betrothal. The second is only a ratification of the first, feasts being provided by the boy's parents on both occasions. While on the approach of the children to marriageable age the final betrothal or *barokhi* is held. The boy's father gives a large feast at the house of the girl and the date of the wedding is fixed.'

III. THE MARRIAGE CEREMONY

The chief actors in the marriage ceremony are the two *dosi* and the two *suāsin*. The *dosi* are usually old men who stand in the relation of father or uncle to the bride and bridegroom; they perform most of the religious rites. The *suāsin* are young unmarried girls, sisters or cousins of the bridal pair. They have to remain in constant attendance.

I will now describe the actual course of a Baiga marriage, the marriage of Kalarin to her Lamsena, Bura, in Pandpur, on March 8th, 1938. As this was a marriage between a girl and her Lamsena who was already living in the house of her father, there was no marriage procession[1] from one

[1] The wedding-procession starts from the bridegroom's house and goes to the bride's village. Ward says that it starts from the bride's house, but this is the Gond, not the Baiga, custom.

village to another, nor did the bridegroom carry the bride home in triumph at the end of the proceedings; but otherwise the rituals did not vary from the normal.

In this wedding, the *dosi* of the bride was her own *mamā*, her mother's brother, who took the place of the bridegroom's father who was dead. Bura's *dosi* was our old friend Dhan Singh (see Chapter IV) who was Kalarin's father's elder brother. But several other old men who belonged to Dhan Singh's generation and were his 'brothers' (*bhai*) acted as *dosi* in the course of the proceedings.

Kalarin's *suāsin* was Chiuli, her *mamā*'s daughter, and Bura's *suāsin* was his own sister Dukli. Bura also had the services of a *suāsa*, poor young frustrated Chandru, who cannot afford a wife himself and had a face of gloom throughout the ceremonies.

The marriage began on a Tuesday morning with the Bichar. The *dosi* went to the shrine of Thakur Deo, offered fire and incense and placed a little lamp before him. The *suāsin* brought a pot of water and some rice. After the usual mantra to prevent the intervention of witches, the *dosi* dropped two grains of rice into the water. They immediately approached each other, the tips met, they swung round and floated side by side. This was an excellent omen: had the grains not come together or had they remained tip to tip, the marriage would not have been successful.

In the afternoon of the same day, the Chiksa was performed. Since both bride and bridegroom were living in the same one-roomed house, they had to sit in opposite corners, wrapped in white clothes, and guarded by their *suāsin*. Bura was watched by his *suāsa* also; when the latter left his post for a few minutes, he was sternly rebuked by Dhan Singh, and returned to duty. In front of both Kalarin and Bura were *kalsa*—earthen pots, cow-dunged and patterned with rice—full of kodon, and earthen lamps on top.

Now each *suāsin* took a dish of *marria* flour and water, and anointed the bridal pair all over till they looked white and leprous. Then they covered them with cloth, and put a little rice in their hands. Then a man picked up Bura and a woman put Kalarin on her back, and they all went out to find an anthill, the *suāsin* preceding them with the *kalsa* on their heads. A chorus of old women sang, "*Tari nāni nāna re teri nāni nāna.*" After some search, we found two small anthills side by side; "one for the Raja, one for the Rani," exclaimed Dhan Singh, pleased. The two *dosi* sat down, traced a little square with flour and turmeric in front of each anthill, and tied a string round each. They offered incense, two pice, some liquor and *chīla roti* (very thin, made of *marria* flour and *gur*, fried in *ramtilla* oil) to each. Then everyone drank a little. Then the bridegroom,

Bura, sat in his mother's lap in front of the anthills, and put his rice before them. Someone put a *mūsar* (rice-pounder) into his hands, and everyone within reach caught hold of it and dug it into the ground. Then the bride, Kalarin, came and sat in her mother's lap, and did the same thing. When she had finished, Bura's men friends and Kalarin's women friends began to fight for the rice-pounder. There was a vigorous and ribald struggle, and Bura's party won. One of them took the rice-pounder and dug with it round the anthills; the women and children took lumps of earth in their clothes back to the house. When the party got home, Bura went inside and shut the door, and Kalarin's friends had to fight to get it open. The earth was thrown down in front of the house. Bura and Kalarin returned to their corners, and the *kalsa* with the lighted lamps were placed in front of them.

Now a party of men went to the jungle to bring the *marua* wood. They found a tall sarai tree (*boswellia serrata*), and a man climbed it and cut a branch. As he went up, he chopped off a bit of bark. They ran to look at it. If it fell *chit*, or the inside upwards, a boy would be born; if it fell *pat*, the inside downwards, it would be a girl. To-day, it fell *chit*. While the man cut the branch, the *dosi* offered incense, *chīla roti* and recited mantra before the tree. They should have tied a string round the trunk, but they forgot.

Out of this wood, they made two little stumps, the *mangrohi*, and two small flat slabs, the *pīdha*. The younger men and boys cut long branches of char (*buchanania latifolia*), thaur (*bauhinia retusa*) and mango, and brought them to a clearing. Here the bride's elder sister's husband, Pindal, brought rice in a *dāli* and *dāl* in an earthen pot, and served it with his own hands on leaf-plates. They all sat there and ate.

Meanwhile in the house, the *suāsin* were bathing the bride and bridegroom. All the *marria* flour was washed off, and they were wrapped in their white clothes, and taken back to their corners.

Unceasingly the chorus of old women sang, "*Tari nāni nāna re tari nāni nāna.*"

And now at sunset a procession of men, bearing the wood and branches for the booth, came singing. The *suāsin* put a *pīdha* before the house, and each man put his foot on it, and she washed it. Every visitor who came that evening brought a green branch, and his feet were washed. Then the men dug holes for the booth, and the *dosi* offered incense and a coconut and put two pice in each hole dug for the *mangrohi*.

In this marriage, both bride's and bridegroom's poles and *mangrohi* were set up in the same booth (*marua*). Normally, one is made in the bride's house and one in the bridegroom's. The *dosi* put two long poles of *sarai* wood and the *mangrohi* into their holes: in the bridegroom's hole they also placed a plantain trunk, and decorated both with bamboo and mango leaves. The *suāsin* came and made a plaster of the mud taken from the anthill and put it round the poles. They also made *sehri*, raised mud supports for the *kalsa*.

Inside the house, the *paili*-divination took place. A *paili* (wooden measure) full to overflowing with *ramtilla* was brought in a winnowing-fan. First the bridegroom (sitting in his mother's lap) and then the bride, took this, emptied the *ramtilla* into the fan, and distributed it to nine people. These then had to return it to the measure. If the seeds still rose above the mouth of the measure, the marriage would be a success; if the level sank, it would be a failure. To-day the omens were again friendly. Someone always keeps back a handful, and there is a cry of "Thief!"

Outside, the younger men were busy completing the booth, giving it a thick roof of leafy branches. Until this was ready, bride and bridegroom, and their attendants, had to fast; now they had a meal of boiled rice and salt.

Everything was delayed because the drums did not appear. Two or three messengers were sent. The interval of waiting was spent usefully, however, in some serious drinking. The bride and bridegroom were anointed with turmeric.

At midnight, the drums (two *nangāra* and a *timki*) arrived, and there was some dancing, After a couple of hours came the Kuara Bhawar. In this rite, bride and bridegroom each goes separately round the *mangrohi* pole, preliminary to the Bara Bhawar when they go round together.

Bura came out first, his *suāsa* in front, his *suāsin* behind with the *kalsa* on her head. When Bura reached the threshold, he 'touched its feet' and threw some rice into the *marua*. Then he walked slowly round his own pole twice, his mother holding him behind. He sat down on a *māchi* which was placed on his mother's *anchra* (end of her *lugra*) which was spread to receive it. The *suāsin* covered him with turmeric, and he was carried on the *māchi* back to the house.

Kalarin repeated the process, save that her mother did not go round the pole with her, but sat weeping loudly. After she had been anointed with turmeric, two men (any two men) picked her up, and swinging her vigorously to and fro, took her round the pole and so into the house.

After this, the *kalsa* with their lighted lamps, were kept in front of the *mangrohi*.

Dancing continued till dawn. The Bilma is danced by men and women together, and is a wildly confused riotous performance. The women held *chatkalia* in their hands, small-handled castanets of wood which they clicked

Marriage. *The bride.*
Digging up earth for the marriage-booth with a rice-pounder.

together. The women danced in a group, sometimes going to and fro, sometimes hopping about in complete disorder.

At dawn, they began to prepare the marriage elephant. In most marriages, it is now that the bridegroom's procession arrives and is met by the bride's brother riding on the elephant. The elephant is made of three cots, one as base and two for the back. Winnowing-fans are the ears, a *dāli* (basket) is put for head, a *kumni* (trap) for trunk, and a bundle of straw for tail. A bell is tied round the neck, and a large gourd and a plantain trunk hung beneath the tail. The whole is covered with a blanket. The bride's brother mounted the elephant, a *pharsa* axe in his hand, and half a dozen men hoisting it on to their shoulders carried it round the village amid scenes of wild enthusiasm. Women followed singing, and men waving axes and sticks in the air rushed on ahead. After the bride's brother, other relations and distinguished guests were carried round. The bride, attended by her *suāsin* (*kalsa* on her head as usual) came to watch, and when all was over she 'touched the elephant's feet'. The elephant itself was put in a corner, and someone gave it a little liquor to drink and removed its left ear.

Now, once again the bridegroom first and then the bride came out of the house, went twice round their respective poles, sat on the *māchi*, were covered with turmeric, and carried back indoors. Drinking, dancing and drumming continued without pause.

There followed the Utar Chadao ceremony. The bridegroom came out again, went twice round his pole, preceded by his *suāsin*, followed by a friend holding a *pharsa* axe over his head to keep away any evil magic. A *māchi* was placed on the end of his mother's cloth which she unwound and spread out before her. He sat on it, placing his feet also on the cloth. The *suāsin* anointed him with yet more turmeric. Then holding a mango leaf in each hand, she dipped them in a pot full of turmeric water, crossed her hands, touched the feet of the bridegroom with the leaves three times, then threw a few drops of water over his head. She repeated this five times.

Then the *suāsin* stood up and put her hands, palms upward, on Bura's head, and the *suāsa* put an arrow (without a head) notch upward on her hand, and poured oil down it. When the *suāsin*'s hand was full of oil, she rubbed it over Bura's head. Then they picked him up and carried him, swinging him vigorously, into the house. They put the arrow by his *mangrohi*.

After this the bride came out, and the programme was repeated except for the arrow ceremony.

Then the *suāsin* coloured two new cloths with turmeric and put them out to dry on the roof of the marriage-booth.

After a pause, the whole party went to fetch the *bijni* (fans) and *parra* (bamboo lids) from the bride's elder sister's husband who had prepared them. The bride's mother sat in front of his house, spreading out her cloth. The *dosi* put the fans and bamboo lids in it. The two mothers gave the drummers a winnowing-fan full of rice, pulse, turmeric and salt. Then the party returned. The bride and bridegroom bathed, and dressed in new clothes and all their ornaments.

Now the bride and bridegroom went out to beg for rice. When they came out of the house, the bride's mother placed their feet on a *parra* and washed them. She kissed the bride, and the bride touched her mother's feet with her hands clenched. Then the bridegroom with his *suāsa*, both covered with a yellow cloth, followed by the *suāsin* with her *kalsa*, and a friend with baskets in a *kāwar*, went off to beg in one direction. The bride, a friend on either side of her, all covered with a yellow cloth, followed by her *suāsin*, went in another direction. Each went to three houses; they stood in a row before the door; the head of the house put their feet on the *parra*, washed them with water from a gourd, 'kissed' them, and gave them a little rice in a winnowing-fan.

Presently both parties returned, and met in the middle of the village. Two boys ran and held a dhoti across the path between them. The men of the bride's party began a mock fight with the men of the bridegroom's party, waving their axes in the air, dancing and shouting.

From time to time, they laid their axes at the feet of bride or bridegroom. Then suddenly Bura broke away from his friends, dashed across the dhoti stretched in his way, seized the bride, threw her on the ground, put a ring on her third finger, picked her up, and covered her with a cloth. As they stood together, the *dosi* tied their clothes in a knot. As they returned to the house, all their relatives came and washed their feet.

Indoors, they sat together. The *dosi* poured a few drops of liquor on the knot and undid it. Bura washed his face and cleaned his teeth with a twig. Then Kalarin did the same. After that, a friend brought a plate of boiled rice and salt and put three handfuls in Bura's mouth. But the woman who fed Kalarin did not put it in her mouth, but in her hand.

At last, they were ready for the Bara Bhawar. The *dosi* brought a bottle of liquor and retied the knot. They all got up. Bride and bridegroom each clasped a betel-nut cutter. They were led by the bridegroom's *suāsin*, who held a pot of water in her right hand, dropping a little as she went. They were followed by the other *suāsin*, and friends, holding axes and sticks above them. On the threshold, they paused, and 'touched the feet' of the door and dropped rice there. Outside, the *dosi* threw rice all over them. Then they went slowly twice round the pole.

After that, they sat on a sack. They should have sat on the *pīdha*, but forgot. They had a dish of turmeric and rice in front of them. (In other weddings, the bride and bridegroom hold a leaf-cup of kodon and turmeric in their hands.) As they sat, the *suāsin* fanned them with the fan. "For two and a half days, we regard them as Raja and Rani, and give them the joys of a court." Everyone now did *tikāwan*, first the *dosi*, then visitors, and lastly, near relatives. Each person washed the feet of the bride and bridegroom with water, then put turmeric and rice, first on the *kalsa*, then on the *marua* pole, then on the *sigh* (liquor-pot) and then on the foreheads of the happy pair. Each put a gift, some gift if only a pice, in the dish.

Last of all, the father of the bride blessed them. "*Sonan dānt khoto, kora me putur, sār me lakshmi, kothi me an, gānth me paisa, lākh barish jiyo.* May you clean your teeth with gold, may there be a son in your lap, may there be wealth in your cattle-shed, grain in your bins, money in your bags, and you live for a hundred thousand years."

Such was the wedding of Bura and Kalarin. May the auspicious omens that greeted it be fulfilled!

Where a marriage party has come to the bride's house, bride and bridegroom go round the pole three times there, and then when they go to the bridegroom's house they repeat the ceremony four times. But the Baiga are very vague about going round the pole; they may go two, three, five or seven times.

At most marriages, gifts are made at the time of the *tikāwan* by the bridegroom's father to the bride's paternal grandmother (*āji-bondri*), to her mother (*mai-odna*), to her brother (*bhai-bānti*), to the *dosi* and to the *suāsin*. But at Bura's wedding, as he was an orphan and a poor Lamsena boy, these presents were not made.

It was formerly the tradition that the newly-married couple must not consummate the marriage in a house, but spend their first night together in the jungle. This is still observed by those who desire a little privacy. On this night the husband must give his bride anything she wants—or he'll be impotent later in the evening!

The next day, they perform the little ceremony known as Beni Chodna. Husband and wife go down to the river, and standing in the water vigorously splash one another. They catch hold of each other, and undo each other's *beni*, or 'plait' of hair. This is a dangerous moment, for if there is a witch about she may put a *bhut* in the hair, and the girl will be childless. Then they bathe each other, and the girl sits in her husband's lap. After a time, she jumps up to run away, and as she goes he hits her as hard as he can.

After this, they make an image of a woman out of mud, and set it up on the river bank. The husband has to shoot at it with his bow and arrow, and if he hits it first shot, they all say that his bride will stay with him. If he misses it, they say she will run away. In parts of Mandla, they make a rough representation of a deer out of sticks and leaves, and the husband has to shoot at it.

During the marriage ceremony a large variety of songs known as Bilma or Birha are sung. Many of these are unusually obscene—others are recorded here.

i

The chicks of the hen are scattered here and there.
The wild cat catches them and eats them one by one.
O *suāsin*, who art taking me round and round the pole,
Thou art my little sister, tell me, O tell me,
Who will enjoy the first-fruits of my youth.

ii

On the hill the mahua tree roars in the storm.
In the valley the wind sounds in the bamboos.
Along the road Bhimsen is shouting.
In the *marua* the drunkards are roaring out a song.

iii

Come along, my parrot, to another nest!
Come along, my parrot, nibbling your leaf!
If you won't, I'll kick your bottom.

iv

It is only four days since we went round the pole together,
And we went to the bazaar together, and bought *chutki*.
Now I have nothing left but the *chutki*.

v

The little girl is coming to her husband's house.
The girl is weeping.
Let us go and see.
Whose friends have come?
Whose friends have gone?
Let us go and see.
The little girl is weeping.

vi

By thinking of you, memory keeps fresh.
By looking at you, love is increased.

Who gives the dish?
Who gives the pot?
Who gives the daughter?
It is the son-in-law that takes them all away.
Our eyes are drowned with tears.
Seeing this our mother begins to weep.
Her brother gives the dish.
His wife gives the pot.
Her mother and father give the girl.
It is the son-in-law that takes them all away.
And our dear mother begins to weep.

vii

On the road-side they are sitting in each other's arms.
Who ground the *haldi*?
Who built the *marua*?
Who beat the drum?
On the road-side they are sitting in each other's arms.
The queen ground the *haldi*.
The king built the *marua*.
The prince beat the drum at your wedding.
O you rascal, what am I to do?

viii

Dum dum dum dum the drums are sounding dum dum.
On every side they are playing the flute.
Two by two the men and women are going along the little paths.
As she goes with her lover, her *chutki* are tinkling.

ix

O girl tie your sari tightly, round and round your body.
Weep in your heart, but keep your secret to yourself.
Let them get the *marua* ready.
Grind the *haldi*, fix the pole.
Sleep with your husband, let your breasts delight him.
But even to him never show the secret that is ours.

x

Cook the lentil, cook the rice!
Prepare the *channa-lapta*[1]
My bride is beautiful,
But her nose is flat.
Alas! Alas! Every night and all night
I'll have to sleep with her.

[1] Curry made of channa-flour with buttermilk.

I have shared the bridegroom's feast.
I have drunk liquor in the house of the bride.
I helped them build the *marua*.
That is all I know; I know nothing more.
Save one thing more—that like the lightning
I will carry her away to Bijagarh.

As we have seen already, the Baiga have no tradition of the avoidance of hymeneal blood, nor have they any ritual for the deflowering of virgins. Very few mature men have ever had the opportunity. On the other hand, the Baiga greatly enjoy intercourse with young adolescent girls, and as it is a convention that every unmarried girl is a virgin, they get a fictitious triumph out of the act which has no basis in reality. It is a triumph, for the man has seduced a virgin; it affords the keenest physical gratification for the girl is immature. "She is very *tip-tip*—greater pleasure in this." "A young girl, if she is a virgin, and before she had given birth to a child, if you go to her, it doesn't exhaust you. If you go to her later, when she is enlarged by contact with many men, she drags your loins to her, and wears you out."

It is the convention that every young wife must pretend to be a virgin, to be ignorant of the methods of intercourse, and to be terrified of going to a man. For days Bugla's wife refused to go near him, although she was already an experienced lover. This was in Amadob. At last the man arranged with two women of his family to go to sleep with the girl in another house, and he himself hid there behind the grain-bin. When they had got the girl inside and half asleep, the two women crept out of the house, and Bugla approached his wife. She began to scream so loudly that half the village gathered outside the door to hear the fun, and encouraged the husband with loud and ribald cries.

Satula had had several romances before she was married to Gumma of Taliyapani, but she had to pretend that she was terrified of going near him. For days he tried to persuade her, but she refused. Then he too resorted to stratagem. He sent Satula with two other girls to watch his field at night, and himself followed quietly. Satula knew perfectly well what was to happen, but she lay down and pretended to go to sleep. Then her husband came and the two women went away. Satula crossed her legs and screamed at the top of her voice. She jumped up and tried to run away. Gumma chased her round and round the field, and at last forced his will upon her. After that, of course, Satula made no more fuss and began to live the normal domestic life with her husband.

Marriage. *The dosi unties the knot.*
The marriage elephant.

"It is dangerous," said Jethu of Bohi. "They shout and scream and let everyone know what you're up to. The next morning all the village laughs at you. So it is best to take the girl to the jungle, to pick mangoes or dig for roots. Then sit down beside her, and pretend to be smoking your pipe, and when she isn't looking, suddenly attack her. She will scream, but who is there to hear in the jungle?"

IV. THE HALDI-PANI MARRIAGE

Such is the official, fully legal, marriage of the Baiga, which can never be repeated, not even after divorce or for a widow. "No man or woman can ever go fourteen times round about the pole."[1] But there is a secondary marriage which is as fully legal, and can be repeated frequently. This is the *haldi-pāni* or *churi-pairāna* marriage. Its children are legitimate and can inherit. No social stigma attaches to it. The *haldi-pāni* marriage is in some ways like a marriage in a registry office as compared to a full-dress wedding in a fashionable church. It is cheaper, quicker, simpler: the divorcee is not refused; above all, it is cheaper.

For the *haldi-pāni* marriage is celebrated with the extreme of simplicity. The apparatus required is no more than a little liquor, a trifle of *haldi* (turmeric) and water, and a few bangles. A carpet is spread on the ground; the happy couple, both of whom may have been married several times already, sit upon it. Their friends anoint them with *haldi*. Then they stand up, they are covered with a new cloth, and the neighbours sprinkle *haldi-pāni* over them, crying "*Bhaigay! Bhaigay!* That's enough!" The husband puts bangles round his wife's wrists and takes her to his bed.

But normally, both parties to a *haldi-pāni* marriage should have been married already by full *sāt-bāwar* rites to other partners. Sometimes, however, the *haldi-pāni* marriage comes first, the fuller rite later. A lot depends on the economic condition of the family, and the temperament of the girl or boy. But nearly everybody, certainly every girl, wants to be married by the full ritual once in life, to know the excitement of that moment, to feel the centre of attention, to realize that this is 'my day and no one can take it from me'. The marriage ceremony is the one grand red-letter day in a Baiga's life.

The *haldi-pāni* rite is used for the marriage of widows. This may take place within a month of the husband's death, or even sooner, especially if a younger brother is waiting to take the elder brother's place. It is also

[1] Very occasionally a woman does get married twice. She is then called Chaudahin, 'fourteen times'. A twice-married man is called Dujaha.

used after divorce, in many cases of elopement, or where the parents are not in favour of the marriage.

If the bridegroom has never been married, but his bride is a widow or has left her husband, the marriage is celebrated with a variation of the regular ceremony. The bridegroom is taken seven times round the pole, followed by the *dosi* carrying an axe to represent the bride, who herself sits looking on. The rest is done according to the *haldi-pāni* rite.

In the case of elopement, the new husband must pay twenty to twenty-five rupees in compensation. This is the rule for a girl's first elopement provided that she was married by the full rites. But there is a sort of sliding scale; a girl after her first elopement is worth twenty-five rupees, as this is the average sum given as bride-price by Baiga parents. But if a girl runs away again, she is assessed at not more than fifteen rupees; a third time, and her price drops to ten.

It is the paying of compensation that really effects divorce both among Gond and Baiga. There is actually a ritual for divorce, but it is very rarely practised. The parties go before the *panch* and solemnly break a straw in half, letting the bits fall separately to the ground. An earthen pot is smashed, and a rupee also dropped on the ground, but quickly recovered by one of the members of the *panch* and used for their refreshment. The *panch* then declares husband and wife formally separated and with no further claims on one another. Any jewellery given to the wife by her husband should now be returned. When a wife runs away, one of the first things the husband does is to recover all the ornaments he has given her. To see this in practice is sometimes pitiable indeed: the husband seems to have no concern about the loss of his partner, no jealousy for his supplanter, but is simply concerned to recover the few pathetically cheap and tawdry ornaments and to extract a few rupees from the man who has cuckolded him. But we must remember that we are dealing with people to whom the price of a cup of tea in a railway restaurant represents a whole day's labour, who think in terms not of rupees or even annas, but of pice and cowries, and to whom these things are of gigantic moment.

V. POLYGAMY

Ek dauki ka rāja, do dauki ka kutta, tīn dauki ka dingra. Of one wife he is the king; of two wives the dog; of three wives the romance (lit. *wanderer*).—Baiga Proverb.

According to the 1931 Census, polygamy is on the decrease among the Baiga. In any case, since there are only 1,007 women to every 1,000 men among the 'Hinduized' and presumably Binjhwar Baiga, and an exactly equal number of men and women among the rest, the opportunities for polygamy on a large scale appear somewhat limited. But for the critical ages between seventeen and twenty-three there are 1,276 Hinduized Baiga and 1,355 'Tribal' Baiga women to every 1,000 men, and it is naturally from girls of this age that men choose their *chhotki* (junior wife).

When a man takes a second—or third—wife, the marriage, if the girl is unmarried, is as expensive and elaborate as any other. A wise husband carefully prepares his *badki* (senior wife) for the coming of the *chhotki*. "You of course are the queen of my house," he says, "and you always will be. But there is too much work for you. Let me bring you a servant. We cannot afford to pay a servant, but I will keep her as a woman of the house. Then you can sit all day talking with your friends, and I'll take her to fetch wood, and send her to fetch water, and abuse her if she fails to husk the kodon." Sometimes the elder wife says, "Very well!" But sometimes she says, "O the work is very light; I can easily do it all myself." Sometimes she loses her temper, and makes trouble; she breaks her bangles and pretends that she is a widow; she sits in a corner and refuses to speak to anyone; she cracks her fingers at her husband and abuses him. "If possible," says Dhan Singh, "it should be done with her permission: if not, it must be done without it. But then there are many quarrels afterwards, and you have to be careful, lest while you are sleeping with your *chhotki*, the *badki* doesn't come and empty the *gursi* full of burning coals all over you!"

At the time of marriage, everything proceeds as usual. The new wife first goes alone five times round the pole with her husband, and then they are joined by the *badki*. The elder wife goes first, then the husband, then the younger wife. The *badki* holds in her right hand a *sarota* which is caught by the husband, and he in turn holds the *chhotki* by the little finger of her right hand. When they have completed the seven circlings of the pole, they sit down for the *tikāwan*, the elder wife on the right hand, the man in the middle, and the younger wife on his left.

If the *chhotki*, however, has been married before, then only the *haldi-pāni* ceremony is performed. The three sit on a bit of sack, and the yellow water is poured over them.

It is correct for a *badki*, whether she approves of the new attachment or not, to make a great deal of fuss at the *chhotki*'s marriage. "He doesn't love me any more," she screams. "He'll drive me out into the jungle; he'll be always beating me; I'll get nothing to eat. Everything will be given to this new girl. Look at these presents; when I was married he never gave me anything like that," and so on. Then her friends come to her and say, "Don't weep, the girl is your sister. She is going to live with you and sleep with you; she will always be with you; what is the use of being angry with her? She will be your servant. Don't be jealous of her. If they sleep in one bed together, if they go to the jungle together, if they go to the well together, don't be angry with them. It is the way of men."

Then the *badki* slowly allows herself to be calmed, and her husband, if he is wise, brings out a new cloth and a few bangles: such gifts make all the difference in the world. Indeed the best husbands give equal presents to the two wives at this time.

Sometimes these polygamous marriages are completely successful. The two wives of Dantar of Karanjia lived contentedly together; they had one great point of agreement—the conduct of their husband who was consistently unfaithful to them both. The two wives of the Dewar of Kotalwahi were very good friends for several years, but in the end they quarrelled and are not now on speaking terms, though still living in the same compound. Timmu, a Muria of Niwas, lived happily with his two wives. "I went twice a day to each of them. They were very happy. I had three children from one, five from the other." Yogi Dewar had six wives at once, and claims that they were perfectly content. Bahadur's two wives seem to be great friends. Rannu, a Bhumia, had three wives at the same time, and they were, on the whole, very happy together. He was an unusually tactful husband: he kept the *manjhli*, or middle wife, living in another village, and visited her from time to time. He had three separate beds for himself and the other two, and he visited one or the other late at night so that no one ever knew which he preferred. Pattu, the headman of Ajghardabra, so the caustic Deo Singh told me, has three wives. "He keeps each in a different village. His eldest son looks after the *badki*; his second son looks after the *manjhli*, he himself sticks close to his *chhotki*. He goes after her like a dog; he runs along behind her with his tongue out. She won't let him go near the other wives. But he is clever: he keeps them

Marriage. *The suasin.*
Bathing the bride.
Carrying out the bride.

all happy: he has had children by all of them. Another man with three wives is Sujji. They live in one house: he runs after all three. They don't quarrel, for he is a rich man."

But it does not always turn out so well as this. Many homes have been broken up when a man has taken a second wife. When Chimdu brought the beautiful Adri to his house, the first wife—after endless quarrels—left him with all her children. When Hagru married Jitho, his *badki*—who was a well-known witch—tried to poison her and nearly succeeded. When Bhola married his *chhotki*, the unusually pretty Cheri, he made things so unpleasant for his *badki* that after a few months of great unhappiness she ran away with someone else. Tiblu had two wives, but he could not satisfy them and they ran away together on the same night. "One sword does not need two sheaths," he said to me regretfully. Dasseru of Bondar told me how difficult it had been to keep the peace in his house. "I first slept between them, with one on either side, and either they turned their backs on me, or they quarrelled over my body. Then I tried sleeping separately, as a Baiga ought to do, and going to one at a time. But then when I went to my *badki*, my *chhotki* sat weeping in the garden; when I slept with my *chhotki*, the *badki* climbed up a tree where she could watch us and shouted abuse at us. At last I sent my *badki* away."

Polygamy, in fact, is only polygamous when it is successful. Where it fails, it usually ends in the divorce or elopement of the elder wife.

VI. THE LAMSENA

The custom of serving for a wife is common to many castes and tribes in the Baiga country. The youth who gives his services is called the Lamsena, or sometimes the Gahania—the man who is 'in pawn'.

By the Gond this system is constantly abused; the Lamsena boy often serves his long seven years for the wife, and at the end of that time is either turned out of the house on the ground that he is unsatisfactory, or the marriage is celebrated and the girl immediately runs away with someone else. No intelligent or influential person would ever be a Lamsena, and so it is very difficult for the defrauded youth to get compensation either through the *panch* or the ordinary courts.

But the more honest and honourable Baiga treat the Lamsena better, and if for any reason the marriage does not take place pay proper compensation.

There is no formal *sagai*, or engagement in these cases, but on the day he begins his work, the Lamsena brings a rupee's worth of liquor to his prospective father-in-law, and he is formally accepted. Now he has to work for any period from two to five years (it is not usually seven years as among the Gond) according to the contract, and during that time he lives as one of the family, and receives food and clothing—one change of clothes every year. If he earns anything during that period, the money must be handed over to the father-in-law.

Sometimes, if the Lamsena is old enough and the girl is willing, they are married first and the boy does his work later. This is done when the girl is suspected of an intrigue with someone, or when she is made pregnant by an unknown lover. The Lamsena is the official refuge of the unmarried mother. His duty is to save a girl's reputation. Among Baiga, though less often among Gond, there grows up a real romance between the Lamsena and his girl. They are not, however, supposed to have intercourse together before marriage. But "if they are both old enough, and their eyes meet, they go together to the jungle". If there is any scandal, they are married immediately.

If the girl runs away with another man, after the Lamsena has done two or three years' service, he should be given Rs. 40 as compensation. This is the official Baiga figure, but I doubt if the boy ever gets more than a quarter of that sum.

A Lamsena cannot serve for a widow, nor indeed would it normally be necessary. If there was a younger brother wanting to marry the widow, he would have to be compensated, but otherwise there would be little or no expense, and the *haldi-pāni* wedding is one of the cheapest in the world. A Lamsena may serve for a married girl who has left her husband; in this case her father undertakes to compensate the husband from the boy's earnings.

VII. THE BHULA CHILD

Illegitimate children are almost unknown among the Baiga. There is in any case no stigma attached to bastardy. The names *bhūla* for the child and *bhūli* for the mother are only given when the father is not known and when no other man is willing to accept the responsibility for the paternity. This happens very rarely. In his long life Mahatu can only remember one example.

The *bhūla* child suffers from no social disabilities. "I would marry my daughter to him," says Mahatu. "We don't think him bad. It was his mother who was bad. But she too did nothing."

When the mother marries and has other children, the *bhūla* child has almost equal rights with them. If it is a boy, he can inherit, and shares with the other brothers—but he gets a little less than they do.

No bastard figures in any of the myths, legends or songs, and the word is not used in Baiga *gāli*.

Chapter X

THE FINAL CRISIS: DEATH

I. BAIGA SENTIMENT ABOUT DEATH

She lies alone in her bed,
For her king has died.

—Baiga Dadaria.

Death is always unnatural. Nanga Baiga would have been immortal had it not been for the treachery of Bhagavan who still to-day holds the keys of life and death in his hands. We will see, in the chapter on Disease, the various agents that contribute to man's dissolution, witchcraft, the envy of ghosts and spirits, the breach of tribal taboos. But before their malice can be consummated in death the permission of Bhagavan must be given. But this belief in the general control of Bhagavan over the issues of life and death is little more than a pious fancy; he is able to cause death, but powerless to prevent it. There is also no such thing as an accident. No wild animal would kill a Baiga unless it was sent by some outside agency; snakes and tigers are entirely benevolent in themselves.

Death is all too tragically common among these people, for the birth-rate is high and the span of life is short. There are some very old men among them, but as with all the primitive tribes in India the proportion of people over forty is low. The figures in the 1931 Census were as follows: Among the Baiga there were 143 men and 136 women per mille over forty. With this we may compare 154 Gond men and 155 women, 100 and 99 Kol, 106 and 97 Maria. The Hindu figures are much higher—171 and 173 Brahmin, 170 and 171 Bania and 196 and 183 Kunbi. At the same time, there is a very high proportion of children under six. 'The Oraons, Marias, Baigas . . . have a higher proportion of children than any Hindu caste except the Dohors, a depressed community.' This will be readily seen from the following table:

Age 0–6.

		Male	Female
Baiga	..	241	258
Korku	..	242	242
Oraon	..	307	322
Gond	..	209	210
Bharia	..	250	237
Dohor	..	242	250
Brahmin	..	160	185
Bania	..	171	188
Bohra	..	141	203

But among all the peoples of India the aboriginals have the lowest expectation of life. Mandla, in which nearly half the Baiga population lives, is one of the worst districts in the Central Provinces and it is closely followed by Bilaspur, another Baiga district.

The age distribution per thousand of tribal Baiga is given by the Census of 1931 as follows:

		Male	Female
0–6	..	241	258
7–13	..	166	139
14–16	..	68	68
17–23	..	98	127
24–43	..	292	282
44 and over	..	143	126

The figures for the ages 14–23 are admittedly deficient.

The Census of 1891 brought out the fact that although more boys are born than girls, the first five years of life are more fatal to boys.[1] Between ten and fourteen the mortality is higher among girls. From fifteen to nineteen aboriginal girls become more numerous than boys and more numerous still between twenty and twenty-nine. After this it is the men who survive more readily, and there is a considerable excess of old men over old women in the tribes.

Throughout the Central Provinces the greater number of deaths occur in September and October, the deadly malarial season at the close of the rains. This is also the time when the largest number of children are born and there is, presumably, a heavier child-mortality. The fewest deaths occur in the healthy bracing months of December and February. I have not been able to obtain separate statistics for the Baiga, but my own observation and the general belief is that in this respect the Baiga do not differ from the rest of the Province.

[1] Major Kendrick, I.M.S. had a theory, and some statistics to support it, that the birth-rate of girls tended to be higher than that of boys in hyper-endemic malarial areas.—Census of India, 1911. Vol. X, p. 118.

The Marghat (burying-place) at Jholar.
Holera Deo on the wall of a Muria house in Niwas.

The Baiga's life is undoubtedly a brief one. The 1931 Census refers to 'the fertility of the aborigines following tribal religion and the comparative brevity of their lives'. The mean age for the Central Provinces is 23·65 male and 23·77 female, and the average span of life is twenty-five as compared to fifty-four in England. The Baiga's average is probably higher than this on account of their many old men.

The Baiga sentiment about death is one of fear for its unseen malignant cause, and of deep sorrow for the dead. They seem to be more afraid of the cause of death than of death itself. A necessary part of every funeral is the divination designed to discover what this was. One method is to carry the body to the nearest stream, where the gunia takes oil in a leaf and puts three drops in the water, one for Thakur Deo, one for Bhagavan and one for 'Sin' (that is, some breach of a tribal taboo). If the drop of oil turns blood-red, they know the dead man has broken a tribal law; if it goes up stream, it is Bhagavan who has called him; if it goes "like crossed fingers" his death was due to a witch. Another, famous, test, common to many tribes, is to look to the level of the grave when it is filled in. If it is level with the surrounding ground, the death was due to Bhagavan. If it rises above, it was caused by a witch. If it sinks below, it was the punishment for the breach of a tribal taboo.

But fear is often entirely swept away by a most genuine sorrow. The custom that demands formal and conventional lamentation round the corpse has largely concealed from alien eyes the real sorrow of the closer friends and relatives. I have often seen faces haggard and drawn with grief. I have watched the wild anxiety of the young husband for his wife, and the frantic solicitude of a mother for her injured child.

Some of the Karma songs deal, rather unexpectedly, with death and these, I think, show a real sense of mortality.

> O friend, when will I sing Karma again?
>
> Father is sobbing *har-hari*.
>
> Mother is beating her head.
>
> The daughter will weep for six months.
>
> I have tried to stop her crying, but she won't listen.
>
> O friend, when will I sing Karma again?

> My father and my brother are all I have
>
> So long as this life remains.
>
> When I die I will be alone.
>
> There is only one thing that goes with us,
>
> And that is wood of sarai;
>
> It is burnt and turns to ashes.

What great sorrow fills the body of man!
Some are carried on a hurdle.
Some are taken on a man's back.
Some are thrown out in a place where crows and vultures eat them.
In the body of man there dwells great sorrow.

Build a palace of hewn stone,
Give it a golden door.
But you'll never be able to live there.
For your life will go down to the dust.
Eat, drink, be happy.
To-day or to-morrow you will die,
And on your body grass will grow.
In this life there is no hope,
And soon you will go down to the dust.

A curious story about Nanga Baiga satirizes the attitude of a widow to her dead husband. A Baiga widow has none of the tragic disabilities of a Hindu widow; she may re-marry within ten days of her husband's death: she need not shave her head or wear a special dress; the only disadvantages of her state are that she must not wear beads or bangles, and she cannot put the turmeric on a bride at a wedding. Otherwise her position is not an unhappy one, especially if her husband's younger brother is waiting to marry her. These facts give point to the following story.

'The wives of Nanga Baiga are the pea-fowl, the salai-bird and the she-frog. One day Nanga Baiga thought, "How shall I know which of these loves me best?" So he went to the bank of a pond and lying down stopped his breath and pretended to be dead. When his wives saw him, they came running to the place.

'The pea-fowl began to weep and cried, "I have cooked rice and vegetables; who will now eat it?"

'The salai-bird, who had just bathed and was settling her feathers, wept and cried, "I've smoothed all my feathers; who now will look at me?"

'But the she-frog said, "He may be dead, but I can still hop. I'll go to the other side of the pond and make a new husband there."

'When Nanga Baiga heard that, he jumped up in rage and hit the frog so hard that ever since she has looked as if she had been squashed.'

But the normal sentiment is one of intense sorrow. Once, when Baisakia was very ill, her husband Mithu came to say she was dying. He was trembling so violently that he could hardly speak; the tears poured down his cheeks.

II. THE DESTINY OF THE SOUL

After death, say the Baiga, the soul goes direct to Bhagavan. For some time I was puzzled by this simple statement because a number of customs and ceremonies seemed to contradict it. For example, the bearers who carry the corpse to the burial-ground take a zigzag course to prevent the soul finding its way back to the house. Again, as the mourners return home after the bathing on the Daswa day, they walk in file. The leader picks up a stone in his right hand and furtively, without looking round, passes it to the man behind him. In this way the stone goes right down the file till the man at the end spits and throws it away. The stone is the soul of the dead man and is thus prevented from returning to the house. This hardly seemed consistent with the belief that the soul had already gone direct to Bhagavan.

But I found an even greater inconsistency than this. After the funeral, sometimes immediately, sometimes ten days later on the Daswa day, the Baiga catch a living frog or fish which they say is the soul of the dead man. They bring it to the house with a black chicken. The dead man's *samdhi* worships the frog and chicken together saying, "Give our brother's soul a place behind the hearth." Then they let the frog go and the chicken eats it. After that the chicken itself is killed.

In other villages, on the Daswa day the women catch a fish or a frog and put it in a hollow mud ball. Then they weep and prostrate themselves before it, and mark it with milk and turmeric as though they were doing the *tikāwan* at a wedding. For it is the man's last marriage rite. They they throw the ball into the river, it breaks and the soul escapes. But the women take a chicken and bring it back from the river saying, "Come, O spirits of our ancestors; we will carry you home and your younger brother and children will ever honour you." Then they kill the chicken near the hearth and believe that the dead man's soul will ever live there.

I was therefore very naturally hard put to it to reconcile these very conflicting ideas. At one moment I found the Baiga taking every precaution to prevent the soul of the dead man returning to the house; at the next I found them bringing it home with every circumstance of respect. And all the time it was supposed to have been carried off to Bhagavan by his chaprasis. But my perplexity was not really my fault. It was due to the loose and inaccurate way in which my Baiga informants used the word *jīv*, or soul, for the Baiga are exactly like ourselves—few inhabitants of an

English village would be likely to give the Pauline *pneuma* and *psyche* their exact meaning in a discussion on religious psychology. It was not until I had thoroughly discussed the matter with the Dewar of Kotalwahi and his two wives that the matter was cleared up, and then mainly through the acute theological perceptions of his junior wife.

After death, man disintegrates into three spiritual forces. The first is his *jīv*, soul or life-essence, which is the life-index of the folk-tales, which is capable of leaving the body in sleep and experiencing what we call dreams, and which may return to earth in some future incarnation. The *jīv* goes direct to Bhagavan. Secondly, there is a man's *chhaya*, or shade, which is represented by the fish or frog, and is brought home to live for ever behind the hearth. Thirdly, there is his *bhut*, or ghost, almost the perpetuation of his lower or evil self, dangerous and hostile to men, whose proper dwelling is the burial-ground, and which must at all costs be prevented from finding its way back to the house. So there was no inconsistency in the various customs and ideas that I had noticed, for they all had to do with the dead man's personality under different forms.

Bhagavan lives on this earth, to the east of the Maikal Hills. He lives in a great palace on an island enclosed by two rivers of fire, Agnadi and Dagnadi. "It is all fire: not a fly or an ant can go there." But Bhagavan is only partly good. "He is half good; the other half is rotten with wounds and disease." Bukwa once saw Bhagavan's palace in a dream. Half of it was blazing with light; the other half was rotting away, the home of death and corruption. For Bhagavan brought death into the world deliberately. By his deception he killed the immortal Nanga Baiga. He is still responsible for all those deaths which are not due to witchcraft or the breach of tribal taboo.

When a man dies, Bhagavan sends his chaprasis to fetch the *jīv*. These chaprasis belong to the Kol tribe. If the dead man was well-to-do, they carry him in a litter; if he was poor, they kick him along the road. When he reaches Bhagavan's island, he finds an exact replica of the house he had on earth. If he had a big house on earth, he will have a big house on Bhagavan's island; if he wore rags in life, he will wear rags after death. The parable of Dives and Lazarus would seem altogether wrong to the devout Baiga. All the food, moreover, that he gave away during life is stored up in his house, and it is on this that he has to live; its quantity determines the length of time that he will be able to stay in this happy place before being sent down to earth again.

There is no hell. But near Bhagavan's palace there is a pond full of crawling worms, and very wicked people are thrown into this. "When the worms begin to eat them, they cry, '*O dai! O dadā!*' When there is just a scrap of them left, they are sent back to earth into the bodies of pigs. When a witch dies, Bhagavan covers her *jīv* with tar, and when she tries to return to earth, he stops her, saying, 'You've done enough evil already, now you must stop here.'"

The Baiga probably did not originally believe in the re-birth of the soul, but many of them have adopted it from their Hindu neighbours, though not in the Hindu form. There is an old song quoted by Russell, which says, 'O girl, take your pleasure in going round the marriage-post once and for all, for there is no second birth.' A pregnant woman or a woman dying in childbirth is not re-born, not is a witch nor a man killed by witchcraft. Many Baiga deny that men can be re-born as animals. The form taken by the doctrine among the Baiga is a simple non-moral one that the souls of the dead return to live among their descendants. It is a sort of corollary of ancestor worship. The Hindu doctrine of transmigration, which is intimately bound up with ideas of Karma and of caste, is entirely different.

The following is a typical statement of the Baiga conception of re-birth. 'If a man has loved his son, his *jīv* will be re-born in his son's son; if he loved his daughter, he will be re-born in her son. Bhagavan sends a man's *jīv* back to wait in the roof of the house until the mourners have given a feast to the village. Then the *jīv* goes again to Bhagavan who decides what he should do. When the time has come, the *jīv* goes to live near a pregnant woman who is related to him, so that he can slip into her womb when it is prepared. The *jīv* always seeks a place of light and warmth where it will be at home and people will love it.'

The *jīv* of animals also go to Bhagavan and may be re-born.

As we have seen, for those who have suffered some extraordinary death, there is no re-birth. A man who has died without tasting the delights of love becomes a *raksa*, a burning angry ghost, covered with black hair, who lives frustrated and confined in a semur tree, always on the look-out to catch some unwary maiden and crop her virgin flower. When a pregnant woman dies or a woman dies in childbirth, she becomes a *churelin*, 'like a black vulture with great wings and peahen's feet turned backwards, fcr ever crying Kai-O'.

When a witch dies, as we have seen, Bhagavan does not allow her to be re-born again in human shape. But even he cannot check her malignant power. 'When they burn a witch, the little bits of wood that remain turn into owls, or the water-pot that they place on the grave becomes an owl. If that owl hoots near a sick man's bed there is no hope for him. If they bury her, then the little bits of mud that are scattered about become owls.'

If a witch succeeds in removing the liver of a man living or dead, there is no more life of his own for him. He becomes a *bīr* or familiar of witches and remains always at their command.

III. THE FUNERAL RITES

The ordinary funeral rites of the Baiga are not elaborate. When they see a man is dying, the relations gather round him, and his wife washes the floor with a cloth dipped in sambhar-dung water. She must do this with single sweeps of her arm; she must not rub the cloth to and fro. Then they lift the dying man off the bed and put him on the ground. If possible they make him swallow a little sweetmeat; sometimes they put a rupee in his mouth—occasionally this hastens his end, for he half swallows it and chokes.

After death, the wife removes his cloth and bathes him. Only his wife may do this, but a son may do it for a widower. If it is a woman who is dying, her mother or sister bathe her, and the parents care for their children. After the bathing they wrap the body in a new cloth if they can afford it, if not in a clean old one. They anoint the body with oil and turmeric. 'As in marriage it was used, so now—that it may go with him beyond death.'

Meanwhile the male relations are making a rough hurdle, and friends have gathered who stand round wailing loudly. Others are preparing the grave or pyre. When the hurdle is ready, the dead man's son, standing with his back to the house, pulls some thatch out of the roof above the door, and they spread this on the hurdle and lay the body upon it.

Then four men lift it up and carry it away, going by a zigzag route and avoiding the main paths as much as possible. They may carry the body down to the nearest stream in order to divine the cause of death; otherwise they take the body direct to the burial ground.

If the man has died suddenly, or after two days' illness, they bury him, for they fear that if they burn him the wind will carry the infection abroad. But if he has 'stuck to his bed' and died after fifteen days or more, they burn him. The old custom was probably to bury in every case. A grave is made waist deep, and the head is towards the south.

The bearers carry the corpse round the grave or pyre three times, then they set down the hurdle on the ground a little way away, pick it up again and bring it by a roundabout route back to the pyre or grave. They lay the corpse face downwards, if a man, and face upwards, if a woman; and the *samdhi* with a sudden movement strips it of the cloth that covered it.

Then the dead man's son, or some other youth of that generation, ties a small bit of new cloth round his waist and plunges into the nearest stream or pond. He comes shivering, and stands with his back to the grave and shovels a little earth into it with his hands. If there is a pyre, someone puts a bundle of blazing grass into his hands, and he lights the wood with it.

Then all the mourners gather round and each throws a little earth into the grave or a handful of twigs on to the fire.

The *samdhi* walks round the pyre or grave with a basket of grain, scattering it on every side.

Someone drags the cot, on which the corpse has been carried, to one side and with a single blow of his axe, breaks one of its legs.

If the dead man is buried, when the grave is being filled in, a handful of the earth is taken to the wife or mother. She touches it, and it is brought back to the grave and thrown into it. When the grave is filled in, the *sābar* or *khanta* which was used for digging it is carried round three times. Sometimes it is thrown to and fro across the grave three times.

Near the grave the mourners put the dead man's *hassia, sūpa, tuma,* baskets or *khanta.* On a child's grave they put his toys. In the grave itself, they sometimes put a man's tobacco, *thaili* and *chakmak.* If he has many bows and arrows and was a good hunter, they hang a bow and arrow on a tree near-by. When the Dewar of Tengradabra died, the sacred pole which stood before his house was taken to the grave and laid upon it.

Later, they make a small circle of stones called the Bhiri above the grave, and cover it with thorns and bushes to keep away the hyenas.

When all is done, the mourners return to the house in file as we have already described, and when they reach there, they find a *samdhi* of the dead man on the roof of his house waiting for them with a pot of water and a gourd. They stand underneath, and he pours water into their hands, and they wash their left feet. The widow brings out oil and turmeric, and they anoint each other 'as if they were bride and bridegroom'. Then the *samdhi* cuts the mourners' hair, and the widow prepares food for them all.

On the third day, the Tijnahawan, the mourners assemble; a few of them go to bathe with members of the household; others sit about and drink. Now the family can once more go freely into the house, take out grain and money, and cook on the hearth—which they could not do hitherto. Even those who attended the funeral could not take grain or money out of their houses, though they were allowed to cook.

On the tenth day is the Daskaram or Bara-nahawan, a feast of goat and liquor. All the mourners bathe. If the dead man has been cremated, his son and his son-in-law gather the ashes from the pyre, and the son ties them in a bundle round his neck and goes to bathe in the river. Sometimes he puts the ashes in a pot, bathes, and fills the pot with water. He takes it home and all the relations have a sip of it.

If the dead man has been buried, the women bring water and sprinkle it on the grave. They may also perform one of the ceremonies with a fish or frog that has already been described.

The *marghat*, or burying-place, is generally on the boundary-line of the village. The *marghat* of Jholar is in thick jungle. Each grave is covered by a heap of stones, surmounted by a carved post and a *tirsul* fixed in the top. When I visited it, Pachlu's son said to me, "I wouldn't spend the night here if I was made ruler over eighteen districts. Once they were our friends, but now they are devils."

The *marghat* in Bohi is in the midst of the jungle, and trees are felled over all the recent graves and allowed to lie upon them in order to prevent hyenas digging up the bodies.

IV. THE MATI UTHANA CEREMONY

When a man is killed by a tiger the rites are much more elaborate and significant. In the middle of October 1937 a party of Baiga came to me from Bohi in the Pandaria Zemindari saying that a man had been killed by a tiger and that on the following Saturday they were going to perform the Mati Uthana ceremony on the spot where he had died. I set out at once, with Sunderlal Mehera and a party of carriers; it was a very exhausting journey, for there was no road and many of the foot-paths had been overgrown by tall grasses during the rains and sometimes disappeared altogether in broad swamps. By nightfall we had travelled some twenty miles and when we reached Tirchula village on the borders of Mandla District my carriers struck. I was determined to reach Bohi that night so as to be in good time for the ceremonies on the morrow, and fortunately we found two men from Bohi who went along with us. It was now dark, but with a half moon, and we made our way across kodon fields and then down the steep hills that lead into Pandaria.

Our carriers were a little drunk and full of what had happened. Two people had been killed. The first was a Baiga boy of about twelve years, the son of Deriya the son-in-law of the lame gunia Jethu. The boy had gone with his little brother to the bewar to pick wild mangoes. There they had separated and he had gone across the bewar cutting at small shoots and shrubs with his sickle as he went. It was then the tiger leapt upon him and carried him off. His little brother ran home and told his father that the boy had run away with a monkey with a big face and stripes and

Hunting the were-tiger at the Māti-Uthāna ceremony.

a long tail. Then Deriya knew his son had been killed by a tiger. He ran alone to the bewar and found a lot of blood on the ground. He was frightened and gathered about eighty men and they went shouting through the forest, but they found no trace of the boy.

The second person to be killed was a Gond. He went with his twelve-year-old daughter Basanta to his bewar. The day before there had been a tiger scare there. A lot of people were in a kodon-clearing and the tiger came by. Some women saw it and began to run away. But the witch who had brought the tiger hid it by her magic, and cried to them, "That's not a tiger, it's only a tree-stump; why are you frightened?" So they looked and there was no tiger there and they returned to their work. But that next day there was only Basanta and her father in the field. At mid-day they rested under a big tree, but Basanta said she would go and put out to dry in the sun some bamboo-shoots that she had gathered. While she was doing so, the tiger sprang on her father, and dragged him here and there about the field, and the child ran home screaming. The tiger ate everything but one hand, a foot and the skull.

'But the shadow of a tiger is so powerful that it stupefies the victim and he doesn't suffer any pain.'

We were very much excited to hear from our carriers that the famous Dewar Rawan was coming to perform the ceremonies on the following day. Rawan is the greatest of the Dewar of Pandaria, a relic of the old heroic age, a great strong man powerful both in body and magic. His life is fully described in Chapter IV.

Late at night we reached Bohi and had a great welcome. The next morning we woke to find large numbers of people, both Gond and Baiga, had assembled from the surrounding villages, and were all sitting round our hut. Everyone was disturbed and annoyed, for Rawan had sent word that he would not come. He had at first promised to come, but the people of Bohi had made a diplomatic error. They sent two ordinary villagers, Baiga of good family and standing but of no ecclesiastical position, to fetch him. Rawan sent a message that he would only come if two Dewar themselves came and fell at his feet with folded hands begging him to come. Also they had not sent enough liquor. So for a long time we sat and condemned this proud and inconsiderate conduct until at about ten in the morning, Jethu the lame Dewar of Bohi gave the signal for a general exodus to the forest, to the field about a mile away where the second of the two victims had met his death.

It was noticeable that although it was a Gond who had died, all the proceedings were in the hands of the Baiga. The Gond did nothing except feed their visitors.

The way to the bewar-clearing was through some magnificent forest, with views on every side of mile upon mile of unbroken jungle. I commented on this to Jethu who was pulling himself along the ground at an amazing rate beside me. "Of course," he said. "Mother Earth blesses the Rani for letting us cut bewar. This jungle where we cut it is far better than in Mandla where the Government has stopped it."

When we reached the field of the tragedy, the whole party of about two hundred men and, curiously enough, two little girls who were unrelated to the dead man, sat down under the tree where the tiger's paw-marks could still be quite clearly seen. The headman showed everybody the marks on the ground which revealed the course of the man's struggle with the tiger, and we saw the cloth and tobacco-pouch and axe lying where they had been left, all that now remained.

There followed a long discussion. It was amusing to see the bovine, placid Gond sitting quietly pulling at their pipes, their faces completely void of intelligence, while the Baiga shouted and gesticulated, arguing with the utmost acrimony the difficult question of what was to be done next. Rawan had not come and there was no Dewar present of sufficient dignity to carry on the proceedings. It was interesting to note that throughout the whole course of the ceremony these discussions continued; the Baiga spectators were continually shouting advice and directions to the main actors in the rite.

At last a *panch* was formed of the five chief Dewar of Bohi and neighbouring villages, but it remained to be decided in whose name the ceremony was to be conducted. The spectators shouted that the *panch* should summon Thakur Deo and ask him about this. So the elders moved away a little to one side of the crowd, but they discovered that no one had brought any fire. This led to another violent altercation, and after a long wait some smouldering cow-dung was brought, and gum from a sarai tree dropped upon it. The Dewar called on Thakur Deo. Suddenly, after about five minutes, the god came upon one of the bystanders who threw himself on the ground, and began to tremble and shake his head in the conventional manner. A few minutes later, the god also caught young Charka who was standing with a group of boys higher up the hill. I shall never forget the dramatic and beautiful sight that this boy made rushing down the hill with his hair flowing about his head and his arms outstretched. He flung himself on the ground with the greatest violence, and after rolling over and over went and squatted before the *panch*, gently trembling in all his limbs.

Then the Dewar began to talk, very gently and familiarly to Thakur Deo in the two men. "Rawan hasn't come. You see our difficulty. We are all in terror of this tiger. What are we to do?" The two *barua* kept on trembling and shaking their heads. At last the older man said, "Bodan Dewar's sons can do this." Bodan Dewar had been a very great Dewar in the old days, but neither of his sons were magicians or knew anything about the business in hand. The elders were rather disconcerted, and they said, "But everything may go wrong, these boys know nothing." "That is my responsibility," answered Thakur Deo. "That is my order." The elders again said, still in that curious familiar style, "Please don't let there be any mistake." Then Thakur Deo saw an axe in someone's hand, and he said, "Whose axe is that?" The owner said, "Mine." Thakur Deo said, "If I take it away, what can you do to me?" The elders said, "He can do nothing." Thakur Deo answered, "Then just so, as I've ordered Bodan Dewar's sons to do this, it will be accomplished through them." Then the *panch* asked Charka the same questions and he confirmed what the other man had said. Thakur Deo left the two *barua*, and they got up and went away. Charka's face was strained and tired. His loin-cloth had become disarranged and his companions greeted him with loud and ribald remarks about his appearance. He had only been possessed by the god once before. Neither he nor the other man nor Bodan Dewar's sons were in any way related to either of the dead.

Then the *panch*, followed by most of the company, went across the field to where a scrap of rag and the blood-stained earth marked the place where the tiger's victim had met his death. The elders sat down in a semi-circle with the two dull and heavy-looking sons of Bodan Dewar, both thoroughly alarmed, sitting in front of them. The rest of the company stood in two long lines between the *panch* and the big tree where we had been sitting. Someone went round with an axe removing any stumps of trees in this space. Then there was another long wait. They had forgotten to bring any chickens. The chickens came, and then it was found that there was no *kodai*. So there was another long wait. At last everything was ready. The Baiga among the spectators had of course been constantly shouting instructions and encouragement to the *panch*. When the *kodai* came, the leading guru, who was Jethu of Bohi, put a few drops of sarai gum on the fire in the name of all the *devata* and the sons of Bodan Dewar. He began to tell the legend of Nanga Baiga and Nanga Baigin who had driven nails into the earth and had become lords of all wild animals. He recalled the first time this rite had ever been performed, when Nanga Baiga had been called in to repair the broken boundaries of a village and had bound the mouth of the tiger. Then a man beat the ground violently with his axe and cried, "Get up, stand up!" Jethu made a little cone of mud to represent a man and set it on the ground. He put some *kodai* into the hands of the two sons of Bodan Dewar, and they waited for a few minutes, but the tiger did not come upon them, and presently they were allowed to get up and go away. Then Baghesur Pat "recognized with delight the body of Deriya", the father of the boy who had been killed, and to the astonishment of everyone, he came upon him, and Deriya was possessed with the spirit of the tiger.

It was an exciting, almost an awe-inspiring sight. Deriya is a slim, rather sinister-looking man, and now with his long hair hanging over his eyes, and his lithe body half bent to walk, he fully looked the part. He began to roar, and run very swiftly all round the field, wherever the tiger had gone. Then he suddenly turned towards the hill and ran into the jungle. A lot of people chased him, they made a regular beat and drove him back. He came creeping through the long grass and then suddenly leapt roaring into the space left by the crowd in front of the elders. He leapt to and fro, dashed himself on the ground, but could not take hold of the little image of the man. For a witch had bound him. He cried out, "I've eaten one, now I'll eat another." Hearing this, Jethu hurriedly made another little image. After that all the elders took tobacco and had a quiet smoke.

Then Thakur Deo and the Mata came on other men, and they too shouted and threw themselves on the ground. For a time nothing happened. Then Deriya jumped to his feet again, and again ran to the forest and returned. But this time when he came he rushed straight to the two little images and caught them both in his mouth. The people seized him and squeezed his throat so that he could not swallow, and one of the Dewar very carefully took the mud out of his mouth and washed it twice with bitter water from a gourd and then with liquor. Jethu took the images and put them in a little gourd and buried it, placing a big stone above it. Then Deriya ran back about twenty yards, and Bodan Dewar's elder son took a chicken and threw it towards him. The first time a man put up his hand and caught the chicken, and Deriya turned on him with such a ferocious snarl that the man ran back to the village. The second time Deriya caught it and tore off its neck. He ran away towards the jungle drinking its blood as he went and chased by many of the people. They caught him and he threw the chick's body away and a Dewar picked it up and buried it with the mud images.

Then Deriya caught a Dewar by the hand and dragged him at a great pace for about half a mile to a rock that overlooked all the valley below. There the Dewar drove a nail into the rock, and Deriya shouted at the top of his voice:

"*Aji-bāgh*, *tāji-bāgh*, break a twig, break the leaves! *Ataria-bāgh*, *lataria-bāgh*, tiger of the nail, tiger of the rocks, tiger with the horns, this is the order of guru Nanga Baiga.

"O tiger, come out, and go away to the thick jungle. Come out, for here there is nothing to eat or drink. You will get nothing here. Away with you to the thick forest! This is the order of Guru Nanga Baiga. Away with you to the thick forest!"

Then we all shouted as loudly as we could, a great shout that echoed through the forest, and then kept silence listening whether earth would answer or no. For if a peacock cries or monkey chatters or deer calls in answer to that shout, the Baiga know that their magic has been successful. But on this day there was no response from the earth. After that Deriya was given liquor and he spat it out on to the nails. The Dewar laid his axe on the top of the nail and muttered a mantra. Then we went round and repeated the ceremony in two other places. Once they drove the nail high up into the tree under which the dead man had been caught. Every time we shouted and listened, but not once did earth reply.

All this time the relatives of the dead man, who hitherto had played no part in the proceedings, had been preparing a great feast down by the bank of the stream. It was now almost sunset and we went down to the stream and sat on a rock overlooking the whole scene. On one side Gond prepared enormous pots of kodon, emptying them when ready on to a bamboo mat. The Gond women sat in a group watching; all the cooking was done by men. On the other side some Baiga youths prepared food for the Baiga women who will not eat from the hands of Gonds. In between sat the visitors smoking and drinking mahua liquor.

When the food was ready, the relatives of the dead man, both men and women together, sat down and were served by a *samdhi*. Bodan Dewar's son, though a Baiga, had to pick up all their leaf-plates and throw them away. Then the Baiga women ate, and when they had done Gond and Baiga ate together.

It was now dark, and everyone busy with food and liquor. No one therefore took very much notice of two other ceremonies that were now performed down on the bank of the stream. The first was the Churi Phodna, or the rite whereby a woman is formally made a widow. The participants in the rite were Gond but they told me that they were following Baiga custom, as is usual where a few Gond live in a Baiga village. The widow stood in the river, her father behind her on the bank, her mother in front of her in the water. Her daughter and sisters stood near by. The daughter covered her mother's head with a fold of her *lugra*. Then one by one the widow's mother broke her glass bangles and let the bits fall into the stream, while the girl wailed dismally. Then she removed the silver ornaments and gave them to her elder daughter. When this was done, the widow's father brought liquor and gave her first and then the mother and then the others. It was a very pathetic scene, the only sign of real sorrow that I observed throughout the day.

After this the Baiga Dewar, the same Dewar who had gone with Deriya to drive the nails, a young and energetic Dewar who seemed to act as a sort of agent for the rest, performed the ceremony known as Bel Todna. This is for the special protection of the dead man's family, and for the reward of the gunia. The close relatives gathered in the middle of the stream, the dead man's father stood in front and behind him his brother, his widow, his daughter and his *samdhi*. The dead man's brother had brought a long thread, and he carefully tied this three times round the little group. The Dewar put a little rice in the father's hand, and brought a chicken and made it eat a little of it. Then the Dewar walked round the group and splashed water over them. When he came back to the front he took the chicken and the thread together in his hand, and with one sharp movement broke the chicken's neck and the thread. He gathered up the thread in his hand and holding it under the water walked down stream for a few yards and there buried them under a big stone.

There was then a pause while some vigorous bargaining followed about the fees payable to the Dewar for their services throughout the day. When this was agreed, the Dewar went and lay flat down in the bed of the stream, while someone covered him completely with a cloth. Then each of the dead man's relatives stepped over him one by one, putting a little money on the cloth, and they went down stream without looking back. Somehow they were to find their way home. When they had all passed, the Dewar sat up and counted the gifts that had been made. On this occasion he seemed well satisfied. By this time everybody else had sat for food and so we went as quickly as possible to join them.

Chapter XI

THE MYTHOLOGICAL BACKGROUND OF HISTORY AND SCIENCE

I. THE FUNCTIONAL CHARACTER OF MYTH

I HAVE put this chapter in the middle of the book as a sort of symbol. For the mythology of the Baiga is the central power-house of the life and energy of the tribe. Those institutions that have a legend to vitalize and control them are living; those that have not are slowly dying out. Myth does far more than explain the Baiga's institutions; it is their motive power and their authorization. When a Baiga is summoned to control a man-eating tiger, he faces this dangerous task with the more courage because he knows that the duty has been his from the beginning. When he comes to perform magic to Dharti Mata and Thakur Deo on behalf of Gond or fellow-Baiga cultivators, he recites the myth of the creation of the world and reminds his hearers of the unique share that his tribe had in it. When he is overwhelmed by his own poverty, he comforts himself and his family by reminding them that to be poor and to live close to the earth was the voluntary choice of his great ancestors, their glory and not their shame. The driving of the nail, the offering of animal sacrifice, the cutting of bewar, the worship of Thakur Deo, the cure of disease, the war against witchcraft, the embarrassments of menstruation, the shame of barrenness, all trace their origin and maintain their credit in what are believed to be historic events which established them as part of the social order.

In this chapter I have gathered together and set out in something like a coherent narrative the various myths that compose the Baiga epic of creation and the biographies of the parents of mankind. The different sources are indicated in the text. I think many Baiga would be able to recount the whole epic, though normally it would not occur to them to go through it all at once; they are more accustomed to recall one incident at a time as necessity demands.

But read this epic through, and you will have a complete picture of the social and religious life of the modern Baiga. These myths are not just interesting stories tacked on to the fringe of Baiga life. They are alive:

everyone of them is continually being put into action. Why does the Baiga eat with the Gond and no one else? He remembers that it was only the Gond who at the beginning of the world would eat with him. Why does the Baiga, the orthodox Baiga, wear so little, why does he not ride on a horse, or touch cow-dung, why did he never practise human sacrifice, why does Narayan Deo live on the threshold of the house? All these matters are not so much explained in the myth, as constituted a part of the social and religious order. The myth breathes life into ancient custom; it makes the unintelligible real. The modern Baiga feels that Nanga Baiga and Nanga Baigin are his friends, he knows them so intimately. The myth makes everything contemporary.

There is an excellent example of this functional character of myth in the Bidri ceremony, when the story of the creation of the world is recited by the presiding Dewar, and especially in the mantra given on page 356. In this mantra, you may find references, just as you might find in any Collect references to the evangelical record, to the birth of Nanga Baiga and Nanga Baigin from the urine of Baba Vasishtha Muni (see page 312 of this chapter), to the Loharsur, Tamesur and Agyasur brothers who assisted the crow to discover the earth (see page 309 of this chapter), to the driving of the nail that held the world in place (again see page 316 of this chapter), to the pilgrimage of Nanga Baiga to the Basor Raja for seed, and the Baiga theory of eclipses (see page 333), and to the discovery of liquor by Bhimsen (see page 311 of this chapter). That is to say, at every turn the modern 'prayer' is related to the ancient legend, and what is more the very mention of the ancient facts has in itself a profound magical significance and power. The touch of the old myth has still its ancient power. The long procession of the years joins hands together and comes to help the Baiga fighting for modern man in his wind-swept field.

The Christian theory, the literature of Breviary and Prayer Book, may be compared to this. The mantra is indeed similar to a Collect, which invariably commences with some reference to a historical or mythical event. The Collect too, though it has its special significance for the day for which it was written, can be used on any other occasion. So the mantra, which is composed for a special occasion, can be used at any other time. But the Baiga do not observe festivals in honour of special events in their mythology as Christians and Hindus do. There is nothing corresponding to Krishna-janmashtmi to celebrate the birth of Nanga Baiga, no Good Friday to remind mankind of his death. The myth, for the Baiga, is not so much an explanation of the origin of modern customs, or something to be remembered with affection and gratitude, as an actual living reality, that is still full of a mysterious potency.

Take, for example, the story of the driving of the nail which is the climax of the story of creation. This legend, in one or other of its forms, is recited along the whole length of the Maikal Range, from the Saletekri Hills to Amarkantak. If a man is killed by a tiger, it is told with certain additions. It is repeated, as we have seen, at the Bidri ceremony, with special reference to Annadai, the goddess of food. It is the basis, the foundation of all the other legends. It gives to the Baiga a position beyond dispute, a priority above all others.

The nail, too, is as important and 'numinous' to-day as it was at the beginning of the world. An earthquake, for example, is due to the crime of incest that shakes loose the nail that holds the unsteady earth in place. When this happens, the Baiga must go and drive a new nail into a stone or tree.

In the myth we read how Nanga Baiga was established as the true Pashupati, lord of animals, with power over them, power to close the boundaries of a village against them. So, whenever a man is killed by a tiger, the Baiga must go and drive a new nail—just as if there had been an earthquake—and thus repair the magical boundaries of the place.

The Baiga must rank among the poorest people in the world. Their tiny huts are often bare of stores: they live from hand to mouth on roots and the produce of the wilds. Contempt and beggary hang upon their backs. Once when I was staying with Bukwa, the Baiga landlord of Ufri, I found the roof of his house fallen through, and the only food he had a few handfuls of gram which his wife had earned by going to grind wheat for a Gond neighbour. Yet he could assure me without any feeling of incongruity, that "the whole world belongs to us; we are the real masters, for the Baiga is Bhumia Raja, lord of the earth".

The problem at once arises: If this is so, how are we to account for the extreme poverty of this Bhumia Raja? But this is no problem to the Baiga. He finds the answer in the myth. He was constituted in poverty by divine permission; it is his privilege, not his shame. He is the child of earth, and must live close to the earth, his mother. "A king cannot live without his kingdom; a merchant cannot live without his riches: a Baiga cannot forsake the earth." What was good enough for our great ancestor Nanga Baiga, he seems to say, is good enough for us. Those who preserve their faith in the blessing of poverty undoubtedly draw comfort and courage from it. For those who live with their ears pressed against the bosom of Mother Earth hear her whispered secrets, secrets about rain and crops and wild animals, which no one else can hear.

These myths then are no mere fairy stories, nor just primitive attempts at a scientific explanation of things. At every point there is the closest contact between them and the daily life of the tribe. To the Baiga they are the records of veritable happenings which set the social order on its course, instituted tribal law, and established him in his unique position as Bhumia Raja, lord of the earth.

II. THE FINDING OF EARTH[1]

'In the beginning there was nothing but water, water, water. There was no voice of god,[2] no voice of *bhut*, no wind, no rocks, no paths, no jungle. As the sky is now, so was water then. On a great lotus-leaf, that drifted here and there on the waters, sat Bhagavan. There was no fruit or flower to his life: he was alone. One day he rubbed his arm, and with the dirt that came off he made a crow, his daughter, Karicag. When she could fly, Bhagavan said to her, "Go and find some earth for me, I am lonely here; I want to make a world."

'The crow flew and flew, flew and flew, who knows where it went. At last the breath left its body and it fell with a thud on the back of Kekramal

[1] A similar myth is common among the Gond of Dindori. But in Betul, Trench found a totally different story current (See his *Grammar of Gondi* (Madras, 1921), pp. 1 ff.). Most of the tribes agree with Hindu tradition about the primæval ocean, but they depart widely from it in their accounts of how the world and the parents of mankind were made. Myths of the creation of the world appear in the Brahmanas and Upanishads as well as in the Epics and Puranas. Apart from the curious legend of the cosmic egg, the conception is highly philosophic. In the Mahabharata, for example, Vishnu the Creator is described as without beginning or without end, an eternal energy, the pervader of all worlds, the unchanging fount of power from whom the whole creation springs, into whom it disappears. The universe is subject to a ceaseless rhythm of creation and dissolution. Each of the four Yugas ends with a general conflagration which is quenched with rain and flood. The world then dissolves once again into a vast ocean. The Supreme Universal Soul, says the Vishnu Purana, which existed alone at the beginning, now reposes on his mighty serpent couch in the midst of the deep. After a time he awakes and becomes Brahma, the active author of creation, who springs from a lotus growing from the navel of Vishnu.

According to the Ramayana, in the beginning all was water, and the earth was formed beneath it. Then arose Brahma and became a boar and raised up the earth. Brahma is called Narayana because the waters (*nara*) were the scene of his birth and first movement.

The Baiga story, especially at the beginning, has probably taken various elements—such as the primæval ocean and the earth below it, the lotus-leaf and the figure of Bhagavan, from Hindu mythology, but later it diverges almost entirely from it. Thy myths of other tribes follow the Baiga pattern rather than the Hindu. Thus the Munda describe how Sing-bonga brooded on the face of the waters, and sent a tortoise, a crab, and a leech to find a lump of clay out of which he might make the earth. The leech succeeded in finding some clay at the bottom of the ocean, and out of this Sing-bonga moulded the world (S. C. Roy: *The Mundas and Their Country* (Calcutta, 1912), App. I, pp. 5–7). The Birhors also give the name of Sing-bonga to the Creator. In the beginning there was nothing but water until a lotus plant grew up to the surface. Sing-bonga was living at the bottom of the ocean, but he climbed up through the hollow stem of the lotus, where he sat and sent the three first-born creatures to find him clay. He moulded this into the world, and scattered seed upon it (S. C. Roy: *The Birhors* (Ranchi, 1925), pp. 400–2).

[2] Throughout the word 'god' translates the Hindi *deo*.

Chhatri, the great tortoise, who was sitting in the water with one arm on the bottom of the ocean and one arm reaching to the sky.

'Kekramal Chhatri said, "What is the matter? Why are you panting like that?" "O elder brother, I was so tired that my life was leaving my body." "Where are you going, little sister?" "I am searching for earth. Where can I find it?" "Go and look for Gichnaraja, the worm at the bottom of the ocean; it is he who has swallowed the earth.[1] I will take you to Logundi Raja who will help you."

'So Kekramal Chhatri took the crow to Logundi Raja and the Raja called the twelve brothers Loharsur, the thirteen brothers Tamesur, and the fourteen brothers Agyasur,[2] and they made a great iron cage with windows.[3] Kekramal Chhatri and the crow got into the cage, and Logundi Raja lowered them down till they reached the bottom of the ocean. He gave them another chain in their hands and said, "When you are ready, pull this and I'll haul you up."

'Gichnaraja was sleeping: the cage landed near his head. Kekramal Chhatri and the crow came out and woke him up. He was very angry. "I've slept for twelve years," he shouted, "and now you've broken my sleep. I've had no food all that time, so now I'm going to eat you."

'Kekramal Chhatri got behind the crow when he heard that. "Whose daughter are you?" the worm asked then. "I am the daughter of Bhagavan." "Why have you come here?"

'"I have come to find the earth."

'"Did your father put the earth here so that you should come and look for it?"

'When she heard that, the crow got very angry and said, "If you don't give me the earth, *bhosri*, I'll beat you."

'That made Gichnaraja frightened, and he said, "The earth isn't here, my daughter, it's over there, but it's guarded by a Dano who will burn you to ashes if you go near him." So said Gichnaraja.

'But Kekramal Chhatri didn't believe this pretence. When he saw that the worm was afraid, he forgot to be afraid himself, and came out from behind the crow's back and jumped on to the worm and seized him by the neck.

[1] In Niwas they say that it was Nal Raja and Nal Rani who stole the earth.

[2] Among the Oraon the beings who first smelted iron are called the twelve brothers Asur and the thirteen brothers Lodha (Cp. Dehon: 'Religion and Customs of the Uraons,' in *Memoirs of the Asiatic Society of Bengal*, i, 9, 128–31).

[3] The Baiga seem to have given a lot of attention to the mechanics of diving, curious in a tribe that has never seen the ocean! In a folk-tale recorded on p. 503 the hero is lowered to the bottom of the sea sitting on a *mächi*. But as he is being pulled up, he falls off and is killed. The Baiga may have observed engineering operations in the Maniari Lake.

'"Give me the earth at once, or I'll cut off your head." So said Kekramal Chhatri.

'So he began to squeeze and squeeze. The worm wriggled and twisted this way and that, and screamed. "My son, my son, wait a moment." He began to vomit then. Twenty-one times he vomited. Each time he brought up some earth, each time it was about the size of a berry.

'His first vomit brought up Dharti Mai, Mother Earth; his second, Piri Dharti, Yellow Earth; his third, Kari Dharti, Black Earth; his fourth, Papi Dharti, Sinful Earth where a tiger can kill you; his fifth, Muhamundi Dharti, arid land where you sow but get no harvest; his sixth, Mudh Maili Dharti, where a woman has her periods; his seventh, Chutahi Dharti, Untouched Earth; his eighth, Dudhia Dharti, earth white as milk; his ninth, Dharni Dharti, the good earth; his tenth, Chamkan Dharti, the earth that quakes; his eleventh, Beri Dharti, where all kinds of earth are mixed; his twelfth, Alo Dharti, red earth; his thirteenth, Nangi Dharti, naked earth; his fourteenth, Gori Dharti, white earth; his fifteenth, Pathari Dharti, rocky earth; his sixteenth, Barra Dharti,[1] red gravel earth; his seventeenth, Sahri Dharti[2]; his eighteenth, Bhairi Dharti, deaf earth; his nineteenth, Anna Kuari Dharti, fertile earth that gives grain; his twentieth, Utkan Dharti, earth where nothing grows; his twenty-first, Kuari Dharti, virgin soil.

'Gichnaraja gave all the earth to the crow, and then Kekramal Chhatri tugged at the chain and Logundi Raja pulled the two of them up. Kekramal Chhatri tied the earth round the crow's neck with rope, and the crow flew away, away, away; she nearly died of weariness; till at last she came home to Bhagavan.

'"Have you brought the earth, my daughter?" he asked when he saw her.

'"Yes, father, I have."

'Then Bhagavan undid the earth from the crow's neck and put it in his lap. Then he called a young virgin. She made a pot out of leaves, and put the earth in it, and she churned it. For eight days and nine nights she churned till all was ready. Then Bhagavan rolled the earth out like a great thin *chapāti*, and spread it on the face of the waters. There it began to grow till it had covered all the waters.[3]

[1] *Barra* is the name given locally to all the poorer soils that cannot bear *rabi* or rice. It is very rocky, but the best soil for kodon and kutki.

[2] *Sahri* is the Baiga's name for an inferior type of black cotton soil, classified officially as *Mund II*. It is suitable for nearly all crops.

[3] The Dindori version of the story is that Bhagavan gave the earth back to the crow and told her to sow it like seed upon the face of the ocean. 'She flew here and there, she dropped the bits of earth in every part of the sea. After a few days the earth began to grow. There was some here and some there.' The account in the text is from Niwas.

'But it was not firm: whenever they tried to stand on it, it ran away; it was slippery as mud in the rains.

'So at last Bhagavan sent his daughter the crow to fetch Pawan Daseri the wind[1] and Bhimsen. The wind, whom Bhagavan had created from the breath of his mouth, came first, flying in great haste. He blew on the earth, he drove some of it up into the air, he mixed it all up, he blew till it began to be hard and firm. But the wind is blind: that is why he is always knocking things over and banging up against people: so the work was not perfect. The earth was hard, but when they stood on one side, the other side tipped up.'

III. THE COMING OF BHIMSEN

'Then came Bhimsen,[2] that great giant, in one mighty stride he came, one foot was in his house, the other came to Bhagavan. But he was very tired and he told Bhagavan that he must have some food before anything else. So Bhagavan gave him twenty-five sacks of rice and twelve sacks of lentils. He ate it all and said, "This is nothing; give me more." Then they gave him twelve sacks of gram. When he had eaten that also, he said to Bhagavan, "Old uncle, you've given me nothing to drink."

'"You must go and find some liquor," said Bhagavan.

'"What is that?" asked Bhimsen.

'"Go and see," said Bhagavan.

'Bhimsen went to the forest and searched and searched. After a long time he came to a mahua tree. The tree was hollow and that hollow was full of liquor. All round on the branches were sitting birds who had been drinking it—haril, phadki, parrots, crows, maina, every kind of bird. They were all nodding their heads. "Why are they nodding their heads like that?" thought Bhimsen. He climbed the tree to see, and there the hollow was full of liquor. Bhimsen dipped his hand in and sucked it.

'"This is liquor! This is liquor!" he shouted, and began to drink. When he had had a bellyful his head began to nod also. He sat down with the birds and they all nodded their heads together.[3]

[1] Pawan Daseri, the Wind, is specially honoured in the little village of Chiraidongri in Mandla, where a strong wind always blows from a hill near the village and drives away every disease.

[2] For Bhimsen, see Chapter I, pp. 59.

[3] The Kol have a legend of the origin of liquor. Sing-Bonga created a boy and girl and put them in a cave to people the world. But they were too innocent; nothing came of it. So Sing-Bonga taught them how to make rice-beer, and in no time they had twelve sons and twelve daughters (Russell and Hiralal: op. cit., iii, p. 508). See Chapter I for a general account of the Baiga's attitude to liquor.

'Then he filled twelve gourds full of the liquor and brought it back for Bhagavan to drink. They sat down, Bhagavan and the wind and the crow, and they drank the liquor out of leaf-cups. Then when their heads were nodding, Bhimsen got up and walked round the earth.

'Where it was thin he put a mountain, where it was too heavy he made a valley. Where it slipped about he put trees to hold it together. But even then the earth was not firm and steady. It still wobbled. It was so scattered and uneven that it was like a broken spider's web.'[1]

IV. THE BIRTH OF NANGA BAIGA

We now come to what, for the Baiga, is the most significant part of the myth. The story of the crow and the worm is repeated by their neighbours, the Gond and the Ahir, though it is probable that it originated with the Baiga Dewar. But the myth of the birth of Nanga Baiga and Nanga Baigin belongs only to the Baiga. It is of great importance; its influence is at least as great as the myth of Adam and Eve.

In the story of their birth there are many variations, interesting and significant. They were born, it is generally agreed, on the Kajli-ban-pahar or Hill of Elephants: though the Binjhwar Baiga of Baihar trace them to Mount Kailas. In several districts, they are associated, for some obscure reason, with Babu Vasishtha Muni. The Muni, according to the Laws of Manu, was one of the seven great Rishi and one of the ten Prajapati. There are many legends about him in the Brahmanas and Puranas. He had a hundred sons. He was a Brahmin. He owned a cow of plenty called Nandini who gave him everything he wanted. There is no apparent reason for connecting him with the Baiga or even with the Maikal Hills. But here he is.[2]

'Baba Vasishtha Muni was sitting in meditation for the earth on the Kajli-ban-pahar. Two drops of his urine, one a full drop, one a half drop, fell to the ground, and from them Nanga Baiga and Nanga Baigin were born. These two lived on roots and their house was a hollow saj tree.'

This comes from Bendi village in Rewa State. From the Baiga Chak in Mandla I recorded a slightly elaborated version.

'Baba Vasishtha Muni was Bhagavan's guru. For thirteen years he passed urine into a gourd. In the thirteenth year the gourd broke and

[1] The Gond, however, say that Bhimsen was able to fix the earth in its place, and it henceforth needed no more attention. Bhimsen is really a Gond hero; the Baiga do not seem to think very much of him.

[2] The Kharia also associate Vasishtha Rishi with the origin of mankind. See S. C. Roy: *The Khārias*, p. 29.

Nanga Baiga came out weeping. When the Baba saw him he was angry, and picked the child up and threw him into the jungle. A black she-cobra caught him as he fell, and gave him two and a half drops of her milk. Then she hid him safely in an anthill. After that the black cobra gave birth to Nanga Baigin. There were two parts of the anthill. The boy lived in one, the girl in the other.'[1]

But in Baihar I was told that Nanga Baiga's mother was Basmoti Kaniya, the bamboo-girl, who fed him with her milk, and gave him a golden axe. These stories, of course, show traces of the Hindu influence which has been slowly penetrating into the Baiga Chak and among the Binjhwar Baiga of Baihar. A much more primitive stratum of myth exists elsewhere. Thus in Pandaria, the Baiga describe how the first gods, being hungry, went to Nangapahar, to dig for roots. They dug up some of them, and out of that hole came a little man and woman, naked, and they all laughed and said, "These are Naga Baiga and Naga Baigin." But afterwards their name was changed to Nanga Baiga and Nanga Baigin.

In Niwas I heard a very similar account of the parents of mankind.[2]

In the *madhuban*, the sweet forest, under a clump of bamboos, were born two children who were to be the lords of the earth. They were Nanga Baiga and Nanga Baigin. They used to play in any pit from which roots had been dug.

Many Baiga say, simply, that their great ancestors were born "from the womb of Mother Earth". We may safely dismiss Baba Vasishtha Muni as an accretion. The genuine Baiga story is invariably concerned with earth, roots, jungle and bamboo.

So there, on the Hill of Elephants, the Hill of Snakes, the Hill of Nakedness, however your fancy takes you, you must imagine the parents of mankind eating their roots and playing in a pit. The years pass and they grow up.

'They were brother and sister. What were they to do? "What is the harm in it?" asked Nanga Baiga. When they were old enough they desired each other. "What need of marriage?" asked Nanga Baiga. They were both naked. Nanga Baiga used to go and bathe in a pond and

[1] Mr. M. Ikramullah, I.C.S., has recorded the following story from the Baiga Chak. 'Bhagnan had a guru. His name was Baba Vishisht Muni. Kari Nagin used to look after him and wash his loin-cloth. One day she found a little semen on it. In spite of her repeated efforts to clean it she could not. So she thought of removing the spot by licking it. The moment she licked it, the cloth was purified but she became pregnant. She gave birth to Naga Baiga.'—*Census of India*, 1931, Vol. XII, p. 404.

[2] The Gond of Betul believe that the first human beings were born from eggs laid by the Singamali birds on the face of the ocean (Trench: op. cit., p. 1). The Pauri Bhuiya say that their ancestors sprang miraculously out of Mother Earth, and so the tribe is called Bhuiya or earth-born (S. C. Roy: *The Hill Bhuiyas*, p. 264). Tota Haran and Tota Buri, the original Munda, were born from the egg of a swan created by Sing-Bonga (Roy: *The Mundas*, App. I, p. vii).

his sister went to watch him. He came to her on the bank and said, "If you're ready, let's do it." She answered, "If you have a mind to it, I'm ready." So they became mated among the trees on the bank of the pond.

'In the place where they lived, there was the stump of a saj tree on one side, on the other side a stone, on the third side bamboos. In the midst sat Nanga Baiga and his sister. Bara Deo was living in the saj stump, Basin Kaniya in the bamboo, Baba Bastar Rai and Baba Karan Rai, sons of Pathar Rai, were living in the stone.'

V. THE SUMMONS TO THE BAIGA

We come now to the calling of Nanga Baiga and Nanga Baigin. When Bhagavan saw that Bhimsen could not fix the earth firmly in its place, he sent the crow to call the two Baiga to come and do it instead.

'The crow flew and flew and flew, at last she saw the smoke from Nanga Baigin's fire rising above the trees. When Nanga Baiga saw the crow, he said, "Here's something good to eat." He was trying to catch her when Bara Deo called out from his saj tree, "Don't trouble her, she has come from Bhagavan." When he heard that, Nanga Baiga took the crow in his lap and fondled her. But he refused to go.

'Then Bhagavan sent Bhimsen, but the Baiga refused. Then he sent Pawan Daseri. When the wind came the Baiga were very frightened, and hid with Bara Deo in the hollow of the saj stump. Nanga Baiga put out his head and peeped at Pawan Daseri, but he wouldn't go with him. Then Bhagavan sent a Brahmin. The Baiga said, "Come and share our food." But the Brahmin said, "I'm a Brahmin," and he ran away.

'Then Bhagavan sent a Kshatriya, and the Baiga said, "Come and share our food." But the Kshatriya said, "I'm a Kshatriya," and he ran away. Then Bhagavan sent a Bania, and the Baiga said, "Come and share our food." But the Bania said, "I'm a Bania," and he ran away. At last Bhagavan sent a Sudra, and the Baiga said, "Come and share our food." But the Sudra too said, "I'm a Sudra," and he ran away.

'In the end Bhagavan sent a Gond who is the younger brother of the Baiga, and he sat down and shared the *pej* and the roots that Nanga Baigin had boiled, and Nanga Baiga said, "We will come with you."

'But Nanga Baiga said, "Look, we are naked as cows—my wife is hiding her privates with her hands; how are we to come and meet the gods?" So the Gond called Bhimsen and sent him to fetch some cloth. Bhagavan tore off half his own *lingoti* and sent it for the Baiga. It was nine hands long, and Nanga Baiga said it was too much. He tore off a hand and a half and gave some to his wife to tie round her waist, and put a small *lingoti* on himself. To honour the earth, Nanga Baigin did not tie the *kānch*, she was naked underneath. Mother Earth looked up and saw her and said, "You must always dress like that."'[1]

VI. THE COMING OF THE BAIGA

'Then Nanga Baiga and Nanga Baigin, with Bara Deo and Basin Kaniya, set out on their journey to Bhagavan.

'On the way, Nanga Baiga wanted to relieve himself and sat down by the roadside. Before he had finished, however, Dharti Mata suddenly shouted, "Come at once!" He only had time to tie his *lingoti*, there was no time to wash. Since then we have never washed after that work.

'Now Nanga Baiga and Nanga Baigin had nothing to sacrifice for the steadying of the world. So they took their own three sons and daughters in a *kāwar*, and were carrying them along. Then they met a jungle hen. "Where are you going?" she asked. And when she heard, "You mustn't kill your own children. Take two pairs of mine. Offer one pair, and keep the other for breeding." So said the jungle hen. Then Nanga Baiga lifted one son and daughter out of the *kāwar* and left them with the hen, and put the chickens in instead.

'A little later they met a sow. She also begged them not to sacrifice their children, and gave two pairs of sucklings in exchange for two more of the children. Then they met a barking deer, and made a similar exchange. The deer that Nanga Baiga kept for breeding grew into goats in later ages.

'Then they came to a bel tree, and she said, "Take my fruits, four of them, they are virgin coconuts, and you must offer them."

'So at last they came to the shores of the world. There was a tall akawan[2] tree growing there. At its foot Nanga Baiga sacrificed a sow to Dharti Mata, a pig to Bageshur Pat, a goat to the Banaspati, and a white cock to Thakur Deo. Dharti Mata was rocking to and fro, but when the blood of the offering fell on her, she stood still. She looked up and said to Nanga

[1] Baiga women always wear the *lugra* or *dhoti* like this. It is the general custom certainly in Balaghat, for a woman to undo her *kānch*, or *kachni* or *pāgi* (as it is variously called) that is, the part of the sari that is tied between the legs, when she meets her *jeth*, or elder brother-in-law, as a mark of respect. Since the Baiga consider the earth to be as honourable as their *jeth*, so they always keep the *kānch* open in her presence.

[2] *Calotropis gigantea.*

Baiga, "When I am angry and will listen to no one in the world, I will listen to you."[1]

'From the Agaria, who was born on the same day as the Baiga, they got four great nails. Nanga Baigin made herself naked, and drove the nails into the four corners of the world. It was very hard, but all the while Gichnaraja was spitting drops of water to make the earth easier. At last the world was steady. Then the two Baiga, being weary, lay down, the man in one corner of the world, his girl in the other. Their feet met in the middle.'[2]

VII. THE CREATION OF MANKIND

Some Baiga say that it was Nanga Baiga himself who created the rest of mankind. "He cut a bamboo and sharpened it, and from the shavings came all the tribes of the world." But the following version is more common.

'When the world was now firm, Bhagavan told the Baiga to go back to

[1] In Dindori, there is another version of the way human sacrifice was superseded by animal sacrifice. A Raja's son was dying, and a Baiga Dewar was called to cure him. He had nothing to offer the offended spirits but his own children, so he brought these. On the way, however, he met the various animals as above and exchanged his children for theirs. As the hen very sensibly remarked, "How can the Baiga prosper if they kill their own children every time anyone falls ill?" During the sowing of the Jawara, as the Baiga do it, they offer half a lemon to Kapardari Mata, and say that this represents a human life which they do not offer in fact. It is probable that the Baiga never practised human sacrifice, though many of their neighbours did.

[2] The Pauri Bhuiya of Orissa have a parallel myth about the steadying of the world. Out of the ocean came a bank of mud, and Dharma created Parihar Burha and Baramani Burhi to live there. 'The mud-bank began to shake and tremble. God saw from heaven that such an earth was not fit for human habitation. Then he made clay figures of a tiger and tigress, infused life into them, and ordered them: "Go, kill the human couple—and put their blood and flesh on the four corners of the earth so as to make it firm."' The tiger and tigress did as they were ordered. The blood and flesh of the original human couple settled down in the four corners of the earth as iron pillars supporting the earth, and the earth became hardened like stone' (Roy, *The Hill Bhuiyas*, p. 263).

The following curious variant on the main story is told by the Baiga of Kabidabra in the Pendra Zemindari. Pendra is a centre of missionary activity, and the tale may owe something to the Book of Genesis. 'At the beginning there was a beautiful Basorin who lived with a young Prince. She made a house of seven stories from a very big gourd. In the lowest story she put water, in the next earth, then seed, then the Banaspati, then pigs, hens and goats. In the sixth story she herself lived with her Prince, and in the top story she put a crow. When she had done this, water came flooding all over the world. There was nothing but water. It was then that Bhagavan was born. He rubbed his body and made a crow out of the dirt. The crow flew away and found the gourd floating on the water. She said "Caw". The crow in the gourd answered "Caw". Now every living thing was in the gourd. The crow tied a rope to the gourd, and towed it along through the water to Bhagavan. When Bhagavan made the world, the gourd settled on the Kajli-ban-pahar, and they all came out. There was Nanga Baiga just going for sacrifice, and they gave him pigs and chickens for it.'

their "Kundmul jungle, the hills where you dig your roots, but return after eight days". Then he said to himself, "In this ocean of the world, how shall I make black men?" He called Rawan, and in Rawan's belly were the Rawanbansi, the Gond. Rawan had no wife. Man was born of man. When the life had quickened in his belly, then the children inside said, "How are we to come out? If we come through your mouth, they will say you have vomited us out. If we come through your eyes, they will call us your tears. If we come through your nose, they will say you have blown your nose. If we come through your fundament, they will say we are your excrement. If we come out of your penis, they will say we are your urine."[1] But at last Rawan's stomach burst open and the thirty-six families of mankind came out. First came the Gond. Then came the Chamar and the Brahmin castes together. Then came the Mussalmans and the English together. And all the other tribes. At last Rawan washed all their bottoms, and out of the mess he made the Panka.[2]

'Then Bhagavan went to the bazaar and opened a shop. Everyone came to buy from him. To the Gond he gave a plough. To the Brahmin he gave a pen, to the Kalar a bottle, to the Bania a pair of scales, to the Dhimar a fishing-net, to the Mahar a loom, until he had given their work to everyone in the world. Panka were told to watch villages and chase thieves. All were given land. But he gave nothing at that time to the Baiga, for they did not come to the bazaar.

VIII. THE BLESSING OF THE BAIGA

'When the Baiga returned from the jungle, Bhagavan called all the tribes together to make them a king. The others came in fine clothes, but Nanga Baiga came clad in leaves, an axe over his shoulder. There were gold chairs, and silver chairs and wooden chairs. The Mussalmans and the English sat on the gold chairs, the Hindus were angry that they could only get the silver chairs but they sat down on them, the Gond sat on the wooden chairs, but Nanga Baiga squatted down on the floor.

'Then Bhagavan took him by the hand and made him sit by his side on his throne, and said, "You are to be king over all the world." But Nanga Baiga said, "No, make the Gond king, for he is my brother." So Bhagavan

[1] A very similar dialogue occurs between Rai Linga and his mother Queen Talko in the Betul legend given by Trench: op. cit., p. 11.

[2] The Panka are usually appointed village watchmen (Kotwar) in the Jubbulpore Division.

blessed the Gond with the promise that they should rule as kings over the world,[1] but he gave a greater blessing to the Baiga.

'"All the kingdoms of the world," so said Bhagavan, "may fall to pieces, but he who is made of earth and is Bhumiaraja,[2] lord of the earth, shall never forsake it. You will make your living from the earth. You will cut wood and carry it on your shoulders. You will dig roots and eat them. Your wife will pick leaves and sell them. You must not tear the breast of your Mother the Earth with the plough like the Gond and Hindus—you are to cut down trees and burn them and sow your seed in the ashes. But you will never become rich, for if you did you would forsake the earth, and then there would be no one to guard it and keep its nails in place."

'Then Bhagavan showed Nanga Baiga how to cut bewar and sow seed in the ashes of burnt trees. When he had taught him everything, he called him to receive a gift of seed. There was a big pillar in the middle of Bhagavan's house, and Bhagavan stood behind it. When Nanga Baiga came for the seed he stretched out his hands, one on either side of the pillar, and joining them made a cup into which Bhagavan put the seed. But then, when Nanga Baiga wanted to withdraw his hands he had to separate them, and a lot of the seed fell to the ground and was lost. Then Bhagavan laughed mightily, and said, "You have lost so much now in the beginning that you will go on losing your seed and harvest to the end of the world. It is good," so said Bhagavan, "that it should be so, for only the poor will ever be content to be servants of Dharti Mata."'

IX. THE ORIGIN OF SEED

I have recorded four different accounts of the origin of seed and the birth of Annadai or Kutkidai, who is the goddess of food. I shall quote them all in full, partly because they show the great importance that the Baiga attach to food and partly because of the light that they throw on allied Baiga institutions. The first account comes from Ajghar village in the Baiga Chak.

'Nanga Baiga made an axe out of wax and went to cut his jungle. He called the five Pandava brothers and took them with him to get seed from

[1] A promise that was fulfilled in the Gond kingdoms of Garha-Mandla, Chauragarh, Deogarh, Kherla and Chanda.

[2] The Sanskrit word *bhumi* means earth or soil. It occurs in many derivatives: Bhumi or Bhui meaning children of the soil, Bhumihar, owners of land and Bhuiya, belonging to the land. The Pauri Bhuiya of Orissa believe that their name means Earth-born. The Bharia-Bhumia of Jubbulpore and Chhindwara have taken the name Bhumia as meaning Lords of the Soil. I have suggested the general term *Bhumijan* as a title for the Indian aboriginals as a whole.

the Old Serpent who lives to the north of the Hill of Elephants. The Old Serpent gave him twelve kinds of seed. They were: *kutki, marria, rasni, sāwa, kāng, arhar, barbati rawās, bedra, jhunjhru, urda, juar, salār bājra.* Then Nanga Baiga by his magic turned the five Pandavas into two bullocks, a yoke, a sack and the *chhai,* the cloth which goes between the necks of the bullocks and the yoke. He loaded them with the seed, and then drove them along, walking, walking, walking towards the great jungle. But the Pandavas got very weary and soon they could go no further. Then they met Raja Bijra's daughter, Basmoti, and said, "We are tired. Keep this seed with you for to-night." Basmoti put all the seed in her belly, and the Pandavas ran away home. In the morning Nanga Baiga came and cut the bamboo and took the belly to his bewar, leaving the head and feet behind, and sowed his seed.'

The next story is from Pandaria Zemindari.

'Banbindra Raja was born without parents on the Hill of Elephants. Rajmoti was born at the same time, and when they grew up she became his wife. Banbindra Raja had every kind of seed in his stomach, and he discharged it through his penis. But his wife could not hold all her husband's seed inside her. She had a daughter, and she sent her daughter to receive part of the Raja's seed. But the girl, Basmotin, thought in her mind, "This is a great sin; why does he come and give his seed to me, his own daughter?"

'Then for shame Basmotin turned herself into a bamboo, and all over her body there grew knots and hollow tubes. In each tube there was a little of her father's seed: it was different in every tube. Then her name was changed from Basmotin to Basin Kaniya. She grew tall and beautiful.

'One day Pahari Bai went to her father-in-law, Nanga Baiga, for a *sūpa.* He went with her to the jungle to cut bamboo to make it. When they came to Basin Kaniya, she said, "Cut me down below, only trim me of my leaves above. Leave the middle part alone." Nanga Baiga did as she desired, and then he found in her body the twelve kinds of seed that her father had given her. So seed was now in his hands and he went and sowed it in his bewar.'

A third story, from Niwas, describes the origin of Annadai, goddess of seed. The Dom, whom Sir G. Grierson believed to have been the original gipsies,[1] are specially connected with bamboos, and one of their sub-castes is known as Bansphor or 'breakers of bamboos'. This is probably why the discovery of seed is attributed to Dom Raja.

[1] *Indian Antiquary,* XV, p. 15. 'Romany is almost letter for letter the same as Domni, the plural of Dom. Romany Rye—"a gipsy gentleman"—may well be compared with the Bhojpuri Domni Rai—"a king of the Doms."' The Dom Raja of the Baiga legend may thus be regarded as linked with the Romany-Rye of European tradition!

'Dom Raja and Dom Rani were living in a village in the heart of the jungle. They dedicated two Laru pigs for the worship of Narayan Deo; they castrated them and removed bits of the ears and tails. The two pigs used to go to the jungle for food. One day they came to a hill covered with bamboo clumps, and they began to eat young bamboo shoots. They had no fear; what forest-guard would arrest a pig? In the bamboo shoots Anna Dai was living. The pigs came home and relieved themselves in front of the house. In their droppings, Dom Raja saw some seeds. 'What are they?' he wondered, 'and where did they come from?' So one day he followed the pigs into the jungle. They again ate the bamboo and as they broke the shoots the grain fell to the ground. Then Dom Raja knew what to do.

'The next day, he and his wife took their *kāwar* and their golden axes and went to the jungle to cut bamboo. But Basin Kaniya said to them, "When you split my body don't hold me with your feet but in your hands." In the seven hollows of her body were the seven kinds of seed—rice, *kodon, kutki, kāng, marria, sawār,* maize. Dom Raja took the seed and went home. In his house he made grain-bins, and put all the seed into them. No one knew that Raja Dom had the seed. But one day he threw his used leaf-platter out into the road, and a crow came and ate what he had left: she got one seed in her beak and carried it home.

'Nanga Baiga and Nanga Baigin were sitting in their bewar, and the crow showed them the seed. Nanga Baiga said, "Come let's get seed from this Raja." So they took their *kāwar* and went to his house. "Certainly I will give you seed," said the Dom Raja, "at *adhiya* rates, but you must stay and join in our feast, for to-day is the Laru-kaj."

'All the gods were there, and Bhimsen. The gods did not want to eat from the hands of the Dom Raja,[1] so they asked Pawan Daseri the wind to come and blow away all the food just after it had been set before them. In that way, the Raja would think they had eaten with him and would be pleased, and yet they would not be hurt by the touch of a Dom. Nanga Baiga cared for none of this, but he sat down with the gods, and soon a great gust of wind blew all their food away. Nanga Baiga was angry at losing his dinner, but he said nothing as he had plenty of liquor in a hollow *thondi* slung from his shoulder. He took Bhimsen into a corner and they both drank.

'But one of the guests ate his food. "Who was it? Who was it?" they all cried. At last Bara Deo said, "Yes, I ate one little bit of the Laru."

[1] The Dom does scavenging work, and the gods would naturally object to eating at his house. So, I fear, would most of the Baiga to-day, though the legend preserves a record of the more liberal attitude of olden times.

Then they were all very angry and said, "From now on you will live separate from us, on the threshold of every house, and when people come in and out, they'll kick you all day long." That is why Bara Deo who is Narayan Deo lives on the threshold. "From that time we Baiga have kept him there, and whenever we go into our houses we give him a hearty kick."

'But from that day onward Annadai who is Kutkidai spread throughout the world. Nanga Baiga and the gods took her away with them that day, and the Sun and Moon stood security for the debt. But they have never been able to repay the Raja, and so every now and then he goes and seizes the Sun and Moon and shuts them up in his house to force Nanga Baiga and the gods to pay their debt. Then they go dark with fear and the world is dark till the gods go and set them free.'

My last story, which is the most significant of all, comes from Dindori Tehsil (Bondar village near Karanjia).

'At first, Annadai lived with all the gods who said to her, "Go down to earth for the enjoyment of man." So Annadai was born, and grew to be as tall as twelve men standing on one another's shoulders. But they said, "We cannot reach you, you are too tall." So she became as high as six men. But they said, "You are still too tall." So she became smaller still, first to the height of three men, then to the height of one, then she was only as high as a man's chest, then as high as his loins. Then when she was so high, everyone was pleased.

'Now as she stood there on the earth, leaves sprouted from her, like the leaves of a wheat-field. The Baiga came running, they caught her and shook her and the grain fell on the earth. So then they began to sow her in their bewar. Near the place where they sowed her was a little pond, on whose banks lived Thakur Deo. He enjoyed the food very much.

'After a time came other Baiga and they saw Thakur Deo feeding and they said, "What is he eating? Let us search and see." They looked everywhere, but they could find nothing, for Thakur Deo's tongue was nine hands long and he fed from a distance.

'There was a Baiga magician there who performed this magic. He said, "If this is the work of some *bhut* or god, then to-morrow morning let there be a dead stag in the field where he is feeding." So saying he clapped his hands and ran away. At cock-crow next morning, he went to the field and there was a stag—dead. The Baiga said, "What I have desired has happened. Now I shall walk once round the field. Let the body of the stag go rotten!" He walked round the field and when he returned he saw worms moving in the body of the stag. "Twice have I seen the power of the *bhut* or gods," said the Baiga. "Now if they show their power a third time I will offer sacrifice. Let this dead and rotting stag rise to its feet and run into the jungle." Immediately the stag jumped up and ran away into the jungle.

'And then the Baiga went to Thakur Deo. "Make my crop grow well," said he, "and I will give you a goat and a pig." Then Annadai grew strong and fat in that Baiga's field. When she was ripe, twelve men had to be brought to cut her down. They worked for eight nights and nine days, and yet the work was not finished. Then they prepared the threshing-floor and the bundles of wheat were brought in. The bullocks trod upon the ears for eight nights and nine days, and when the work was done the goat and the pig were killed. A little was offered to Dharti Mata and the rest was cooked and eaten. Then when all was over they started to carry the grain to the house. But Thakur Deo was angry because they had forgotten to give him any offering, and he brought all the chaff back on to the threshing-floor and said, "I will not remove it till you sacrifice to me." The Baiga said that he would give his first-born child if Thakur Deo would remove it. Then Thakur Deo called for Pawan Daseri, and he blew all the chaff away. The Baiga brought his son and made him sit in the midst of the threshing-floor, by the pillar, and Thakur Deo came in with his bow and arrow and shot the child. The boy died there in the place where he was sitting. When the villagers came and saw the boy dead, they all began to weep. They carried his body to the jungle and burnt it on a pile of wood.

'Bhagavan called all the *devata* to give each his work. He made Thakur Deo the lord of villages and gave him Babu Gunshian as his *mukthyar* (agent). To Dharti Mata he gave the whole world. Khalsahin got the Jawara festival. Dulha Deo was given the marriage-bed, Paniharin the water-pots, Khut the cattle-shed, Baghesur Pat the jungle. Bhagavan said, "Wherever you go, men will honour you."

'But Thakur Deo thought that he was not properly respected and he got very angry. Bhagavan sent Brahmins, Kshatriyas, Banias and Sudras to worship him, but he took no notice of them. At last Brahma himself came, but he took no notice. Then Bhagavan called Nanga Baiga and Nanga Baigin. They had gone to relieve themselves when they heard Bhagavan shouting for them. They quickly dressed in saj leaves and came running to Thakur Deo. On the way, Nanga Baiga went again. He had no water, so he came all dirty as he was to Thakur Deo.

'Now Thakur Deo had turned his back on all the Hindus. But when Nanga Baiga and Nanga Baigin came he turned round and squatted down beside them. He began to joke and laugh and he patted Nanga Baiga on the back. Nanga Baiga had some liquor in his *thondi*, and with this he made great friends with Thakur Deo. Presently he wiped his dirty funda-

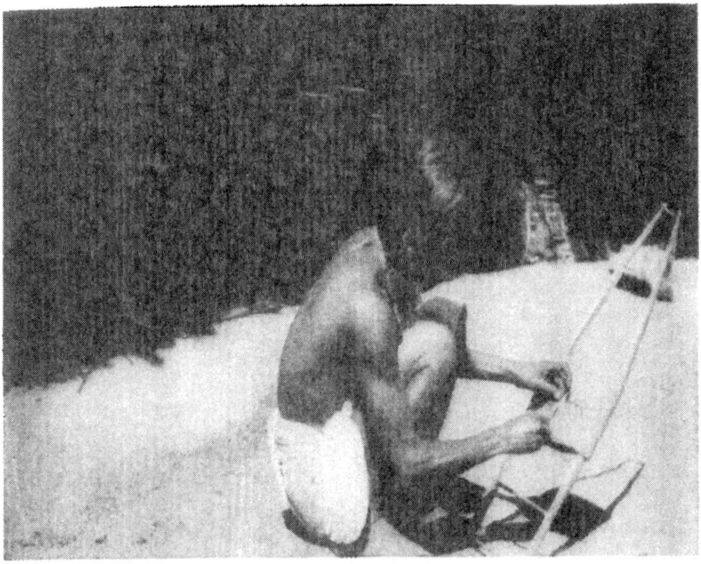

Making a tobacco-pouch.
Making a kumni fish-trap.

ment with a leaf and put it in front of Thakur Deo. That old god began to roar with laughter. Nanga Baigin laughed so much that she was sick. Then they all laughed again, they could not stop laughing. They held their sides and rolled on the ground.

'At last, Thakur Deo said to Nanga Baiga, "Because you have made me laugh and given me good liquor, now if ever I am angry and will listen to no one else, I will always listen to you. I am the lord of all villages, and you are to bring to me everything that concerns my villages. You may bless the seed and cure the sick." So said Thakur Deo and went away. From that time, we Baiga have always gone to Thakur Deo at the Bidri to bless the seed.'[1]

X. THE CHILDREN OF NANGA BAIGA

There is a good deal of variation in that part of the myth which deals with Nanga Baiga's children, for all the different divisions of the tribe naturally want to trace their origin back to their great founder. I quote three typical accounts, one from Niwas, one from Rewa State, and the third from Pandaria. Accounts of the origin of the *goti* are decidedly weak and not very widely known, which, in view of the decay of the strictly exogamous rules of the tribe, is what we would expect. My first account, then, is from Niwas.

'One day Bhagavan said to Nanga Baiga, "You will have two sons." He said to Nanga Baigin, "You will have two daughters." Then said he, "Call your sons Bharotia and Binjhwar and your daughters Baigin and Bhumnin. Let the Binjhwar boy marry the Baigin girl, and the Bharotia boy marry the Bhumnin girl. The Bhumnin may make *sūpa, dauri, jhāpi* and all things with bamboo, but the Baigin may not. They may kill every kind of animal, but they are not to touch a horse, or move a dead cat or dog. They must not clean their houses with cow-dung: that is a sin. They must find the dung of the sambhar, put it in a pot, and when it is ready clean with that. Every man is your brother: you are not to observe untouchability." So said Bhagavan. It is only since all the Hindu

[1] The Santal Thakur Deo is more like a Village Uplift Worker than the Johnsonian figure of the Baiga legend. In the old days the Santal enjoyed many blessings; rice grew ready husked, cloth grew on bushes, men's skulls were loose and could be lifted off and cleaned. But one day a girl went to a field to relieve herself and as she did so she picked and ate the rice that was growing near her. This annoyed Thakur Baba and he deprived mankind of its privileges. In those days the sky was very near the earth, but people threw their used leaf-plates out into the road, and one day the wind carried one of these up into the sky. Thakur Baba was annoyed, and lifted the sky to its present height above the earth. Bompas, op. cit., p. 402. By comparison the primitive character of the Baiga story stands out strikingly.

castes increased that we have observed it, and begun to clean our houses with cow-dung.'

My next example is from Rewa State.

'Nanga Baiga had a son and a daughter, and their names were Gunshian and Gunshiain. These two married each other although they were brother and sister. Then Nanga Baiga sent a dream to the girl saying, "You will have twelve sons, and you are to give each a different name." When she awoke she had twelve sons, and she gave them these names—Binjhwar, Chituria, Damgarhia, Gangarhia, Dawaria, Pachgaiha, Salgaia, Kumaria, Sawat, Masania, Chandania, Chandgarhia. Then she had twelve daughters, and she gave them names after her fancy. She said to her sons, "As your names are, so go and make your homes. Binjhwar must live in Bij Garh, Chituria must live in Chitra Garh, each must live in his own *garh*." Then said Nanga Baiga to them, "You are all brothers, but you are of different *jāt* and *garh*. You must always marry someone of a different *jāt*."'

The Pandaria story is hardly complimentary to the gods.

'At the time of the first sacrifice when Nanga Baigin fixed the earth in its place, she gave birth to four-and-twenty children together. There were twelve sons and twelve daughters. When Bhagavan saw this he was frightened and said, "How are we to marry all these? Unless we do something, they will marry each other, brother with sister, and there will be a great earthquake." So Bhagavan thought and thought, for twenty nights and one-and-twenty days he thought: all that time he never ate. Then he caused all the twelve girls to die and called their *jīv* to him.

'He sent for Mahadeo and Parvati and said, "You must take the form of a Baiga and a Baigin: I will take the form of a sadhu and we will go with these twelve girls to Nanga Baiga and Nanga Baigin."

'So away they went to the jungle on the Hill of Elephants and there they found Nanga Baiga and Nanga Baigin sitting on their thrones of mud, eating roots. Bhagavan came first as a holy sadhu and said, "From to-day your *jāt* will be Deoaria and your *goti* Baghel. Three of your sons belong to the Seraria *jāt* and the Morabi *goti*. Three belong to the Pachgaiha *jāt* and the Durwa *goti*. The other six are Deoaria and Baghel like yourself. I will find twelve girls for your sons to marry."

'Just then came Mahadeo and Parvati looking exactly like Baiga: Parvati had her *kānch* undone and there was no hole in her nose for ornaments. They had the twelve girls with them.

'"We are Baiga," they said, "and we want daughters for our husbands. Marry your sons to our daughters." Then Nanga Baiga said, "But what is their *jāt*?" They answered, "Our *jāt* is Binjhwar and our *goti* is

Nangbansi." Then said Nanga Baiga, "Good, we can marry our sons to your daughters."

'Then Nanga Baiga and his wife went to the jungle and they dug every kind of root for the marriage. Bhagavan came then in his proper form, and at the marriage he made a gift to all the children. He gave them the earth. He said, "You may always take what you will from the jungle. Kings may lose their kingdoms, but you will never lose your jungle."'

XI. THE TRUE PASHUPATI

Nanga Baiga and his consort have returned to the jungle. The great nails that hold the world in place (unless incest frets its stability with earthquake) have been driven into place. Nanga Baiga has been given the jungle as his home and bewar as his livelihood. He is supplied with seed. What of his subsequent adventures?

A very important story that relates the origin of menstruation is given in full in the chapter on that subject. Similarly I give here a shorter version of the origin of witchcraft and a fuller account in the chapter on Magic. With these exceptions such legends as I have been able to record about the parents of mankind are given here.

It is now that we make the acquaintance of a new and somewhat different cycle of legends concerned with two mysterious beings whom, for want of better names, the latter-day Baiga have called Mahadeo and Parvati. But they bear no resemblance to the august and splendid deities of Hindu theology. Mahadeo is not a Baiga deity. "Mahadeo comes from afar, he is a stranger," said Thuggur the Dewar to me. In the legends, Mahadeo and Parvati are simply a typical couple who get the better of the Baiga at every opportunity. They might almost symbolize a conflict of the Baiga with civilization.

'Mahadeo was the son of Amardevi who lived in a lotus that floated on the surface of the ocean. When he grew up he desired his mother, and married her, changing her name to Parvati. Mahadeo took his wife to Nanga Baiga's jungle, and there they lived on roots—it was while they were searching for *kanhia-kānda* that they came to know Nanga Baiga.

'They used to play hide-and-seek together in the jungle. Mahadeo would hide something and they all had to find it. Then Parvati would hide something. Nanga Baiga would call out the name of a tree, and they had to try to find it. Nanga Baiga and his wife always won the game, because their eyes were white and they could see everything. So

Mahadeo and Parvati said, "We must put an end to this!" Parvati said to Nanga Baigin, "Why not get some bhilwa fruit? If you put its juice in your eyes, it will make you very beautiful." So Nanga Baigin went and got some of the fruit and put it in her eyes, and some also in her husband's eyes, but it only burnt them and that is why the Baiga's eyes to-day are so black and they can see no more than other people.

'Then Mahadeo and Parvati made birds and animals out of mud and they gave life to them. Nanga Baiga and his wife gave them their names. They all decided that the Baiga should not eat tigers, jackals or hyenas. They also made the *goti* which are to stop brothers and sisters living together.

'After a time Parvati became pregnant, and went away to her own house. For twelve years Mahadeo lived alone in the jungle and worked as a carpenter. Parvati felt very lonely: every day she used to ask, "When will he come?" At last she made a tiger from the dirt she rubbed from her breasts and sent it to frighten Mahadeo, hoping that he would then run home to her.[1] When he heard the tiger roaring, Mahadeo said, "For twelve years not even a bird has dared to twitter near me and now what is this?" He threw wood-shavings all over the tiger, and turned him into a jungle-dog. The tiger-dog ran home and sat in Parvati's lap. She put fire in a stick and thrust it into his mouth, and he ran back to Mahadeo, turning into a tiger again as he went.

'Then Mahadeo called Nanga Baiga and Nanga Baiga said, "What's the matter now, Mahadeo?" Mahadeo fell at his feet and said, "Do go and kill this tiger for me." Nanga Baiga picked up his axe, he went into the jungle, and threw his axe at the tiger and killed him.

'There was a banyan tree twenty-four *kos* long. Nanga Baiga buried the tiger under the tree. But as he was digging, he cut one of the roots, and the tiger drank milk from the root and returned to life. He went again to trouble Mahadeo. Mahadeo called Nanga Baiga and was very angry. They had a quarrel. Nanga Baiga at last went back to the jungle to kill the tiger a second time. He raised his axe to hit him, but the tiger lifted up his paw, and said, "Wait, listen to my story." So Nanga Baiga sat down on the stump of a tree and began to smoke his pipe.

'The tiger said, "Whenever I catch men, goats, cattle, chickens in a village, all the people will call on you to help them. You won't get gold or silver—that is for the Hindus. But wherever you do your magic in a village or forest, there I will never come, and the people will trust you and will give you enough for your livelihood."

[1] In the Birhor legend, Parvati first makes mosquitoes, then a tiger, and then snakes. But Mahadeo is a match for her: he creates *dulü* which eat mosquitoes, dogs to chase the tiger, and a vulture to eat the snakes. He has no need of a Birhor to help him. The Baiga story shows a far lower estimate of Mahadeo's powers (Cp. Roy: *The Birhors*, p. 403).

'When Nanga Baiga heard this, he thought, "What has this Mahadeo done for me? If I make a pact with the tiger I will always have enough to drink at least. For food I can get roots. I will do what the tiger desires." So he let him go.

'One day soon after this the tiger killed a Gond, and the headman of the village sent for Nanga Baiga to protect the village. They agreed to give Nanga Baiga a goat and one rupee's worth of liquor and two coconuts. So all night he sat 'looking' in his *sūpa-tuma* and in the morning he went to the Agaria and had four nails made. He called everyone to the place where the man had been killed. The ground was red with his blood. Nanga Baiga made two little images, one of the sin that had killed the man, the other of the *banaspati*.

'Then Nanga Baiga called on all the tigers in the world by name—the white Shet-bagh, the horned Singh-bagh, Lataria-bagh the hyena, Jalaria-bagh, the cattle-eating Dhor-bagh, Kowachi-bagh the leopard, Bundia-bagh, Gul-bagh, the small Lorcha-bagh, the tiny dog-like Bhusur-bagh, Dandhia-bagh, the tailless Buchi-bagh, the small-eared Tajia-bagh, the magic, wooden Khunta-bagh, Tendua-bagh the panther, Chita-bagh and Son-chitti-bagh.

'The *barua* entered into him and he trembled all over. He leapt in the air and caught hold of the Sin-Image. Then they understood that that man had broken a law of the tribe; perhaps he had been to someone in his own *goti*—no one could say—and so he had been standing on *pāpi-dharti*, and the tiger had been able to kill him. Then Nanga Baiga drove a nail into a tree, and they all shouted, "Be off, be off, Buchi-bagh!" Then he went to another tree and drove a nail into that and they all shouted, "Be off, be off, Bundia-bagh!" He went again to a third tree, and now they all shouted, "Be off, be off, Jalaria-bagh!" At the fourth tree, after he had driven in the nail that should close the tiger's jaws in that place, Nanga Baiga himself said, "O Dharti Mata, O Banaspati, to-day I Nanga Baiga have fixed the boundary of this village. I Nanga Baiga, make it free from every kind of tiger!"

'From that day Nanga Baiga has been lord of all wild animals.'[1]

XII. THE GIFT OF MAGIC

Phulmat, the old sorceress of Kotalwahi, told me how Nanga Baiga once had a different kind of encounter which gained for the Baiga the power to promote childbirth and remedy disease.

[1] That is to say, it is Nanga Baiga and not Mahadeo who is the true Pashupati, lord of animals.

'Beyond the Seven Seas and the Sixteen Rivers lived the seven Samduria sisters. None of them had either child or husband. They said, "We must find a guru." They searched and searched, but could not find one anywhere. Then the youngest sister went wandering along the shores of the ocean, and one day she found Nanga Baiga sitting there eating berries. She touched his feet and said, "Come, I'll make you my guru."

'"What are you talking about?" asked Nanga Baiga. "What do you want with a guru? Tell me what you really want."

'"I want you to give me a child," she said at last.

'"That is easy," said Nanga Baiga.

'Soon there was a child in the girl's belly, and she went home to her sisters, after hiding Nanga Baiga in the depths of the jungle.

'The sisters had never seen a pregnant woman before, and they did not understand what had happened. "How fat you've grown!" they said. "You must be eating too much." So said the six sisters. "No, no," said she, "it's not that. I've found a guru, and he's given me a child." "Where is he?" they all cried. "Oh, he's gone away," she said.

'After twelve months a boy was born. The six sisters were so jealous that they could not speak a word. The youngest sister went to Nanga Baiga and said, "Give me some good food or the child will die."

'Nanga Baiga said, "I'll bring some magic herbs from the jungle for you, then you'll be all right." So Nanga Baiga brought a twig of katai, and the root of the chhindi tree and kassi bark and gave them to her. When she had taken the medicine, she felt well again.

'Guru Nanga Baiga went on living in that jungle. Now one of the Samduria sisters was a very powerful witch. She said, "Now let all childbirth cease throughout the world!" And it was so.

'Nanga Baiga took his *sūpa*, and Nanga Baigin took the *tuma*, and they sat down to see what was the cause why no children were being born. He saw all the *devata* sitting in his *sūpa*, and he saw also the Samduria sisters sitting there to do evil to men. So he offered them a pig and two coconuts and childbirth began again.

'So nowadays, when a woman has no child, the Baiga looks in his *sūpa* and if he sees those six jealous Samduria sisters dancing there, he knows that it is they who have done the mischief.'

XIII. THE DEATH OF NANGA BAIGA

Now comes the myth of the end of Nanga Baiga and the coming of death to the world.[1]

[1] A fuller version of this story is given in Chapter XII.

'Bhagavan grew tired of the Baiga. He wanted other *jīv* in the world. But he could not kill Nanga Baiga. So he made the sensation of itching and Nanga Baiga began to scratch. All day and all night he scratched till his nails were all worn away and his skin torn to threads. But there was one part of his body that he couldn't reach, the small of his back. He used to pick up sticks and scratch himself there.

'One day, when Nanga Baiga picked up a stick to scratch himself, Bhagavan turned it into a cobra. It bit him and he died. We would never have been subjects of death if Bhagavan had not tricked us.

'As Nanga Baiga was dying he said to his sons, "Don't bury my body or throw it away, but cut it up and put it in an earthen pot and boil me and then eat my flesh." So his sons did this, but Bhagavan seeing what would happen if they ate their father's flesh was frightened, and came to them disguised as a sadhu. "What is this?" he asked.

'"We are cooking Nanga Baiga," they answered, "and we are going to eat him when he is ready."

'"But that is a great sin," said Bhagavan. "You had better throw the pot into the river."

'They were afraid of the sadhu, so they did as he told them. But a little of the steam escaped from the pot and entered the nostrils of the youngest son, and he became the first gunia. But all the rest of Nanga Baiga's magic was lost to us through this Hindu god's deceit. Down the river, three women ate Nanga Baiga's flesh and became witches.'

XIV. ASTRONOMICAL MYTHS

It is in their astronomical beliefs that the Baiga have chiefly felt the influence of Hindu ideas.

Yet even here they have not actually borrowed more than a few stories and some names. Their myths gain a spurious theological respectability by the use of such names as Lakshman, Bhimsen, the Pandava, Sesh Nag, which cover entirely non-Hindu ideas. It is always necessary in India to burrow underneath the actual words and names to the ideas below them.

The Baiga, of course, are not astronomers. Their sphere is very definitely the earth. I once asked Mahatu if the markings on the moon represented Nanga Baiga. "Certainly not," he answered in a shocked voice. "Nanga Baiga belongs to the earth; what would he be doing in the moon?" The Baiga do not use the stars for divination. The moon has an influence on the menstrual cycle of women, but otherwise is mainly important as a light to dance by.

The Baiga believe that the world is surrounded by clouds, clouds above and clouds below. It is flat and round like a great *chapāti* and rests on the surface of the primeval ocean where it has been fixed in place by nails driven by Nanga Baigin at the beginning of the world. Earthquakes are due to the loosening of these nails as a result of incest; they are warnings; one day if incest continues—so say the stricter Baiga—the world will break up and sink again into the ocean.[1] Whenever an earthquake occurs a Baiga Dewar must go and drive a nail into the earth to fix it once more in its place.

Above the earth pass the Sun and Moon in orderly procession. The Sun is male, the Moon female.[2] "We know the Moon is a woman, for she retires for her period every month." There are many and various stories about the Sun and Moon, and I will now quote half a dozen which I have recorded in different districts. There is no one account universally believed. My first story is from Pandaria.

'Nanga Baiga was born from a black anthill growing on the head of Dharti Mata. One day he climbed to the top and looked all round. Then he pissed into the anthill. At once, from the belly of Dharti Mata the Sun and Moon were born in a blaze of light. Nanga Baiga and Nanga Baigin were very frightened at this sight and hid behind Dharti Mata. When the Sun saw the Moon, sin came into his mind, and he caught hold of her. When Bhagavan saw that sight, he cursed the Sun. "Once you had two eyes," he said. "Now may one of them burst open." He said to the Moon, "You be lord of the four quarters of the night," and to the Sun, "You be lord of the four quarters of day, but you will have to go burning, burning in the pain of burning." It was then that Dharti Mata began to grow very large and to demand food-worship.'[3]

Another account, told me by Dandi Bhumia of Rewa State, also links the Sun and Moon with Nanga Baiga.

[1] The popular Hindu explanation of earthquakes is that the great boar Varaha who holds up the world is shifting the load from one tusk to the other. Mahatma Gandhi takes, like the Baiga, a more ethical view. He attributed the Bihar Earthquake of 1934 to the sin of untouchability.

[2] In Hindu mythology the Moon is generally male. The Purana call him the son of the Rishi Atri by his wife Anasuya. The Moon marries the twenty-seven daughters of the Rishi Daksha (these are the twenty-seven lunar asterisms). But his affection for Rohini makes the others jealous, and Daksha curses him with consumption, though his wife obtains the boon that his wasting away will only be temporary and periodic.

[3] General tribal tradition agrees with the Baiga in making the Moon female. The Munda, for example, regard Chando Omol the Moon as the wife of Sing-Bonga the Sun (Dalton: *Descriptive Ethnology of Bengal*, p. 186). The Korku also hold the Moon to be female (Russell: II, p. 559). The Pauri Bhuiya, however, regard it as male, and the younger brother of the Sun (Roy: op. cit., p. 279). The Santal say that the Moon is the wife of Sing Chando, the Sun (Bompas: op. cit., p. 402). In order to appreciate the very wide gulf between the Hindu and the Baiga beliefs about the Moon it is only necessary to read Crooke: op. cit., p. 12 ff.

'The world was dark, dark as a night when two lovers run away together. The old cobra, on whose head rests the world, called for Bhagavan and said to him, "How can mankind endure this darkness? Take the *dhār* from my ears and they will shine." Now as she was taking the *dhār* from her right ear it hurt her, and she got angry with it, and said, "Away with you, *bhosri*, go away and burn yourself!" But the *dhār* in her left ear came out easily, and she said, "Your light will be mild and gentle.[1]"

'As Bhagavan was taking them home, the Moon lagged behind. They came to the jungle where Nanga Baiga had his bewar. It was a noble jungle; after the bewar was finished it grew up again; there was no loss. There were very many little paths. Bhagavan and the Sun went one way, the Moon went another. She wandered here and there; she saw Nanga Baiga digging roots and talked to him; he showed her the fine crops in his bewar; she went on and lost her way; at last she returned and found the right path. Then Bhagavan said, "You will always wander in the sky; first you will go one way, then another!" So it has ever been. The Moon is truly a woman, she can never make up her mind or keep to one plan.

'Then said Bhagavan to the Moon, "You travel by night," and to the Sun, "I will give you a horse; you travel in the day and watch the world." He said to the Moon, "Every day you must do an hour's work more, then you may do an hour's work less, until you have your period."'

We come now to stories which relate the Sun and Moon to their children the stars. Very similar accounts are current among the Santal, the Oraon, and the Turi, a small tribe living on the Chota Nagpur plateau. This is only one of many instances where the Baiga appear to have closer cultural contacts with the tribes to the east of their country than with their immediate or western neighbours.

From Mandla comes the following legend.

'In the depths of the great ocean below the earth, Aginjar the father of the Sun and Phulmotia the mother of the Moon were living together. These two were brother and sister, but they were married.

'The Sun had a bed; they were sleeping together. Suddenly the Moon said, "But I'm your sister." The Sun said, "No, you're my wife." Now the Moon had given birth to hundreds and thousands of children. "If you're not my wife," cried the Sun, "where did these children come from?"

'"They were given me by my mother. Are you blind of one eye that

[1] The Baiga wear the *dhār* without its characteristic chains, so that it appears as a simple circular shield.

you can't see I'm your sister?" As she said this, one of the Sun's eyes broke open.

'The Sun said, "We will have a test. If these children are not mine, you'll be able to eat them. If they are mine, I'll be able to eat them." Now the Sun and Moon had each their own children. The Sun ate all but two, which he kept in his cheek. The Moon stuffed them all into her mouth, but didn't swallow them, she kept them in the pouch of her cheeks like a monkey.

'Then said the Moon, "Bring out your children." But the Sun could only bring out two which became the morning and the evening stars. The Moon brought out her thousands and scattered them all over the sky.

'Thus they quarrelled and decided to live separately. Their bed said, "I am a bed of sin," and she ran to hide under the sea. But Nanga Baiga was cutting his bewar and he saw her running away in the distance. He threw his axe at her, and then tossed the bed and the axe together up into the sky.'

The Baihar version of the story attributes duplicity to the Sun instead of to his wife. 'The Sun had eleven brothers, the Moon had eleven sisters. They wanted to marry them all, but couldn't afford it. So the Sun said, "Let's eat them all." The Moon ate her sisters, but the Sun hid his brothers in his cheeks. Then he went to the Moon and said, "Where are your sisters? Have you been foolish enough to eat them? You are as stupid as a Baiga! Look at my brothers." He brought them out of his mouth. Then the Moon tried to bring up her sisters but she had digested them by then. She spat, and her spittle went all over the sky and became the stars. From that day the Moon has to work all the year round, with only one day for her periods: but each of the Sun brothers works for a month and plays for the other eleven months. If all twelve brothers worked at once, the world would be burnt up by the heat. The Moon is wife to all twelve brothers and they have her a month at a time.'[1]

The marks on the Moon are variously explained. In Baihar the Binjhwar

[1] The Oraon say that there were seven Sun brothers who were melting the world by their heat. The Moon pretended to be eating the stars her children and persuaded the Sun to boil his six brothers and eat them (*Census of India*, 1931. I, B, p. 116). The Santal describe how Ninda Chando the Moon covered up all her children in a basket and smeared her lips with red. She went to Sing Chando the Sun and told him that she had eaten all her children and he had better eat his. This he did, but kept two alive to play with, and these are the morning and evening stars. When the Moon let her children out of the basket, the Sun saw them and rushed at them to destroy them, but they scattered all over the sky (Bompas, op. cit. p. 403). The Turi tell almost the same story save that they make both Sun and Moon female, they are two sisters and the Moon was afraid that her sister's heat would kill her children, so she arranged that the Sun should kill her own children instead. The Sun was so angry that she swore she would never see the Moon's face again, and that is why the two never appear together (Russell and Hiralal: IV, p. 591).

Baiga, as we would expect, have adopted the Hindu belief that they represent a hare (which gives the Moon its name of Sasadhara[1]) though they add some characteristic tribal details. "Nanga Baiga was working in his bewar when a hare pricked his feet with its horns, for in those days hares had horns on their heads. Nanga Baiga was annoyed and caught the hare by the horns and threw it into the air. The horns came off and fell down on to the head of a stag where they have remained ever since. The hare ran away and took refuge in the moon. If only the hare could be coaxed away, the moon would be as bright as the sun."[2]

Bukwa of Ufri, however, told me that the Bhumia believe the Moon to be covered with tattoo marks. "She is a woman, fair-skinned and beautiful; it was necessary for her to be tattooed.[3] So she called the Badnin. 'I want you to tattoo me.' So said the Moon. 'How much will you give me?' asks the woman. 'I'll give you one rupee,' says the Moon. 'No, I must have four rupees,' says the other. 'Very well, I'll give you three rupees.' 'But I must have two annas for heating the needles,' so said the woman, 'and food for one day while I'm doing it.' So it was agreed, and the woman tattooed a hare, a scorpion, a deer, a liquor-still, a phadki and two eggs all over the Moon's body. Now she only needs some bangles to make her really beautiful."

Although generally throughout India as in Europe, eclipses in the sun and moon portend no good to men, the Baiga do not regard them as ill-omened. After all an eclipse takes place high up in the sky; so long as the earth remains steady, it is no concern of the Baiga. A pregnant woman, however, should take the elementary precaution of staying indoors. She should hold her breath, take the black dust from the underside of an earthen cooking-pot and put a little of it on her left buttock. She is then safe from any possible danger.

The Baiga theory of an eclipse may be paralleled by ideas common among the Ghasiya of Mirzapur, the Mehtar, the Teli, and the Birhor of Chota Nagpur. The Baiga probably had no tradition of their own and simply borrowed from their low-caste neighbours. The following story is from Rewa.

'Once at the beginning of the world the gods found they had nothing

[1] Another common Hindu name for the Moon is Mriganka, marked like a deer.

[2] The Bharia-Bhumia believe the marks are caused by a banyan tree which Bhagavan planted there to diminish the Moon's light and thus give a chance to their tribe to do some successful stealing (Russell and Hiralal: II, p. 248).

[3] 'A dark girl needs a bright *phundara* and silver ornaments; a fair girl must be tattooed,' is a very common saying.

to eat and they grew very hungry. So they went to a Basor[1] to beg for food. The Basor said, "I will give you what you want, but you must eat from my hands first." What could the gods do? They had to agree. Now the Basor had a great bin full of grain and he told the gods to remove the grain through the hole at the bottom of the bin. When they had taken it all out, the Basor took enough for their meal and made it ready.

'But the gods sent Bhimsen secretly to fetch Pawan Daseri the Wind. When he came they told him that when they sat down to eat, he must come and blow all the food away, for how could they eat from the hands of a Basor?

'And so it happened. The Basor put the food before the gods and went away. Then the wind came in a great gust and carried it away, and when the Basor returned and saw the plates were empty he supposed they had eaten their food. But when the gods were removing the grain, the Basor said, "Who is going to repay me?" "Oh, the Sun and Moon will do that," they answered. The Basor said, "Well, they must fill the bin through the hole in the bottom, not from the top. That is my rule." Then all the gods went away.

'After some time the Basor sent for the Sun and Moon and they came and tried to fill the grain-bin from the bottom upwards. But they couldn't do it. So the Basor caught hold of the Sun and Moon and kept them in his house till the gods came and set them free.

'Again, after a time, the Sun came, and at another time the Moon came, each bringing sacks of grain and tried to fill the bin. Each time the Basor caught them and kept them in his house until the gods came and released them.

'And so it continues for ever, and that is why the Sun and Moon sometimes go dark with the shadow that is cast on them by the walls of the Basor's house. Nor can the debt ever be repaid, for who could fill a grain-bin through the hole in the bottom?'[2]

[1] The Ghasia say the lender was a Dom, the Mehtar say it was Rahu. The Basor are workers in bamboos, and their name is a corruption of Bansphor which is the title of one of the sub-castes of the Dom. They are generally regarded as untouchable, and one of the reasons why the Baiga are now giving up working in bamboo is probably a fear that they may be identified with Basor. Curiously enough, Basor women, like Baiga women, are forbidden to wear a nose-ornament; the penalty for doing so is a tribal dinner.

It is significant that Mehtar, Dom, Basor and Baiga are all called Bansphor, breakers of bamboo.

[2] 'During an eclipse the sweepers reap a good harvest' for 'the sun and moon are in Rahu's debt, and he comes and duns them, and this is the eclipse: and the alms given to sweepers are a means of paying the debt' (Russell and Hiralal: IV, p. 232). The Birhor say that the Sun and Moon have stood security for the debts of the poor, and the creditors come from time to time to take them into custody (Roy: *The Birhors*, p. 495). The Ghasia say that the Sun and Moon once borrowed money from a Dom and failed to pay it back. Now in revenge a Dom occasionally devours them and vomits them up when the eclipse is over (Crooke: I, p. 21). The Teli story is that 'the Sun is indebted to a sweeper. The sweeper has gone to collect the debt and the Sun has refused to pay. The sweeper is in need of money and is sitting *dharna* at the Sun's door: you can see his shadow across the Sun's threshold. Presently the debt will be paid and the sweeper will go away' (Russell and Hiralal: IV, p. 550).

The Baiga have only the roughest knowledge of the stars. They say, "Why should we study the sky? All we need to do is to put our ear close to the bosom of Mother Earth and she tells all the secrets that we need to know." Stars are the Moon's spittle or the children whom she spat out of her mouth. The morning and evening star belong to the Sun. "The stars," said Dhan Singh, "come down to earth whenever they can for food and drink. Sometimes they go right under the earth. Above and below us are great clouds. The stars are the trees growing on the clouds." And Phulmat once told me that the stars were made of diamonds, though what the old lady knew of diamonds I am at a loss to say.

It is, of course, the Great Bear which is most familiar to the Baiga. "It is a bed on which a corpse is carried out. When they bring it out, it is night; when they put it back, it is day. When we carry a corpse, we always smash the bed with our axes. That is why bits of the bed are scattered all over the sky."

In Baihar, however, they say that there was once a King and a Queen. "They quarrelled and the Queen ran to kill herself in the star called the Tank. The Kotwar ran to stop her. The King was sitting on his bed and when he saw the Queen running towards the Tank, he jumped out of bed so violently that one leg of the bed broke—that is why you always see one leg in the wrong place." The aristocratic Binjhwar Baiga would naturally make the hero of the story a King and Queen, but in Mandla the same story is told with a Bhoi (Gond) and Bhoin as hero and heroine.[1]

A group of five stars is called the Nangar (plough). Five others, close together (Orion?) are called Kutela, the wooden rod used for levelling earth, cleaning hemp, or washing clothes. Venus is the Chowkidar—at midnight the night-watchman, at dawn the cock-crow watchman. The evening star is the Machhritarai (the Fish Star). "As long as it is in the sky, fish come to feed, afterwards they sleep. Dhimar only fish till then."

"Once when Guru Mahadeo was ploughing, a phadki laughed at him. He threw her into the sky. There she is. And two eggs. But she's not sitting on them for fear of Mahadeo. The Nangar is Mahadeo's plough The Kutela is the stick he threw at the phadki. The Tengra (hoe) is what he cleared his field with."

There are also in the sky the Chirai (bird) and the Barewa Tura, the boy who roasted it for supper. There is a Barhai or Carpenter and a Dhimar or Fisherman who throws the net (Jhal) to catch the Fish (Machhri). There are

[1] The Santal call the Great Bear the old woman's bedstead and the fire-pan thieves. The star furthest off is kept far away because he is always laughing and might give the thieves away (*Census of India*, op. cit., p. 101). The Dhiri of Chhattisgarh say that the Great Bear is a bed with three thieves tied to it. They came to steal the bed from an old woman, but were caught and tied there for ever (Russell and Hiralal: II, p. 529).

also the Dhanu (Bow), the Ban (Arrow) and the Sap (Snake). "The Scorpion came into the sky like this. Dharti Mata was digging white mud, when her cloth fell down and she swung it back over her shoulder. There was a scorpion in the folds of her cloth, and it flew into the air and stuck there."

Shooting stars are variously described as "a *jiv* sent down by Bhagavan to live again on the earth" (Mandla), "star excrement" (Baihar), "the spirit of a sinner burning" (Rewa), "a spirit coming down to earth to make a woman pregnant" (Dinḍori) or "a star that has come down to graze" (Kawardha). It will be noted that almost every district has its own and separate explanation.[1]

The rainbow is the horse of Bhimsen, who is always connected with rain by the Baiga. "It is the water horse," I was told in Baihar. "It has jumped out of the water across the sky to tell us that rain is coming. It has only two colours, black and red. When there is more black than red, it means that there will be rain also the next day."[2] In Kawardha they said that the rainbow comes out of the anthill. "At the bottom of the anthill is a tiny gourd. The rainbow goes up into the air and across the sky searching for another anthill, and when it sees one descends into it. Only a great gunia can find the gourd, which is the *singi-tuma* of Bhimsen. If you can find it and give it to a barren woman, she'll have a child." It is generally believed that it is dangerous to point at a rainbow, as the pointing finger may become crooked. The Baiga always, therefore, point with a clenched fist.[3]

Thunder and lightning is also connected with Bhimsen.[4]

'The Pandava wanted to know what was underneath the earth, and they fell at the feet of Bhimsen and begged him to go down and see. So they tied him to a *māchi* and let him down by a rope. He went down down down for eight nights and nine days. Then the Pandava out of mischief let the rope go and he fell to the bottom. He began to weep, wondering how he was to get back. But the old cobra who lives there gave him the horse of lightning and he sat on it, and before he knew what had happened

[1] The Santal call shooting-stars star-dung. So do the Maria of Bastar State. So do the Lakher and Sema Naga, and no doubt many other tribes also. The Thado Kuki say that shooting stars are going to the bachelors' hall, and have a song which represents them as calling to the other stars to join them there (Hutton: *The Sema Nagas* (London, 1921) p. 251).

[2] Hindus generally regard the rainbow as the bow of Rama or Indra. Sometimes it is called the Paniharin, the water-carrier.

[3] The Birhor have the same tradition (Roy: *The Birhors*, p. 380).

[4] The Baiga do not regard thunder and lightning as ill-omened; the Hindus do. Thunder is the voice of Indra, or the roar of the wheels of the Chariot of Bhagavan. Lightning is a little girl whom Raja Kansa tried to murder, but she escaped him by taking refuge in the sky.

he was back home. He has never ceased wondering at his wonderful ride.

'Now Bhagavan keeps Bhimsen as his servant, and when he wants to give the world water he sends Bhimsen to give it. Bhimsen drags it along in the skin of a rat and as the skin rubs along over the air, it makes the roaring noise of thunder. Bhimsen rides all over the four corners of the world on his horse of lightning dragging his rat-skin behind him.'

Chapter XII

THE MAGICIAN AND HIS CONTROL OF THE NATURAL WORLD

Whoever destroys is a witch: whoever protects is a gunia. Who knows whether Bhagavan is good or no; but we do know the gunia is good. —Baiga Proverb.

1. THE BAIGA MAGICIAN

THE Baiga regard themselves as the most powerful magicians in the world. They are regarded with awe and veneration by other tribes and communities. Even the Brahmins who live in their neighbourhood consult them in every crisis, for the fertility of a barren wife, the success of an intrigue, the ripening of the harvest, the recovery of stolen goods. 'The Baigas or Bhumias,' says Sterndale, 'are reverenced by more than the mere aborigines, but chiefly on account of their reputation for casting the evil eye, being able to assume the form of wild beasts, and various other uncanny practices, which their isolated habits and wild appearance give colour to.'[1] The Baiga's charms are necessary for the growth of the crops, the potency of the bridegroom, the frustration of witches, the protection of the village against bears and tigers.

The magic of the modern Baiga is, of course, a weak and beggarly thing compared to the magic of their ancestors who could make the dead to live, turn themselves at will into wild animals, call the hosts of heaven to their aid, wield monstrous weapons, walk on the water, fly through the air, and win whole villages of girls by their love-magic.

But even to-day, the Baiga is a match for anyone. Magic is the most vital and potent reality of his life. If he cannot always raise the dead, he can at least ward off the demons of disease. If he cannot raise crops without seed, he can at least whisper the secrets of fertility into the seed he has. If he cannot attract the love of a whole village of maidens, he is quite competent to seduce them one by one. His magic, in fact, covers every

[1] Sterndale: *Seonee* (Calcutta, 1887), p. 304.

aspect of his life; without it, existence would be unbearable, lacking all spice and flavour, without vitality.

It would also be extremely dangerous. For magic is a necessity in a world where nothing happens by chance, where every happening derives from some secret supernatural cause. If the milk turns sour, somewhere a witch has cast a spell upon it. If a child falls ill, some hostile spirit has attacked him. If a tiger kills a bullock, it has been sent by some enemy of the village. Nothing happens by chance; nature has always something up her sleeve.

It is essential therefore that the village magicians should control every aspect of village life, so that it may not be disturbed by the wanton rage of witch and spirit.

It is impossible to read through the autobiographies recorded in Chapter IV without being struck by the enormous importance of magic in the everyday life of the tribe. The primary duty of the magician is, of course, to fight disease and death, to diagnose its cause and then defeat it. But he must also make the course of love run smoothly; he must stimulate the growth of crops and protect them from hail, storm and jungle pig; he must keep cows from straying; he must direct the arrow to its mark; he must lay the ghost of the dead, shut the mouth of the tiger, protect from snake and scorpion, and even save the villagers from the exactions of officials. Thus regarded, the religion of animism[1] takes on the new aspect we have suggested in the first chapter; we can see it as a valiant battle against all the mysterious enemies of mankind, enemies that lurk in every tree and behind every stone, and the gunia or magician assumes heroic qualities. The gunia stands between mankind and all the malignant forces of nature and super-nature; his only weapons are a frail stick of straw and a winnowing-fan; but he has authority handed down to him from remote antiquity, and his knowledge is more than a match for all the hostile powers.

We may take, as example of the old type of gunia, Banga Baiga, Lahakat's maternal grandfather. "Wherever he went, a tiger followed him. When he went to his bewar the tiger sat and slept by his side. But when any woman came there, the tiger was shy and slipped away into the jungle. Banga always put a basketful of rice-water out for the tiger in the evening, and at midnight it used to come and drink it. When Banga couldn't go to his bewar, the tiger used to look after it for him. One day his wife said, 'What is that line of footprints between our house and the bewar?' 'That's only a dog; come and see for yourself.' So she went, but when

[1] Hinduism has been described as a combination of pantheism with transcendental metaphysics, animism as a blend of materialism and magic. The most characteristic belief of Hindu magic—that penance may force the gods to do the ascetic's will—is unknown to the Baiga.

she saw the tiger, she flung her arms round her husband, trembling with fear. 'Don't be afraid,' said Banga, and he called the tiger to him, and began to pat and fondle it. Then his wife did the same, and was no more afraid."

Banga also had the power of stopping fires. If a fire broke out on one side of a house, he could draw a line beyond which the fire could not spread. He could bring rain by offering a cock to Bhimsen. He could cross a flooded river. He used to take off his dhoti and throw it across the water. It would stretch to the opposite bank and stand solid as a plank.

Others had even greater powers.

"My grandfather couldn't do it," admitted Lahakat. "But he used to tell us how the Baiga of his generation would sit on a pole and fly through the air."

A Brahmin in Baihar told me that once on a journey he was benighted and took refuge in a Baiga's house. There was no food there at all, save one root "thin as your finger" and some milk. The Baiga put the milk on the fire, and held the root above it. Immediately, from the tip of the root, there poured a shower of flour. The Baiga mixed it with the milk, and gave the Brahmin a delicious gruel for his supper.

II. THE MAGICIAN'S HERITAGE

The Baiga magicians derive from the old guru who succeeded Nanga Baiga. There is very great confusion about the original guru, and how he was actually related to Nanga Baiga, but there is general agreement that there were originally four great Baiga guru—Daugun, Nindhan, Danantar and Madhakawar, all four brothers. Daugun was the eldest and the other three used to serve him.

'In those days Nanga Baiga was living in Nanga Pahar. Bhagavan had given him this boon: "From your left side will flow black blood, from your right side will flow red. Whoever drinks the black blood will be a witch; whoever drinks the red blood will be a gunia."

'One day Nanga Baiga said to the four brothers, "Take me beyond the seven seas and the sixteen streams." So they took him there and Nanga Baiga sat beside the Seven Seas. At night blood began to flow from both his sides. A snake came to drink the black blood. Its name was Ajghar. A mongoose came and drank the red blood.

'Nanga Baiga heard that a man was dying in a village near by, and he sent one of the brothers with a little of the red blood. He touched the dying man with it and he recovered.

Mahatu's shrine at Chauradadar.

'Many little animals came and drank of the black blood and they turned into poisonous snakes and scorpions.

'Then Bhagavan, being jealous of Nanga Baiga, sent a snake to bite him. Nanga Baiga wanted to scratch his back, and thinking the snake was a stick, picked it up, and it bit him and he died.

'As he was dying, Nanga Baiga told his sons and disciples not to bury him, but to divide his body into twelve portions, put them into twelve pots and cook them for twelve years. At the end of that time, they should eat him, and all his magic would pass to them.

'But this was just what Bhagavan was anxious to avoid. So when the twelve years were over, he came disguised as a Brahmin sadhu, smeared with ashes, a gourd in his hand, and told the sons what a great sin it would be to eat their father's flesh. They thought it over and agreed, and at last decided to throw the twelve pots into the river. But as they were doing so, one of the brothers got a whiff of the steam (or, according to other versions, one scrap of the flesh) and he became the first gunia.'

There is, unfortunately, no real agreement as to who this first gunia was. Some think it was the youngest of the four guru—Danantar; others say that it was the youngest of Nanga Baiga's own sons. But whoever it was, he only got a sadly attenuated portion of Nanga Baiga's magic, a mere whiff of the steam of it in his nostrils.

'But the twelve pots floated away down the river. There on the bank Kani Gondin, Sukhi Chamarin and Langri Dhobin were bathing naked. Some say they were playing in the water with the seven Samduria sisters. They saw the pots floating down and waded out to get them. When they brought them to the bank, they found them full of meat. They tasted it, and it was sweet and good. So they ate it all. The Chamarin ate the head and became the first *tonhi*. The Gondin ate the chest and became the first *sodhe*.

'Then they were filled with Nanga Baiga's magic, but it had turned evil. They looked at a fig tree growing on the bank of the river, and with the poison of their gaze it withered away. Then came Bhagavan to them and told them how to make an image of Hilauran Bir out of their excreta, and a pond out of their urine, how to make a knife out of a bamboo, and from the dirt of their bodies the image of a man. Then he went away. So the witches composed two-and-a-half mantra and became naked and let down their hair and danced before the images. They put life into the mud image of the man, then killed him with their knife and drank his blood. After that they went to the burial-place and found the graves of seven men. Seven times they went round each grave, and made a pond of urine. Here they made images of Parvati and Mahadeo out of their excreta. They dug up the dead bodies and restored them to life, but they so bound them with their mantra that they couldn't move. Then they bathed them in the pond of urine and cut off their heads. They removed the livers and ate them, and drank their blood. Then they buried them again. The seven corpses became ***bīr*** (familiars) of the witches and troubled the villagers in their turn.'

Such was the beginning of witchcraft in the world and of the age-long struggle between the forces of good, the red blood, embodied in the Baiga gunia, and the hosts of evil, embodied in the witches of all the other tribes, the children of the black blood.

The Baiga had suffered a great blow in the death of the father of the tribe, and the loss of his magic. Almost at once the witches commenced their offensive, they assailed the twelve brothers and turned them into parrots, making them sit ridiculous, in a row, on a tamarind tree. But the young guru Danantar who had become the first gunia was, for all his depleted magic, stronger than the witches and he turned the twelve parrots back to men. Ever since there has been a ding-dong battle between the magicians and the witches.

This account of the origin of witchcraft may be paralleled by the tale of Dhanwantari, the physician of the gods, who went to treat Raja Parikshit. Parikshit had been deceived and bitten by Takshaka, the king of the snakes. But it was Dhanwantari himself who died, and he asked his sons to cook and eat his body, and thus take his magic into themselves. But Takshaka stopped them, and they threw the cooking-pots into the Ganges. There the notorious Lona Chamarin found them and ate their contents, and so gained all Dhanwantari's magical powers, and especially his power of curing snake-bite.

The obscurity and confusion in which the origins of the guru and the gunia are concealed is reflected in the mantra. Many guru are named in these and survive in the muddled memories of the older people. But no one really knows anything about them. Such are the four already named, Daugun, Nindhan, Danantar, Madhakawar. Then there are Goraknath Guru, Basmasur Guru, Agyasur Guru, Jolamukhi Guru, Tapasri Guru, Nangasur Guru, Tadasur Guru, Makkhi Guru, Dhudhiasur Guru, Boran Guru, and a score of others. Three brothers are specially prominent, Supet Guru, the eldest, who lives in a dry place where no rain can fall, Kari Guru, and Seth Guru.

The thread of gunia-ship is carried on from father to son. Dhan Singh was initiated by his father-in-law, Thaggur by his own father. Mahatu has taught all his sons, so that if one forgets the others may remember. Jethu was initiated at the age of twelve by his paternal grandfather. Jogi

Dewar succeeded his father, who in his turn succeeded his father, as the gunia of Karanjia. Young gunia are taught as if they were in a school, and for the first two or three times that they practise *sūpa-tuma*, an elder man sits by them to see that they make no mistakes.

One of the most common complaints of the younger generation of gunia is that their parents have not told them everything. Mithu darkly suspects his father of holding back vital information. The sons of Bodan Dewar are almost wholly ignorant. When I was in Bohi I was puzzled by the position of a rather bovine-looking youth who was constantly referred to as the *mukhia*. I discovered that he was the son of an old and famous Dewar of that village who had, however, failed to pass on his knowledge to him. But he retained sufficient authority as his father's son to be regarded as the chief of all the Dewar, and everything had to be done in his name, even though he himself was unable to take part in a single rite.

Sometimes, gunia are appointed by the direct action of the *devata* in dreams. Mahatu became a magician in this way, so did Phulmat.

Initiation consists in taking the master's leavings. The older man takes liquor in his mouth, spits it back into a leaf-cup and gives it to his disciple to drink. At Hareli, it is the custom for the disciple to take his teacher a coconut. At Diwali, he goes with a *sūpa*, a dhoti, coconuts and liquor and offers the gifts to his guru. The guru takes a little rice and puts it in the *sūpa*, saying: "From to-day the Mata will visit you; from to-day you will be a gunia. Now you will be able to 'see'."

A Brahmin once asked a famous Baiga Dewar to initiate him. "Go and make *chapāti* from my excreta and eat it," said the Baiga. "Then I'll teach you, you Brahmin!" Mahatu once offered to make me a gunia if I would drink his blood.

'The Baiga medicine-man,' says Forsyth, 'fully looks his character. He is tall, thin and cadaverous, abstraction and mystery residing in his hollow eyes. When wanted, he has to be sent for to some distant haunt of gnomes or spirits, and comes with charms and simples slung in the hollow of a bottle-gourd. A great necklace, fashioned with much carving from the kernels of forest fruits, marks his holy calling.' The highest grade of medicine-man is the Dewar. The name is probably derived from Diabar, lighter of a lamp, and refers to the practice of divination by a lamp, though curiously this method is not common among the Baiga Dewar. There is actually a small tribe of musicians called Dewar, probably descended from Gond and Kawar, who live in Chhattisgarh, but these are now devoted mainly to the *sārangi*, and only secondarily to the practice of magic. The Baiga Dewar is treated with the greatest respect; he is competent to perform the Bidri and other agricultural rites; he can close the boundaries of villages against the man-eating tiger; he can stop earthquakes by driving a nail into a tree. He can perform any magical rite within the limits of his jurisdiction. The whole countryside is divided up into circuits, and though a Dewar may be called for consultation into another circuit, there is a regular etiquette of the business, and he must not do so without permission.

An ordinary gunia confines his activities mainly to the war against disease. He must be content with his *bahari-kāri* and *sūpa-tuma*, and the occasional sacrifice of a pig or chicken to the household gods.

Among the Baiga, the Panda is of no special importance. "The Panda is only of yesterday and the day before." He has no pedigree. But he is on the right side.

A Jan Pande is a clairvoyant. He divines by dreams and visions. The spirits whisper him in the ear. He has no need of any apparatus. He is credited with considerable powers, and is feared because there is no means of checking his decisions.[1]

We will now proceed to consider the various fields in which magic plays its part. We will take love-magic first, because of its great emotional significance for the Baiga. Then we will describe the control of the Dewar over rain, hail-storms, the crops, and all wild animals. In the next chapter we will discuss fully the large subject of the cause and cure of disease.

III. THE MAGIC OF LOVE

The unsuccessful lover turns instinctively to magic for relief. Magic is indeed the artistic touch added to an intrigue, it increases its romance, it gives it supernatural, if not social, sanctions. Girls are delighted when a man prepares love-magic for them; it proves the seriousness of his intentions; it makes the whole thing much more exciting. Magic is thus a vital part of the grand business of love.

The love-magic gains its effect partly by suggestion. It is generally necessary for a go-between to put the *mohini* on a girl's shoulders or in her food, and though it is often said that she mustn't know about it, this rule is rarely followed in practice. When a girl knows what is being done, it not only kindles her passion, but it proves the importance of the intrigue. It is not an easy thing to make a love-charm, and no one would do it unless he meant business.

[1] Among the Santal, the Jan Guru detects witches by gazing on a leaf smeared with oil (Bompas: op. cit., p. 419).

The effect of love-magic on a girl is to make her 'restless as parched gram in the pan', uneasy as 'a fish stranded in a dried-up stream', wretched as 'wood being devoured by white ants'. She is visited every night by her lover in dreams; he enjoys her and she is powerless to prevent it. A Karma of Silpiri describes the feelings of a man who sees his girl enchanted by a rival.

Ho ho ha re! I'll find another girl as beautiful as you.
Last week you went to buy a pot in the bazaar,
And since then you have been restless,
For that boy's *mohini* is working in you.
All night you dream of him, but I don't care.
I'll find another girl as beautiful as you!

Knowledge of the most efficacious love-magic is generally confined to the chief Dewar, though a few old women may also know some of them, and sell them at a price. Not all *mohini*, however, are worth having. Mahatu's are considered almost useless, a waste of time and money. Dhan Singh's are powerful and expensive. When Halku, a Pardhan of Patan village, wanted to win the beautiful but bashful Kanni, he summoned two very important Dewar from Rewa State, and promised to sacrifice a white goat to Lingo, god of the hill that overlooks Patan, if they were successful. They were. A very charming youth from Silpiri boasted to me that he had won three girls in this way, and offered to provide ten for anyone who would care to have them. The headman of Morndar also boasted that if he put a *mohini* in a pebble and threw it at a girl, he could always get her. "My *mohini* are so strong that if a girl sulks with everyone else, she'll laugh with me; if she crosses her legs for others, she'll spread them out for me." The crippled Jethu of Bohi who is not physically adapted to a very ambitious erotic life, has won girl after girl by the power of his love-charms.

One of the most remarkable successes of Baiga love-magic occurred in our own Leper Home. Baisakiya, middle-aged, stout, a leper, with two children, was left a widow in Chauradadar. After her husband's death, she set her heart, as she was legally entitled to do, on his younger brother, the young and attractive Mithu. But he did not respond to her advances; she was much older than him, and very plain. Besides, Mithu already had an attractive young wife whom he had only recently married.

But Baisakiya prepared a *mohini*, and put it in the boy's food. Half-way through supper, he felt an access of sexual excitement. He realized what had been done to him. He accepted his fate philosophically. He would have to marry Baisakiya now, or he would have no peace. But he decided that if he was going to marry, he might as well have a devoted wife. So he proceeded to turn the tables on her, and return the love-magic. When she was out of the room, he chewed a mouthful of rice and spat it back into the pot from which, he knew, Baisakiya would eat later on. He did this five times, and then stirred up the rice in the pot so that no one could see what had happened. Baisakiya came in for her supper, ate the magic dish, and was immediately entranced, far more than ever before. The next morning, she saw Mithu going with his wife to the fields. "May a tiger kill her!" she muttered. But she was not a witch, and her curse had no power. The girl was spared, but within a week, Mithu had deserted her, and was living, madly in love, with the stout, coarse-featured, middle-aged, and leprous Baisakiya.

I will now give a few specimen *mohini* and the mantra which must accompany them. The first is one of Mahatu's supposedly inefficacious charms.

"Get the bones of a crane or a black jok-insect. Burn it and mix it with cow's butter, dirt from your own chest, and some dust from the right footprint of your girl.[1] You may either mix this in her food, or else send it with a go-between and let her smear it on the girl's hair and shoulders. The best plan is to take the girl down to the river, and when she stoops to wash, suddenly to rub it all over her back and hair. Then promise the *bhut* of Samaliagarh that if she stays with you for ten years, you'll give it a goat." While mixing the *mohini*, the following mantra is to be repeated.

> *Domi sisi vidya khāo. Baith bharosē rāj karo. Soya ho hi uthāya ke lānbē. Baithē ho hi uthāya ke lānbē. Lāg lāg re sanna sai mohini. Vokē bāp mahatāri bhai dai ghar dwār pāni panghat dongar pahār ke māya moha la tor ke lān be. Dekh beta chukka na lagai.*
>
> *Domi sisi vidya khāo.* I sit in faith and rule my kingdom. If she is sleeping, wake her and bring her. If she is sitting, wake her and bring her. Seventeen hundred *mohini*, go and work, work. Let her leave her love for father, mother, sister, house, door, water, the bathing-ghat, forest and hill. Let her leave desire for these, and bring her to me. See, son, make no mistake.

This charm, Mahatu tells me, is often used by husbands who want to recover errant wives. But the only two husbands who have consulted him assure me that it is unsuccessful.

[1] Footprint dust is always powerful. The Chero used to injure their enemies by measuring their footprints with straw and muttering mantra over them. This caused wounds and sores in the feet. Note also an incident recorded in the *New Statesman*, Vol. XIV, No. 337, p. 211. 'Women who fill small tins with sand from the footmarks of the Duke and Duchess of Kent's children (on holiday near Sandwich) are worrying the police.'

In Mandla Tehsil, I was given what I was told was a much more useful charm. "Get hold of the girl's menstrual cloth (which will be hung out to dry somewhere). Then get a black chicken, a bottle of phuli liquor, a coconut and some oil of the castor tree. On a Sunday morning, without seeing anybody's face, go to a cross-roads and give incense in the name of Bhavani Jogini. Break the coconut and kill the chicken. Put a drop of the chicken's blood on the cloth and cross it with the oil. Then repeat the mantra. After this, take the cloth to the girl's house, wait till no one is about, then hold your breath, draw a line with the cloth across the threshold and walk away, with face averted, to your own home. Within a day or two she will follow you."

The mantra is as follows.

> *Ursē mohini, khursē mohini, jor mohini, kon mohini? Bhāvan jogini mohini. Khāka jā mohini? phalānē ke pās. Ola ātho ang ma paith ke moha darbē phalānē dauki la phalānē dauka ke lānē. Dusar la gāli dē phalānē la dekhē ta hansat hansat ghar me ā jāy. Tab to jāno debi sarda. Kon hānktai? Nāga Baiga nāgin Baigin, guru mahadeo, parvati, nidhān guru, guru danātār, jekhar chela main hun. Guru mor hānkē phalānē dauki la lān de ta. Jāno debi sarda bhāvan jogini.*

> Ursē mohini khursē mohini! The mohini that joins together. Whose mohini? It is Bhavani Jogini's. Where are you going, mohini? To a certain girl. Attack her eight limbs and fill them with lust. Bring a certain (here give the name) girl to a certain boy. If she now gives *gāli* when she sees me, let her come henceforth laughing to my house. Then alone will I believe in you as Sarada Devi. Who sends this *mantra*? Naga Baiga Naga Baigin, Guru Mahadeo Parvati, Nidhan Guru, Guru Danatar, whose disciple I am. O Guru, according to my saying, bring this girl. Then I will believe in you, Sarada Devi, Bhavani Jogini.

The most elaborate of all the *mohini*, which I heard in Pandaria, but which is known to the most expert Baiga (as well as to many a Brahmin) everywhere is this.

"On a Wednesday, at sunset, dig up the corpse of a young virgin boy and remove the skull. Take it away and wash it in twenty-one streams. Then find a cow which has a calf of the same colour as herself. Milk the cow into the skull, and mix into the milk fresh oil of ramtilla, cow's butter, the blood of a black chicken, and twenty-one grains of rice. Cook it over a slow fire. Go with it to a pipal tree and throw the mixture over the tree. Wherever the grains stick to the tree, gather them carefully and mix them into the food of the girl you desire. Keep also the grains that have fallen to the ground. You will need them when the time comes to remove the charm." The accompanying mantra is suitably elaborate.

Kuar kotli tola dekho. Bāra kasht ma, tola sowat nindra ma jagāyo. Tilmoti chāurmoti, tola dekh ke rāja mohais jaisē. Dekho, gāy ke neona milāyo. Bāra baris guru ke seva karaiyo. Jā dekho guru ke bachan lāgai. Apan ghar ke lāj marjād rākhbē. Māta jogini, bhāvan jogini, bāvan bīro, mai sirseti, jā dekho phalānē dauki la phalānē dauka ke lānē. Atho ang ma paith ke, hāda hāda por por ma paith ke, moha dār moha ke hansāwat kudāwat le lān. Wirān ke ghar tor ke apan ghar jor lāj marjād rākhbē. Khairo māta, tola lāgai. Banaspati, tola lāgai. Mohini pāhu, ta kari murga jora nāriyal dehu.

O virgin skull, I see thee. In twelve trials, in thy deep slumber, I wake thee. O Tilmoti, Chaurmoti, as the Raja fainted when he saw you, so also. See I have mixed in the butter of a cow. I have served a guru for twelve years. May that guru's promise hold good. Preserve the credit of your house. O Mata Jogini, Bhavani Jogini, Bhavani Biro, Mai Sirseti, go and get this girl for this man. Settle on her eight limbs, enter into every bone. With your lust bring her laughing and jumping. Let her break that other man's house, and come to this house. So may you preserve your credit. O Khairo Mata, O Banaspati, if I get her I'll give you a speckled cock and two coconuts.

The reference to Tilmoti and Chaurmoti is to a well-known Baiga folk-tale (see p. 502). This charm almost comes within the category of a prayer, with its petitions to the various goddesses. But the manual acts which accompany it are regarded as forcing the goddesses' hands, and enabling the magician to have his way with the universe, which is a mark of true magic.

A much simpler method has often served Jethu very well. "On a Wednesday," he says, "I take the dust from the girl's right footprint without her knowing it. On the following Sunday, I mix the dust with some powdered coconut oil of the castor tree, and the blood of a black chicken, repeating the mantra as I do so. Then I mix this in her food or throw it on her hair. I got that girl in Silpuri by this mohini, and later another girl in Belki." The mantra is much shorter.

Mohini mohini kon mohini? Ankhi chimkāwan mohini, musikyāvan mohini, man mohan mohini, ghar paithāran mohini, battisbandhan mohini, khair bhavāni mohini.

Mohini! Mohini! What mohini? The mohini that makes her eyes wink, the mohini that makes her smile, the mohini that captures her heart, the mohini that brings her to the house, the mohini of the thirty-two corners of the roof, the mohini of Khair Bhavani.

But it is not enough to put your mohini on a girl, to detach her from all other loves, to bring her jumping and laughing to your house. A mohini, like all magical apparatus, is a very dangerous thing. If it fails, it may give the girl an attack of menorrhagia that will persist for months; if it succeeds and is not removed before the first child is born, then so powerful is the magic that works within her that the mother will eat the child.

To remove the mohini from a girl, her husband or lover must sit down before her, blow ashes all over her body, and repeat the following mantra.

> *Timan moti, brahma kanthi, dedh bānk,* moonlight night! The goddess of England, Sarada Mai, removes this. Who removes it? The guru removes it. I the guru's disciple remove it. At my wish, O mohini, leave this girl entirely.

IV. THE CONTROL OF THE WEATHER

To those who depend on the earth for their livelihood the weather is of the first importance, and the Baiga takes care to keep it, as far as possible, under his control. There are recognized methods of making and stopping rain, or driving away hail, in all of which the Baiga is adept.

First of all, when the rains have failed, says Phulmat, "we prepare a patch of ground with cow-dung for Bhimsen, and make on it a square of flour. The four corners are for Bhimsen, Bara Deo, Bhagavan, and Nanga Baiga. Then we throw dung at each other and afterwards we attack the Ahir. When he has had enough, he cries out that it will rain on such and such a day". Another method is to send a naked little girl, a virgin, before dawn when no one can see her, down to the river to bring water. When she comes back her family sprinkle water over her body, "and Bhagavan sees the sight and gives rain".

Some of the Baiga who have taken to the plough use the method common among the Gond of taking two naked girls to the river where there is a strip of sand. They take a plough, tie them to it, and make them drag it along. They use the goad till they bleed. But the girls must be careful not to touch the plough with their hands or the charm will be spoilt. This is not a real Baiga custom, however, and I doubt if it is at all common.

To stop rain, the gunia catches the first drops in his hand and buries them. Sometimes they take the *mai* (the long log of wood with which they break up lumps of soil) and put it crosswise in a stream. They promise Bhimsen anything he wants if the rain stops within fifteen days. They let the log float down the stream. If it goes straight down, the charm will be successful.

The stopping of hail is generally a very urgent matter. The magician takes a hailstone in a straw and says to it, "Go away to another king's country!" Then he blows it away. If it does not go in one puff, there will be a very bad storm.

Sometimes the magician stands on one leg with a hailstone in his hand, and recites a mantra.

> Raja Ram has climbed on a stone.
> Above him is an arrow.
> *Ari ari jimi pari pari bhum*!
> Who drives the hail away?
> The guru drives it and I the guru's pupil.
> By my order, go away!
> Go to the Renjawad-benjawad jungle!
> Go to Ghaili-kachar, the jungle where no man can go!
> Go search for birds and eat them!
> But if you return here, you'll have to eat the excreta of a Rakshasa.
> I drive you away from here.
> *Ari ari jimi pari pari bhum*!

I was once held up by a hail-storm in Jankhi village, and we took refuge in the house of Patanga. I was sitting by him reading, when a movement attracted my attention. I looked round and found him unconcernedly blowing the hail away, and muttering mantra under his breath. Nobody took the least notice of him, and he himself performed the rite with complete casualness. But the hail did go away, and caused a heated quarrel later. For Patanga by accident blew it towards our own village Sanhrwachhapar, and the storm broke over my garden and ruined the flowers. The epileptic boy Tutta, a Gond, was furious at this, and himself blew the storm on to another village, standing out in the hail, and shooing it violently before him as though he were driving a herd of buffaloes.

In other parts of the Province, this duty is performed by the Garpagari, who is a recognized public servant and paid in kind by the villagers. There were 954 Garpagari in the Province in 1881, but the present figures are not available. 'The Garpagari,' says the *Bhandara Settlement Report* of 1867 'is a sort of magician, and his peculiar business is to avert hail-storms and atmospheric calamities of all kinds from the village. The general belief in their power seems not to have lessened and the record of their dues has been everywhere cheerfully recorded.' What was written of the Garpagari seventy years ago would equally apply to the Baiga of to-day.

V. THE CONTROL OF ANIMALS

There is a special intimacy between the Baiga and all wild animals. In the old days, the chief Dewar always went abroad in the company of a tiger. Even Lahakat can remember that when he was a boy, his mother used to put what was left of the evening meal in a pot behind the house, so that the tigers and other animals could enjoy it. "We are too poor to do that nowadays," he says. In Dindori they talk about Dugru Baiga of Barangi who used to spend whole nights alone in the forest. "Three or four tigers would come and lick his hands and feet, and stroke him with their paws. He sometimes got tired of them, and said 'Go away.' Then they would run away into the jungle, but they always returned."

Another powerful magician of the same type was Ballia Bhumia. "One day he was going through the jungle and met a tiger in the middle of the road. The tiger rushed at him, roaring; it was about to kill him. Ballia caught it by the ear and said, 'What! Are you going to eat me? Am I not your guru?' And he slapped him on the face. Then the tiger crouched down before him and began to lick his feet. It lay there till Ballia told it to go back to the jungle."

A Brahmin landlord told me how once a Baiga had become indebted to a Brahmin money-lender. When the interest had sufficiently accumulated, the money-lender demanded a bullock in payment. The Baiga said he would bring it the following morning. So during the night the Baiga went to the jungle and caught a huge tiger, and brought it and tied it to a stake in front of the Brahmin's house. Then he lay down to sleep beside it. In the morning he called to the Brahmin, "Come and see your bullock." When the Brahmin saw the tiger, he fell at the Baiga's feet and returned his bond on condition that he sent the tiger back to the jungle.

Another story relates how a Baiga girl once went out of her house at night in the dark to relieve herself. She wanted a leaf according to the famous Baiga custom and put out her hand to pick one. A tiger had been sitting beside her all the time, and she caught hold of its ear and tried to pull it off. The tiger was terrified, and crouched down before her, begging to be allowed to return to the forest. When she had finished, the girl let it go.

Such stories are constantly repeated and firmly believed by everyone. I found, however, that the Baiga were very frightened of my pet leopard

Singaru and not one of them would enter her cage. On the other hand, I was once going from Chauradadar to Karadih with Mahatu, and we came across a very large tiger sitting in the middle of the road. I was unarmed, and the tiger began to walk towards us. But Mahatu was not at all put out. He began to mutter some incantations, and after a few minutes the tiger yawned lazily, and strolled away into the jungle. Mahatu claimed the entire credit for its departure.

A tribe that can control tigers is not likely to find any difficulty in handling cows. The Baiga is generally called in to perform his magic rites whenever a man or bullock is killed by a tiger or a leopard, when the jungle pig begin seriously to damage the crops, and where a cow refuses to stay with its owner. In the myth recorded in Chapter XI we have seen how animals were originally created, and how Nanga Baiga was made lord of the jungle and the jungle folk. This tale is generally recited when the Baiga comes to perform his ceremonies.

If a man buys a new cow or bullock, and it is bad-tempered, and refuses to stay in its new house, but is for ever straying away to its old home, then the Baiga calls it back with the following mantra:

> O Lame Tiger! O Lachi Ahir! Dalaiha Khut! Goraiya Khut! Khairkondi! As you give food in the house for the cow of plenty, so bring back this cow, and I will give you a new black blanket, and a small *khumri*, and a *seer* and a quarter of *khīr*.

If the jungle pig have grown very troublesome, the Baiga goes to the fields, and after offering chickens or coconuts in the usual manner, he recites this mantra, standing on one leg, and waving his hands before him as though he were actually driving the creatures away:

> Let the fire cease to consume the pyre. Let the dead body of the river be carried away. Tandiamal Dano has come, with one tooth in the sky and one in hell. May the feet of the dun sow be bound, may her hair be bound, may her ears be bound, may her thirty-two teeth be bound, may her mouth be bound! Look, my son, drive the Dano away, so that they may all go far away.

When a tiger or leopard enters the fields or bewar and kills men or bullocks, it is considered that the boundaries of the village have been broken and must be repaired. The *mero* is a very sacred and significant spot to every Baiga. Once in Sanhrwachhapar, in May, 1937, a leopard killed a number of bullocks. Dhan Singh was called to repair the magic boundaries of the village. He took us all out into the jungle and chose a tall tree.

Ramsden

Shrine of Baghesur Pat at Kodri.

He offered coconuts and the gum of the sarai, and walked crouching and growling round and round the tree. Then he took a nail and drove it into the wood, at the same time shouting a mantra which bade all the tigers run far away to another country. He gave me the following curious mantra for 'binding the jungle':

> Dongra Pat, Nangbansi Pat, Baghesur Pat, Moon and Sun, Mother Earth. You alone exist. And after you Nanga Baiga and Nanga Baigin, the Bhumraja and Bhumrani. You alone exist. To you I give fire. While going, remain in front; coming, remain behind. Come when you have killed. Then I will not push you into the pit of hell. But if you come I'll make you drink water from the Chamar's tanning-pot.

In another chapter I have given a full description of the rites attending the death of a man who has been killed by a tiger. But I will record here two other mantra for driving away or closing the mouths of tigers.

i

O the wood of the castor tree!
O the garden of the tiger!
A brother and sister have married one another.
Come out O tiger and away with you to the thick forest!
This is the order of Guru Nanga Baiga.
Awake O hill! Run away O death! O rocks be overturned!
A brother and sister have married one another.
This is the order of Guru Nanga Baiga.
Come out O tiger. There is no home for you here.
Run away to the dense forest!

ii

O dead *bhut*! O *bhut*, away! I will beat the privates of the *bhut*.
If he is a sinful *bhut*, make him run away! If he is a good *bhut*, make him run away!
I drive away Budia-bagh, Kawachi-bagh, Gul-bagh, Dhor-bagh, Seth-bagh, Dudh-bagh, Buchi-bagh, Sing-bagh, Dadhia-bagh, I drive them all away.
Twelve kings I drive away.
O tigers, if I am a true guru, then go away!
O tigers, even if I am a false guru, go away!
There is no place for you here. Away with you to the thick jungle.

VI. THE BIDRI RITES: THE CONTROL OF FERTILITY

Even more important than the banishing of tigers is the blessing and protection of the crops. Both Mahatu and Jethu claim that after they had performed this magic in any village, the harvests have been always good.

Every year, in the sacred month of Jeth, when Mother Earth lies ready to be impregnated, and men everywhere gather and prepare their seed, the Baiga are in great demand to perform the Bidri ceremony. In 1937, on June 17th I myself, as landlord of the village, assisted Thaggur the Dewar at this ceremony at Sanhrwachhapar.

In the morning, in a burst of sunshine just before the rains, we all went to a great pakri tree outside the village which is the *madhia* or seat of Thakur Deo. The celebrant was old Thaggur Dewar of Bahapur, small, wizened, chapfallen, with beautiful manners and great dignity. He seemed very conscious of his awful duties, and before the ceremony began was very silent and reserved.

The proceedings opened with an incident of good omen. We gathered round the tree, and Thaggur fished about inside the hollow trunk to find the Three Stones of Thakur Deo. When he removed his hand, however, he revealed not three, but four, small smooth round stones. This miracle was greeted with the utmost enthusiasm, and old Thaggur himself beamed from ear to ear as though he himself were personally responsible—as no doubt he was.

The original three stones were Thakur Deo, Annakuari and Badauna Deo. The newcomer, declared Thaggur, was Mahadeo.

In front of the tree, where we now took our places, a small patch of ground had been prepared with cow-dung, and another patch about three feet square had been roughly dug up, first with the *sābar* and then with the *bakkar*, to represent a field. Where bewar is practised, this patch is prepared to resemble a bewar-clearing. All the villagers had brought little baskets full of every kind of seed, and they now emptied these in a pile in the middle of the cow-dunged square. Somebody brought a pot of milk, and the stones of Thakur Deo were dropped into it. A smouldering lump of dry cow-dung was placed before the pile of seed, with neat little leaf-cups of turmeric and *ghī*.

Then Thaggur got up and went round the tree, dabbing turmeric on the trunk at every step. When he sat down again he put some incense on the fire. Then he called for chickens. The Gond, who all this time had been laughing and joking with complete indifference to the solemn nature of the rite—Thaggur and I were the only serious people there—produced a number of diminutive and scraggy creatures. But they were adequate. Thaggur chose a black chick for Dharti Mata, a brown one for Nanga Baiga and Nanga Baigin, a speckled one for Badauna Deo and his tigers, and a white cock for Thakur Deo. A little pile of rice was then prepared and dedicated.

Thaggur took a chick in his hands. He washed it, held its mouth to the rice, and stroked and fondled it in a very gentle and soothing fashion, until it began to peck at the rice. Directly it did so, it was held that the sacrifice had been accepted, and immediately Thaggur plucked two or three bits of hair from the back of its neck and threw them on to the pile of seed. He then with a firm quick movement twisted off the head. He killed the cock by pressing it down on the ground and constricting the windpipe. In every case he let a few drops of blood fall on the pile of seed, and then threw the body away.

All this time Thaggur was reciting mantra at a furious rate and relating many of the traditional myths—for the sacrifice of the chickens took a long time: each of them had to be persuaded to eat in turn—about the birth of Nanga Baiga, the discovery of liquor by Bhimsen, the first driving of the Nail, the discovery of seed.

Meanwhile the villagers were busy making little models out of leaves, leaf birds, leaf pigs, leaf sambhar and leaf chital. This afforded them great amusement, and was profitable as well, for as they threw them in a pile in front of Thakur Deo, they declared that all that year the fields would be free of those birds and animals.

Then Thaggur took a rupee and washed the silver above the pile of seed, letting the water drop upon it, and then, with my assistance, he poured liquor and milk all over it. He filled my hands again and again with liquor, and made me scatter it over the seed.

Then the old magician turned his attention to the square of ground that had been roughly ploughed. He was not satisfied with it, and made a Gond boy do it all over again with a ploughshare held in his hands. When it was ready Thaggur very solemnly sowed some of the blessed seed in the little furrows. After that, everyone presented his basket and received a share of the seed to be mixed with the rest and thus impart blessing to the entire crop.

Thaggur's work was over, and his eyes began to move anxiously towards three bottles of liquor that rested, invitingly, against the tree. These were the contribution, of the village. I added three more, and we all went home.

The following were the chief mantra used at the ceremony.

i

'Come, let me go and see. When Bhagavan makes the earth, let me go and see them. From the urine of Baba Visisht Muni, Nanga Baiga and Nanga Baigin were born. Let me go and see them. The twelve Loharsur brothers, the thirteen Tamesur brothers, the fourteen Agyasur brothers, I will take them with me. Nanga Baiga drives the nail in the earth. I go to see Bhagavan. Nanga Baiga has gone to the Basor Raja for seed: Dharti Mata is the debtor: the Sun and Moon have stood bail for her. Let me go and see. Bhimsen goes to find liquor carrying a great pot. Let Nanga Baiga go! Let him go to the temple of Thakur Deo. They have collected all the seed. Nanga Baiga has prepared the place, he has brought fire. O Thakur Deo, thou art master of the village, we trust in thee to free it from disease. Let there be a great harvest at reaping time and threshing. I offer chicks to Thakur Deo, to Dharti Mata, to Nanga Baiga and Nanga Baigin. I make a pile of their heads and bodies. I make a river of blood. Our trust is in thee.'

ii

'O the eight parts Dharti, and nine parts Prithwi, know this! I see thee, O Thakur Deo. Thou art known to be the greatest of the gods. O Baghesur Pat, thou art believed to be king of the jungle. I see thee, O Raksin Mata. Bring us prosperity from the boundaries of other villages. May their gain decrease and ours increase! I see thee, O Annakuari; make every grain into twenty-one. I see thee, Meghraja! Let the crop grow well. Let even the widow be able to have guests; in the married woman's house let the drums sound for joy. Let there be no hunger or thirst any more. May the grain grow even on the *kuta* (pegs for tethering animals). Let all the children dance for joy, each holding his penis in his hand! Then we will know that Nanga Baiga and Nanga Baigin, with Jilandhar Guru, have indeed helped us.'

VII. PROTECTION DURING THE DANCE

For protection during the Karma special songs against witchcraft and evil are sung at the beginning of the dance. Here are two typical songs of protection.

i

First I sing to Mother Earth.
Then in Panghat where they draw water
I offer the jurji bird.
There I bind the witch's *bīr*,
The *bīr* that bites and scratches.
More than this I cannot say.

ii

Everyone of you listen! Little gods, great gods, all of you listen!
May the *tonha* and *tonhi* be bound!
May the *guru* and *guruain*, may the *sodhe* and *dain* (woman without husband) be bound!
May Chitawar Deo of the chhindi tree (a snake-god) be bound!
May *bhut* and *massan* be bound!
Everyone of you listen! Both great gods and little gods, obey!

VIII. THE DANGERS OF MAGIC

All transactions with the world of magic are highly dangerous. The least mistake in the ritual, the failure to fulfil a promise made to the gods or animals, the omission to remove a love-charm, may have disastrous consequences. Mahatu once had a violent attack of fever as a result of sacrificing a cock of the wrong colour to Dharti Mata. It is generally believed that if a man leaves a love-charm on his lover, its effects are so powerful that it may drive her to eat her own children. Most serious of all is any failure to implement a promise made to the unseen powers.

For example, Samrat Bhumia, of Achera in Pandaria, promised Baghesur Pat, Nangbansi and Marra Deo that if the crop in his bewar was good he would give them a goat, a pig and a chicken. "If I cut the crop without making this offering," he declared, "you may take my own body!" He had a bumper crop that year, but he thought it was not really necessary to go to the expense of fulfilling his promise. On the last day of the harvest a tiger came and carried him away.

Dehra Bhumia made the same mistake in Jimor. He promised Baghesur Pat that if he found a good piece of jungle for his bewar, he would give him a cock. He found the plot, but forgot to give the cock. When his twelve-year-old son went to the bewar to help cut the trees, he too was carried off and eaten by a tiger.

It is so risky to make any promises in connection with the bewar, that many Baiga have given up the old rites connected with the cutting, firing and sowing.

I add a few more examples that illustrate the dangers of playing with magic.

Baisakin's husband promised a speckled cock if his cow recovered from an illness. He failed to give it, and within three days had died from a painful disease.

In Belki there was a Baiga witch. She promised her Massan (familiar) a *jīv* at the next Nawa festival. The following day a tiger came and seized her sister. The old woman rushed to the rescue and saved her, then went with all speed to offer another *jīv*, a cock, in her place. So necessary is it to be explicit and exact in all magical dealings.

Baghela Muria of Barkera forgot to give a goat to Dulha Deo at his marriage as he had promised. He fell very ill, and only recovered when he implemented his vow.

In Chati (Niwas) a Dewar, called to perform the Bidri rite, failed to put the blood of the chickens on the seed. As a result, when the crop had grown up a little, insects began to spoil it. Another Dewar was called: he repeated the ceremony; a little of the new seed was scattered in every field, and all was well.

Kauru Dewar made a *mohini* for a girl, and her lover forgot to remove it. She went mad, ate her own hand, and went wandering in the jungle.

Finally, we may note how very easily the gunia's own powers are lost or diminished by some breach of the rules of magic. Phulmat is less successful than at first; since her husband's brother's wife went to her shrine during her period "the god has been dim". Pachlu has lost his power, since his wife woke him at a critical moment when his *jīv* was talking to Bhagavan in a dream. Bansi has not only lost his power, but has seen madness and death invade his home because his wife unwittingly entered his *madhia* during her period.

Chapter XIII

THE CAUSE AND CURE OF DISEASE

While the gunia lives, the gods are well fed and happy. But when a witch arises, the world perishes.—Baiga Proverb.

I. PHYSIOLOGY AND ANATOMY

THE anatomical interest of the Baiga centres round two things, the function and location of the *jīv*, or soul, which animates the entire organism, and the psycho-physiology of sex. We have dealt with the latter fully in another chapter; here we may briefly describe the Baiga's theory of the soul.

The *jīv* is the source of life. 'As water lives in a pot, and the pot feels full of water, so is this body full of *jīv*. If the pot breaks, the water runs out and disappears into the earth. If the body breaks, away runs the *jīv* and disappears.'

About the exact location of the *jīv* inside the body there is considerable disagreement. Lahakat says it is like a little fly and lives in the hollow above the stomach where it makes a put-put-put noise. On the other hand, Mahatu declares it to be a glow-worm or small grasshopper, which lives in the tongue and eyes. For it is the eye that tells us ourselves and the tongue that tells other people that we are alive. "The *jīv*," says Dasseru of Bondar, "has its playground in the space between the eyes and the tongue." Hothu of Taliyapani and old Thaggur, however, are quite clear that the *jīv* lives in the testes. "We know it is in the testes, for if we squeeze them, we feel the life going out of us." But the whole body is its parish. "There is a path from the testes that leads all over the body. The *jīv* goes to and fro, giving life to everything."

The *jīv* can also leave the body, and normally does so in sleep, in the shape of a little bird or grasshopper, and its adventures are what we call dreams. In the folk-tales, the *jīv* is often kept permanently outside the body, in a place of safety, in an arrow, an iron grain-bin, or even far away in charge of 'a parrot in a golden cage hanging from a kadam tree on an isle beyond the seven seas'. I have only found one reference to this belief outside the realm of fiction, and that is in a Jharpat song from Baihar.

> Where shall I hide my *jīv*, O friend?
> If I put it on the bank of the swift-flowing river,
> The Singni fish might find it and carry it away.

The Baiga appear to confuse the heart and liver, and to be ignorant of the functions of the kidneys. Thaggur once explained his theory of metabolism: "When we eat, the food goes straight into a little chamber. There is a separate pipe for water. In the chamber are many worms, and these devour the food and turn it into excrement. Sometimes the worms come out with the excrement." Yet, though he admitted that "if we ate more, we would have more blood," he could not tell how the worms turned the food into blood. He had, however, some idea of the circulation. "The blood," he said, "is made in the liver, and goes round and round the body."

Rawan's description is fairly typical. "The heart (or liver) is on the main road by which the food goes down. Food and water travel together as far as the heart. When the water in the heart dries up, the heart beats rapidly, for all water goes to the heart. When we drink, then we are at peace. From the heart, two roads go downwards, one to the house of water, one to the house of food. Here water is turned into urine—it is made yellow by the heat—and the food is devoured by worms and made into excrement. The water-house is near the opening, the food-house is distant; so urine always comes out first."

II. DISEASE DUE TO NATURAL CAUSES

The rough and inaccurate character of Baiga physiology and anatomy is of very little importance in their general medical theory, which considers that hardly any diseases are due to natural causes. Most disease has its origin either in witchcraft or in the spontaneous and inexplicable hostility of unseen beings.

The Baiga has no conception of natural infection or contagion. He has no fear of contact with a leper, and will unhesitatingly have intercourse with a woman suffering from an acute vaginal discharge. "Disease," says Hothu firmly, "is not caused by dirt, or bad water, or food. It is always the work of witches or evil spirits."

I did once think that I had found Hothu with some theory of infection, when he told me that if one man in the village got a cough they all got it; and that in the old days the Baiga never suffered from cholera. It was only when they started visiting the villages in the plains that they brought it back with them. But later he revealed that what he meant was that when Naksurki Mata came into a village, she was not content with one victim, but went round giving colds to everybody; and that Baiga who were foolish enough to go down to the plains were haunted by Murri Mata and brought her back with them.

The Baiga do, however, in some cases admit a possibly natural cause for disease. Thus fever may sometimes be caused "by drinking a lot of water when you are cold". Headache may be due "to a hot breeze blowing into a man's nose and ears". Itch comes from lying naked on the earth—or by laughing when a horse breaks wind. Venereal disease, specially, is apt "to come from our own bodies".

The Baiga have developed a fairly elaborate theory of venereal disease, though this is not endemic among them as it is among their neighbours. To the Baiga all venereal disease is one infection. A man first catches *thanki* (gonorrhœa); if untreated, this develops into *garmi* (syphilis); the next stage is variously described as *parmi*, *sujāg* or *dhāt* (various forms of chronic gonorrhœa including gleet). At last comes *patthari* or stricture, when "the mouth of the penis is shut, and all the urine flows back into the stomach. It swells and swells—the man dies in agony". Epididymitis is not connected with gonorrhœa, nor is locomotor ataxia and other advanced complications with syphilis; these are always due to witchcraft. Arthritis, however, is sometimes related to gonorrhœa. Leprosy and yaws are, correctly, regarded as distinct diseases.

"Syphilis," says Lahakat, "lives in a woman's vagina, and by going to her, you get it. Woman is the real danger, and brings these sores upon us." Gonorrhœa is sometimes induced by excessive intercourse. Jethu agreed that syphilis came from connection with infected women, but it might also be caused by eating hot things and by drinking too much *mahua* liquor.

The Baiga do not suffer very greatly from syphilis; their special scourge is gonorrhœa. This is not caused by sexual intercourse except in one special case. "You don't get gonorrhœa by going to a girl," said Jethu, "but through drinking hot water and going about in the hot sun. Then the urine turns yellow and it burns us. When a man goes every day in the sun he gets fever and this turns into gonorrhœa. *Thanki* gets its name because when a man urinates, he bites his arm and says *than than than*, because of the pain."

Another way of catching gonorrhœa is to step over a place where someone has urinated. "You can also get it from a witch. She puts

Samduria Deo in the stone where they wash clothes; then even if thirty-six families wash there, every one of them will get it."

Gonorrhœa may also develop after a man has been to a woman during her period, a belief which is confirmed by modern science. To cure this, it is necessary for a man to take a menstrual cloth full of blood and wring it out in a bowl full of water. Then he must wash his penis in the mixture.

It is dangerous to go to a woman when there is blood in the urine, perhaps due to cystitis. On the other hand, when the urine is simply burning, the pain will be relieved by intercourse. Coitus with a virgin is a very valuable cure. In Bohi I heard of a man who had been suffering (apparently) from an acute prostatitis, who went to a virgin and was cured.

III. DISEASE DUE TO SUPERNATURAL BEINGS

Disease may sometimes be due to natural causes; it may sometimes be aggravated by cold or heat; but at the same time it may be traceable to some supernormal agency. We will first consider those diseases that are due to the hostility, often the quite haphazard and irresponsible hostility, of unseen supernormal beings. Later we will deal with the large and absorbing problem of witchcraft.

There is hardly a god or spirit in the entire Baiga pantheon who may not sometimes be moved to send disease upon mankind. Even Bhagavan the Creator may do so. Perhaps this is not surprising when we consider the way he tricked the first Baiga and sent death into the world. Bhagavan is indeed the friend of the Baiga, and once gave them many blessings; but his friendship is a 'policeman's friendship'—at any moment he may decide to act in his official capacity.

It is hard to explain the widespread belief that Bhagavan himself sends worms into a wound. This idea is common all over the Central Provinces, though it may well have originated with the Baiga, and it is very moving to see the horror and despair with which the discovery of this complication is greeted. The whole family is excommunicate. They are shunned by men; the curse of God is upon them. There is no remedy. Only an expensive tribal dinner will free them of the deed.

Again, in common with most of village India, the Baiga believe firmly in the activities of the Mata or Mothers of Disease. These fearful beings, to whom by a curious twist of fate, has been given the sacred and beautiful name of Mother, attack both men and animals. The following story of their origin comes from a Baiga village in Rewa State.

The magician's ladder.
The magician's swing.

'Murra Deo was born in Madhogarh. Piri Deshahi was born in Deohaveli. Then these two arranged to marry, and Murra Deo's marriage party set out for Deohaveli, and when the marriage was done, came home with the bride and her seven sisters.

'But as they were on the road, night fell, and they prepared to rest. Piri Deshahi said to her sisters, "Go to my lord, and massage his limbs; care for him, for he is tired." But Murra Deo said to them, "Go away. I want my wife." But they said, "No, we are all your wives. You can do anything you like with us." Now the prettiest and the youngest of the sisters was Hinglajin, and Murra Deo cast his desire upon her. He took her to his bed and the others, mad with jealousy, ran away to tell Piri Deshahi.

'When Piri Deshahi heard this, she was so angry that she took an axe and killed the whole of Murra Deo's army. She cut off their heads and made a great mound of them like a mountain. In the morning, Murra Deo looked out and saw all his army dead. He called his wife and said, "What a great wrong you have done me." Then said his wife, "What need of an army? We are going to travel through the world."

'Then Piri Deshahi brought twelve hundred bullocks from her father's house and twelve hundred men to drive them. They loaded them with all their goods and started on their journey.

'First they came to Songarh. There was a lake there. They unloaded the bullocks by the lake and sent them to the jungle. In the middle of the night, Piri Deshahi went to the lake and stirred up all the water and made it muddy. That night Chilkin Piri was born. In the morning the villagers went for water, but when they had drunk it, they fell ill with vomiting and many motions. They had griping pains all over their bodies and many died.

'Then the Raja of that place came and fell at Piri Deshahi's feet and cried: "Whatever you want to load on your bullocks I will give you. If you want men for human sacrifice I will give you twelve hundred of my own subjects." So Piri Deshahi loaded the bullocks with men, to each bullock a man, and the disease stopped.

'The next day they went to Haldinagar. Here Piri Deshahi did the same things, and that night Bai Haldahin was born. In the morning the people fell ill of a yellow vomit, and the Raja gave the party twelve hundred sacks of turmeric to go away. When they left the village the people recovered.

'The next day they reached Ramnagar. Here Dispiri Mata was born and all the people of the place were attacked by syphilis. They offered twelve hundred goats and Dispiri Mata went away.

'Then they came to Lamanagarh. Here Mirgi Devi was born, and the people fell down in fits. For this, Piri Deshahi took from the Raja twelve hundred horses.

'At Naikagarh, Naikin Bai was born, and a plague attacked the cattle. So the Raja gave twelve hundred buffaloes, and Piri Deshahi agreed to leave that place.

'Then at Hasnagarh, Hadphoran Marhi was born. Smallpox broke out that night, and hundreds of the people died. The Raja there was very poor; he had nothing to give, so he said, "I will give myself." And he became the *panda* of Piri Deshahi.

'They went on to Kairagarh. Here Kairadeshahi was born, and all the unborn children died as they were being delivered. The Raja offered twelve hundred speckled chickens, and all was well again.

'So they went through the world, till all the twenty-one sisters who give disease to men were born. These are the sisters who dance by night in the gunia's *sūpa*, whom only he can see.

'These then are the twenty-one sisters, the diseases they give and the gifts they require.

'Chilkin Piri gives pains that grip the stomach. She must be given a black pig, three chickens, coconut and incense.

'Bai Hardahin causes a yellow vomit; she may be satisfied with a pig.

'Dispiri Mata gives syphilis. She must be given the ears of a buffalo.

'To Mirgi Devi, the bringer of epilepsy, the tongue of a horse must be cut out for sacrifice.

'For Naikin Bai, who attacks the bullocks of the Lamana, a black goat should be given.

'Hadphoran Marhi gives the smallpox which breaks out of the marrow of men's bones. She must have a *sarria* (rosary), black bangles, a *bandan* such as is tied round the head, and a *tikli*.

'Kairadeshahi causes children to be still-born. She requires a speckled she-goat. On the goat they must put *tikli*, *sarria*, *bandan* and black bangles and let it go free in the jungle.

'Durpatta Mata prevents a child being born at all, and thus kills both child and mother.

'Maura Mata gives children fits. She must be given a black chicken and coconut.

'Ghatchindan catches cattle by the throat. She must be offered a black chicken and coconuts.

'Baihi and Bauri Bai drive men mad. The man cannot speak, he bites his hands and feet. She demands a spotted goat and a black she-goat.

'Kapni Piri gives ague. This may be cured by a coconut.

'Chingan Mata cripples a man's hands and feet with rheumatism. She must be given chickens of five different colours, a young pig, coconuts and liquor.

'Dhahu Dhukan causes sudden pains in the chest. She must be offered a black chicken and coconuts.

'Raksin Mata causes itch with large sores. She wants chickens of seven different colours and a coconut.

'Galadevi brings mumps, a swelling of the neck and cheeks. This can only be cured by offering a black she-goat.

'Churelin Mata goes to young men in their sleep and robs them of their seed, making them impotent. She can be sent away with a black chicken with a black bangle and red *sarria* round its neck. Or, sprinkle parched rice round the bed at night; she will come and eat it, and forget to go to the boy.

'Rahabasin Mata startles people and makes them ill with fear. Offer her a black chicken.

'Pharka Undharan Mata is the opener of doors. She opens the door and comes into the house, and makes all the vessels rattle. To stop her, tie two little gourds over the door. She will play with these and not come in.

'Phoki Mata attacks the cattle with dysentery. She must be offered a goat and a pig.

'Jappi Mata is the sleeping disease. She demands *ghī* and a little *gur*.

'These were all born as Piri Deshahi and Murra Deo went on their journey through the world. At last they came to Bhairat on a hill far away in the forest. Here from Piri Deshahi and Murra Deo was born their son Dhau Bundela. Then Piri Deshahi called all her people together, and told them what they should do. She told them to wander through the world, each giving her disease wherever she went, and only going away when she received the proper gifts.

'When all this was done, then Piri Deshahi and Murra Deo made a great sacrifice for all the Mata and Devi in the world, and for the twenty-one sisters. First they sacrificed the twelve hundred men whom the Raja of Sonnagarh had given them. They had no axes or knives, so they killed them with their diseases. When they were dead, the sisters drank their blood. After that they killed all the animals in the same way.

'When the sacrifice was over, Piri Deshahi sent the twenty-one sisters out into the world. They went everywhere and from that day the world has been filled with disease.

'These are the sisters who dance in the *sūpa* of the gunia, but the gunia always tries to speak with Piri Deshahi herself, for she tells without error or deceit what gifts must be offered, and at her command, the Mata goes away.'

This story is of very great importance, for it gives the theoretical background for the most important part of the *gunia's* work, which is the task of diagnosis. Once a diagnosis has been made, treatment and cure are matters of pure routine. But the diagnosis is vitally important, for if a man offers to Hardahin Mata the offerings due to Chilkin Piri, she will refuse them, and he will get worse. We will consider this point at length a little later.

Among the *devata*, Narayan Deo is apt to catch a man by the throat and prevent him swallowing. When this occurs a Laru pig must be dedicated and sacrificed after three years. Baghesur Pat is lord of the jungle; he often takes the form of a tiger, and punishes those who have failed to implement their promises when praying for a good crop. Sometimes he is sent by a witch to injure her enemy. Chitawar Deo is another dangerous godling, who lives in the chhindi palms of Bilaspur, and when annoyed, or incited by a witch, assumes the form of a snake, and bites his enemy.

V. THE BHUT

We must now describe some of the ghosts and familiars who can be equally dangerous to mankind. These are often known by the general name of *bhut*, which in Baiga usage may cover jealous ancestors, the ghosts of women dying in childbirth, the spirits of unmarried men, the whirlwind, and such familiar demons as the *mua* and *massan*. Even the *guru* or the *devata*, even the ghost of a wife or husband, may be found in the enemy's camp, among the beings hostile to mankind.

In Hindu tradition, as the Vishnu Purana tells us, the *bhut* are fierce flesh-eating creatures who were made by the Creator in a fit of temper. They are the sons of their mother Krodha, Anger. But to the Baiga they are no more than the possibly dangerous ghosts of the departed. The whirlwind is also a *bhut*, and no one should ever use a piece of cloth that has been carried by it up into the air. Marki is another very troublesome *bhut*, recognized by ripples on a stream, who causes vomiting and dysentery. In most tamarind trees and pipal trees, *bhut* are living, and it is dangerous to sit beneath them at night.

For example, when Gahania, a Dudh-bhaina of Bilaspur, was a child, a *bhut* caught him and hid him in a hollow tree. The parents found him, but the *bhut*'s power was so strong they could not remove him. A *gunia* came and bound the *bhut*, but the child was blind, deaf and dumb. But when proper offerings were made, he recovered.

V. THE CHURELIN

But chief among the dangerous spirits of the other world is the *churelin*. The *churelin* is the ghost of a woman who has died in pregnancy or child-birth. She takes the form and size of a peahen, with her feet turned back-wards.[1] Lahakat once saw 'with his own eyes' a *churelin* with a face like a monkey and a peahen's wings, sitting on the top of a tree crying *karil charil*. This vision was followed by an epidemic in his village. Mahatu also saw a *churelin* near Chauradadar, in the thick jungle, sitting on a tree. Another time he saw one in a cave with water falling in front of it.

There are two kinds of *churelin*, the *pāpi churelin* and the *dharmi churelin*. When the *dharmi churelin* comes to a village, the sick recover and children are born without pain. But when the *pāpi churelin*, like a black vulture, comes and cries *Kai O! Kai O!* all the sick die, and parturient women cannot be delivered.

The *churelin* is thus not necessarily malicious, but she is always dangerous. She provides young men with exquisite and thrilling experiences, experiences which may be pure delight—though they may also bring death. It is the *churelin*'s habit to seek for lonely men. When she finds one, she takes the form of a beautiful girl, naked, alluring, and lies down beside him in his empty hut. "She comes in the shape of his mother, sister, aunt, sometimes his lover, and sleeps with him." But when a man dreams that he is with someone he knows, it is generally assumed that this is not a *churelin*, but a girl who is making love-magic for him. "Men grow very weak through this. To drive her away, a man prepares parched rice and scatters it all round his bed. So when she comes, she sits down to eat the rice and forgets all about him." Such is Dhan Singh's account.

Mithu, however, scouted the idea that anyone would want to drive a *churelin* away. "She flew into my house like a little bird. Then she changed into a lovely naked girl. Three times I went to her. In the morning I could see that my seed had fallen on the ground, but there was no one there."

Lahakat was once visited by two *churelin* in a single night. The first was very lovely, with a little child in her arms. She flirted with him, laughed, talked, made him smoke and drink, massaged his legs, and then gave herself to him. She went away and another, not quite so beautiful,

[1] This is a feature common to demonic beings in India. The *yaksha* has its feet turned backwards. So does the *kichin* of Bihar which probably corresponds to the *churelin* (Grierson: *Bihar Peasant Life* (1st Edition), p. 408).

came. He had coitus with her also. On both occasions he experienced orgasm. "We know it's a *churelin* when we've never seen the girl before. My wife knew of it. She had just given birth to a child. She was not angry. But if it had been a girl we knew, then there would have been a great quarrel."

The *churelin*, like mortal women, is subject to the revolutions of the moon, and suffers a regular menstrual period. At such times, she approaches her victims with her hair loose and tangled. If this sign is ignored, she makes herself ugly and terrible, and tries by all means to avoid intercourse with the man whom she is yet driven to approach.

In Jamunpani, there was a man who slept with a *churelin* every night. She was very beautiful. One night he caught her and said he was going to keep her with him for ever. "Let me go," she cried. "I'm naked." "I won't," he said. "Then all your family will die." So then for fear he let her go. "But if you can keep a *churelin*," he said, "it is a great advantage. She will bring you everything you want, and make you wealthy and famous."

Mahatu, in fact, has succeeded in domesticating a *churelin* who has made him famous, though hardly wealthy. He had taken the precaution of offering annually—for many years—a black chicken, a pair of black bangles, a coconut and some *sendur*, to *churelin* generally. At last one *churelin*, flattered by these attentions, came to live in the *kinnāri-bāja* (a sort of banjo) which hangs on the wall of his house. She has been specially useful to him in helping his wife through her confinements. Once when all the village women failed, the *churelin* came and massaged his wife till his child was born. Again, on October 29th, 1937, she came all the way from Chauradadar to Sanhrwachhapar, a distance of twenty miles, to help his daughter-in-law Baisakiya through her travail.

In other parts of India, the *churelin* is regarded less optimistically. To answer her night-summons means death; the mere sight of her may bring on a wasting disease; the youth who is so rash as to be seduced by her is carried away to the underworld. If he eats the food she gives him there, he must remain till his strength and beauty is gone, and he only returns to earth, broken and white-haired, when all his friends are dead.[1] The Santal, when a pregnant woman dies, drive long thorns through the soles of her feet in order to prevent her running very fast. For if the Santal *churelin* catches a man, she gives him no pleasure, but licks the flesh from his bones with her rough tongue.[2]

Elsewhere there are special death ceremonies for pregnant women: the Bhandari of Bengal, and sometimes the Gond, cut the belly open and

[1]Crooke: op. cit., I, p. 269 ff. [2]Bompas: op. cit., p. 411.

remove the child in order to bury it separately. The Majhwar of Mirzapur bury the corpse intact, but fill the grave with thorns and pile heavy stones upon it to keep down the ghost.

The Baiga have no such customs, and this confirms the fact that they are not especially afraid of *churelin*, but look upon them as affording novel and exciting sexual experiences. The older men, however, agree that to be visited by a *churelin* is what we would call a deviation, it is a compensatory experience like masturbation or bestiality. Thus it probably does harm.

VI. THE RAKSA

The *raksa* is a much more unpleasant being. He is the ghost of a man who has never experienced coitus. His face red and burning, his body covered with thick black hair, he lives in a semur tree, waiting for an unwary village maiden to pass his way. "He comes and presses a girl while she is asleep; she can neither move nor speak while he is covering her; he takes her like a husband and cries Ai ai ai, and goes away." It is fashionable, of course, for girls to regard these visitations with horror and alarm, but my own impression is that they no more dread them than men dread the coming of the *churelin*. Unfortunately, it is possible to contract gonorrhœa from coitus with a *raksa*; this is perhaps the most fruitful source of venereal infection among women.

Dhan Singh, however, has tamed a *raksa*, and this affable familiar ghost now lives in his house and guards his grain-bins, but makes himself troublesome to any young woman visiting the house.[1]

The Tembu and Fingo tribes of South Africa, as Dr. Laubscher has recently informed us, have similar erotic phantasies.[2] The Impundulu commonly features in the delusions of female schizophrenic patients. He sits on their chests and tries to choke them if they refuse him sexual liberties; I have heard of *raksa* attacking women in the very same manner. I have found nothing among the Baiga, however, to correspond with the rather coy and amorous attitude of Tembu women towards the Tikoloshe. It is the erotic snake-demon, the Ugatya, who gives venereal disease and then not to the woman, but to her husband.

Roheim has complained that anthropologists are inclined to neglect the phallic attributes of demons.[3] This is certainly true in India, and an investigation of Indian phallic demons, especially as these appear to schizophrenic patients, along the lines of Dr. Laubscher's book, would be of great value.

[1] See p. 165.
[2] Laubscher: *Sex, Custom and Psychopathology* (London, 1937), p. 8 ff.
[3] Roheim: *Riddle of the Sphinx* (London, 1934), p. 41.

VII. THE MUA AND MASSAN[1]

The *mua* is the ghost of a child who has died before learning to talk. There are not many stories about the *mua*, but he is sufficiently important to require special mantra to check his activities. *Massan* is another mischievous spirit, and often acts as the familiar of witches. To Hindus, *massan* belongs to the Smasana or burial-ground. He causes wasting diseases such as tuberculosis in children. Sometimes he takes the form of a bear and wanders in the hills. The Baiga do not connect him with the burial-ground, but locate him under stones by the road-side, or behind trees in the bewar, whence he may suddenly pop out and steal the peasant's food. *Mua* and *massan* may be sent by witches to catch or possess a man, and may give him almost any disease. They are not associated by the Baiga with any specific illness.

VIII. DISEASE DUE TO WITCHCRAFT

Baiga life is heavily overshadowed by the dark cloud of witchcraft. For although many diseases and disasters are caused by the hostility of the unseen *devata* and *bhut*, yet probably the majority of evils are due to witchcraft. If a man is killed by a tiger or bitten by a snake, if a mother cannot be delivered of her child, if a boy's limbs wither and he goes lame, if a storm destroys the crops, if the milk curdles or the meat goes bad, the Baiga immediately look round for a witch or sorcerer who might have reason to wish them harm.

These disasters may be ultimately due to natural causes, but it is the witch who makes them happen now and to this particular person. 'We shall give a false account of Zande philosophy,' says Dr. Evans-Pritchard,[2] 'if we say that they believe witchcraft to be the sole cause of phenomena. This proposition is not contained in Zande patterns of thought, which only assert that witchcraft brings a man into relation with events in such a way that he sustains injury.' This would be equally true of the Baiga mind.

The Baiga witch differs from the European in being solitary. Although,

[1] Among the Kharia, the *mua* holds a more important place. He is the spirit of anyone who has died a violent death. The Katal Mua is a man killed by an axe, the Bhokal Mua was stabbed to death, the Tangal Mua was hanged, the Pasal Mua was beaten, the Baghout Mua was eaten by a tiger. The *mua* misguide and tease human beings, but do them no serious injury (Roy: *The Khārias*, p. 317).

[2] Evans-Pritchard: *Witchcraft, Oracles and Magic among the Azande* (Oxford, 1937), p. 68.

Charka possessed by Thakur Deo (as described on p. 300).
*Yogi Dewar divining by the kāri.**

as we have seen, at the very beginning there was something like a college of three witches, this never developed; there is no Sabbath or Esbat, no flying through the air to the assemblies, no renunciation, no vows, no covenant. The Baiga witch is unutterably lonely, practising her art in secrecy and terror. Nor are there any special marks by which a witch may be known, except that possibly her eyes may shine red in the dark. I have been unable to find any trace of a tradition of polymastia (extra breasts) or polythelia (additional nipples).

The rigour of the witch-trial and the punishment for witchcraft has been considerably modified in recent years. I have not met anything that can match the savagery of the Middle Ages in Europe. Now and again a witch is treated with great cruelty, but she generally now escapes with little more than a beating. In Bohi, I was asked to make a report to the Government against a witch and get her punished by a magistrate, and in Karanjia recently (in January, 1937) a man was taken to the police-station on a charge of attempting to turn himself into a tiger. That is not how the ancient Baiga would have dealt with such offences!

How does the Baiga witch set about her business? She may injure her enemy in many different ways; she may affect him directly and immediately by the power of her eye; she may destroy him by a curse; she may invoke the aid of the *bhut* or *devata* to bring disease to his house; she may send a snake to bite him or a tiger to kill him; she may herself come by night and drink his blood; she may send her magic flying through the air on a leaf, a pebble or a bat.

Let us consider the last method first. It has, of course, parallels in many parts of India and the world. The Angami Naga believe in a certain kind of pebble which will bring illness on the man at whom it is thrown. The Sema Naga ascribe a similar power to a berry. The Bharia of Jubbulpore and Chhindwara in the Central Provinces believe that they can kill a man by sending what is known as the *muth*, or handful, of rice, kodon, lemon or *urad* seeds, through the air towards their enemy. Somewhat similar is the *tamatatikwa*, or ghost-shooter, of the Melanesians of the Banks Islands and the bone-pointer of the Malays and Central Australians.[1]

Here is an incident that occurred not very long ago in Tinsatola. 'A Baiga couple were living in the village. He was a gunia, she a witch. They had three sons and two daughters. She had had five husbands; one by one she had killed them all. She married this man, not knowing that he was a gunia. One day he went to his bewar to cut the trees. She put

[1] Compare Hutton, *Angami Nagas*, p. 242; Russell and Hiralal, op. cit., ii. 248 and iii. 581; Skeat and Blagden, *Pagan Races of the Malay Peninsula*, ii. p. 199; Rivers, *Medicine, Magic and Religion*, p. 13; and Spencer and Gillen, *Northern Tribes of Central Australia*, pp. 531, 553.

her magic (*jādu*) in a leaf, and ordered it to go to the bewar and kill this man also. Unseen by anyone, the leaf flew through the jungle; it hit her husband on the chest; he fell down. But he was a magician; he had already seen the wickedness of his wife. He had nothing with him, only some cotton to make fire to light his pipe, and the hollow bamboo *tondhi* in which he kept his money. He took his wife's magic and put it on the cotton; he stuffed the cotton into the bamboo; he pointed it towards his wife, where he thought she was; he sent it away from him. Soon he was well again and came home with a bundle of roots on his head. But his wife had been struck by the returning magic and was hiding in terror in the house, for she knew that now she had a master who was a stronger magician than herself.'

Jethu gave me these three mantra which he said were used on leaves and stones. The stones were then thrown in the direction of the man whom it was intended to injure, and the magic would fly through the air, and attack his liver.

i

Arise in this necessity of mine, O Muali, O Jhinjhi Kal, O hundred-footed Padgani. Let the poison go like an Elephant swaying to and fro. Where the poison falls, there eat his liver.

ii

The seven hundred poisons and the nine hundred kinds of wisdom! Who sends this? The guru sends it. I the guru's pupil send it. May this sending of the mantra make a deep wound in his life.

iii

Goddess Kinkin and her mother with loose bangles! Chamkan Bir! Bhavan Bir! Kalkaldevi! Go, go, my warriors! Break into his liver and eat it! Obey my word! Break his waist! Break his back! Take his life out! Go, my poison!

Sometimes the witch catches a bat and holds it in her hands muttering a mantra over it. Then she lets it go in the direction of her enemy. The bat may turn into a leaf and flutter away until it falls on the enemy's head or chest, when it will infect him with the magic, and return. Or it may retain its own shape and after dark fly to the man's house, and sit on his chest or flap his head with its wings. This will put the deadly magic upon him. The following mantra is to be used:

Alpat guru! Champat chela! My disciple has gone to the forest.

> Often, often he asks for knowledge. Go, go, my knowledge, to my enemy and ruin his family. Even if he hides under the water, let him not be saved.

The witch commonly makes a snake out of the dirt of her body and sends it to kill someone. The witch Maniaro killed Mahatu's father Punna in this way. In Jethu's life-story there is a dramatic account of his encounter with a magic snake and the disaster that befell. Mahi was bitten by a magic snake and nearly died. The witch also sends tigers. She calls Baghesur Pat and persuades him to take the form of a tiger and kill her enemies. Bukwa's mother's sister was a witch and sent a tiger to kill him near Ufri. The tiger that killed two people at Bohi was sent by a witch, who was so powerful that the Dewar could not properly perform the rites that would bind the creature's mouth.

These animals may be either real animals who come at the witch's bidding or magic animals who are specially created. Mahatu told me how this was done. "The witch gets a chip of wood from a tree or a house that has been struck by lightning. She buries it. At cockcrow on a Sunday she goes naked to the place, walks round it twice and then, in the middle of the third round, jumps over it. Then the chip of wood pushes its way out of the ground. She asks it, 'Will you become a snake?' If the chip is ready, it wriggles along the ground. If not, it stays still. She says, 'Will you become a tiger?' If it is ready, it jumps along the ground. 'Will you become a lawa?' The chip flies into the air. Then she tells it where to go, throws black and yellow rice at it, utters a mantra, and the chip becomes a snake or tiger and goes away.

A witch may also turn herself into a lawa, and frighten her victim into a decline. "A Kol girl," says Binjha Muria of Niwas, "made love-magic for me, but I threw it away. Then she became a lawa by her magic and as I was going home flew ahead of me, and sat by the road. When I came by, she flew violently up into the air, struck me on the chest, and disappeared. I was very frightened, and was ill for many weeks."

If a witch can get hold of the leaves on which another woman has eaten, she can give her a long attack of mennhoragia, though this may also be caused independently by a disease godling called Baisasur Banjari, who must be appeased with the ear of a buffalo.

At a wedding a witch may throw evil magic on the bride to make her childless, or put it on her while they are undoing the *beni* down by the river.

The direct curse of a witch is very powerful. The first witches had so much poison in their eyes that when they looked at a tree it immediately withered away. The Baiga dread the Evil Eye in much the same fashion as the rest of India. Mithu refused to accompany me into Pandaria for fear some witch might come and watch him eating. "If she watches me and counts each mouthful, one, two, three, four, then I will get terrible pains in my belly."

A witch may take some dust from her own left heel and put it on her left eye. When she wants to injure someone she flicks a little of it towards him with a curse.

My friend Mahatu once had a painful attack of epididymitis (which was actually as far as I can discover a normal complication of gonorrhœa from which he was suffering at the time) as a result of a witch's curse. "I went to Bukwa's house for a funeral. I was very drunk and I abused his mother's sister. It was that same woman who once brought a tiger to Ufri to eat Bukwa. She was very angry. She said, 'You impotent fool! I'll see you going, but I'll not see you returning!' I went away, I was rolling like an onion for drunkenness, I thought nothing of it. I went down the river for a few miles, and then suddenly my testes swelled to an enormous size. I was alone. I sat weeping by the river. At last I crawled home in agony. I went to an old gunia. He offered a pig for me. After eight days my testes became small again, and I gave a rupee's worth of liquor to the gunia for saving me. But he was very angry with me for my folly in abusing a witch."

Bisram, a Binjhwar Baiga of Niwas, had a similar experience. He had two wives, one a Muria, the other a Binjhwar. By marrying a Muria, he exposed himself to the hostility of witches. His Binjhwar wife one day laid her hand on his thigh, and at once his testes swelled up. Later, she sent a snake to bite the Muria girl, who died. At last, the villagers caught the witch, and the gunia urinated in her mouth and thus deprived her of her power.

Bhangi Muria was cursed by a witch, and was impotent for three months.

My next example illustrates both the power of a curse, and the Baiga's method of dealing with the crisis. "In Tilinkirwa there was a young Baiga girl called Sukwaria, a young girl with breasts that every man there longed to fondle. One day in the early morning, three cows came and two of them rubbed against the wall of her house, and knocked off some of the plaster. 'Let a tiger kill them,' cries the girl in a temper. And sure enough, that very day, by noon, all three had been killed by a tiger. The Ahir came in from the forest, and told the villagers, and a man who had heard the girl's curse reported it to the village. She swore that she had never said anything. But they dragged her out of her house, began to beat her, threatened to put salt and chili in her vagina. When she heard that she said, 'Yes, I did say it, but I am not a witch, so how could my words have such power?' They went on beating her. 'Yes, yes, I am a witch,' she confessed at last. Then they beat her so much that in five days she had swelled to twice her size, and she was ill for a month and lost all her beauty."

When a witch dies, her *jīv* goes to Bhagavan. He refuses to let her be re-born in any human being, holding that she has done enough harm already; instead he lets her *jīv* take possession of the feebler body of an owl. But even then her capacity for mischief, though limited, is not ended. If she can sit, in the form of an owl, on a house where a child has just been born, the parents—if they are foolish—may throw stones or sticks at her. The owl picks up the missile and dips it in the nearest stream, then puts it in the sun to dry. Then as the stone or stick dries, the child's body will also wither with the wasting disease that they call *sukhi*. If you do want to throw anything at an owl, it is safer to use clods of earth, as these will either break at once or at least melt when dipped in the water.

IX. DISEASE AS A PUNISHMENT FOR BREACH OF TRIBAL LAW

In addition to the causes of disease that we have already discussed, we must add the breach of tribal law. Incest, for example, may bring leprosy, blindness, or worms to devour the hands and feet. It is curious, however, that lepers and the blind are not regarded with reproach. The Baiga have no fear or horror of leprosy[1] and do not segregate lepers in any way. In Bohi I found three brothers, all of whom had been born dumb. This was ascribed to their parents' incest, and in this case I did find that the boys were regarded with distaste as something monstrous.

Breach of the rules of exogamy are officially supposed to have the same effect, but no one really believes this.

Another fruitful cause of disease is plough-cultivation. "I have used the plough," says Hothu. "But my children have always been weak and sickly on account of it. If even one Baiga in a village uses a plough, every one of us is affected." And Mahatu tells how, when bewar was first stopped in Blocks 64 and 52 of the Raigarh Tehsil, and the Baiga Chak was formed, a child died in every house.

To ride on a horse, or even to wear shoes is dangerous. "In the old

[1] The Hindus generally attribute leprosy to non-natural causes. Often it is due to eating beef or to an offence against the sun. In Mathura it is believed to be caused by telling lies in one of the sacred groves of Krishna. The Chasa believe it is a punishment for injuring the totem animal. See Russell and Hiralal: ii. p. 425, iii. p. 347; Forbes: *Ras Mala* (Oxford, 1924) i. p. 59; Mills: *The Lhota Nagas* (London, 1922) p. 198.

days, Bhagavan told Nanga Baiga that he and his children were not to plough, nor ride on horseback, nor touch horse-dung, nor wear shoes. Now we do all these things, and they have brought poverty and sickness upon us."

"There was once," says Jethu, "a Baiga called Sansai living in Kairabaora in Pandaria. He rode one day on a horse. Immediately a tiger came and ate him in front of his own house, and two or three days later ate the horse also."

Mistakes in ritual and the failure to implement promises made to *bhut* or *mata* may also bring disease. Mahatu once had a severe attack of fever as a result of offering a cock of the wrong colour to Dharti Mata. We have already described a number of deaths due to failure to pay what is owed to the *bhut*. Blindness may be caused by eating the first mouthful from the hands of an excommunicated person.

Itch comes as a result of laughing when a horse or cow breaks wind. No penalty seems to attach to a giggle when a human being does so.

In conclusion it is important to bear in mind that all animals and snakes, as well as many spirits, are purely neutral in character. They will never do harm unless they are incited thereto by a witch, or unless their victim is standing on *pāpi dharti*. If a man has broken some tribal taboo, if he is in fact in a state of mortal sin (which is practically what *pāpi dharti* means) then he is in a very dangerous position. "A tiger," says Dhan Singh, "can only kill a man if there is a *bhut* in the house who orders it to do so, or if the man is standing on *pāpi dharti*. Tigers will only kill bad men. For tigers and snakes have no evil in them. They are good. Snakes only bite us when an enemy compels them."

X. THE DUTIES OF THE MAGICIAN: DIAGNOSIS

When a magician is called to the bedside of a sick man, his first and most important task is that of diagnosis. In many cases, the cure follows a correct diagnosis as a simple matter of routine. If, for example, the gunia sees in his *sūpa* that the illness is due to one of the twenty-one 'Mothers', the official and standardized offering will be made, and the patient will recover. If he does not, it means that there has been some complication, the additional malice of witchcraft has perhaps been added to the original malice of heaven. Or again, if the magician is of opinion that the sick man has been caught by Narayan Deo, there is no question about treatment; the family must immediately dedicate a Laru pig.

There is, however, no standardized treatment for diseases caused by

The gunia at work in the Bida rite.
*Phulmat, the woman gunia, divining by sūpa-tuma.**

witchcraft, and here the magician must use his own judgment; in such a case indeed everything depends on his courage and decision. And it is no light matter to enter the lists against the powers of evil; the gunia is a noble and heroic figure fighting an unseen enemy who may be allied with all the hosts of heaven, and he himself armed only with the uncertain and depleted knowledge that has come to him from the past. The magician combines the duties of doctor and detective. He has to track down a public enemy in the interests of public health. In his person, Scotland Yard is combined with Harley Street.

In his task of diagnosis and detection, the classic methods are the *bahari-kāri* and the *sūpa-tuma*. Both these methods resemble European table-turning. When using the *kāri*, the magician asks it a number of questions, to which it answers "yes" or "no" by altering its length. When he uses the *sūpa-tuma*, the magician sits down opposite a 'control'. As he himself stirs the rice in his *sūpa*, he asks question after question, and the 'control' replies by shaking the *tuma* (gourd) in his hands in different ways. In both cases, therefore, the only way of reaching a conclusion is by asking a great number of questions which will allow no other reply than a simple affirmative or negative. But sometimes a spirit rides upon the gunia and speaks to him directly in the depths of his soul. This naturally greatly accelerates the process of detection, but it happens only to experienced magicians. So far as I know the Baiga never fake this experience.

The *bahari-kāri* is simply a piece of *chir* or *chirra* straw pulled out of a broom or the walls of the house. It should be twelve fingers' breadth long. It is held in the hands and first pointed down to the ground to the accompaniment of a mantra. Then the question is asked, and it is measured by the hand, four fingers at a time. If its length increases to the breadth of thirteen fingers, the answer is affirmative and favourable; if it decreases to eleven, the answer is negative and dangerous.

The *kāri* is generally used for matters of less importance, to detect minor crimes of theft, to trace straying cattle, to decide whether the day is favourable for an enterprise. But it is also used as a preliminary to the more serious business of the *sūpa-tuma*. The gunia tries to discover through his *kāri* whether or no it will be safe for him to start on the cure of the sick man, or whether he too will be caught by the prevailing evil. He also asks whether he is likely to be successful. If the *kāri* gives a favourable reply by elongating itself, the magician proceeds. The following is a specimen of the mantra that are recited during the measurements of the *kāri*-straw:

> Daugan Guru, Guru Danatar, Nidhan Guru, Aginjar Guru, Loharjar Guru, Okan Guru, Jokan Guru, come my Guru! Do penance. In all

the eight doors and nine pathways of my house, do penance. When I go away, I bind the village boundary; when I return I bind the cattle's resting-place and the open field. I bind with the immortal nail, the immortal word. Come, Guru, stand!

Sirseti sarwa seti! I am responsible. To your understanding, the gift should be as a pearl. I honour you. Come guru, stand! I have said that I am binding the boundary, the cattle's resting-place, the open field. Let no evil enter them. I the guru bind them. If evil has already entered, let it turn into water. I the guru bind the seven witches.

Who is that evil one who has caught the man? I will look and see. In my hand is Chir-bhavani. Jaldevata Rani is standing near. See, this man is sick, did it come from the east, the west, the north, the south? Was it the work of *bhut* or *mata*, of *mua* or *massan*, of witch or wizard? Does the evil one live in this village or Jimor, in Taliapani or Ajghar, in Rupnidadar or Chakmaktola? Is it Adri or Phulmat, Baisakin or Mahi, Jitho or Sukho, Jethia or Singaro?

Hinglajin Mata, go and search for it! If it is true, grow one finger! If it is false, decrease one finger! I am known to be the disciple of twelve guru. Let not my word be false. If my word is found untrue, then all I will give you are my pubic hairs and the dirt from my body.

For the next part of the proceedings the apparatus again is of the simplest kind. All that is needed is the *sūpa*, the winnowing-fan that is used for magic all over the world, a *tuma* or gourd with a long handle, a little fire, the gum of sarai which is used as incense, and some rice or kodon. The magician goes into the sick man's house with a disciple or other 'sympathetic' person who will act as his 'control' and sits down in a corner of the room. He takes the rice or kodon out of the gourd with an open hand—the hand must not be clenched over the gourd or fan—and going to the sick man, waves the rice over him from head to foot. He returns to his place, puts the rice in the *sūpa* and the gourd on top of the rice, and makes the usual offerings of sarai gum and fire before them. The disciple, or *tumhār* as he is called, washes his feet and comes to sit in front of the gunia. The gunia removes the gourd from the fan, and the *tumhār* 'touches its feet' and takes it in his hand. He places the handle on the ground and sits silently taking the names of all the guru and gods known to him. The gunia picks up a few grains of rice and throws them at the gourd. This has the effect of sending a *māta* into the gourd and making it vocal. Then with a mantra he 'binds' any witch who might try to interfere with the proceedings.

Now the gunia, taking the *sūpa* in his left hand, begins to rub the rice round and round with his right, at the same time reciting long strings of mantra in a curiously soothing sing-song tone. I was seriously ill in October 1937, and I asked Mahatu to perform this rite in my room and diagnose the cause of the illness. I found the rhythm of the rubbing of the rice and the singing extraordinarily comforting; its effect was no doubt partly hypnotic. The gunia begins with 'Sirseti Pat', then takes the names of all the gods, and sends them out to search for whoever is causing trouble. The gods go out and search everywhere, and when they are done they come back again, marking their return by jerking the gunia's hand violently off his *sūpa*.

Now the tone of the rite increases in urgency. The gunia begins to ask his 'detectives' what they have found. Question after question pours from his lips, and the *tumhār*, who has hitherto sat silent, begins to take an active part. When an affirmative answer is given, he shakes his gourd vigorously backwards and forwards. When the gods answer no, he shakes it to and fro. There is a little rice in the gourd which makes a sudden, startling rattling noise.

Now the process which was begun in the *kāri* is practically repeated. The gunia has to ask an endless variety of questions to discover the cause of the trouble. He can only get an affirmative or negative answer. Often he gets no answer at all. I do not think that the divination is often faked. The *tumhār* is perfectly genuine. A strange atmosphere surrounds the rite; the gunia certainly have the power of creating the impression that they are in touch with mysterious other-worldly beings, as indeed they believe themselves to be. Often the rite lasts all day and sometimes far into the night. Now and then, the spirit comes and rides on the gunia, and he drops his *sūpa* and falls into convulsions, shaking his head desperately to and fro. Sometimes he sees directly in his *sūpa* the seven Samduria Sisters dancing or the one-and-twenty Mata. No one can tell what will happen when the magician has been thoroughly hypnotized by the rhythm of his own movements.

For the most part, the gunia improvises as he goes along, and often conducts a curiously intimate conversation with the spirits who are dwelling in his *sūpa*. But there are certain formulae which are always repeated. One of these is the Sirseti Pat, with which—in one form or another—the proceedings are normally begun. The gunia were very reluctant to tell me this, but Mahatu could not resist the claims of friendship and gave it to me.

The Sirseti Pat

Sirseti timān beti, gaddi māro, uttam kiri rigi chhigi, sarab set bindhi ghālo. I hold the gourd in my hand. I have put sarai gum on the knot that ties my dhoti. Outside, the court is full of knives and salty seeds.

You are the master of knowledge! You are the temple of knowledge, O Mai Sirseti! Come, come, sit on my tongue, sit on my throat.

The road and the Samur Tank are full of water. I have shoes on my feet, a stick in my hand. I have come to see the road. O Siddha Mai and Gundain! O son, you are right. The knowledge of the twelve pots of good! The knowledge of the twelve pots of evil! O Mai Gundain, come and stand before me. O golden bamboo! O silver pit! O Mai Gundain, declare plainly in the *sūpa* who is troubling us.

Later, the gunia uses a great variety of mantra, and often, as Mahatu has admitted to me, says anything that comes into his head. But where the head is the head of a Baiga, even its improvisations are of interest. I once recorded such an improvisation in the course of the rite:

Khairbhavani of the corner, stand! Sun and Moon, stand still! Ghatwahi of the mountain! Merai of the boundary-line! Paniharin of the watering-place! Galiyain of the road! Phatakin of the gate! The four corners of the house! The eighty-four Banaspati! The thirty-two bindings of the roof! Stand! Stand!

Ojha guru! Bojha guru! Be ready! Moon and Sun and Water-god! Guru and Gurain of both our arms! Twelve hundred cow-horns! Sixteen hundred Chitawar! Eighty thousand Dungarin! Nine hundred drunkards!

XI. DIAGNOSIS BY BAN-BATI AND PIDHA-GUMANA

The Bhaina Baiga employ the *bān-bāti* method of divination. The disciple places a small earthen lamp in a net-work of string and holds it up before the Dewar. The Dewar repeats a mantra and proceeds in the same way as in the *bahari-kāri*. The only difference is that then the answers were given by the varying length of a bit of straw, and here they are given by the waving of a lighted lamp. When the answer to the Dewar's questions is an affirmative, the lamp swings towards him; when it is a negative, it swings to and fro. When the real culprit or cause of the disease is named, the lamp swings with great vigour. If it goes out, it means that a witch has interfered with the rite.

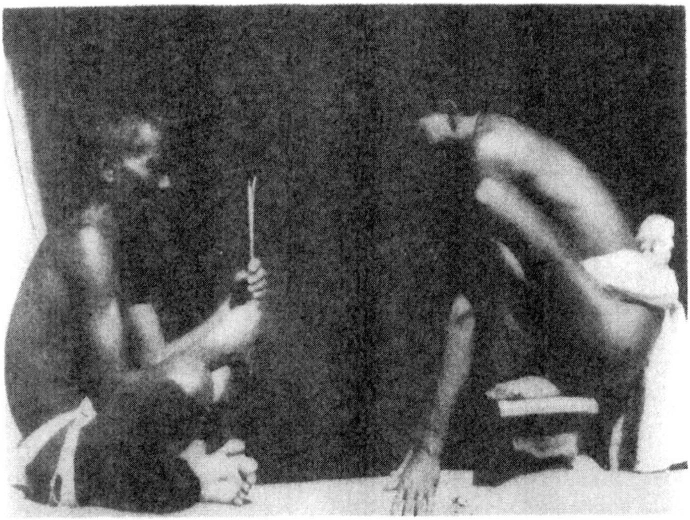

*Divination by the whirling seat (pīdha gumāna).**
*Divination by the swinging lamp (bān-bāti).**

The Dudh-bhaina Baiga practise *pīdha-gumāna*. They put a little *kodai* on the ground, on that a drinking-pot, on that a flat wooden seat called *pīdha*. On this the disciple or 'control' is seated. The Dewar sits in front of him with a *kāri* or a lighted lamp. The control leans forward with his hands on the ground, and as the Dewar puts his questions he is whirled round and round by the spirits. If the answer is yes, he goes anti-clockwise; if no, he goes clockwise.[1]

XII. DIAGNOSIS BY THE BARUA AND THE DHAM

But there is another very important type of divination where the god speaks directly, through the mouth of a man or woman who has passed into a state of dissociation. In every village there are a number of people known as *barua*, those on whom 'the god can ride'. During most ceremonies, and indeed at any time of quickened religious excitement, these persons are liable to fall into a sort of frenzy—they throw themselves on the ground, their limbs twitch spasmodically, they wag their heads desperately to and fro (this is called *jhūpna*), they beat themselves with iron scourges, they thrust iron spikes through tongue or cheeks. The god is riding upon them. At such moments, he often reveals secrets that have not been discovered by the ordinary methods of the gunia.

Some gunia or *panda*, in fact, trust to this as their usual method of divination. They fix a day when their clients are to visit them—every Monday is a common choice—and regularly fall into trances and prophecy. This is known as *dhām*. The *dhām* requires a certain amount of apparatus. The *panda* builds a little *madhia* (shrine) for himself, and erects a couple of poles before it. He may furnish it with a wooden ladder, with a *jhūla* (swing), with a *barāhi* (a rope studded with iron spikes), a *gurud* (an iron[2] chain, spiked, having a knob at the end), a *pīdha* (a flat board studded with spikes), and a pair of *karauth* (shoes also covered with spikes). When the god rides upon the *panda*, he may rush up the ladder—not touching it with his hands, he may beat himself with the chains, sit on the *pīdha*, swing violently in his *jhūla*,[3] or walk about on the spiked shoes. He may tie branches of thorns round his body. He does undoubtedly achieve a certain degree of

[1] In the plates facing page 380 which illustrate these rites, the actors are a Gond and a Pardhan, not Baiga, but I have included them to illustrate this kind of divination which these tribes all practise in the same way.

[2] For the power of iron to frighten away evil spirits, see Frazer: *Golden Bough*, iii., p. 234 ff. It is worth noting that the only metal for which there is a Gondi word is iron.

[3] And for a full account of "Swinging as a Magical Rite", see *ibid*, iv. pp. 277–85.

anæsthesia. Then from the top of the ladder, or from the spiked seat, he utters his oracle with great authority.

Phulmat has a shrine of this kind, and people go to her for *dhām* every Monday. Bansi had one till tragedy fell upon him; the childless visit Pachlu every Sunday.

Sometimes, the magician can diagnose witchcraft by the methods we have described, but finds the powers of evil opposed to him too powerful to go further. In such a case he has to employ other means to bring the crime home to the actual culprit. Sometimes "the gunia heats oil on the fire; then he puts a pice into the boiling oil. All the women must come and pull out the pice one by one. If their fingers are burnt, they are innocent; she who feels nothing is the witch".

Lahakat's aunt was a witch. When she was living in Amanala, there had been a lot of sickness and the magician decided that it was due to witchcraft, though he could not name the culprit with any certainty. "He put *marria* flour ready; he gave a mohlain leaf to every woman, and a little flour on every leaf. He told each woman to spit into the flour and mix it into a ball. My mother's sister could not spit properly. Had she spat blood that would also have proved it. So they knew she was the witch. They beat her with branches of the castor tree, for that is the only wood that can hurt a witch, and drove her out of the village."

XIII. THE DUTIES OF THE MAGICIAN: CURE

TREATMENT BY MAKING THE APPROPRIATE OFFERINGS

When the gunia has diagnosed the nature and cause of the disease from which his patient is suffering, he must immediately proceed to take the proper remedies to ensure his recovery. If he diagnoses a definitely supernatural cause, his task, as we have seen, is easy. He asks the sick man to make the offerings prescribed by long custom for every separate spirit of disease; if the sickness is due to Narayan Deo, he fixes a day for the dedication of the Laru; sometimes even the promise of an offering later on, when times are better, is sufficient.

In cases of hernia, it is believed that the swollen member makes a creaking noise, *chi-chi, chuur chuur*, like a man calling for a pig. Once a year, therefore, a pig should be sacrificed to satisfy its demands.

XIV.

TREATMENT BY DRIVING THE DISEASE AWAY

Where witchcraft is diagnosed as the cause of any sickness, and the witch is known, she herself is forced to remove the evil and send it out of the village. This is done in various ways. The most common method is to place the disease or the evil spirit who brought it on a goat or hen, and drive it into the jungle. The same theory underlies the Bida ceremony when all the diseases of the village are carried out in a little cart beyond the boundary line.

Mahatu's experience as a gunia is instructive. "A child in the neighbouring village of Karadih had been very ill for eight days. They sent for me. That night, in the *sūpa*, I compelled the Deshahi to come to me and confess. She said, 'I was playing like a child with a golden *sūpa*, a silver basket and a copper broom, when the witch sent for me. She was a Gondin. She said that she would carry me on her head, and would give me four goats. So I said I would go if she told no one it was me. She swore that she would eat the flesh of her own sister, if she told anyone. Then she took me to the village and made me attack the child.' That was how I discovered that the sickness was due to the Deshahi. But she was angry and escaped me, and attacked everyone so that the whole village fell ill. Then I called her again, and this time she said, 'I am angry because the witch promised me four goats and has only given me two.' When I heard that, I took everyone to the village boundary and promised to punish that deceitful witch and give the Deshahi what she wanted. I went home. All that night I measured my *kāri* and at cock-crow when the cows were loosed and the crows began to caw, at that moment, the Deshahi gave her body to ride upon me. She asked me to give her a black goat, a pig, a necklace and a *tikli*. So I promised her all those things. In the morning, I took a black goat; I put a *tikli* on its forehead and a necklace round its neck. I made it eat some rice and we drove it out of the village. It took all the disease away and the Deshahi too went back to play with the golden *sūpa*, and the silver basket and the copper broom. We killed and ate the pig ourselves."

Note the curiously intimate relations between the gunia and the spirit of disease against whom he is fighting. Note also the normally neutral and innocent character of the Deshahi, playing like a child with her toys, happy and contented, till the witch sent for her and forced her to do mischief to mankind.

Another example comes from Kannat in the Dindori Tehsil.

"Bunbunni Baigin lived in Dumgarh. She came to Kannat, and on her way home took the *bhut* of a pakri tree in Pakrisoda, tied it up in a cloth and kept it for five days in her own house. On the fifth day, five boys got fever and by night they all were dead. There was a famous Dewar in the village, named Solu, and he saw in his *sūpa* that it was Bunbunni who had done this evil, and he named her before all the people. She denied it. But they cut branches of the castor tree, and beat her, until at last she confessed. Then they said she must send the *bhut* away. She asked for four hens and some rice. She fed the hens, and killed three and let one go outside the village. She put the *bhut* on that hen and drove it away."

Colonel Ward found this method used in Mandla seventy years ago.

'Among all the people of Mundla, the Bygas are supposed to have the power of removing diseases from any place. For instance, when a town or village is attacked with cholera, the Bygas are called to the rescue at once; and the people have a thorough belief in their efficacy in cholera epidemics. I have seen the very greatest benefit follow a visit of the Bygas; the people have such confidence in their powers and ceremonies that they lose half their fright at once, and are consequently not so much predisposed to an attack of the disease.

'The proceedings commence by the shrine of Kair Mata being cleaned up for the occasion, the ground freshly plastered with cow-dung, and the stones anointed with vermilion. After sunset the Bygas go round the whole village, through every street, draw from the thatch of each hut a straw, and are supposed to have collected beforehand a sufficient number of young chickens to represent every house; the proper number is one for every house, but much less than that generally suffices. After perambulating the place, they go to Kair Mata's shrine, generally nothing more than a heap of stones under some tree two hundred yards or so to the east of the village. Here the straws drawn from the thatch are laid on the shrine and set fire to with a little ghee, rice, and tumeric; the chickens are touched with vermilion (sendur), offered up on Kair Mata's altar, and driven away in the smoke and darkness; the disease is supposed to follow them.

'If this remedy fails the same ceremonies are gone through, only goats are substituted for chickens; and lastly, as a forlorn hope, pigs are tried, and, as a rule, never fail. The reason of which success is sufficiently obvious, as, the people having to subscribe the articles necessary for the poojah, some little delay always occurs, and then time must be given to watch the effects: so that by the time the pig sacrifice is determined on, the disease has pretty well worn itself out. No animals are killed as sacrifices on these occasions; they are merely let go, and no one knowingly will ever have anything to do with wanderers of this sort: they are left to wander in the wilderness as scapegoats: to meet them on the night they are driven off is supposed to be certain death.

'A great deal of ceremony is attached to their priestcraft, and, as might be expected, considerable expense. For instance, in Mundlah itself, a town of some 8,000 inhabitants, a sum of eighty rupees had to be paid down before the Bygas would undertake the work. It was subscribed readily. Next came a request that the people might be ordered not to leave their houses on the night the Bygas made their rounds, as those who did would surely die. Nothing was done officially, but the people sent the public crier round, and the notice was almost universally respected—only two people venturing out of their houses between sunset and sunrise. It was a strange coincidence that they were the only two people who died of cholera that night, and, naturally, it was a great source of capital to the Bygas, although I believe they do thoroughly believe in their own ceremonials. Their theory is that the devil and all his evil spirits, who are in the habit of spreading cholera, are bound to accompany the Byga priests, to whom certain powers are given over them; and woe betide any person not so gifted who meets the Byga procession, he at once feels the power of the devil, already wroth at having his actions restrained in any way by the Bygas.'[1]

Three other rites are associated with this policy of direct action, *jhāt-pūja* and *jūa-pūja* and the making of a *thūa*. In this case, after the gunia has discovered that a witch has sent the disease whose origin he has been asked to investigate, he proceeds, not to offer sacrifice (as he would if he had traced the disease to some purely supernatural source) but to direct and drastic punishment of the witch, and to a form of sympathetic magic which is expected to remove the evil influence from the victim. I will describe the rites in the very words of my informants.

"In Ragda, an old Baiga had a son in his age and loved him greatly. He had an enemy who was a witch. She hated the boy because he was beautiful. She made magic against him and the boy fell ill. The father called many gunia but they could do nothing. The boy's chest was burning, burning: he could not breathe. At last he died.

"At that very time, one of the gunia told the father that the cause of the boy's illness was this woman, who was indeed his own mother-in-law. When the father saw his beautiful child lying dead, he thought in his mind, 'If she doesn't bring him back to life, I'll kill her.' So he took his bow and arrows and went to his mother-in-law's house and said, 'Make my boy alive again, or I'll kill you.' She cried, 'I'm not the witch. I know nothing about this, or of magic either.' The Baiga was about to shoot her, when the neighbours came running in and stopped him. Then he

[1] Ward: op. cit., pp. 158 f.

took a cudgel of castor wood, and began to beat her. She screamed and wept and at last she promised that the boy would live, 'but first I must do *jhāt-pūja*'.

"So they all went to the house and stood round the child's body. The woman removed some of his pubic hairs. She made a little fire and offered the hairs to the fire, saying, 'Accept this offering; let the boy live.' At once he began to breathe; in an hour's time he was crying for food; in three days he was well.

"This story is true. All of us in Rabda have seen it."

This is an excellent example of what we may call magical procedure, the preliminary consultation with the gunia, his discovery of the culprit, her punishment and promise to undo the wrong, and finally the ceremonies that set things right. This is the normal procedure in all such cases. What varies is the ritual at the end. This may be the sacrifice of a goat or cock; it may be the recital of mantra, the driving of a nail, or some such bizarre and curious rites as these.

Jūa-pūja is apparently quite as effective as *jhāt-pūja*. In a village of Niwas Tehsil we were told how a gunia saved his own son.

"The wife of that gunia was a witch. They had three daughters and two sons. She was always troubling the neighbours, and they often beat her, but it was no good. At last she killed her own eldest son by her magic. The father went away by himself to see who had done this evil. He soon saw in his *sūpa* that it was his own wife. But he could not see what he was to do.

"He came home and tried every kind of offering, but his child lay still and cold. Then at last he saw that he must do *jūa-pūja*. He took lice from the boy's hair, and taking the creature in his hand, nipped off its head between his nails. He had put a fire there, and he let a drop of its blood fall on the fire. Then he wrapped its body in a leaf and carried it to the nearest stream and threw it in. The magic that had killed the child had entered the body of the louse, and it was carried away by the water. When the father returned he found his son breathing and the next day he was well again."

The making of a *thūa* is an important element of Baiga magic. The expression seems to cover any kind of sympathetic magic that aims at removing an evil from a person or a place.

Thus, if anyone is suffering from fever, his neck should be lightly pricked three times with a thorn. The thorn is then taken to a cross-roads and thrown away.

Similarly, if a child cries continuously, or shivers, or has sores in the mouth, the gunia takes a lock of its hair and a little rye in a bit of broken earthenware, waves it round the child and carries it to the nearest cross-roads. He puts it down there, and orders whatever *bhut* was causing the trouble to go away and not return. Then he comes home without ever looking behind him.

Or again, suppose you have a fine pumpkin-bearing creeper, and one of the pumpkins rots and you are afraid the infection will spread, you may make a *thūa* by taking little bits of the rotten pumpkin and mixing them with ash. Then walk towards the sunrise in the early morning, and make seven little heaps of the ash at about twenty yards' intervals. The infection will pass away along the line thus made.

To cure a bubo on the loin, stand the patient in the doorway of his house. Take an axe and touch the bubo and the door-post alternately, five times each. Touch the place once with a burning bhoir stick. Then let the patient cut the stick in half with the axe, and all cry, "Now his disease is cut."

To cure a tertian fever, a woman takes a pot full of rice-water. She tips up the pot, with the lid on, three times and then throws the water away. A neighbour must ask, "What are you doing, mother?" To which she replies, "I'm throwing away the fever."

To cure boils, take the patient to a cross-roads. Collect twenty-one little pebbles. With your eyes shut, touch each boil with a pebble, spit on it, and throw it away. Then go home without looking behind you.

To stop a baby crying, take a black chick to a cross-roads and let it go. The chick cries *chi chi chi* instead of the child.

A *thūa* should always be made on a Sunday or a Wednesday.

One other method of getting rid of an evil magic is to return it to the sender. We have already seen how a gunia who was attacked by his wife's magic in the jungle sent it back. If a witch sends a bat to injure a man, he can likewise return the magic by catching the bat, uttering the proper mantra, and releasing it in the direction from which it came. I have recorded two of these mantra.

> I break its wings.
> I join the broken veins.
> I put Dharma, heavy as a stone, upon it.
> O Pangan Deo, go back, go back.
> Who sent you here?
> Go back, O Pangan Deo, stay here no longer.
> If you don't go back, you will eat the flesh of your guru's wife.
> Who drives him away?
> Daugan guru drives him, and I the guru's pupil.

ii

Atla-damla, ād-bhairo, bād-bhairo!
Another's girl, another boy,
A little girl, a little boy!
Away, away, O horse, and Sahadeo![1]
I will make you fly away.
Go back whence you came.
Do not break any fence on the way.
O Vidya,[2] go back whence you came.

Exorcism is also practised. Where a *bhut* has possessed a man, Jethu recommended the following treatment.

'When a *bhut* attacks a man, take pig's dung and dehwan[3] leaves and rotten coconut, mix them together, put the mixture in a pipe and light it. Let the gunia fill his mouth with smoke, and then blow it up the nose of the victim. Soon the *bhut* begins to feel uneasy. "Yes," he says, "I admit it. I am so-and-so. My home is in such-and-such a place. Forgive me. This is no place for me. I'm off."'

XV.

TREATMENT BY BREAKING THE POWER OF THE WITCH

After the witch has been detected and forced to repair the evil she has done, it is essential to prevent a repetition of the mischief by breaking her power. This is done by defiling her in every way possible.

This is the reason for the rather disgusting treatment of witches, common in the last century, now less frequent, but still occasionally inflicted. She must be made to drink urine from a shoe, her nose is slit—for this inhibits the power of her evil eye, her tongue, breast, thighs may be pricked. She may be forced to eat a mixture of blood and rice, with some pig's dung added; often burning chili, salt, human hair or horse hair, and kodon husks are thrust into her vagina.

The conclusion of the story about Bunbunni illustrates this:

"The villagers slit her forehead, and made her drink her own blood. They put pig's dung and man's dung and a bit of leather into an old shoe with urine, and made her drink it. After that there was no more trouble."

Another curious instance comes from Niwas.

[1] God of horses.

[2] The word *vidya* is used by the Baiga to denote any form of words that has magic properties.

[3] *Cordia macleodii.*

"In Bilgaon was a famous Baiga witch. She came from Chhattisgarh. She could not bear to see a fine young man. She used to turn herself into a tiger or a snake and kill them. When many young men had died in her village, they called gunia but no one could tell who was doing the evil. Then they sent for Baghu Muria, offering him two coconuts and three bottles of liquor. When that witch heard Baghu was coming, she turned herself into a tiger and hid by the way. As Baghu came out of his house, he sneezed, and understood that there was danger. He took his *kāri* and learnt where the witch was hiding. He bound that jungle with mantra, and went on to Bilgaon. Behind the house where Baghu sat with his *sūpa*, the witch sat in her tiger-form, but Baghu bound her with his mantra. When the people saw her, they shouted and ran into their houses, and shut the doors. Baghu came out and cried, "This is not a tiger, this is the murderer. It is a Baigin who has killed your young men." Then he changed her into her own shape, and broke her eyes with his fingers, and urinated in her mouth. She ran into the jungle, and died."

Less drastic treatment was undertaken by Bahadur. He drove the evil magic out of the body of a witch in Baihar.

"I placed a stick of castor against each of her eyes, and made her hold them there. Then I struck her knees three times, twice on the left knee and once on the right knee, with a tamarind stick, and as I did so all the magic passed out of her body into the sticks. Then I tied her eyes with her own *chindhi*. I urinated through the hollow castor sticks, and threw them all away into the river."

XVI.

TREATMENT BY THE USE OF MANTRA

The simple recitation of mantra, without any ceremonies or apparatus, is often effective to defeat the nefarious activities of witches, to drive away troublesome ghosts, to save a man from snake or scorpion bite, or to undo the evil effects of the blistering juice of the bhilwa. In Rabda village in Kawardha State, the Baiga still remember an incident of twenty years ago, which vividly illustrates this point.

"In Rabda there lived a famous Dewar. In the same village was a witch who was continually trying to injure her neighbours. But the Dewar always saved them, and so she began to hate him greatly. One day that witch turned herself into a tiger, and came to kill him when he was working in his bewar. But he bound her by his mantra so that she could not move.

"Another day she changed herself into a snake and went to bite him, but he bound the snake also by his mantra.

"After a time, the Dewar went to visit another village; in the evening he was returning. The witch took the form of a lawa-partridge, and collected many other lawa. They all waited for the Dewar by the side of the road. When he came they all flew into the air with a great whirring noise, and so frightened him that he fell ill and the witch's magic stuck in him.

"After a little while the Dewar died, and was buried. The witch went by night and dug up his body. She made herself naked and let down her hair. She had with her a pot pierced with six holes and a light inside.

"Now the Dewar had two brothers. They learnt in a dream what the witch was doing. They got up and ran to the place and climbed a tree above the grave. But the witch saw them and bound them with her mantra so that they couldn't come down.

"The witch went round the grave five times and danced. She pulled the body out. With her excrement she made an image of Daugan Guru. She made the corpse sit cross-legged, and washed it with her urine. Then the corpse came alive. But even now the Dewar was more powerful than she. She tried to bind him with her mantra, but she couldn't, and he bound her instead.

"Then he freed his brothers and sent them to find his *tuma* which had been hung on a tree near the grave. With this he bound the witch more strongly than before. Then he went to the village and called the people, but when they heard the dead man's voice they dared not come out. The Dewar supposed that they were all bound by the witch's mantra, so he too made mantra to wake them up. Then at last they came and caught that witch by the empty grave.

"They beat her then, and cut open her forehead with a black bangle and gave her water from a shoe to drink. So was that Dewar restored to life and the witch lost all her power.

"Everyone in Rabda village can testify to the truth of the story."

I have recorded the following specimens of mantra used to bind or banish *bhut* and other evil spirits. I am told that by changing a few words they can also be used to bind witches, and of course they are efficacious charms against the witches' familiars.

i

I bind the sharp end of a knife.
I bind the glow-worm in the forehead.
I bind the magic of nine hundred guru.
I bind the familiars of nine hundred witches.
I bind the fairies of the sky.

I bind Samduria of the ocean.
I bind Meraria of the boundary line.
I bind Paniharin of the bathing ghat.
I bind Ghataria of the hill.
I bind Nar-singh of the road.
I bind Kohaiya of the pathway.
I bind the Churelin of the lanes.
I bind Thakur Deo in his shrine.

As I take the net to catch fish, so will I catch all witches.
I the guru's pupil catch them.

Let the sky turn upside down, let the earth be overturned, let horns grow on horse and ass, let moustaches sprout on a young girl, let the dry cow-dung sink and the stones float, but let not this charm fail.

ii

I bind the glow-worm of a virgin.
I bind every kind of *massan*.
The nail of bone!
The lamp of flesh!
Who binds the spirits?
The guru binds and I the guru's pupil.
May the waters of the river flow uphill! May the dry cow-dung sink and the stones float!
But let not my words fail.
See, O see, O mantra, my own child, my mantra!
Endure strong as a mountain!
May there be no error in my words.

iii

The blanket of the *bhut*! The bedding of the *bhut*!
The food of the *bhut*! Away with it!
O *bhut*, away, away!
May he be crushed by my teeth!
May he be drowned in twelve pots of water!
That water I will drink.
O *bhut*, away! away!!
I am coming! I the son of Daugan guru!
I will be there very soon.
The earth trembles beneath me, the earth quakes at my coming.
O *bhut*, become a rabbit and run away!
Become a deer and run away!
For I am coming without delay.

Recitation of these mantra is generally accompanied by a simple ritual. The gunia offers fire and incense, and perhaps a coconut. He treats the coconut as if it were a living creature, holds it between his hands and rubs its 'nose' in a pile of rice. After a time he picks up a little rice and, pulling back some of the hair of the coconut, slips the rice beneath it as if he were feeding it. Then he pulls off two or three tufts of hair from the back of the coconut's 'neck', and smashes it on a stone. This is exactly how he prepares a chicken for sacrifice.

Then the gunia stands on one leg and recites his mantra, frequently repeating parts of it, especially such expressions as "Go away!" or "I drive you away!" Then he cries out loudly, claps his hands, and shoos the unseen herd of spirits from before him.

Sometimes, when matters are very serious, the gunia drives a nail into the ground, just as if he were stopping an earthquake or repairing the magic boundaries of the village. He may perhaps sacrifice a goat or pig. Then he uses the following mantra.

A broken shoe!
The nine iron needles!
With these I bind the spirits.
I bind the *bhut*, the *pret*, the *mua*, the *massan*, the *deo*, the *pangan*.
Who binds them?
The guru binds them, and I the guru's pupil.
Immortal nail!
Immortal charm!

There are a number of mantra for use on special occasions.

INJURY BY A MUA

When the gunia traces the origin of a man's disease back to a *mua*, the ghost of a child who has died without speaking, the following mantra are used.

i

Come Aghori Baba, Tapsi Baba, Latadhari Baba with matted hair, Gola Bharati Baba! Come, run to the front! The guru binds! I the guru's pupil bind! May the immortal nail I drive be never loosed. The never-dying speech, the never-dying Moon and Sun and Thakur Deo! O Thakur Deo, thou art master of the village. Do not allow *bhut* or *pret* or *mua* to come into this village. I will now test thy power, and then give thee an offering of a speckled goat. I will make the blood flow. I will give twelve cart-loads of incense and thirteen cart-loads of offerings.

ii

Come, Dongra Pat! Come, Dharti Mata! Come, Nanga Baiga and Nanga Baigin! Come! I drive the nail. Come Pira Pat! I remember Dharti Mata and Moon and Sun! Don't let my words be falsified. This is the service of the five fingers. This is the prayer of the ten fingers. Thy sputum is my feast, thy urine is the gargle of my throat, I am the dirt and dust of thy body. I have said that I am thy slave.

SCORPION-BITE

During the recitation of this mantra, the patient's limb should be carefully massaged towards the extremities in order to bring the poison down.

Come, black scorpion! Come, red scorpion! O scorpion looking like the tail of a hen! Let the poison come down, O scorpion! Let it come down, wandering. Your bite is of gold; we are bringing you down with a silver broom. Come down from the bones. Who brings you down? The guru brings you down, and I the guru's pupil. Let no poison remain in the whole body!

TO STOP BLEEDING

When a man is cut by an axe or knife, this mantra should be used to staunch the flow of blood.

Ram aims at a phadki, but Lakshman binds the bow. Who binds? The guru binds, and I the guru's disciple. As a leaf flies into the air, so let this injury fly away. As a stone sinks in water, so let it sink. Let the poison go to its own place.

TO CURE BHILWA-BLISTERING

A rather unexpected mantra is used to counteract the effects of the *semicarpus anacardium*, the bhilwa or marking-nut. The juice of the pericarp of the bhilwa is frequently used by the Baiga, as indeed all over India, as a counter-irritant. In unskilful hands, its use leads to serious blistering. Some people are said to be affected by the smoke of the burning wood, or even the shadow of the tree. It is used medically on the abdomen for affections of the spleen and liver, in the lumbar region, and on the shoulders and limbs, specially in the sterno-clavicular articulations, for rheumatism, generally some form of gonorrhœal arthritis which is common among the Baiga. Persistent application of the expressed juice or frequent rubbing with the bruised pericarp 'leaves a smooth cicatrice of satiny texture, without raised edges'.[1] The Baiga have possibly an additional reason for disliking

[1] See Codrington: *The Use of Counter-Irritants in the Deccan*, J.R.A.I., Vol. LXVI, 369 ff.

the bhilwa, for it was the means by which Mahadeo and Parvati tricked Nanga Baiga and Nanga Baigin, and made their all-seeing eyes as weak as those of other men.

The following mantra is used:

> I pick the bhilwa, I remove the stone, I take out the seed! The guru sows it and I the guru's disciple sow it. By my sowing it will be sown. I blow the seed away. The guru blows it and I the guru's pupil. By my blowing, let it not ripen; by my blowing, let it not increase! May it stick to the tree like *lac*! May it quickly wither! When it grows, may the flower be broken; when it comes to fruit, may the branch fall. When it dries, let it wither away!

BURNS

In cases of burning, Jethu has found the following mantra efficacious:

> Come guru, guru my servant, come guru. Who binds? The guru binds. Whom does he bind? He binds the God of Fire (Agindeo). As I bind the hand of the God of Fire, so bind the fire in his (the victim's) hand. I bind the burning fire. As I wrap him in cloth, so in the cloth let him be cooled. As the sea is cold, so let this burnt man be cold. Who cools him? Lanjha Guru cools him, whose disciple I am. I rouse Aginjhar Guru. By my aid, let this sick man satisfy his hunger, let him sleep his fill, let him have no pain. I bind the poison, I bind the fire. As water cools, so let the sick man cool.

XVII.

TREATMENT BY THE JAGAR

This is the classical treatment for snake-bite. A number of men gather round the victim and begin to sing mantra. As they continue, the rhythm of the music affects the more sensitive among them and Nag Deo climbs on one of the *barua* who falls on the ground, and contorts himself in the usual manner. Presently he goes to the victim, sucks blood and poison from the wound and spits it out into a pot of milk. Then he throws himself on the ground and counts very quickly, "One, two, three . . ." up to twenty and cries, "*Hāk pare Daugan guru ke jāg chēt samhār.* (This is the bidding of Daugan Guru! Arise! Attend! Beware!)" Then he jumps up and sucks the blood again, repeating the whole process three or four times. While he is doing so, the onlookers sing with increased vigour and play on the drums.

Baghela Muria was cured of the bite of a witch-snake by this method.

The following mantra are sung at the *jāgar.* They are also used privately and can be repeated as a protection when one is going through the jungle.

Kos! Kos! Twelve *kos!* Twenty-four *kos!* Fifty-two *kos!* At the fifty-second *kos* was found the *kurupbān*, the *aginbān*, the *chakarbān*. O snakes, your god is the lawa-titur! My guru is the chechan eagle (who kills snakes). When it flies, I destroy its flesh; when it sits, I cut off its legs. May the one and a quarter *seer* of poison turn into water for me!

ii

In the Kajli-ban-kachar may the snake be crushed and killed! If any poison yet remains, I have wisdom. May my cry reach the god who breaks stones. Here am I, O Guru Dhan Singh! May the *seer* and a quarter of poison come out, and go down into the earth with Buddha Nag!

iii

May the poison come out and his body grow cool as water!
May the aches in every part of his body,
And the pain in his belly be stilled!
May he once more bathe his body!
May he once more take his food!
May he once more walk in his courtyard!
May he once more walk in the forest and the open field!
There may the tiger and the bear
Turn into stones before him!
May every snake become a stick!
May thorns and stubble melt like wax!
When he walks by night, let him not go as an ant,
Stumbling on his way!
May light dawn on him!

XVIII. PROPHYLACTIC MAGIC

Many charms are used for prophylaxis. They are then generally called *dawai*, medicine. The *bach*, a jungle herb, is worn round the neck tightly wrapped into a little bundle with a bit of cloth, to stop fever. Or a small piece of the bone of a jadhdhu snake may be strung on a thread and worn round the neck.

For preventing cough, some smoke-black from the kitchen roof is mixed with turmeric and tied up with a rag, and put round the neck.

Over the doors of houses in Bohi I observed a number of charms. Deriya, who is subject to bad dreams, had tied the *takri* (Fig. 21) over his

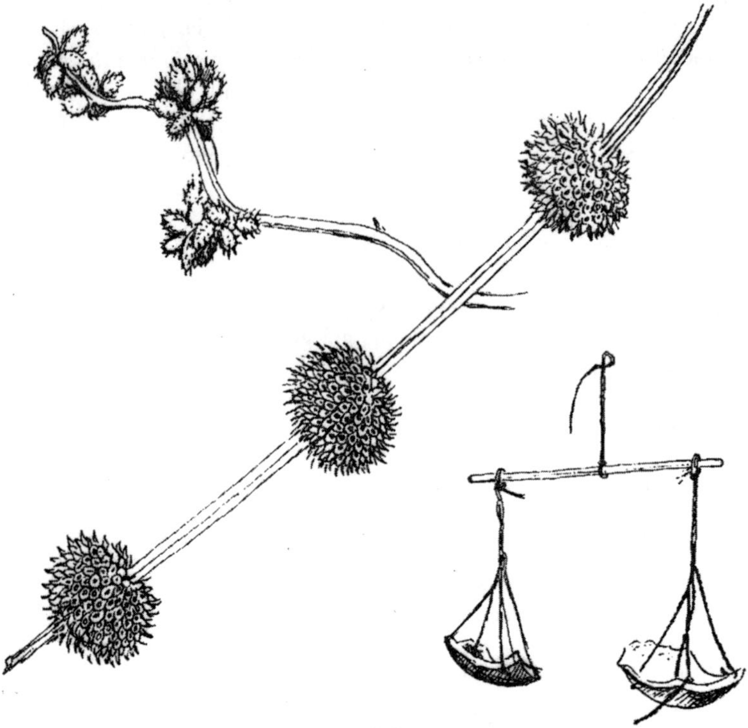

FIG. 21. *Prophylactic charms.*

door—a tiny pair of scales made from a gourd. The idea is that when the *churelin* or other spirit enters the house their attention is caught by the toy, and they begin to weigh themselves in it, and soon forget all about their original purpose.

Jethu had a round spiky ball, like a great thistle, over his door. This is the *gohana* which prevents fever entering the house. In another building I saw a spray of the herb they call *chula kānta* and in another a branch of *satbela* to stop arthritis (Fig. 21).

In the house of a Binjhwar Baiga of Niwas, I saw an eagle's feather above the door. The bird's bones were ground and a little tied round the neck of a child to ward off magic and disease. In Jholar (Baihar) I saw a very large wild onion hanging from the roof of the cattle-shed. This was intended to keep away foot-and-mouth disease.

A woman who wishes to suckle her child on a journey can protect it by squeezing out a little milk and spitting on it three times.

For a protection against snakes, there is no better method than to tie a mantra in the little tuft of hair that is always allowed to grow on the back of the head. The tuft must be knotted in one breath, the mantra being repeated mentally at the same time.

> *Sirseti gur gur chanda tap karē tap ki massan.* Where Basuk Nag sways to and fro! Bhawar Nag! Kesra Nag! Come, my guru! May the *seer* and a quarter of poison turn into water before me! Let it turn into pure water! Jadhdhu Nag! Kala Nag! Sua Nag! Bhuiludi Nag! Go away to Buddha Nag!
>
> I bind *andhan*! I bind *bhandan*! Beat the life in the head! O guru, Hansan Thakur! Come guru, remove the poison!

In March, 1938, Mithu's house was the target of a good deal of hostile magic. His wife fell very ill, and his fruit-tree withered. So he made a monkey out of straw: it looked like the combination of a lizard and a goat; it had a beard of black goat's hair. The 'monkey' was hung up in the garden, in the belief that when the magic saw the black beard of the monkey, it too would become black, and thus powerless. The Baiga have many other ways of protecting the *bāri*. They stick an old broom and a charred log in the middle of the tobacco patch. Then as the log is black, so any magic that comes near will turn black and disappear. The head of a dead buffalo also frightens away magic which would be defiled by touching bone. To protect fruit or creepers on the house, the people draw patterns in white and red dust on an old earthen pot, and put it on the roof. When the evil magic comes, it plays with the different colours and forgets to do any harm.

Mantra can also be used to ward off evil and disease.

To prevent a dog-bite, this mantra is repeated hurriedly as the animal approaches:

> The snapping of the dog's jaws! I break the nails in its four feet. Into its privates I thrust a handful of iron nails.

Another mantra prevents an epidemic of *dhuki*, which may be cholera or influenza.

> Bind them body and soul! Bind Jalhain, goddess of water! Bind the *bhut*! Bind the *pret*! Bind the *mua*! Bind the *devi*! Bind the *massan*. Bind the *dhuki*! Bind the *bīr*! Bind the evil eye! Bind the *dīth*![1] Who binds them? The guru binds them! I the guru's pupil bind them!

[1] A *dith* is a squint, for one of the eyes of a squinting person is always full of magic.

XIX. PRESCRIPTIONS

The supernatural remedies that we have described are nearly always enforced by jungle medicines. The Baiga have a very large number of these at their disposal, and I will quote some of them in a moment. A great many of the herbs used by them have long been recognized in Indian medicine.

The large number of remedies for venereal disease may reflect its widespread incidence. The use of black pepper as a cure for syphilis may have a magical significance, a hot remedy for a hot (the word *garmi* simply means heat) disease. Other medicines are certainly based on imitative magic—the use of the spotted leaves of the *phadūkanār* to cure the bite of the spotted *jadhdhu* snake[1]; the use of a twig of pipal, whose leaves tremble even when there is no wind, to rouse a man who suffers from excessive sleepiness; the tying of a gaily-coloured girl's *phundara* round a scorpion-bite.

The advice to put some of the medicine up the nose in case of snakebite is widely observed in India.

These remedies have been collected from all over the Baiga country, except from Balaghat and Jubbulpore.

For syphilis

1. Roots of ban semar (*galactia tenuiflora*), hasiyadaphar (*baliospermum axillare*). Grind these up together and make the powder into pills with *gur*. Give one every morning for twenty-one days.

2. Fruit of bel (*aegle marmelos*), bark of dudhia (*holarrhena antidysenterica*), seeds of ghol (*portulaca oleracea*), some black pepper. Dry, grind and mix together. Put in milk and drink. This is an excellent remedy for the gummata, but for a permanent cure:

3. Gum of dikamali (*gardenia lucida*) put on the wounds.

4. Root of indravan (*coccinia indica*) cut up and made into pills with *gur*.

5. Root of kachnar (*bauhinia purpurea*), black pepper, the tongue of a tiger. Dry, grind, and make twenty-five pills with *gur*, to be taken twice a day.

6. Root of akol (*alangium lamarckii*), black pepper. Grind, strain, drink in water twice a day for a week.

7. Bark of anjan lokaria (*tephrosia purpurea*), black pepper. Dry, grind very fine, mix with water and strain. Drink twice a day for a week.

[1] Perhaps the *daboia elegans*.

Milward

The magic monkey described on p. 397.
Woman at Lamni drying harra. (Note the pīdha seat in the left foreground.)

For gonorrhœa

1. Steep the rhizome of kurkoti (*pachystoma senile*) for a night in water. Add sugar and black pepper.

2. Root of bhawarsal (*hymenodictyon excelsum*), the ripe fruit of dhanbaker (*cassia fistula*). Crush them together, mix the expressed juice with water.

3. Root of ramdatan (*smilax macrosphylla*), seeds of lalphatta (*panicum crus-galli*). Grind together, boil in water. Cool and drink for three days.

4. Grind the seed of chandarjot (*jatropha curcas*); add sugar and water. Filter through a cloth and drink.

For dhāt (gleet) and parmi (chronic gonorrhœa)

1. Bark of dudhia (*holarrhena antidysenterica*), root of khamer (*gmelina arborea*). Grind and give to drink in milk.

2. Bark of behera (*terminalia belerica*), tendu (*diospyros melanoxylon*), a little plant called muhmundi (*thespesia lampas*) that grows in swamps. Mix, dry, grind, make pills the size of a *tikli* with *gur*.

For restriction of urine (patthari).

The stone in the head of a saur fish. Grind this and give in water for five days. Without it, there is no hope for the patient.

For itch

Dig a hole in the ground and put a pot in it. Cover its mouth with a dish which has a hole in the middle. Put some dry gum of the sarai (*boswellia serrata*) tree on the dish. Cover this again with another dish and place glowing coals upon it. The gum melts and drips slowly into the pot, after which it may be rubbed into the affected parts.

For diarrhœa

1. Bark of saj (*terminalia tomentosa*), tinsa (*ougeinia dalbergioides*), karar (*bauhinia purpurea*). Pound up together with water. Let it stand all day. Drink in evening.

2. Kadadhari plant (*eleusine aegyptiaca?*). Grind it, mix with buttermilk and drink.

3. Chew the bark of karikorai (*holarrhena antidysenterica*).

4. Root of kassi (*bridelia retusa*). Give it to eat. It is very good for stomach-ache.

For sleepiness

Take and use a twig of pipal (*ficus religiosa*). Then as the leaves of the pipal tremble without wind, the patient will be alert and awake always.

For impotence

1. Tuber of black musri (*curculigo orchioides*). Give to eat on an empty stomach.

2. The liver of a sparrow, or other small bird, eaten daily.

For sore eyes

Fruit of the aonla (*emblica officinalis*). Grind it up and make a poultice for application to the eyes.

For cough

1. The expressed juice of harra fruit (*terminalia chebula*).

2. Once when I was suffering from a very bad cough, Mahatu recommended me to take turmeric and chillies in a pot of boiling milk.

For headache

1. Leaves of amli (*bauhinia malabarica*). Grind, mix in cold water, and apply to forehead.

2. Leaves of jhunjhunia (*phoenix acaulis*). Crush the leaves and make a poultice for the head.

For broken bones

1. Take the creeper called harsingri (*nyctanthes arbor-tristis*) and apply it to the fractured part, tying it on firmly. Also give a little of it to eat.

2. Make some *pūri* (flat wheat cakes) and take the bark of bija (*pterocarpus marsupium*) and tie it on affected part.

For the paralysis called by the Baiga chingran bād, where the patient sits all day hunched up and cannot stretch himself.

1. Bees' wax, fruit of the pipal (*ficus religiosa*), fruit of the karaiyu (*miliusa jelutina*). Mix and grind. Make an ointment with ramtilla oil (*guzotia abyssinica*).

2. Bhimka roots and karela (*momordica charantia*). Dry, mix, grind. Make into pills with ramtilla oil, and give five a day for three days.

For nausea

Kosanar plant (*coix lacryma-jobi*). Grind, and give to drink in water.

For fever.

1. Take the leaves of the gurbel creeper (*tinospora cordifolia*), pound them, and boil them in water. Bathe the patient in this, and also give a little to drink. "When the evil spirit sees the water of gurbel, it leaves the sufferer."

2. Take twigs about a hand long from near the trunk of the bara osai (*vitex peduncularis?*), pound them up, and boil all night in water, which becomes red. Bathe the patient in this, and give some to drink.

3. Grind up the root of tikur (*curcuma angustifolia*). Make poultice and apply to head.

For rheumatism

Rub ashes on to the painful place and drink as much liquor as possible (Pachlu's remedy).

For scorpion-bite

1. Ground flowers of mahua (*bassia latifolia*) applied as a poultice, and some mahua liquor taken internally.

2. Roots of the birhol (*indigofer pulchella*). Pound them up, and apply to the place. After a time apply a bit of old coconut.

For centipede-bite

Tie a girl's bright-coloured *phundara* round the place.

For snake-bite[1]

For a black snake. 1. The seeds of karu turai (*luffa acutangula*) ground and made into pills with *ghī*.

2. The bark of tendu (*diospyros melanoxylon*), and char (*buchanania latifolia*). Grind and give some to drink in water. Stuff a little up the nostrils.

3. The root of the chandar-nar (*ficus hispida*). Grind and give to drink in water.

For a putki snake (a small jumping snake). The root of the chandar-nar.

For the jadhdhu snake (long, khaki-coloured, with spots). The leaves and roots of the phaduka creeper. These leaves have spots on them like the spots on the snake. Pound them up and drink them in water.

For the dandarkarail snake (a black snake about three feet long, black with white bands). Take sukla grass (*andropogon contortus*) which is growing on a stone. Add the root of the daukidoto creeper (*vitis latifolia*) that is growing out of an anthill. Grind, give to drink, and stuff some up the nostrils.

XX. THE BIDA RITES

Two important public ceremonies are connected with the prevention and cure of disease, the annual ritual at the Dassera Festival, and the occasional ceremony of the Laru-kaj.

The Baiga celebrate Dassera in October, but not on the same day as their Hindu neighbours, and with a wholly different purpose. For the Hindus, the Dassera Festival is the autumn Saturnalia celebrating the return of fertility. It is associated with Rama's conquest of Ceylon, and the triumph of Kali over the buffalo demon. Every caste worships its implements; they look out for the nilkanth, and compose their quarrels.

For the Baiga, however, apart from general dancing and jollity in sympathy with their neighbours, the Dassera ceremony is associated with public health. It is the great prophylactic, a sort of sanitation drive along the super-normal boundaries of the world. The experiences of the past

[1] In the folk-tales there is a legendary cure of snake-bite by stuffing the root of the phang creeper (*rivea hypocraterformis*) up the victim's nostrils.

year are recollected; the gunia recall all the *deshahi, piri, bhut, pret, churelin, raksa, mua,* or *massan* that are suspected to have visited the village in the past year, or may even now be haunting its borders. On the Dassera day, a Dewar comes to advise on the correct offering to be made to these hostile powers in order to persuade them to leave the village. In any case, offerings must be made to Thakur Deo, for he is the protector, and with a chicken to the *deshahi* and a coconut for the *bhut*, the village is spiritually disinfected.

I have assisted at this ceremony many times, in Karanjia, in Sanhrwachhapar, in Bohi. In Bohi, at the end of October, 1937, the Bida, as it is called, was celebrated in the early morning of the day after the funeral ceremonies described in another chapter. A few people gathered in front of Jethu's house, and prepared a little cart made of bamboo sticks and wheels of sarai bark. Round it they set up a number of *tirsul*, bamboo sticks shaped to represent the tripod. Some of these had a few peacocks' feathers tied to the top, all were liberally plastered with sendur. They tied a black bangle, a *sarria*, and a *tikli* to the cart.

Gradually most of the villagers collected; there was at least one representative of each house—though no women were present—and each brought a small leaf-cup of parched gram, and a broken broom. Into the cups they had put whatever spirit had been troubling their house in the past year. These were all placed round the cart.

Then Jethu's son took a large earthen pot, or rather the broken lower section of one, and put fire in it. Jethu came and sat by, and after saying a number of the customary mantra, offered *ghī* and coconut to the broken pot, which is called the *khappar*. Afterwards he pulled up one of the *tirsul* and planted it in the pot.

On this occasion, the *barua* did not come upon anyone. Sometimes, the god rides on a man in the usual fashion, and then everyone goes to him, and offers him coconut, begging him to save them from their diseases.

But as this did not happen, Jethu's son picked up the *khappar*, and another boy pulled the *tirsul* out of the ground and laid them with the little leaf-cups on the cart, and picked it up. Then these two went ahead, a third youth sweeping the path as he went along with one of the old brooms, and the rest of us followed out through the forest to the boundary mark to the east of the village. The main party did not actually go very far, but the three youths went away to the boundary, and there threw away the little cart and the broken pot, with, of course, all the little leaf-cups containing the various spirits that had been invading the village. These were now banished. The path had been swept clean. The three youths returned, taking care not to look behind them, for fear that they should bring the spirits along with

Panku of Bohi carrying the khappar to the village boundary at the Bida ceremony.

them back to the village. Sometimes, the gunia also goes to the boundary and drives twenty-one nails, either iron or bamboo, into the ground, and buries a coconut there. But this was not done at Bohi.

When the three boys returned, the Dewar Jethu and two or three assistants proceeded to sacrifice a number of chickens to Thakur Deo, Dharti Mata, and several other deities. This was done in the usual manner to the recitation of the following mantra:

> Barahin of twelve villages! Galiain of the road! Deshahi who wanders through every village! Sadakain of the highway! Phatkahin of the gate! O twelve hundred dancers of the Dassera! O sixteen hundred breakers of bamboo! O Khairkoti Khair Bhavani! You know the evils that threaten us. We black-faced men know nothing. You alone can drive away all evil. Away! Away!! Away!!!

When the chickens had all been killed the older men got up and returned to the village. I was following them, when I noticed the boys scrambling for the bodies of the chickens. When they had all been collected—and they were very tiny chickens—the boys made a fire, and began to roast them. Even the heads were roasted—a twig was stuck into the head (which had been twisted off) and it was held over the fire. The bodies were held in the flames, first to singe off the feathers and then, more slowly, to cook the flesh. The boys were tremendously excited over this. Jethu's son and the others who had just taken a leading part in the most solemn rite of the year, went to it with as much enthusiasm as the children of six and seven. When the chicks were ready, a boy collected them, and distributed them on little leaves. We each got a small bit of burnt and smoked flesh and bone. But the boys were delighted, and chewed everything up, even the heads and bones.

XXI. THE LARU-KAJ

The Laru-kaj is probably the most ancient of all Baiga rituals; the method of killing the pig by crushing or bumping it to death suggests that it originated at a time when the tribe did not possess cutting instruments of iron. The aim of the rite was to appease by a kind of bargain a demon of disease who, formerly free to travel about the world with his fellows, was confined by them for misbehaviour in the threshold of men's houses. But he was no household god like Dulha Deo, trusted and revered; he was placed on the threshold and everyone who went in or out was to give him a hearty kick. The full story is given in Chapter XI where the demon is called Narayan Deo or Bara Deo, these two being often identified in the modern Baiga mind. Narayan Deo is, of course, a name of the Sun, but the Baiga, who in any case are never much interested in extra-mundane phenomena, seem to have adopted him quite fortuitously without any special reference to the Sun, in the same way that they have now identified him with Bara Deo.

I think it is likely, in spite of Russell,[1] who seemed to regard it as a form of Sun-worship, that the Laru-kaj has nothing whatever to do with the Sun. From time to time the unpleasant disease-demon called Narayan Deo-Bara Deo attacks a man or woman; it seizes them by the throat and prevents them from swallowing food. The gunia is called in and 'looks' in his *kāri* and *sūpa-tuma* to see what is the matter. If the gunia sees that it is Narayan Deo-Bara Deo who is causing the trouble, he at once—and this procedure must invariably follow such a diagnosis—proceeds to make a bargain that if the sufferer recovers but not otherwise, he will dedicate a Laru pig to the honour of the despised demons. A pig is not, of course, an unclean animal to the Baiga, but the most useful and favourite of his pets.

If the sick man recovers, his family at once, but on a Monday, take a pig to the threshold of their house and cow-dung the ground. They make a small square with wheat flour and spread some rice, cooked and uncooked together, upon it. A smouldering lump of dry cow-dung is put by the side. They hold the pig in front of the square and drop a little *ghī* on the fire, saying, "With a happy mind eat this rice. We put our trust in you. From to-day may our children live happily."

If Narayan Deo intends to give more trouble, the pig refuses to eat the rice that is in front of it. It is then necessary to produce liquor and coconuts. It is sometimes the most tedious business waiting for the pig to eat. The gunia holds it in his hands, stroking and coaxing it with a stream of mantra, he rubs its nose in the rice, he adds a little *ghī*, sometimes a handful of kodon, he pours water on it to make it more appetizing, but the frightened pig often takes no notice, and it may be an hour or two before it swallows a little of the rice. Directly the pig has eaten, the people take two *mūsar*, or rice-pounders and crush the creature's testicles between them. They cut off a bit of the tail, and sometimes a bit of the left ear, and bury these in a little hole in the middle of the square; this is filled up with mud, and liquor is sprinkled over it. Then the pig is carried to the rice-bin and touched with it three times.

Now the pig is Narayan Deo's *sawāri*, on which he can ride, and must be carefully guarded. It is often kept shut up—at least, that is the modern

[1] Russell and Hiralal: op. cit. ii. 85 and iii. 101.

custom—and given the best food. It must never be given leavings from the household table.

When three years have passed, the household prepares plenty of *kodai* and rice, and gets in a store of liquor. They invite their friends and relations, and on a Saturday begin the Laru-kaj.[1]

On one side of the courtyard of the house, a big pit is made with some logs across its mouth, and a small hole about a foot square and a foot deep is dug before the door. These are both known as the *narda*. Inside the house, a *samdhi* of the man who was sick prepares the *phulera* with bel leaves. This is a sort of swing which is tied with *haldi*-coloured thread to the pole in the middle of the house. Immediately below it, the women cow-dung the floor and make a square with flour, tracing round it all kinds of fantastic designs, and in the middle of the square they put rice and a small fire.

The chief actors in the drama nearly all stand in some special relationship to the man who was formerly sick. The Dewar gunia may, of course, be anyone, but the *kamri* who will be the first to touch the flesh of the pig must be the man's *samdhi*; the *barua*—who should be three in number, and must be men liable to spirit-possession—must belong to the same *goti* as himself, and the two old people who will handle the *phulera* should if possible stand to him in the relationship of classificatory grandfather and grandmother. All these people have to fast declaring, "To-day we do the Laru-kaj in truth." And when the ceremony is over and the feast begins, these must eat last of all.

The pig is caught and dragged squealing to the door. Once more rice is put before it, and the Dewar cries, "Look, *mahārāj*, to-day we give you rice. Don't give us any trouble." Directly it eats even so much as a mouthful of the rice, it is lifted up and its front legs are tied. A lighted lamp in an iron vessel is waved round the creature three times. Its mouth is forced open with two bamboo sticks and more rice is pushed into it. Boiling water is poured over its phallus, and allowed to run into the hole in the ground before the door. Then three men, holding the pig by its two hind legs and buttocks, push the pig's head into the hole which is now half full of water. Earth from the sides is shovelled in so that no air can reach its nostrils. The squealing stops abruptly though the animal's struggles are redoubled. Then the men begin to bump it up and down in the hole. The bumping is not sufficient to cause death, which is due to suffocation,

[1] Should the pig die before the three years are concluded, another must be given. Should someone kill it by mistake, he must replace it, or Narayan Deo will attack him. It goes without saying that Narayan Deo keeps his part of the bargain and refrains from troubling any member of the household during the three years of the pig's dedication. The Laru-kaj is thus a prophylactic against disease, as well as a cure.

and in about ten minutes the pig's struggles cease and it is carried out to be washed and singed. While this is going on, all the women present throw wet cow-dung and other refuse over the men, and scream insults at them, and they sing what Russell calls a sacrificial hymn.[1] This is the hymn:

Ter nā ni nā O! Ter nā ni nā O!
Make a hole in the big gourd. I will go for water.
The old mother blows me out of the house.
O ter nā ni nā O!
The leaves of the parsa tree have long stalks.
You've been lying with your son.
I am going to cut my bewar.
You've been sleeping with your brother.
I am busy making rope.
You've been lying with your sister's son.
I am roasting gram.
I am lying with you, and your mother's watching us.
I am cutting wood for the fire.
You've been lying with a little boy.
Ter nā ni nā O! Ter nā ni nā O!

When the pig has been washed and its hair singed off over a fire, they drag its body to the larger *narda* and cut it up, allowing the blood to fall into the pit. The grandfather and grandmother wrap up the head and the liver in mahua and bel leaves and put the bundle in the swing. As they do so, they sing:

Bring water, bring water! I'll wash his feet with water.
Bring oil, bring oil! I'll wash his feet with oil.
Bring milk, bring milk! I'll wash his feet with milk.
Teri nā ho! Nā nā re nā! Teri nā nā mor nā nā!
To-day is Saturday, this is the night for the Laru!
We put the *belwanti* on the feet of the god.
I make a square of pearls.
O master, sit here on your throne.
Tare nake nāmāre nāna saheb! Tare nake nāmāre nāna!

When the *phulera* begins to swing of its own accord, they know that

[1] Another method, which is the one described by Russell, was to crush the pig to death. This is still sometimes followed. "The pig is laid across the threshold of a doorway on its back, and across its stomach is placed a stout plank of *saja* wood. Half a dozen men sit or stand on the ends of this, and the fore and hind feet of the pig are pulled backwards and forwards alternately over the plank until it is crushed to death, while all the men sing or shout a sacrificial hymn." Russell and Hiralal, op. cit. ii. 85: My own informants tell me that it is a log of *char* wood which is invariably used, but this doubtless varies from place to place.

. *The sacrifice of the Laru-pig.*
Feeding the pigs at Bohi.

Narayan Deo has come. They shout with triumph and throw a lot more dung about and sing:

Ter nāna ke nāno ho!
Where were you born? Where is your dwelling-place?
I was born down below. I live on the fence.
I am going to live with you.
Then I'll sleep with your sister.
O Phulera, dance and dance again.
Are you cooking in your kitchen?
May a cat dishonour you!
Don't have an old woman, she looks so very dirty.
By enjoying young girls, my life is satisfied.
Bring the root of adrak: may your father have you!
Where are you off to, girl?
May your brother dishonour you!

Then the pig is cooked, and the *kamri* makes divisions of the flesh in the names of all the *devata*, in the name of Narayan Deo, of Mai Dharti, of Bara Deo, of Bal Raja and Bal Rani, of Bala Bhimsen, of Ugat ka Raja, and of Nanga Baiga and Nanga Baigin. While this is going on, excitement outside has gradually been increasing. The three *barua* are being 'ridden' by the gods and are dancing, shaking their heads and throwing their arms about with convulsive gestures. Everybody is singing, screaming *gāli*, and getting drunk.

A plate of meat and a basket of rice is placed beneath the swing. Eight men come in and sit all round and leaves are put ready on the floor. Then the old woman and the *kamri* and any strangers present distribute the meat, a share of rice and four scraps of meat for every household. Then they all have their supper, and when everyone else has eaten, the Dewar and those who have been fasting with him have their share. At the time of eating, they sing another song.

First you enjoy her, and then you regret it.
But why be angry with me,
For am I not your husband?
On the black bitch's neck there is a ring.
Ter nāna ke nāno ho!

After supper, there is generally dancing throughout the night.

The Laru-kaj is thus not a form of Sun-worship: it is a valuable prophylactic and cure of certain diseases. It belongs to the medical science of the Baiga rather than to their theology.

Chapter XIV

DREAMS

1. THE ADVENTURES OF THE JĪV

LIKE many other primitive peoples the Baiga enjoy a double experience of reality, both entirely 'true' as they say, though never confused, experienced by the self under different forms. When a man dreams, his *jīv*, the life-principle which is the immortal part of him, capable of reincarnation, which resides in his body as a little fly or glow-worm, leaves his body lying still in the dark secrecy of his hut, and flies out in search of adventure. Sometimes the *jīv* takes the form of a grasshopper, sometimes of a little bird. "It flies here and there," says Pachlu. "It perches on a tree, gets frightened, flies away; it floats on the water, it doesn't sink. I feel very happy as I fly about." The separation of body and soul presents no problem to the Baiga. Some of the heroes of the folk-tales keep their *jīv* permanently outside their bodies in a secret place for safety.

The dream adventures of the *jīv* are never confused with those of waking life, yet they are entirely real and significant. The *jīv* sits and talks to people; it searches for food and enjoys it; dead parents come with warning and advice; and if there is any disdainful hostile girl, the *jīv* goes to her and wins in sleep what it could never gain by day. Should the *jīv* be caught by a tiger, the man will die. Sometimes people wake aching all over with the wounds that their *jīv* have suffered during a dream. But there is a clear distinction. No one will be taken to court for giving an enemy a beating during a dream. There is no punishment for adultery or incest committed by the *jīv*. There is an obvious difference between a dream tiger and a 'waking tiger'. Perhaps the distinction is not so much in the tiger as in the seer. In both cases the tiger is real—there it is—you can see it But in a dream only part of the man has the experience; in the waking state both body and soul enjoy it.

At all events, whatever the *jīv* sees in a dream has significance, sometimes it is a symbolic, sometimes a prophetic significance. There is a regular code of interpretation.

II. PROPHETIC INTERPRETATION

Many dreams, for example, go by contraries. If I beat someone, someone will beat me. If I go to another man's wife, my wife will go to another man. If I steal something, someone will steal from me.

Other dreams are prophetic 'warnings'. Some of these seem to have gained their meaning in a quite arbitrary fashion, simply by observation of the sequence of events. A man has a dream. The next day something unusual happens. The two things are connected. The dream caused or at least was a warning of the event.

Sujji of Kawardha told me that this was actually how he had evolved his scheme of interpretation. One night he dreamt of a pile of silver; the following day there was a death in the village. So he deduced that silver was prophetic of death. Another time he dreamt that he was building a house, and again someone died and now he had to dig the dead man's grave. So to dream of building a house is a warning that you will have to dig a grave.

I have collected the following prophetic interpretations:

If you see a sambhar killed, it means that a man of your own family will die.

If you see a snake, it means that a relation is coming to visit you[1] or—more optimistically—that a pretty girl is coming to the village.

If you kill a man and burn the body, it means that if you go out to hunt you will get a sambhar.

If you drink a lot, you will get a bad cold.

If you see a garden, it means that a sahib is coming.

If you pay money to anyone, it means a visitor is coming.

If you smoke and drink with a sadhu, beware of tigers in the way.

If a girl 'kisses' you on the cheek, a snake will bite you.

If you see a cow coming from the north, it will rain.

If you kill your mother or father, you will shoot a sambhar.

If your son marries, both you and he will get smallpox.[2]

If you show your penis to a friend and he spits on it, it means that you are going to fall ill, but that someone will give you medicine.

Interpretations vary from place to place. This is the scheme of Thaggur Dewar:

[1] So also among the Kharia. (Roy: op. cit. p. 444.)

[2] The Birhor think that to dream of anyone's marriage means that he is going to fall ill.

If a dog barks in your dream, it means that someone in your house will die, for Marra Deo is on the way and has frightened the dog.

If you see someone burnt, it is no good going to him with your *sūpatuma*, for nothing can save him.

If a snake bites you, you will get a new wife.

If a scorpion bites you, beware—for someone is waiting to beat you with a stick.

If you scratch your foot with a straw, you will get worms in a wound.

I collected these interpretations among Bhaina Baiga in the Bilaspur District:

If you have someone else's wife in a dream, you will get a meat meal the following day.

If you beat a drum, leaping up and down in the dance, you will meet a tiger.

If you see a fire in the jungle, there will be a quarrel in the house next morning.

If you see a pond with broken banks, there will be a theft in your house.

If you see rain, a guest will come.

If you see a cow with buffaloes, there will be clouds and rain.

If you have a wound in your right hand, you will get a lot of money.

It is curious that none of these things serve as omens in the ordinary sense. There is nothing sinister about hearing a dog bark in the day-time, and a wound in the right hand in your waking hours has no bearing whatever on your fortunes.

Here are some examples of prophetic dreams. Dallu of Bangaora (Kawardha) saw in a dream a very famous old Dewar called Dursu, long since dead, who declared that *he* had had a dream of a horse standing in the road.[1] This means, said the Dewar, that if you go into the jungle to-morrow, you'll meet a tiger, so beware. The previous night a traveller had come to Dallu's house. In the morning, Dallu told him the dream and begged him not to continue his journey, but the man laughed at him, went on his way, and was killed and eaten by a tiger. The horse is always regarded as bad by the Baiga, and it is unlucky to tread on horse-dung. The traveller, therefore, should have been doubly warned.

Sujji once dreamt that a cobra (which is universally regarded as the custodian of hidden treasure and thus a natural symbol of wealth) visited his house—a good dream suggestive of wealth to come. And he did in fact become rich with much grain and many cows. But after some years he had another dream, and now the cobra left his house. Almost immediately,

[1] The Bhuiya regard the horse dream as lucky, the Kharia as unlucky.

his house was burnt down, his cows died, and he was in distress for some years till he rebuilt his fortunes.

Mahi once dreamt that she was picking mangoes and eating them. A tiger came by, and she was very frightened and climbed up the tree. Soon afterwards, as she expected from the dream, she became pregnant.

III. SYMBOLIC INTERPRETATION

In these dreams there is only rarely any connection between the dream and its meaning. But in many other dreams, there is an obvious symbolism which is interpreted as we would expect. Thus, to dream of a stick means, obviously, a snake, and vice versa. To see a rupee in a dream warns you of the jadhdhu snake which has small circles like rupees all over its body. If you dream that your house has fallen down—a symbol of the broken home—it means that your wife will run away. If you see a broken earthen pot—to break a pot is part of the ritual of divorce—it means that two lovers or two friends will part. So Thaggur told me that he once dreamt of a broken cooking-pot and soon afterwards his wife ran away.

In Belki village of Pandaria, I found these interpretations:

If you dream you are cutting *chir* grass, it means you will see a tiger. For you tear your hands when cutting *chir* grass and this is a terrifying thing, as terrifying as seeing a tiger.

If you hear the noise of a drum, you will hear the roar of a tiger the following night; and if you see a round earthen cooking-pot, you will see the tiger's head.

To see red water means that you will pass blood in the morning.

A char tree covered with its little round fruits indicates an attack of smallpox.

A pile of rice means worms in your body.

Many fish in a field foretells a bumper crop.

A tree falling warns you of a death in your house.

To dream of excrement signifies that someone will give you honey or *khīr* (a great luxury). Gahania once dreamt that his hands were covered with cow-dung and when he went to wash them, they turned into gold.[1]

To see a fruit means that your wife is pregnant, to see a cucumber means that you are going to have a son.

[1] In other countries the excrement dream is often connected with money. *Khīr* or honey would have the same emotional significance as money to a tribe which commonly resorts to barter. The Birhor also believe that to dream of excrement is prophetic of honey the following day. But the Bhuiya regard this as an unlucky dream, a warning of illness to come.

A river in flood is a sign that your wife will begin her menstrual period the following day.[1] If you are swept away by the flood, however, your wife will have a premature delivery, and if you are drowned in it, you will get a pretty girl on the morrow. Hironda, the old Barotia woman of Jholar, dreamt that she was being carried away by a flooded river, and was only just saved in time. The next day she began her period. This was in her youth.

IV. TYPE DREAMS

The following type-dreams are worth recording in order to illustrate the similarity in the manifest content of dreams throughout the world, for they may be paralleled almost anywhere.

Loss of teeth and hair

Mahatu once dreamt that he "went to the jungle and saw a red fruit. I picked it, and as soon as I put it in my mouth, all my teeth fell out, and the hair from every part of my body. Blood poured out of my mouth. I don't know what the dream meant". But the very important Yogi Dewar told me that this dream was good and quoted one of his own. "My teeth all fell out, and they offered me meat, but I couldn't eat it and asked for rice instead. This was a good dream; it means that in my next birth I shall be a Brahmin." The interpretation here is probably due to the association—inability to eat meat through loss of teeth, vegetarianism, Brahmin. Generally the Baiga do not attach any meaning at all to dreams about the loss of teeth or hair, flying or falling. The two last dreams are, of course, natural adventures of the *jīv* in its bird or grasshopper form.

Dhan Singh tells me that he has never dreamt of losing teeth or hair, but he has nightmares about his eyes. "Both my eyes fell out; they spouted out from the sockets on to the ground. I wandered about blind, stumbling against everything. At last a man came to find me, and put my eyes back. Then I woke. Another time, I dreamt that blood poured from my eyes. I wept from pain and fear. Someone came and rubbed medicine on them, and the blood ceased to flow." Dhan Singh, however, has excellent sight and has never suffered from any disease of the eyes.

Flying dreams

"There were fifty men with me," said Dasseru. "They were all flying: I was in front; I had no companion. I went up and up and up till I touched the sky. It was like a stone, cold and black. The

[1] In Nyasaland, if a man dreams of a flood it may mean that his wife is about to begin her period. (Hodgson: "Dreams in Central Africa", *Man*, April, 1926.)

stars are also black, each star is big as a house. They are black, but their hips flash with light. There are little hills on the sky. I sat on one of them. None of the others could fly more than half-way. When I came down, they flew after me, but none of them could go so fast as I could."

"Feathers sprouted on my arms"—this is one of Mahatu's dreams—"and I flew up into the air. A *bhut* was carrying me. Someone else was flying, but I went faster. Suddenly the *bhut* dropped me. I fell with a thud and woke."

Phulmat once dreamt that her "*jīv* went flying up into the sky to catch the sun. It had nearly reached it, and I was stretching out my hand to grasp it and pull it down when I fell, right down into a lot of mud."

Yogi Dewar dreamt that "a house somewhere caught fire. I rushed into the fire and sat down on top of a big flame. Many people came to save me. Then without wings, as the fire blew upward, I went up, up, up into the sky—and then fell down, down, down, right down below the earth."

Climbing and falling dreams

"I was climbing a mango tree with both hands. Suddenly I fell with a great crash. As I fell, my *jīv* ran back to my body and I awoke. My legs and back were aching, and they continued to ache all day." Another informant described how "I dreamt that I had gone to pluck mangoes. I tried to catch the mangoes that were growing on another branch, and I fell. As I fell I shouted for my mother. But it was too late and I died. I don't know what this dream means."

Dreams of raw meat

1. "Our hut was so full of the raw flesh of the sambhar that there was no room for us to sit down. I said, why don't you take it out and burn it, then we'll have cooked meat." 2. "We never see raw meat in our dreams. Only witches eat raw meat." 3. "To see raw meat is bad: it means someone will die."[1] I do not think this symbolism is to be connected with death ceremonies, for the Baiga do not usually indulge in much meat-eating at funerals; but there may be some connection with cannibalism. Most probably, however, it is the association with witchcraft that stamps this dream as bad. Witches drink fresh human blood and consume raw meat: their eyes are like fishes' eyes. Hence to dream of raw meat or fish is dangerous.

[1] Dr. Seligman has collected examples from Europe, Africa, Borneo and China which illustrate the universality of the belief that this dream is bad—a curious belief in view of the primitives' love for meat. But at least in Africa there seems a clear connection between this dream and death ceremonies, and hence 'repression with persistence of the affect is what might be expected'. See *British Journal of Psychology.* (General Section), Vol. XVIII, pp. 378 ff.

Dreams of fire

"In my house I had much rice and many calves. In my dream I saw it catch fire. I rushed to and fro in the village. Some brought water, others beat it with sticks. I was flying about like a grasshopper, weeping and crying, 'Save it, save it.' The people threw out the charred rice, but everything else was burnt save my earthen pots. When the fire cooled, I went round the village begging for new seed and bullocks. I promised them wine. The young men ploughed my field, there was a fine harvest, and I built a big house in place of the one that was burnt. Then my *jīv* returned to my body, I awoke and went to my wife for comfort."

Dreams of death

These dreams are common, but do not appear to be ill-omened.

"I had died, and three spirits—Rikhi, Keora and Bhagat—caught me and carried me away to the house of Bhagavan. When Bhagavan saw me, he folded his hands and said, 'I never sent for you. They have brought you by mistake.' So he put me in a litter and sent me home. When I got back everyone was weeping for me. I gave my wife a kick and said, 'What are you weeping for? Look at me, I'm alive.' By my kick I disturbed the fire near which I was sleeping, and some fell on me and woke me." (Pachlu.)

"I was wrestling, in a rage, with my father. Then a tiger knocked me down and killed me. I went down below the earth, and there I turned into a tiny man only a foot high. A great snake saw me and said, 'I'm going to eat you.' I said, 'Open your mouth,' and in I went and came out the other end. And at once I flew away; up to my own house." (Pachlu again.)

"Four thieves caught me and hanged me on a tree. The rope cut my head off. Then came the twenty-one sisters and the nineteen Rikhi Muni and danced under the tree. One Muni gave my head a kick and it flew up and stuck on my body again. The Muni took me from the tree and was going to give me something. I put out my hands for it—but I really put them out into the fire. That woke me." (Pachlu.)

"In my dream two men beat me so violently that I died. My wife began to weep, but I sat up saying, 'Don't cry, I am alive.'" (Lakgan Muria.)

"I died and they took me out to bury me. But on the way I sat up alive, so they took me back to the house, and put a *dhoti* and a turban on me. A new *jīv* came into my body and a woman took me in her arms and rocked me to sleep." (Buka.)

"I was dead. Twenty-one women and two men were fanning my

body. Then I got up and climbed on to the roof. Someone blew a conch. When the women heard it, they began to dance. One of the girls caught me and squeezed me in her arms till the blood flowed from my body." (Pandu Kath-bhaina.)

V. CULTURE DREAMS

It is possible to tell with some degree of certainty from the manifest content of a people's dreams how far the old culture holds and how far it is disappearing before alien influences. It is very striking to compare the dreams of Baiga who live on a main road with the dreams of those who live in the heart of the forest some miles even from a regular foot-path. The former have dreams of 'sahibs,' motor-cars, policemen, Hindu sadhu and Hindu gods and goddesses; I have hardly found one dream of this kind among the latter. Pachlu, who lives in the remotest jungle, is no real exception, for he is a travelled man and on familiar terms with many 'sahibs.'

I will give a few examples of the more civilized and Hinduized dreams from Baiga living on or near the main roads. The first two are from Bahadur, who lives at Hirapur on the main Baihar-Balaghat road.

"A sadhu with long hair and a spear in his hand came to me and thrust his spear into my stomach so that I died. Two boys came to him with crowns on their heads and said, 'You villain, why did you kill this innocent? Take out the spear.' So he did, and I lived again. Then I put my head on the feet of the boys, and knocked my head really against the side of the bed, and woke.

"Durga Bhavani came and cut off my head and ran away. Then Tapsi Muni came and stuck my head on again, struck me once on the back with his stick and I awoke—alive."

The next is from Ketu living on the Jubbulpore–Dindori road, an ex-landlord who had many and unhappy dealings with sahibs.

"I fell under a motor and was groaning. Two sahibs came, pulled me out and threw me into a ditch at the side of the road. I got up and began to give them *gāli*. One of the sahibs ran towards me brandishing his stick—when I woke."

Changna Muria lives in Berkera, also on the Jubbulpore–Dindori road.

"I sat in the Deputy Commissioner's motor and went touring in the jungle. We met a tiger. The D.C. shot at it, but missed and the tiger leapt on the D.C. I ran far away till I fell into a stream. There was a witch busy bringing back life to a corpse. I was terrified and ran away again, and now climbed up a tree. There was honey there but the bees came to sting me. I tried to beat them off—and woke."

Siram Binjhwar also lives near the Jubbulpore–Dindori road in Niwas. He is despised by his fellow Binjhwar because he has married a Muria girl.

"A sahib came to see me in his motor. I turned the sahib out of his motor, and got in and drove it. I came to a river, and there the car turned over and sunk into the water. I was inside the car under the water. I tried to look out—and awoke."

It is fairly safe to say that such dreams are not experienced by the Baiga of the wilds of Kawardha and Pandaria—at least I have found no trace of them.

VI. OFFICIAL DREAMS

'The dreams and visions of so-called primitive peoples,' says Dr. Lincoln, 'always fall into two distinct classes, the unsought, or spontaneous dreams occurring in sleep, here called "individual" dreams, and the sought or induced "culture pattern" dreams of special tribal significance.'[1] The Baiga do not seem actually to distinguish individual and official dreams, but the latter are fairly common, specially as means by which the gunia is called to his high office. In the old days also, when ritual abstinence was practised before a hunt, an 'official' dream revealed where the game was likely to be found. And still to-day, there are gunia who sleep on the left side, and expect and receive dreams which reveal to them the diagnosis of a complaint, or the probable time of the conception of a child.

A glance at Chapter IV will show the very great importance that these dreams have in the life of the people. I have preferred to leave them there in the midst of the life-stories, rather than assemble them here, for thus their associations are more clearly seen. But we may note how Rawan's prowess in the hunt came to him through a dream, how Bansi was set on his career as a gunia, and how he was removed from it, how Pachlu gained his secret knowledge and how he too lost it because his wife woke him at the wrong moment, how Mahatu was initiated by a human sacrifice offered in a dream, how Phulmat was commanded to adopt the profession of a gunia and was ill till she obeyed. Often jungle medicines and mantra are revealed in dreams. Mahatu, for example, has received many revelations of this kind. "Once Nanga Baiga came to me in a dream and showed me the *jaribhuti* (jungle herbs of any kind) for curing leprosy and *dhuki* (possibly influenza)." And again: "I met a tiger in my dream. It chased me. I screamed for my mother and father and all my friends to help me. But the tiger caught me and before they could save me, it had broken my arm and leg. They took me home, and brought some *harsingri*. They cut it up, and then tied it to

[1] Lincoln: *The Dream in Primitive Cultures* (London, 1935), p. 22.

my arm with strips of bark, so that the arm became straight. But the wound remained. So then the bark of saj, sarai and tilwa was brought and burnt. While it was still burning they pounded it up and put the powder on my wound." Another type of treatment was used for bear-wounds. "In my dream my *jīv* left my body and went to collect roots for food. Suddenly a bear saw me and before I could escape, it had caught me, bit my hands and chest and most of all scratched my face. I screamed to my father and mother for help. They came and drove the bear away. 'Are you still alive, my son?' cried my mother. They made a bamboo litter and brought me home. 'He will die unless we can make medicine of *kirchichia*[1] roots,' said my mother. So they got the roots, pounded them up and put the powder dry on the wound. Then they slung my cot to the roof, off the ground, for if a brown jungle ant bites a man after he has been injured by a bear he is certain to die.' At the time when Mahatu had the last two dreams, his parents were dead.

VII. THE PARENT IN DREAMS

The intervention of parents, however, is very common. 1. "My father comes and takes my bow and arrow and shoots sambhar and gutri (barking deer) for me. Then I go to the same place the following day, and I am able to shoot them myself." 2. "Three months after my father died, he came to me in a dream and told me the best place for me to take our bullocks to graze." 3. "My dead father sometimes comes and says: 'Sow your kodon in this field, and your rice in that.' Once I did as he told me and had a very good crop."

Visitations of dead relatives are very important for the correct naming of a child. "When the dead man's spirit comes to the house of a pregnant woman of his own family, then his son sees him in a dream." The father says: "I am going to be born again in your house." After a child is born it refuses at first to drink its mother's milk. But when the son tells the gunia of his dream and they all know who the child is, and name it, then the child goes to drink. Another Baiga told me how he had seen his dead father in a dream. The father told him that he was returning to earth again. The very next day his wife became pregnant. So then they knew that the child would be a boy and that it was their father returned to earth.

Mahi described how her *jīv* left her body in sleep and went to visit her dead parents. They were sitting by the fire in their little hut (an exact replica of the hut they had on earth) near Bhagavan's palace. Her father

[1] *Gloriosa superba.*

was putting fuel on the fire, and her mother was warming her hands at the blaze.

Jethu told me how he had once seen his dead parents.

"One day I saw in my dream that my mother and father came and talked to me. After a few days, while we were celebrating Nawa, I went to Dulha Deo near the hearth and was giving him incense. When I turned round I saw my father and mother, but I didn't recognize them. They were sitting on either side of the door. My mother said, 'Son, give me some water. I am thirsty.' My father said, 'Son, give me some tobacco.' I said, 'Who are you?' They answered, 'We are your mother and father.' I said, 'My parents are dead. Tell me who you really are.' Just then a neighbour came by and cried out, 'Jethu, your parents have come to see you.' I thought he was joking and said, 'Go away, I'm busy.' Then my mother took the bangles from her arm and laid them on the threshold, and my father put his pipe there, and they disappeared. When I came out, I saw the pipe and bangles and I began to weep. My parents were here and I did not go out to greet them. But whether this was dream or waking I cannot say."

Sometimes it is Dharti Mata, or Mother Earth, who is the same as Thakurain, who comes and reveals the right medicines to use, and the proper place to sow the seed. The most powerful mantra, or spells, are usually revealed in dreams.

Mahatu is perhaps rather exceptional in his dependence on dreams. His whole life is controlled by them. "All my magic comes from dreams," he says. "I am always talking to the spirits." Other Baiga, however, have assured me that dreams do not play a very great part in their lives, and that their magic and charms are not derived directly in this way, but are handed down from father to son in the ordinary manner.

VIII. SEXUAL DREAMS

We must now turn to a consideration of sexual dreams. These are greatly modified by the extraordinary freedom that is allowed to children and young people, which is fully described in Chapter VIII. The account given in that chapter of the free life of children, the almost complete lack of sexual inhibitions, the comparative indifference to the rules of exogamy, the mild and tolerant rule of the father, makes it evident that the sexual background of the Baiga is very different from the middle-class Puritan European atmosphere in which Freud formed his theory of repression and the interpretation of dreams. This is far too big a subject to be compassed here, but it seems to me probable that the Oedipus-complex, though it exists, does not have dominant importance in Baiga family life. Baiga society is patrilineal, but the father is in no way a tyrant, and the Baiga child grows up to dread, at least in consciousness, quite other authorities, the gods, ghosts and devils, the police, the forest officers.

In the Baiga version of the original parricide, we have indeed a father and a group of brothers, but these are represented as in no way divided among themselves but united against the hostile and domineering authority of the gods. The father of mankind, Nanga Baiga, is dying, killed by the treachery of Bhagavan who created him. He tells his sons to cut up his dead body and cook it for twelve years. At the end of that time they are to eat it, and all his power and magic will pass to them. But Bhagavan tricks them again, and only the youngest son gets a fragment of his father's flesh and an attenuated portion of his power.

Here is a remarkable resemblance to Freud's 'great event' which was 'the foundation of all culture', and yet everything is different. It is not the sons who slay their father, but their common enemy, a jealous Urizen of a deity. It is their father himself who bids them eat his body, but they do not even accomplish that, only one of them obtaining a tiny fragment of the flesh. I shall suggest presently that this legend does in fact give the key to the whole family sentiment of the Baiga which inevitably differs from that of the middle-class Puritan household of Europe.

It is obvious, however, that in any patrilineal society, there will not be a uniform feeling towards all fathers, however 'kind' they may be; and I must now quote one dream of Mahatu's which does seem to illustrate exactly 'the typical father-sentiment, full of contradictory emotions, a mixture of reverence and contempt, affection and dislike, tenderness and fear' as it is known in Europe. "I went with my father to the jungle with my bow and arrow. My father shot at a sambhar, but hit and killed me instead. The arrow made a hole right through my body. I fell down. My father ran and cut some bark, made it into fine threads and with a bamboo needle pushed it into the wound and filled it, stopping up both the ends with sarai gum. After that we both lay down and slept, but I couldn't sleep. All the time I was saying to myself: 'He killed me purposely, so I must kill him.' So I took my axe and cut his head off. But then I felt very sad and wept bitterly. As I was weeping, Maswasi Devi came and asked me what was the matter. I said: 'I have killed my father, and here I am all alone in a thick jungle.' So Maswasi Devi took magic herbs and stuck my father's head on his body, tied it with cloth and spread cloth all over the body. Then she repeated some mantra and my father came back to life. He sat up and said: 'My dear son, why did you kill me who gave you life?' Then we went home together." When I asked him the meaning of the dream, Mahatu said he could not understand it. "My father never beat me. I used to massage him, so he loved me specially. My father was dead at the time of the dream."

But to return to general sexual dreams. If dreams are mainly the expression of repressed desires, then we would expect to find very few sexual dreams, either overt or symbolic, among the Baiga, for they generally give free rein to their desires. And this is in fact precisely what I have found.

For example, the Baiga have a very full scheme of sexual symbols which are expressed in the Dhandha, or Riddles, the posing of which is a common form of entertainment. There are hundreds of these riddles and among them the following symbols of the genital organs or the sexual act frequently recur. The sexual act is symbolized by a piece of cotton being threaded into the eye of a needle, making a string of beads by pushing a cord through them, putting bangles on the arm, pushing the body into a shirt, slipping the foot into a shoe, pounding rice—the long rice-pounder falling regularly into the little cavity in the ground, grinding corn—the upper grindstone working on the passive lower stone. Ploughing and sowing seed is a common symbol, for the earth is woman and woman is the earth. The phallus often appears in the riddles as a sword, a plough, a stick, 'a gun that eats living flesh'. The female genitals appear as a sheath, a pot of curds, a mouse's hole covered with grass. The child in the womb is 'a fish in the river; white ants cannot harm it'. A famous riddle is—'Three brothers went to rob a house. One brother went inside, the other two sat by the door'. The word 'rob' suggests adultery! Deflowering a virgin is symbolized by iron in the blacksmith's forge—'Black when it goes in: red when it comes out'. A Binjhwar Baiga told me that he had dreamt that he had pushed a stick into a small earthen pot and splashed the water out violently, and that this dream symbolized intercourse with a virgin.

Thus sexual symbolism is familiar to the Baiga,[1] yet, as we should expect, it is only rarely to be discovered in their dreams.

Overt sexual dreams, however, are less uncommon. I will give a few typical examples.

"I was catching fish in a lonely part of the river. Two girls came to fetch water. Then ran to me, and put their arms round me. I went to both of them. Afterwards I opened my arms to hold them, and I awoke." (Bahadur.)

"A very beautiful girl was sleeping with me. Who she was I don't

[1] Curiously, the symbolism (common in ancient India) of the fire-drill is not used by the Baiga. Cp. Held: *The Mahābhārata* (London, 1935), p. 140.

Binjhwar making the bamboo lining of a cap.
Bharotia starting work on a bamboo mat.

know, but she had many ornaments. Afterwards she went alone to the bazaar. Four constables came and threw her on the ground." (Bisram.)

"I went to the jungle for a hunt. I killed a sambhar. Another sambhar rushed at me and caught me with its horns. Bhagavan was sitting on the horns. As they struck me, he turned into a girl. I stretched out my arms to take her, and fell off the horns into a pond. In the pond was a big house with a golden door. I tried to open the door, but as I touched it, my hand was burnt and I awoke." (Bisram.)

"I was sleeping with four girls at once. One of them was very beautiful and I went to her. The others caught me and made me naked. Then all four climbed on to me. As they did so, I turned into a girl, and they into men. Then a dog came and bit them." (Yogi Dewar.)

Lahakat seems to have scores of such dreams, thrilling and romantic adventures that match his waking exploits. He is not a bit ashamed of them, and his unconscious has no need therefore to serve them up, as it were, in a symbolic form. The Baiga's freedom from repressions does not result in their having no sexual dreams at all, but it means that they do not have to be disguised.

The symbol of the earth, representing woman, however, is fairly common, but not always sexual. Thus to touch the earth with the hand means that you will meet a girl on the morrow, and to see a woman carrying water means that this year the crops will be good. When a woman comes to a man in a dream and says, "Protect me, keep me", that woman is Mother Earth herself coming to the Baiga for her protection against disease, fire or earthquake.

IX. THREE KINDS OF SEXUAL DREAMS

There are three other kinds of sexual dream common among the Baiga. The first is the dream of visitations by the spirits of the dead, for in Baiga villages even unsubstantial death is amorous. We have already described fully the encounters of human beings with the *raksa* and *churelin*.

We have also described elsewhere the effects of love-magic. If a man finds a girl indifferent to him, he performs magic to make her dream of him and the dream invariably kindles her desire.

If he himself can manage to dream of her and have intercourse with her in the dream, he seems to get a sort of right over her, and when he tells her about it, the girl usually responds. Dasseru Bhumia had the following experience. "I was in love with the headman's wife, and during the Karma dance I trod against her heel to show that I wanted her, but she took no notice. So at night I went to her in my dream. The next morning I met her as she was bringing water from the river, and I said: 'Last night I was with you.' She answered: 'If you really want me, then we'll go to the forest together.'"

Lahakat told me that whenever he had to sleep alone his *jīv* went out to seek romance. "It finds a girl, and touches her breasts. If they are strong and firm, it fondles her throat. It sees her whole body, looks at her bangles, her anklets, her earrings. Then she yields to him." His marriage was achieved by love-magic,[1] not on his part, but through the enterprise of the girl. "She sent her *jīv* to me at night. I caught her breasts and they were good. So I enjoyed her in my dream. Then the next day I met her in the forest. I told her: 'I had you in the night.' 'Yes,' she said, 'I sent my *jīv* to you because I love you.' Then my love for her blazed up, and we lived together."

Mahi also once told me how she called her lover to her in sleep. "He would stay with me all night, and in the morning when I woke up and found him no longer there, I would feel very lonely." And the quiet and dignified Dhan Singh prefers to take his erotic pleasures in dreams. Somehow or other he induces them, and enjoys himself immensely. "My *jīv* goes to a girl. We sit together and eat gram. Then there is nothing I don't do to her. That's when I'm really happy."

The third kind of sexual dream is not so pleasant—it is the castration-anxiety dream. This, in view of the family sentiment prevailing among the Baiga, may be connected simply and directly with the fear of impotence. That is their own association to it, and I do not see why we should go any further. For here again the social and psychological setting is different from the European. The family sentiment is different. The fear of impotence is far more common, and gives rise to an acuter conflict. For the Baiga is especially proud of his sexual powers. In the folk-tales the Baiga's phallus is always the largest of all. He boasts that in youth he has four or five, and even in age at least two, connections with his wife every night. If he fails in his duty, his wife accuses him of being unfaithful to her, and may run away with someone else. At the same time, venereal disease—though not endemic as among the Gond—is fairly common. The Baiga is under-nourished, and he begins his sexual activities at a very early age. There is the constant fear that he may be deprived of his sexual energy through witchcraft. These facts, combined with the enormous strain put upon him

[1] 'Most love-magic,' says Malinowski, of the Melanesians of the Trobriand Islands, 'is supposed to produce a dream which awakens the amorous wish. Thus these natives, remarkably enough, reverse the Freudian theory of dreams, for to them the dream is the cause of the wish.' (*Sex and Repression in Savage Society* (London, 1927), p. 93.) As a Baiga told me: "Girls can give us dreams to make us desire them."

by continual sexual intercourse, make impotence a far from rare occurrence and set up an acute psychological conflict.

During the Karma dance the women often shout taunt-songs at their lovers, and these illustrate the scorn with which sexual inadequacy is regarded. "Even in a plough the nails are hammered straight and strong," they cry. "The branch of the tamarind sways to and fro, but it never breaks."

> In Srawan flowers the *sawan*,
> In Bhadon blooms the *kasi* grass.
> Whenever he sees a girl,
> How he longs to take her.
> But his loins are powerless.
> Yet when he sees a girl,
> How lustily he swaggers.

Under these conditions, we would naturally expect this conflict to find some outlet, and what is more natural than that it should be expressed in castration and multilation[1] dreams? The following are examples of such dreams.

"In a dream I went to my wife, and to my horror I found that she had teeth in her vagina. She closed them and bit off my penis and blood poured out. The next day I found that I had got gonorrhœa." (Bukku Binjhwar of Kanhari.)

"One evening I was going for a bathe in the river. As I went into the water, someone cut off my penis with scissors sharp as the claws of a crab. When I came out of the water, it was all burning, and when I touched the place there was nothing there. I began to weep and beat my head against a stone. Now what makes me a man has gone, so I had better die, I cried, and I jumped back into the river and was drowned. When I woke up, the first thing I did was to feel my penis and see if it was there. I found a small sore on it." (Dasseru.)

"One night I caught hold of my friend's penis and cut it off. I said: 'You have slept with your own sister, and when we asked you for a penalty feast, you refused to give it.' This I did in my dream. My friend had really been to his sister. The next day when I met him, he said: 'I don't know what is the matter, but my penis is hurting me.' I said: 'When did it begin to hurt?' 'Last night at midnight.' 'I sent my *jīv* to you to punish you and it cut off your penis in the night. That is why it is hurting now.' Then he was ashamed and left me." (Dasseru.)

[1] Dasseru knew of an actual case where a girl's nose and clitoris were cut off by a jealous husband. In the folk-tales, there are several examples of the mutilation of the clitoris or of the labia majora.

"We were ducking each other in the river. As we played, a crocodile caught my leg. The others tried to save me, but they couldn't get my leg out of its mouth and I died." (Putua, a notable gunia.)

"A tiger chased me through the jungle. I shouted for help. But before I could be rescued, it had eaten one of my arms. Next day I found it hurt so much that I wept and had it burnt." (Rawan.)

The following probably belongs to the same order of dreams.

"I married a Kol girl and slept with her. But when I wanted to take her, I could not find her vagina. I was very angry and made a hole in her body with my nails. She died. I ran away for fear, weeping as I ran. I fell into a pit, where four constables were waiting for me. They arrested me and began to beat me." (Changna.)

We have already quoted Mahatu's dreams of mutilation by tiger and bear.

Closely related to these dreams is the curious and widespread legend of the Vagina Dentata. It is known, of course, that it is distributed throughout North America. It has been found in Samoa; it occurs as a legend among the Ainu; it has been discovered as an individual dream among the Kiwai.[1] But so far as I know its existence has hardly been suspected in India. A common theme in Indian folk-lore, however, is the Poison Damsel. In some stories, she is said to poison her lovers not only by her look and breath, but by intercourse. The evil effects of her bite are mentioned, and this is believed to refer to an amorous kiss on the lip. Penzer thinks that the legend of danger of death and poison as a result of intercourse may have arisen from recognition of the effects of venereal disease.[2]

In my own opinion the legend of the Poison Damsel, like the Vagina Dentata legend, must be associated with the fear of impotence.

Among the Baiga, the Vagina Dentata legend is as common as the dream. I have found it in Kawardha, Pandaria, Mandla and Niwas. The stories[3] vary greatly, are related with great gusto, and are generally exceedingly amusing—at least to the Baiga. They are generally on the lines of this story from Kawardha State. A Brahmin girl goes to stay in a Baiga's house, and persuades his two sons to visit her at night. The boys were very jealous of each other. "She spread her bed and called the eldest boy to her. She made him lie down and sleep with her. In her vagina were teeth, and when the boy went to her, she closed them on his penis and cut it off. He was so angry with his brother that he stopped himself from crying out, thinking: 'Let my brother have the same fate.' So he bore

[1] Lincoln, op. cit. p. 108.

[2] *The Ocean of Story*. By Tawney, revised by Penzer. (London, 1924), ii. p. 305.

[3] These are being reserved for separate publication later. See also story on p. 483.

the pain in silence. Then the Brahmin girl sent him away and called his brother. She cut off his penis also, and both of them became impotent." After many adventures, the girl's own husband returned and removed the teeth with a pair of pincers.

Another of these tales (from Mataval village in the Mandla District) shows a clear connection between the Vagina Dentata fears (for the noose in the story is equivalent to teeth) and the cannibalistic impulse.

"An old Baiga and his wife had two sons and a daughter. All three were married. One day the two boys went with their father to dig for roots in the forest, and the old mother and her two daughters-in-law were left in the house. Presently a Brahmin came to beg. The mother said to the girls: 'Give him something or other.' But they thought she meant that they were to give him everything. So they said to each other: 'See, we are two, he is only one. I'll go to him to-day, your turn will be to-morrow.' Thus it was arranged. So the first girl called out: 'Come and get your present, *mahārāj*.' He said: 'Give it to me in the courtyard.' He went and sat there, and she sat down before him. He said: 'Give it to me.' She said: 'Take it from me.' Then he understood. He was without a wife. Strength came to him, and he took his present, and went his way. At night, the two husbands came home. The girl who had given herself said to her husband: 'A Brahmin came to-day and took something or other.' But he didn't understand. The next day also the husbands went out to the forest, and the Brahmin came again. This time the second girl said: 'I'll give him to-day.' She took him into the house and gave herself to him.

"Then the husbands came home with bundles of roots. One the way the Brahmin met them and begged for some roots to eat. The Baiga said: 'Why do you look so thin to-day'? The Brahamin said: 'Because of something or other.' Then the Baiga understood and quickly went home. At night, the second girl said to her husband: 'I gave the Brahmin something or other to-day.' When he heard that, the husband thought: 'I'll make a trap for the rascal.' So with hair-string he made a noose, and put it into his wife's vagina, tying the end of it to the string round her waist. His brother did the same. They said to their wives: 'Don't tell the Brahmin that we have done this.' The next day the Brahmin came. 'Give me something or other,' he begged. That day the old mother was sleeping inside the house. The Brahmin took the girl inside and shut the door. Then when they were fairly at it, the mother awoke, and the Brahmin, frightened, hastily withdrew. The string tightened round his penis and cut it off. But he did not cry out. He said to the girl: 'Look, I have dropped my medicine on the floor. Give it to your husband to eat and it will give him a lot of strength.' So the girl hid the penis in her sari. That day the husband brought a basket of fish. The girl put the penis in with the fish and vegetable, and gave it to the men to eat. As they were eating, her husband found the penis. 'This is a fine fish,' he said, as he picked it up. But it jumped out of his hand and fell on to his brother's plate. His brother picked it up, and thought it looked a good bit of fish, and ate it. He didn't bite it, he swallowed it whole.

"At night the penis broke out through his stomach and went into his wife's vagina. Then he got up and went to his wife. The cut-off penis stuck on to his own so that it became double in length. It was so long that it killed the girl. He didn't know that she was dead, but he felt very pleased that his penis had become so long. In the morning the old mother came to wake the girl, and saw the blood flowing. Then they knew that she was dead and they buried her."

There is very little evidence of the cannibalistic impulse among the Baiga, though in another folk-tale five brothers kill and eat their little sister who had cut her hand while cooking and had allowed the blood to fall on to the food. That day they enjoyed their dinner so much that, when they discovered that its improved taste was due to human blood, they said: "If blood tastes so good, how much better will be the flesh." And so they killed the girl and ate her.

Mahatu once had a cannibalistic dream. "I went with my father to the jungle, and there we saw a man, a Baiga, lying dead, and all his blood had been drunk by a tiger. When I saw him, I said: 'Let's eat him; we never get meat nowadays.' So we both ate him. When I got home, I began to vomit. 'It's very bad to eat man's flesh,' I said. 'No,' said my father, 'that is not the reason. You are vomiting because you ate so greedily.' But I asked for some very hot *pej*, and when I had drunk that, I felt better."

The following dreams are not connected so much with fear of impotence as with the dread of menstrual blood.

"I was drinking milk from the udders of a cow. As I drank it turned into blood. I went to throw myself and the blood-milk into the river. On the bank of the river two snakes coiled round my legs. I fell down and a girl came and drove them away. She tied my penis with a string to a tree." (Buka.)

"I was having intercourse with a girl during her period. Two men came by and saw us. They tied us together with our own clothes, and dragged us to the river, and threw us in. Then fish came and bit off my penis and the river was full of blood." (Maru Kath-bhaina.)

To dream of blood flowing from the penis is a warning that a man may go to a woman during her period without realizing it. We have already seen the horror with which such an act is regarded and the very great danger, both social and supernatural, that attends it.

X. INCESTUOUS DREAMS

Incestuous dreams are not common and seem to be lightly regarded. This is what we would expect. Dasseru, Mahatu and his sons, Dhan Singh, Hothu, Lahakat and others all admit to occasional dreams of incest which they find depressing. But they do not speak of them with special horror, nor do they have to pay any penalty for them. Bhangi Muria, though I was a stranger to him, described quite calmly how:

"I slept with my sister and took her as we slept. You are my wife, I said."

And Pandu Kath-bhaina said:

"I dreamt I was sleeping with my sister and did all that a husband can do. Then she said, 'Come, let's run away together.' But my father saw us, and beat us both. My sister went to the jungle and hanged herself, and I ran away."

In this last dream we have evidence that the conventional attitude does exist alongside the more 'modern' and liberal view. This corresponds with what we have already seen in Chapter V.

XI. DREAMS OF FOOD AND FEAR

Although I have given them a good deal of space I do not think that dreams of a sexual character are the most important to the Baiga mind. Food is more important than sexual satisfaction—for one thing, it is far harder to obtain. And chief of all the psychological tensions is anxiety. Fear compasses these people like a blazing forest fire. Their lives are shadowed by the uncertain weather, by their reluctant crops, by witches, ghosts, landlords, police, forest-guards, by capricious and malignant deities. From his earliest days, the Baiga child finds himself in a menacing and hostile world. The gods are jealous of him. The Creator himself compassed the death of the first Baiga and robbed the tribe of all his magic. A host of Mata are busy spreading disease throughout the world. Every tree and stone conceals a malignant spirit. The child's own mother may be a witch, planning to eat her children. If he lives in a forest village, it is the range officer or forest-guard who represents authority. If he lives in an ordinary village, it is the landlord or the *patwari* (revenue officer) whom he grows up to fear. Officials extract *begar* (forced unpaid labour) from him, the money-lender cheats him and extorts extravagant interest. The whole world is against him. Only the family and the tribe provides some kind of refuge. In comparison with these fearful and menacing authorities, the father represents protection and security, he is the support of tribal integrity against the outer world. This is vividly reflected in the Baiga version of the original parricide, where it is not the sons who kill the father, but God himself. The family is bound together by far stronger ties than in Europe, a small strongly cohering unit valiantly opposing a hostile world. Under these conditions, the Oedipus-complex is not likely to be the dominant family sentiment.

We would, however, expect anxiety dreams to be common, and so they are. In their own system of interpretation, the Baiga declare that a tiger represents, not the father, but the forest officer, who is lord of the jungle; the cruel and stupid bear is the constable; the leopard, swift in pursuit and swift to show its claws, is the forest-guard; the crocodile with its large mouth ready to swallow everything, is the money-lender; fish are witches; bullocks are merchants.[1]

The following are examples of anxiety dreams. "To dream of fish is very bad. If you sleep near a witch, if she's your enemy, she gets up in the night, pats your head and says: 'Make him dance and let him see the *bhut*.' Then after ten days you begin to dream of fish. You catch thousands and thousands, but when you come home there is nothing there. That means that you are yourself turning into a fish and become a witch, wanting to eat anything and everything. Your eyes become like a fish's eyes glaring hungrily at everything." (Putua.)

"I went to have a bathe. Everyone else only went a little way, up to their knees. But I went deeper and deeper till I came to a great sea, where the crabs' claws were thick as a man's thigh and huge fish swam to and fro. I tried to catch them, but they slipped through my hands. Then I saw great crocodiles in the water. One of them chased me round and round, all over the sea. It tried to eat me. But at last it got very tired and returned to its hole." (Dasseru.)

"I was bathing in the river. I looked down, and there was a huge fish, large as a man, swimming silently in the water. I tried to kill it with a stone. But it swam up and down and round and round me, and I couldn't catch it. It was the *bīr* of a witch." (Dhan Singh.)

"I went to the bazaar. A bear chased me. I went into a stream, and the bear came and sat on top of me." (Bhangi Muria.)

[1] The Kharia believe that if they dream of a tiger it means that a court bailiff or policeman is coming to their house. (Roy, op. cit. p. 444.)

"A tiger carried me off from the field into its jungle, and put me in a cave with a big stone on my chest. Then a ghost came and put a flower in my mouth and went away. I saw a pig go into my field and began to shout and so woke." (Baghela.)

"I had a fight with a tiger. I killed it, but two more tigers came. I ran away screaming and fell into a ditch. In the ditch a boy was having a girl. The girl caught me but the tiger came and caught me also." (Ketu.)

"I jumped into a blazing fire. When I began to burn, my wife pulled me out, and dragged me to the river to cool me. When I came out of the river, I went to the jungle and saw a horse. But when I got nearer I saw it was a tiger. I ran home shouting for fear." (Har Bhajan.)

"I was sent by a merchant to find his horse. I took the bridle and went into the jungle. I met a tiger, but I thought it was a horse, and put the bit in its mouth and got on its back. At once it ran away into the jungle, but I caught the branch of a tree, and climbed up into it. Then two other tigers came and were going to climb up after me, but I urinated into the tiger's face—and awoke and found that I had really done so in my bed." (Lahakat.)

"I was going along the road and suddenly turned into a tiny little girl. Then I went home, and found no one there, and all my house tumbled down. A bullock with a crumpled horn rushed at me." (Hironda.)

"I was sitting on an elephant. But it hit me with its trunk and I fell to the ground. Then two bullocks charged me—neither of them had eyes or ears. Soon after many men came and I got up and ran away." (Rawan.)

"I was in the jungle, picking mangoes. I picked many, but I didn't eat them. Then a tiger came and jumped on me, and I was terrified. I woke screaming." (Murwa Muria of Niwas.)

"A *bhut* was chasing me in my dream, and I screamed with fear. I had gone to fetch roots from the jungle, then I saw the ghost with great branches in its hands. It chased me and tried to beat me. But wings sprang from my shoulders and I flew away." (Dasseru.)

"Many bullocks laden with wheat came to our village. When they were unloaded, two of the bullocks came charging violently at me to gore me with their horns." (Murwa.)

"I saw my house absolutely dark. All the lamps went out, and there was no fire. This dream meant that our house-gods were angry with me. The following day I fell ill." (A Binjhwar Baiga.)

"I saw the stump of a saj tree turn into a tiger, which chased me. This meant that Bara Deo (who dwells in the saj tree) was angry with me." (*Ibid.*)

Mahatu and his sons have many dreams of bears and tigers, which they associate with their fear of the police and forest officers. Such nightmares are the commonest of all dreams among the Baiga.

Food and hunger dreams are also common.

In dream after dream we find the Baiga hunting the sambhar, shooting birds, eating the fresh green bamboo shoots (also a forbidden food) gazing with longing eyes on their bewar green and fresh with a bumper crop. The worst of all dreams is to see a wanton woman display her privates to you, for that dream means that you will go hungry on the morrow.

Here are a few specimens of hunger dreams. "We all said: 'Let's go to the jungle and hunt.' As we went we saw a sambhar. We surrounded it, and I killed it with a shot from my bow. But when it fell down, it began to talk, and to curse us. We were all astonished, and I took some thread and sewed up the wound so that it recovered. Then the sambhar told us that she was Maswasi (goddess of the chase). She took us to a hill, and we surrounded it, and a whole herd of sambhar ran out, but we didn't kill one. Then we were very angry, but Maswasi took us to another place, and there we killed a fine sambhar and divided it up. But we left nothing for the goddess. She was very angry and said she would kill us. But I gave her a goat instead, and then she gave us this blessing: 'May you always be able to kill sambhar.'"

"My dead mother and father come to me and say: 'We are all together in a big village and Bhagavan is with us. He gives us as much *dāl-bhāt* as we want. We eat all day long.'"

Only a trained psychiatrist could draw the right conclusions from the evidence assembled in this chapter, but for the moment I think it is safe to suggest that the Baiga attach considerable, but not excessive, importance to dreams, that their culture is both expressed and reinforced by their manifest content, that the unusually small amount of sexual inhibition saves them from the conflicts that would be normally expressed in disguised and symbolic sexual dreams (though these do sometimes occur), that the Oedipus-complex (in the form of the father-murder in the primal horde or of the father-murder and mother-incest type) does not represent their dominant family sentiment, and that their most tormenting and readily remembered dreams are the nightmares of anxiety and hunger.

Chapter XV

DANCES AND SONGS

1. DRESSING FOR THE DANCE

THE Baiga dance whenever the season or their loves invite; give them a bright moon and a little liquor, and their feet begin to move unbidden, and their hands stray towards the drums.

The Baiga are better dancers than the Gond. They take the art more seriously, and dress better for it. Men put on ornaments, tie big round turbans and stick tufts of peacocks' feathers in them. Girls put on every ornament they have, they often tie pretty red and orange shawls across their bodies, they bind their hair in loose pigtails with strings of mauve wool and little rings of *bīran*[1]-bark. In their hair, they put tufts of peacocks' feathers tied at the tips with bits of coloured wool pulled out of a *phundara*. They often use wooden clappers called *tiski* (Fig. 22).

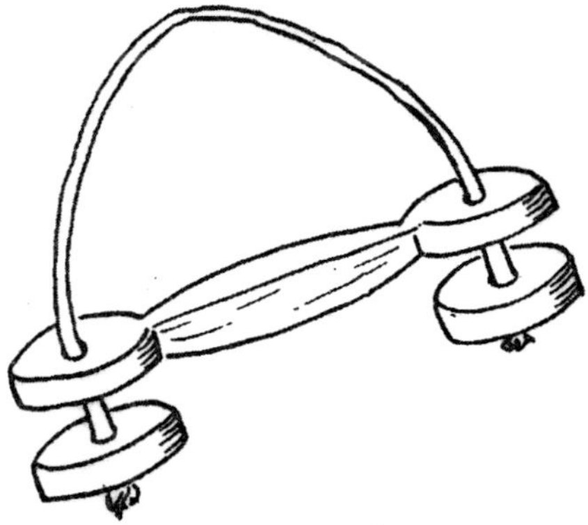

FIG. 22. *Tiski.*

Four different drums are used. The most common is the *māndar*, a long drum generally made of earth, faced at either end with bullock-skin, hung round the neck and played with both hands. The *dhōl* is a large

[1] Perhaps the *chloroxylon swietenia*, a small tree with thick corky bark.

wooden drum, skin-faced at either end, played with the hand at one end, with a stick at the other. The *nangāra* is a conical earthen vessel bound with leather strips. Cow's skin or goat's skin is stretched across the top. It is played on the ground, with two sticks, at weddings. The *timki* is a small earthen hemispherical drum, played with two sticks.

The Baiga do not seem to attribute any magical efficacy to dancing, though once in Baihar I found an idea that the Karma helped the crops to grow. The dance is generally simply a recreation, almost the only recreation, where friends and lovers meet, and the heart is warmed.

II. THE KARMA DANCE

The Karma is the central Baiga dance, of which all the others are but variations. It is the great dance of the tribe, in which men and women, young and old, can all share alike.

The Karma has two main formations—both centring round a group of men singers and drummers. This group stands in the middle of an open space, two or three men have the long *māndar* swung round their necks. They begin to drum, and the others start singing. Gradually, the girls collect and stand in a line a few yards away from the men. The men do not face the girls, but stand in a clump, often facing each other. At the beginning of the dance season, after the rains, they perform the *tikāwan*. Somebody brings a plate with a small lighted oil lamp and a pile of rice; he dips a finger in the oil, then in the rice, and dabs this on the foreheads of the dancers. They greet him and touch his forehead in return.

When sufficient girls have assembled, the men begin to sing. When they have finished the first 'verse' of a song, the girls take hands and try to repeat what the boys have sung. If they succeed, the drums begin and the dance is on. If they fail, they have to go on trying till they get the words correct. Sometimes, the girls begin and the men have to repeat the song.

Now, according to the numbers present and their inclination, one of two things may happen. In the first formation, the girls stand in a straight line, swaying slightly, and singing rather softly. Then suddenly they bend down, and begin to dance. The drummers give a loud yell, jump in the air, run towards the girls, crouch down before them. The girls recede three steps, the drummers following them, then advance, recede and advance. The central bunch of men remains still, and the line of women

Bhumia with māndar (standing), timki (left) and dholki.
Men and women about to dance the Dassereliwar.

and the drummers gradually work round in a large circle. The dance, therefore, looks like this:

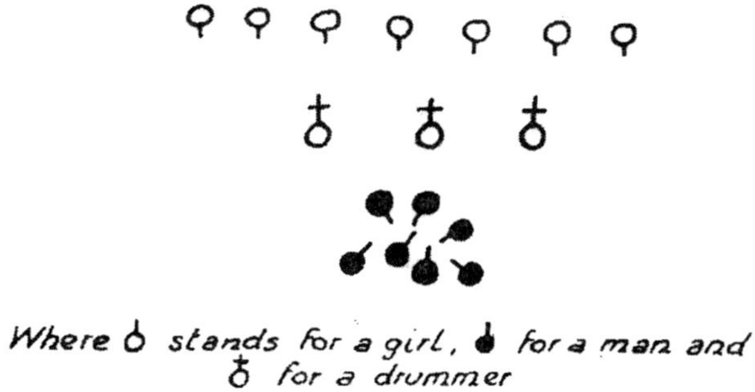

FIG. 23.

But there is another formation:

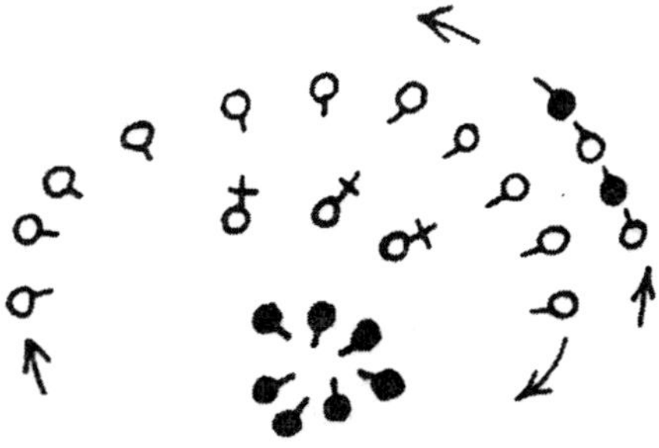

FIG. 24.

Here the women go round in a large circle, sometimes clockwise and sometimes anti-clockwise, and a line of boys and girls with the *tiski* in their hands go very fast round the circle in the opposite direction. They dance with great vigour and bang the *tiski* clappers as loudly as they can.

The women in the Karma dance always circle round the men, but in the first formation, the circular movement proceeds very slowly, all the stress being either on the movements of the feet, or on the advancing and receding line; while in the second, the women go round rapidly.

A third formation, which is regarded as a separate dance though it is really part of the Karma, is called the Dassereliwar. The notable thing about this is that it is the only dance in the neighbourhood where men and women hold each other. The line is formed by alternate men and women—the men have their arms round the women's shoulders, the women clasp the men by the waist. They form a long line and dance slowly in a wide circle. Half a dozen boys and girls go round quickly in the opposite direction, and the drummers and a number of old women hop about by themselves with great energy.

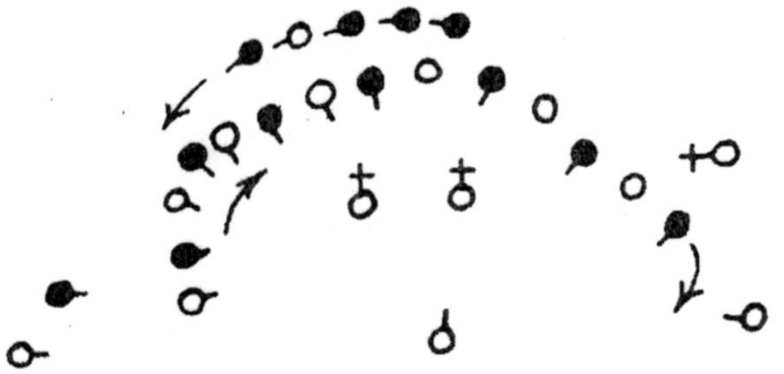

The Dassereli war

FIG. 25.

There is a very great variety of steps used in the Karma, some of which are named.

The circular movement, for example, is most commonly effected in the Khalha Karma. The woman advances the left foot, brings the right up to it and swings it back and to the right, brings the left foot back a little to the right of its original position, and bows, then repeats.

Another circular movement is this: Bring the left foot forward and across the right, then back but a little to the left of the original position; then bring the right foot forward and across the left, then back, this too a little to the left.

Straightforward advancing and receding movements may be made in the Tadi, Lahaki or Jhumar Karma. In the Tadi, there is a quick left, right, left movement forward, then the right foot is brought up to the left, touches the ground with the toes, and is taken back at once. The left follows, then the right, then a bow, and the steps are repeated.

The Lahaki Karma, which is generally sung to rhymed songs, and has a powerful effect on the emotions, is a jerky, rather suggestive movement. The women stand in line, each lifts the left leg by bending the knee a dozen times, then puts the left leg a little forward, bends the knee, brings the right foot up beside the left, puts the left forward again, bends, brings up right, and so on. Or the line may go round and round: in this case, the right foot is moved first but to the right, the left is brought up to it, but always a little in front. In this movement, one foot only takes the lead, and the other follows, and at every pace the body is jerked from the knee.

The Jhumar Karma is a very pretty rapid movement, in which the feet are alternately brought forward and back very quickly. The right shoots forward and is back in its place immediately, and the left is out and back as quickly. A line of women doing this in perfect time is a delightful sight: the line gradually works forward, or round and round.

Other steps that I have noticed are these:

1. Sway left leg, then, suddenly and very quickly, dart it forward, bring up the right foot, touch the ground near the left foot and at once swing it away to the right, bring the left leg back, bow, and repeat by beginning with the right leg, and so on.

2. Take left foot over in front of the right, bring up the right foot to the right side of the left foot, take left foot back to the original position, carry the right foot with a flourish over to the left and in front of the left foot, bring the left foot up and across the right again, and so on. This is done bending, quickly and vigorously.

When the main attention of the spectators is diverted to the drummers who squat on their heels and hop vigorously about, drumming furiously as they do so, the dance is known as the Khalti Karma.

III. THE JHARPAT DANCE

This is a development of the Karma. In this the men singers do not stand bunched together in a little group, but in a line, holding hands and facing the girls. The drummers leap to and fro between the two lines, which advance and recede by a simple movement, left foot to right, right foot to right, left foot to left, right foot to the left behind the left foot, or by an even simpler left right left backwards and forwards. The lines of dancers generally bend as they dance, but from time to time stand still and sing loudly.

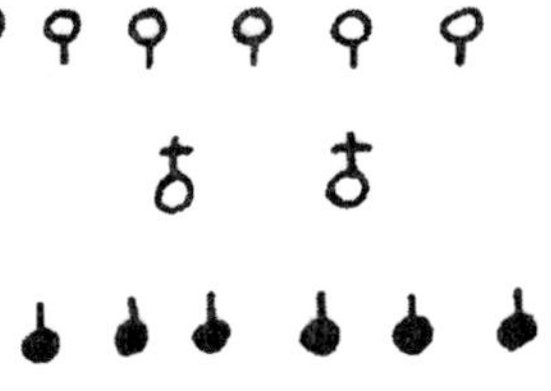

The Jharpat

FIG. 26.

This dance is usually confined to the young.

IV. THE TAPADI DANCE

The Tapadi is a dance for women only. It is formed in three ways.

Two lines of women face each other, not holding hands, but clapping them bending low, and moving their feet with a very simple left right movement, pausing at each step:

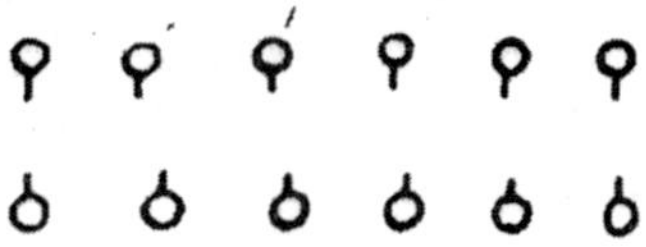

FIG. 27.

After a time one line turns its back on the other, then both lines go down on their knees, and clap their hands vigorously, swaying to and fro.

FIG. 28.

Finally, both lines join together, and go round in a big circle, all facing inwards, bending down, and clapping their hands.

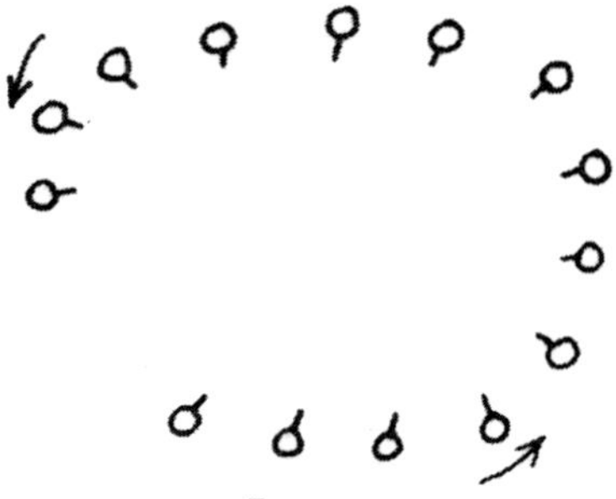

FIG. 29.

The Tapadi is danced without drums.

V. THE BILMA DANCE

The Bilma is the marriage dance. It differs from the Karma and Jharpat which are danced to the *māndar* drum, and the Dassera which is danced to the *dhōl* drum, by being accompanied by the big deep *nangāra*. Like the marriage itself, it is exciting and confused. The dancers gather near the drums, and when there are enough they cry "*Kiring, kiring*", the drums begin, and everybody begins to dance just where they are, men and women mixed together, bending low, stepping up and down very fast. Sometimes, the men make the obscenest gestures, and the girls are not behindhand in imitating them.

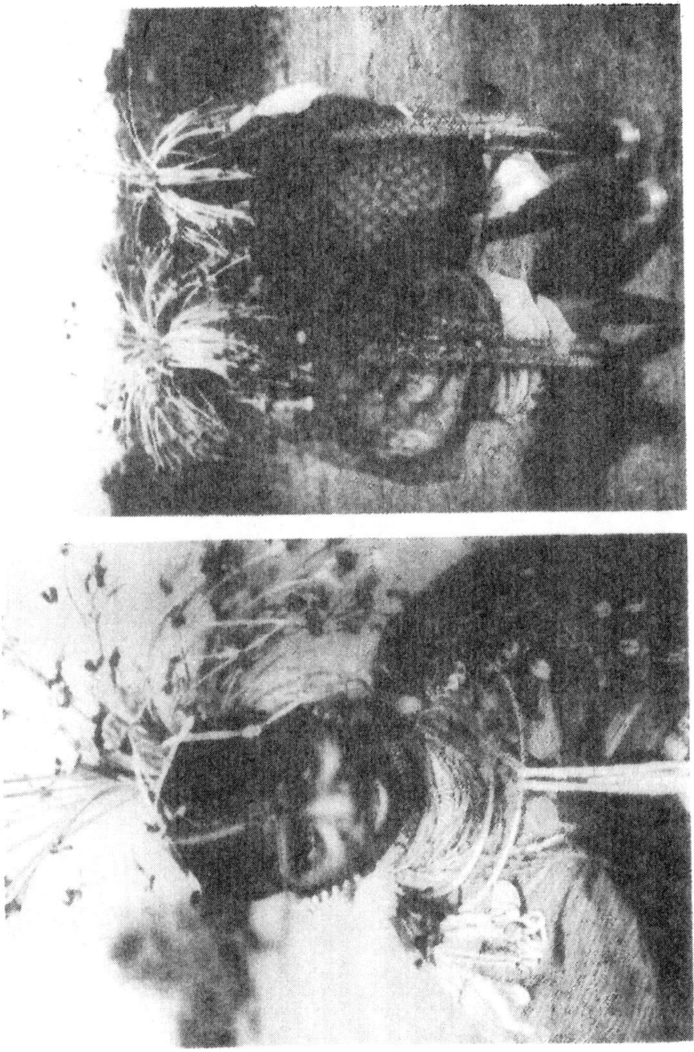

Girls dressed for the dance.

VI. THE DASSERA DANCE

The Dassera is the dance for men only. The Baiga do not seem to be very good at this, at which the Gond excel. A drummer sits with the *dhōl* and beats it monotonously, and a few men run round and round in a circle. Now and then they change their direction and every time they do so they utter a thin weird bat-like cry. Danced in complete silence, under a moon, it is rather impressive, but it has none of the variety and excitement of the Gond Saila.

VII. THE SONGS

There is, of course, no corpus of Baiga poetry. Their songs and music belong mostly to the dance, and often are composed to suit the day. Other songs are traditional, and are used with extempore variations. A few belong to gifted individuals: they are not exactly copyright property, but they are generally associated with the owners' names, and normally sung only in their presence. Thus, the beautiful Pharria of Amtera has her own Karma, which she introduces whenever she goes to the dance: she used to sing it quietly to her husband in the early days of their affection, and it bound her strongly to him. This was the song:

Sanjha saberē surta āthāi mor jodi ke nīta duppar ō sanjha sabera re.
In the evening and the morning, comes a longing for my love,
In the mid-day and at evening and the morning.

In this book I have recorded Karma, Jharpat and Bilma songs among those that are associated with the dance. There are also songs for the Tapadi and Dassereliwar, but they are not sufficiently distinctive to be recorded separately. The Baiga do not often sing or dance the Saila: their corresponding men's dance, the Dassera, is performed in silence to the rhythmic throbbing of the drums. The Baiga only rarely sing the satirical Sajani popular among Gond, but they are very fond of the Dadaria, the one great kind of song that does not take its origin from dancing.

The form of the songs depends so entirely on the dance or the tune to which they are sung that it is impossible to give standard measures for each kind. Words are clipped, altered or repeated, quantities are changed, meaningless ejaculations are inserted with complete freedom in order to fit the main burden of the song to the tune.

I will now give a brief account of the main types of song.

VIII. THE DADARIA

The Dadaria, or Salho as they are called in Chhattisgarh, are the true *ban-bhajan* or forest-songs. They are sung by the Baiga and other hill-tribes as they go to their work in the forest. A group of Baiga by the fire often suddenly burst out singing—and it is Dadaria that they sing. Young lovers sing them to each other, and many a proposal has been made and elopement aranged in verse. It is always a delight to hear Dadaria sung; from the depths of the forest comes a song fresh and thrilling, with a lilt, a joy, an excitement that never stales.

Each verse of the Dadaria is very short; sometimes many of these verses are strung together to make a long poem, and they are then sung antiphonally. I have already quoted in Chapter VIII the most complete long Dadaria that I have been able to record. In this chapter, I have collected a number of isolated themes: these may be said to form the floating reserve of Baiga verse—any dozen of them may be selected and sung without particular reference to their sequence.

The general plan of the verse is a first line referring to some homely familiar object of the countryside, the creeper climbing up the wall of the house, the mango tree silhouetted against the sky, the *pej* cooking in the pot. The second line, which is nearly always about love, has often no connection with the first. In many Dadaria, the lines rhyme, and in many each ends with the word *dos* (friend). The three songs that follow will give some idea of their general form.

Tel la chupar ke nikārē pāti mola bara nīk lāgē dos
Kaisē sauro ke chhāti re mola bara nīk lāgē dos.

When she puts oil on her hair and makes the parting, I feel very happy, friend.
How (lovely are) the breasts of my beloved. I feel very happy, friend.

ii

Gayela dongar kātela karela,
Tor hoti bai chhodē haun gharela re dos.

To go to the forest to cut *karela*!
For you, O girl, I have left my home.

iii

Gayela dongar mārela khūsera,
Tor pet ke darad la batāvē dusera—ga tor pet ke darad la re dos.
To go to the forest to kill the *khūsera*!
You show the pain of your heart (lit. stomach) to someone else, O friend.

iv

Kharē majhania nikar pania,
Dāgnī bidh dolai tor kanhia.
Just in the mid-day, you went out for water.
Like a thin bamboo sways your waist.

I now give a number of translations from Dadaria which generally follow the above models.

i

Round are the horns of the black buffalo.
When we lie down together, we feel drowsy.

ii

Your belly is so full of *pej* that you are sure to feel sleepy.
But when you don't talk to me, I begin to cry.

iii

In the new house they have made mud figures on the wall.
You may give me every *gāli*, so long as you do not attack our love.

iv

When you have a pipe between your lips how quiet you are.
Come to the river or the bed of a dried-up stream,
And I will show you what is in my heart.

v

As water from a well is drawn out and thrown away,
So how great a waste for a girl to see her lover from a distance.

vi

The parsa tree has grown as high as a man can reach.
O girl, it is a long year since I saw you last.

vii

The gossips have all gone to bed,
And everything is put away.
I have looked for her in the verandah,
I have looked for her in the courtyard.
But I can't find her anywhere.

viii

I have set my *jhitka* in the Banjar river.
Is there any girl who loves me enough
To give me some *gānja* to drink?

ix

That garland of beads does not become you.
When you are distant from my heart, how sad I feel!

x

My axe has felled the first tree in the bewar.
My eyes are broken through looking at the girl
Who has carried my *pej* to the forest.

xi

The bullocks are going home,
But I don't hear the trampling of their hoofs.
I am leaving life itself for this girl.

xii

I have put a bullet in my new gun.
Come on, my bed, I will put a new girl on you.

xiii

He is whirling his stout stick in the air.
Without a wife, a man pines away, O friend.

xiv

The kachnar tree blossoms by mother Narbada.
O girl, if you love me, let me sleep with you.

xv

The stalk of the creeper is twining upwards.
The girl I've just enjoyed is sitting by my side.

xvi

Against the sky swings the mango fruit.
O my sweet enemy, take my life and I will take care of yours.

xvii

The room is freshly cleaned with cow-dung.
The rat runs across the floor.
My love, you go ahead and I will follow.

xviii

You catch the fish and I will cook it.
The love of my friend takes me out of the world.

xix

A little boy is playing in the sand.
O my friend, how could you have forgotten the passion of our love?

xx

How high the duba grass has grown!
Come to a deep stream and take a vow,
Holding water in your hands.

xxi

Honour to thee who made the moon.
There was none to help thee make it,
But only black clouds girt about with swords.

xxii

O Creator, honour to thee who didst create the folds of the dress,
Where lovers meet.
She whispers, Go and tell your brother,
He can meet me in the folds of my dress.

xxiii

The stars are scattered here and there about the sky!
O my brother's friend,
Tell me the secret about his wife.

xxiv

The village street is deep in mud.
The girl's chin is smeared with dirt,
For her lover has deceived her.

xxv

The girl has taken her *khanta* to the forest.
But she does not know how to dig a single root.
Take the *khanta* from the little fool,
And hit her with it!

xxvi

Come my girl, and help me cut this wood.
If you can't do it, I'll hit you with my axe.

xxvii

At summer noon we peep down the well
To see if there is any water there.
What did you see that you so shyly hid your face?

xxviii

I am killing a snake.
Why are you afraid of me, my love?

I am killing a rat.
Come, my friend, follow after me.

I am killing a monkey.
The whole village is blind.
Don't be afraid, my love.

xxix

For me she dressed herself with care:
She tied her sari tightly round her body.
But when she came to me she never smiled.

xxx

How ripe are this year's mangoes!
O girl, I will catch you somehow: you won't be able to save yourself.
Even if you hide beneath the water, I will drag you out.

xxxi

I am rubbing my body with *arsi* oil.
When will I be able to sleep with my young love?

xxxii

I have killed a peacock, I have cut shoots of green bamboo.
Tell me, my young love, when will you sleep with me?

xxxiii

They have all gone away to the bewar.
O my love, meet me down by the river.

xxxiv

I am wearing a turban,
Its tail is hanging down.
O girl, look behind you,
And your life will be changed.

xxxv

You wear your cloth too tightly round your body!
I have never made love to anyone before.

xxxvi

We put long poles across the roof
To save it from being blown away.
O girl, give me what you promised last year
Before you leave me this time.

xxxvii

The bear is eating mahua, the camel eats the pipal,
The boy is winking at his girl.
But her breasts are hurting her, O friend.

xxxviii

I went to the jungle for kachnar fruit.
O girl, dance slowly, slowly,
Or else the drummers will carry you off.

xxxix

The fire is blazing *jugor jugor*.
The girl peeps *mutur mutur* from her house, O friend.

xl

O the heavy sacks of salt
Coming from the lowlands!
Who remembers a forgotten friend?

xli

From childhood we were friends.
But now half-way through life,
We're parted, friend.

xlii

There's boiled rice in the dish.
There's oil in the little pot.
I've lost my *jawāra*,
And how lonely I feel without him!

xliii

O your fate is written in the tamarind leaves.
Hai! hai! you are weeping because your love has run away.

xliv

We are drawing water from the well.
From a distance my friend is looking at me.

xlv

The *pej* is cooking in the pot.
Without seeing my love, I find no happiness, my friend.

xlvi

There is fire in the dry cow-dung.
I am but a stranger here,
But take me to your heart with fire.

xlvii

My lover's mind is fickle as the ripples
Of a stream broken by a stone, O friend.

xlviii

The branches of the lime tree are heavy with fruit.
So sleep with me to your heart's content, O friend.

xlix

I've bullocks and a cart, but I haven't got a yoke.
I've wandered all over the world,
But I've never yet seen a virgin, O friend.

l

I went to the jungle and got some poison.
I am singing Dadaria; listen with your left ear, O friend.

IX. THE KARMA SONGS

The Karma songs are much longer than the Dadaria; they are generally sung at a dance, but sometimes privately between lovers or carelessly as a man might sing a refrain from an opera. They are occasionally rhymed and are then called the Lahaki Karma which are able to tear a man away from his family and make him forget the whole world in the wonder of the rhythm. The form of the Karma varies greatly and there is more delightful onamatopoeic nonsense in these songs than in any others. But they all begin with a phrase which indicates the tune to which they may be sung. The following are four different Karma themes:

i

Ho ho re, hansna batāna kaisē man ko milāna re.

ii

O ho ho re, bālam jī ke man murajhāni man me rākho dharī re.

iii

O ho ho re ha, ghunghur dhundhar dikai maidāna re.

iv

Ho re hai, āso ke girāni ma akila be rayē.

I will give a fifth in full and translate it.

v

Ye hai, rāti ke choli saberē chhabilia, chalti ke bera odha de chūnaria hai re.
Chhūm chhana nāna ho gay chalti ke bera, odha de chūnaria hai re.
In the morning, my beautiful girl (asks for) her dress of the night (before).
Time is passing (she says). Dress me in my flowered sari.

The scene is a hut where a girl has visited her lover and spent a night with him. But now their 'enemy the dawn' is coming, and she is begging him to dress her and let her go. But note how this simple theme is expanded by repetition and a phrase like *chhūm chhana nāna* which echoes the sound of *chūnaria.* There is no rhyme and yet the whole song rhymes.

I now give a selection of fifty Karma songs, translated as literally as possible.

i

A little bird is flying round her head,
Its wings fall over her eyes.
Look! Look! and see, her lover said.
But she replied, In the dark how can I see?
    Where can I find a lamp?
    Where can I find a wick?
    Where can I find the oil?
I will give you a golden lamp.
I will give you a silver wick.
I will give you *arsi* oil.

ii

At sunset I was parted from my love.
O Earth, break and take me in.
I have no mother or father, I am alone in the world.
O Earth, break and take me in,
For at sunset I was parted from my love.

iii

How thrilling Hindu girls are!
This girl here is a Kalarin.
Watch her sitting in the still
Cooling the pot of mahua.
She takes *johār* from everyone that comes.
How thrilling Hindu girls are!

iv

It was dark in the jungle when my love's *barāt* came.
The tiger was roaring Ao Ao; the bear was growling Kao Kao.
But I thought of only one thing,
How could I go to my beloved.

v

I have come, O I have come, for love of you.
I have left father, mother, all my family.
I have even left the baby at my breast,
For love of you.

vi

O girl, you torment me, you are so deceiving!
And you stand there beautiful as the moon.
Yet as a deer is snared and killed,
So will I snare you, for I have caught a thousand so.

vii

The well is shaded by the trees.
Don't go alone for water, wait for me.
    Where is your pitcher?
        Where is your *gundhri*?
    Golden is my pitcher.
        Silver is my *gundhri*.
Don't go alone for water, wait for me.

viii

O love come silent as a thief.
The door is shut, come silently.
I open it, come silently.
O love, you take me as a thief.

The Jharpat dance.
Baiga Saila, or Dassera, at Silpiri.

ix

The rain is pouring down,
The lotus blooms on the water.
There is a dark mango tree,
The bees fly in and out.
A girl stands beneath the tree.
The rain is pouring down.

x

O my soul be patient, she is very beautiful.
But this lovely treasure belongs to another.
How wonderful she is! When you see her your mouth waters.
But she is not for you. Be patient.
Ah! she has come out of the house,
She peeps out from the verandah.
Tears fill my eyes, for she is not for me.

xi

Why have you called me into the jungle?
Well, here I am, busy picking leaves.
What now?

xii

Alas! alas! you have forgotten
What happened underneath the banyan tree.
O my love, you are leaving me,
But never forget what happened
Beneath the banyan tree.

xiii

My water-pot is made of brass,
My *kalsa* is made of silver.
As the *kalsa* cracks, so cracks the love within me.
When love is broken, how can you save the body?

xiv

Take me to some country that I have never seen,
Where, O my love, the thunder roars,
Where, O my love, the lightning flickers,
And the rain pours down.

xv

Why did you go to the wooded hill?
Why did you wander in the rice-field?
I went to chop wood in the jungle.
I went to cut rice in the field.

xvi

O lover, we all know it, your life is leaving you for love of your girl.
Many girls have gone for water.
They are saying by the well
That your life is leaving you for the love you bear your girl.

xvii

O girl, your eyes are fixed on me to bewitch me.
O whence is the magic of your eyes?

xviii

O my love, let's go and bring leaves from the forest.
  Who will make them into platters?
  Who will make the platters round and large?
My younger *bhauji* will make them into platters,
But the elder will make them round and large.
  Then my younger brother will eat off one,
  And the elder will eat off the other.

xix

You can see me from a distance,
But you cannot touch me.
He has gone to his bewar,
But he has locked me in.
The door is wood, the lock is iron,
The door is strongly made.

xx

I am going to dig for roots.
  A-re-re-re, re-re!
Take your *khanta* and *kudāri*,
Climb the hill and dig a basketful.
Who will divide your roots?
Your uncle will divide them.
  A-re-re-re, re-re!

xxi

You went to the market and brought new bangles.
You have made this young girl ready to go with you.

xxii

Bring your axe, bring your spear, and climb the hill with me.
But if you are my true love, save O save your body.
For above your head there hangs a sword.

xxiii

As the green bamboo bending lightly to and fro,
In whose arms is my love's body bending?

xxiv

In the middle of the court grows the pipal.
Pick the fruit and eat it.
And now, my girl, I feel very thirsty.
Tell me where can I get water.
My love is going to the well for water.
Her lover catches her and steals her water.

xxv

I have left my love in Serguja.
Day and night my life thinks of her.
O where is the half of my life?
How can I pass my days and nights without her?
When I lie down to sleep the memory returns.
Sadly, sadly through the night I console my mind.

xxvi

Without you my life is empty!
My heart is eaten by desire.
The *ghun*-insect eats the *channa*,
The frost kills the *masuri dāl*,
The *senduri* weed grows up amid the wheat.
Without you my life is empty.

xxvii

Let us spend this night in sin!
She comes from her house and stands in the door.
When she sees her lover, no one can check her love.
O let us spend this night in sin together!

xxviii

There are figs on the tree in the middle of the court.
The girl is eating them, she plucks them one by one.
She has eaten so many that she is very thirsty.
She says to her boy, Come with me to the river.

xxix

My girl cut thorns and made a fence for my garden.
She planted onions in the furrows,

And every day she watered them.
Quickly the onions sprouted.
She dug them up and tied them in a bundle.
I made a big load of them and put it on her head.
She carried it to the Hardi bazaar.
There she spread the onions on a sack before her,
And began to call their price.
Their price was tinkling rupees.

xxx

O my love, you were coming, what has stopped you?
For you, my life is wretched.
O love, you were coming, and I was going with you.
Why don't you hold your life and mine together?
For you my life is melting away.

xxxi

The phadki bird cries *gutur gutur*.
The lover puffs at his pipe.
  Where does he get his *sulki*?
  Where does he get his black *gānja*?
The lover is smoking *sulki*,
His girl is smoking the black *gānja*.

xxxii

In the middle of the court a lovely girl wriggles her body like lightning
  to and fro.
On her toes the *chutki* tinkle and the *pairi* round her ankles.
Sometimes she glances at me.
O she's swinging her body to and fro.
I asked her for the ring from her finger as a token of love.

xxxiii

My friend said he was sitting over there preparing his pipe.
But life always chases youth.
O friend, when it was all over, I said to him,
Take another pipe. Smear the ash on all your eight parts and escape.

xxxiv

I never said anything, my girl.
Why did you run into the jungle to weep?
I never cursed you, nor spoke roughly to you;
I never turned you out of the house.

So why did you run to the jungle and weep?
    It was your mother cursed me, your father spoke so roughly.
    Your young brother turned me out of the house.
    That's why I went to weep in the jungle.

xxxv

The rain is falling *sitpit sitpit*,
The *musel* grass is growing high.
The cows that were grazing in the *musel*
Are returning home in the evening.
A tiger is chasing the calves—
And a lover follows his girl in the evening.

xxxvi

O she has flown away like a swan in the wind.
She has left me alone and my life is restless,
For my own life has left me.
When first she came to my house,
She sat in the doorway.
She wouldn't talk to me,
She wouldn't sleep with me.
And now my swan has flown away.

xxxvii

I have made a cup of sarai leaves,
And filled it to the brim with pipal-leaf curry,
But I cannot swallow a mouthful without my love.
O friend, where can I find comfort?
Sobbing *kalap kalap* I let my life go from my body.
There is no rest for me without my love.

xxxviii

My bed is lonely now.
What can I do but run away?
For this bed, I left my mother, brother and all my family.
For this bed I left the two babies at my breast,
And they wept after me.
And in the end he left me.
I will run away again, for this bed is lonely now.

xxxix

The clouds are dark and full of rain.
How will you journey to that far-distant land?
The red turban of my love is getting wet,
The long hair of his girl is drenched.
How will you journey to that far-distant land?

xl

The sun is rising from below,
And the light has come.
But my life cares not.
From dawn to sunset I sit on my bed,
Wiping away my tears.
There is the bed, all silent now.
When the sun sets, it is time to sleep.
The night passes and the sun comes again.
I sit and wipe away my tears.

xli

She has lit a fire in her courtyard.
She has run weeping out into the road.
Her blanket is over her head.
Why has she gone into the road to weep?

xlii

O girl, you have forgotten me.
But whenever I play on the drum,
I remember you.

xliii

Look, there are three men on the bank of the river
They are travellers, run and see who they are.
Light your lamp to show the way.
Go to the river and see if they are for us or no.

xliv

She is very beautiful,
But her young breasts are fallen.
He fondles them no longer
That once were his loved playthings.
Youth passes quickly, quickly;
But a girl's youth endures
The shortest time of all.

The Tapadi dance.
The Karma dance.

xlv

Long brinjal grow in the garden.
A thorn has pierced my breast,
For my love will not come near me.
No more he sleeps with me at night,
And another thorn has pierced my heart.
A-re-re le-le bo-bo bo-bo!
So she seeks another love, le-le bo-bo bo-bo!
Come to me, my lover, come!
Le-le bo-bo bo-bo!

xlvi

O girl, my cows are grazing,
Scattered through the forest.
With them are buffaloes with heavy horns.
In your house is a girl, in mine a boy.
They are sitting together, and her leg is on his thigh.

xlvii

In every lamp the wick longs for oil;
My eyes long for your bed.
My youthful heats desire the play of love.

xlviii

In the midst of the river grows a pipal thick with leaves;
Among the leaves monkeys are hiding.
O my love when will I meet you
And hold you close amid the leaves?

xlix

In the midst of the river grow the rushes, my young darling.
From one there grows a thousand.
If a man deserts his love, what other end but sorrow?

l

Hold your love in your mind,
But never speak of it.
Try to console your heart.
His sinful eyes will never listen:
They will go where they desire to go.

X. THE BILMA SONGS

The Bilma songs are given in Chapter IX, but here I will give a specimen of them in the original to illustrate their metre and technique.

Maiya bāp ghar rahē
Sāngo khelē kodaiya re khay,
Māmi mama ghar rahē
Sāngo roi roi kodaiya khay,
Ye jauni hāth ma kaura uchay
Derin ansuwa ponchay. *Kir-ing!*
When she stayed in the house of her mother and father,
My love ate *kodai* happily.
When she stayed in the house of her husband's mother and father,
My love ate *kodai* weeping.
In her right hand she lifted up a morsel.
With her left she wiped away her tears. *Kir-ing!*

XI. THE JHARPAT SONGS

There is little to distinguish the Jharpat from the Karma songs except that they are sung to a different dance measure, and lack the characteristic Karma introductions. Like all the other songs, they give us vivid, intimate pictures of Baiga life, such as no study or questioning could elicit. They illuminate not only the love affairs, but the ordinary details of everyday life—the man weary after the long labour of clearing his bewar, the girl making a fence of thorns round her garden, creaking shoes that ruin an elopement, the planting of chili seedlings by digging with the fingers holes in the soft earth, the scorpion that interrupted a romance with the sudden anguish of its bite.

Many Jharpat end with a cry like *Bhallē bhallē bhallē*! Good! good! good! or *Le bolo le bolo*! These I will now illustrate.

i

Berin berin kānta layē gharik rundhē bāri,
Bāri la jhank dekhai duno muthiari.
Nandia ke khalē dongi ma girāi pāni. *Bhallē bhallē bhallē.*
Many times I have brought thorns and quickly fenced the *bāri.*
Across the *bāri* the two lovers peep.
Down by the river water falls into the dongi. Good! Good! Good!

ii

Bar tari soyē pipal tari gōde, ke pairi la lai-bhagin chor,
Jarai jindgāni jarai tor nind,
Le bolo le bolo.
She sleeps beneath the bar tree, but her legs are under the *pipal.*
The thief took away the *pairi.*
May your life burn, may your sleep burn,
You have lost them.

iii

Dagar dagar jāt rahē
Goti kābar māre,
Gathrin ma dām nāhi
Najar kābar māre.
Bhadera ma wo bai marai habera.
As I was going along the road,
Why did you hit me with a pebble?
There is no money in your bundle,
Why did you wink at me?
Then why, O girl, did you nudge me on the hill.

I add a selection of translations from my collection of Jharpat songs to illustrate their scope and significance for Baiga life.

i

As I clear my bewar, my head nods for weariness.
O girl, when I see you, how happy I feel!
When the flood comes down, it breaks the river bank.
If I don't see you, my heart will break.

ii

Come, my girl, and meet me in the dried-up stream.
There's a ripe jamun tree there, boy.
A jackal comes to eat the fruit.
While you are on me,
It may hit you with its long tail.
But I will be underneath, it won't hurt me.

iii

The saj tree is thick with blossom.
O girl, you are going to your mother's house.
Come back again, when you've captured the heart of your boy.

iv

My love is playing on a fiddle.
He is hiding behind a tree.
O broken and blind may be the eyes
Of any girl that looks at him!

v

O my lover, take your sickle, and go and cut bark in the forest.
Make a rope with it, cut wood for a bed,
And we'll sleep on it together.

vi

Pluck a bundle of castor leaves,
And make a place for us to sleep.
But when she lay down a scorpion bit her.
O my *gondelaphūl*, was it a scorpion that bit you?
Why did you lie down on the ground,
When you had just tied your hair so beautifully?

vii

The *motiāri* brings thorns from the jungle,
She makes a fence for her garden.
She peeps through it at the river,
Looking down at the running water.

viii

The palace of the Raja glitters in the sun.
Dipē dipē dikā rē.
Inside is silver and gold, bright as the fire.
Dipē dipē dikā rē.

ix

Come, my love, let's run away.
Let's escape from this country.
Your *pairi* are sounding *chunu chunu*,
Take them off and carry them in your dress.
Your *chutki* are sounding *chunu chunu*.
Take them off and carry them in your dress.
She says, Your shoes are creaking *rutch mutch rutch mutch*.
Take them off and carry them.

x

The parrot talks in its swinging cage,
The maina sings on the mountain.

The sal tree reaches up to the sky.
From of old I have loved you, O girl.
And so I now have hopes of you.
The parrot talks in its swinging cage,
And the maina sings on the mountain.

xi

Under the pipal tree how sweetly sings the haril!
Chunur munur sound the *chutki* on her feet.
My heart is filled with joy as I hear that music.

xii

They are cutting the bewar, they cut down all the jungle.
I can hear them shouting, they are cutting all the jungle.
O girl, your husband is away in the bewar.
Roast some mahua and take it to your husband.
You are my *lālbhāji* and I your *jāmundāra*.

xiii

I have planted chili seedlings,
I dug holes with my finger in the ground.
They have grown very well.
O my *bhauji*, give me that stick.
I will hit the plant with it and the chili will fall.

xiv

O my love when I see your beauty,
I laugh aloud for joy.
You have put a pitcher on your head.
You are carrying a basket on your hip.
I look back to see if you will come or no,
O beautiful love of mine.

xv

O love, regard my sorrows, my unhappy fate.
I work all day to fill my belly.
I have no clothes for my body.
All my life is wasted caring for my husband.
O love, regard my sorrows, my unhappy fate.

xvi

O my sinner, let us spend this night together
My mind whispers, Come, let us run away.

But I am afraid of that long journey.
I look at you and long to live with you for ever.
But at least, my sinner, we will spend to-night together.

xvii

Under the ber tree they are playing the drum.
How good it is to hear.
O sister, give me my *pairi*,
And I will go and listen.

xviii

I was looking for you everywhere, but I couldn't find you.

But when you were in the jungle
Firing your bewar,
I sent a girl to call you,
But you took no notice.
It is because you love an old woman.
So why should you desire a child like me?

Who says I love an old woman?
It is you I love.

I too am an old woman now.
Get an unmarried girl, she will suit you better.
What will you do with me?

Chapter XVI

GAMES AND RIDDLES

I. CHILDREN'S GAMES

LIKE everybody else, what Baiga children like most is jumping off things and rolling about. They can spend a happy morning climbing on to a fallen tree and leaping down to the ground. They adore rolling over and over in the soft warm sand of a river bed. Their most successful games are improvised, like Bazar-bazar, when they perform miracles of imaginary bargaining with leaves, stones and bits of stick, or Rehechi-khel, played by placing one log of wood across another. Two children sit on it, and the others spin them round.

What is probably the most famous game of all, Ghar-gundia or Houses, has no rules at all, and is played according to the inspiration and opportunities of the moment. This game takes the place, in the sex education of children, that is held by the Bachelors' Dormitory elsewhere. People never forget it; they talk of it with wistful regret; many Baiga had their first shy erotic experiences while playing it. It can never be recaptured. You can never play Ghar-gundia once you are grown up.

It is a very simple game. A group of children wanders off into the jungle. They build some rough shelters with branches and leaves. They pair off, little girl with little boy, and each family sets up house. A few stones make a hearth, some leaves and sticks are food and vegetable. The boy goes and fetches wood for a fire. The girl pretends to cook. They divide the house into kitchen and bedroom, and after their meal they creep together into the inner room.

Once, coming home from picking mangoes, Charka was 'married' to a little girl. The customary rites were properly observed, and the two children began their 'married' life together. Day after day they went to their shelter. Charka was not more than twelve, it was his first experience of the kind. Panku was more ambitious. He had two 'wives' from the beginning. "My *badki*," he told me, "was very shy, she made me blindfold my eyes before doing it. But my *chotki* didn't mind." Phagnu was about eleven, and the girls eight or nine at this time.

Gai-gai and other animal games like Horse and Mare, Goats, or Cock and Hen, generally lead to the same conclusion. The boy gives a realistic imitation of a bull or goat and the girls, screaming with delight, resist his onslaughts, but not for ever. More innocent animal games are Kukur-bilai and Hati-khel, but neither of these are specifically Baiga. In the Kukur-bilai game a circle of children join hands, one child is inside and one out. The child inside is the cat and the one outside is the dog. The dog chases the cat in and out of the circle, which joins in the game by preventing the dog getting through, until the cat is caught. In Hati-khel, two boys get down on their hands and knees, a third lies across their backs, and a little girl sits on top of the elephant thus made. But these two games are played all over the world.

The Dhulahi-putari game gives Baiga children a lot of pleasure because of the extraordinary interest which they, in common with their elders, take in family relationships. In this game, they make dolls out of mud, bits of wood or torn scraps of cloth, and with great zest and excitement marry them off to each other, create and settle family quarrels, arrange intrigues and dispose of divorce proceedings.

In the Baiga Chak I once saw a bunch of a sort of maidens-hair on a pole tied to the topmost branches of a semur tree. The boys had put it there, on the most difficult branch they could find, and a girl had to climb the tree and bring it down, spit on it and throw it away. Failure was likely to expose her to obvious penalties. This is called Dauki-chundi khel.

The Sadhu-khel is a vulgar and very popular game. Two boys decorate themselves as sadhu with ash, begging bowl and stick. They pretend to be in the jungle. The first sadhu asks the second sadhu all the names for the different parts of the body: the second gives the usual names, but the first rejects them, and suggests synonyms, dancing jerkily as he does so. As he gradually approaches the more critical and intimate regions the excitement becomes intense, and his arrival there is greeted with uproarious applause. The dialogue goes something like this:

First sadhu, pointing to his eyes: "What are these?"

Second sadhu: "*Ankhi* (eyes)."

First (dancing): "You're a fool. They are *jugum dāni tinko bīja haran ko* (the things that shine and dance). But what is this?" (points to nose).

Second: "*Nāk* (nose)."

First: "Not for a moment. (Dancing again.) *Suruk dāni tinko bīja haran ko* (the thing that sniffs and dances). But what is this?" (points to mouth).

The Cat-and-Dog Game.
The Root Game.

Second: "*Mūh* (mouth)."

First: "No, no. *Gap gip tinko bīja haran ko* (the thing that gabbles and gobbles)."

And so through all the parts of the body. The arm is *kela kām tinko* (the thing like a banana); the stomach is *basam dāni tinko* (it turns all to ashes); the legs are *tāma thūnhi tinko* (standing poles); the more intimate regions are described variously as *bug bāg tinko, ting tāng tinko* and *turuk tayya tinko*.

Another popular game is Luka-Puka. This is simply Hide and Seek.

Dandati-bha-rati is a sort of Oranges and Lemons. Two boys stand facing each other and hold up their arms to make an arch. The others form a line, each holding the waist of the boy or girl in front. They go round and round, in and out of the arch, singing "*Dandāti-bha-rāti todi ai bāsuri!*". From time to time the 'arch' collapses on to the procession and its members are caught one by one. Those who are caught 'turn into cats' and lie down holding the feet of the boys who make the arch. When all are caught, these try to run away, but as their feet are tightly held, they fall over on top of a struggling heap of laughing children.

In Kaprel-narvel, one child covers his eyes, and the others hit him until he has guessed correctly who did it.

Nawan-goti is a sort of Hunt-the-Slipper. The children sit round in a circle passing a stone secretly from hand to hand. The child who is 'out' has to catch the stone in someone's possession.

Chango-khel is on the same principle, but more elaborate. The children sit in a circle each clasping his right knee with both hands, the thumbs sticking up. One boy with eyes blindfolded is set down in a corner to make cow-dung pats. Another boy takes a little pebble and goes round the circle touching each knee in turn. He slips the pebble under someone's thumb and cries out that everyone should close their thumbs. Then the cow-pat boy gets up and his eyes are uncovered, and he goes round singing "*Ela chāngo! Ela chāngo!*" to find the pebble. When he thinks he has found it, he cries: "This boy has a swelling on his head!" If he is wrong he has to try again. If he fails five times, a couple of boys jump up and blindfold him again. They fill his hands with dust and the pebble. Then they drag him round the circle and he gradually drops the dust and at last the pebble. Then they take him off outside the circle, loose his eyes, and send him back to find the pebble by following the trail of dust. If he finds it—not a very easy matter—they make him Raja; if not, he must go back to his cow-dung.

Kukri-chu is a game in which the cock, by hens attended, singles them from the crowd one by one. A boy stands alone facing a group of children, preferably girls, and cries "*Kukri chū kukri chū*". Someone in the group calls out, "Whose cock are you?" He names someone, perhaps his prospective father-in-law, but at least someone who will cause amusement. Then, "Where do you come from?" ask the crowd. He tells them. "What do you want?" "I've come for a hen!" he says. "Which would you like?" He chooses one of the crowd, and she at once runs to him, and her fellows try to stop her. If she gets away, the dialogue is repeated and continues till the cock has carried off all the hens.

The Phugri game is also played by Hindu children. The players squat on the ground, their arms resting on their knees, and hop along as far as they can, crying:

Chena bar kīra
Bhaiya mānge pirha
Chena bar kīra la
Kā kar bo
Kābo konda roti
Ama ma hudda ma
Mai kela phūgri
Phur pup phur pup.

Or:

A re dhān chiraiya
Kābo konda roti
Rai bhūj ke goch mūde
Mamā ke dulāru
Phur put phur put.

Another Hindu game played by the Baiga is Nun, or the Salt Game. Three long lines are made with ash or dry white earth, and these are intersected by short lines dividing them up into a number of rooms. In a room at one end is a store of salt, and in alternate rooms are placed police and

Police	Thief	Police	Thief	Police
Salt	Police	Thief	Police	Thief

FIG. 30.

thieves. The thieves have to get into the store of salt and pass it down the line to one another without being captured by the police as they pass from room to room. Each player must keep to his own room.

Chipo-gadi is played in this way. A boy goes down on his hands and knees and a boy lies down on his back on either side of him and puts his legs across his back. They put the soles of their feet against each other and push the boy in the middle to and fro.

Bel Sataka is a game of the same pattern. Two boys sit opposite each other and put their feet on one another's shoulders. Two other boys sit, one on each side of them. They put their legs under and above those of the first two boys, who then lower their legs till they are all interlocked in a sort of ball, when they begin to sing "*bel satāka bel satāka*".

The Tapori game is very amusing. The hands are clapped and the elbows and head touched in rapid, complicated and rhythmic succession while the performer sings a song which had better remain in the indecent obscurity of the Chhattisgarhi language.

The most characteristic and important of the Baiga games is the Kanda-khel. A number of boys sit in a line, each between another's legs which are extended. Little bits of wood, the roots, are put between the toes. This is the *kānda-bāri*, or garden of roots. Three boys are chosen to be the husband and wife who own the bari, and a chaprasi. First of all the husband and wife go round the line waving their hands above it; this is the watering of the field. Then the husband hops round on one leg shouting, "I'm putting up the fence." The wife follows on both legs crying, "I'm pulling it up." He gives her *gāli*, and they have a pretty quarrel to the delight of all. Now when roots are half-grown, the custom is to bend the shoots over and set them in the earth so that they will take root again. So the husband and wife pick up a small boy—he holds one leg, she takes an arm and the head—and they drag him down the line, his buttocks press down each head in turn. Sometimes, a long bamboo is used instead. Then they come to pick the *kānda-bhāji*, the shoots that can be used as vegetables. They squat for this and the 'roots' pinch their bottoms. They jump up shouting, "The ants are biting me!" Now the chaprasi comes along, and shouts at the boy to bring him a handful of roots. The husband says he's sorry, but they are not for sale. Then the chaprasi says, "Do you know that your cow has just had a calf. I saw it as I came through the village. You had better go and look at it." Husband and wife are very pleased and run away to see. When they have gone, the chaprasi pulls up one of the roots and makes off. The husband and wife return and count the roots. They find one missing. The chaprasi returns and sends them away on some other pretext, and steals another root. After this has been repeated three or four times the couple return while he is actually pulling up a root, and they all cry "Thief! thief!" and the roots jump up and they all pursue him, and so the game ends.

II. RIDDLES

A more intellectual type of game which, like most of the tribesmen of Chhattisgarh and the Satpura Mountains, the Baiga are fond of playing, is Riddles. I have collected a large number of these, and a selection is given in this chapter. These Dhandha, or Janauwal (as they are called in Chhattisgarh) throw many a curious and interesting sidelight on tribal life. They are obviously the fruit of keen observation, and reveal a power of grasping a connection between things not usually associated. Some of them are rich in humour—the razor as the little plough that wanders fearlessly through the jungle of the beard, the fly as the beggar-boy who sups with the king, the hen as the little old woman with a load of rags on her back, the baby as the frog drinking from two tanks, are all delightful.

Especially neat also are the descriptions of fish in a river—'where the creeper goes, the beans follow'; cracks in the sun-parched earth—'in summer there are rivers everywhere: in the rains they are dried up'; a lighted lamp—'from one grain of rice, there is a houseful of husks.'

Some of the riddles have a double, and highly vulgar, meaning. These are the most popular, not for their coarseness, but because Baiga humour is always delighted to find wickedness behind a mask of innocence.

There is no need for further comment. Most of the Dhandha explain themselves.

i

No one can touch the stars in the sky;
And no one can touch this golden pendant.

A hanging wasp's nest.

ii

A beautiful girl with a black spot on her face.

The flower of the parsa tree (*butea frondosa*).

iii

You stay behind; I am going away.

A man speaks to his footprint.

iv

Hundreds of leaves huddled close together; the fruit is like a ball of *laddu*. If you can't answer this, it shows your husband is a pimp.

The aonla tree (*phyllanthus emblica*)

The Elephant Game.
The Bel-Sataka Game.

v

They go and come as often as you wish; but when they see water, they shiver.

A pair of shoes.

vi

Its mouth dances along from one place to another.

A cow grazing.

vii

Wherever the creeper goes, the beans follow.

Fish in a river.

viii

The ox is tied in its stall, but the yoke walks away.

A creeper.

ix

You can't put one of the queen's pots on top of another.

Two eggs.

x

A king's stick that no one will lift.

A snake.

xi

A little plough wanders fearlessly through the jungle.

A razor.

xii

One dung-hill for a hundred cows.

A honey-comb.

xiii

In her father's house she is in torment; but when she goes to her mother-in-law she is happy.

Iron in the forge.

xiv

You need not mix the mud with straw or water, and yet the palace is ready.

An anthill.

xv

Eight legs on the ground; four legs point to the sky. There's only one tail to the twelve legs.[1]

A dead bullock carried by four men.

xvi

The mother is a dwarf, and her child is red.

The ber, a small tree with red fruit (*zizyphus jujuba*).

xvii

The mother is empty, the son is full.

The mahua (*bassia latifolia*), whose flower is dry, though the corolla are full of juice.

xviii

The black cow lays hundreds of eggs, and though she doesn't sit on them, the children are born.

Flies.

xix

Soft when it is unripe, hard when it is ripe.

An earthen pot.

xx

Many windows, but one door.

The *kumni*, a trap for catching fish.

xxi

Touch one and you know the secret of them all.

In cooking rice, you test one grain to see if all are ready.

xxii

In front, how beautiful! But when you look behind it's ugly.

A girl's shadow.

xxiii

You can't lift up this royal necklace and put it in your hair.

A procession of ants.

xxiv

You can see it in your mother, sister, aunt or niece, but not in your own wife. If ever you do see it, it means you're impotent.

Broken bangles. Only a widow breaks her bangles.

[1] For some interesting remarks about riddles which are concerned with legs, see Roheim: *Riddle of the Sphinx*, p. 21 (quoting A. Aarne).

xxv

A tree springs up when it hears the music of the sky, but it has no branch or leaves.

A toadstool growing after a thunderstorm.

xxvi

I was going to fetch you; but you have met me on the way.
Let me alone; and I'll take you home with me.

A woman going for water gets caught in a storm.

xxvii

It curls round like a snake. It is white as milk. Solve my riddle and I'll carry you off with me.

Sutia. A circular silver ornament for the neck.

xxviii

A little brat that feeds with a king.

A fly.

xxix

A little girl makes the king weep.

Chili.

xxx

He makes a belt out of his own sinew. He cuts off his own head and shoves it into his stomach.

A leaf-pipe.

xxxi

You sow it in water, and it fills the whole river. But when you reap it you can hold it in one hand.

A fishing-net.

xxxii

White water in a black tank. In it dances a queen.

A churn in a pot of curds.

xxxiii

All night he stands wakeful; all day he sleeps.

The door of a pig's house, which by day is detached and laid on the ground.

xxxiv

A threshing-floor upside down.

A toadstool.

xxxv

You've hands like a man; you've feet like a man.
But for four months you sit quiet.
Why didn't you make a house for yourself?

A monkey in the rains.

xxxvi

All day it was swollen; in the evening the swelling went down.

A bazaar.

xxxvii

In summer there are rivers everywhere; in the rains they are dried up.

Cracks in the dry earth.

xxxviii

Ten brothers beat her; five brothers laid her down on the ground.

A *chapāti* kneaded with two hands, put down with one.

xxxix

Six girls have only one pair of buttocks between them.

A basket carried in the six cords of a *sikka*.

xl

It is born without help of water; it grows in the hot sun; it dries up in the wind.

Perspiration.

xli

It has neither bone nor flesh; it does the work of a sword, and it lives in water.

The potter's string.

xlii

It was a beautiful baby; in youth it lived in the midst of a crowd; in age it rattled as it shook to and fro.

Channa.

xliii

Rub against the thigh.
See a hole and go inside.

A needle and thread.

xliv

Mother lies still: father moves about on top of her.

A grindstone.

xlv

A beautiful tree, the tree grows high.
The bird sits there, and the tree sings.

Hemp.

xlvi

The mother has a root. The daughter has a hole inside. The grandson is a hunchback.

Mahua. Seed, flower and fruit.

xlvii

No leaves, no branches, this tree stands solitary.

A column of smoke.

xlviii

One crooked well. One hill of kachnar trees. Thirty-two pipal trees. One leaf.

Throat, mouth, teeth, tongue.

xlix

In a small block of forest, a barking-deer dances. Ten went for the beat, but only two did the killing.

A louse in the hair.

l

The walls of the well are made of wood. In the water swims a crocodile.

The mouth.

li

A boy dances and as he dances ties a turban on his head.

Parched gram.

lii

Catch hold of its tail—and it growls.

A grindstone.

liii

Say *sheo sheo*, and the branch begins to quiver.

The tail of a dog.

liv

She lays her eggs, then covers them with a stick.

A cow relieves herself, raising her tail, and then lowers it over the place.

lv

A dried-up frog carries a load on its back.

The cross-beam of a house.

lvi

It travels everywhere, but when it returns home, it takes no room at all.

A spear.

lvii

A little piece of wood climbs a huge mountain.

A hare.

lviii

A flying gaur settles on the ground; it has a lot of money on its back.

A peacock.

lix

Thirty-six creepers and one fruit.

A bazaar

lx

The python wriggles through the water.

A boat.

lxi

A girl with her breasts on her back.

A *sūpa* which has bulging corners on the back.

lxii

An old woman with teeth in her belly.

A leaf basket with the stalks sticking out inside.

lxiii

At the least touch it growls.

A drum.

lxiv

How easily it runs to and fro!

A bamboo door sliding on a pole.

lxv

Get up, you *bugli* (girl with swollen cheeks) and do a little work.

A measure for measuring grain.

lxvi

It falls from on high. Pick it up and lick its buttocks.

A wild mango.

lxvii

The earthen pot has a lid of wax.

The fruit of the tendu tree.

lxviii

I have grown and grown, but I never visited another village.

The earthen bin, which is gradually built up, but can never be moved from its place.

lxix

On the fence a drum is hanging.

An ornament in the ear.

lxx

He makes it straight with his spittle. He finds the hole and pushes it in.

Threading a string of beads.

lxxi

The bark is fresh, but the bark-cord with which we tie it is old.

A leaf-plate.

lxxii

He carries a full pot to the jungle; he leaves a root behind; and brings the pot back empty.

Defecation.

lxxiii

A little old woman with a load of rags on her back.

A hen.

lxxiv

A cow with a crumpled horn goes into the deepest jungle.

A scythe.

lxxv

The palace has many tiles on the roof, many windows in its walls. But there is only one big door. When the king enters he cannot get out again.

A fish trap.

lxxvi

He climbs and he burns; he looks like a girl carrying water.

The sun.

lxxvii

The music drops from heaven, but who is the player?

Lightning.

lxxviii

From the wet tree, dry chips of wood.

A man cutting his nails.

lxxix

One sword, two sheaths.

A man with two wives.

lxxx

It survives even after drinking water through its vent.

The *bissera*, a fishing trap.

lxxxi

A king's turban that cannot be measured.

A path.

lxxxii

Touch the place and a spring gushes out.

The eye.

lxxxiii

He weeps sitting in the river.

A frog.

lxxxiv

The creeper is in the cave underneath the hill. But the flower is on the summit.

The wick of a lamp.

lxxxv

The little yogi comes whence we know not.
Put him in anything and it will die. And then we eat him.

Salt.

lxxxvi

A tank-dweller says to a land-lubber, O you who eat making a *crus-crus* noise, why have you trodden on my moustache?

A prawn and a rabbit.

The Phugri-phu game.
Playing with the ghadli.

lxxxvii

When the yogi from the East is on his way, his disciple slaps his thighs and blows the conch.

Cock-crow.

lxxxviii

Cut the crop and let the field go for grazing.

A sheep.

lxxxix

Sow black seed in a white field; cut the crop and it awakes and sings.

A song written on white paper.

xc

The marigolds are blossoming; there is none to pick them. The golden stick is on the ground; there is none to pick it up. The big horse is standing ready; there is none to ride him.

The sun. A snake. A tiger.

xci

In the thickly-wooded fortress the thief is captured. He is executed in the City of the Nail, Nakanpur.

A louse.

xcii

From under the ground he speaks to her who is hanging above. The dead are making a great din.

The *sakla* root tells the brinjal that they are playing the drum, which is made of a dead bullock's skin.

xciii

The stump cut by a woman never grows.

Umbilical cord.

xciv

A roasted *kotra* went to the forest and made a *poh-poh* noise.

An axe.

xcv

The bullock has a pair of bells; at ploughing time it doesn't care whether the ground is *barra* or *māti*.

A man who is indifferent whether he ploughs in unmarried or married flesh.

xcvi

The *chukchirai* bird rubs its buttocks on a stone and hides itself in its nest.

A razor.

xcvii

A mouse's hole is covered with grass.

The vagina.

xcviii

The man sleeps. It is the girl who shakes him.

Grindstone.

xcix

In the valley is a temple. On the temple sits two fireflies. Above the fireflies is a hill. On the hill are tigers and bears.

Mouth, nose, eyes, head and bugs.

c

Yellow rice in a black earthen pot.

Honey in the hive.

ci

A boy with a big stomach cries all night. He has no mother or father.

The *māndar* (drum).

cii

Red shirt—black cap.

Flower of the semur (*bombax malabaricum*).

ciii

O son-in-law, go and plough—when rain falls on the stony earth, return.

Perspiration.

civ

The roasted *bāmi* fish is going into the depths.

A ploughshare.

cv

A frog drinks the water of two tanks.

A child at the breasts.

cvi

Black when it goes in, red when it comes out.

Iron in the forge.

cvii

A red crane stands in the valley. Suddenly, it climbs the hill with a great crackling noise.

Fire.

cviii

The *kāri* fish is inside the river; the ants can't spoil it.

Child in the womb.

cix

How quickly the yogi climbs the hill. His pubic hairs are nine yards long.

Peacock.

cx

Sleep my girl and I'll put my needle into you.

Foot and shoe.

cxi

Plant them close together. Tie them close together.

A comb.

cxii

One pillar and two doors.

The nose.

cxiii

The tiger roars in the ant's hole.

A gun.

cxiv

The tail of the black hen is sweet.

The black fruit of the bhilwa tree (*semecarpus anacardium*).

cxv

Mother, O mother!
What is it, my daughter?
My father is coming.
Let him come, my daughter, my cunnus is strong enough.

The *mowa* grass says to its root, "The jungle fire is coming." "Never mind, my root won't be spoilt." The root remains after the fire, and springs up again.

cxvi

How it hurts while it is going in! But what joy when it is there inside!

The arm of a girl on to which bangles are being pushed.

cxvii

One stick beats two *nangāra* (drums).

The tail of a cow.

cxviii

The root is in the river, the flower is on the hill.

An earthen lamp.

cxix

It is round when it comes from the forest.
We make a hollow of its body.
It eats curd and milk.
Then it goes to the rubbish-heap.

Mohlain leaves made into a leaf-cup.

cxx

Man gives birth to the child, his wife gives it milk.

The *pitla* basket (see fig. 13a), made by men and used by women.

cxxi

All the women have only one navel between them.

The pit where the women go to dig earth.

cxxii

Three brothers have only one nose.

The fruit of the *ricinus communis*, the castor-oil plant.

cxxiii

Where it tickles, there you press it.

A bug.

cxxiv

The poor man throws it away; the rich man puts it in his pocket.

Blowing the nose.

cxxv

Body like a grain-bin; eyes like a *til* seed.

An elephant.

cxxvi

Squashed flat when it goes, squashed flat when it comes.

The *gundhri*, a roll of cloth placed on the head under a pitcher.

cxxvii

Drive the plough, catch hold of the yoke.

Man and wife.

cxxviii

Why do you look backwards as you go?

A man has struck his foot against a stone.

cxxix

Beat it jumping up and down.
Keep an eye upon the hole.

Pounding rice.

cxxx

As long as you hold me, I'll stand up.
But when you let me go I'll sleep.

A broom.

cxxxi

We throw away the flesh and eat the bones.

Grain.

cxxxii

You may go to eat, but unless five of us help you, you can't.

Five fingers.

cxxxiii

A roasted chicken climbs a tree.

An axe.

cxxxiv

He is brought and hung up. When the crowd gathers, they beat him.

A drum.

cxxxv

A beautiful palace without a door.

An egg.

cxxxvi

Three *jīv*, four horns.

Two bullocks in a plough.

cxxxvii

No one is afraid of you, yet your daughter is eaten and they take oil from your son.

Mahua.

cxxxviii

A thorn-covered bull with a single horn.

Brinjal.

cxxxix

Outside it is beautiful. It goes to and fro. But open it, and there's nothing but the mouth of a well.

Woman.

cxl

It is as long as your arms. It has a door in its breast. But the king enters through the cunnus.

A shirt.

cxli

Wave it to and fro, and draw it in.

Pej.

cxlii

Three brothers go to rob a house. One brother creeps inside, and two sit by the door.

Adultery.

cxliii

Without feet it climbs: without a tongue, it eats: if it drinks water, it dies.

Fire.

cxliv

The whole jungle is ablaze, but the sadhu's loin-cloth is untouched.

A path through the forest.

cxlv

When I was a virgin they were always beating me and I didn't mind. But now I am married I can't endure even a slap.

An earthen pot.

cxlvi

The load goes out to graze, but the bullock remains in the house.

A man and his bed.

cxlvii

It has a neck but no head. It has an arm but no hands.

A shirt.

cxlviii

From one grain of rice there is a houseful of husks.

A burning lantern.

cxlix

In four it boils, in four it cools, in four it sinks into the water.

The year and its seasons.

cl

Who would sleep on a moving bed? Who would weep for a dead king?

A flooded river and the death of a tiger.

Chapter XVII

FOLK-LORE

A.—ANIMAL-LORE

THE Baiga are surprisingly poor in animal-lore. The reason may be that so hungry a tribe prefers to see a bird in the pot rather than in its nest, to watch an animal being skinned rather than to observe its manners in the jungle. It is possible too that the harsh administrative measures of recent years have made the Baiga feel less at home in the animal world. But whatever the cause, I have not been able to collect more than a handful of aetiological tales, and a few curious stories all centring round one theme, the coitus of an animal with a human woman.[1] There are half a dozen songs about animals.

i

O monkey, the mango-days have come again!
Where will you get an axe-head? What wood will you use for the haft?
How will you cut the branches,
And bring the mangoes to the ground?

ii

O dry is the river,
And dry is the stream!
Beneath the stones the thirsty crab
Is sobbing *kalap kalap*,
And at last sends forth his life.

[1] There is a widely spread belief that animals abduct women and that women may have animal lovers. There is a Chinese tale of a monkey stealing a man's wife and carrying her away: the husband follows and rescues her. Many African tribes and the Dyaks believe that baboons and orang-outangs carry off girls, though the Kafirs think the baboons are friendly and protect women from lions. (See Tylor: *Primitive Culture*, i., p. 286; and Macdonald: *Folk-Lore*, iii. p. 355.) The Eskimo believe women may find lovers in dogs, eagles and even whales, and may give birth to puppies and bears. (Rink: *Tales and Traditions of the Eskimo* (London, 1875), p. 126.)

iii

The queen of the red ants says *chit chit chit.*
The queen of the white ants has made a fort.
The queen of the prawns broods over the earth.
The queen of the birds cries from the sky.
The parrot with red wings is working magic.

iv

The hornless bullock is afraid to bear his load.
How many sacks are you going to put on my back?
You have filled one sack with roots.
You have filled the other with rice.
How am I to carry such a load?

v

The phadki's wing is broken.
It came to Mandla and sat in my lap.
All around us is a wooden wall.
The mice and cats are playing hide-and-seek.
The hare is hopping about.
All around us is a wooden wall.
The barking-deer has broken its legs.
The goats are jumping up in the air.
The mice and cats are playing together.
All around us is a wooden wall.

I will now quote some of the tales, and first those of an aetiological character; these are nearly all to do with birds and describe why they sing as they do.

There is a phadki who says, "*Utur putur phuris phuris phuris*," or "Come down children, it's now full." The reason is that once the female phadki collected some *til*, washed it with water, and measured it in a measure. Then she went out of her nest, but before she went she said to her children, "None of you are to eat the *til*." Now the *til* slowly dried, and as it dried, its quantity seemed to decrease. The phadki came home, and measured the *til*. Some of it had gone! She was very angry, and killed all but two of her children. Then she thought, I'll wash it again, and now when she measured it she found the measure full. So ever since she cries for sorrow to the children she had killed.

The pihu-bird, sometimes called the bird of sin, because she once put ashes instead of flowers on her husband's head as he was setting out on a journey, is described by the Baiga in a pathetic light.

The pihu-bird is always saying, "*Mor pihu mor pihu*, my love, my love," because her husband was taken by the police to jail and died there. So she now searches for him day and night, in vain.

Another story describes the relations of the peacock and the kussera-bird. 'The kussera-bird used to be a Pathan. The peacock was a wealthy merchant. One day a Raja sent his chaprasi (the Pathan) to call the peacock. The peacock said, "You go ahead, and give the Raja my greetings!" Then the peacock called the Sonar to make ready a dress for him covered with ornaments. The Pathan sat on his horse and went away. But as he went along, he turned into a kussera-bird. Then just as a chaprasi bothers everyone, the kussera seized all the little birds along the road. When the peacock had put on all his ornaments, he turned into a bird also, and began to say, "*Rāja la rām rām kehan kehan kehan kehan!*"'

The three stories that follow are in the form of fables.

i

There was a contest between the fox and the wind, which could go the fastest. The fox won. How did he win? The wind began first and he made a loud roaring noise in the trees. But the fox lifted up his head and cried, and another fox in the next field heard it, and he too cried, and again another fox further on heard it, and cried. So the cry went away, away, away, and the wind panted behind, but could never catch it up.

ii

One day a fox said to himself, "We are the greatest tribe in the world, and nowhere is there a tribe so numerous and powerful as we." He sat down, well pleased with himself, and at that moment an ant bit his backside. He jumped up and went to sit somewhere else. But there too an ant bit him. He went to a third place, and a fourth, but everywhere he found ants. Then he knew that there were more ants than foxes in the world.

iii

Once the bees, which were born from a bull's ears, went and sat on the food of a great Dewar. In that food was poison. The Dewar said, "As there is poison in my food, so will there be poison in your teeth. And for troubling me, you will have to live, seven hundred thousand of you, in one house. And you will eat your own children." So from that day, bees eat their own children, and those who are left survive.

I have also recorded a number of longer stories, the leading characters of which are animals.

1. THE HARE WHO SERVED AS A LAMSENA

One day in the heart of the forest Chirbu met a hare. The hare was sitting absorbed in magic. He was a great Dewar. Then said Chirbu to the hare, "You may be a great gunia, but I am going to kill you for my supper."

"No, don't kill me," said the hare. "I'll get you a wife."

"I have plenty of people like you who are ready to get me wives."

"Ah, but I will get you a really beautiful one."

So then the hare and Chirbu went to the village. When his sister Chirki saw the hare, she was very pleased. "My brother has brought me something to play with," she cried. She washed the hare's feet and gave him food and water. Then said her brother Chirbu, "I am going to keep this hare as your Lamsena."

One day the girl said, "I want to eat some mangoes." So Chirbu and the hare, each with his axe over his shoulder, went to get mangoes from the forest. There was a Dano watching the mango trees. He had a beautiful daughter who lived in the hollow of a mango tree. When the Dano saw the two friends, he said, "I have been hungry for many days. Now I'll eat both of you!"

But the hare hit the Dano with his axe and killed him. Then he cut down the mango tree, and out came a lovely girl. The hare gave the girl to Chirbu and went and picked many mangoes.

They went home, and Chirki ate the mangoes, and Chirbu married the Dano's daughter. Chirki and the hare were married at the same time. After their marriage they went away to the jungle to find a bewar where they could earn their living. They found a huge rock with a cave in it and they made their home there.

When the hare went to sleep with Chirki, he put his paw in her vagina and scratched it and it bled. The hare sniffed at it and a little of the blood went up his nose. He sneezed and scampered away to clean his nose. Then he came back and mounted the girl. But she squeezed him between her legs till he cried, "Let go, let go, I'm dying."

But she would not spare him and squeezed and squeezed him till he died.

II. THE THREE BABIES

One day a fox came to visit a Baiga household. The mother washed the fox's feet with water and made him sit on a seat. "It is a long time, nephew," said the old woman, "since you have been to see us."

"What shall I say, mother, I have been waiting all this time for your daughter to be ready to come and marry me."

"But our daughter is still too young. She has never yet been to a man. How can we marry her?"

"I swear to you that I won't touch her. Only let her come and live in my house."

Then the parents brushed their daughter's hair, and smoothed it with oil, and put on her a new sari, and sent her home with the fox.

They went through the forest together. When they came to a stream the fox took his bride on his back and carried her across. At midday they rested under a tree and took their food. Desire came to the fox and he embraced the girl with his paws. But she said, "No, I'm too small. Besides you are a fox and I am a human being. How can you love me?"

Then they both lived there together under the tree. One day a Baiga came by carrying a chicken. When the man saw the girl he desired her. He let the chicken go and the fox ran after it, and the man ran away with the girl.

As they were crossing a river, a crab caught hold of the girl's clitoris and she began to scream. The Baiga pulled the crab out and put oil on the place, and when she was well took her to his house and married her.

One day when the man had gone to his bewar and the girl was alone in the house, the fox came to see her, and brought a dog-friend with him. They both went to her. Then her husband came to her, and that day she became pregnant.

When she was delivered, she gave birth first to a fox, then to a puppy and thirdly to a boy. The man kept all three in his house with great care. But one day the Raja came to their village and he saw the beautiful fox and dog and bought them, and took them home.

After some time the fox and the dog had a quarrel and the dog killed the fox. Then the Raja being angry had the dog killed. The Baiga and his wife came weeping to the palace. "Why have you killed my children?" cried the girl, and she told the whole story. Then the Raja was very sorry, and he gave the Baiga a good job in his house, and he himself kept the girl.

So they all lived very happily in the Raja's house.

Dressed in thorns—sometimes for divination, sometimes for fun.
Throwing a spear.

III. THE CRANE AND THE FOX

A crane and a fox were great friends. They went everywhere together for food, and whenever they found any dead thing they ate it. The fox used to nibble round the edges, but the crane with his long beak used to go right into the stomach and bring out the entrails.

One day the fox said, "Friend, who taught you so much wisdom?" The crane said, "Bhagavan himself taught me." Then the fox said, "Take me to Bhagavan so that I too can learn wisdom." The crane said, "Come along then. I will fly into the air and you catch hold of my foot. Only you must not look down."

Then the crane flew up into the air, carrying the fox with him, and flew and flew and flew, higher and higher. The fox said to himself, "Why did he tell me not to look down. I will look down." And so he did and at once he fell down, down, down head-first into a deep pool of mud. He was entirely buried, only his hind-legs and tail were left sticking out.

On the bank of the river there was an Ahir and his daughter grazing cattle. The Ahir saw the fox's tail and thought that here was a good dog, so he pulled the fox out of the mud. The fox pretended to be angry. "Why did you pull me out, I was busy digging for rupees. If you don't put me back I'll call for my uncle the tiger and he'll eat you."

Then the Ahir was frightened, and he said, "Don't call the tiger. I'll marry you to my daughter." So the fox said, "Very well. Tie your daughter to that tree." The Ahir tied his daughter to one tree and a calf for the wedding feast to another. But when the fox tried to kill it, the calf kicked him far away. The fox went rolling over and over and over.

Then the girl said, "If you are so impotent that you can't kill a calf, what will you do with me?" The fox said, "It didn't kick me. I just felt a tickling in my back and I was rolling over and over to scratch myself."

The night came. The fox was very hungry. He went to the village and stole a chicken. He brought fire and gave half the chicken and the fire to the girl. She roasted the chicken for her supper. Then they slept together.

Presently the girl said to the fox, "Why do you sleep so quietly and do nothing?" Then the fox tried to go to the girl, but she kicked him and he went rolling over and over and over down to the river. But the fox came back and said, "I have just seen my uncle the tiger sleeping down by the river. If you don't let me do it, I'll call him and he'll eat you." Then the girl was frightened and let him do what he pleased. But the fox tore her with his claws and the girl began to scream. The tiger heard the noise and came to see what was the matter.

The fox was frightened, and said, "Look, uncle, I've brought a calf for you." The tiger killed it immediately, and drank some of the blood. Then he pulled out the stomach and sent the fox down to the river to wash it. The fox hid half under a stone, and brought back the rest for them to eat.

Presently the tiger saw the girl and asked who it was. The fox said it was his wife. "Well, I shall eat her," said the tiger. "No, no, uncle," said the fox. "You can't do that. Come, wait for to-night, and to-morrow I'll get you a wife." Then the tiger said, "I feel thirsty, let's go down to the river." So they both went to the river and drank some water.

The fox sat down on the stone under which he had hidden the calf's stomach and pulled it out and began to eat it.

"What are you eating?" asked the tiger. The fox said, "I am eating my own stomach. I pull it out through my vent, and eat it and so it goes back through my mouth. In this way I never need be hungry." When he heard this the tiger was very excited, and asked the fox to teach him to do it also. The fox told him to go and get some rope, and when he had it, he tied the tiger up. He put his paw up through the tiger's vent and pulled out his entrails and ate some himself and offered some to the tiger. But the tiger was almost mad with pain and very quickly died.

The fox went on eating and eating, and presently he pushed his head right inside the tiger's body and the door closed upon him and he couldn't get out.

A young Baiga had come to the jungle to gather leaves. He saw the girl tied to the tree. She had gone thin for fear and hunger, and looked like an old woman. But when the Baiga saw her, desire entered his body through his eyes and passed into his mind. He said to himself, "When a man is hungry he will even eat uncleaned rice, and cares nothing for the little stones. So when a man is in heat, he will go even to an old woman." So thinking he went to the girl and caught her in his arms.

But she said, "Brother, first give me something to eat and some water to drink. Then you may do with me what you will."

The tree to which she was tied was a char tree. The Baiga climbed it and picked some fruit and went down to the river and brought her water. Then after she had eaten, he went to her. He saw that she had been torn by the nails of the fox, and asked her what had happened. She told him the whole story. Then he took her home and married her.

IV. THE FOX AND THE FROG

A fox and a frog lived together. During the rains, the fox couldn't get any food. The frog stayed in the water and was very happy. Then the fox said, "I'm going to eat you." "No," said the frog, "Don't eat me. I'll get you a wife." So the fox let her be.

The frog went hopping along to the house of their Raja, and greeted him. "*Mamājī*," she said. "*Rām rām!*" The Raja gave her a seat to sit on and the frog asked the Raja to give her his daughter for his friend to marry. The Raja had great faith in the frog who always warned him about the rain, and he sent his daughter with her.

The girl went on ahead and the frog hopped along behind. They went on and on till they came to the fox's house. The frog cried, "Brother, I've brought you your wife, come out and see her."

When the girl heard this she was very angry and she stamped on the frog and killed her. The fox ran out to bite the girl, but she cried, "What! would you bite the girl who has come to be your wife?" Then the fox took her with him to the jungle.

They went for a very long way and at last the girl felt hungry and sat down under a tree. The fox went to a village near-by to try and find some food. There, in a Baiga's house was a pot of *pej* and the fox picked it up in his mouth and brought it to the tree.

Meanwhile the girl had fallen asleep. The fox hid the pot and went to the girl. Just then a young Baiga came by, and when he saw the fox he threw his axe at him. He missed the fox, but he hit the pot and broke it. The fox ran away.

Then that young Baiga came and looked at the Raja's daughter. He thought she was dead. But when he saw she was living, desire came into his mind through his eyes, and he went to her.

When the girl saw that young Baiga above her, she put her arms round him. The boy was very frightened when she did that.

Afterwards, the Baiga took the Raja's daughter to his house and gave her a lot of *pej* to drink. He married her, and daily they went together to the jungle to cut their bewar, and to dig roots.

V. THE KINDLY COWS

An old Baiga widow had one son. He used to take the cows of the other villagers out to graze. One day he led them far into the jungle.

He came to the edge of a stream and there he saw a tiger going for water. The tiger put his nose into the water and sniffed at it, and a huge crab that lived there caught him by the nose. The tiger was very angry, and looking round saw the boy. He beckoned to him and said, "Come and set me free." The boy hit the crab's claws with his axe and broke them. Then the tiger said to the boy, "Tell no one about this or I'll eat you." The boy ran away in fright.

But that night the boy told his mother all about it. Then he was frightened and he tied his bed up to the roof and slept there. The tiger had been listening behind the house and he heard the boy telling his mother and was very angry. Then when everyone was asleep, the tiger crept into the house and pulled down the bed and carried it off with the boy in it towards the jungle. Half-way along the road, the boy woke up. There was a big tree by the roadside and as they went beneath it, the boy caught hold of the branches and pulled himself up into it. The tiger went on his way with only the bed on his back. When he reached his den and found the boy was gone he came back to look for him, but couldn't find him anywhere.

Under that tree lived Surigai and a great pile of dung that she had been dropping for twelve years. No one ever cleared it away. So in the morning, the boy came down from the tree and cleared away the dung and washed the calves, who were all covered with filth and dung. In the evening Surigai came home and instead of dung, dung, dung, found everything was clean. She cried to the boy, "Come down, I won't hurt you." But for fear the boy refused to come for two or four days. Then all the cows licked him and said, "Look, here are two pots for you." Then Surigai filled the pots with milk, and the boy drank the milk and washed all the cows and lived with them for some time.

But later the boy wanted to go away. So Surigai gave him two flutes, one for Dukh and one for Sukh, one for sorrow and one for joy. She said, "When you play on Sukh-basseri, we'll graze happily, but when you play Dukh-basseri we'll all come running to protect you." So the boy went home. One day to see what would happen, he played the Dukh-basseri, and all the cows came rushing to his house and frightened his mother and trampled down the *kānda-bāri*. His mother asked him never to do that again.

One day the boy went to the river to bathe. One of his hairs fell out and he wrapped it in a leaf and threw it in the river. It floated down the stream to where a King's daughter was bathing. She picked it up and when she saw the hair she fell in love with it and refused to eat or drink till her father sent a Dhimar up the river to find the boy. The Dhimar brought the boy and he married the Princess. But his father-in-law was unkind to him and wanted to kill him, so the boy played on Dukh-basseri and all the cows came and surrounded him and his wife. Then he went back to his own house taking his girl with him.

B.—FAIRY-TALES

The Folk-tales (of which the following are a small selection) have been collected from all over the Baiga country and, no matter where they come from, show a remarkable family resemblance to one another. They are not quite what we would expect from the Baiga, but then fairy stories never are what we would expect from anyone, and these tales are not so distant from the actual life of the tribe as we might suppose at first sight—for example, the tale of the king's son breaking the pots of the water girls is exactly paralleled in Rawan's life-story: he used to make friends with girls by breaking the water-pots on their heads with his arrows.

I have, however, omitted tales that are common among Hindus, and as far as I can discover these are genuine Baiga stories. They are told simply and solely for recreation. They are a way of escape from the harsh realities of everyday existence: that is probably why they are so unlike it. The Baiga tell their stories with great animation; they act parts of them, burst into song at others, whisper the secret bits and weep at the sad ones. It is a delight to listen to them round the fire in the long winter evenings.

It is worth noting the important place given to magic, to the separable soul and life-index, and to some tradition of a former Baiga kingdom.[1]

I. THE CLEVER POTTER

A potter had thirteen sons, twelve of them were married, all but the youngest. The twelve took earth and made pots, but the youngest boy stayed at home and did nothing. One day the brothers thought, "Why should our little brother be so idle? Let us compel him to do some work." So they ordered him to bring twelve cart-loads of mud. "You must drag them yourself, there's no need of buffaloes." So the youngest brother went, filled the carts with mud and dragged them to the house. When

[1] 'In Mandla the Baigas sometimes hang out from their houses a bamboo mat fastened to a long pole to represent a flag which they say once flew from the palace of a Baiga king.' —Russell and Hiralal, ii., p. 79.

the other brothers saw how strong he was, they were afraid that he would use his strength to kill them, so they drove him from their house.

The potter boy went to the jungle and there he found a Baiga who was ploughing with a tiger instead of a bullock. Then the potter said, "I've never seen anyone so strong as you." The Baiga said, "I'm not so strong as the boy who dragged twelve cart-loads of mud." Thus they became friends and they went on together to find a living.

Presently they met a Lohar who was shaping red-hot iron by bending it with his bare hands. "We've never seen anyone so strong as you," they said. "O, I'm not so strong as the Baiga who ploughs with a tiger," said he. Thus they became friends. Then the three of them went on their way together.

Soon they met an Ahir who was making rope out of the dry dust in the road. "We've never met anyone so clever as you," they all said. "O I'm not so clever as the Lohar who bends red-hot iron with his bare hands." So they became friends. Then the four of them went on their way together.

Then they saw a Teli who was pressing out twelve measures of oil without the help of bullocks. "We've never met anyone so clever as you," they said. "O I'm not so clever as the Ahir who makes rope out of the dry dust," said he. They made friends with him also, and went on with him to the Kajli-ban-pahar. There they found a good clean spot to live in, and they arranged that every day one of them should stay at home to cook while the others did the hunting.

One day, when it was the Teli's turn to cook, a Rakshasa in the shape of a little boy came to him and asked for something to eat. The Teli gave him a bit of *marria* bread. The boy begged for more. "No, that's plenty," said the Teli. "Be off with you." But the boy took rice from the pot uninvited. The Teli got angry and began to beat him. Then the Rakshasa, with one tooth in heaven and one in hell, began to fight. At last the Teli was beaten. Then the Ahir came home, and began to fight, and he was beaten. Then came the Lohar and he was beaten. Then came the Baiga and he was beaten. At last came the potter and he killed the Rakshasa. Now the Rakshasa had five daughters, very beautiful. The potter took one of them. "Who will marry her?" they all asked. "You are the best," they said at last to the potter. "You marry her, and we'll all call her *bhauji*." So the potter kept her, and all five of them went to her in turn. But the girl herself loved the Baiga, and she said to him, "I want to live only with you, and not have to sleep with any of the others."

So when the potter went to her, she wept and said, "I don't like living with such a lot of men. Let me live with the Baiga and you bring my four sisters for the rest of you." So the potter went and brought the four sisters and gave them to his four friends. After a time they went away to a village, but the Baiga and his girl stayed in the jungle. There they made a little hut, and got all they wanted without toil from Dharti Mata.

One day the Baiga's wife went to bathe in the river. As she washed her head a few of the hairs fell out.[1] She wrapped them up in a leaf and threw them into the river and went home. The hairs went floating down the river to where a Gond Raja's son was bathing. When he saw the hairs he fell madly in love with them. "If the hair is so lovely what will the face be like?" He went home and said to his father, "I must marry this girl or I will die." His father was so anxious that he sent an old Malin up the river to find the girl. She went in a boat till she found the girl bathing in the river. The Baiga had gone to hunt sambhar in the forest. The Malin said, "O my lovely child, I am your mother's sister, and I've come all this way to see you." So the girl was pleased and took the old woman home and gave her the best food they had. Then the Malin plotted how to kill the Baiga. She asked the girl, "When your husband goes to hunt in the jungle, where does he keep his *jīv*?" She said, "In his arrow." The next day the Baiga went out to hunt again. The Malin collected a pile of wood and put the arrow in it, and burnt it.[2] Directly the arrow began to burn, fever attacked the Baiga far away in the jungle. He came running home. He kicked his wife in the breast and cried, "You've killed me." The mark of his foot always remained on her breast. Then he died. But the girl put his body in a box and filled it with oil. After a few days the Malin took the girl away saying that the Raja's son wanted to marry her. The girl said, "My Raja is dead. I won't marry again for twelve years." But as she was being dragged to the Raja's house, the four friends met her. She told them what had happened, and they killed the old Malin and took the girl back with them to the jungle. There they searched in the ashes and at last found a tiny bit of the arrow. The Lohar made it afresh, and they opened the box, and the Baiga returned to life again. Then they lived happily with their wives in the jungle, and Dharti Mata gave them all things that they needed.

[1] A common motive in Indian folk-lore. In Bompas, op. cit. p. 29, there is a tale of a boy who went to bathe, and sent some of his hairs floating down the river in a leaf. Two princesses found them, and the younger refused food till the boy was found. A parrot and a crow brought him to her, and they were married. See also Steele: *Tales of the Punjab* (London, 1894), p. 42.

[2] For the 'separable soul' see Macculloch: *The Childhood of Fiction* (London, 1905), p. 118; and Steele, op. cit., p. 55. In the latter, Punjabi story, a prince's life is kept in his sword. This is placed in the fire, and he feels a burning fever. It becomes red-hot, and a rivet falls out of the hilt—and his hand comes off. At last, the sword is repaired and repolished, and the prince comes back to life. Many other references, with a full discussion, will be found in *The Ocean of Story*, op. cit., i. pp. 129 ff.

II. THE BEATING OF BHAGAVAN

A Raja ruled over a town where lived an old Baiga and his wife. The Baiga had been in the Raja's service for many years, and to reward him the Raja gave him a large block of gold and sent him home to enjoy the remainder of his days. On the way home the old man came to a river. He put down the gold upon the bank and went to bathe. But a dog came by and stole the gold. The old man thought that Bhagavan had taken it, and he got very angry and said, "I'll kill Bhagavan for this." He shouldered his axe and went down the road to search for Bhagavan. Soon he came to a great tank that a Seth had made. It was very deep, but there was no water. "Where are you going?" asked the Seth. "I am going to beat Bhagavan." "When you see him tell him that there's been no water in the tank for five years."

Then the old man came to a field and saw a horse standing there "Where are you going?" asked the horse. "I'm going to beat Bhagavan." "Then when you see him, tell him that no one has ridden me for twelve years."

Then the old man came to a village where a Gond was living. He had five wives, but they all had run away. Only his sister was with him. Then Bhagavan came in the form of a Dewar and said to the old man, "Where are you going, father?" "I'm going to beat Bhagavan." So Bhagavan said, "Why do you trouble to go further? Go home and you'll find the gold in your own house." But the old man said, "I must first write a letter." So Bhagavan wrote it for him. In the letter the old man told the whole matter of the Seth, the horse, and the Gond. Then said Bhagavan, "Tell the Seth to bury a ring in the tank and water will spring up. As you go, saddle the horse and it will carry you home. Take the Gond's sister with you, and all his five wives will return to him."

So the old man did as he was ordered, and everything happened as Bhagavan had said. At last when he came to his own house, he found that the dog had carried his gold home. So he married the Gond's sister and they lived happily together.

III. THE GIRL AND THE JACKAL

An old Baiga and his wife had seven daughters. They were very poor and had no food for the girls, save some roots and a few handfuls of gram.

At night, they put all the children to sleep, and then they took a cock and killed it, thinking to eat it all by themselves. But one of the girls was sleeping near the hearth, and she woke up and said, "I'll light the fire for you, mother." Then they all woke up and the old people had to share with them.

One day the father went to get wood in the jungle. He got some char fruit, and put it in the cloth tied round his head. When he got home, he said, "Come, my girls and look at my head." But only his youngest daughter came. He scratched his head and some of the char fruit fell out. "Look what big lice are falling out of my head," he said. Then all the children came, laughing and fighting for the fruit. "Father, take us to pick some more." "No, no, it's too hot." But at last they made him take them and they carried water in a gourd. The father took them all to Kajli-ban-pahar. There he showed them the char trees, and stuck the gourd of water in a branch of the tree. The father loved his youngest daughter very much and kept her with him. While the others were scattered through the jungle eating char, he went with the little girl and drank all the water and broke the gourd. Then he and his favourite went home.

The six sisters began to feel very thirsty. There was a tall semur tree there. At its foot were two leaf-cups. In one of them was a man's urine, in the other a jackal's. Two of the sisters were so thirsty that they drank them. There were still four left who had had nothing and they went to and fro.

But the two who had drunk went to a village and lived there. They both became pregnant. One gave birth to six boys, the other to a jackal.[1] When the boys grew up, there was lots of food in their house, but there was none in the jackal's house, for the boys were able to cut bewar, but the jackal could only sometimes catch a hen. So the jackal began to steal from the boys' house and give the food to his mother. One day the boys discovered him stealing. So they set a trap by making some rice-paste with a bit of dry cow-dung in it. Presently the jackal was caught in it and they threw him with the trap into the river. It floated down, down to a place where an Ahir was grazing his cows on the bank. When he saw something floating down the river, he thought it might be valuable so he got hold of it. But there was only the jackal, the cow-dung and the paste. The Ahir

[1] Stories of women who give birth to animals are common throughout the world. (See Macculloch, op. cit. p. 262 ff.) The Aino have a tale of a girl who gave birth to a snake as a result of the sun's rays shining into her as she slept. (Chamberlain: *Aino Folk Tales*, p. 43.) The Dyak and Silakan refuse to kill the cobra, because one of their women once gave birth to twins, a boy and a cobra. There is a similar belief in Java about the crocodile. The Eskimo seem especially fond of animal lovers, believing themselves descended from the union of a woman and a dog. Women may bear puppies and bears. (Rink, op. cit., pp. 77, 126, 412.)

threw away the cow-dung, kept the paste, and let the jackal go. The jackal went home and asked his mother to make him some bread. "Tie it round my neck with an axe," it said, and his mother did so. Then it went to the jungle. The jungle was full of rats. The jackal caught an old rat and said, "I'm hungry, now I'm going to eat you." The rat said, "Don't eat me, master. Let me serve you instead." So the jackal said, "All right, cut all this jungle for me." The rat did so. When it was cut, the rat set fire to it, and the jackal sowed gourd seed in the ashes. When the crop was ready the jackal again caught the old rat and said, "Open a gourd for me." When the rat had opened it, the jackal caught a sparrow and said, "There are six brothers. They have much rice in their field. Fill this gourd with their rice." The sparrow went and brought the rice, and so did other sparrows, till every gourd in the jackal's field was full.

Then the jackal went to a Gond's house and said, "O *mamā*, lend me your cart." The Gond gave him the cart and the jackal brought all the gourds and put them in his house. Then the jackal asked the Gond for his daughter. "But you're a jackal, how can I give you my daughter?"[1] "Well, I've a lot of food here. At least she won't starve." The Gond said, "Give me a gourd and I'll make curry." The jackal gave him one and when the Gond saw that it was full of rice, he was pleased, and gave his daughter. Then the jackal went to his mother with his wife and the cart-load of rice. The six brothers had no rice at all, and full of anger they killed the jackal. The eldest brother kept the girl, but they all had her.

IV. THE BAIGA KING AND THE GOND GIRLS

In Garha Haveli there was once a Baiga Raja. He had one son. He was a great hunter. He had a great tank made, but there was no water in it. One day two Gond girls went to get water to drink, and when they could not find any, the elder girl said to her little sister, "Give me that ring off your finger, and we'll throw it in the tank and then there'll be plenty to drink." They threw it in the tank and a lot of water sprang up and they were able to drink. Then the elder sister wanted to go home, but the little girl said, "I want my ring," and she began to cry. Then the big girl went into the tank to get the ring. She went up to her knees, and cried out, "I have gone up to my knees, but I haven't found the ring." But the little girl wept and cried, "Bring it, bring it to me." Then she went further and she cried, "I am up to my chin in the water, but I've not found the ring." But still the child cried, so the girl went right under the water and called out, "Is it me you love or your ring?" But the child only cried, "I want my ring." At last the girl found it, and threw it on to the bank, but she herself was drowned.

When her little sister had picked up the ring, she began to cry out, "Come, come out of the water." But when she saw that her sister was drowned, she began to weep bitterly. There was a tamarind tree on the bank of the tank, and the child climbed up into this.

Presently, the Baiga king came by. He had five sepoys with him. The first was lame, the second was deformed, the third was deaf, the fourth squinted, and the fifth was blind in one eye. The king went to relieve himself by the tank, and said to his sepoys, "Here is a good shady tree. Let us rest here." So he lay down under the tree and one of the girl's tears fell on him. He jumped up and said, "What is this that is throwing water on the king? Is it a *bhut* or a *pret* or a bird or a human being? What is it?" He looked up but could see nothing. Then they all looked up, but no one could see the girl, until at last the one-eyed man saw her.

The king sent him up into the tree to bring her down. When she came down, she seemed so beautiful to the king that he fainted away. His sepoys threw water on him, and he recovered. That day he didn't go hunting, but went home, taking the girl with him. There he gave her a bath, put on her the best clothes and spread before her a wonderful meal. When his son came in and saw the girl's beauty, he too fainted. When she saw him, desire came to her and she longed for him. Then the boy went into the village to play with his friends, and he told them, "My father has brought me a good girl." So they all came running to the house to look at her. When they saw her they all fell to the ground in a faint. But the father thought, "I must have this girl." And his son thought, "I must have this girl." But the king married her. His son thought, "You may be my father, but one day I'll carry off your wife." The girl also didn't want to marry the king, but loved his son.

Now no one knew that the king had married the girl. In the house there was a large iron grain-bin, and the king's *jīv* was kept in an axe which was hidden inside the bin. The boy discovered this, so he waited until one day his father went into the bin to see his *jīv*. At once the boy shut the door and locked it. Then he brought a lot of wood and put it all round the bin and poured oil on it and set fire to it, and burnt his father to death.

Then he took the Gond girl, and after he had given a tribal feast he made her a Baiga, and they both ruled the kingdom.

V. THE MONKEY BOY

A Gond Raja had seven sons, of whom six were married. The youngest boy was very mischievous and there used to be many quarrels between him and his brothers' wives. The youngest wife said to him one day, "Why do you bother us? Get a wife for yourself and bother her." Hearing this the boy got very angry and went to the Kajli-ban-pahar and began to live there. He got no food and grew very angry. He used to live in a tree. In that jungle there were nine lacs of monkeys. He went to them and told them his story. When they heard it, they thought for a long time, and at last they decided to kill an old monkey and dress the boy in its skin and let him live with them. So they did this.

In that jungle lived an old Baiga with his wife. The boy sat in a tree near-by. The monkeys used to steal from the Baiga's bewar kutki, maize, and other things, even rice and kodon. The Baiga and his wife got very angry and they made a trap. One day the boy got caught in it. The old Baiga was about to kill him, when the boy said, "Don't kill me, I'll live with you and serve you." Then they thought, "We have no child. This monkey talks like a boy. Let us keep him with us." So they adopted him as their son and he worked for them.

One day the Raja sent his *kotwar* with a drum nine hands long and a stick seven hands long to call all the villagers for *begār* to cut his rice. Shouting for them, he came to the Baiga's house. The boy said, "I'll go. Don't you go." They answered, "Don't go, you'll get into trouble." But he went. All the people were standing round. He went to where the women were standing. They sent him back to the men. The men sent him back to the women. They all roared with laughter. When the *kotwar* saw what was happening, he sent the boy to work in a separate field. This field belonged to the Raja's daughter. It was a field of twelve *khandi*. In two hours the boy cut all the rice, tied it in bundles, made a pile of it, and sat on the top of the pile. Everyone came to look, they were all astonished, and someone was sent to tell the Princess that her field was ready. The Princess was very pleased and cooked a great feast for the boy. Before the girl saw him, the boy went to the river to bathe, and to do that he removed his monkey-skin. As he was doing his hair, four or five of the hairs broke; they shone like gold. He hid the hairs in a leaf on the river bank. When the Princess went there with the food, she found the leaf. She undid it. When she saw the hairs she fainted with joy.

Then when she recovered she went to the field, taking the hairs with her.[1]

There she gave the boy a gold dish, a silver pot and the food she had prepared. The boy said, "I won't eat off this, but only off leaves." The Princess thought, "He must surely be a Prince." She brought him a leaf-plate and he ate. He began to throw away his leavings, but the girl said, "Don't throw it away. I'll take it home with me." The boy said, "If you touch my leavings and my father hears of it, he'll kill me." But she took his plate and went home.

Then, for love of the boy, the Raja's daughter went to sleep in a tumble-down house on a broken bed. Everyone went to look for her. After searching for a long time, at last they found her. But she refused to say a word to anyone. A thousand men asked her what she was doing there, but she refused to say a word. At last a clever old Malin came. She took a very long sari, some black *til*, some white *til* and a baby pig. The Malin hid the black *til* in her hair, the white *til* in her sari and the pig in her lap. Then she sat beside the Princess. Presently she pulled the black *til* one by one out of her hair and ate them, saying, "How horrid these lice are." She pretended to vomit as she ate them. Then she picked the white *til* one by one out of her sari. "How horrid the bugs are," she said, eating them one by one. Then she squeezed the little pig till it squealed, and she cried, "O la-la, how full of wind I am to-day!" At last the girl burst out laughing, and said, "Go away, old mother, or I'll hit you." But that clever Malin said, "I won't stop breaking wind till you tell me what's the matter."

So at last the Princess said, "I'm unhappy because I want to get married." When the Raja heard that he held a court. Everyone came for it. The monkey-boy also came and sat on a tree. The Princess went with the garland, and when she had looked at everyone she put it round the monkey-boy's neck. Then the Raja said, "This is no good, we must try again." Three times they tried. But every time the girl put the garland round the monkey-boy's neck. Then the Raja got very angry and said, "Give this mad daughter of mine and this monkey a handful of gram and drive them away and let them live in a hut in the jungle."

They went and made their home there. Every night, after the girl had gone to sleep, the boy used to creep out of the hut and go to the village, and throw gram at all the horses that were there. He wanted to see which of them would awake. There was a mare who always woke. He used to

[1] Bompas (op. cit., p. 451) contrasts the Bengal tradition that it is the girl's hair which floats to her lover with the Kolhan stories in which it is always the long hair of the hero which inspires love in the heart of the Raja's daughter. The Baiga know both forms of the tradition.

saddle her and ride round and round the village for hours. Then he would let her go and come home. One night, his wife awoke and found that he was away. She discovered his monkey-skin lying on the floor. She was angry and burnt it. When the boy returned, he felt very sorry but there was nothing he could do. So he went to another village and they built a fine palace. The news of it came to the girl's father. He sent men to call them. But they refused to go, they were afraid. Then he brought them by force and gave them his kingdom. And the boy took his wife home to show her to his six brothers.[1]

VI. THE DISPUTE

Once the Cow was disputing with the Wind who was greatest.

Then Nanga Baiga came by and asked them why they were fighting.

The Cow said, "I am the greatest, for all over the world the crops grow by the help of my dung."

Then Sorrow and Sleep came to that place. Sleep said, "You are both wrong. I am the greatest, for whatever trouble or sorrow you have during the day, I can cure it at night."

The Wind said, "Yes, I am not great, for without the help of the clouds I cannot move."

At last Wealth joined them. He said, "I am the greatest, for where I live there is no need of dung, and the Wind cannot harm me, and Sleep comes unbidden, and no Sorrow can remain where I am."

Sorrow said, "He speaks truly. For where Wealth lives, I cannot live."

Nanga Baiga heard them all, and he said, "Truly there is none greater than Wealth."

VII. THE MAGIC FRUIT[2]

Out of five Baiga brothers, four were married. The youngest had

[1] The skin-dress is a common feature of folk-tales. The Dove-maidens of the *Arabian Nights* had a feather vest which they removed for bathing, and without which they could not fly. A Santal tale describes a boy who had a caterpillar skin. One day he took it off, and put two of his hairs in a leaf and sent them floating down the river. A princess found them and refused to eat till she met the boy. At night, when he removed his skin, she burnt it, and thereafter he retained his proper shape. (Bompas, op. cit., p. 228 ff.) See also Frere: *Old Deccan Days* (London, 1868), pp. 183, 193—the king who had a coat of jackal-skin; Stokes: *Indian Fairy Tales* (London, 1880), p. 41 ff.—a prince with a monkey-skin; *Folk Tales of Hindustan*, pp. 54 ff.—a princess with a monkey-skin which was burnt by the hero; Thornhill: *Indian Fairy Tales*, p. 67; Steele, op. cit., p. 185; Behari Day: *Folk-Tales of Bengal*, (London, 1889), p. 86; Knowles: *Folk-Tales of Kashmir*, 2nd ed. (London, 1893), p. 20.

[2] The Ho story of the Belbati Princess presents several points of comparison with this tale. Bompas, op. cit., p. 461.

not yet got a wife. The other brothers were all afraid that the youngest would be after their wives. They said, "Go, and find a wife for yourself." So away the boy went.

As he went, away through the great jungle of the Kajli-ban-pahar, he came to a village where there was a great Dewar magician. He decided to become his disciple until he could get a pretty girl to marry. After he had served the Dewar for some time, the Dewar became very fond of him and said, "Whatever you desire, I will give you."

The boy said, "I have everything in the world, save a mate."

The Dewar said, "That is nothing. Ask for something more."

"No," said the boy. "All I want is a wife."

Then the Dewar said, "You must stay with me for four days more." The Dewar went out to his bewar and brought sweet roots and fruit and fed the boy. Then the boy promised to do everything that the Dewar told him.

Then said that Dewar, "In the jungle is an anar tree. Beneath it is a spring of water. There live the twenty-one sisters, and the youngest of them is Anarjodi who lives in the fruit of the tree. Before cock-crow every morning she comes out to bathe, and the twenty sisters wash her and rub her with oil and clothe her with lovely clothes and put her back again." Then the Dewar gave the boy a *bel dhanda* and *amarkand* water and fed him on sweet roots, and said, "Don't be afraid. Go at night and hide behind the tree. Then when Anarjodi comes out, look at her, and just as she is going back, beat the tree with your stick, and the fruit in which she lives will fall to the ground."

So that very night the boy went and hid behind the tree and did as the Dewar had told him. He knocked down five fruits from the tree, but Anarjodi wasn't there. So he came again the next night, and this time when he struck the tree Anarjodi's fruit fell down. The boy picked it up and ran away as fast as he could go. But the twenty sisters saw him and they chased him right up to the Dewar's house. There they stopped, for they were afraid to come near the Baiga Dewar. Then the Dewar made the boy rest for two days, and after that he said, "Go home now, but don't break open the fruit until you get there. When you go to bed in your own house break the fruit open against the leg of the bed." He also gave the boy some ashes. "When you're in trouble," he said, "eat the ash and call for me, and I will help you."

Away went the boy towards his home. The sun was very hot and on the way he came to a well. He was thirsty and after drinking lay down to rest. As he lay in the shade of the trees by the well he began to wonder if it really was the right fruit that he had brought with him. He broke it open to see, and out came the loveliest girl in the world. When he saw her, that poor Baiga boy fainted. The girl poured water on him and he recovered. She sat down and he put his head in her lap and slept.

The girl had a flower tied in her hair. In that flower was her *jīv*. As the boy slept, a bumble-bee came and carried off the flower. It flew over the mouth of the well and dropped it in. Directly the flower touched the water the girl disappeared. When the boy woke, he saw that the girl was gone and he wept for a long time. Then he ate some of the ashes that the Dewar had given him and called on him for help. Then once more the fruit appeared, unbroken, in his hand.

At last the boy reached his home. His four brothers welcomed him, but they wondered why he had not brought a wife with him. The boy made a strong house, fenced it well and said that no one was to enter it. His sisters-in-law were very curious, but he would not let them see anything. When all was ready, he broke open the fruit against the leg of his bed, and his girl came out and he slept with her with great joy.

Now one day a Chamarin came to his house. The boy had gone with his brothers to cut bewer. She went up behind the girl and snatched the flower from her hair and put it on the fence. The girl at once disappeared and the Chamarin dressed herself in her clothes and ornaments, and cooked food for the boy. But though she was in every other way like Anarjodi, one of her eyes was broken.

The boy came home and ate his supper. He didn't realize that this was a new girl. One day the villagers said, "Our brother has brought a beautiful new wife. Let us go and see her." When they saw her, they all began to laugh. "It's only that one-eyed Chamarin," they cried, and declared that he must give a feast as penalty for taking such a girl to his house.

The boy was filled with shame by this, and again ate ash and called on his Dewar for help. When he did so, Anarjodi returned and he killed the Chamarin. At that the villagers were very pleased.

One day a Raja, hearing of Anarjodi's beauty, sent his army to fetch her. But the boy blew his ashes at them, and the ashes turned into bees, wasps, scorpions and snakes and drove the army away.

After that they lived very happily together. But one day a Brahmin sadhu came to their house at the very moment when the boy was with his girl and loving her with great passion. When the sadhu saw this love-making, he cursed them: "Next time you lie together, may you both die!" and went on his way.

The next day the boy again went to Anarjodi, and as he put his arms around her, they both died.

The villagers thought they were so deep in love that they were sleeping together all day long. None liked to disturb them. But the days went by and there was no sound from the house. At last the brothers went in and found them dead. They carried them out and buried them as they were in each other's arms.

VIII. THE PRINCE AND THE BAIGA GIRL

A Gond Raja had one son. After his marriage the boy brought his wife home. He used to go daily to hunt. When he came home she used to put a pot of water on the threshold so that he could wash his feet, but she was too shy to come before him. So many days passed.

Then one day the Raja's son killed his wife in a tank. When the Raja heard it, he called the boy to him and said, "How many marriages do you want?"

"I'll marry as many girls as you will give me," said the boy.

"Very well," said his father. "Have as many as you want."

So the boy saddled his horse, and took food and a lot of money and rode off into the jungle to find wives. Presently he came to a Baiga village. There was a lake there. He lay down to rest on its banks.

In the evening a Baiga girl went to get water. When the Prince saw her, he fell in love with her immediately. He followed her back to her house, and going in asked her father if he might stay there. After a few days the Prince said to the old Baiga, "Give me your daughter, and you can have anything you want."

The Baiga answered, "I am only a man of the jungle, and you are a Raja's son. How can you marry my daughter?"

"If you don't give her to me," said the boy, "I'll die here."

So they were married, and the Prince took his girl home. The girl's *jīv* was kept in the hollow trunk of a babul tree on an island beyond the seven seas and the sixteen rivers. The Prince went there and saw his wife's *jīv*, that all was well with it, and returned.

One day the Baiga girl said, "I want to go to my mother's house to see my brothers and sisters." So they went to her house. Now that girl had three sisters more beautiful than herself. The Prince stayed there and all three fell in love with him.

At night they said, "You are to sleep in this room. Don't go outside, don't open the door, don't come into our room." Then after they had gone to bed, all four sisters sat on a bed, and it flew into the air, and took them to Bhagavan. Then they began to dance before him.

At night, the boy's desire grew for the three sisters, and he got up to go to them, but could not find them anywhere. In one room there was a horse, whose name was Bendul. He fed the horse and sat on its back and it carried him up to Bhagavan's house, and there he secretly watched the dance.

In the morning the three sisters asked their elder sister to let them also live with the Prince. But she was angry and refused. "He is your *bāto*," she said. So the three sisters took her out into the bewar and killed her there, and the Prince took the three of them home instead, and they lived with great happiness in the Raja's house.

IX. THE MAGIC POT

A Brahmin and his wife went daily begging and every evening they saved a little and put it by. They had two pots, one for *til* and one for rice. After a time, both pots became full. One day there was very heavy rain and they couldn't go begging. So the goodwife said, "I'll go to bathe. You take some rice out of the pot and get it ready." She brought both the pots and put them before him. But as he was about to take some rice out of the pot, a voice came from it.

"Take me out gently, father, or you'll hurt me."

The Brahmin was very frightened and he went to the other pot, but from this too a girl's voice spoke. So he went outside and waited for his wife. When she came, he told her what had happened, and she very carefully took some rice out of the pot and there was a lovely girl. Her name was Chaurmoti. From the *til* pot, they took another girl, even prettier than the first. She was called Tilmoti. The Brahmin and his wife were very pleased at this. They made a swing in front of their house and every day set the girls on it.

One day a Baiga and his wife came to that village to sell roots and little baskets. When the Baiga saw the girls he fell down senseless. His wife threw water over him. When he recovered he sold his roots and then went quietly to tell their Raja. "Their heels are as delicate as your tongue," he told him. The Raja was very excited and went with the Baiga to the Brahmin's house.

When the Raja saw the girls, he too fell senseless. When he had recovered he asked the Brahmin to give him Tilmoti as a wife. He gave the Brahmin his weight in gold for her.

After some days, Chaurmoti went to see her sister. Tilmoti had many ornaments. Chaurmoti asked her to go and bathe, so they went to the well together. When they got there, Chaurmoti persuaded her sister to let her put on her ornaments, and then both leant over to see their reflection in the water, and Chaurmoti threw her sister in and drowned her.

When Chaurmoti went back to the palace, the Raja seeing her with all her sister's ornaments thought she was Tilmoti. But during the night, Tilmoti became a *bhut* and sat in a mango tree outside and called loudly:

"O my Raja, has our little son drunk his milk to-night? O my Raja, have you had your proper food? Tilmoti sits on the branch of a tree; Chaurmoti is in the Raja's bed. The Raja has gone mad, he sleeps with his wife's elder sister."

The next day, the Raja sat all day beneath the mango tree, wondering what it was he had heard. At night Tilmoti again became a *bhut*, and said the same thing. Then the Raja caught hold of her. "Let me go," she cried. "I'm naked." But he wouldn't let her go. So Tilmoti said: "Bury my sister in earth and put wood over her, and on the wood a lighted lamp. Then I can come back to you."

So the Raja hastened to do as she said, and Tilmoti came alive from the well, and they lived happily together.

X. THE ISLAND IN THE SEA

There was a Gond Raja who used to go every day to bathe before cock-crow. One day he said to his Rani:

"Is there anyone in the world who bathes earlier than I?"

But she was angry because he always left her so early, and she said, "Why not? There are thousands of such bathers in the world."

Her Raja got up and came to her, saying angrily, "Who are they? Find them for me and show me. If there are any such, then you can go back to your mother's house. I don't want you any longer."

So the next morning the Raja went to bathe and his Rani went with him. There they found a fox and a dog washing themselves in the lake. When the Raja saw this he had nothing to say, but his wife was afraid and she ran away. The Raja took another wife.

The Rani went away, away, away, till she came to the Kajli-ban-pahar. There was the house of the twenty-one sisters. They had all gone to the jungle to get wood, and had left the door of the house open. The Rani, seeing the house was empty, went in and found a lot of things to eat. She cooked herself a meal and slept for a time, after locking the door from the inside.

In the evening the twenty-one sisters came home and found the door was shut.

"Who is there?" they cried. "Is it a *bhut* or a *pret* or a *churelin* or a *rākshasa* or a *chorchandāl*? Open the door."

"No, I'm afraid to open it," answered the Rani. "You will eat me."

"If we eat you," replied the sisters, "let us all turn to ashes."

So then the Rani opened the door. When the sisters saw her, they were very pleased, and kept her with them as their servant. After some days they gave her a gift, and a child was born to her, although she took no seed from a man. They called the child Deokuar. The sisters used to play with him and feed him, but soon he grew up. His whole body was golden.

In a neighbouring village lived two Lamana brothers. One day they came with their bullocks past the sisters' house. When they saw the boy they thought they would like to have him as their servant, so they went to the house and said: "The Raja cannot eat since you left him. He has sent us to fetch you. Come with us at once."

So the Rani and her boy at once left the house and went through the jungle with the two Lamana. As they went, desire came into their minds for the Rani. They beat the boy and sent him ahead with the bullocks and when he was gone they went to her. The boy was beaten in this way every day and grew very thin. At last they came to the village where the Raja was. The Rani was married to the Lamana. They kept their bullocks by the edge of the sea. They made the boy go and graze them there.

In the middle of the sea there was a small island. The boy drove the bullocks into the water and made them swim with him out to the island. He stayed there all day long. In the evening he made the bullocks swim back home, but he himself remained.

During the night the lovely daughter of a Dano came and wandered to and fro about the island. The boy watched her from behind some bushes. She had gold *pairi* on her feet. As she went one of the *pairi* caught in the bushes and was torn off. At last she dived into the sea and went down, down, down to where her mother lived at the bottom of the sea.

The boy took the *pairi* and gave it to the Lamana. They took it to the Raja and sold it to him for three-quarters of a hundred rupees. The Raja gave it to his new wife and let her wear it but when she went to get water from the well, the other women said: "Aren't you ashamed to wear a gold *pairi* on one leg and a silver one on the other? How many husbands have you that one should give you gold and the other give you silver and a third will be giving you brass and a fourth iron?"

The Rani said nothing, but when she returned home, she went and lay down in a broken hut. When the Raja got back from his court, he found that his wife had cooked no meal for him. When he found her, he asked her what was the matter.

She told him all that the women had said, and he was very angry. "Never mind," he said. "I'll get you another gold *pairi.*"

Then his Rani was pleased. She got up and hastily prepared *pej* and fried some roots and promised to make *lapsa* in the evening.

The Raja called the Lamana and threatened them that unless they brought the pair of the *pairi* he would kill them. They were very frightened and sent the boy back to the island to try and find the *pairi* if he could. The boy asked the Lamana to bring a long rope and a *māchi.* Then they all went to the island.

Then they tied the *māchi* to the rope and the boy sat on it and the Lamana lowered him over the edge of the island into the sea.

Down, down, down he went till he came to the house of the Dano's daughter. When she saw him she was very afraid for him. "Why have you come?" she cried. "My mother will eat you if she sees you."

"I have come for love of you," said the boy. "Whether they eat me or no, I must be near you."

Then the girl was very happy, and she turned the boy into a parrot and put him in a cage. When her mother came in she roared, "I smell the smell of a man. Where is he? I must eat him."

"There's no one here," said her daughter. "You can eat me if you want to."

So the Dano went away grumbling to herself. When she was gone, the girl turned the parrot back into a boy, and he said, "Ask your mother to tell you where she keeps her *jīv.*"

When the time for food came, the girl went and sat quietly in a corner. "Why aren't you eating?" asked the Dano.

"You go everywhere in the world, and I have to stay here. Tell me at least where your *jīv* is."

"I have never told anyone," said the Dano. "But you are my daughter, and I will tell you. Beyond the seven seas and the sixteen rivers is an island. There guarded by a tiger, a Dano, a snake, a horse and an elephant, is a kadam tree. From the tree hangs a cage. In the cage is a parrot. In the parrot is my *jīv.*"

"But how do you get there?" asked the girl.

"I take a goat to feed the tiger, some milk for the snake, some parched gram for the Dano, grain for the horse, bread for the elephant. While they are eating these things I go past them to the tree."

When her mother had fallen asleep the girl went to the boy and told him all that her mother had told her. Then secretly, unknown to the girl, the boy got a goat and milk, grain and bread and parched gram and set off across the seven seas and the sixteen rivers. When he had passed the guards, he reached the cage. He opened it, killed the parrot and took the *jīv* away. Then he went back to the girl.

The Dano had died when the boy took the *jīv* from the parrot, and the girl cooked a great feast for him and then begged him to take her to his own country and his mother's house. So she put on all her ornaments, and they sat on the *māchi* and pulled at the rope for the Lamana to haul them up. The girl sat on the *māchi*, and the boy held on underneath. But he let go and fell, fell, fell down to the bottom of the sea and was killed.

Then the Lamana took the girl with her ornaments to the Raja and he was very pleased and wanted to marry her. But the girl said, "I'll only marry the man who can tell the story of Deokuar."

In the meantime, the boy had come back to life and had swum up through the water back to the island. Presently he came to the Lamana's house. The Raja was going everywhere trying to find someone who knew Deokuar's story, but no one could tell him what it was, until he called the boy who at once began to tell him.

When the girl heard it, she knew that her lover had returned. "This is Deokuar himself," she said, "and it is he that I am going to marry."

When the Raja knew the whole story, he had the two Lamana killed and he called his old Rani back to his house. He gave the gold *pairi* back to the Dano's daughter and she married Deokuar and they had a great feast and a hundred rupees' worth of liquor.

XI. THE CONSCIENTIOUS DANO

An old Baiga had seven sons, and six of them were married. The brothers went to cut their bewar, and when they had fired it and the rains came, they sowed their seed. When they had done that they were tired and they refused to go to the bewar any more, but sat quietly at home.

The old Baiga and his wife became anxious about their crop, and when in response to all their abuse not one of the brothers would go, they went themselves to see to it. When they got to the bewar they found that rats had eaten the whole crop. They put a trap for them and went home.

The next morning they found that a fox had stolen all the rats and they were very angry for they had looked forward to a good feast of rat's-flesh. They had a dog with them, and sent it to catch the fox. The dog ran to the fox's burrow, but there the dog and the fox fell in love with one another, and began to live together.

From them was born a beautiful girl. The fox said, "Now I want clothes and ornaments for our daughter." The dog went to the bazaar and stole some cloth from a shop and some ornaments from the goldsmith. He carried these things to the burrow.

When the seven brothers went to cut their crop in the bewar, they found the girl there with the fox and the dog. The girl went to the youngest brother and snatched the sickle from his hand and began to cut the crop for him. They all began to laugh, but they took the girl home and the youngest brother married her. They taught the girl to cook and do the duties of the household.

But the other wives got jealous. One day the girl went to gather mohlain leaves. Then the other wives plotted to tell the old Baiga and his wife that the girl had said that mohlain leaves make very good plates for eating the flesh of one's parents-in-law. When the old Baiga heard this he was very angry, and told the boy to take the girl to the jungle and bring him her eyes, ears and fingers. The youngest brother went with the girl to the forest, and said, "Why should I kill you? Run away from here. We will meet again." He found a corpse, and brought its eyes, ears and fingers to his father, and the old man was satisfied.

In the forest was a Dano. He had many cows, with a Surigai to look after them. The girl came there and when the cow saw her she hid her. The Dano came and said that he smelt human flesh. The cow said, "If there was a human being here, wouldn't I have eaten her myself?"

The Dano prepared and ate buttermilk, and went to sleep. But the cow prepared *khīr* and *puri* and gave it to the girl. But she kept a little and went and smeared it on the Dano's buttocks.

In the morning the Dano awoke and found his buttocks covered with *khīr* and *puri*. "How is this?" he thought. "I ate *maheri*, and I have relieved myself of *khīr* and *puri*!" He turned round and spoke severely to his backside. "If you bring *khīr* out of buttermilk again," he said, "I will know what to do to you."

That night he again had buttermilk, and the cow again prepared *khīr* for the girl's supper. She again smeared it on the Dano's backside. In the morning, the Dano found he had *khīr* all over him, he tasted it to prove it. "It really is *khīr*," he cried, and so to punish his backside, he got a tin of boiling *ghī* and sat in it. "Do you want me to cut you off altogether?" he said to it. "Why are you hurting me like this?"

The third morning when the Dano awoke he found that he had done it again, and now in despair he decided to punish his backside properly. So he sat in the fire and was burnt to ashes.

After this the girl went home. She gave *pej* to her brothers and rice to her own husband, and *khīr* and *puri* which she had learnt to make in the Dano's house. Whenever she made *khīr* she used to laugh, and at last her husband made her tell the whole story. Then the brothers were very angry with their wives and beat them so much that they ran away, each to her mother's house.

The youngest brother and his girl lived happily in the forest, and every day they put a basket of the food that was left behind the house for the dogs and foxes.

XII. OLD MOTHER'S BUTTOCKS

An old Baiga and his wife cut their bewar and sowed kutki in the ashes. When the kutki was ready, the pigs came and ate it. They were very sad, but the old woman said, "Let's dig a well, and I will watch with a rice-pounder and you with your axe and we'll soon kill these creatures." This is what they did. When the pig came to drink water, the old man struck it, but only wounded it, but the old woman pushed it into the well. When the pig was drowned, they pulled it out and got it ready for cooking.

The old man said, "You cook the pig and I'll go and have a bath." So the old woman roasted the pig over the fire, and as it was cooking she took first one bit and then another, and it tasted so good that she had soon eaten the whole pig. Then she was very frightened, so she cut off one of her own buttocks and filled up the place with white earth and cow-dung, and cooked the buttock instead.

When her husband came in, she cried, "Come along, my old one. All is ready and getting cold." He sat down and began to eat with great pleasure. But a cat came into the house, and sang:

"The pig was all eaten by the old woman,
The old woman's buttocks are being eaten by her man."

The old woman tried to drive the cat away, but her husband heard it and made her show him her buttocks. When he saw one was missing, he began to beat her, and she ran away. Now the old woman had two sons, one was a gourd and one was a brinjal. She went to the gourd but it was broken. So she ran to the brinjal field instead. The brinjal took his mother back and they found the old man weeping. They made him go on with his dinner, but again the cat came and sang the same song, and the old man got angry and beat his wife again.

This time she ran away to the house of Dundi Rakshasin, the demon without fingers. The old woman asked her to help her to go to her mother's house. "How can I pass through the jungle so full of tigers and bears?" The Rakshasin gave her a lot of parched gram which fills the belly with wind, and a pot full of ashes.

Then on the way whenever a tiger attacked her, the old woman sat in the pot and her wind blew the ashes into the tiger's eyes and it went away. This happened many times, and the old woman had nearly reached home, when a bear came. The old woman blew the ashes into his eyes as usual, but his hair saved him, so he seized her and ate her up.

But as she was dying, she cried, "Eat me if you will, but you don't know what a plump old man there is over in my bewar."

So when the bear had finished the woman, he went to the bewar, and ate her husband also.

XIII. TOMATOES

An old Baiga woman had one son. There was no food in their house, the grain-bin was always empty, but they went every day to work and so got something to eat from day to day.

One day the old woman said to her son, "I am going to cut rice in the Raja's field: you stay at home, and get the *pej* ready, and make some curry with *kirchi kānda*." After she had gone the boy made some *pej* and drank part of it, but there were no *kirchi kānda* to make the curry. So the boy relieved himself and made curry from his excrement. Then he went to sleep.

His mother came home in the evening, very hungry. She drank the *pej*, but when she opened the pot of curry she found flies sitting on it and a foul smell. "Chi! chi! chi!" she cried, and threw it away. She woke the boy up and abused him and beat him.

The next day the boy went to work and the mother stayed at home. The boy went to a very big field all by himself, and worked so hard that he had cut half of it by evening. Then the owner of the field came, and the boy hid his sickle behind him. "Who told you to cut all this?" asked the man. "Nobody," answered the boy. "The sickle cut it of his own accord." When the man heard that he was very excited and he said, "Give me this sickle." The boy said he could have it for a hundred rupees. The man brought the money and the boy gave him the sickle and went home well pleased. All night mother and son laughed together over the trick the boy had played.

But the next day when the landlord went to the field and put the sickle on the ground and found that nothing happened, he sent his agent to arrest the boy. When the boy heard that he was coming, he ran away into the jungle with all the money tied in a cloth.

On the way the boy met a bear, and the bear chased him. At last the bear caught him in his two paws and all the rupees fell to the ground. Just then a merchant came riding by. His horse had a bit of gold, a gold saddle and a silver whip. "Look," cried the boy, "this bear has passed rupees." The merchant was very excited when he heard this. "Hold the bear for me," he cried. "I will keep it and it will bring out rupees for me also."

"No," said the boy. "I want the bear myself. But if you will pick up all the rupees for me, I will give him to you." Then the boy let the bear catch the merchant instead of himself, and taking his money, jumped on to the merchant's horse, and rode away.

Next he met a wedding-party of Gond. He offered the girl his horse, and she sat on it and he carried her off. They made a house for themselves at the foot of a mountain. One day the husband and a party of his friends came to take the girl back. The boy welcomed them, but in the evening as they went to bed he warned them that it was the law of that place that anyone who relieved himself in bed would be given six years' imprisonment.

When they were all asleep, the boy got *ramtilla*, pounded it and put in small tomatoes. Then he smeared the mixture on the buttocks of all his visitors. When they woke in the morning, they felt cold, and they looked and saw the little tomatoes, and thought they had relieved themselves in the night, and for fear they all ran away.

So the boy kept the girl and they lived happily together.

Chapter XVIII

THE FUTURE

It is not the business of the scientist to concern himself with moral or political questions; it will be obvious to readers of this book that I do not even think that the field-worker should concern himself with anthropological theories, but should confine himself to recording evidence. But the problem of the Baiga and allied tribes is of such great urgency, and is so greatly neglected in India, that I have decided to discuss it briefly in this concluding chapter. Those who have come to know and love Mahatu and Phulmat, Jethu and Charka in these pages will, I have no doubt, be equally anxious to see their future assured.

It is not yet too late to save the Baiga from the fate which an over-hasty and unregulated process of 'uplift' and civilization has brought upon peoples in other parts of India. We should do well to lay to heart the warnings of responsible observers like Dr. J. H. Hutton and Mr. S. C. Roy. Writing of the nomadic Birhor and Korwa of Chota Nagpur, Mr. Roy points out how they still live as far as possible on forest produce and the spoils of the chase. But 'with the opening up of the country by roads and railways under British rule and the gradual deforestation of the country and ever-increasing restrictions on the use of the forest, these forest tribes are slowly but surely dying out, partly from famine and partly from loss of interest in life'.

Dr. Hutton strikes the same note of warning in the last Census Report. The semi-civilized aboriginals, he writes, 'may retain a sort of emasculated tribal life, deprived of the customs and festivals that gave it meaning and cohesion, and fall into that psychical apathy and physical decline which has decimated so many tribal communities in the Pacific and elsewhere; and this decline is accelerated in another way by the opening up of communications. Many new diseases are imported against which no immunity has been evolved, since they did not form part of the environment to which the tribe is adapted, and the result is a staggering mortality from which there may be no recovery. The rapidly approaching extinction of the tribes of Great Andaman has largely been due to diseases imported into the penal settlement and communicated to the Andamanese by convicts'. I may add that the importation of venereal disease into the tribal districts of the C.P. by outsiders has resulted in a disastrous infection of the Gond in that area.

In an admirable article in the last Census, Mr. J. P. Mills discusses the evil effects of a narrow Christian Missionary policy. He points out how the American Baptist Mission in Assam has suppressed all the ceremonies of the Naga such as the great Feasts of Merit and all sacrificial feasts. 'The place of these is not adequately taken by small parties meeting to drink tea.' This is a great loss, especially to the poor, 'who always get their full share of good cheer at Animist festivals. To abolish these feasts is to do away with the very few occasions on which the awful monotony of village life is broken'. Singing and dancing have also been suppressed among the Ao, Lhota, and Sema Christians. Their ornaments have been removed, 'their beads stripped from their necks, their ivory armlets from their arms, and even the cotton wool from their ears'. Wood carving, intimately associated with the festivals, is disappearing. 'The suppression of the wearing of all ornaments or tribal finery, of dancing, of singing (except hymns), of village feasts and of all artistic outlet is spreading an unspeakable drabness over village life. . . . Told year in and year out that all the past history, all the strivings, all the old customs of his tribe are wholly evil, the Naga tends to despise his own race, and no night of the soul is blacker than that.'

Note one point of agreement in each of these three passages. Dr. Roy speaks of 'a loss of interest in life', Dr. Hutton of 'psychical apathy and physical decline', Mr. Mills of 'the awful monotony of village life', of an 'unspeakable drabness'. It is this drabness and deadness that will destroy the tribesmen of India.[1]

Unfortunately, the Indian aboriginal is all too ready to respond to the slightest hint that he should abandon his old culture and interests. Mr. Grigson describes how many Maria 'almost as in obedience to some decree' abandoned the rib-dress, shield and gaily-coloured head-dress and skirt that had made their dances a delight to watch.

Again, 'in 1932 a rumour went through all the tribes of Jeypore and spread thence into Bastar that a god had descended on one of the mountains

[1] 'The undermining of old-established authority, of tribal morals and customs tends on the one hand completely to demoralize the natives and to make them unamenable to any law or rule, while on the other hand, by destroying the whole fabric of tribal life, it deprives them of many of their most cherished diversions, ways of enjoying life, and social pleasures. Now once you make life unattractive for a man, whether savage or civilized, you cut the taproot of his vitality. The rapid dying out of native races is, I am deeply convinced, due more to wanton interference with their pleasures and normal occupations, to the marring of their joy of life as they conceive it, than to any other cause.'—B. Malinowski, *Argonauts of the Western Pacific* (London, 1922), p. 465.

of the Eastern Ghats and commanded all men to give up keeping black poultry and goats, wearing clothes or using umbrellas or blankets with any black in them, and using beads or articles made of aluminium alloy'. Soon black goats, cocks, hens, umbrellas, blankets, beads, were littering the road. Mohammedans began to make a good thing out of slaughtering the goats or exporting them.[1] Probably the rumour originated in some such interested source.

Organized 'social uplift' movements have an equally mischievous effect. In 1924 the Hos of Kolhan met at Lumpunguto and decided to stop the ancient songs and dances because 'they were looked down upon by their cultured neighbours as very low and degrading', because the boys' health was damaged by late hours and their morals injured by dancing, and because they involved unnecessary waste of time and energy. Women were also forbidden to work in the bazaars, and the Hos were ordered to become teetotal.[2]

I have seen the thing happen, not yet to the Baiga, but to the Gond, in my own district. At the end of 1936, a Raj Gond reformer made an expedition into the wilds of Mandla. He was accompanied by three or four 'chaprasis'—one of them was a hard-drinking Mussalman adventurer—and carried some large books containing the Hindu scriptures which he apparently had not studied. The party went from village to village holding meetings. The reformer stated that he had the authority of Government behind him and that failure to obey his orders would be punished officially. He promulgated the new Gond religion. He pointed out, almost in the manner of the Christian missionaries described by Mr. Mills, that the old life of the Gond was altogether bad and caused the tribe to be despised by their Hindu neighbours. Everything, therefore, that the Hindus despised must be abandoned. The great Karma dance, the one surviving instrument of Gond culture, must stop. Men and women must not sing the 'immoral' Dadaria together. In practice this meant that all singing and dancing would stop—for the Gond always likes to be on the safe side. Pigs and chickens, the only tax-free domestic animals, must be destroyed. The Gond must become teetotal. Women must be put in purdah. The rules of untouchability must be strictly observed. Children should be married young in Hindu fashion. Cows must not be yoked to the plough.

Breach of these rules would involve the offenders in serious penalties which would be enforced by Government. For dancing the Karma a fine of Rs. 50, for drinking liquor a fine of Rs. 50, for keeping pigs Rs. 25, for yoking cows to the plough Rs. 10, and so on. A Brahmin sub-inspector

[1] Grigson, op. cit., p. 76.

[2] D. N. Majumdar in *The Modern Review*, (March, 1925), p. 285 ff.

of police gave his support to the movement, and started a story, which gained wide currency, that Government had recently fined a Gond Rs. 50 for shooting a crow; how much more, then, would they penalize the killing of chickens?

The movement spread like wildfire throughout the District, and hundreds of Gond donned the sacred thread and paid a four-annas subscription to the reformer. An 'unspeakable drabness' settled down on the reformed villages. In the long evenings the men had nothing to do save quarrel with their wives who were greatly affronted at the restrictions proposed on their liberty. Those who were sick and had hitherto turned in convalescence to a little liquor as tonic were now barred of that remedy. The 'kick' had gone out of tribal festivals, the flavour from tribal feasts. "What are we but animals?" said many a Gond to me, "but we used to have just a few things that made us men, our beautiful dances, our songs, our liquor. Now these are gone, and we have sunk down below the animals. Even our food is taken from us."

But the seed has been sown. The life has gone from many villages. Child-marriages have started, untouchables are despised, in some villages the women have lost much of their freedom. At the very moment when India is rousing herself to banish these things from her borders, they are being introduced into her remoter areas where they have not been known hitherto.

So far, nothing of this kind has happened to the Baiga, and even the supposedly reformed Binjhwar tribe of Chhattisgarh are freer than the Gond. But the tendency is there. It is most instructive to go straight from a bewar-cutting jungle village in the wilds of Pandaria to a village by the roadside in Mandla or Niwas. In the former, tribal life and organization still retains its old vitality; you enter the village and at once you feel the stir and throb of communal energy; tribal life is an integrated whole, it makes sense, there are no gaps in it, it has no insulated spots, everything is related and functions in its proper place. The people are vigorous, independent, happy. But go to a semi-civilized village of Binjhwar in Balaghat, Mandla or Niwas. The people might belong to another race. Servile, obsequious, timid, of poor physique, their tribal life is all to pieces. Parts of it, like the right to hunt and practise bewar, have been torn out by the roots. Some of their simple and innocent dances, under Hindu influence, have been given up. The souls of the people are soiled and grimy with the dust of passing motor-buses. In the village, you are in the midst not of a living community, but of a collection of isolated units. Tribal life and tradition appears slightly ludicrous, even to the tribesmen themselves. And once that point is reached, there is no hope for the tribe.

It is not too late to save most of the Baiga from the psychical apathy and physical decline that otherwise awaits them. What might be done?

The first necessity is the establishment of a sort of National Park, in which not only the Baiga, but the thousands of simple Gond in their neighbourhood might take refuge. A line drawn round the Mandla District (excluding Mandla town and the country west of the Nainpur-Mandla road), Baihar Tehsil, the north-west jungles of Kawardha, the mountains and forests of Pandaria, the Lormi Range of Bilaspur, the parts of Pendra Zemindari contiguous to it, would enclose a wild and largely inaccessible part of country that might have been created for the very purpose.

This special area should be under the direct control of a Tribes Commissioner. I see no reason why the tribal areas should be 'excluded' or 'partially excluded' as they are under the present Government of India Act, but it is obvious that some expert should stand between them and the Legislature.

Inside the area, the administration should be so adjusted as to allow the tribesmen to live their lives with the utmost possible happiness and freedom. Courts and lawyers could be largely superseded and wide powers given to the old tribal panchayats. The headmen should be leaders of the tribe, not agents of Government. Non-aboriginals should be required to take out licences; the scores of vagabond adventurers that wander through the country exploiting the people should be removed, and others only licensed on condition of their behaving properly towards the aboriginals. No missionaries of any religion should be permitted to break up tribal life.

The idea of a 'National Park' does not mean the same thing as an 'Anthropological Zoo'. Many people in India suffer from the curious and rather puerile belief that the anthropologist wishes to keep primitive people 'as they were' as materials for his research. But this is not so: the scientist is not interested in any particular grade of civilization: he is concerned with things as they are: the semi-civilized Gond is just as interesting and important as the wilder Baiga. But the anthropologist who has come to know and love the people he has studied will naturally desire the best for them, and his views on that may well clash with those of the politician who merely desires to exploit them in the interests of his own party.

The anthropologist will not be untrue to science if he urges that everything possible should be done for a tribe's progress and advantage provided that the quality of tribal life is not impaired, that tribal culture is not destroyed, and that tribal freedom is restored or maintained.

There is wide scope for economic betterment. Special arrangements might be made for the marketing of Baiga produce. If education is introduced, it should be on the lines of what is known at present as 'the Wardha scheme', simplified and adapted to the use of primitive people. Education based on spinning, wood-carving or the growing of vegetables and fruit trees would be of real value. The old type of literary education, its regimentation, its exams, is useless to a tribe that will never be able to buy books or subscribe to newspapers.

It has often been noticed that the Indian Penal Code, as applied to aboriginals, needs considerable modification. But only in Bastar State, which has had the advantage of a series of enlightened administrators, has this been done. Especially the matrimonial sections of the Code are totally unsuited to tribal society. It is Baiga custom to change your wife frequently, and the old ideas of marriage by capture survive in the theory that the best wife is one with whom you have eloped. To apply Sections 366, 497 and 498 to these people is little less than ludicrous. What happens among Gond, and what may begin to happen any day among Baiga is this. The great majority of these cases are settled amicably by the tribal *panch*. The lawyers in the Tehsil towns who sometimes do not get more than Rs. 30 worth of business in a month feel rather restive about this, and send their touts up into the tribal areas. I have seen the ravages caused by these touts in three or four villages, the suspicion, the hostility, the unsettling of all accepted standards that they create. Even more than the law, the lawyers need to be amended.

For the Baiga, however, the law will probably always be little more than a distant bugbear. For even the lawyer is not anxious to bring a Baiga to the courts. As a lawyer at Baihar once frankly told me: "When we see the opposite party has called a Baiga witness we give up the case—for we know he will be incorruptible"—a curious sidelight on the character of the Baiga—and of the lawyer!

What the Baiga needs above all else is the restoration of the freedom of the forest. After all, the forest did originally belong to him. At the time of the first settlements, everybody else was established in his property, but the Baiga was not permitted to own anything. I find it hard to write temperately when I think of the injustice that has been done them. The forest was their home, they were the true *pashupati*—the masters of the wild beasts, they were the natural lords of the forest—and now their once proud-quivered loins must tremble at the lash of every little whipper-snapper of a forest-guard!

The Baiga still, as a reference to the life-story of Rawan will show, enjoys the freedom of the forest, but he does so with a guilty mind. It seems to me essential that this feeling of guilt should be removed. The Game Act has pressed heavily upon the Baiga and has served still further to devitalize tribal life. It is a shame and a disgrace that a tribe that has lived for millennia by hunting should now have to witness the spectacle of any townsman who can afford a licence coming into its country and slaughtering its animals for pleasure, while they who depend on their bows and arrows for food should have to hide them in their huts.

It would be a very good thing if the Baiga were at least allowed an annual hunt. The annual hunt probably has a magical purpose, 'possibly a survival from the hunting stage of society, when it was thought expedient to perform at the beginning of the year a rite which would ensure good luck for the season'. The Bhatra used to have a ceremonial hunt in March preliminary to the Bijphutni festival in honour of Mati Deo, god of hunting. The Gadba do the same even now and cook the game in the presence of Mati Deo; if they fail their women pelt them with cow-dung. It is during the tribal hunt that the Santal come together as a tribe and settle their major problems. One of the chief Rajput festivals was the Aheria, the spring hunting. So is the Sekrengi of the Angami Naga, the Jur Sital of Bihar, the hunting festival of the Halrakki Vakkal of Kanara. If the Baiga were allowed one great annual hunt, this would have a revivifying effect on tribal life and might even benefit the game in the long run, for they would be less likely to poach at other times. The killing of hares should in any case be permitted, and it should not be illegal to carry bows and arrows.

Fishing also should be freely permitted throughout the Baiga country. At present, subordinate officials get many a good meal by confiscating the Baiga's catch.

The dictatorship of these subordinate officials must come to an end. I cannot think of anything more shameful, anything meaner, anything more disgraceful to an administration that claims to be enlightened than the way subordinates[1] openly rob these poor people, some of the poorest in the world, of the few goods they have and of many hours of labour. *Begār* is the curse of tribal India. Nearly every subordinate thinks it is his right to exact free labour from the aboriginal, and to take free of charge whatever food he needs. Again and again I have seen the poorest people robbed of the chicken that they have been saving up for a festival, of the pot of *ghī* that they had treasured against a marriage, of the fruit that with difficulty they had raised. When I have tried to introduce fruit trees into the villages, I have usually been met with the objection, "What is the use of our growing fruit trees? the officials will take the fruit away from us." Let me quote an unimpeachable witness. The Hon. J. W. Best, late of the Indian Forest

[1] In 1890 a Conservator of Forests wrote: 'No rules, no expenditure, no supervision will keep out fires so well as the presence near the forests of villagers who, owing to their being liberally and judiciously treated, are on good terms with the forest department.'

Service, has some very strong words to say about the *begār* practised among the Baiga of the Lormi Range.

'Each policeman, tehsildar, revenue inspector, and anyone else with power to twist the wretched villager's tail, made his demands on the village. He demanded guides and transport to the next camping-ground for himself and his servant, the collection of firewood, the cutting of grass, the carrying of water, the supply of ghee . . . the greater part (of which) is not paid for. . . . The very men whose business it is to check these abuses themselves benefit from them, and are the last to stop them. . . . The lower the rank of the government servant, the more oppressive he is. . . . Let the reader imagine himself with a precious garden as his sole property and means of livelihood. You start the day meaning to do some digging to get in your early potatoes. A uniformed policeman turns up and compels you to carry his bedding to another village ten miles away. Next day you start on your work again. This time you have to stop so as to bring firewood for the tehsil. Another day it is a matter of carrying water, or hewing wood, or doing odd jobs for somebody's servant. And so it goes on, until the sensible man leaves the village for a place where these tormenting officials do not come. People say, "Why do the villagers do it?" They are compelled to by the tradition of ages, and they know that it is far worse to refuse than to obey.'[1]

Every Government in turn has tried to check this abuse, but far more vigorous and urgent measures need to be taken than any tried hitherto. *Begār* would to some extent disappear if a new attitude were adopted towards the tribal areas. At present they are the *Kāla-pāni*, the Andamans of the official world. Any subordinate who has proved himself a black-guard or incompetent elsewhere is sent off to a tribal area as a punishment. When it is regarded as a high privilege to be given the delicate and difficult task of developing and administering a primitive area, and subordinates are paid accordingly, much of this trouble will automatically disappear. That *begār* is not a law of nature that cannot be evaded is shown in the lives of many officials, especially police officials, whose integrity and kindness have made them loved by the tribesmen they protect and serve.

But to the Baiga the most important need of all is a more liberal policy with regard to bewar. As we have seen in Chapter III bewar is for the Baiga a fundamental social and religious need. It was established by divine mandate; it is part of the very stuff of the tribe's mythology, folk-lore and poetry; to abandon it is to commit mortal sin. Wherever bewar is permitted you will find the old culture vital and energetic; where it has been stopped, the Baiga have sunk down to the dead level of futility,

[1] J. W. Best: *Forest Life in India* (London, 1935), p. 134 ff.

mediocrity and apathy of the rest of village India. So long ago as 1880, the Deputy Commissioner of Mandla reported as a sort of triumph that the new plough-using Baiga village of Chaugaon was 'quite indistinguishable from an ordinary village of the district'.

And that is indeed the fate that threatens the Baiga, unless the administration take a bold and generous line.

They will become indistinguishable from ordinary villagers! Their fine physique will be sapped by the introduction of child-marriage; their generous hearts constricted by a belief in untouchability; their happiness and freedom lost in the practice of purdah; they will sink from their proud office of lords of the jungle to the very bottom of the social scale; half-way between civilization and an emasculated tribal life, they will practise the worst features of both.[1]

This gloomy future could be averted by the creation of the National Park that I have suggested, or at the least by the handing over to the Baiga part of the great tracts of forest that can never be exploited commercially. So remote and inaccessible is this forest that it can be of no value to the State, yet it might be of the highest importance in saving from extinction one of the most interesting, most delightful and most ancient of all the peoples of the Central Provinces of India. Those who believe in 'Home Rule' for India should at least see to it that the original owners of the country are given a few privileges.

But if any further tracts of forest are handed over to the Baiga, it should be done generously. The strict regimentation of the Baiga Chak is neither desirable nor necessary. No official should ever be stationed in a Baiga village. A forester should visit the tract from time to time to teach the Baiga those better methods of bewar-cutting which I will describe in a moment, and to supervise the allocation of the fields, though these should first be chosen by the village elders and only afterwards approved by him.

The policy of 'weaning' the Baiga from the axe has completely failed. Many of them have yielded to official pressure and taken to the plough. But in their hearts they all—with the exception of a few Binjhwar—long to return to their jungle. Such a state of things cannot be regarded as a success. The 'weaning' policy should now be definitely abandoned, and a new policy of bewar-education adopted in its place. For if there is anything at all in the survey of shifting-cultivation in other lands, and the opinions I have collected in Chapter III, it is that the harm done by bewar can be

[1] Some of the Weddids "have already been completely assimilated into the caste-system of the Indids. In this way they became low-caste, the dregs of humanity. . . . The contrast with the free jungle tribes is very characteristic. With the surrender of their weapons and the freedom of the forests, and just in the degree to which they gave way to the attractions of a foreign and 'higher' civilisation, they sank to the very bottom of the social scale." Von Eikstedt: op. cit., p. 25.

greatly modified by the observance of certain conditions, especially by the introduction of the *taungya* system which has proved so successful in West Africa.

My proposal is, therefore, that new tracts of comparatively worthless jungle should be given to the Baiga, and that they should be allowed great freedom within their borders, provided that they observe the following conditions—which it should not be beyond the wit of man to instil into their minds.

1. Bewar should only be cut in mixed forest or bamboo forest, more or less clear of sal.

2. It should be cut only on hill-tops and the middle and upper slopes of hills, and a protective belt should always be kept between the forest-zone and the bewar-area line. The Baiga to be responsible for seeing that fires do not spread beyond the bewar.

3. Each hill-slope should be laid out in small alternated strips, leaving untouched jungle in between. Then when the bewar had grown up sufficiently, the strips omitted could be worked.

4. Bewar should not be cut on ridges enclosing the head waters of important streams.

5. A rotation of ten years should be observed.

6. No bewar should be used either more or less than two years at a time.

7. The trees should be cut flush with the ground, and with a clean, not jagged, section.

8. The stools should be kept clear of combustible matter when the bewar are fired.

9. A number of trees should be left. They may be stripped of their branches, but a tuft of green should be left at the top of the tree.

10. At the end of the third year, every Baiga should undertake to plant a number of trees of special selected varieties in the bewar before he leaves it, and Professor Stebbing's suggestions regarding *taungya* should be generally observed.

Many of these rules are enforced by the forest authorities in different localities. Others will be suggested by silviculturalists. It will be difficult to persuade the Baiga to observe them—but not so difficult as 'weaning him from the axe'.[1]

[1] Conditions in Africa suggest that the amount of land required need not be very great, provided that a regular system is followed. In the Southern Provinces of Nigeria each family of 3·6 persons (the size of a Baiga family is about 3·7 to 4·0) cultivates two acres annually, and the land rests for seven years against one of cultivation, hence each family requires sixteen acres. In the Northern Provinces each needs twenty-four acres. (Stamp: op. cit., p. 35). Prof. Daryll Forde has studied this question in a Cross River village and found the ratio of cultivation to fallowing was 1:4 and the area cultivated in any one year to be less that 1·5 acres to a family. (See C. Daryll Forde, *Land and Labour in a Cross River Village*, Geographical Journal, Vol. XC, pp. 31 ff). The Baiga ratio would be 10:2 or even 10:3, which would be more economical.

At least, this remarkable tribe deserves more kindness and consideration than it has hitherto received. The grim example of the fate of the Australian aboriginal is before us.[1] The findings of scientific anthropology should save India from repeating the mistakes of other nations. I will bring this chapter to a close by quoting some striking remarks of Colonel Bloomfield in 1881. Bloomfield, it may be remembered, was strongly opposed to bewar, but he cautions those who 'entirely forget, if indeed they are not ignorant, of the rights which these Baigas might in all justice claim. For generations untold, probably from the time when the ancient Britons were yet clothed in their original garments of skins, the ancestors of these Baigas have lived, died, and been buried on the slopes of these hills and in the fastnesses of these jungles. They have supported themselves, their families and their aged parents without the aid or interference of the State, or poor laws, or anything else, thereby setting a good example to the more civilized poor of the British Isles and other countries.

'They have managed their own affairs without the aid of judge, jury, police or any Government officials; until the last few years they have escaped the grasp of inexperienced Extra-Assistants and over-officious police subordinates.

'Surely then these Baigas might fairly claim absolute occupancy rights of the land they have held so long, or even be considered sub-proprietors of their holdings. They have not, however, in their wild ignorance, put forward any claim whatever. . . . The stopping of bewar-cutting was the very taking of the bread from their mouths, yet they have hardly so much as grumbled: they have given no trouble at all, but have quietly and cheerfully submitted themselves to their fate, and with no State aid worth mentioning, earned a hard though honest livelihood in their own quiet way.

'Had the Sonthals or Bhils, or the tribes on the Assam borders been treated in this way, there would have been a very different story to tell; bloodshed and jungle fighting would have been the order of the day.

'This being the case, I cannot doubt that you will agree with me that the Baigas are entitled to all credit and consideration at our hands.'

[1] A study of Schapera's admirable *Western Civilisation and the Natives of South Africa* (London, 1934), and Mrs. Bates's *The Passing of the Aborigines* (London, 1938) will throw much light on the administration of tribal areas in India.

Appendix I

DISTRIBUTION OF THE BAIGA

TO-DAY the Baiga number some 40,000 persons. According to the 1931 Census there were 37,086 of them—excluding those who lived in the Central Indian Agency. They were distributed as follows:

Jubbulpore	2,665
Mandla	19,938
Seoni	659
Chhindwara	52
Nagpur	3
Balaghat	5,640
Raipur	386
Bilaspur	2,404
Drug	255
Bastar	397
Kanker	420
Kawardha	3,074
Raigarh	791
Changbhakar	162
Udaipur	97
Korea	108

In addition to these, Rewa State returned a total of no less than 35,813 Baiga, an increase of 35·3 per cent on the 1921 total and almost as great as the entire strength of the tribe elsewhere. But these figures cannot be accepted. 'The true strength of the Baigas,' as the Report itself admits, 'is never recorded, as they get mixed up with the Gonds in South Rewa and also their exact affiliation with certain allied tribes . . . is not yet known.'[1]

Indeed it is not possible to trust any statistics about the Baiga, for, in the first place (as we have seen) the name Baiga is given to many village priests who are not members of the tribe, and in the second place, there are allied tribes like the Binjhwar, Bhumia and Bhaina who are so similar that they are often not distinguished. Thus, there are Binjhwar Baiga and Baiga Binjhwar—Baiga who are members of the Binjhwar sub-division of the Baiga tribe proper, and members of the Binjhwar tribe who are called Baiga because they act as sorcerers. There are Bhaina-Baiga and Baiga members of the Bhaina tribe. There are Gond-waina Baiga who are quite different from Gond who are simply fulfilling the functions of a Baiga; Bhumia-

[1] *Census of India*, 1931, Vol. XX, p. 227.

Baiga who must not be confused with the Baiga members of the Bhumia tribe. It is impossible to expect uninstructed Census enumerators to observe these subtleties.

The figures—for what they are worth—for the variations of the Baiga population are these:

1881	38,883
1891	21,336
1901	23,471
1911	27,274
1921	25,078
1931	37,086

These fluctuations may be due to the rules governing bewar-cutting which drove many Baiga out of British India, but it is more likely that they were caused by confusion as to what a Baiga really was. This confusion is more clearly seen when we examine the statistics for the various districts. The Baiga of Bhandara dropped from 1,887 in 1881 to 138 in 1901, and there are no Baiga there at all to-day. The Balaghat Baiga decreased from 7,737 to 3,863 in 1891 and 3,442 in 1901. This was undoubtedly due to emigration into Kawardha State. It rose slowly again to 5,640 in 1931. In Bilaspur the fluctuations were extraordinary:

1881	8,433
1891	794
1901	2,716
1911	157
1921	405
1931	2,404

In Bilaspur there are many Bhaina and Binjhwar, and these variations are probably due to confusion of the Baiga with them.

Mandla has steadily increased its Baiga population from 11,493 in 1881 to 19,938 at the last Census.

The real tribal Baiga live in a compact block of country with Mandla District as its centre. It is almost safe to say that a return of Baiga from any district or state not geographically connected with Mandla is probably for persons of other tribes holding the office of Baiga in their village, but does not refer to members of the actual tribe.

Leaving these aside, we find the Baiga concentrated in the following Tehsil and States. Throughout this book I refer to the distribution of the Baiga by Tehsil and, in the case of Pandaria and Pendra, by Zemindari, rather than by districts.

Jubbulpore	2,500 (approx.)
Mandla	7,000
Niwas	6,000
Dindori	7,000
Baihar	5,500
Pandaria	1,500
Bilaspur	1,000
Kawardha	3,000
Rewa	3,000

We may summarize the distribution of the sub-divisions of the tribe as follows:

In Jubbulpore and Mandla: mainly Binjhwar and Bharotia.
In Niwas: Binjhwar, Bhumia, Muria, Bharia and Kurka.
In Rewa: mainly Bhumia, but some Binjhwar and Bhaina.
In Baihar: Bharotia, Narotia, Binjhwar, Gond-waina (?) and Kondwan (?).
In Bilaspur: Bhumia, Binjhwar, Dudh-bhaina, Rai-bhaina, and Kaṭh-baina.
In Dindori: Bhumia and a few Bharotia.
In Pandaria: Bhumia.
In Kawardha: Bhumia, but on the western borders a few Bharotia and Kondwan (?).

There are no statistics to indicate the present relative strength of these sub-divisions, but in 1891 the Census gave these figures:

Bharotia	8,327
Binjhwar	7,768
Muria	3,347
Narotia	2,037
Bhumia	6,085
Others	8,447
Total	38,011

Exactly ten years earlier, in 1881, Colonel Bloomfield made a record of the tribal divisions of the Balaghat District. He noted the three main divisions:

Binjhwar	671
Nahar	1,139
Bharotia	596
Total	2,406

It is obvious that these figures, specially as regards the Bharotia (who were then living in such inaccessible regions as would make accurate enumeration difficult) are quite inadequate. The Census of 1881 gives the total number of Baiga in Balaghat as 7,737.

Appendix II

LIST OF GARH

The following is a list of the exogamous *garh* into which the Baiga are divided. It is not complete—completeness would only be obtained by a village-to-village Census of the whole country—but it will give some idea of the variety and range of these *garh*, in contrast with the dozen or so *goti*, and the half-dozen *jāt*.

Mandla Tehsil

Kakuria	Timania
Phalturia	Baradakia
Murakia	Pachgaiha
Udaria	Palia
Upharia	

Dindori Tehsil

Bararia	Kaharia
Telasia	Kotdaria
Kukaria	Ataria
Bidhia	Kordia
Rathoria	Kewatia
Chithuria	Pachgaiha
Bindhia	Chamaradaiha
Saria	Chapuria
Ghatia	Ninguria
Daria	Machia
Chanaria	Kamania
Nandia	Niguria

Niwas Tehsil

Bagdaiha	Pachgaiha
Kisunia	Sarjania
Dhobia	Bassania

Pandaria

Jajulia	Chachhuria
Upharia	Amdaria
Mudakia	Rathoria
Babulia	Saradia
Odaria	Kusaria
Ghatia	

Baihar Tehsil

Kewaria
Pachgaiha
Chamaradaiha
Chapuria
Ninguria
Chithuria
Bindhia
Saria
Ghatia

Rewa State

Chithuria
Ghangharia
Pachgaiha
Kumania
Chandaniha
Bhainoti
Aduria
Upharia
Saradia
Lamoriha
Masaniha
Poria
Mahataria
Nangbansia
Ghusaria
Badgaria
Dhobia
Basaria
Damgadia
Dewariha
Salgaiha
Sawat
Chandgaria
Damadia
Chapuria
Paria
Saria
Dhijoria
Bagdaria
Jhimor
Sarjaniha
Amgaria
Dhodhia
Kisaniha
Mangaria

Kawardha State

Kusaria
Kachnariha
Surakia
Bagdaria
Kawathia
Gondia
Ghangharia
Niguria
Duria
Jhimuria
Chithuria
Mahagia
Satkuria
Koharia
Gutalia
Chaharia
Nadia
Amthuria
Dewariha
Rathoria
Jajulia
Dimuria
Odaria
Pathaniha
Pachgaiha
Mundaria
Bindhia
Languria
Lakhia
Ghatia
Jhimuria
Chandarania

Appendix III

BAIGA RELATIONSHIP TERMS

THE terms of description and address are normally the same, though often the personal name is used: where they differ I have noted the term of address in brackets. The genealogies from which these terms are taken have been omitted for lack of space.

Father's father	Dādi
Mother's father	Budhā
Father's mother	Āji
Mother's mother	Budhi
Father	Dadā (Babā)
Mother	Dai
Father's elder brother	Bara Babā
His wife	Bari dai
Father's younger brother	Kakā
His wife	Kāki
Father's sister	Māmi
Her husband	Mamā (Māmu)
Mother's brother	Mamā
His wife	Māmi
Mother's elder sister	Bari Dai
Mother's younger sister	Mosi
Mother's elder sister's husband	Babā
Mother's younger sister's husband	Kakā
Wife's father	Mamā
Wife's mother	Māmi
Wife's father's father	Budhā
Wife's mother's mother	Budhi
Husband's father	Mamā
Husband's mother	Māmi
Husband's father's father	Budhā
Husband's mother's mother	Budhi
Elder brother (M.S.)	Dāda
Younger brother (M.S.)	Bhai or Dau
Elder brother (W.S.)	Dāda
Younger brother (W.S.)	Bhai (Dau)
Elder sister (M.S.)	Bahin (Bai)
Younger sister (M.S.)	Bahin (Noni)
Elder sister (W.S.)	Bai (Bai)
Younger sister (W.S.)	Bahin (Noni)

Father's brother's son	Bhai
Father's brother's daughter	Bahin
Father's sister's son	Mahina bhai
Father's sister's daughter	Mahina bahin
Mother's sister's son	Bhai
Mother's sister's daughter	Bahin
Mother's brother's son	Mahina bhai
Mother's brother's daughter	Mahina bahin
Husband	Dauka
Wife	Dauki
Wife's brother	Sāra
Wife's elder sister	Dedsās (Bai)
Wife's younger sister	Sāri (Noni)
Husband's elder brother	Jeth
Husband's younger brother	Dewar (Dau)
Husband's elder sister	Ded sās (Bai)
Husband's younger sister	Nanand (Noni)
Wife's elder sister's husband	Sadhuā
Wife's younger sister's husband	Nānsādhu
Husband's elder brother's wife	Jethāni (Bai)
Husband's younger brother's wife	Dewarāni (Noni)
Wife's brother's wife	Bahin
Husband's elder sister's husband	Sadhua
Husband's younger sister's husband	Bhai
Elder sister's husband (M.S.)	Bhatua
Younger sister's husband (M.S.)	Bahin damānd (Babu)
Elder sister's husband (W.S.)	Bhatua
Younger sister's husband (W.S.)	Bahin damānd (Babu)
Elder brother's wife (M.S.)	Bhauji (Bahu)
Younger brother's wife (M.S.)	Bhai-bahu (Noni)
Elder brother's wife (W.S.)	Bhauji (Bahu)
Younger brother's wife (W.S.)	Bhai-bahu (Noni)
Son	Beta (Dau)
Daughter	Beti (Noni)
Elder brother's son (M.S.)	Bhatija (Dau)
Elder brother's daughter (M.S.)	Bhatijin (Noni)
Younger brother's son (M.S.)	Bhatija (Dau)
Younger brother's daughter (M.S.)	Bhatijin (Noni)
Elder sister's son (M.S.)	Bhācha
Elder sister's daughter (M.S.)	Bhāchi
Younger sister's son (M.S.)	Bhācha
Younger sister's daughter (M.S.)	Bhāchi
Elder brother's son (W.S.)	Bhācha
Elder brother's daughter (W.S.)	Bhāchi
Younger brother's son (W.S.)	Bhācha
Younger brother's daughter (W.S.)	Bhāchi
Elder sister's son (W.S.)	Bahin beta (Dau)
Elder sister's daughter (W.S.)	Bahin beti (Noni)
Younger sister's son (W.S.)	Bahin beta (Dau)

Younger sister's daughter (W.S.)	Bahin beti (Noni)
Wife's brother's son	Bhācha
Wife's brother's daughter	Bhāchi
Wife's sister's son	Beta (Dau)
Wife's sister's daughter	Beti (Noni)
Husband's brother's son	Beta (Dau)
Husband's brother's daughter	Beti (Noni)
Husband's sister's son	Bhācha
Husband's sister's daughter	Bhāchi
Daughter's husband	Damānd
Son's wife	Bahu
Son's son	Beta nāti (Dau)
Son's daughter	Beta natmin (Noni)
Daughter's son	Beti nāti (Babu)
Daughter's daughter	Beti natmin (Noni bai)

Appendix IV

BAIGA NAMES AND THEIR MEANINGS

THIS collection of names is gathered chiefly in the Mandla District. The meanings of the names are those given to them by the Baiga of the neighbourhood; they may not always be linguistically accurate. The spelling also represents the pronunciation of the local Baiga: it probably differs from that of the general population.

The reader will easily be able to distinguish those names that are given to a child as a baby, and those that he wins for himself when he has grown up.

Adri (f.)
Agaria. Member of the Agaria sub-tribe of Gond, given to a boy to lower his value in the eyes of the *bhut*.
Agāro (f.). Eldest.
Aghnu. Born in Aghan.
Aitwāri. Born on a Sunday.
Ajeb. A portent.
Akla. The name of a large male jungle pig.
Amru. Immortal.
Andha. Blind.
Andhri (f.). Blind.
Asād. An idle boy.
Asādhu. Born in Asadh (June—July).
Asru. Born in Asadh.

Bachgār. A reader.
Bādi. He was visited by a magician on his birthday.
Bahabal. He often trembles.
Bahādur. Brave and strong.
Bahōran. A previous child who has now been reborn.
Baihar (f.). The wind.
Baiju.
Baisa.
Baisākin (f.). Born in Baisakh.
Baisāku. Born in Baisakh.
Bajāri. Born on the bazaar day.
Bamūtia. He is always urinating.
Banariha. He plays the *bāna*.
Bānda. He has small hands.
Bānga. A prattler of nonsense.

Bania. A merchant came to the village on his birthday.
Baranu. One who has been burnt.
Baredi. One who watches cattle.
Barju. He loves to contradict.
Bartu. One who has been burnt.
Batbanna. He always has an excuse when you give him work.
Bhadi. Ugly.
Bhādu. Born in Bhadon (August—September).
Bhagēla. He will run away with another man's wife.
Bhaira. Deaf.
Bhakoṣi. He eats too much.
Bhālu. A bear came by on his birthday.
Bharia. One who fries gram.
Bharju. He puts anything he can get into his cooking-pot.
Bhasku. He sucks violently *bhas bhas* at his pipe.
Bhāt Khāwa. An eater of rice.
Bhimsen. The old hero of the Mahabharat.
Bhitu. Born near a wall, or while his parents were building a wall.
Bhobha. Silent.
Bhōbla. Without teeth.
Bhoin (f.). A rich man's wife.
Bhola. Simpleton.
Bhukhau. Always hungry.
Bhursi. He has hairs on his body.
Bhūta. A whirlwind passed by on his birthday.
Bidru. Born during the Bidri ceremony.
Bigāri. On his birthday an official took his father for begar.
Bilra. As a baby he made a noise like a tom-cat.
Bir Singh. Strong.
Birghu. Bold.
Birja. He cries for everything as a child; when grown-up he fights for it.
Biru. Strong.
Bisu. They spent Rs. 20 on him.
Bōdra. With a big navel.
Bōdri (f.). The same.
Buchhul. He always pushes himself forward.
Buddhu. Stupid.
Bugla. With plump cheeks.

Chaitu. Born in Chait.
Chammu. A small brass pot.
Chamra. The [untouchable] shoemakers' caste, given to anyone whose children die.
Chandia (f.). No hair on her head.
Chariha. He always repeats scandal.
Charka. White. Given to a boy of light brown colour.
Charwa. Tender of cattle.
Chatla. He plays with mud.
Chattu. He talks very quickly, chat chat chat, in fact he chatters.

Chharaka. A tender of goats.
Chhēri (f.). She eats all day and wanders from house to house like a she-goat.
Chhita (f.). One of twins.
Chhōta. Small.
Chirbhu. He is easily excited in argument.
Chutti. He has a long top-knot.

Dādhi. The bearded man.
Daglu. He has spots on his face and body.
Dal Singh. A champion.
Dallu. Fat.
Daphru. As a baby he beat with his hands as on a drum.
Darbāri. A lazy man who sits in the darbar talking.
Darōga. Born on the day an inspector came to the village.
Dasru. Born during the Dassera festival.
Dauri. The mother's pains began when she was outside the house, and she hurried in.
Dāya Singh. The merciful.
D.F.O. The District Forest Officer came to the village on his birthday.
Deo Singh.
Dhāndu. Fat.
Dhania (f.). Rich.
Dhan Singh. Rich.
Dharmu. Religions.
Dhimar. The caste of fishermen.
Dhirat. Born on the bare ground, without even ashes under him.
Dhōdhi. She gives misleading information.
Dhōla. A drum.
Dhulia. The caste of musicians and bamboo-workers.
Dhunda. A child that plays with dust.
Dhurri. He throws his lies about like dust.
Diwar. A great magician. Also spelt Dewar.
Dogla. Deceiver.
Dokra. A small and wizened child, like an old man.
Dongru. One who was born when the mother came home from the forest.
Dukalu. Born during famine.
Dulari (f.). A darling.

Gajru. A hungry man who chews carefully whatever he gets.
Ganga. Sometimes given to a twin, the other is called Jamna.
Garbhia. Proud.
Ghinu. Filthy.
Ghisa. He shuffles along.
Ghotri. Tiny.
Ghughsi (f.).
Gidha. Swift as an eagle.
Gitgār. A good singer.
Gobarchhattia (f.). With big breasts, as big as cow-pats.
Gondu. Gond.

Goti. A breaker of small stones.
Gubra. He plays with cow-dung.
Gugli (f.). A girl with a dour and sneering expression.
Gumma. Dumb.
Gupau. Beautiful.
Gutanu. Deformed.

Hadaraha. He is always asking for more.
Hagru. Excrement, a name intended to give a false impression of the child's value.
Halku. He can only say ba-ba-ba.
Hattu. He fights over everything.

Jaighuria. He plays with little toys. Also Pachguria.
Jalsain. A child born during a dance which was held at Sanhrwachhapar in April, 1937.
Jamādar. On his birthday an official came to the village.
Jangi. A fast walker. Also a quarrelsome man.
Jangli (f.). Born in the jungle.
Janhar. The mother's pains began while she was eating.
Jantri. He pretends to superior knowledge.
Jatka. His two fingers are joined together.
Jethia (f.). Born in Jeth (May—June).
Jethu. Born in Jeth.
Jhadu. Born in a thicket.
Jhagru. Quarrelsome.
Jhitka. Thin.
Jholti. A loafer.
Jhulan. He walks with a swing.
Jhupru. Sleepy.
Jiddi. He goes to all lengths to get his own way.
Jitram. With tousled hair.
Jogi or Yogi. On his birthday a sadhu came to the village.
Johan. The boy stares at everyone.
Jonhi (f.). Born in moonlight.
Jonhu. He observes everything even far away.
Juggunu. A child who is always blinking.
Jugei. A child who is always looking for things.

Kalangiha. He ties his turban with a flourish.
Kamod. A flower.
Kāna. One testicle is larger than the other.
Kandāh. He has discharges from his eyes.
Kāri (f.) Black.
Kariya or Kāru. Black.
Karra or Kanja. He has light eyes.
Katarni. One who always interrupts a conversation.
Katewa. He is always cutting things.
Kaura. He takes big mouthfuls.

Khajju. He is always itching.
Khasār. He suffers from asthma.
Khetu. Born in a field. Or Khet Singh.
Khokha. A Bengali term of affection.
Khumān.
Khursa. One who will live long.
Kōdu. Born while the mother was gathering kodon.
Kolhia. A jackal howled as he was born.
Kohura. Born in the morning mist.
Konda. Stupid, deaf or dumb.
Kopa. Angry.
Kota (f.). A pair of twins, with Chhita.
Kubri. One of the buttocks bigger than the other.
Kulbul. When he was in his mother's womb, he was always turning over and over.
Kuaaria. Born in Kuar.
Kumaru. A boy.
Kurmi. On his birthday a Kurmi came to the village.
Kurri. When he was born his father was putting kurri planks across the hollows in his field.

Lachhi. A bunch of flowers.
Lāda. A boy with a huge stomach.
Lahakat. His penis swings to and fro as he walks.
Lamia, or Lāmu. The name given when a child is conceived immediately after the birth of another, before the mother has had time for a menstrual period.
Lamru. Tall.
Lamsena. A boy who serves for his wife.
Lamua. Tall.
Lapsi. A sweetmeat.
Latti. Perhaps his father had a long pig-tail (*latti*).
Lawa. He runs quietly along the ground like a lawa.
Lēbhaga. He always runs away with other men's wives.
Likhāri. A writer.
Lodha.
Lothāra. The boy is always rolling about in the mud.
Luddhor.

Māghu. Born in Māgh.
Mangra. Named after the crocodile.
Mahaku. He has a bad smell.
Mahatu. Wealthy.
Māhu. Born in Mah.
Mālho. One who wanders from place to place.
Mallu. Looks like a monkey.
Mandal. A well-to-do person.
Mandha. A drunkard.
Māndro (f.). She always goes calling on the neighbours.
Mandru. One who plays a drum.

Mangadhia. He is always thinking of something new.
Mangal or Mangli (f.). Born on a Tuesday.
Mangnu. A beggar.
Maniari. The river of that name.
Manjhlu. The second of three brothers.
Mān Singh. A respected man.
Manua. He is very silent.
Marhu. A helpless inactive person (f. Marghūl).
Māria.
Mechia. He has a fine moustache.
Midru. He looks with half-shut eyes.
Milāp or Milān. One who brings people together.
Mukkhi. A leader.
Munda. With shaven head.
Mungia (f.). Red beads. Given to a pretty child.
Munshi. A clerk.
Mutru. He wets his bed.

Nachkār. A dancer.
Nāla. Born in a little stream.
Nandu. Small.
Nanku. Small.
Nanua. Small.
Narri. A deceiver.
Nāru. Born with a long umbilical cord.
Nathū. He has a hole in his nose.
Nawasin (f.).
Niyāki. A settler of disputes.

Padru. He often breaks wind.
Pakra. He has white hair.
Paltu. He was born with feet first.
Pancham. He was the first son after five daughters.
Panku. Member of the Panka caste of watchmen.
Panga. He cannot walk—perhaps he has no feet.
Parsu. He serves wine to the whole party.
Paterin. She was born in the forest while her mother went for wood.
Pathān. A Mussalman came to the house when he was born.
Pathardabki. Nickname, meaning squashed by stones, given to a short, stumpy girl.
Pathāri. Named after the Pardhan caste of musicians.
Pejkhāwar. An eater of pej.
Pesgi. On his birthday his family successfully negotiated a loan.
Phadal. Fat.
Phaggu. Born in Phag (January—February). Or Phagnu.
Phalangia. Jumps as well as a monkey.
Phannu. Always looks as if he were about to cry.
Phanja. A forcible character.
Phirtū. A wanderer.

Phitkiri. Nickname for a fat girl.

Phulia (f.). When she was born the placenta did not come out till later. But, often, Phulia is simply a term of affection.

Pittu. Small.

Potha. Given to a fat girl. 'A hen about to lay an egg.'

Punuwa. Born at the full moon.

Pūtu. He is very fond of little mushrooms.

Ramli (f.). She forgets herself and wanders about.

Ranger. A range officer visited the family on his birthday.

Rasri. A rope.

Rassia. A lover in a bad sense. 'The young man carbuncular' of T. S. Eliot.

Ratnu. A jewel.

Raunu.

Rigla.

Rijhu. Popular among the girls.

Ruksa. His body is always dirty.

Rūpi (f.). Beautiful.

Rurha. Thin.

Sahanāo. You use this to address someone with the same name as yourself.

Samāru. Born on Monday.

Sargu. He was unconscious after birth, but revived, and they said his life has returned from heaven.

Saunu. Born in Shrāwan.

Shikāri. A hunter.

Singaro. Adorned.

Singlu. He has a bump on his forehead.

Sira. Thin.

Sitaha. Suffers very much from cold.

Sukha. Born on a Friday.

Suklu. Beautiful.

Sumri. One who remembers.

Sūna. Born in an empty house with none to help.

Sundaha. He is very fond of meat.

Sūrta. Remembrance.

Tahālu. A wanderer.

Tantu. Thin.

Taranga.

Tedha. Hunchback.

Thaggu. A cheat.

Thakku. He is always tired.

Thākūr. A rich man.

Thangu. A sick, tired man.

Theki (f.). She is very obstinate.

Thigli. Full of humour.

Thuggūr. Short or dwarf.

Thumtha.

Thurri.
Tiketa. A parasite on other people's hospitality.
Tikarām. The eldest son.
Tikhru. He stays, though all others run away.
Tiktu.
Tiku.
Tilha. Born in a til field.
Timāli. Proud.
Timānu. Small.
Tingāli. Lustful.
Tirchu. With crooked buttocks.
Tirri. He gets angry quickly.
Titri (f.). A girl born after three boys.
Titru. A boy born after three girls.
Totra. A stammerer.

GLOSSARY

Words that are explained in the text are not included.

Akri-kodai. Half-husked kodon, 50.
Amarkand. Water to make a man immortal.

Badki. Senior of two or more wives.
Bahari-kāri. Divination by measuring straws, 377.
Bakhar. Barrow.
Bālpos. An adopted child, 99.
Banaspati. Magic herbs of the forest.
Bān-Bāti. Divination by the swinging lamp, 380.
Barāt. Marriage-party.
Bāri. Garden enclosure near house.
Barua. A man or woman liable to be "ridden" by the gods, 381.
Begār. Forced unpaid labour.
Bewar. Shifting cultivation, or a clearing made by this method.
Bhauji. Elder brother's wife, traditionally free with the younger brother.
Bhosri. A common term of abuse, 72.
Bhut. A (generally dangerous) ghost or spirit, 366.
Bichhia. Toe-ring like a scorpion, probably intended to protect against scorpion-bite.
Bīr. A witch's familiar.

Chakmak. Flint for lighting pipe.
Channa. *Cicer arietinum*.
Chapāti. A flat circular cake of wheat-flour.
Chaprāsi. A subordinate official, often a messenger.
Chaura. A mud platform in a shrine.
Chhotki. Junior wife.
Chungi. Leaf-pipe.
Churelin. Ghost of a woman who has died in childbirth, 367.
Chutka, chutki. Toe-rings.

Dadaria. Songs sung, often antiphonally, in the jungle or round the fire, 438.
Dāl. Lentils of various kinds.
Dāno. Ogre.
Deo. A god.
Deshahi. A god, often a disease-giving god.
Dewār. A magician, 343.
Dhām. A form of divination, 381.
Dhār. A silver ornament for the ear, 13.
Dhol. A wooden drum, 431.
Dhoti. Man's loin-cloth.
Dosi. A master of ceremonies at a wedding.

Gāli. Abuse.
Garh. An exogamous division of the tribe.
Ghī. Clarified butter.
Goti. An exogamous sept.
Gundhri. A roll of cloth placed on the head to balance a load.
Gunia. A magician.

Haldi. Turmeric.
Harra. *Terminalia chebula*.
Hawel. A neck ornament of coins.

Jāt. An endogamous sub-division of the tribe.
Jawāra. (i) A sort of harvest festival (ii) A type of friendship.

Jeth. The sacred month, May-June.
Jhāt. The pubic hairs.
Jīv. The soul.

Kalsa. Decorated earthen pot with lamp used in weddings.
Kānch. The end of the woman's cloth tied between the legs, 12.
Kānda-bāri. Root-plantation.
Kāwar. A pole with a net (*sikka*) at either end, for carrying loads.
Khandela. The end of the girl's cloth which is thrown over the right shoulder at puberty.
Khandi. A measure equal to 20 *kuro* or 100 *seer*.
Khandlāhin. A girl who has passed the age of puberty.
Khanta. A spud.
Khappar. Broken earthen pot used at the Bida ceremony, 402.
Khijri. Rice cooked by steaming kept very moist, 48.
Khīr. Milk boiled till it solidifies.
Khumri. A wicker hood lined with *mohlain* leaves, used in the rains.
Kodai, Kodon or *Kutki*. Cleaned and husked ready for eating.
Kōdon. The small millet *paspalum scrabiculatum*.
Kos. A measure of two miles.
Kudāri. A hoe.
Kuro. A measure equal to 5 *seer*.
Kutki. *Panicum psilipodium*.

Lāl-Bhāji. A sort of spinach.
Lamsena. A youth who serves for a wife, 287.
Lingoti. Small strip of cloth tied between the legs.
Lugra. Strip of cloth worn by Baiga women instead of *sāri*.

Māchi. A small seat.
Madhia. A hut dedicated to the gods.
Mahārāj. Respectful form of address.
Mahua. *Bassia latifolia*.
Mālguzār. Landlord.
Māndar. Earthen drum, 431.
Manjhli. The second of three wives.
Mantra. A magic charm.
Marghat. Burial ground, 298.
Marua. The marriage-booth.
Mero. Village boundary.
Mohini. Love-charm.
Mohlain. *Bauhinia rahlii*.
Motiāri. A lover.
Mukkadam. Village headman.
Mūsar. A rice-pounder.

Nangāra. Earthen drum played at weddings, 432.
Narja. A balance, 40.
Nilkanth. The blue jay.

Pairi. Anklets.
Panch. A village council with a quorum of five.
Panda. A magician, 344.
Pej. A gruel which is the staple food of the Baiga, 50.
Phundara. Coloured wool for tying the hair.
Pīdha. A wooden seat, sometimes spiked.
Pret. Properly a corpse, used by the Baiga for a ghost.
Pūja. Worship.
Pujāri. Celebrant.
Puri. Flat wheat-cakes fried in *ghī* or oil.

Raksa. Ghost of an unmarried man, 369.
Rākshasa. A legendary ogre.
Roti. Wheat-bread also called *chapāti*.

Sābar. A long pointed iron rod for digging.
Sādhu. An ascetic.
Sagai. Engagement, 272.
Samdhi. A relation by marriage, 179.
Sārangi. A fiddle with horse-hair strings, played with a bow.
Sāri. Woman's cloth.
Seer. A measure equal to 80 *tola*.
Sendur. Red powder off the fruit capsules of *mallotus philippinensis*.
Sikka. String nets for carrying loads.
Sodhe. Witch.
Srāwan. The Hindu month corresponding to July-August.

Suāsīn. Unmarried girl who attends bride or bridegroom at a wedding.
Sūpa. A winnowing-fan.
Sutia. A silver torc worn round the neck.
Swarāj. Home-rule.

Taccāvi. A Government loan to cultivators.
Tehsil. The sub-division of a district.
Thaili. Bag for money or tobacco.
Thondi. Hollow bamboo used for keeping money or tobacco, 15.

Tikli. A spangle worn in the middle of the forehead.
Til. *Sesamum indicum.*
Timki. Small earthenware drum, 432.
Tirsul. Iron or wooden trident.
Tola. A measure equal in weight to a rupee; 80 go to a *seer.*
Tonhi. Witch.
Tuma. Gourd.

Vidya. Knowledge, applied by the Baiga to any kind of magical formula.

INDEX